* * * *

THEATER
AND REVOLUTION

ALSO BY FREDERICK BROWN

An Impersonation of Angels: A Biography of Jean Cocteau

Père-Lachaise: Elysium as Real Estate

THEATER
AND
REVOLUTION

THE CULTURE OF THE FRENCH STAGE

* * * *

FREDERICK BROWN

Vintage Books
A DIVISION OF RANDOM HOUSE, INC.
NEW YORK

First Vintage Books Edition, May 1989

Copyright © 1980 by Frederick Brown

Library of Congress Cataloging-in-Publication Data
Brown, Frederick, 1934–
Theater and revolution.
Reprint. Originally published: New York: Viking Press, 1980.
Includes bibliographical references and index.
1. Theater—France—History. 2. Theater and society—France.
3. France—History—Revolution, 1789–1799. I. Title.
[PN2631.B7 1989]   792'.0994   88-40509
ISBN 0-679-72253-X (pbk.)

Page 492 constitutes an extension of this copyright page.

Manufactured in the United States of America

10 9 8 7 6 5 4 3 2 1

TO HILTON KRAMER

ACKNOWLEDGMENTS

✦ ✦ ✦ ✦

A fellowship from the National Endowment for the Humanities relieved me of teaching duties during the 1975–76 academic year and enabled me to pursue my subject without interruption. The University Awards Council of the State University of New York provided me with a grant-in-aid to do research in Paris.

The staffs of the Cabinet des Estampes at the Bibliothèque Nationale and of the Bibliothèque de l'Arsenal were indispensable, the one in arranging to reproduce illustrations, the other in helping me interpret the catalogue of the Rondel theater collection, where I found much useful material.

For their cooperation I should like to thank Yves Bonnat of the Centre Français du Théâtre, Gerhard Vasco of the SUNY at Stony Brook Library, and Charles Webber, director of the photo-optics laboratory at Stony Brook.

I owe a debt of gratitude to Jennifer Snodgrass and to Georgette Felix for the valuable assistance they gave me at The Viking Press.

This book profited enormously from conversation with friends and, in particular, from conversations I have had over the years with my colleague Carol Blum. To them and to her I am deeply grateful.

It was, finally, my good fortune to be able to rely on the editorial wisdom of Elisabeth Sifton, who offered me guidance when I needed it and read my manuscript with fine critical intelligence.

PRELIMINARY NOTE

✦ ✦ ✦ ✦

When Louis XIV chartered the Théâtre-Français, otherwise known as the Comédie-Française, his decree provided that under normal circumstances it alone should have the right to perform spoken plays in the city of Paris. This provision begot not only an official stage but a cultural pariahdom governed, theoretically, by the interdiction against dramatic discourse. With the Revolution, the Théâtre-Français surrendered the monopoly it had enjoyed since 1680, which is to say that the boundary line between culture's preserve and the culturally disenfranchised was abruptly erased. In due course Napoleon redrew that line, quarantining theaters associated with *le peuple* inside genres deemed childish or archaic and, on occasion, silencing them altogether lest the vulgar tongue "contaminate" the mind of France.

It is this world "outside" as it survives even in our own day that constitutes the material of my book. How, in modern France, the theatrical avant-garde has consistently evoked and used the popular tradition; how it has incorporated the latter into radical aesthetics and bestowed ideological virtue on forms born, in part at least, of necessity; how the "high" and the "low" impinge on each other—these are among the central issues to which I address myself.

Rather than speak about the avant-garde in disembodied terms, I have elected to present my argument biographically, to carry it forward from pre-World War I Paris to 1968 through the lives of Jacques Copeau, Charles Dullin, and Jean-Louis Barrault. These three directors represent generations of a clan for whom theater was a realm inherently at odds with the bourgeois world, and whose modernism expressed a yearning for some primitive, if not indeed religious, order of human experience. The works they staged command my attention only insofar as close attention to a given work may elucidate the ideal they served. I am concerned here, above all, not with texts but with the diminished role of the written text, not with playwrights but with the nature of dramatic ritual, with the social implications of structural change in the theatrical arena itself, with the significance of the director's ascendancy in modern Europe. Although a biographical approach forbade me from covering this ground comprehensively (a prominent innovator such as Gaston Baty hardly enters my narrative), the limits it dictated were, I felt, rewarded by the opportunity to show theory evolving in the complex interplay between social tradition and the personal history of theatrical ideologues.

If the subtitle I chose were reversible, it would convey more explicitly the fact that my book deals as much with the staging of culture as with the culture of the stage. From the Revolution on, rulers succeeded one another like theatrical impresarios eager to make Paris a universal showcase, to display their magnificence or their social philosophies in *mise en scènes* that involved casts of thousands. Each regime trooped across the Champ-de-Mars with its own scenario. Each removed the other's names from institutional façades and obliterated the effigies of heroes or saints its predecessor had erected on city squares. When, after World War I, the Surrealists held séances the point of which was to let the Unconscious desecrate Paris's sacred monuments, they were, through their very desecrations, affirming the historical piety that in France one did not exercise power until one had dreamed up the capital. What follows may be read, then, as a play within a play, with ideological images revolving on a fixed stage.

F. B.

CONTENTS

✦ ✦ ✦ ✦

A CHRONOLOGY

✦ ✦ ✦ ✦

1402: Formation of the Confrérie de la Passion
1486: Charles VII establishes the Paris fair on land belonging to the Saint-Germain abbey
1548: Completion of the Hôtel de Bourgogne
1570: First mention of Italian *commedia dell'arte* troupes in France
1635: Richelieu charters the Académie Française
1661: Louis XIV assumes personal power after Mazarin's death
1680: Foundation of the Théâtre-Français, also known as the Co-médie-Française
1697: Expulsion from France of the Italian comedy players
1701: Louis XIV appoints an official censor for theaters
1705: The Boulevard du Temple is completed and soon becomes a fashionable promenade
1715: Death of Louis XIV and proclamation of the Regency
1731: Louis XV reaches his majority
1760: First fairground theater is established on the Boulevard du Temple
1762: Saint-Germain fair buildings burn to the ground and are rebuilt in 1763
1774: Death of Louis XV
1789: The French Revolution; a national assembly convenes
1791: Theater censorship is abolished and prerogatives of the Co-médie-Française revoked

1792:   Abolition of royalty
1793:   Execution of Louis XVI and Marie Antoinette
            Festival of the Constitution, also called the Festival of Unity
               and Indivisibility
            The Convention replaces the Legislative Assembly
            The Revolutionary Calendar becomes law, with 1792 as
               Year I
1794:   Festival of the Supreme Being
            Fall of Robespierre (9 Thermidor, or July 27)
1795–99:   The Directory
1799:   The Directory overthrown on 18 Brumaire, and a Consulate,
               including Napoleon Bonaparte, formed in its place
1800:   Guilbert de Pixérécourt's *Coelina* opens on the Boulevard du
               Temple, establishing him as the foremost writer of melo-
               drama
1804:   Napoleon has himself consecrated emperor
1807:   A Napoleonic decree classifies the repertoire of Boulevard
               theaters
1812:   Statutes are drafted for the Comédie-Française
1815:   Napoleon suffers defeat at Waterloo
1815–30:   The Bourbon Restoration; Louis XVIII is succeeded by his
               brother Charles X in 1824
1816:   The Odéon Theater is rebuilt after a fire destroyed the origi-
               nal structure
1827:   Publication of the preface to *Cromwell*
1830:   After the July Revolution Louis Philippe is enthroned as
               constitutional monarch
            Performance of Hugo's *Hernani* at the Comédie-Française
1832:   A cholera epidemic sweeps Paris
1833:   Frédérick Lemaître creates Robert Macaire
1846:   Death of Jean-Gaspard Deburau
1848:   Uprising ends the July Monarchy and leads to the creation
               of a republican government, with Louis Napoleon at its
               head
1851:   In December Louis Napoleon dissolves the Assembly and as-
               sumes dictatorial powers
1852:   A plebiscite confirms Louis Napoleon in his new title of em-
               peror of the French, Napoleon III

The stage version of Dumas's *Camille* has its premiere

1853: Work begins on the reconstruction of Paris

1862: Almost all Boulevard du Temple theaters are demolished

1869: Emile Zola publishes his first novel, *Thérèse Raquin*

1870: The Franco-Prussian War, which formally ends with signing of the Treaty of Versailles in January 1871. The Commune of Paris continues to resist until May 1871, when it is suppressed by regular French forces.

Napoleon III flees to England

1871: Formation of the Third Republic

1879: Birth of Jacques Copeau

1885: Birth of Charles Dullin

1886: André Antoine organizes the Théâtre Libre in Montmartre and brings naturalist aesthetics to the French stage

1906: Antoine is appointed director of the Odéon

1908: With Jean Schlumberger and André Ruyter, Jacques Copeau founds the *Nouvelle Revue Française,* which he directs until 1913

1910: Birth of Jean-Louis Barrault

1911: Firmin Gémier launches the Théâtre National Ambulant

1913: Establishment of the Théâtre du Vieux-Colombier

1914: In August war breaks out

1917–19: The Vieux-Colombier has two seasons in New York

1921: Establishment of the Théâtre National Populaire, with Firmin Gémier as its first director; Charles Dullin founds the Atelier

1936–38: The Popular Front

1939–40: The year-long nonengagement between French and German troops known as the "Phony War"

1940: In June Marshal Pétain concludes an armistice with Germany and takes office as chief of state at Vichy

1944: Paris is liberated after four years of occupation

1949: Death of Jacques Copeau and Charles Dullin

1968: In May insurrection of students and workers against the de Gaulle regime

* * * *

THEATER
AND REVOLUTION

CHAPTER I

✦ ✦ ✦ ✦

ON BOURGEOIS
THEATER

In April 1867, Louis Napoleon, who had been at work reinventing Paris ever since he proclaimed himself Napoleon III, emperor of the French, fifteen years earlier, inaugurated a Universal Exposition that would, before it closed in October, attract over six million people to his splendid new capital. Among those who came by special invitation were the Tsar and the Tsarina, the King of Prussia, The Khédive of Egypt, the Mikado's brother, the Sultan of Turkey, the Hapsburg Emperor, and—no stranger to Paris—the Prince of Wales. During seven months, hardly a week passed that Louis did not have occasion to greet some panjandrum alighting at a railroad depot and lead him in military pomp to the Tuileries Palace, where gala after gala preempted other, more banal affairs of state. All along the boulevards, theaters, restaurants, and boutiques drove a thriving trade as Paris mobilized its vast pleasure industry for visitors who arrived by the trainload or boatload from every quarter. "French is the language least heard on Paris streets," declared one Frenchman, Henri Darbot, and, true enough, this polyglot horde was ubiquitous. It filled the Théâtre des Variétés when Offenbach's *The Grand Duchess of Gerolstein* opened there on April 12. It fed its eyes on women dancing the cancan with total abandon at halls like Bal Mabille (to which it found its way by following a guidebook published under the title *Parisian Cytheras*—a kind of erotic Baedeker). It oohed at fireworks staged in the Tuileries Gardens and aahed at gorgeous carriages in the Bois de Boulogne, where Society paraded its

wealth every day. Gravitating to light, to movement, to fanfare, to novelty, it did not neglect Paris's venerable monuments, but beheld them in
the spirit of that innocent abroad Mark Twain, who wrote: "We visited
the Louvre at a time when we had no silk purchases in view, and looked
at its miles of paintings by the old masters." How could old masters
compete against Blondin waltzing on a tightrope with blazing Catherine
wheels fastened to his body? When the great aerialist performed in a
suburban pleasure garden, the horde flowed away from Paris like the
sea at ebb tide. And when, come October, this horde left Paris for good,
laden with silk from the great textile mills at Lyons, the image graven
upon its mind was more likely to have been of machines displayed in the
Palace of Industry than of paintings hung in the Louvre.

The Palace of Industry occupied the Champ-de-Mars, where the
Eiffel Tower was to rise on the occasion of another Exposition held
twenty-two years later. Standing amid gardens and grottoes laid out by
Adolphe Alphand, architect of the Bois de Boulogne, this "bourgeois
Colosseum," as the Goncourt brothers dubbed it, was an immense iron-
and-glass oval whose bulk dwarfed the minarets, the pagodas, the
domes, the cottages, the kiosks built to represent national states for half
a year. Unlike the Eiffel Tower, the Palace of Industry did not survive
the abuse cast at it by those who, with that French penchant for giving
native diseases foreign names, lamented France's "Americanization";
but while it stood, it embodied more ostentatiously than any American
structure the materialist world view to which Pius IX had addressed
himself in the encyclical *Syllabus of Errors*.

Had Pius ever seen it, its six concentric galleries might indeed have
put him in mind of Dante's Hell, especially by day, when a roar of machinery drowned the hub bub of the crowd and vapor from stationary
steam engines billowed toward the glass roof. To tour these mile-long
galleries was, if one believed in progress, to rejoice in man's victory over
nature or, if one did not, to witness the spectacle of pride running
before a fall. Here, industrial Europe displayed itself at its most vainglorious. There were machines of every order and dimension: textile
machines, compressed-air machines, coal-extracting machinery, railway
equipment, electric dynamos, hydraulic lifts. There were locomotives
and large-scale models of those railroad stations that bespoke the nineteenth century's architectural bewilderment. There was an exhibit on
the History of Labor, where proletarian visitors were given to under-

stand that they did not lack basic necessities but had, on the contrary, prospered well enough since 1848 to afford the clothes, utensils, and gadgets laid before them in grotesque profusion. Beneath this glass roof, nothing could contradict Louis Napoleon's optimism, not even a fifty-eight–ton steel cannon manufactured by Krupp of Essen for King Wilhelm of Prussia. "A writer for the official bulletin wondered what earthly use it could have beyond frightening everyone to death. More offensive to Parisian sensibilities was the fact that it was remarkably ugly, though in the end [the jury] did give the cannon a prize," notes one historian. With political reality suspended for the moment, inklings of doom were as unwelcome on the Champ-de-Mars as were the paintings of Manet (who exhibited his work in a shack outside its perimeter, charging fifty centimes' admission). Only boorish folk dared to suggest aloud that a fifty-eight–ton cannon was not a stone lion, that a medal would not render it inoffensive, or that its jury might soon become its fodder. And when such folk spoke, it made no great difference, for tourists pressed on heedlessly, orbiting through Wonderland until their journey led them to the outermost ring, where they restored themselves in cafés and restaurants, one more exotic than the next. At night, the Palace's wall shimmered with gaslight as women in native costumes from all over the world brought forth native dishes and scarlet-clad gypsy bands played czardas and French flower girls selling Parma violets mingled with the crowd.

To Epicurus Rotundus, nothing about the Palace of Industry was so revealing of its nature and purpose as the garden around which it had been built. "My dear Sir," this pseudonymous Englishman told the editor of *Punch,* "the heart of this garden, the center of all these monster rings, which made you feel as if you had got into Saturn, was a little money-changing office. I liked this cynicism." What fortunes of irony might he have reaped from the knowledge that in Robespierre's day Parisians gathered two hundred thousand strong to worship the Supreme Being on this same Champ-de-Mars. Where formerly there stood a Revolutionary altar known as "the Sublime Mountain," now, like the hub of some immense carousel, there stood a "Money Pavilion." In supposing that the latter reflected cynical intentions, Epicurus Rotundus was, however, quite mistaken, for if he was not, then one would have reason to conclude that Napoleon III spoke cynically when he stated that "a government can often get away with violating legality or even liberty, but will be shortlived unless it places itself at the head of civilization's larger interests." An unwarranted conclusion it would be. Since money made the world go round, humorless believers like a cousin of the Goncourts who prayed each night as follows—"Oh Lord, may my urine be less cloudy and my hemorrhoids less painful. May I live long enough to make another hundred thousand francs, may the Emperor stay in power so that my income will increase and may Anzin Coal continue to rise on the stock market"—found it altogether suitable that money's temple should occupy dead center at the Exposition of 1867.

In a state governed as much by the technocrats bred on Saint-Simon's philosophy as by Napoleon III himself, "civilization's larger interests" coincided with those of the entrepreneurial class furiously at work laying railroad tracks, stringing up telegraph lines, digging canals, mining coal, smelting ore, building factories, launching steamships, founding department stores, and, as if it were the Grand Army of a new Empire, opening markets far beyond the confines of France. Although businessmen had received blessings from on high before 1848, when Prime Minister François Guizot issued the famous edict *"Enrichissez-vous!,"* "Enrich yourselves!," not until Napoleon III's ascendancy did government predicate its very *raison d'être* on the idea that capital must at all costs flow, and flow, wherever possible, into public works of a magnitude previously unimagined, that obstacles to indefinite growth were harmful to the common weal. "Government exists in order to help society overcome the obstacles to its progress. . . . It is the beneficent mainspring of every social organism," declared Louis, whose liberal philosophy may be said to have reflected, in part, the animus of a "bastard" and "adventurer" at odds with tradition. Recognizing that economic life could not accommodate modern technics unless it burst the financial structure constrained upon it by the old regime, he presided over a financial revolution, which J. M. Thompson describes in his biography of Louis Napoleon:

The government loans of the old regime had been taken up, right down to 1847, by private banking firms, of which the Rothschilds were the most famous, and the use to which the money might be put was limited by their interests—those of an international plutocracy in close touch with the old dynasties of Europe. . . . It was for this purpose that in 1852 the Brothers Pereire—a name not unknown in the financial affairs of the Revolution—founded the first *Crédit mobilier,* which did not limit itself to state loans, but laid itself out to finance industrial societies: and, in order to extend its influence beyond anything attainable by the old-fashioned family banks, offered its shares to the general public.

The danger was of overexpansion. And when overexpansion led to a crisis in 1867, conservative financiers like the Rothschilds did not lose the opportunity to remind Europe that they had prophesied it. But for fifteen crucial years, the Crédit mobilier and its partner, the Crédit foncier, together with the Comptoir d'escompte and numerous Sociétés de dépôt, all backed by the Bank of France, financed industry and agriculture, making Paris the financial center of the Continent.

What this revolution brought about was a state of affairs succinctly described by Dumas *fils* in the play *The Question of Money,* where one character says: "Business? Why, it's very simple: business is other people's money." With other people's money, the Pereires, for instance, made millions financing the Austrian State Railroad, the Imperial Ottoman Bank, the Compagnie Générale Transatlantique, the Grand Hôtel, public utilities and transportation companies in Paris, the Louvre department store. Money borrowed from the Pereires or raised by public subscription enabled zealots like Baron Haussmann and Ferdinand de Lesseps to reconstruct Paris and to dig a canal across the Isthmus of Suez. Credit sponsored lesser visionaries than these and, indeed, thrived on dream; credit begot credit, disproving (or so it seemed in the heyday of Emperor Napoleon III) King Lear's arithmetic proclamation that "nothing will come of nothing."

To believe the Goncourts, Second Empire France was a nation remarkable for its venality, with everyone in it either taken or on the take, from ministers of state and generals and members of the imperial entourage down to *chefs de bureau.* "France is like Molière's miser, closing its fingers around dividends and property, ready to submit to any Praetorian or Caracalla, ready to endure knowingly any shame—so long as its profits are safe," they wrote. "Orders and casts have disappeared in a rabble-route where, like two armies fleeing confusedly, two kinds of men crush each other: those, the clever and the bold, who want money *per fas et nefas*, and the comfortable, who would keep their gain at any price." These liverish voyeurs often exaggerated a truth so as to have bourgeois society warrant the opprobrium they heaped on it, even when extenuating circumstances might have been found; but it is undeniable that the industrial revolution bred not only industrialists but speculators and peculators who swam in great schools toward the smell of instant profit.

Conspicuous among the latter was Louis Napoleon's uterine brother Charles, duc de Morny, a *bon vivant* utterly without scruple in peddling the influence he enjoyed to satisfy his immoderate appetite for every pleasure gold could buy. But Morny distinguished himself at court only by the extent and flagrancy of his machinations. Unlike General de Saint-Arnaud (whose debts Louis Napoleon erased on hearing him declare that "Fould counts on the market's decline while I, who have confidence in your star, Sire, invest on the principle that it will go up. Yet I am the one who has been hurt!"*), Morny frankly honored greed above all sovereigns and seized every occasion to prove his allegiance. It is characteristic of the man that after representing France at Tsar Alexander's coronation he should have brought home from Moscow an eighteen-year-old bride, Princess Troubetzkoi, and, along with her, a paper granting Crédit mobilier rights to construct a Russian railroad system. Louis Napoleon built a Roman capital in Paris, so Morny built a Pompeian resort in Deauville, where courtiers, bloated with money made on real-estate investments, spent their summers gambling some portion of it away.

The disease to which Deauville bore witness, or the fever on which it thrived, was epidemic. It raged in cafés and restaurants where as often as not talk revolved around stocks, bonds, mortgages, debentures. It beset the "little people," the cooks, water carriers, street vendors, clerks who queued up outside Parisian town halls on the eve of national loan subscriptions and remained queued up all night long—hoping that this one might see them treble or quadruple their mite. It greeted de Lesseps in the person of a cabby who, after dropping him at the Compagnie

---

* To understand the full import of General de Saint-Arnaud's plea, one must bear in mind that Achille Fould, a banker and, until 1852, Louis Napoleon's finance minister, was a Jew. Thus, the general's stock-market speculations reflected his patriotic ardor, his innate Frenchness, his willingness to immolate himself at the altar of *la patrie,* while the Jew's derived from pure self-interest.

Universelle du Canal Maritime de Suez, announced familiarly: "Monsieur de Lesseps, I am one of your shareholders." It drove beyond exhaustion uniformed messengers who would spring with telegrams between the Stock Exchange and the Central Post Office like a flying phalanx of yo-yos unreeled across Paris by an officer corps of brokers. It made itself felt everywhere, but nowhere more irresistibly of course than in its very seat, the Bourse, from which there rose a din that could be heard at night (for although the great hall closed at 3:00 p.m., trading would continue until 10:00 p.m. in the arcades outside) by strollers on the boulevard des Italiens, quite some distance away. Zola describes it vividly in his novel *Money*:

> It was the active hour when the life of Paris seems to rush toward the central square between rue Montmartre and rue de Richelieu, the two choked arteries that sweep the crowd forward. From the four intersections at the four angles of the square carriages flowed in uninterrupted waves, furrowing the pavement amid eddies of pedestrians. The two lines of cabs stationed along the gates would break and reform incessantly while on the rue Vivienne the victorias of commission men stretched out in a tightly packed row with cabbies sitting on high, reins in hands and whips ready to crack at a moment's notice. The steps and peristyle of the Bourse were black with the swarm of tailcoats and from the wings, beneath the great clock, there rose the clamor of bids and offers, the tidal roar of speculation that drowned out the muffled noise of the city. Passers-by turned their heads out of desire and curiosity, baffled by what was happening there, by the mystery of financial operations which few French brains can fathom, by the ruins or sudden fortunes that emerged from the gesticulation and from these barbarous shouts.

What is suggested in *Money* is that this fever had become a substitute for religious exaltation, the Bourse a profane temple, the broker a priestlike figure invested with magical power, financial jargon an incantatory language, and the mass of French a worshipful throng. Other, more conservative writers did not quarrel with his metaphor, inclined though some might have been to turn it against him, or, rather, against the scientific-materialist doctrine from which Zola would extrapolate the grand design of his fictional enterprise *Les Rougon-Macquart*. And why indeed would they quarrel? Tradition had unquestionably been dealt a serious blow by circumstances beyond anybody's control. Where bourgeois tradition held that the virtuous man planned, labored, saved; that he found the reward for all he begrudged himself in his children's advancement; and that he set posterity a shining example of the golden rule—circumstances now invited men to believe that the magic attending stock-market quotations augured a new dispensation, that one shrewd guess, one coup, "killing," or break might rescind the curse put on them at birth. Paris swarmed with immigrants from provincial France who had come by railroad seeking fortune in the capital, only to end up in some squalid tenement outside the customs barrier eating dust all the days of their life. But a gambler could always cite that other swarm on whom fortune had smiled, the golden dustmen who had struck it rich, the parvenus who justified Alexis de Tocqueville's contention that "there is no longer a race of wealthy men just as there is no longer a race of poor people; the former emerge every day from the bosom of the crowd and constantly return to it." Not since Revolutionary days, when the Convention decreed *sang*, or aristocratic blood, and *naissance*, or high birth, obsolescent in decreeing 1792 Year I, had Frenchmen with nothing to lose (but something to wager) greeted so warmly the prospect of losing their past. One such Frenchman even became emperor. When Louis Napoleon, whose patronymic may be said to have constituted his first imposture, declared in an unguarded moment, "We are all of us newcomers," he spoke as the emperor of parvenus.

To what extent sudden wealth fostered conspicuous consumption was most apparent on the Boulevard, the district that encompassed the large theaters, operas, elegant cafés, and luxurious restaurants of Paris. Dignitaries came from every quarter to feast at the Café Anglais, the Café de Paris, the Café Riche, or La Maison d'Or as the financial center of Europe became its gastronomic capital and chefs like Dugléré recaptured a position France had lost under Louis Philippe's July Monarchy. "The Second Empire was for French cuisine what the reign of François I was for the fine arts, a renaissance," wrote a culinary historian of the *belle époque*. "Weary of the superannuated, bourgeois cuisine of the previous regime, the new court spent without counting in its pursuit of luxury and its infatuation with appearances. Important households made themselves known by sumptuous receptions where the table had pride of place. The Court, ministries, embassies, and many town houses became the school at which great artists, exclusively French, received their training. All foreign courts were our tributaries."

ON BOURGEOIS THEATER 9

Nineteenth-century gastronomic literature supported imperial pretensions insofar as great meals would often figure therein as martial encounters between a chef and a diner, the implication being that *retenue*, the power of "retention" by which perfect courtiers formerly distinguished themselves, had shifted its seat from the heart to the gullet. Zola, Maupassant, and the Goncourts took a more jaundiced view, stating at every opportunity that the gullet was just another credit bank, that Epicuri Rotundi of the Second Empire frequented the Boulevard not so much to savor the remarkable inventions brought forth by Bignon at the Café Riche or Pascal at the Restaurant Philippe as to flaunt their substance, to fatten themselves against potential disaster. In Zola's *Pot-Bouille*, for example, the food Uncle Bachelard devours at Foyot evokes the merchandise that gluts his warehouse. A saturnalia at the Café Anglais, in whose private rooms royalty used to dine with harlotry, determines the career of Guy de Maupassant's unconscionable opportunist, Bel Ami. Restaurant lore often enters the Goncourt *Journal*, as here:

> The Café Anglais sells eighty thousand francs worth of cigars a year. The cook earns twenty-five thousand francs. His master owns a large estate, horses, a carriage, and belongs to the Council of State. There you have Paris at the height of folly.

And here:

> The talk of the town is de Goy, always dreaming about millions. . . . The other day, he really did inherit some sixty thousand francs, gambled and lost forty thousand in one evening at the Maison d'Or; availed himself of this sudden and fugitive prosperity to foot the dinner bill of perfect strangers, offering them money for dessert. Busquet accepted a five hundred franc note while Murger claims that he took no more than a louis.

And in another passage where the brothers explain that their maid, as she was passing the Maison d'Or one morning, saw a nun with a little cart, collecting table scraps from a masked ball that had taken place there the night before.

Nothing these writers wrote tells us more, however, than the tale told about Viel-Castel, a viscount who enjoyed considerable prominence at court during Louis Napoleon's reign. According to Jean-

Paul Aron, the author of *The Nineteenth-Century Eater,* he wagered that in one hundred and twenty minutes he could polish off a dinner worth five hundred francs (nine months' wages for the average worker):

> When seven o'clock chimed at the Café de Paris, he was served twelve dozen Ostend oysters, which went down so easily that he had another twelve dozen, and watered down the lot with a bottle of Johannesberg. But oysters don't count. Dinner began with the soup, bird's nest soup as it happens. Carried away by the game, he ordered, on the spur of the moment, a beefsteak with potatoes. Then the meal unfolded as planned: a splendid *féra* from the Lake of Geneva, which he stripped bare; an enormous pheasant stuffed with truffles; a salmi of ten ortolans, which disappeared in ten bites; asparagus, green peas. The dessert was simple: a whole pineapple and strawberries. With the *relevé* and *entrée,* Viel-Castel drank two bottles of Bordeaux; then a bottle of Constance with the roast and of sherry with the dessert. Naturally liqueurs after coffee. He payed 518 francs 50, finishing just under the wire, and at nine o'clock excused himself, fresh as a rose.

Given a society in which conventional wisdom had it that time was money, Viel-Castel's feat may have been the perfect parody of a capitalist *tour de force*, a parody illustrating, moreover, those hidden rapports between excrement and gold soon to be exposed by Doctor Freud.*

If restaurateurs became millionaires, far greater wealth accrued to the courtesans known as *lionnes* or *demi-mondaines* whom Zola portrayed so well in *Nana.* Exempt from the punishment that bourgeois law visited on common whores and from the corset it imposed on proper matrons, these women, some of whom had "fallen" but most of whom could not have fallen lower than the basement in which they found themselves at birth, queened it over the Boulevard. However else one may characterize her, the *lionne* was, above all, the delusion of an inflationary world. Having acquired titled clients whose titles gave her

---

* Then there was the Club of Large Stomachs, which met every Saturday at Restaurant Philippe. Its members would remain at table from six in the evening to noon on Sunday, ingesting, during that interval, three meals: the first from six until midnight, the second from midnight until six in the morning, and the third from six until noon. The array of dishes and volume of wine were staggering.

her credit, she came to embody in the eyes of nouveaux riches a sexual magic inseparable from the lust for patents of nobility, or from the dream these evoked of aristocratic license, of pleasure uncontaminated by mundane responsibilities. What led the parvenu financier to invest in a dubious venture that carried Morny's endorsement led him to crave, no matter how much it might cost him—and, indeed, the higher the stakes the better the game—a share in Morny's latest concubine. Gilding this idol of brass, he rewarded her not for her solicitude (idols don't solicit), nor even for her expertise (expert though she was in the venereal arts) but for her narcissism. Did Cora Pearl, a Cockney lass *née* Emma Crouch, who had her breasts reproduced in plaster, complain, when some lover shot himself in her living room, that "the pig has ruined my beautiful carpet"? Did La Païva, an East European Jewess *née* Theresa Lachmann who married a Portuguese marquis, dismiss her husband after their nuptial night with the explanation that she was content to be a whore and had ceased to find him amusing? True or apocryphal, such stories, far from compromising the lioness, earned her fresh tribute, for even as they bespoke her animality, they argued a hardheartedness congenial with the mineral world in which idols were expected to feel most at home. "If the Frères Provençaux served an omelette garnished with diamonds, Cora would be there every night," said the Duc de Gramont-Caderousse of Cora Pearl. Men, certain men, fancied the idea that nature had given this glittering creature, whatever her name, a born affinity to diamonds, silver, gold, pearls, crystal.

And the lioness did not disappoint them—not La Païva, for one, in whose establishment at 25, avenue des Champs-Elysées they were shown a staircase made of pure onyx, a ceiling of naked nymphs (including the mistress) painted by Baudry, bathroom walls tiled with mirrors and agate, a tub of marble and silvered bronze into which water flowed from gem-encrusted faucets, a bed that cost one hundred thousand francs, and finally La Païva, who wore cheap garments the better to proclaim that the jewelry in which she draped herself was, thank you, clothing enough. "Marvelous thing, wealth! It pardons everything," wrote the Goncourts after dinner with her. "Nobody who comes here notices that there isn't a house in all of Paris more uncomfortable than hers. At table, drinking a glass of watery wine is quite impossible as the bottles and carafes dreamed up by her are cathedrals of crystal it would take a water-carrier to lift." Despite their crankiness on this occasion, the Goncourts would, on any other, have thought it self-evident that the

Hôtel de Païva enshrined not only the flesh of a courtesan but the egregious materialism of a whole society, and would have been the first to declare that man an arrant fool who entered a temple expecting all the comforts of home. Indeed, several years before, during the Exposition of 1855, when people were queuing up to see the crown jewels, they observed in their journal that "if it were possible to give them Rembrandt's light or Hugo's poetry in material form, to make it visible and tactile, they would spurn it for a diamond like 'The Regent,' the diamond being the most concentrated essence of wealth."

Fascination with "the most concentrated essence of wealth" was, as the Goncourts knew full well, by no means peculiar to the *profanum vulgus*, however. The first stanza of Baudelaire's "The Jewels" will suffice to represent a hundred others that declaim his erotic investment in jewelry:

> La très-chère était nue, et, connaissant mon coeur,
> Elle n'avait gardé que ses bijoux sonores,
> Dont le riche attirail lui donnait l'air vainqueur
> Qu'ont dans leurs jours heureux les esclaves des Mores.*

Among Parnassian poets such as Théophile Gautier (who frequented La Païva's), poetic practice became a lapidary art and the gem an object lesson. *Salammbo* and *Hérodiade* attest to the lapidary in Flaubert, whose imagination ran riot with scenes of orgiastic violence while girdling them in the inertness of a mineral landscape or in palaces of precious stone. When Arthur Rimbaud broke free from the Parnassian school, even then the "alchemist" he fancied himself—the alchemist transforming language into something more concrete than words—held him hostage to metal. And further ahead loomed the bejeweled Sphinxes of Art Nouveau.

Propriety dictated that the poems in Baudelaire's *Flowers of Evil* be expurgated by the Imperial censor, but Offenbach's *La Gaîeté Parisienne*

---

* "The precious one was naked, and, knowing my wish, / Wore only her resonant jewels, / Of which the rich regalia gave her the conquering air / That Moorish slaves have in their happy days."

drove a thriving trade on the Boulevard, where impresarios exploited the public craze for spectacles of never-never land, feats of magic, displays of material wealth, glimpses of female crotch. Dramatic art went into serious decline as interest shifted from theater per se to conjury, with playwrights relying more and more on the technician who devised special effects. One such, Jean-Pierre Moynet, wrote:

> When it comes to mounting a new *féerie*, an enterprise into which a director does not throw himself lightly, a great bustle is produced in the theater. The machinist, the designers, the property man and the maker of papier-mâché costumes and props rack their brains to find sensational *trucs*. A special effect often saves a play of this kind when the literary elements in it are not sufficient to do so. Authors demand the most impossible things, yet stage artists strive to realize them. Also, the manuscripts of these plays teem with ideas, each one more extravagant than the last. It is necessary to balance an extravagant idea with simple and perfectly performed execution in order that the *truc* does not get stuck in the middle of its operation.

Victor Séjour's *The Madonna of the Roses*, for example, owed its entire success to a fire simulated with bengal lights, bellows, "spark," and lycopodium. When Dennery's *The Battle of Marengo* played at the Châtelet, the manager requisitioned several four-inch artillery pieces from the War Ministry and arranged to have their gun crews fire blank shells without any assurance beforehand that the theater's glass roof could stand the acoustical impact. A production of Meyerbeer's *The African Woman* at the Opéra took place on a stage transformed into an enormous ship that was made to rock fore and aft by hands working machinery underneath it. *King Carrot*, a *féerie*, or fairytale play, written by Victorien Sardou and Jacques Offenbach, in which an old magician who is dismembered and burned piecemeal emerges from the fire a young man, inspired devices of the utmost ingenuity. "The machinist's art uses all its resources in the construction of *trucs*. Some of them are veritable masterpieces," declared Moynet. "The machinist is at once a carpenter, a cabinetmaker, and a mechanic. The study of design and of dynamics is indispensable to him. Physics and even chemistry furnish him many effects. We will return to this when we develop more fully the subject of scientific progress applied to the modern stage." While the Church was accrediting Bernadette's vision at Lourdes in hopes of recovering from science something of its cognitive eminence, theater was discrediting occultism with *trucs* that enhanced the prestige of the engineer. Those who did not fancy pilgrimages to Lourdes got all the magic they wanted on the Boulevard, where, like everything else, the supernatural became big business. Behind the backdrop and beneath the floorboards of several dozen stages (especially the Opéra's) machinists and electricians, scene painters and upholsterers, tailors and seamstresses, locksmiths and blacksmiths, smoke- and fire-makers, fountain keepers and lighting masters all did yeoman work in the service of yet another industry, the entertainment industry, which manufactured fairytale scenes for the carriage trade, manufacturing them with the same fastidiousness that Viollet-le-Duc applied to his pedantic restoration of medieval fortresses and Napoleon III to the trappings of Napoleonic glory.

Just as Aristotle's pieties, after having served heroic drama during the seventeenth century, came to tyrannize imitations thereof, like a frame that grew ever more ornate while the image it surrounded grew increasingly hollow, so Victor Hugo's defense of historically accurate decor came to justify virtuoso exercises in local color. Latter-day mechanics exploited all the technology at their disposal for *féeries* and constructed Romantic environments from which the Romantic hero had disappeared. This disappearance was symptomatic. When Jules Goncourt wrote, "Money is a very big thing that leaves men greatly diminished," he voiced the opinion held by many contemporaries that affluence had cost France her soul, that greatness had become the confection of newsmongers or paid auxiliaries, that the missing numeral between Napoleons I and III denoted a spiritual abyss in which the fallen soldiers of *la grande patrie* had somehow fathered a nation of wee opportunists rising rank upon rank toward self-aggrandizement. Nothing was what it used to be, they mourned—not even opportunism. How could the writer create a Rastignac when Rastignac's counterpart in modern France would have succumbed to the devil without making overtures to some loftier principle? How could he create a Vautrin when the devil, far from exerting animal magnetism, had acquired a respectable paunch? "Ah, it is very difficult indeed nowadays to find a man whose thought has some space in it, who ventilates you like those great swells of air one breathes at the seashore," sighs Norbert de Varenne, the poet in Maupassant's novel *Bel Ami* who sells his talent to a newspaper mogul. "I knew several such men. They're all dead."

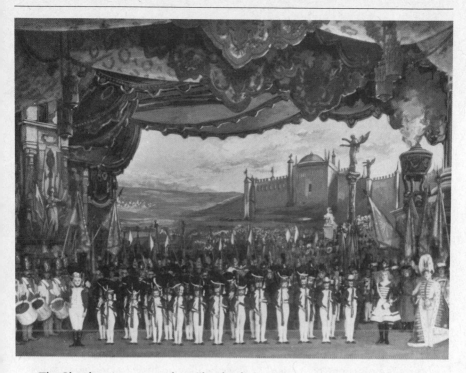

The Châtelet, circa 1900, where "local color" ran riot in extravaganzas of the sort illustrated here. From Le Théâtre

Prominent among the hero's executioners was the playwright Eugène Scribe who, during the 1820s, had created in the "well-made play," the *pièce bien faite*, an instrument wonderfully compatible with the values or prejudices embraced by bourgeois eager to lord it over history. Historical drama served him as a means of demystifying the past, of banalizing exalted figures and exalting banality, of having Great Shades unmask themselves before a bourgeois tribunal. Consider, for example, *The Glass of Water*, in which Lord Bolingbroke is made to tell his interlocutor:

You shouldn't despise the little things; it's through them that one achieves the great things. You think perhaps, like everyone else, that political catastrophes, revolutions, the fall of empires, come from deep, weighty, important causes. . . . What an illusion! Nations are subdued or governed by heroes, by great men; but these great men are themselves led by their passions, their whims, their vanities; that is, by the most wretched and trivial things in the world. I am sure you don't know that one window of the Trianon, criticized by Louis XIV and defended by Louvois, started the war that is raging through Europe at this moment! The wounded vanity of a courtier has been responsible for the kingdom's disasters; an even more trifling cause, perhaps, shall be responsible for its salvation. And without looking any further . . . I myself, I, Henry St. John, who up to the age of twenty-six was regarded as a fop, a fool, a man incapable of serious pursuits . . . do you know how I suddenly became a statesman, how I got into parliament, into government affairs, into the Ministry? I got to be minister because I knew how to dance the sarabande, and I lost power because I came down with a cold. . . . The secret is not to try to compete with Providence and manufacture events, but to profit from events. The more trivial they appear, if you ask me, the more consequential they are.

This peroration ends with Scribe's single most famous line: "Great effects from small causes . . . that's my system."

Where the climactic moment in, say, Corneille's theater turns upon a feat performed by the hero—whose irreducible *virtu* (his "metal") places him above the flux of time, enabling him to shape history—the turning points or "peripéties" in a Scribe play adduce a world governed entirely by Providence, that is, by the playwright, who manipulates his dramatis personae as a puppeteer manipulates puppets. Where the hero exercises his immutable will upon the course of events, the man Scribe would have us admire is an opportunist who rides an arbitrary contraption to a rational denouement, who profits from tricks of fate that coincide with the *trucs* of the well-made play. As previously the hero conquered all, so now did the well-made play. Keeping its audience intrigued, then wrapping itself up neatly like some guest at a proper salon, it left behind no residue of doubt and no hint of unfathomable depths. Mystery is what it meant to abolish, and to abolish through plots that substituted their own devious logic for human pithiness, that simulated depth the better to expose depth as a simulacrum hiding some all-important whim or momentous trifle. Scribe's theatrical enterprise may thus be said to have constituted a perversion of Diderot's justly famous witticism: "Behind every great idea there is a little bit of testicle." The great became commensurate with the little bit—Versailles, for example, with a single window of the Trianon, with a common cold, a dance, a glass of water.

✦ ✦ ✦

What Scribe called his "system" would hardly warrant commemorating if it did not illustrate so well the distance between the profane theater and the Comédie-Française, between entertainment and culture, between the pleasure that the bourgeois sought on the Boulevard and the education offered their children in *lycées*, where "greatness of soul" was very much in order. The more acquisitive and mobile French society became, the more emphatically did its conservative elements insist upon classical humanities as a prerequisite for admission to the cultural body politic, this initiatory program reflecting a belief—a belief shared by "new men" eager to have their children quickly naturalize themselves—that culture would not deserve its name when it acknowledged the physical life or had material *use*. Culture was *désintéressée*— "selfless." It raised its proprietor above nature; it established an inner distance that guaranteed his virtue; it forged an essence impervious to "motives"; it sanctified power. Where the average man—say, one of the provincials who, motivated by money and the main chance, trebled the capital's population during the mid-nineteenth century—spoke from *within* himself, men bred on the ancients spoke from outside, their education having in fact made it imperative that they do so. One historian of French pedagogy, Antoine Prost, explains as follows how this classicization took place:

> To write an oration was to put noble words in the mouths of great personages. Maximian writes to Diocletian imploring him not to renounce the Empire, Francis I to Charles V complaining of his incarceration, et cetera. The subject who spoke was always a great one: king or emperor, saint, learned man, or poet. And what did one have these personages say? To be sure, nothing one might have chanced to hear in everyday life but, rather, sturdy aphorisms. As in Corneille and Bossuet—who became classics for this very reason—one exhaled only great sentiments. "What pure and virtuous souls!" Villemain exclaims. These princes are oblivious to reasons of state, jealousy, deceit. . . . Honor, dignity, nobility, virtue, courage, sacrifice, repudiation of the world: on these heroic summits, generosity was the air one breathed.

Until quite late in the century, the subject that crowned the academic curriculum was rhetoric. *Lycées* reserved highest honors for the pupil who had written the most eloquent *discours* (oration), and done so in a language no longer spoken.

Lower-class boys aping students of rhetoric. Lithograph by Honoré Daumier.
Bibliothèque Nationale

Latin antiquity furnished most of the paragons, much as it had during the French Revolution when Jacobins compared their leaders to Greek and Roman worthies. Lest a student discover that Horace and Tacitus could themselves fall short, on occasion, of Horace and Tacitus, pedagogues either expurgated the Latin work or else wrote a new literature submissive to contemporary bourgeois ideals, a literature which they taught along with the *selectae* and *excerptae* of original texts (*De viris illustribus* was one such forged antique). Latin served to hallow patriarchal authority, to enthrone virtue in history, to reestablish, in secular terms, a Beginning from which mankind had fallen. It was the premise of *rhétorique* that a child who "put noble words in the mouths of great personages" year after year would, by virtue of this theatrical discipline, transcend himself the better to possess himself; that idealized antiquity represented an external model, but an external model containing the *real* interior. When François Guizot said, in eulogizing Casimir Périer, that this representative of France's *haute bourgeoisie* was "real and serious to the core," he meant to deny him any little vestige or corner of childhood, to argue his timelessness, to present his case for membership in the Pantheon. "Without Latin, one is but a parvenu as regards intelligence," he declared on another occasion. Whatever qualities had enabled men to succeed in business, they would remain "subjects" since they lacked the objective musculature developed in rhetorical *progymnastica*. "Our bourgeoisie, even the most humble members of it, holds Latin and Greek dear," wrote a candidate for election to the High Council on Public Instruction in 1891. "They are the hallmark of a true high-school education. When most of our *collèges*, when several of our *lycées* will no longer teach them, the bourgeoisie will remove to Church institutions. . . . How will one make it understood to those who accept this mutilation of the curriculum that a house in which one learns only French does not differ significantly from primary school?" Latin separated the men from the boys, not to say the upper classes from the lower (until several decades into the twentieth century, *lycées* charged tuition far beyond anything the average laborer could afford).

This bourgeois pedagogy suggests a parallel with the therapeutic regime devised by certain alienists of the eighteenth century. Like privileged schoolboys, inmates of enlightened lunatic asylums were treated as actors cast in a morality play and made to perform it without respite, the theory being that their roles would thus supplant their unruly nature, that objective discourse would silence their native voices, that the alien within would capitulate to the real self outside; cued and coached by a director who deleted vulgar *ad libitums* from their text, they formed a model society, a society saner than the sane. "The students are not to say what they are thinking as they think it, but that which it behooves them to say, by applying the rhetorical rules. . . . An oration is the 'development' of some long and detailed 'matter' dictated by the master in which nothing may be altered. . . . The dissociation between form and content is thus the foremost axiom of this pedagogy," wrote Antoine Prost. In Latin antiquity, schools of rhetoric had proliferated when forums of debate disappeared (Quintilian, for example, wrote the *Institutio Oratoria* under Diocletian, whose reign, as we know from

Tacitus, brought fifteen years of enforced silence); a similar paradox proved to be the everyday experience of children in bourgeois France. Even those who are thought to have rebelled—Mallarmé and Rimbaud, for instance—bore witness to the efficacy of their education in fabricating hermetic languages, making an ideal of *poésie pure*, or leaving the page blank. Had Flaubert written the book he wanted to write, "a book about nothing, a book without any external support, held together only by the inner strength of its style, the way the earth hangs suspended in space, a book which would have almost no subject," he might have found himself elected to the Académie française instead of dragged before a court of law.

Indeed, Flaubert's project calls to mind Edouard Herriot's epigram: "Culture is what's left when one has forgotten everything." Mastering the formal properties of the "objective" language sufficed in itself to teach virtue and lend authority. What made an eminence intrinsically worthy of the station he occupied was his classical architecture. "The ruling classes will always be the ruling classes," declared a politically powerful cleric, Monsignor Félix Dupanloup, "because they know Latin." If pedagogues who shaped France's elite cadre judged students on their ability to elaborate in Latin verse or prose an adage dropped from above, allowing literature itself a subordinate role and discouraging the interpretation of it, they regarded Latin not as contents with which to fill containers but as armature on which to scaffold façades. The patrician head, like the patrician language, was a *chose en soi*, a form self-centered and all-inclusive. It would therefore not avail philistines to read Latin literature in translation; they would remain philistine even when they grasped its ideas since Latinity resided in a structural soul rather than in literature, philosophy, history, lives.

That soul created an essential distinction between the French spoken by cultivated men and the French spoken by men affiliated with nature, between true French and French redolent of patois, between head French and manual French.* "Children think, imagine, feel, write never

---

* Those deemed "foreign" because of race or religion could never truly initiate themselves. When they had overcome one barrier, they found themselves excluded by another, even more mystical. Jean Renoir puts this across most effectively in his film *The Grand Illusion*, where the German (though he could as well have been French) aristocrat who discovers a Jewish POW reading Pindar in the original laughs at what he considers a ridiculous intermarriage.

more vigorously than in Latin, and, what is more, in Latin verse,"
wrote Dupanloup in 1873, defending Latin rhetoric against the most
recent assault launched against it by liberals. "In French, they are almost always common, vulgar; the reason for this is simple—they do not
speak very well and are fluent only in the French of their re-creations.
The easy style and familiar everyday conversation are scarcely fit to ennoble speech. . . . In Latin, it is otherwise: there they have conversed
with none but men of genius, they know only the language of Cicero
and Vergil, along with that of Plato, of Homer. Indeed, they know them
at their most elevated and generous: their compositions necessarily
show the effects of it, and attain such perfection as they cannot attain in
French, *but which subsequently infiltrates French itself*" (italics added).
Enlarging upon the metaphor contained in *culture*, a word that signifies
both intellectual culture and tillage, Dupanloup promotes the study of
Latin as a devotional exercise or stoic discipline:

> The point of it all is to reach not the vain and banal word, but *the true
> word*. . . . To do that, the primitive, natural, vulgar word must be broken
> and grafted, through art, through true art, through the true culture and the
> great education, it must be given a kind of new form, nobler and more
> elevated. Vergil's word must be applied to the soil of the mind.
>
> Et qui proscisso quae suscitat aequore terga
> RURSUS IN OBLIQUUM verso perrumpit aratro.*
>
> It is the second line that must be observed in cultivating the word.

Like the medieval bishop hallowing a new church by spreading ashes on
the floor and tracing in them the Greek and Latin alphabets, the
nineteenth-century prelate would have re-created young heads pure by
having them internalize a sublime language.

This pedagogical model influenced even renegades from the
Church, men such as Ernest Renan, a defrocked seminarist of great
brilliance whom Napoleon III appointed to the chair of Hebrew and
Chaldaic languages at the Collège de France, despite ecclesiastical objec-
tions. His most famous work, *The Life of Jesus*, in which he brought
the tenets of natural science to bear upon Christ's life, begins with the

---

* "Much service, too, does he who turns his plough
   And again breaks crosswise through the ridges he raised."

contention: "Humanity is so weak-minded that the purest thing needs the cooperation of some impure agent. . . . *Science alone is pure, for science has nothing practical about it. It does not touch men* [italics added]. Propaganda does not concern it. Its duty is to prove, not to persuade nor to convert." Taking great religious phenomena (Chartres Cathedral, the Fête-Dieu, the Franciscan order, Islam) back to root delusions fostered by men who knew no better, or else to ancient hoaxes sprung by knaves who knew what they were about, he postulated a future in which the intellectual vanguard would transcend childhood embroilments and, through science, "purify" itself. So it was with the historian Hippolyte Taine, whose dictum that "every man and every book can be summed up in three pages and those three pages can be summed up in three lines," implies a process leading at infinity to some quintessential distillation, to the apotheosis of scientific knowledge in one Word.

Scientific progressivism saw its hierophants establish between the *faible d'esprit*, or "weak-minded," and the *tête forte*, or "tough-minded," a distinction equivalent to that which Christians made between heathens and themselves. The tough mind was consubstantial with laws that governed reality, while the weak mind was built for dreaming. The strong mind fathomed the internal mechanism of things, while the soft mind played dupe to appearances. The strong mind turned matter and events to its advantage; the weak mind wrought havoc or cringed inside chimerical prisons. Claude Henri de Saint-Simon, the philosopher whose writings became gospel to France's technocratic elite, founded a world-view on this distinction, extending it backward in time and outward in space. About history he wrote: "It does not seem to me particularly interesting or instructive before Socrates. Doing research into the events that preceded his advent is, in my view, as vain as taking pains to recall all that one thought while one was being nursed, during one's weaning, during the years one spent learning how to read and write, in short, until one reached the age of puberty. . . . [By the same token], research into the history of Chinese and Hindus ought not occupy the strong-minded, for it is obvious that these peoples have never emerged from childhood."

Some fifty years later, Renan, though far more knowledgeable about matters Oriental (having spent several years in the Near East on an archaeological mission), echoed him in his biography of Jesus, where the reader is warned that "our conscientious distinctions, our cold and clear-headed thought processes" are inapplicable outside Europe. "People would have it that Jesus was a sage or a philosopher, a patriot or a just man, a moralist, or a saint. He was none of these things," declared Renan. "He was a charmer. Let us not re-create the past in our own image. Let us not believe that Asia is Europe. Among ourselves, for example, the madman is a being out of order. . . . In the Orient, he is a privileged creature who enters the highest councils without anyone daring to stop him. He is listened to and consulted. He is considered next to God because it is thought that, his individual reason having been extinguished, he participates in divine reason." With Unreason plighted upon the distaff side of earth and to a past of Asiatic remoteness, the strong head could then be born potent *ab origine* and objective by nature, an Athena-like epiphany having eradicated from it traces of childhood.

If the female Liberty who once presided over the guillotine with spear and Phrygian cap strongly resembled Athena, Athena's immaculate conception in Zeus's head was a myth ready-made for "new men." When Alexis de Tocqueville observed, some four decades after the Terror, that "there is no longer a race of wealthy men, as there is no longer a race of poor people—the former emerge every day from the bosom of the crowd and incessantly return to it," he might have observed further that the bourgeois who had risen, but risen ever fearful of falling into bosoms and crowds, was eager to sanctify his altitude, to make his head a fortress well secured against threats from below. Thus may we understand the eulogy in which Guizot declared of his confrere, Casimir Périer, that he was "real and serious to the core." Such qualities denoted aristocratic birth in an officially egalitarian society, or salvation in a materialist age. Under the old order, "bred" (*nés*) were those whose bloodlines argued their purity; under the new, breeding acquired an abstract vocabulary. Lineage had vouched for the aristocrat's *virtu*; impersonal law vouched for the bourgeois' tough-mindedness. When, in accordance with one system or another (he could choose from among Saint-Simonianism, Cousinian spiritualism, Comtian positivism), he had outgrown his personal anecdote and draped himself on rational form, then he would have become "real," establishing an identity that transcended revolutions past and future.

Indeed, rational theologies were made to obviate vicissitude, to banish the memory of a nation sans-culottes, and to systematize bourgeois power. Here again, Renan emerged as the most articulate spokesman for a class torn between its revolutionary origins and its aristocratic temper, its progressive faith and its social conservatism. "To form, through the universities, a rationalist head of society ruling by science, proud of this science and ill-disposed to see an ignorant crowd despoil it of its privileges; . . . to uplift the populace and revive its enfeebled faculties, a patriotic clergy inspiring it to accept a superior society, to revere science and virtue, to embrace the spirit of sacrifice and devotion: that would be the ideal state of affairs," he declared in *The Intellectual and Moral Reform of France*, a work written shortly after the Franco-Prussian War, when the ruins of the Paris Commune were still smoldering. "The Church made the mistake of believing it is well to impose upon men adherence to formulas they don't understand," he went on to say in *Philosophical Dialogues*, another work written during that period. "The conduct of science, which reigns triumphant now, will, perhaps, bear a closer resemblance to that of Islam than of Christianity. Christianity was persecutory because it understood belief as something that acts *ex opere operato* upon the individual who does not understand it, like a pill one swallows without knowing its content. Islam, on the other hand, took scarcely any pains to convert the impious. . . . We, too, see no great advantage in winning adherents to science from among those who don't understand it. It is sufficient that they serve it and bow to its incontestable strength." Unlike the soul, which enjoyed citizenship in a classless society ruled by Faith, the strong head was the impersonal monarch of an ideal state in which the aptitude for abstract thought distinguished Athenians from helots.

Science as taught in *lycées*, in *collèges*, and in the universities was a stepchild of the rhetorical curriculum; while addressing itself to the physical world, it dealt more with the symbolic design of it than with its stuff, more with a hermeneutics that conferred transparency and syntax on matter, than with matter. Had the bourgeois Establishment claimed as its own the accomplishments of Pasteur, Berthelot, and Claude Bernard, the only plausible grounds for its suit would have been that necessity mothers invention. "Who will believe me when I affirm that in the budget of public instruction not a farthing has been appropriated for the progress of science through laboratories!" exclaimed Pasteur in 1858—Claude Bernard appending to this the bleak conclusion that "laboratories are the tombs of scientists."

Notwithstanding the Palace of Industry, and an emperor who had the imperial household eat from dishes made of that wondrous new metal, aluminum, efforts to legitimate a scientific bachelor's degree, to acquaint students with their hands and their eyes proved largely futile until 1870 and France's military debacle at Sedan. Germany furnished *les modernes* the weapon they needed in their struggle with *les anciens*. And yet, even wounded national pride could not profoundly alter a formalist disposition to segregate mind from matter and culture from the everyday.* Holding theoretical work in much higher esteem than experimental science, the culture that produced such great mathematicians as Viète, Descartes, Pascal, Lagrange, Laplace, Cauchy, Hermite, Henri Poincaré, Lebesgue, and d'Ocagne produced no comparable family of Franklins, Faradays, and Joules. When, in the early 1880s Jules Ferry, a minister of public instruction bent upon changing this state of affairs, declared: "la leçon des choses à la base de tout," (let us learn all our basic lessons from things), he knew that to juxtapose "lesson" and "things" was to invite failure in rhetoric for having perpetrated an oxymoron.

Mounted on pedestals of Latin grammar and scientific logic, the *tête forte* was disposed to take a condescending view of women in general, to regard himself as the bearer of a rational design and womankind as innately mobile, unfinished, weak. "The weakness of woman's

---

* It could, on the contrary, reinforce it. Renan's pronouncement that "it was not, as has been said, the German grade-school teacher who prevailed at Sadowa but German science" hints of the feeling that science had plighted its troth with Germany, that it was not so much at home in France as across the Rhine. To what extent the formalist tradition permeated military minds may be judged from the belief in magic borders (the Maginot Line, the *cordon sanitaire*, the myth of an "impenetrable" Ardennes Forest), in a priori, geometrical constructions that made mobilization and movement supererogatory, costing France the offensive in three successive wars with Germany. Likewise, ballistic power. Paul Valéry did not much exaggerate when he said, by way of praising Pétain, the "hero of Verdun," who welcomed him into the French Academy: "You discovered simply this: *that gunfire kills*. . . . I am not suggesting that this was until then unknown. Only there was an inclination to ignore the fact. How could this have come about? Simply because theories can never be elaborated without some cost to reality. . . . It became clear to you that the prevailing tactical rules tended to give scant importance to this idea that *gunfire kills*."

brain, the mobility of her ideas, the social role she was destined to perform, the necessity of constant and perpetual resignation along with a kind of easy, indulgent charity: all this demands religion, a charitable, soft religion," proclaimed Napoleon Bonaparte, whose maxims formed an army that survived Waterloo intact and held sway through every subsequent reformulation of the French polity. During Louis Philippe's regime, Eliza Guizot, the prime minister's wife, wrote (on her husband's behalf no doubt) that for woman to "surrender" herself to "the pleasures of the mind, intellectual pursuits" was "dangerous," although "the pleasures of interior meditation, of pious contemplation cannot be taxed with frivolity or slackness." When a woman demonstrated intellectual power and political astuteness, she would more often than not earn the scorn of men who found such intellectuality to be a perversion of female nature (for example, in Daumier's album on "bluestockings" and "women socialists," the women are always portrayed as harpy-like) or else a masculine suit of clothes that exemplified the female's genius for dissemblance. "I had a strong prejudice against Madame Sand," Tocqueville declared in *Recollections*, recollecting his first encounter with the transvestite lioness of French letters, "for I detest women who systematically disguise the weakness of their sex, instead of interesting us by displaying themselves in their true colors."

The myth had it that woman's "true" self was an invalid better spared pleasures and exertions of the mind, an organism whose fragile constitution would experience some fundamental derangement in absorbing "strong" material or in ruminating ideas other than those characterized as soft. Did men prove their manhood by feats of retention? Woman, on the contrary, suffered comparison to a leaky vessel that sailed through life discharging sentiment and alms, blood and progeny. Without the iron hull that made men men, she could safely transport nothing but ethereal goods, baby flesh, or faith. "Woman was the giver of life, she was also the guardian of its refinements and amenities," wrote Esmé Wingfield-Stratford in an essay on Victorian England that summarizes attitudes prevalent across the Channel as well. "In consequence, among the middle and upper classes at least, it was designed to keep her out of the hurly-burly of the struggle for existence. Hence the fiction of a delicate, fairy-like creature on whom no wind must be allowed to blow too roughly. Hence too the idea that it was degrading for a lady to go out and earn her own living." Tradition deemed it appropriate that she bring her husband not only a dowry at marriage but a readiness forever after to dress the wounds dealt him in his daily campaign for advancement. *Parisian Letters*, a book co-authored during Louis Philippe's regime by Madame Emile de Girardin and the Vicomte de Launay, stated that "woman is not made to share the pains of man! No, she is made to console him for them, that is, to distract him from them." *

Woman's physical invalidism was not without certain moral implications that further justified her living as a legal minor under the government first of her father, then of her husband, and always of her Church—for in the "mobility of ideas" imputed to her by tradition, her protectors saw a generic inclination to stray, to "err." "Of all the avenues that lead to happiness, the surest for a young girl just out of convent school is the one chosen by her provident father," wrote Sainte-Beuve, suggesting with priestly unction that when given her own way a woman would likely desert the straight and narrow path. (Sainte-Beuve's own preference, incidentally, was for the *Vénus de carrefour*, or streetwalker.) "A young lady always knows too much," says Madame Vuillemain, the fanatical mother in Zola's novel *Pot-Bouille*. "Modesty above all," she continues, by way of describing her pedagogical regime:

No games in the staircase, the little girl always at home and in view, for little hoydens think about nothing but evil. The doors closed, the windows shut tight to keep out drafts, which bring nasty things in from the street.

---

* Ideally, then, she would perform much the same function that Renan ascribed to Christ, of whom he wrote in *The Life of Jesus*: "The Gospel was the supreme remedy for the troubles of vulgar life, a perpetual *sursum corda*, a powerful distraction from the miserable cares of the earth. . . . Thanks to Jesus, the most barren existence, the life most absorbed by sad or humiliating tasks looked out on a patch of heaven. In our busy civilizations, the memory of the free life of Galilee was like the perfume of another world, the 'dew of Hermon' that kept drought and vulgarity from parching God's preserve."

Religion was conventionally called *une affaire de femmes*, even by otherwise progressive-minded men, though on the whole those who sought to have science legitimated in the school curriculum struggled to have women freed from her sentence of life imprisonment in piety. In May 1870, Jules Ferry, for example, declared, in a speech given at the Sorbonne (a speech interrupted by frequent applause on the Left and frequent laughter on the Right): "Today there is a barrier between woman and man, between wife and husband, as a result of which many marriages, harmonious in appearance, cover the most profound difference of opinion, taste, feeling. Such marriages are not true marriages, for the true marriage, gentlemen, is a marriage of souls. Now then, tell me, how common is this marriage of souls? . . . The Church means to possess woman, and for that reason democracy must free her from its grasp. Democracy must choose under pain of death— woman must belong either to Science or to the Church."

Outside, never release the child's hand, accustom her to keeping her eyes lowered, so as to avoid unseemly spectacles. Where religion is concerned, nothing in excess, but as much of it as is needed to enforce moral curbs. Then, when she has grown up, engage schoolmistresses, don't put her in boarding school where the little innocents are corrupted; and attend her lessons, be eternally vigilant that she not know what she ought not to know, hide newspapers of course, and lock the library door.

A prenatal receptivity to whatever corrupts body and soul required that this porous being go forth, when forth she went, swathed in veils, imprisoned in trusses, and stuffed with precepts; that she live hermetically sealed, if not from the world outside, then from the secret intelligence given her by nature. It behooved young girls, who always knew too much, to unlearn what they knew and strive for innocent womanhood, just as it behooved fallen women to regret a childhood innocence not of this world. ("For a moment I built a whole future on your love, I longed for the country, I remembered my childhood—one always has a childhood to remember, whatever one may have become since then," declares "the lady of the camellias" on her deathbed; similarly, Emma Bovary puts on a white confirmation dress before she dies.)

At convent school, where nuns taught the demoiselle such skills as would serve the future wife in running a proper household, she spent some portion of the day, every day for five or six years, performing devotional exercises. Not until 1867 did there exist an alternative. And when, in that year, Victor Duruy, a remarkably courageous minister of public instruction, had prefects throughout France organize secondary-school courses for women (allowing mothers to sit beside their daughters in class as guardians of morality), the Church, including even liberal clergy, closed ranks against what it considered a threat to *féminité*, a doomsday assault on female ontology. "Young girls are reared for private life in private life; I demand that they not be led to the courses, the examinations, the diplomas, the award ceremonies that prepare men for public life," proclaimed Bishop Félix Dupanloup from his diocesan pulpit in Orléans, where Duruy struck the first blow, enrolling fifty-seven young women. "The secondary-school education of young women has remained for the most part religious, and the family, shaken to its foundation, owes to this education what purity it still possesses. . . . I demand that the state not encumber the future with female freethinkers." Nearly half a century later, Roger Martin du Gard com-

The drawing room in a fin-de-siècle Boulevard drama. From Le Théâtre

memorated the efficacy of this resistance in the novel *Jean Barois*, whose hero succumbs to the Catholicism of his provincial wife after epic struggles to free himself from Old France through socialism.

It would have been perfectly in character for a Frenchman who urged modesty on a wife who needed no such urging to seek on the Boulevard excitements irreconcilable with life *en famille*. Let us not assume, however, that champions of the family shrank from making themselves heard in this sphere where the fallen and the low otherwise reigned supreme. There was, for one, Alexandre Dumas *fils*, Dumas *père's* playwright son. So strenuously did he deplore irregular liaisons of the sort to which he owed his own illegitimate birth that the Académie française elected him an immortal. "You will use any weapon at your disposal to punish unfaithful wives," said the gentleman who welcomed him into France's most august assembly. "Let them beware, henceforth, of those pretty jade-handled knives that loiter on tabletops, of those pistols their husbands have been toting in their pockets and those shotguns forgotten in convenient corners. . . . Surely those women are stout-hearted indeed who would not recoil before this formidable apparatus of moralization." With Dumas *fils* the "well-made play" became indeed an apparatus of moralization, so constructed as to bring "the social law" home victorious while taking, en route, devious turns that gave the outlaw (courtesan, adulteress, rake, embezzler) a momentary but illusory advantage. Never was his audience allowed to emerge from the theater without the ruins of some foiled plot or the corpse of some illicit passion.

It could be said that Dumas wrote plays to purge theater, for his plots are typically "plots" against bourgeois order, his antagonists impostors who lead double lives or harbor dirty secrets, his denouements trial scenes in which the actor finds himself (or, more often, herself) unmasked, and his hero Society as represented by a stock character rather like the sleuth of modern detective novels, who unravels ill-begotten schemes with remarkably lucidity. This sleuth, whom Dumas called "the Reasoner," stood guard between stage and audience. However immoral a drama, the Reasoner was always there, orienting the public's moral perception from inside the play, assuring bourgeois spectators that they had the upper hand, distancing them from their own dark side with urbane analyses that reduced the "underworld" to something predictable, mechanistic, and, above all, weightless.* Familiar with the machinations of Sodom and Gomorrah as only he could be who had seen them rehearsed often before, he did not censor what occurred on stage but filtered it through his cynical intelligence, or tamed it in neat bons mots, in set speeches made to be taken home and quoted verbatim.

---

* At one point in *Le Demi-Monde*, the Reasoner, momentarily outwitted by the courtesan with whom he is vying for the moral well-being of a friend, says to her: "Vous êtes d'une jolie force, vous!" Even in acknowledging her "power," he reduces it with *jolie* to the dimensions of a toy. He is, in short, toying with her.

"They quote his repartees and peddle his aphorisms. The number of people reputed for their wit who plagiarize him every day is countless," observed one critic, Hippolyte Parigot. "When he mints an image in one of his plays . . . this image becomes common coin, however banal and complicated it may be," wrote Zola.

The evidence suggests that if officialdom had had its way, it would have required every published plot to come equipped with some Reasoner. When, for example, the government brought a charge of immorality against *Madame Bovary* in 1857, the imperial prosecutor arguing to have Flaubert's novel banned from circulation declared: "Who in this book can condemn this woman? No one. Such is our conclusion. In this

---

Before 1914, heavies from the Comédie-Française starred every summer in classical spectaculars at the Roman arenas of Nîmes, Arles, and Béziers. Shown here is a scene at Béziers, with the classical cityscape reconstituted in cardboard. From Le Théâtre

book there is not one character who can condemn her. If you find a single wise character, a single principle in virtue of which adultery is stigmatized, then I am wrong. But if there is not a single character who can make her bow her head, not an idea or line in virtue of which adultery is scourged, then it is I who am right—the book is immoral." It seems likely he had in mind one incarnation or another of the Dumas custodian who upheld Society's best interests in the playground, taking care that children not be left to their own devices, that the imagination not run amok, that virtue always win the day. What he voiced was a fear prevalent among bourgeois that without some such figure anything might be possible, that *tout serait possible*. And, indeed, time proved him right, for time would see the formula Dumas *fils* deployed on behalf of a rational order turned to the account of an epistemological wilderness by playwrights like Luigi Pirandello. In *Henry IV, Six Characters in Search of an Author*, and *It Is So (If You Think So)*, the Reasoner became the sleuth of an insoluble mystery, or the advocate of madness who indicts the criminal audience, proclaiming private delusions more real than the so-called real world.

Flaubert's prosecutor said in his brief against *Madame Bovary* that the novel was "a painting admirable from the point of view of talent, but a painting execrable from the point of view of morality. . . . Monsieur Flaubert can embellish his paintings with all the resources of art but without any of its caution; there is in his work no gauze, no veils— it shows nature in the raw." His metaphor made it plain that it was incumbent on the Reasoner to supervise painted images as well as stage pictures. An artist who brought off technical tours de force equivalent to the well-made play, who fashioned antiques, and gave female nudes the prophylactic air of soap carvings, could anticipate handsome rewards. If he aspired to the Prix de Rome (or even if he did not) he would spend long hours copying paintings in the Louvre, whose dimly-lit galleries were obstacle courses where young men sat at wooden easels propped three-deep. Like the ideal wife, the ideal artist served a purpose nonetheless significant for being largely decorative. He couched his patron in refinement, he dowered him with classical allusions, he consoled him for the hardships he endured with pastoral *féeries*. In an address to England's Royal Academy in 1840, François Guizot left no doubt that the bourgeoisie required not original eyes but, on the contrary, erudite and skilled forgers. "The statues of great men have come to populate public squares," he said, as though such statues constituted the oligarchy of a stable civilization. He added: "It is a happy thing, gentlemen, [in] the [era] and [present state] of modern societies. What would you do, what would any of us do with these hordes incessantly raising themselves to the level of civilization, of influence, of freedom, if they were so consumed by thirst for material well-being and by political passions as to have nothing in mind but thoughts of enriching themselves and fighting for their rights? They need other interests, other sentiments, other pleasures."

Now distracting middle-class condotierre from issues of pith and moment, now carving effigies of them, the artist was implicitly there to proffer a mirror from beyond the grave. Art had no official status except *outside*, which is to say that officialdom shook none but dead hands. As for those who detested the "other interests, other sentiments, other pleasures" of the bourgeoisie's trompe-l'oeil Otherworld, they were banned from the Salon, an annual bazaar organized under official auspices. And when, in 1863, Louis Napoleon gave them leave to hang their work in separate premises, the critical brotherhood lost no time comparing this Salon des Refusés to Charenton, the French counterpart of Bedlam. How undignified of the State to conduct itself like a fairground entrepreneur who displays freaks in his booth and charges admission! declared Maxime du Camp with mock charity. Better that "monstrosities" (among them, paintings by Manet, Pissarro, Whistler, Cézanne) be kept quarantined lest the canvas end up contaminating the social fabric.

Guizot at the Royal Academy spoke on behalf of men who feared the socioeconomic vehicle they themselves had made and ridden upward. As the vehicle accelerated, with new money aging in a generation and poor men waxing rich overnight, their apprehensions increased. Change, or the feeling that any trick of fortune might end their reign, induced them to stultify themselves for dear life, to celebrate stultification and embrace rigid forms. Under the absolute monarchy, no word could be uttered as theater, no line shown as painting, no note played as music without the king's leave. Theoretically, art sprang from his head and existed as art insofar as it reflected or commemorated him. When the king was beheaded, his authority devolved on neoclassical conventions to which the *haute bourgeoisie* could not have clung more tenaciously had it been a candidate for the guillotine. Academic art, like the

(LEFT) *The stance of a tragic heroine, and* (RIGHT) *a convincing rock about to be hurled by a* monstre sacré. *Both at the Comédie-Française, circa 1900. From* Le Théâtre

implacable face worn by hysterics, shielded its champions against the specter of alienation. Did they feel invaded by masses from the countryside? They could rejoice in old classical company. Had the shape of life become tentative and its rhythm breakneck? The more reason to take solace in meticulous lines and glassy finishes that reflected the world as distantly as a monocled eye. "No modern nuance alters their faces . . . wrapped in an atmosphere of the past," wrote an admiring critic about the figure in one of William Bouguereau's decorative allegories.

What such bourgeois found lunatic about Impressionist art (and in academic circles Impressionism became synonymous with mental degeneration) was its lack of "finish," the shimmer of life or process that it often embodied. Théophile Gautier, whose idealist slogan "Art for Art's sake" endeared him to the upper classes, could write, a propos of a Barbizon painter [Daubigny]: "It is really too bad that he . . . should be satisfied with an impression and should neglect details to the extent that he does. His pictures are nothing more than rough drafts left in a very unfinished state." Some thirty years later Monet, Pissarro, and Sisley escaped him altogether. Those who shared his incomprehension shared his view that through art one found asylum from the *horrible quotidien* and from the rambunctious century. To abolish detail, to leave brushstrokes on one's canvas, to take pleasure representing things familiar or ephemeral was to profane the temple.

In this sense no one expressed the relationship between artist and bourgeoisie more naïvely than Napoleon Bonaparte, who would sometimes have his portraitist, Jean-Baptiste Isabey, impersonate him at masked balls so that he could behold himself from outside. "Were I not a conqueror," he once declared, "I would like to have been a sculptor." Conquest was the quest for an absolute self; in conquering the world he would have immobilized it, or won that vantage point from which he yearned to contemplate his imperial "I" after the fashion of a believer contemplating a votive image. Indeed, Napoleon founded a necropolis, Père-Lachaise, where eminences similarly interned by history would keep the Academy's sculptors well employed throughout the nineteenth century, like actors hiring impresarios to carve them roles more durable than any to be had on the world's stage. Even when outside Père-Lachaise the ever more rapid revolution of Fortune's wheel made it necessary to build a *cimetière de monuments*, a storage shed for statuary commemorating events and figures weathered by ideological storms, there at least they could exult in their healthy patina.

While the custodians of aesthetic order held the Impressionists responsible for corrupting morals, moralists held "provincials" or "foreigners" responsible for transforming a once virtuous capital into an Impressionist canvas. To the moralist, the villain was anyone who blurred social boundary lines, who skewed proportions, who celebrated fugitiveness, who glided through France as an epiphenomenon of the general havoc spread by railroads. Railroads came to represent, in didactic commentary, the preeminent symbol of an erotic force that would, unless stringent measures were taken, humiliate the French paterfamilias, destroy the French family, usurp the French mind, and substitute for France itself a mongrel pornocracy governed by queens all in the image of Manet's *Olympia*. "The railroads, exercising a bizarre influence on the intellectual as well as the economic state of society, pour into Paris every day a mobile but tightly packed mass of bustling provincials whose literary culture is, to say the least, slapdash and vagrant," wrote a critic named J. J. Weiss in *Theater and Mores*, referring to the exodus from rural France that saw Paris' population increase, between 1830 and 1880, from one million to nearly three. Dumas *fils* also arraigned the railroad network. In *Francillon*, he had a Reasoner, Henri de Simeux, blame society's ills on "the invasion of women from abroad, the glorification of courtesans, the daily trainload of exotic mores that enter the city on every line, hastening local degenerations," and he reiterated this diagnosis in his preface to *La Dame Aux Camélias:*

> Railroads were created. The first rapid fortunes made by the first speculators seized upon pleasure, instantaneous love being one of the first needs. . . . The new transportation facilities brought to Paris a host of rich young people from the provinces and from abroad. The newly enriched, most of whom had risen from the lowest classes, did not fear to compromise themselves with such and such a girl who had won herself a name at the Bal Mabille or the Château des Fleurs. It was necessary to provide for the sensual appetites of a progressing population, as well as for its physical nourishment.

It would seem inevitable that after Sedan, when Ernest Renan conferred Prussia's victory on German science, Dumas *fils* should have ascribed France's debacle to what he called *La Bête* (The Beast), to the conquest of the French head and capital not by foreign soldiers but by resident aliens.*

---

* Note, too, that Zola entitled his novel about railroads *La Bête humaine*, intending to depict, as he put it, "the transit of the entire world, the opposition between these trains moving toward the twentieth century and the dark drama played out there, the fauves squatting underneath civilization."

"Quos Deus vult perdere prius dementat" summed up the wisdom with which conservative bourgeois prosecuted courtesans, usurers, and immigrants from the hinterland: "Whom God wishes to destroy, he first drives mad." Anticipating Vichy, whose supporters would likewise hold the homebred foreigner (Jew, Socialist, female militant) responsible for France's downfall, they were, though they would not often admit it, of the opinion that in Kaiser Wilhelm Providence had dispatched an agent to punish France, to cleanse the body politic, to restore the bourgeoisie its reason, to deliver Paris from corruption. By the same token, when General Weygand made Hitler a gift of Paris rather than arm working-class Parisians, he obeyed a centenarian call to defend the seat of bourgeois power, propriety, and tradition against the enemies besieging it from within.

What dictated the surrender of Paris in 1940 was the same fear that had prompted such academic luminaries as Meissonier, Bouguereau, Charles Garnier, and Dumas *fils* to declare war on the Eiffel Tower fifty years earlier in a "proclamation of artists" worth quoting at length:

Writers, painters, sculptors, architects, passionate lovers of the heretofore intact beauty of Paris, we come to protest with all our strength, with all our indignation, in the name of betrayed French taste, in the name of threatened French art and history, against the erection in the heart of our capital of the useless and monstrous Eiffel Tower, which the public has scornfully and rightly dubbed the tower of Babel. Without being blind chauvinists, we have the right to proclaim publicly that Paris is without rival in the world. Along its streets and wide boulevards, beside its admirable riverbanks, amid its magnificent promenades, stand the most noble monuments to which human genius has ever given birth. The soul of France, the creator of masterpieces, shines among this august proliferation of stone. Italy, Germany, Flanders, so legitimately proud of their artistic heritage, possess nothing comparable to ours, and Paris attracts curiosity and admiration from all corners of the universe. Are we to let all that be profaned? Is the City of Paris to associate itself any longer with the baroque, mercantile imaginings of a builder of machines, and thus dishonor and disfigure itself irreparably? For the Eiffel Tower, which even commercial America would not have, is without a doubt the dishonor of Paris. . . . When foreigners visit our Exposition they will cry out in astonishment, "Is it this horror that the French have created to give us an idea of their vaunted taste? . . ." All one must do to understand our case is to imagine for a moment a dizzily ridiculous tower dominating Paris like a black and gigantic smokestack crushing beneath its barbarous mass Notre-Dame, the Sainte-Chapelle, the Tour Saint-Jacques, the Louvre, the dome of the Invalides, the Arc de Triomphe, all our humiliated monuments, all our raped architecture disappearing in this stupefying dream. And for the next twenty years we will see cast over the entire city, still trembling with the genius of so many centuries, cast like a spot of ink, the odious shadow of the odious column of bolted metal.

The tower thus stood condemned as a vulgar solecism upon which Paris's stately proportions would come to grief, as an infringement of the modern world on an historical canvas awarded first prize by the Academy, and finally, as a tower of Babel garbling with foreign languages the mind that had elaborated in pure French or pure Latin a classic urban oration.

This document calls to mind Zola's novel *L'Assommoir* where, in one magnificent scene, workers who wander down from Montmartre during a wedding celebration erupt upon the Louvre and Tuileries, which they had never seen before, like Vandals suddenly introduced to Rome. But an equally pertinent, indeed a companion, footnote would be the exchange that took place between Matisse and Picasso in May 1940, just as France's General Staff, who feared the Commune of 1871 more than the imminent German occupation, was preparing to surrender Paris without a fight. "Our generals, what about our generals? What are they doing?" Matisse asked Picasso. Picasso answered: "Our generals, why they're the professors of the Ecole des Beaux-Arts."

Needless to say, the courtesan would not have seemed so invasive had art for art's sake not been something very like a clandestine apology of pleasure for pleasure's. Nor would the *fils de famille*, the playboy son, have cut quite so dangerous a figure in homiletic theater had he not clung to his mythic counterpart, the *père de famille*, as inseparably as madness to pure reason, or sumptuous baubles to a categorical imperative of toil. Dumas *fils* perhaps fancied himself the prophet of an inherently bourgeois *fait accompli* when he concluded his preface to *Camille* with the admonition that "if woman is allowed to go on doing what she does, in fifty years at most our nephews (we will no longer have children, only nephews) shall see whether anything remains of the family, of religion, of virtue, of morality, and of marriage in your beautiful land of France whose cities will have broad streets that converge at circles and circles built around squares in one of which it will be appropriate to erect a statue commemorating useless Truths."

The well-made city designed by Louis Napoleon, who once declared that "I want to be a second Augustus because Augustus made a city of marble," was only two decades old when Art Nouveau invaded it, junglelike, wilting its patrician façades and planting stalks of lily on either side of the portals to its subway. Rome, even Roman-alphabet letters, succumbed to a Levantine force of gravity. The Académie des Beaux-Arts, which had kept its custodial eye on architecture for nearly two centuries, rang in the new one by awarding the First Grand Prize to a student who had submitted plans for a casino and thermal bathing establishment of Caracallan proportions. For all the energy Dumas *fils* expended against the Furies, after 1906, the year theater censorship was abolished, they would return vengefully and, borne aloft by playwrights like Henri Bataille and Henri Bernstein, find themselves acclaimed by a public that found nothing more pertinent than the consummation of marriage in adulterous beds, except the consummation of adultery in incestuous cribs. Still worse lay in store. Where Guizot, Comte, and Renan had hewn a statue of man real through and through, their twentieth-century *fils de famille,* the Surrealists, would, on page one of *La Révolution Surréaliste,* festoon passport photographs of themselves with their eyes shut tight around a naked Madonna, announcing that they meant to restore the soul by sanctifying the Unconscious.

In December 1896 the Boulevard staged a gala for its most celebrated heroine, Sarah Bernhardt. Although time had caught up with her, so had the age—a new *fin-de-siècle* generation that paid homage to the ideal of epicene beauty she could no longer quite embody at the age of fifty-one, after a stomach operation. Hipless and supple, like the African cat she kept in her town house, she still insisted, as she always had, that "I am a woman for whom common sense does not exist." Five hundred people gathered at the Grand Hôtel, among them numerous dramatists and men of letters who held forth during pauses in the banquet. When they had done eating and orating, a caravan of one hundred hackney coaches transported them across town to the Théâtre de la Renaissance. There, in her own palace, Bernhardt performed excerpts from Racine's *Phèdre,* singing French with a voice of silvery resonance, and afterward reappeared on the stage to mount a throne. Twenty poets stood at her feet, each in turn delivering a sonnet written for the occasion. It was generally agreed that Edmond Rostand, whose lovelorn rhetorician Cyrano de Bergerac was to take Paris by storm several months later, had quite the better of rivals with verse like:

> Queen of attitude and princess of gestures,
> In times like these, devoid of madness, you, ardent soul, protest;
> You speak verse, you die of love, your flight lifts
> You out of sight. . . .
> You extend arms of dream, then arms of flesh,
> And when Phèdre shows, we are all of us incestuous.

The well-made world was decidedly coming undone. Dumas *fils's* moral fervor had given way to a spirit that embraced Rostand's campy classicism, and the defense of family had broken down before the unabashed adoration of *monstres sacrés*. When Orestes strode down a Spartan boulevard, surrounded by loose women, singing—

> With these women Orestes
> Makes papa's money dance;
> Papa laughs, however, as
> It is Greece who will pay.

—what critic would have dared to rebuke Offenbach for profaning antiquity, as critics had done during the hey-day of *La Belle Hélène*? At Boulevard theaters Parisians indulged their taste for sexual promiscuity without receiving absolution from a Reasoner. Which is not to say that Reasoners did not abound elsewhere in France. By 1896 Alfred Dreyfus had spent a year on Devil's Island and Picquart, chief of Military Intelligence, pieced together the special-delivery letter that would plunge the country into civil war.

CHAPTER II

✦ ✦ ✦ ✦

THE SPEECHLESS
TRADITION

L ike the courtesans who queened it over the *fin-de-siècle* Boulevard under aristocratic pseudonyms, the Boulevard itself concealed common origins, for originally that term designated the Boulevard du Temple, a thoroughfare on the Right Bank between Paris's northeast wall and the Saint-Antoine ghetto, where theaters of every shape
and description stood side by side. The Théâtre de la Gaïté, the Théâtre
Lyrique, the Théâtre du Cirque, the Funambules, the Petit-Lazari, the
Théâtre Historique—these establishments, of which the first had risen in
1760, catered more to the plebs than to the middle class, their stock-in-
trade being mime, tightrope acrobatics, puppet shows, performing animals, and, above all, melodrama. As a consequence of the blood profusely shed on stage every night, of virtuous maidens wronged and
knaves brought to justice, the Boulevard du Temple was styled "Boulevard of Crime." Here Alexandre Dumas set up house when he was
made unwelcome by the Comédie-Française. Aristocrats who liked to
slum it found ample opportunity to mingle with lowlives in outdoor
cafés like The Turkish Garden. To the bourgeois, however (not to all,
but certainly to those who set store by their reputations, or those for
whom the expression *épater les bourgeois* had been custom-tailored), it
was a place best shunned. Proper folk did not necessarily rejoice when
Baron Haussmann reduced most of its theaters to rubble in 1862; nor
did they mourn their disappearance.

Lying outside the cultural boundary line that had been drawn by

seventeenth-century grammarians and garrisoned ever since by monar-
chical institutions like the Académie and the Théâtre-Français, this original Boulevard was a barbarian purlieu, a foil to classical France, a
subliminal zone where popular forms—forms outgrown and despised—
survived unofficially. Extending back to the commercial fair from which
it descended in a direct line, its history had been one of incessant guer-
rilla warfare against the Comédie-Française, of skirmishes with a censor
determined that it should remain dumb and antic. Jean-Jacques Rousseau went so far as to say that it did not even exist in the eyes of *le
monde* (a word signifying either "high society" or "the world"), that
"spectators . . . have become so delicate they would be afraid to compromise themselves at certain theaters as in certain homes, and would
not deign to see performances given by people of lesser condition than
themselves. It is as if they were the only inhabitants of the earth; all the
rest is nothing in their judgment. . . . Those who go by foot are not of
the world (*monde*); they are . . . men of the lower order, people of the
other world." But exist it did. Indeed, the aesthetic conventions by
which the ruling class enshrined its culture enshrined what it sought to
exclude, conferring upon the lower world, the "other" world, or the
nonworld a kind of sacred ignobility.

The Saint-Germain Fair, which took place in a vast enclosure on
the Left Bank bounded on the south by the Church of Saint-Sulpice and
on the north by the huge Abbey of Saint-Germain, was an event of
tremendous importance, economically and socially, from the fifteenth
century until its decline in the 1780s. Every year, for some three hundred, it would open to fanfares on the morning after Candlemas, February 3, and close just before Christ's arrival on Palm Sunday, spanning
the Lenten season. Merchants hawked their wares morning, noon, and
night until ten o'clock, when the innumerable candles that lit the pavilions—and occasionally, in 1762 for example, set them ablaze—were extinguished in observance of curfew. Although pedestrian and horse
often collided near the gateway, owing to the fact that the carriage
trade would habitually enter the marketplace at full gallop, once the
customers found themselves inside, rich and poor thronged together—
remarkably unmindful of their social differences, like passengers setting

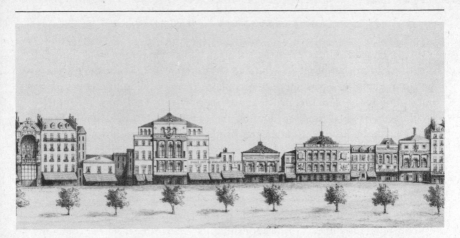

The alignment of theaters on the Boulevard du Temple before the reconstruction of Paris under Napoleon III. Bibliothèque Nationale

sail on a ship of fools. "There, everyone mingles pell-mell, masters with valets and lackeys, rogues with honest folk," wrote one chronicler. "The most refined gentlewomen, the most fetching doxies, the most subtle cheats are, if one may say so, intertwined."

The first to profit from this kermis was the Saint-Germain Abbey that towered overhead, reminding entrepreneurs—those entrepreneurs it could license—that some portion of their earnings should be set aside for their salvation. In the words of a Montmartre whore who together with her sisters migrated across the river every February, "fairtime is the vintage season," and everyone—both buyers and vendors—worked the vineyard of The Lord. To tumblers, puppeteers, magicians, actors who lived betwixt and between, now wandering through the countryside, now holding forth on the Pont-Neuf, the abbots of Saint-Germain gladly extended their hospitality. During this one season, business came before theology, and the *comédiens forains* (foreign actors) drummed up a great deal of it, attracting crowds wherever they set up their platforms (called *tréteaux*, literally "planks"), whether on the fairground or on the narrow streets and culs-de-sac surrounding it.

Any attempt by these *comédiens forains* to make their platforms something more than a basis for acrobatic feats and interludic quips, to elaborate a regular farce or to construct a theatrical abode would have brought them trouble from the Confrérie de la Passion, the Brotherhood of the Passion. Older even than the fair, this association was the off-spring of Parisian burghers who had chartered it in 1402 for the purpose its name implies—to stage religious plays. In 1518, King François I gave it a monopoly on acting in Paris, a monopoly it upheld long after it deserted its original function. During the 1530s and 1540s, when Reform tore Catholic Europe asunder, the Brotherhood fell into a slough, muddling the sacred and the profane so completely that its biblical entertainments could not be told from low farce. Though nominally faithful to the emblems of Christ's Passion that ornamented its lintel, between its lintel and its stage it somehow got everything confused. By 1548, when an archdiocesan order forbade it to perform plays that touched upon religious subjects, thus abolishing its repertoire, it had become all but senile and might appropriately have died a natural death but for its splendid theater, the Hôtel de Bourgogne (which was situated on the Right Bank, just north of the central market), and for its feudal monopoly. It rented the one to traveling companies; it availed itself of the other to amass great wealth, levying imposts on every performance given in Paris. A tax farmer more than a patron of theater, the Brotherhood held fast to its preserve, suing poachers and invariably receiving favorable judgments. Not until 1595 did Parlement find against it. In that year, the fairs (for Paris boasted more than one fair, if none quite as large as Saint-Germain) were thrown open to provincial actors who had made good their case that the fairground, constituting an island within the city, a legally idiosyncratic enclave, ought to protect them from the Brotherhood's venal clutches.

There matters rested for eighty-five years. While the Hôtel de Bourgogne's stage became increasingly elevated, rising from the level of early-seventeenth-century buffoons like Bruscambille and Fat William to that of Corneille and Racine, the smutty farces otherwise known as *parades* staged at fairgrounds year after year evoke a mental region by and large innocent of civilization. Some other civilization might have tolerated such innocence but not the French, whose sovereign, calling himself as he did the *Rex Christianissimus,* voiced a certain weakness for hyperbole, a repugnance for disparate modes, contingent forms, the imperatives of custom, the accidents of time and space. Thus, when the Brotherhood of the Passion expired at last, its orphaned monopoly languished only two years before finding embodiment in a new, far more powerful institution. On October 21, 1680, Louis XIV affixed his signature to an edict that brought into being the Comédie-Française:

His Majesty, having deemed it suitable to unite the two companies of actors, one established at the Hôtel de Bourgogne, the other in the rue de Guénégaud in Paris so that henceforth there be a single company in order to render more perfect the performance of plays . . . has commanded and commands that they be united into one and the same company . . . and, so as to give them the means of perfecting themselves ever more, His Majesty wishes that this company perform plays in Paris, forbidding all other French actors to establish themselves in the city and faux-bourgs unless expressly granted authorization to do so by His Majesty.

To be sure, the perfection thus enjoined upon the Comédie-Française had a moral sense consonant with Catholic usage. But, in addition, the Oneness that was both a sine qua non and inherent attribute

The Saint-Germain-des-Prés fairground in the seventeenth century.
Bibliothèque Nationale

of such perfection bespoke rational ideals applied by the new age to beauty as well as to kingship, to the small stage and to the large one, to the King's Players and to the monarch himself (described by one contemporary as possessing the "solemnity of a *roi de théâtre*"). Malebranche, writing in *Christian Meditations*—"It is true the visible world would be more perfect if the continents and seas had more regular shapes than they do . . . if they were not so disorderly"—was not more a child of Cartesian perception than Louis. Like his vassals sequestered at Versailles, where a geometrical landscape coerced the eye to sight an absolute point on the horizon, Louis's actors, disporting themselves before a Serlio backdrop (whose perspective lines made all viewpoints relative to One and conferred upon the stage a universal dimension), *necessarily formed a single company.*

To suggest that Louis conceived this theater, as he did Versailles, in the service of a cognitive or meta-cognitive design, that dramatic art was a dream reflecting the dreamer's will to see all and know all, that "One Stage" argued "One Spectator" might seem exorbitant were it not for his legion of spies, for his daily correspondence with informers, for his avowal that of all things nothing gave him greater pleasure than to have "eyes open all over the earth, to learn the news of provinces and nations, the secrets of all the courts, the humors and failings of princes and their ministers, to be informed of the infinite number of things that one thinks we do not know, to see around us that which people strive to hide . . . to discover the true views of courtiers, their hidden interests." Nowhere and everywhere, he would, it seems sufficiently clear, have occupied a viewpoint where all lines of perspective converge, like the puppeteer manipulating strings.* As power was one and indivisible, so was the geopolitical and aesthetic space of its manifestation. "Le goût est un," declared the Marquis d'Argenson, an eighteenth-century statesman and memorialist whose father was the first to occupy the post of theatrical censor created by Louis XIV. "Taste is singular."

The censor's office was as much a guardian of absolute taste as the

---

* By the same token, Louis XIV translated social rank into an order of cognition, and the solar emblem into real sight, declaring in a memoir written for his son: "As he [the king] is of a rank superior to all other men, he sees things more perfectly than they do, and he ought to trust rather to the inner light than to information which reaches him from outside. . . . Occupying . . . the place of God, we are sharers of His knowledge as well as His authority."

Théâtre-Français, and the circumstances that led directly to its creation by Louis help to elucidate further the principle it served. In 1697 Paris's chief constable boarded shut the Théâtre Italien on orders from Versailles, deporting the Italian comedy troupe whose forebears had first come to Paris a century before, lured there by France's Medici queens. "So long as they were content to wallow in ordure on the stage and sometimes in impieties, one did nothing more than laugh at them. But they took it into their heads to stage a play entitled *The False Prude*, wherein Madame de Maintenon was easily recognized. . . . After three or four performances they received an order to close their theater and leave the kingdom within a month," wrote Saint-Simon years later. Guilty though they were of having planned to stage *The False Prude* (Madame de Maintenon's piety, it should be said, made people the more disposed to see this former governess of the royal bastards as a female Tartuffe), the Italians never in fact did so. Exile was therefore punishment incommensurate with the crime, unless it were suited not to their offense alone but to the comic form itself—not, in other words, to a specific indiscretion but to the socio-aesthetic postulate of Italian comedy. High and low were born to share a single stage, for *commedia dell'arte* had one parent in popular tradition (the Roman Atellanes), the other in classical literature. Even when they exercised forbearance with regard to Versailles, zanni or valets could not but twit gentlemen in the scenario, just as gentlemen could not but suffer their physical presence. Actors recruited by troupes like I Comici Gelosi and I Comici Confidenti had to play not only hoi-polloi but artistocratic love duos, whose rhetorical improvisations were contrapuntally indispensable to the valets' slapstick. A Renaissance critic who praised the "Ciceronian fluency" of one actor and the gestural, often obscene *lazzis* of another did not admonish them to keep separate company.

High and low, the rational and the ludic became incongruous only later, during the Counter-Reformation, when a couth God and a couth Muse enjoined Churchmen to purge animals and nudes from religious iconography, and the upper classes to excommunicate the lower from dramaturgical rites. In 1639, La Mesnardière, an aesthetician of note, upbraided the sixteenth-century commentator Castelvestro for having dared to speculate that poetry was entertainment originally conceived (in La Mesnardière's words) "not only to divert, but to divert the common people and not only the common people but the vile, crude, igno-

The horseplay (lazzi) of commedia dell'arte zannis. Before he became the pretty simpleton of Marivaux's polite comedy, Harlequin wore a cat-faced mask and carried a lath or slapstick (at left).

rant, stupid populace." Should a play express noble sentiments, the common herd could grasp it only visually, he claimed, stigmatizing by implication that other herd—the herd of low words fated to be driven from French like demons from Gaderene. "The crude multitude can derive no pleasure from a serious, solemn, truly tragic discourse and . . . this many-headed monster can know at most only the ornaments of theater." *

---

* A passage from Corneille's *Horace* is interesting in this connection. The titular hero, defining aristocratic *virtu*, says: "Rarely does an issue arise / That displays the virtue of a great heart in all its scope. / According to the occasion it acts more or less / And appears to its witnesses strong or weak. / The common man, who sees only the bark of things / Judges its force by measuring its effect." Whereas the aristocrat is always equal to himself, which is to say that he owns himself and owning himself, owns

What did this contempt for lower-class "sight" signify? Clearly, the function of illusionist paraphernalia, which took firm hold in France somewhere around 1640—the stage curtain, the deep perspective backdrop—was to chasten the eye rather than to delight it, to frame a noble image rather than to stir the senses, to enforce belief in an ideal world, where figures deploying themselves ceremoniously and using language estranged from everyday life became artifacts of *le style noble,* that is to say, incarnate emblems of rhetorical movement. Here again, Versailles and the classical stage reflect each other. Just as Madame de Maintenon, who wrote reproachfully of Louis that "he wishes to observe all the externals [of religion], but not its spirit. He will never miss a station or a penance, but he will never understand that it is necessary to humble himself and enter into the true spirit of penitence," did not surmise that the gestural vocabulary of religious observance might be for Louis what the clockwork movement of Creation was for rationalist divines, neither presumably did she understand that classical stagecraft sought to illustrate a state of Grace. Louis, ever fearful of things buried from view—whether in the mind, in the city, in the wood, or in the future—built a formalist paradise whose ritual externalized and codified court life, making of it a theatrically legible surface. And his Théâtre-Français, where etiquette forbade nature to throw violent scenes, to use crude words, to prompt brusque movements, to extemporize in any way, was equally the ritualistic celebration of absolute power. Here, something rather like Descartes's distinction between the fantasmagoria apprehended by our senses and objective, measurable expanse came to form a proscenium border, a "fourth wall" immuring the hieratic yonder from a world in flux. The lower classes—that clamorous, "many-headed" monster—might converse anywhere but on a Parisian stage, or use any language on stage: except French. Dramatic dialogue was assigned quasi-liturgical significance, and drama became a representation of Order that for all its Aristotelian pieties was nonetheless magical, the stage a culturally exclusive neighborhood, and the actor a transcendent

the power he exercises over others, the *peuple,* the common people, are outsiders judging the world by its changing aspect or "effects" (a word that was to enter theatrical parlance. Purists of the nineteenth century would decry theater that endeavored to capture the audience by spectacular "effects"). Where aristocrats were heir to a *moral tradition,* commoners were children of nature, living in a perpetual present, apprehending the world through their senses alone.

marionette. Whatever forces raged "outside," they would remain contingent, "unreal," or foreign so long as they lacked a tongue to articulate and thus legitimate themselves as theater. Conversely, the powers-that-were availed themselves of their religio-theatrical monopoly to project into the scenic box an image that time could not usurp, to fashion an identity that was proof against historical estrangement. Like the bishop, the general, and the judge in Genet's play *The Balcony*, they idealized authority beyond the mere exercise of power, making themselves unassailable inside a theater.

During the 1690s, the Italian comedy troupe had begun more and more to embroider scenarios in French. Among other factors that accounted for its deportation was, paradoxically, its assimilation. Where Arlecchino always wagged a phallic slapstick with impunity, he lost his innocence once he took the name Harlequin, and forfeited any claim to moral allowances made for those of foreign birth. Culturally, lackeys and instincts had no place in France; theirs was silent country. Given their due by the censor provided they kept dumb or spoke gibberish, directly they ventured to express themselves in French they threatened to suborn the mind of Culture.

Driven off the legitimate stage, *commedia dell'arte*'s stock characters went underground, so to speak, entrenching themselves in the Saint-Germain and Saint-Laurent fairs from which vantage point they would snipe at officialdom for half a century. Although the battle had already been joined there (a puppetmaker named Alexandre Bertrand had dared in 1690 to erect a small theater on the Saint-Germain fairground and to stage a play with human actors; outcries by the King's Players brought about its demolition), it would no doubt have ended soon enough but for Harlequin, Mezzetin, Polichinelle, Crispin, and Scaramouche. This rabble helped focus and sustain dramatic energy by providing a tradition, by constituting inherently resilient types, by being

An eighteenth-century harlequinade entitled Harlequin, King of China. *The placard with writing on it was used to circumvent the interdiction against speech.* Les Théâtres de la Foire (*Maurice Albert*)

LE ROY DE LA CHINE

Frappons l'Insolent qui m'outrage.
Mais je ne le vois plus. O Dieux!
Il trompe ma fureur. J'enrage.
Quel autre Objet s'offre à mes yeux.

to the lower class what heroes of classical antiquity were to the upper. While the King's Players—or "Romans," as they were called in fairground parlance ("Curse the Romans, and repeat after us: May the Great Devil take them away!")—spent their stage lives modeling Jean Bérain's plumed helmets and martial tunics, the zanni had the ductile nature of survivors. Men for all seasons, they were putty that virtuoso hands like Alain René Lesage and Alexis Piron, who wrote innumerable satires for the fairground, could shape to any fantasy or polemical occasion: Harlequin particularly. Harlequin emerged as the quintessential non-Roman, the supreme antihero of a subversive culture.

Harlequinades, like Harlequin, assumed as many forms as the imagination could devise to skirt censorship, prefiguring in certain ways what has come to be known as absurdist theater. The law of silence made every such spectacle something in the nature of a prison-house drama; every actor in it became a child condemned to express himself through physical signs, and the French language was the freedom denied him. However vigilant they were, those who upheld that law—the constabulary, representatives of the Comédie-Française and of the Opéra—could no more contain those who sought, by every ruse imaginable, to violate it than could King Pentheus immobilize Dionysus in Euripides' *The Bacchae*. When his mouth was forcibly shut, the fairground actor would carry rolled-up sheets of paper—as many sheets as the scenario had lines—and unfurl words from his pocket. When his pocket was emptied, words written on a blackboard flanked by cherubim would descend from the rafter like a Tiepolo cloud. When he was forbidden blackboards as well, even then Harlequin contrived to "talk," for in the *pièce à la muette*, or dumb show, which was one genre among numerous others born of enforced silence, actors would recite gibberish while conveying the sense of it pantomimically. Any concession made above became a new foul line to be trespassed below; any inch given there a foot taken here. Did the censor at one moment sanction monologues? The fair trumped up one-man dialogues, with Harlequin reading aloud the lips of a dumb interlocutor. Did the censor relent so far as to tolerate brief skits? Three of these performed seriatim with diversionary breaks or "floor-moppings" would suffice to constitute a play, though not a play easily recognized as one by some examiner numbly reverent of Aristotle's unities.

And so it went. Depending on political whim or circumstance, the disenfranchised might gain or lose, and lose in a single season all they had nibbled from the pie in ten, only to recommence, nothing daunted, their furtive litigation. Bertrand's was not the unique example of an enterprise launched with puppets that got transformed, as discreetly as possible, first into children, then into adults, before waking the Master, who would straightaway render them inanimate once again. (In the worst of times, even the puppet—the French puppet, that is—became an ontological threat, whereupon fairground entrepreneurs countered with *marionnettes étrangères*.) To dare to grow up, to articulate thoughts lacking in taste, represented an infringement on the premises of Roman humanity. Indeed, no word spoken by the fairground actor, who spoke it every chance he got, could more predictably stir his audience to sympathy and anger—as though it were a *cri de guerre*—than the word "taste." "J'aime l'arlequinerie, oui, je suis dans ce goût-là," asserts a character in one of Lesage's prologues: "I love harlequinery. Right, that's to my taste"—suggesting a mental caste rather than some random trait (i.e., "I am *made* that way"). In *The Quarrel of the Theaters*, personifications of the Comédie-Française and of the Fair argue as follows:

> *Comédie (raising her eyes to heaven)*: What bad taste Paris displays
>   nowadays!
> *The Fair:* You find Paris sensible
>   When it seeks diversion with you
>   But when it resorts to us
>   You call its taste deplorable.

For which impudent remark, and others, fairground troupes did penance of total silence from 1718 until 1721, the Duc d'Orléans—a regent favorably disposed, on the whole, toward his basest subjects—capitulating to pressure brought upon him by his court.

A typical *parade* like Grandval's *Syrup up the Arse, or, The Happy Deliverance: An Heroi-Magnifishit Tragedy* will, by virtue of its title, spare us from having to belabor the point that pieties mouthed by one class were in due course excreted by the other, that a religion of taste inevitably polarized worship and blasphemy at either end of the digestive tract. But eighteenth-century "harlequinery," while it anticipated such notable petards as the *Merde!* hoist to scandalous effect in Alfred Jarry's *Ubu Roi* and the farts that André Malraux, minister of cultural

An acrobatic intermezzo at Nicolet's theater, which was established on the Boulevard du Temple in 1760. Bibliothèque Nationale

affairs, wished to silence before they could be let loose by Jean Genet's Arab in a state theater (*The Screens*), anticipated avant-gardism no less in its celebration of metamorphosis, of change, of dissemblance than in its scatology. Where the classical stage stood architecturally still, the "other" stage could afford to take exotic voyages through time and space, being innocent of the unities. The aristocratic hero was inherently selfsame, his identity residing in his *virtu* or his mettle, but

Harlequin answered the little man's dream of diabolic versatility: having no virtuous core, he was, like an onion, the sum total of his skins. Nor did he have cumbrous principles and sacred bonds to hinder him from racing after opportunity. Now the ruler of an island kingdom where foreigners are crowned then cooked (*Harlequin King of Serendib*), now a panderer in Islam (*Harlequin Hulla*) or Muhammad himself, now a mountebank in China, a surgeon in Barbary, a Grand Mogol, an Emperor of the Moon, a court jester, a palace laundryman, an astrologer, Harlequin emerged from Paris fairgrounds as the local prankster he had always been, no doubt, but distended almost beyond recognition. The universe had become his locality. What with the newly published translation of *The Arabian Nights* at their disposal, and numerous accounts of life in hitherto unexplored regions of the world, Lesage and Piron churned out tales that anticipate the future exploits of Rocambole, the adventures of Fantômas, and even the perils of Pauline.

Though harlequinery remained a staple item of marketplace theater throughout the eighteenth century, economic prosperity and the social changes attendant upon it whet the appetite, in those who were rising, for somewhat more delicate fare. Indeed, even harlequinades, when they took the form of parody (as in *Harlequin Deucalion* or *Harlequin Homer's Advocate*), served to educate the plebs, to acquaint it with the mythological figures they ridiculed, with the refined manners they aped, with the bones worried by cultivated folk: what men parody, they internalize willy-nilly. As open-air platforms became wooden barracks, barracks regular theaters, and one such theater the Opéra-Comique, humor tended to evolve likewise. This development was anything but fluent, however. The "Romans," defending not only their theater but an Order, one of whose symbolic mainstays was taste, begrudged the vulgus every inch of elevation won beyond the common measure, every word spoken in a polite cause. After it found itself hopelessly overwhelmed at the barrier set up between silence and French, officialdom beat a tactical retreat under Louis XV, condoning dialogue outside the Comédie-Française *provided only that it be distasteful*! Judgments delivered by the censor, who was, as we infer from various memorabilia, more tolerant of smut than of literate badinage, would seem perverse if understood otherwise than in light of a desire to keep high *essentially* distinct from low, to safeguard the one in preserving the other. Should the lower world prove capable of rising, what would prevent the higher from falling? Polite society therefore protected itself as much by the vernacular as by "native" euphemisms, with the police making certain that *le peuple* and *le monde* acted each according to its "nature." Though Voltaire inveighed against "les misérables bienséances françaises" (those wretched French proprieties), nonetheless he invoked them when he said of Shakespeare that "it seems as if Nature had amused itself by assembling in his head the greatest imaginable power and grandeur, and the lowest and most detestable forms of witless vulgarity," implying that in France Nature didn't dare play jokes. Like the botanical garden Bernard Jussieu designed for Louis XV, wherein every French plant exclusive of wild vegetation enjoyed its logical place, the Théâtre-Français was a taxonomist's Eden, weeds having been rooted out of it and consigned to namelessness in the fairground. However genteel those English gentlefolk were who set store by Colley Cibber's adaptation of *Richard III*, their sensibilities, next to the French, were as homespun to gossamer, or so one would judge from the example given by a woman of quality who, on hearing King Lear declare, "J'ai besoin d'être père," exclaimed: "Fie! How indecent of him!" Clytemnestra's screams in Voltaire's *Electra* afflicted such high-strung nerves that to save his play from closing straightaway he dashed off a second, bromidic version of the murder scene. Similarly, the first performance of *Eugenia* in 1767 would, by all accounts, have been its last had Beaumarchais not purged, overnight, "base and trivial expressions which caused displeasure."

Not that legitimate theater was devoid of unmentionable things; only that a certain linguistic code made it seem so. Who but the initiate could have known that "a secret marriage," for example, invariably meant a sexual liaison in eighteenth-century drama? By appearing to shun its own most beloved obsessions, by constituting a duplex reality, this language allowed those who understood it both the honor of virtue and the pleasure of vice. Figuratively scabrous in its meaning, it was literally blameless. Small wonder, then, that Churchmen, particularly Jesuits, proved to be among the most energetic apologists of *le beau style*. Father Bouhours, for one, declared style "the effect of exquisite discernment, the mark of our good taste," and Father Rapin, for another, boasted that "this purity of writing has so firmly established itself, he would be foolhardy who dared to make verse in a century as delicate as ours without perfect knowledge of the language." As theology had always furnished power a transcendent justification, so now, increasingly, did aesthetic doctrine. The knack of divorcing words from thoughts, or container from contents, of vouchsafing the mind something like *pro forma* virginity, characterized France's Jesuitical elite, a class deeply religious to the extent that it made French its gospel and rhetorical *politesse* its virtue. That this knack brought quite considerable rewards would seem self-evident; equally evident was the forfeit paid—paid to the "lower" world—in artistic scope and vigor. Jean Chapelain, a charter member of the Académie française, wrote in 1668 that "versification, good or bad, does not necessarily figure [among those things essential to the constitution of a poem] and [can] be altogether absent without a poem being the less a poem," but it was the spirit of Madame de Rambouillet's precious salon rather than this school of thought that finally won the day. Whereas Corneille's theater and even Racine's owe their greatness to the tension between verbal restraint and an age in which half-savage aristocrats thought nothing of using their swords to drive home mortal repartees, by 1712—the year Palaprat wrote that "those stormy times have passed, our police enforce a calm atmosphere for which spectators are most grateful"—such blood as flowed flowed less profusely than tears, while points of etiquette drew more of it than points of honor.

Stiff outside and melting soft within, gentlefolk often had the consistency, if not the flavor, of a Brie. Long before nineteenth-century bourgeoises embodied it to perfection, virtue was all embonpoint in wire hoops. "Monsieur," said the famous playwright, Prosper Crébillon, addressing himself to an Englishman at the Café Procope shortly after the failure of his tragedy *Atreus and Thyestes* in 1707, "*Atreus* is a tragedy too strong for the character of our nation. It would have done better in your country. It was made for men, whereas in France we have nought but women." Should one ascribe his remark to wounded vanity? But Voltaire poor-mouthing his own *Zulima* as a sop that reeked of French ladies' rosewater did not do so out of wounded vanity; nor, for that matter, did Grimm when he commented, some years later, that "our facile taste . . . sanctions egregious absurdities in the name of what we call *beaux vers*."

The same ideals and fears to which the comic genre lost its guts claimed tragedy's as well, with tragedy surviving but only as a pedantic rite, a grammatical simulacrum of itself, a protostructuralist exercise. If word and thought belied each other onstage, the king's player was the living image of their discrepancy, saying one thing and doing quite another. Bound by inflexible conventions, he could neither raise his arms above eye level, nor run (whatever the circumstances), nor speak except in certain prescribed cadences. Panard, a fairground wit, did not exaggerate when he wrote these couplets:

> J'ai vu des guerriers en alarmes,
> Les bras croisés et le corps droit,
> Crier plus de cent fois aux armes,
> Et ne point sortir de l'endroit.*

And Favart did so only slightly in his classic caricature of the *style noble*:

> Je prends une attitude, et fort bas je commence;
> Ma voix en même temps s'élève par éclats;
> Je balance le corps et j'agite les bras. . . .
> Tantôt de mes deux bras décrivant un ovale,
> J'en impose aux humains du ton sacré des rois,
> Et je mugis des vers, en étouffant ma voix.†

Efforts to silence the lower world met with success, though not necessarily in the booths of Saint-Germain. While the fairground grew more human, the Théâtre-Français turned to wood, its actors, the hierophants of impersonal virtue, moving hither and thither like marionettes jerked by a hidden hand.

In a sense the hidden hand was joined, beyond the grave, to Cardinal Richelieu, whose Académie française institutionalized his belief that ruling France meant ruling French. Richelieu chartered the Académie (1635) in an age of polyglot chaos brought about by dogmatic schism, by world exploration, and by technological progress. The Reformation had made Rome's voice but one among others, explorers had unwittingly merged Europe with a world of different alphabets, and technology had created a vast new vocabulary—the effect of all this being com-

---

* "I have seen warriors at the ready / Arms crossed and body straight, / Shout a hundred times over, Let's charge! / And never take a step."

† "I strike an attitude and nearly scrape the floor; / My voice meanwhile peals upward; / I balance the body and wave the arms. . . . / Now describing an oval with my two arms, / I adopt, to intimidate mere mortals, the solemn tone of kings, / And bellow verse, while smothering my voice."

parable to the effect upon Pantagruel of those words, frozen since time immemorial, that thaw and burst noisily round his ship as he sails the Northern Sea in search of the Oracle of the Holy Bottle. Secular babble filled the liturgical void. Who better than a prince of the Church could appreciate that the temporal power he served would bolster itself by elaborating a new *lingua sacra*, one whose authority derived not from above but from within, not from ecclesiastical canon but from its structural logic, not from "things" but from its own grammar? "To labor with all care and diligence to give our language certain rules, to render it pure, eloquent, and capable of treating the arts and science; . . . to cleanse the language of impurities contracted in the mouths of the common people, the jargon of lawyers, the misusages of ignorant courtiers, the abuses of the pulpit": thus did the Académie, whose forty members set about compiling an official dictionary, formulate its chartered purpose.

Grammarians, aestheticians, lexicographers were not long in forming a priestly caste and men of parts—the *grande bourgeoisie*, the *noblesse de robe*—in appropriating a language inherently congenial to their administrative and juridical functions. What lent authority to those who wielded it was the linguistic code they knew in common, or rather, the rhetorical virtuosity with which they employed a mandarin designed to make the speaker deny himself common words and build abstract edifices, to hobble the mind by way of forging an intellectual counterpart to the balletic body. Indeed, participation in a "new body"," in a "second nature," was the ultimate reward those otherwise hardheaded gentlemen foresaw; directly French was at issue, they contrived to sound like religious zealots. The essay on "Rhetoric" written for Diderot's *Encyclopédie* suggests that its author, outlining a pedagogical method for the elite cadre, did so as a rationalist believer who would have had no quarrel with Descartes's gnomic observation that *mundus est fabula*— "the world is in our words for it," or "the world is a play." Proclaiming that "rhetoric, of all parts of literature, demands the most knowledge and enlightenment of a teacher, the most perspicacity and application of a student," he prescribed exercises wherein a student, with rhetorical tools in hand, would bring them to bear on noble orations, reconstructing the latter under close guidance. Once his education was complete, he would, like adepts of talmudic *pilpul*, find himself possessed of sublime virility, or clothed in spiritual flesh:

Moved to enthusiasm by this intoxicating study, by the beauty they will have admired in the movements, thoughts, language of the orator, while being struck by his reasons, they will have been even more profoundly affected by the passion that animated him, exhausted by the ideas and sentiments he will have transmitted to them, they will burn with desire to disseminate them; and if they have, within themselves, some seed of natural eloquence, these seeds will burgeon in the live and deep heat with which he will have penetrated them.

The puberty these images evoke is an apostolic event, as if to say that Eloquence weaned its sons from raw nature and *wrote them anew*. It distinguished the mandarin from inhabitants of "the other world," from zanni whose dialects rooted them in some one province, whose archaisms held them hostage to the dead, whose jargons narrowed the mind to shop, field, or tool.

That the distinctions Roman France made between itself and Harlequin's constituency were modeled after theological ones, that Catholicism permeated linguistic speculation, becomes abundantly clear in various treatises that enjoyed a considerable vogue during the eighteenth century—Charles de Brosses's *Mechanical Formation of Languages* and Court de Gébelin's *The Primitive World Considered in the Natural History of the Word*. Taking for granted a paradigmatic language, or original Word, in different ways they imply that language, like man, had fallen from Grace, growing ever more corrupt, disintegrating, losing its objectivity. If Court de Gébelin deplored "the frightening specter presented by the multitude of languages," his phrase, which echoes La Mesnardière's "the many-headed monster," flies beyond reason and carries him into a penumbral area where linguists, along with aestheticians, upheld the sanctity of power. Excommunicated from true French, the plebs became the ontological outsider, whose very being was fortuitous. Hemmed in by patois, it came to figure as Nature's human analogue, as a Protean species incapable of thinking without multiplying, of formulating concepts, of attaining that vantage point from which the mind extends beyond the senses. Did the upper class predicate its authority on its rhetorical virtue? By the same token did it predicate servility upon a lack of such virtue and declare it self-evident that vulgar tongues give the lie to a vulgar essence. "Partout le goût du peuple est grossier," wrote the celebrated critic, La Harpe, in *Lyceum*: "Wherever there is a plebs, its taste is coarse."

So deep-seated was the belief in a holy tongue that even those who championed the lower order would, many of them, labor to redeem it by abolishing its diverse idioms and forcibly teaching it French. Thus, in 1794, during the Terror, a Revolutionary bishop, Grégoire, urged the National Convention to have dialects extirpated from France, telling it that "where language is concerned we are still, with our thirty different patois, back at the Tower of Babel while in the matter of freedom we form the vanguard of nations." Indeed, the people's censor proved to be far more ruthless than the king's:

Probity, virtue are the order of the day, and this order must be eternal. The theater would seem to be unaware of it for I am told that morals are by turns exalted and insulted. . . . Let us drive immorality from the stage; further, let us rout jargons by which a kind of line dividing equal citizens one from the other is still preserved. Under the despot, impresarios like Dufresny and Dancourt could, with impunity, bring into the theater actors who excited laughter or pity by speaking a *demi-patois*: propriety now ordains that this tone be forbidden. In vain will you object that Plautus had characters who spoke the barbarous Latin of Ausonian mountain people, or that the Italians—and quite recently Goldoni—produce upon the stage their Venitian merchant and the bergamask dialect of Brighella, et cetera. What is quoted as an example worthy of imitation is but an abuse to be reformed. . . . I would have it that all municipalities conduct their discussion exclusively in the national language; I would have it that a vigilant constabulary set to rights the host of signboards that represent an outrage to grammar.

Most such felonious signboards stood corrected, but some few at least escaped notice and held out long enough to have their day, not only in antiquarian shops but in avant-garde literature—in *A Season in Hell*, for example, where Rimbaud, who dreamed of reinventing language, wrote that he "loved idiotic paintings, mountebanks' dropcloths, signboards, popular engravings, erotic books with misspelled words . . . fairy tales, the little books from childhood . . . silly refrains, naïve rhythms." By then, anyone who could read omens would have foreseen that low culture—the primitive and the popular—was destined to form the basis of high, that hermeticism of a new kind lay in the offing.

But in eighteenth-century Paris, returning there if we may, plebeian entertainment, language, and society exercised a fascination not so

much upon disaffected sons of the bourgeoisie as upon the jejune aristocracy. To believe Lessing, who observed that "the Nation is too vain,
too infatuated with titles and other obsolete prerogatives—everyone,
down to the most ordinary man, would sport insigniae of rank, and
company kept with one's own kind is poor company indeed," a class in
the ascendant consecrated itself with the stays and ruffs jettisoned by a
class bound for the grave—death, like love, releasing those it chose
from aesthetic pieties, from formal attire, from grammar itself.

As a rule, men and women of blood still endeavored to save face
even though this meant stifling yawns at the Comédie-Française, but
many were the exceptions who unashamedly frequented the fairground
at Saint-Germain or Saint-Laurent. "Ladies are running like crazy to
fairground spectacles; how it delights me that they should share the
taste of their lackeys and coachmen!" gloated Lesage in 1709, some five
years before Louis XIV departed this world in an odor of sanctity that
did not linger behind him. Under the Regent and Louis XV, licence
reigned as it had not since Henry IV's lifetime, when three valets could
perform a cuckold farce for the five-year-old heir-apparent without its
being thought unseemly. "Taste has fallen so low that Lully's operas are
no longer held in consideration and people prefer little ballets fit for the
fair or tightrope dancers," Marin Marais noted in the 1720s. (Marais
had figured among the elite of musician-composers attached to Louis
XIV's household—one of those summoned almost every Sunday after
mass to give little concerts for the king.) What would have been his dismay had he survived to witness Louis XVI's brother taking lessons from
Placide, a fairground acrobat, in the Petit Trianon, then demonstrating
the art of tightrope walking before peers of the realm! Stranger still,
when, round about 1750, harlequinades were momentarily eclipsed by
crude farces whose chief dramatic raison d'être was to bawl in different
slangs—charwomen would speak the charwoman's vernacular, peasants
the peasant's, wigmakers the wigmaker's, et cetera—this linguistic slice
of life otherwise called a "fishmonger play" enjoyed as much popularity
among the titled as among fishmongers. Marie Antoinette's model farm
was only one, rather sedate, manifestation of loftiness abasing itself, of
a flight into fantasy that saw the aristocratic class lose its head to the
populace onstage before it lost it on the scaffold. Gentry who delighted
in parades need not have visited the marketplace; they could find it at
one another's town houses and at country villas like the one near Pantin
owned by Marie Guimard, first dancer of the Opéra, in which actors—

Madame Saqui, famous at Vauxhall and on the Boulevard du Temple for her tightrope dancing. From an engraving done in 1820. Bibliothèque Nationale

some recruited from fairs, others from the streets nearby—wore nothing but figleaves.

Théâtres de société having become an upper-class craze, the Nero of these amateur theatricals was Louis Philippe I, grandson of the Regent, who after 1789 would style himself Philippe Egalité. In addition to his theater opposite the Saint-Laurent fair, he built four more on estates he owned outside Paris, where, from time to time, there took place Lupercalian orgies supervised by his Petronius, Alessandro Cagliostro. That the first drama ever staged in a Saint-Germain booth, something called *The Forces of Magic and Love,* curiously prefigured these graveside celebrations of the aristocracy, that *The Marriage of Figaro* had its premiere in a nobleman's private theater, that countesses found a vocation, in extremis, as soubrettes or country maidens and counts as acrobats, did not stay the executioner's hand during the Terror to come. On the contrary, Revolutionary theater would observe the proprieties in an inverted form, forbidding any reference onstage to aristocratic rabble, shedding blood under the moral aegis of classical antiquity, and dividing head from body.

When Louis XIV opened the Boulevard du Temple in 1670, little did he suspect that one day this wide, gravelly thoroughfare which had been reclaimed from marshland along the city's northeast rampart would accommodate throngs of pleasureseekers or that inmates of the Bastille—those free to use the terrace—would train spyglasses upon it by way of providing themselves daily entertainment. And yet, even during his lifetime, it had evolved into a far more hospitable place, with five rows of shade trees rising higher than the adjacent wall. A "turn round the ramparts" became the fashionable exercise among aristocratic blades, who would congregate there toward late afternoon, whether to prance up and down its center lane or to wander promiscuously out of sight. They were joined, in due course, by alert entrepreneurs from the nearby Saint-Antoine ghetto—cocoa vendors, trollops, and, finally, publicans who divided this arboreal strip into concessions bearing names evocative of Fragonard or Watteau: "Paphos," "Hebe's Garden," "Apollo's Café," "The Bower," "The Turkish Garden," "The Blue Sundial." By 1770 the promenade resembled London's Vauxhall. It

A *typical* baraque foraine—*the wooden playhouse of eighteenth-century fairground theater. Shown here is the one belonging to Nicolet.*

had its fireworks, its fortunetellers, its balladeers accompanying themselves on hurdy-gurdies, its circus strongmen. Crowds ebbed and flowed from a "Cabinet of Electricity" at one end to a display of mechanical gadgets at the other. Before long, Curtius, whose wax museum was among the capital's most popular attractions, established here, at the city limits, a branch featuring notorious scoundrels. It remained only for these scoundrels to come alive, as indeed they would, every night, on the melodramatic stage.

The Boulevard's theatrical existence is often said to have begun in 1760, the year Nicolet, a tightrope-walker-turned-puppeteer, set up his platform there. In 1764, when the Provost of Merchants gave Nicolet permission to build a permanent structure, he straightaway cast aside marionettes in favor of human actors, calling his theater "The Hall of Great Dancers" (like the frog of the fable, the "little folk" had a penchant for self-inflation). Inevitably, officialdom took umbrage at this encroachment upon its domain. Struck dumb, Nicolet avenged himself upon the Théâtre-Français by recruiting a remarkably clever ape, to whom he taught the mannerisms of a famous tragedian, Molé, and staged mock-heroic pantomimes that drew some twenty thousand spectators every Sunday. News of the triumph spread throughout the fairground community, whence there soon emerged a rival, Audinot. More cautious than Nicolet, Audinot, who graduated by small degrees from the articulate puppet to the mute child, proved, in addition, to be rather more literate. Where Nicolet's motto was "De plus en plus fort," (More and more action), Audinot's, which appeared on bills promoting his pantomimes, could have been devised by the very Romans to whom it was addressed: "Sicut infantes audi nos," which means "Hear us speak as children speak," or—*infantes* having two meanings—"Hear us speak as those who possess no words speak." *

What multitudes came to hear Audinot, Nicolet, and those others who subsequently established themselves on the Boulevard may best be judged from the *Complaints and Grievances of His Majesty's Players*, an appeal made by the Comédie-Française to the National Assembly in 1789. "Despite the great lessons in patriotism and virtue which our masterworks offer abundantly, there is no taste for them [nos chefs-d'oeuvre dégoûtent]; people spurn our performances," they declared, justifying their enmity in language that anticipates the nineteenth-century bourgeoisie's poorhouse sermons: "Being insolent, lazy, and corrupt, the *petit peuple* of Paris are drawn by the minimal price of admission to fairground theaters, which superabound, and fuel the spirit of dissipation, the distaste for work, the refinements of corruption."

Similar appeals made during the Old Regime had fallen on deaf ears. Versailles had considered it expedient to distract the Parisian mob from hunger and cold—"The populace must have spectacles," declared a cabinet minister—and its politics suited its aesthetic affinities. Did the King's Players imagine that Louis XV, who slept in his final bed with a daughter of the streets, was likely to take sides against street theater? Were they not more dismayed than shocked to learn that the king, after watching Audinot perform at court, had endowed him with the privilege of speech? "Little spectacles" tickled society as much in its upper-

---

* The motto also contains a pun on his name: *audi nos,* Audinot.

most reaches as in its lower—a state of affairs that prevailed from Louis to Louis, from Madame du Barry to Marie Antoinette. In 1777 *Dom Japhet of Armenia,* Scarron's vulgar comedy, which the Théâtre-Français ritually performed at Shrovetide for the delectation of the plebs, was held over through Lent because of the applause it got not from the parterre below but from the royal gallery above. "The play has had extraordinary success this year and has delighted the queen and royal family," wrote Bachaumont in his *Secret Memoirs.* "They performed a divertissement called 'The Cavalcade,' embellishing it with picturesque tableaux, such as horse-races, which are all the rage among princes and our young lords." Two years later, when *The Beaten Pay the Penalty,* a farce even more unredeemably coarse, filled one of the little Boulevard theaters month after month, great and small alike were drawn to its premises. "Not only the populace but the city and the court are running there *en masse*," wrote Bachaumont. "The grandest go mad over it; dour magistrates and bishops sit in screened loges. Ministers of state have attended, especially the Comte de Maurepas, an avid connoisseur of farces. There are people who claim that the play is Maurepas's handiwork, and this rumor has had a part in sustaining and increasing its vogue." *

Where else, then, could the Théâtre-Français turn in defending its moral and aesthetic custodianship if not to an assembly of cultivated bourgeois? Its appeal must have seemed altogether plausible in 1789, a year during which high-mindedness begot numerous diatribes against Boulevard theater. Among these, one entitled *Letter to a Family Man on the Little Spectacles of Paris* bears home what had long been evident, that the paterfamilias stood four-square ready to uphold cultural institutions once upheld by the king; that Rome rested, then more than ever before, upon a middle-class back. "Monstrous pantomimes, a mixture of buffoonery and heroism, featuring duels, cannonades, torture scenes, and men metamorphosed into cats, dogs, bears, apes . . ."—thus did many Parisian burghers view the goings-on round about them. At the city's rim, in the faubourgs and in the hustings beyond there lurked a Protean enemy, the *infantes.*

With each successive step leftward, the Revolution drew that much closer to its virtuous epiphany in Year I, immolating one by one all

---

* Maurepas was Louis XVI's leading minister of state at the time.

symbols of rank, erasing personal imprimaturs, undermining the very basis of individual discrimination, judgment, and taste; creating here a God there a mass of anonymous celebrants; razing walls inside France while sealing her from the world outside. Before it absolved itself of history, however, it monopolized the past by building museums in which to house artifacts looted from châteaux or town houses; before it made Nature its theater and mass festivals of self-celebration its art or text, it built theaters in the Roman style and seized the classics, distributing Corneille, Racine, Molière, and Crébillon among the plebs, like royal jewels. In 1791 Chapelier, a delegate in the Assembly, warned his fellow legislators that the theater would "become a school of virtue and patriotism" only when they bestirred themselves to repeal laws that set one house above every other. Mirabeau thereupon submitted a proposal whose main stipulations were that:

> Any citizen can establish a public theater and present in it plays of any kind, by making a declaration to the municipality before its opening.
>
> The works of authors dead more than five years are public property and can, former privileges notwithstanding, now be presented in all theaters indiscriminately.
>
> The works of living authors cannot be presented in any public theater without the formal consent in writing of the authors, under penalty of confiscation of the total receipts for the benefit of the author.
>
> The directors or members of the different theaters will be, by reason of their position, subject to the inspection of the municipality. They will receive orders only from the municipality, which can stop or forbid the presentation of any play except that which conforms to the laws and to police regulations.

By 1792, more than two hundred theaters sprang up throughout the city, twenty-three of them on or near the Boulevard du Temple, not counting cafés, where a beer entitled patrons to a dramatic presentation. "If this goes on," wrote one critic, "Paris will have a theater in every street, an actor in every house, a musician in every basement, and an author in every garret."

Although theatrical entrepreneurs continued, for the moment, to suspend performances at Eastertime, before and after Holy Week they flogged the Church indefatigably, staging plays like *The Husband Con-*

fessor, The Convent, or *The Fruits of Education, The Cloistered Victims, The Capucins, Amelia,* or *The Convent* in which monks and nuns assumed every sin of which the Catholic imagination could unburden itself (by 1794, the populace, as we shall see, would have *hallowed* its own natural impulses). "The performers at every one of the theaters, great and small, soon found it necessary to include among the articles of their wardrobe the chasuble, the surplice, the coif, and the girdle of Saint Francis," the classical actor Fleury observed some years afterward.*

Despite conceptual grids laid upon Paris by Revolutionary administrators, it was as if the ship that symbolized the city on its coat of arms had been ripped loose from moorings in this world and cast adrift, its fixtures rolling fore and aft with every successive wave. Had some Parisian fallen asleep on Good Friday, 1789, when France traditionally observed "The Repose of the Good Lord," and reawoken two years later, what would have been his amazement to find *Horace* or *Phèdre* being performed in Nicolet's theater (with Harlequinades filling the interval between acts) and Boulevard repertoire drawing crowds to the classical stage! Indeed, Fabre d'Eglantine, whose masterpiece was to be the Revolutionary calendar that made Holy Week anachronistic, wrote a play along these very lines, *The Convalescent of Quality,* or *The Aristocrat.* "The whole state is changed. Men are equal;/There are no more lords, no more vassals./Parlements are dead, the high clergy too,/The army has sided with the highest law,/The King, agreeing with all, is honored in our hearts,/And is, moreover, the father we have chosen," someone informs the titular aristocrat, whom gout had kept housebound from 1789 to 1791. Soon enough, *citoyen(ne)* would replace Monsieur, Madame, and Mademoiselle; the polite form, *vous,* would become suspect; the calendar would revert to nature à la Rousseau, elapsing without Sundays; the king would lose his head, and what had taken place "before," during 1792 years, would constitute a temporal ruin, an Old Regime. By the abolition of a vocabulary that had ancestrally oriented people—of words that assigned each man his place, that

---

* Fleury had been a tenured member of the Comédie-Française. It is worth noting here that until well into the twentieth century actors on the European stage were expected to provide their own costumes. This practice disappeared with the advent of ensemble theater.

stood guard between subject and object, that linked present tense to past—the pre-Thermidorian Revolution sought to revise the very grammar of civil existence.* Divorced from his own history, exiled from his personal experience, on what basis could the individual predicate a self? Theaters multiplied, as though all society were being resolved into theater.

With the censor gone, the lower world straightaway rid itself of paraphernalia that hobbled its movement and obscured its nakedness. "The famous decree has just appeared," wrote Madame Fusil, wife of a royal actor, to Madame Lemoine Dubarry in Toulouse. "You cannot imagine what a revolution it has produced. The gauze behind which they'd act and sing at one of the Boulevard theaters called the Délas-sements-Comiques was torn to shreds by young people. It's as if they've gone berserk." Like the veils of polite language and the screened-in loges from which high society beheld scatological farces, a semi-transparent curtain, or scrim, in use since Louis XIV's reign, served to fuzz the reality of forbidden images, to hold high apart from low, to maintain a barrier, nonetheless effective for its flimsiness, between *infantes* and respectable folk. Letting the vulgar disport themselves on a stage, but a stage made foreign or remote by this euphemism, ostracizing them while keeping them in view, the scrim was a Jesuitical device that suited to perfection the apostles of *le beau*, the cultural absolutists who peered through their fingers to save face. So long as it hung where curtains hang, the space behind this nominal fabric lay "outside," segregated, if only in the literal sense (curtains are curtains, whether transparent or opaque) from a region whose exclusiveness, "objectivity," and taste the Comédie-Française upheld. When it fell, language itself tended to crumble, with one form of total theater—the theater based on Aristotelian orthodoxies—making way for another. Long before Antonin Artaud declared the stage to be "a physical and concrete place that demands one fill it and have it speak its concrete language," his vision was fully accomplished in exorcistic rituals by means of which the populace legitimated itself as a physical mass, as a global collectivity, as a *monde*.

---

* That a playwright named Dorvigny could stage his comedy *Perfect Equality, or The Thees and the Thous,* one month before 9 Thermidor might have been construed as prophetic of the Fall, for humor was anathema to Robespierre.

By 1794 culture had become the nation's official nemesis—a possession, but one which its new proprietors could not possess (except to bury it), manifesting itself as it did in language that evoked something inherently outside them, something *other* than them. What a liberal, meliorist regime made universally available was seen by the demotic order that followed as containing a threat of alienation. Not only did tragedies of Corneille, Racine, and Crébillon all but disappear from the stage, having been banned outright or mutilated beyond recognition, but those who had once monopolized the classical repertoire, the King's Players, found themselves thrown into prison. "These gentlemen, by taking on the costume of martial heros like the Duc de Vendôme and the Sieur de Bayard, or the glittering garb of the *Glorieux,* and by stepping into the red-heeled pumps of little marquesses, have foolishly identified themselves with their parts, imagining themselves to be noblemen," wrote Plancher-Valcour, former director of the Délassements-Comiques. "Plays recalling the Old Regime should no longer be given, even if they attack it, recall its vices, its follies, and its monstrous abuses," he continued. "It is not enough to decree that counterrevolutionary plays must not be given. We should dispense with all classics for at least half a year. When simplicity and republican fellowship have replaced the folly and ostentation of the Old Regime, our children can again laugh at our fathers." To mock the literary tradition was, he implied, to keep it alive, to acknowledge antecedents, and venerate the father, albeit perversely. Holding forth in the name of illiterate sans-culottes who found the classical theater largely incomprehensible, Jacobins and Jacobin sympathizers like Plancher-Valcour would have extinguished its very memory.

The campaign against dramatic literature of the Old Regime thus reached beyond the social prejudices this literature embodied. Its ultimate object was the mnemonic faculty itself, the mind in its power to distinguish self from other and "now" from "then," to perceive change and to apprehend the past as something independent of moral imperatives legislated by the State. It could be said that seditious thought lay hidden not in this character or that one but in the aggregate of features and responses we designate a "character." Where each character, by definition, addresses every other from behind eyes that see the world according to a perspective determined by history and nature, architects of the Terror hoped to create a chamber without partitions, a republic of objective expanse and transparent depth, a global interior echoing one voice. Nothing is more instructive in this regard than the *Plan of National Education*, which Robespierre read before the Convention on July 13, 1793. "The totality of the child's existence belongs to us," he declared. "The matter, if I may say so, never leaves the mold. No external object can enter and distort the form we give it. Prescribe, and the execution is certain; imagine a good method, and it is instantly followed; create a useful concept, and it is practiced completely, continually, effortlessly." Created all in the same mold, like those manikins who recited propagandist tirades on the Revolutionary stage, future citizens would emerge as hermetic agents of civic virtue, or as paradigms of a moral archetype whose dictates replaced historical consciousness and personal judgment.

Utopia could not accommodate more than one. Compressing disparate individuals into a singular called *le Peuple,* it abolished the conceptual basis of exchange—the ground "in between" where parliaments convene. "To be good, the people need only prefer itself to what is not itself; to be good, the magistrate must immolate himself to the people," declared Robespierre. "To love justice and equality, the people does not need any great virtue; it suffices for it to love itself." Republican virtue became an instrument of the desire for total control, self-effacement the predicate of absolute cognition, and transparency the principal mode of an hermetic ideal. Did France "propagate light"? Then everything around it must be pitch-black, Robespierre proclaiming in one speech that "half the globe lies plunged in shadows whilst half is brilliantly lit," and, in another, that Sparta—the Republic's paradigmatic model—"shines like a lightning bolt in the immense shadows," as if to say that the sun were pleased to lavish its undivided attention upon this sacred pale, or that *le Peuple* were its transcendent cynosure. Did the imperative of virtue incriminate sanctuaries, and most especially the individual mind, where each keeps his own council? Vice constituted a belligerent "outside," an occult "foreigner" who entertained only one design—that being to expel from Eden the collective Adam of Year I. "The two opposite genii . . . contesting the empire of nature are in this great period of human history locked in a mortal combat that will determine irremediably the destinies of the world, and France is the stage of this awesome struggle," Robespierre proclaimed. "Without, all tyrants are bent upon encircling you; within, all the friends of tyranny are banded together in a conspiracy: they will go on plotting until all hope will have been wrested from them."

Individual structures were torn down the better to immure, beyond penetration, a collective body. Incorporating all private space (not even land so much as the psyche: Jacobins like Saint-Just denounced "factionalism" and "difference" and "division" for being doctrinally incompatible with freedom), terrorism made private the whole, isolating France from non-France by a metaphysical no-man's-land that could not be crossed except at risk to one's identity, if not one's life. To be a selfless and impersonal citizen, a receptacle for the Objective Will or the Supreme Being—this was to be. Death and unreality lurked outside, in the subjective netherworld where evil passions motivated men.

Just as the world outside posed a mortal danger, so did the memory of what came "before." And just as the purlieu of France was villainously dark, so was the expanse of time during which kings begot kings. Indeed, a *citoyen,* should he deserve that crypto-religious title, would expect to find purchase nowhere but in the corporate state whose epiphany was his: not in the pluralistic wilderness beyond, nor in personal experience, in familial custom, in the proverbs of mankind. By terrorist lights, the past represented another mode of externality, another foreign body to be cast out (or else indoctrinated with the present), another threat of alienation. "Nature tells us that men were born for freedom, and the experience of centuries shows us man enslaved; his rights are written in his heart, and his humiliation in history," observed Robespierre, speaking here as an apostle of Jean-Jacques Rousseau. Though Jacobin leaders were, to be sure, steeped in classical antiquity, the allusions they made to it scarcely reflect a historical consciousness. To them, Sparta and Republican Rome were not moments in the human continuum but chapters of Gospel, not mundane communities but images on a scriptural backdrop that lent authority to the Revolutionary drama whose protagonists it idealized. Rather than commemorate the old, what Robespierre and Saint-Just did was to divinize the newborn, invoking antiquity as ventriloquists "throwing" their word or will across the ages into golden mouthpieces. History thus became one more metaphor of the virtuous plenum—the house without inner walls.

In accordance with Robespierre's belief that the people, to be good, need only prefer itself to what was not itself, history constituted the stage for an all-inclusive, all-exclusive self-embrace.* By the same token, theater enforced a total appropriation of the past. No matter what their role or historical context, all *dramatis personae* wore tricolor costumes, so that Phèdre, for example, did not dare to appear onstage without a red cockade pinned over her breast (until the Commune forbade performances of Racine's masterpiece in March 1794). "Greeks, Romans, medieval knights, Turks, Arabs, Peruvians, Parsees, Byzantines all grind out the same speeches. And the public, which is devoid of historical feeling, expresses no surprise. . . . In man there is seen nothing but a reasoning reason [*raison raisonnante*], the same in all eras, the same in all places," wrote Hippolyte Taine in *The Origins of Contemporary France.*

Everything forefathers had done and wrought—the rules, measures, scrims, boundaries that oblige each to perceive reality in plural terms—now represented an ontological sin for setting man at odds with his nature. Once the king—or the father, as he was often called—had been removed and the weight of history alleviated, it is as if all were possible. Those who severed his head crowned the Collective Body, objectifying instinct in a way that brings to mind the Surrealists venerating a Delphic Id. While Robespierre declared to the Convention, "Woe unto him who seeks to dampen this sublime enthusiasm and to stifle with disheartening doctrines *the people's moral instinct* [italics added], which is the principle of all great actions!" the secret police, whose ubiquitous ears pricked at the least whisper of contradiction, wrote, in a report that epitomizes the Terror:

> The small theaters frequented by the less well-to-do citizens, show in the spectators and those who entertain them a patriotic spirit pleasant indeed to the true republican; while the more elegant houses, excluding all but the rich by their high prices, receive only the enemies of liberty and those indifferent to it. But, as previously mentioned, these are general observations and there are exceptions, such as the Theater of the Republic. This theater

---

* Rousseau formulated this idea explicitly in his essay on the origin of languages. History, he contends, has reduced the volume and stamina of a public voice, creating the babble of private voices and a maze of obscene interiors. Thus, "among the ancients, one made oneself easily heard to the people on a public square; one could speak all day long with ease. . . . Herodotus used to read his history to the peoples of Greece assembled in the open."

truly deserves its name; the most ardent patriots gather there to applaud the smallest action, the least reference favorable to patriotism. Last night this theater gave *Robert, the Brigand Chief* [written by La Martelière], and one might say that no play is more in tune than this one with our present spirit. It exhales virtue, true republican virtue worthy of the founders of Rome.

What passed for patriotic was a play whose titular hero, driven from home by his knavish brothers, meets outlaws in the forest and becomes their leader after demanding of them blind devotion in a war he declares against corrupt society. Not only did this proto-Western (modeled, it is said, on Schiller's *Robbers,* but very much in the tradition of outlaw romances that had, for centuries, regularly appeared in cheap pulp magazines) raise the roof with violent clashes, defeating, whether by volume of noise or by sheer suspense, anything like a thought; the roof it raised had, until recently, given cover to the King's Players. And not only did the fairground tribes occupy a temple of high culture, renaming it first Theater of Liberty and Fraternity, then Theater of the Republic, but they arrogated to themselves the cognomen of its priests. When "instinct" became moral, low high, and virtue a function of the senses or a communal outpouring rather than a capacity for "holding in," then the *infantes* could, by the same logic, become founders of Rome.

Insofar as the Terror may be said to have begotten a theater consonant with its doctrinal postulates, that theater resided in the *fêtes*, the great pageants of 1793 and 1794, which David designed as *tableaux vivants* marshaling all citizens into Jacobinism's social cosmos. Some years before the Revolution erupted, Rousseau, whose own theatricality made him a sworn enemy of Parisian theater (where actresses, as he said, "bewitched" men like himself, filling them with thoughts otherwise alien to them and tarnishing their innate virtue), wrote that a republic ought to abolish all spectacles except contests held out-of-doors, in the Spartan tradition:

This great and superb spectacle, given beneath the sky in the presence of a whole nation, offered nothing but combats, victories, prizes, objects apt to inspire in the Greeks a spirit of ardent emulation and to warm their hearts with feelings of honor and glory. It was in the midst of this imposing apparatus, so well engineered to elevate and stir the soul, that actors, animated by the same zeal, would share, according to their talents, such honors as were conferred upon victorious athletes, often upon the first men of the nation. I am not surprised that, far from abasing them, their métier, exercised in this manner, gave them a pride of courage and noble disinterest that seemed at times to make the actor as lofty as his role. All this notwithstanding, never was Greece, except for Sparta, cited as an example of good morals; and Sparta, which did not tolerate theater, withheld honors from those who attended it.

With what rapt attention Robespierre had studied Rousseau's *Letter to d'Alembert on Spectacles* becomes apparent in a speech he gave about national festivals—a speech that carries Rousseau's idea one step further, or rather, drives home its solipsistic message. "Man is the greatest object to be found in nature; and the most magnificent of spectacles is that of a great people assembled," he declared. "Never are Greece's national festivals described except with enthusiasm; and yet their object

The Fountain of Regeneration near the ruins of the Bastille, where the populace gathered before marching across Paris during the Festival of Unity and Indivisibility. Bibliothèque Nationale

consisted in little more than games that showed to brilliant effect the strength, physical dexterity, or, at most, the talent of poets and orators. But there was the grace of it; one witnessed a spectacle greater than the games, the spectacle of the spectators themselves." Where the rational conventions that governed polite theater (or what has come to be known as "the closed stage") maintained, however gauzily, a barrier between actor and role, between audience and dramatis personae, between language and nature, with perspective lines theoretically vouchsafing the king an absolute viewpoint, the Terrorist festival laid low that barrier, sanctifying the mass of its celebrants, the collective body, or the universal *presence* that had no need to look beyond itself. Did Robespierre define the people as virtue incarnate, and Saint-Just the people's republic as "one and indivisible, quite apart from place and persons"? In a state which its dictator-theoreticians claimed to have been founded not by ordinary mortals bringing to bear their experience but by nature (like a prodigy child whose knowledge issues from its own "objective" substance rather than from an elder's lessons), such antinomies as appearance versus reality, mask versus face, role versus actor became obsolete. The *fête*, whatever its immediate goals, had, above all, a religious function. It celebrated a plenitude of Being. It nullified what lay beyond and came before. It severed the head each time anew, with tribal impunity.

Never was this symbolic *raison d'être* promulgated more clearly than during the Festival of the Constitution, otherwise known as The Festival of Unity and Indivisibility, which took place on August 10, 1793, exactly one year after the National Guard had invaded the Tuileries, bringing down the monarchy and starting time from Year I. According to David's minutely calculated *mise en scène,* all Frenchmen were to rise before daybreak "so that the sun's first rays . . . [which were to] be for them a symbol of Truth to which they might address their paeans, would illuminate the gathering place." They gathered, some two hundred thousand strong, where the Bastille once stood, at the city gate, milling over rubble-strewn ground to the foot of a *fons juventatis*—a colossal statue of Mother Nature squeezing jets of water from her breasts.* Amidst "fraternal kisses," "salvos of artillery", and "joyous songs," the president of the Convention, holding high an antique cup,

---

* In one engraving that commemorates the occasion, she is depicted as having multiple breasts, like Diana of Ephesus, though in fact she had only two.

delivered an invocation that began as follows: "Oh Nature! receive this expression of the French people's eternal attachment, and may the fecund waters that spring from thy breasts, may this pure liquid, which quenched the thirst of the first humans, consecrate, in this cup of Fraternity and Equality, the oaths that France swears to thee this day, the most beautiful day ever lit by the sun since it was hung in the immensity of the firmament." Thereupon envoys from all quarters of France drank (in alphabetical order), among them an old man who exclaimed: "I near the edge of my grave, but in pressing this cup to my lips, I feel that I am reborn with the human species, which is regenerating itself." With this act, a huge parade commenced, moving for sixteen hours along the boulevards, from one totem to another, much as on Palm Sunday (when bishops customarily set token prisoners free) the faithful reenacted Christ's triumphal entry into Jerusalem, proceeding from station to station while intoning hosannahs.

Although the popular clubs and legislators formed a vanguard, what the official record of this cortege dwells upon is its main body, which David had organized with a view to blurring not only signs of rank but the very *perception* of difference, of an heterogeneous world outside, of an outside:

> In one stroke, the Orderer of the Festival imprinted upon it its single most beautiful trait [wrote the government propagandist]. After the delegates from primary assemblies, there is no division whatever of persons and functionaries, nor even a trace of some deliberate order or prescribed regularity in the march. . . . All were equal as men, as citizens, as members of the sovereignty; everything became confusedly merged in the presence of the People, the unique source of all powers which, while emanating from it, remain subject to it; and in this social and philosophical confusion, the spectacle of which words, chants, instruments, and cries of joy mingling in the air made even more thrilling, holy equality—that eternal imprint of nature—became something visible and palpably felt.

Festooned with three-color ribbons, liberty caps, fasces, sheaves, and olive branches, it must have resembled a Bacchic throng invading the polis as it marched to the rhythmic beat of drums and the blare of trumpets. While here and there, around republican maypoles, sans-culottes joined hands with actors wearing the costume of Harlequin or Polichinelle, it swept forward relentlessly, beneath images of severed heads drawn on the Arch of October 6, past the place de la Révolution, where, in the guillotine's shadow, he who had recently extolled Mother Nature now set fire to a heap of aristocratic oddments, to the Champ-de-Mars, where eighty-seven departmental commissars scaled a huge artificial rock that symbolized the Sublime Mountain.

Should there linger any doubts that this procession solemnized the epiphany of a new *corpus mundi,* or that it may plausibly bear comparison to such rituals as primitive man held to mark the birth of a Year God, David's final touch will suffice to dispel them. Bringing up the rear was a tumbril laden with royal accoutrements, while miles ahead those in the vanguard held high a banner showing an eye—an eye that, so the caption gave everyone to understand, stood for "the eye of surveillance piercing a thick cloud." No longer did the guardian eye belong to kings. Brought out-of-doors and hung, as though it were the sun, over a stage commensurate with nature, it belonged now to that self-fathered prodigy, *le Peuple,* whose instinct or feeling was its objective virtue and whose ken was totality in the shape of itself. Now blind, now all-seeing, this organ had a constitution as paradoxical as the ideal it mirrored. Though it proposed to guard the festive throng against despotism from without, it was also there to expunge men's hidden resources, to abolish the complexity that attends human being, to make certain that the nation should become an altogether legible surface, and thus to implement what Robespierre called "the despotism of liberty." Its emblematic connection with the Enlightenment sanctioned a censorial regime even more ruthless than that which had obtained before 1789, a regime bent on transforming "the wordless ones" into divine puppets. In a report dated July 11, 1793, David set forth plans for "a vast theater" where, once the ceremony of August 10 was over, "the chief events of our Revolution shall be represented in pantomime."

Long after it was officially over, the *fête* would continue on the Boulevard, where scenes from it, warmed over again and again, and spiced ever more violently, provided the bulk of theatrical fare to be had during the Terror. As in a former age Piron and Lesage furnished polemical skits on a moment's notice, so now playwrights, whether they chose to or not, delivered themselves of pretexts for sound and fury that bore names like "historical fact," "patriotic fact," "patriotic divertissement," "patriotic comedy," "republican impromptu," "patriotic tableau," "patriotic vaudeville," and finally, *sans-culottide.* Those

gymnastic frolics by means of which the *infantes* had held their clients
fast in between acts, though they still served, often gave way to diversions rather less benign, or so one gathers from the Abbot
Grégoire, who reported in his diary that "during the entr'actes, an actor
would step forward to tell the audience the number of victims who had
died that same day on the place de la Révolution; and this announce-
ment would be accompanied by a song during which, as often happened
in the prisons, the singers imitated the heavy sound of the ax and the
contortions of the dying while singing the praises of liberty."

There survived a slender population of *connaisseurs*, as people
were known who could quote Corneille, Racine, Crébillon, and Voltaire
or, indeed, distinguish them from one another. The Terror had more
than fulfilled Plancher-Valcour's wish that classics be dispensed with
until "our children can again laugh at the folly and ostentation of our
fathers," for even as they chopped off their father's head, the children
triumphantly buried themselves in their bodies, forgetting how to laugh,
forgetting how to remember. Where under the Old Regime, *infantes*
fought for speech, under the new they avenged themselves upon the
proprietors of French, using language to intone their omnipotence, or
abolishing it altogether, in patricidal mummery. "The theaters are still
encumbered with the rubbish of the Old Regime, feeble copies of the
masters, wherein art and taste are set at naught, of ideas and interests
which mean nothing to us, and of customs and manners foreign to us,"
declared Joseph Payan on 5 Messidor 1794, one month before this ardent Jacobin lost his head along with Robespierre. "We must sweep this
chaotic mass out of our theaters. . . . We must clear the stage, and
allow reason to enter and speak the language of liberty, throw flowers
on the graves of martyrs, sing of heroism and virtue, and inspire love of
law and the *PATRIE*." When, in one of his last public acts, Robespierre
decreed that the place de la Révolution be converted "into a circus open
on all sides and consecrated to national festivals," it was fitting that the

---

(ABOVE) *The opening ceremony of the Festival of the Supreme Being on
June 8, 1794. An amphitheater was constructed in the Tuileries Gardens.*
(BELOW) *The culminating ceremony of the Festival, at the "Sublime Mountain"
on the Champ-de-la-Réunion, formerly Champ-de-Mars.*
Bibliothèque Nationale

site thus proposed for a national theater should have been the site on which ritual executions of the past took place every day, with tumbrils incessantly depositing fresh supernumeraries at the guillotine.

It could be said that the Davidian parade foreshadowed the march as glorified by Leni Riefenstahl in *Triumph of the Will,* or those other marches choreographed by Sergei Eisenstein in *The Battleship Potemkin, Alexander Nevsky,* and *Ivan the Terrible,* where a plot reaches its climax the moment individuals are swept up in a collective surge directed against Russia's enemy. The *fête* did not stop with 9 Thermidor. So inexorable was its progress across the nineteenth century that those who exercised power came to view *le Peuple* as a species indescribable except in terms of movement and roads, of emotion and drive. "In democracy, dramatic pieces are listened to, but not read," wrote Alexis de Tocqueville during the 1830s. "Most of those who frequent the amusements of the stage do not go there to seek the pleasures of the mind, but the keen emotions of the heart. . . . You may be sure that if you succeed in bringing your audience into the presence of something that affects them, they will not care by what road you brought them there, and they will never reproach you for having excited their emotions in spite of dramatic rules."

CHAPTER III

✦ ✦ ✦ ✦

THE BOULEVARD
OF CRIME

On September 21, 1800, one year into Napoleon's Consulate, a play entitled *Coelina, or The Child of the Mystery* was given its premiere performance at the Théâtre de l'Ambigu, on the Boulevard du Temple. That Parisians attended it in droves was not in itself unusual, for Paris during the Directory and the Consulate could not have enough of spectacles and food. "The taste for theater, which has spread throughout all social classes in recent years, seems to have become a mania even more than a need," wrote Grimod de la Reynière, himself an epicure in the old tradition. After famine, gluttony reigned supreme. Goldsmiths, jewelers, and tapestry weavers ruined by the Revolution began life over again, many of them as restaurateurs catering to peasants who had grown rich speculating in paper currency (*assignats*), provisioning the army at blackmarket rates, or looting seigneurial estates. Their good fortune went hand in hand with the theatrical community's. Where under the Old Regime, dinner was eaten early in the afternoon and digested during an interval of repose introducing the day's second half, which would end quite late at supper, by 1798, when the *Journal de Paris* observed that "the nature of public occupations and the economy have brought about a different division of the day's moments," dinner had become a prolonged repast and supper a brief collation. "Half of Paris," reported the *Journal*, now found itself released from its labors by six o'clock and sought whatever amusements might help fill the evening hours, whether it was loitering among notorious

83

harlots known as *Merveilleuses* at the Palais-Royal, mugging die-hard Jacobins, or attending plays. "Our boxes and orchestras are now occupied almost exclusively by shopgirls, apprentice locksmiths, and market porters who come to kill time, and not infrequently to display their jewels," wrote one gentleman clearly old enough to have admired those same jewels hanging from other necks.

Nor did such as count themselves lucky to be sitting in the Théâtre de l'Ambigu on September 21 anticipate some profoundly original work. Based upon a best-selling novel of that era, the play held few surprises in store. Coelina, the audience knew beforehand, would be innocence itself, a rich orphan, born des Echelettes, who had been reared from infancy to nubility by her father's modest, untitled brother, Monsieur Dufour. Do Coelina and Monsieur Dufour's son, Stefany, regard themselves each as the other's born mate, in the style of Bernardin de Saint-Pierre's Paul and Virginie? Monsieur Dufour, sooner than profit from any occasion in life, or let a venal thought enter the altruistic chapel of his mind, refuses to join them in marriage. No such qualms inhabit Truguelin, however. The villain of this piece, the evil countervailing Dufour's good, Truguelin, like Dufour, is Coelina's uncle, and, like Dufour, has a son. Having demanded the heiress's hand for this son of his, Truguelin arrives to claim it, whereupon a fourth, hitherto shadowy member of the Dufour household, Francisque Humbert, springs to life. If Coelina is bereft of parents, Humbert is bereft of speech. Found one day outside the village of Sallenches, near an escarpment where assassins had left him for dead, though not before ripping out his tongue, the poor old man needs no other reason than his wound to explain his presence under Dufour's roof. The sight of him there makes Truguelin recoil. Coelina presently overhears the following conversation between the villain and his robotic servant, Germain:

> *Truguelin:* Dost thou know where the wretch is sleeping?
> *Germain:* Here.
> *Truguelin:* In this very room?
> *Germain:* He was moved so as to make room for you.
> *Truguelin:* Let us enter my quarters and . . .
> *Germain:* When everyone will have retired. . . .
> *Truguelin:* At midnight. . . . If he resists . . .
> *Germain:* He's dead. . . .
> *Truguelin:* Let us withdraw.

Coelina (aside): The monsters!
Truguelin: I hear a noise.
Germain: Someone's coming. . . . It is he.
Truguelin: He! Why postpone it any longer?
Germain: The time is not yet ripe; let us hide.
Truguelin: Thou shalt keep watch.
Germain: You will act.
Coelina (aside): The knaves!

But for Coelina, Humbert would be taken unawares; instead, he foils their plot, letting loose gunblasts that waken the household. Dufour straightaway drives Truguelin out, and betroths Stefany to Coelina—an engagement no sooner resolved upon than celebrated by villagers who materialize onstage with bagpipes, hurdy-gurdies, and tambourines.

The couple, whose marriage heaven itself devised ("Coelina," et cetera), must, alas, endure further trials here-below before consummating it. As stubborn of purpose as a weed or a mole, Truguelin has Germain deliver a baptismal certificate that proves Coelina to be the adulterous issue of Isoline Truguelin and Francisque Humbert, that the old man who sanctifies Dufour's hearth once violated the sanctity of des Echelettes'. Even as the village's jubilation over her engagement reaches fever pitch, Coelina loses a husband—gaining, in the process, a father, whom she embraces tearfully. "Go, quit my presence and take with thee the fruit of thy guilty love," shouts Dufour, condemning the mute and the bastard to wander homeless, like another Lear and Cordelia.

Surprise follows on the heels of surprise. Directly Humbert has made good his exit, there arrives out of the blue a witness to the crime that left him speechless, who has just recognized in Truguelin its perpetrator, and so informed the constabulary. Truguelin, now a hunted man, seeks refuge in that same little corner of France to which Providence has guided Humbert and Coelina; for however wide the hinterland, good and evil travel together dialectically. Again, Truguelin would kill Humbert and again misfires. Everyone bursts in on cue—constables, Dufour, Stefany—whereupon Coelina's mystery is laid bare. Not a sinful liaison but a marriage kept secret from all but Truguelin united Humbert and Isoline. Learning that his sister was with child, the irrepressible villain made her wed, bigamously, Baron des Echelettes with an eye to the fortune he himself would some day contrive to embezzle. And the baptismal certificate? Humbert, it seems, stole Coelina from the cradle if only to set the record straight and have her baptized Humbert—a nominal consolation that earned him Truguelin's undying hatred. "I know the rest," Dufour says to Humbert, waving away the unexplained and inexplicable. "You are a doughty man, and I give you back my esteem."

On this tale, told to an audience nonetheless prostrate for knowing in advance what twists and turns it would take, there hangs a moral, which one minor character delivers, singing it to the folk tune "Un rigodon, zig, zag, don, don":

> Now you see, dear friends,
> That in vain with darkness one covers
> The evil one has done,
> Sooner or later Truth will out.
> Let's be good, open, virtuous,
> Let's make others glad,
> For then one dances gaily
> The rigadoon
> Zig, zag, don, don;
> Nothing quickens the beat
> Like a good deed done.

What makes *Coelina, or The Child of the Mystery* so particularly noteworthy is the fame it conferred, overnight, upon its author, Guilbert de Pixérécourt, a native of Nancy whose own life rivaled for implausibility the plays he wrote. Born to a family of Lorraine bourgeois ennobled by Louis XIV, he had just completed law studies, at the age of seventeen, when the Revolution broke out, repealing the laws he had studied. Despite a violent Jacquerie that laid waste to the family estate, he would have chosen to remain in France, he claimed, had the choice been his. Like other wellborn youths, he joined, at his father's behest, the flock of émigrés who had found sanctuary beyond the Rhine, particularly in Koblenz, where titled Frenchmen were so numerous and scandals so rife that it resembled Versailles in miniature. After a year, during which he learned German, saw battle against Revolutionary forces, and fell in love with a rich orphan, homesickness drove him back to France. One narrow escape persuaded him that in the beast's maw there was greater safety from its teeth than near its extremities, and so he made straight for Paris.

Louis XVI had fallen from his throne. In September the prison massacres would take place. Young Pixérécourt did not witness these, but he witnessed enough besides to beggar the most sadistic imagination. While tumbrils were rolling through the streets of Paris, high up in a garret that somehow escaped the eye of surveillance, he read Hervey's *Meditations* and English poetry of the graveyard school, notably Young's "Night Thoughts on Life, Death, and Immortality." At length, general conscription, or the *levée en masse* of which David's summer festival was a prelude, offered him the opportunity to join a Nancy brigade and thus win citizenship in the beleaguered Republic. All might have gone well if citizenship had not required attendance at meetings of the local Jacobin club, if the Jacobin assigned to Nancy by the Committee of Public Safety had been someone other than Marat Maugier ("a vile scoundrel," as he was described by one fellow Revolutionary, "spreading terror throughout the region, exacting sexual favors from women whose husbands were held in detention and from young virgins soliciting the freedom of their fathers"), or if the playwright in Pixérécourt, choosing this perilous moment to emerge, had emerged with some rudimentary sense of discretion. A satirical skit blatantly entitled *Marat Maugier, or The Jacobin on Mission* brought in hot pursuit of him agents dispatched by the Committee of Surveillance.

Once again he made for Paris, arriving there only days before a decree was issued banishing foreigners and nobles from the capital. Now twenty-one years old with nowhere to turn in a world seemingly devoid of reason, he let the spirit of paradox guide him and, as was his wont, sought freedom not by fleeing the trap but by walking into it. Thus, he revealed his predicament to none other than Bertrand Barère de Vieuzac, a Revolutionary of the most violent hue. Improbable though it would seem, Pixérécourt contended that Barère recommended him to Lazare Carnot, who was masterminding France's national defense from his post in the Committee of Public Safety. But undeniably the last month of the Terror did find him employed as assistant chief clerk under Carnot. One year later, when all signs indicated fair weather ahead, Pixérécourt crept out from the bureaucratic shelter, took a wife, and began to write.

As if his head had suddenly been uncorked, there came pouring from it comedies, *opera buffa*, parodies, pantomimes, vaudevilles, dramas, even tragedies—a veritable tide that would have swept him, along with his wife and infant child, into the poorhouse but for 40 sous a day he earned decorating ladies' fans. At length, fortune smiled. In September 1797 the Théâtre de l'Ambigu staged a comic operetta entitled *The Little Auvergnats* and several months later, *Victor, or The Child of the Forest,* a drama formulated to satisfy the public's new craving for Gothic tales. By 1800 Pixérécourt had transcended Grub Street once for all. Until *Coelina,* however, nothing suggested that he would become the sovereign font of melodrama, that he would write some 120 plays during the nineteenth century's first quarter, that these, taken all together, would receive over 30,000 performances (in an age when 100 constituted an exceptionally long run), or that the Boulevard public would accord him such respect that one critic, Charles Nodier, could observe without exaggerating: "Pixérécourt's theater, in the absence of worship, made up for the rules of conduct laid down by a mute pulpit."

Literary historians concerned with the genealogy of melodrama bring to mind the parable of blind men guessing the shape of an elephant. Some, who note the prevalence of things that go bump in the night, of *memento mori,* of brooding castles and dungeons that conceal ghastly instruments, of priapic monks and monasteries given over to unspeakable ceremonies, claim its true parent to have been Gothic fiction translated from the English, especially Mrs. Radcliffe's *The Mysteries of Udolpho,* which appeared in 1794 and Lewis's *The Monk,* which appeared one year later. Others, noting the strawberry marks and variations thereof (Coelina's birth certificate, for example) that restore orphans and waifs a lost identity, have traced its parentage to the eighteenth-century bourgeois drama of Nivelle de la Chaussée, Sedaine, Diderot, and Mercier. Others still, noting its convoluted structure, its poverty of language, its ceaseless movement, its belligerent roars and tremolos, its exotic habitat, would have it that melodrama descended from fairground pantomime and bandit folklore.

Where they seldom look, however, is to life itself, or, rather, to the public Pixérécourt addressed. "The entire people had just enacted in the streets and on the public squares the greatest drama of all time," Nodier observed from the eminence of mid-nineteenth-century France. "Everyone had been an actor in this bloody play, everyone had been either a soldier or a revolutionary or an outlaw. These spectators, who smelled gunpowder and blood, required emotions analogous to those from which they had been cut off by the re-establishment of order. They needed conspiracies, dark cells, scaffolds, fields of battle, gunpowder, and blood." Bearing in mind, too, the swift, inflationary turn of Fortune's wheel, the mortal danger that attended every word and move, the venerable conventions—among them, the Gregorian calendar —repealed as if by magic, the lightning fall from Grace of Revolutionary saint after saint, one may venture to say that experience itself had begotten melodrama. Though the Directory and the Consulate restored order, they did not by any manner of means extinguish the Terror, which survived, in those who survived, as a still point of the mind, a fulcral memory around which dreams would never cease to revolve. *Le Publiciste* made the point in 1804 that "the spirit, the tone, the methods of Revolutionary anarchy have passed from political clubs (Cordeliers, Jacobins, et cetera) to theater; here people listen, judge, condemn with the same coarseness, the same blindness, the same fury." It could have driven home this point again in 1814, at the conclusion of Napoleon's reign, and again in 1824 at the conclusion of Louis XVIII's. Where time marched forward in other respects and places, on the stages of the Boulevard, Parisians observed year I, year in and year out.

Melodrama ritualized the Terror. Its very core was a world view that allowed of no profane middle ground between virtue and evil, that pictured innocence hard put by enemies whose deviousness and implacability constituted a kind of brute nature transcending the merely human, a diabolical underground. Robespierre had declared, in "Administration of the Republic," that "we want an order of things where all base and cruel passions would be chained, all generous and beneficent passions awoken by the laws." So, in melodrama's universe, life is all passion and all humanity pressed into an armed camp or a frontier village devoid of anything like a diplomatic principle that could acquaint the outlaw with a conscience or the lawful with an unconscionable impulse. Did Robespierre sanction terroristic acts in the name of self-defense, suggesting, whenever he spoke, that past, present, and future were incessantly at stake, or that the world's virginity—the innocence of year I—were cause sufficient to justify a war without constraints? In the melodramas Pixérécourt wrote with the sincere intention of drumming scruples into an audience half-savage and half-pioneer, enemies expunge every issue but themselves, like spouses so faithful to a grudge that death alone can part them. (The Freudian, considering these plays radically bereft of psychological nuances, might ascribe such poverty to a feud between Tweedle-dee and Tweedle-dum; the Superego, or lawful persona, shoots silver bullets, and the Id, or hardened criminal, shoots lead ones.) Notwithstanding Pixérécourt's animadversions against the *régime sanguinaire*, the "bloody regime," whose leaders never grew weary of extolling peace, the Just Society defended again and again by melodrama proved as costly to stage lives as had the Robespierrian republic to real life and limb. A statistical compilation published in 1826 by a journal entitled, appropriately, *La Pandore,* may represent the most eloquent summation of a dramatic age:

> From October 15, 1825, to October 16, 1826, 107 suicides, 3 poisonings, and 9 arson attempts took place on the stages of the Opéra and the Théâtre des Italiens; 50 poisonings, 19 assassinations, 43 suicides and 37 arson attempts on the stages of the two Théâtres-Français; 175 assassinations, 55 thefts, 45 arson attempts at the Porte-Saint-Martin; and finally, on the stages of the Ambigu and the Gaîté, 195 assassinations, 300 poisonings with arsenic, corrosive sublimate, and other substances, 400 arson attempts, 780 robberies—150 of them armed, 200 by ladder, and 300 with skeleton keys.

At the very least, it suggests that language emanated from the stage—as from our comic-strip characters—in succinct puffs, that a subordinate clause would have tried the patience of spectators requiring from theater something other than food for thought. "I write for people who cannot read," declared Pixérécourt.*

What they sought was the thrill of precipices, the collective self-abandonment to pity and fear and rage, the atmosphere of *fêtes* which had transformed them into an emotional mass or an apostolic family capable of getting drunk on virtue. Just as Pixérécourt's rhetoric echoed Robespierre's—the essence of it being the cliché wherein an adjective

---

* Some years later, when Pixérécourt, having made his fortune, sought to ennoble his *oeuvre,* he wrote: "Melodrama purified the language of the people who, after seeing it played, borrowed it for two sous and read it until they knew it by heart. Poetry, that language of the gods, could be understood only by enlightened and educated spectators; tragedy is not in harmony with the education of the people. The great political interests which almost always constitute the basis of tragedy require, to be appreciated, long study and deep, extended, varied knowledge. Needed was a theater made specifically for the common people." There may, however, be no contradiction with his earlier remark in the sense that "people who cannot read" were people unable to read the language of cultivated men.

A scene from Alexandre Dumas's Antony, *with the caption:*
"She resisted me . . . I assassinated her!" From a lithograph by A. Johannot.
Encyclopédie du Théâtre contemporain

deals summary justice to a noun ("Virtuous woman!" "Inhuman monster!" "Vile seducer!" "Respectable old man!")—so his plots, like those
malignant "intrigues" to which Robespierre constantly made reference,
served to keep the public in suspense, to relax its grip on everyday reality, to make it desert its critical sense and plunge naked into a world
bereft of neutrality, where everything is as irrational as it is imbued
with moral purpose. Above the doorway to the Théâtre de l'Ambigu,
Pixérécourt might have written: "Relinquish common sense, all ye who
enter," or, "Here, everything is possible," for in the melodramatic
beyond, appearance always belies reality: the dead may spring to life,
and protagonists, whether heroes or villains, avail themselves of a thousand masks. Lured by some "mystery," that is, by some forbidden fruit
irresistible to the beast in him, what departure from rhyme and reason
would the average spectator not gladly oblige? For the privilege of committing incest, burning houses, eating human flesh (Pixérécourt's *Robinson Crusoe*), exerting superhuman strength, seeing in the dark, finding
treasure troves, and then emerging from this debauch in an odor of
sanctity, would he hesitate to lay his mind in forfeit? He inclined,
rather—as who does not once sleep descends?—to the wisdom of the
Fathers: Credo quia absurdum.

Thus did Pixérécourt build a parish more numerous, not to say
more lucrative, than any curate's in France. Provided by nature and history with believers, he led them wherever he chose, multiplying *coups
de théâtre,* one more exorbitant than the next, like a conjurer or like the
demagogue whose magnetism resides in the key he (and he alone) possesses to a world of semblances. In much the same way that the Terror
evoked an inimical "outside" dark beyond the power of ordinary reason and experience to penetrate it, marshaling the populace behind the
eye of surveillance before having them worship a Supreme Being, melodrama made reality something occult, portraying the world as a theatrical surface, an absurd fantasmagoria whose deeper design the lone spectator could not apprehend, or as a place not to be understood by
ordinary men but to be exorcized by the Playwright-Redeemer—a place
possessed.

The playwright's surrogate was usually (though not, as it happens,
in Pixérécourt's most famous melodrama, *Coelina*) a hero endowed
with remarkable powers of metamorphosis and with energy far beyond
the common measure who, but for the grace of God, might have be-

come a villain. Indeed, villains or "brigands" made popular in folk song and halfpenny rural magazines like the *Bibliothèque bleue* (which even Pixérécourt's nonreaders read, if they read nothing else) furnished the traditional mold. "The celebrated Cartouche had qualities that could have made him an admirable man, he did have: much wit, vivacity, and memory," wrote an eighteenth-century embellisher of the legend— Cartouche being one among others (notably Mandrin, Fanfan la Tulipe, and Compère Guilleri) who, for all their otherwise unpardonable mischief, gave the poor what they stole from the rich. "Great presence of mind and judgment and intrepidity. But wrongheaded ideas about honor, ostentation, and vainglory proved to be his undoing." Cleansing this heroic ore of its sensual impurities, La Martelière created Robert de Moldar, titular hero of *Robert, The Brigand Chief* which, it will be recalled, the Revolutionary secret police found unimpeachably 'Roman" in spirit despite La Martelière's declaration that "as a stranger to all the sects which have in turn appeared on our political horizon, I have never embraced any opinion or party other than that of law and justice." "Rousseauian" would have been the more felicitous designation, for Robert, prefiguring Pixérécourt's "Vivaldi, the man with three faces" (not to mention Dumas's Count of Monte Cristo, Balzac's Vautrin, and even, in a certain sense, Stendhal's Fabrice del Dongo) must, by whatever means, set to rights the corrupt society that wronged him.* With him, criminality became a calling, the criminal's mark or brand or signature a transcendent stigma, and his gang, if gang he leads, a community of militant disciples.

The melodramatic superman who evolved from Robert de Moldar, having no such mundane allegiances as may compel *hommes moyens sensuels* to bargain with justice or postpone its consummation, does not operate inside the confines of a social identity. Both his fluent disguises and his immutable essence, the magical transformations he works upon himself and the Fate branded in him betray the God-child who, to save, need only materialize. A Presence, or an Absence, he is born each time anew, emanating immaculately from nowhere (forest, mountain, desert) whenever called to redress some wrong—then evaporating. No cognitive process such as would involve doubt, ratiocination, and inquiry can

---

* It was in fact Rousseau who coined the term *mélodrame*, using it to define his play *Pygmalion*.

solve the riddles of melodramatic society; only passion—the absolute, instinctive passion for justice embodied by the hero, who is as mysterious as he is coefficient with his name. His name suffices. It heals, mends, sheds light on darkness. It transcends all knowledge and experience. It spells Truth. Exempt from rules of reason and laws of nature, he does not explain himself; rather, he identifies himself, affixing his mark to his deeds like an illiterate king issuing fiats, or a celebrity signing blank checks.

And whom does he save? Only those who cannot help themselves; for as misery loves company, so superman loves the infirm. Though Vivaldi's confession in *The Man With Three Faces*—

> There is perhaps beneath my coarse envelope a heart more tender and a soul more generous than yours [the Doge's]! . . . That is the goal toward which I lean, the glory I mean to acquire. These run-of-the-mill men, these beings one sees loitering by the thousands through the streets of Venice resemble insects creeping beneath our feet: one crushes them, or if one spares them it is because one despises them, and one sees them expire every day without having so much as suspected their existence. Not for me the shame of such a destiny! Only what is rare and extraordinary has a claim to the esteem of our contemporaries and the admiration of posterity.

—would not appear to speak well of the hero, his experience of demagogic psychology told him that children fearful of being trodden underfoot readily identify with ruthless giants striding overhead. Like the great summer festival of 1793, which saw floats honoring the aged, the blind, and foundling children in white bassinets lumber through an arch gory with paintings of severed heads, melodrama could mix—as if this were its ultimate formula—the tears of compassion shed by "the little people" for themselves and the blood of *les grands* shed by their transcendent justiciar.* When seen from close up by sympathetic eyes, what came to be known by the bourgeois as the "Boulevard of Crime" resembled a boulevard of walking wounded.

No less various than the crimes perpetrated by melodramatic villains were the afflictions endured by melodramatic innocents. Good old Werner, in Pixérécourt's play *The Woman with Two Husbands*, is

---

* The blind were positioned around a woman who personified "Misery Crowned."

blind, as is good old Albert in *Valentine*. Philippe, an old sergeant who makes the heart bleed in *The Fortress on the Danube* has only one eye, and Dufour in *Coelina*, lest we doubt his virtue even for an instant, proves it a priori by suffering from gout. On the amputated limbs of Pixérécourt's personae, Napoleon could have mounted another Grand Army. As for parents, to judge from the orphans who abound, parenthood would appear to have been a peculiarly suicidal enterprise. Highest among martyrs, however, ranked the Mute. That no one brought tears to Boulevard eyes more readily than he who had been, in Pixérécourt's pompous expression, "deprived of the Word," accounts in some measure for the popularity won by *Coelina* and, fourteen years later, by *The Dog of Montargis* (in which, once again, a mute wrongly bears the onus of someone else's crime). What is the mute, indeed, but the hero himself turned round about? Where the hero's name has the force of magical incantation, the mute's aphonia translates his anomia: speechless, he is nameless. Where the hero administers justice summary and absolute (reminding us by the way that Pixérécourt was a barrister *manqué*), the mute's inability to plead his case, to make himself heard, to answer his accusers, is a nightmarish precondition of injustice summary and absolute. Where the hero lives outside society, the mute is an alien or a prisoner within it. More clearly perhaps than any of melodrama's other traits, this particular idiosyncrasy revealed it to be religious in nature, to consist of moralities whose very subject was the cultural schism between those who possessed the Word and those who did not. Now a mute victim of evil tongues, now a supreme actor whose gift of self-transformation evokes the glossolalia of Jesus' ignorant zealots, the *infantes*, having struggled for generations against the Roman establishment, were canonized as melodramatic saints.

Pixérécourt wrote for "people who cannot read." This category embraced not only the very poor but the very rich, or in any event the *new* rich whose favorite address, the Chaussée d'Antin, became, during the Directory of 1795–99, synonymous with their lack of breeding. "Ladies from the Chaussée d'Antin push and shove in the Boulevard crowd right alongside rustics from the faubourg Saint-Antoine," observed one commentator in 1809, while another marveled at the women

*A theater on the Boulevard du Temple during the Napoleonic period,
showing three actors performing a* parade *to whet the public's curiosity.*
Bibliothèque Nationale

who came dressed to kill, as it were, taking cosmetic measures "worthy of the Opéra in its prime." When Fay (administrator of the Marseille theater and author of a *Plan for the General Organization of all the Theaters of the Empire*) considered the Boulevard, what he saw from his Mediterranean perspective was a combination zoo and corrida (indeed, bullfights were staged near the Boulevard du Temple in the 1820s and 1830s) which reduced all spectators, both the grand and the humble, to their lowest common denominator. "The coarse populace, seduced by a bogus magic that dazzles it while playing tricks with its reason, and even high society, excited by the attraction of and need for novelty, would throng to these monstrosities, as one goes to see some hideous animal on public exhibition," he wrote.

That a raw society may resemble nothing quite so much as a jaded one is borne home by the evocations of Byzantium and third-century Rome in Balzac's novelistic cycle, *The Human Comedy*. According to the actor Fleury, who narrowly escaped death during the Terror only to be slain by indifference during its aftermath, the new patricians, like the old, put in appearances at the Théâtre-Français, as it behooved them to do, but otherwise frequented the "little theaters," some of which were palatial: "The ladies of *new France* led the charge [to the Boulevard]. They'd rent a box for the season in our Théâtre-Français where they would come and spend an hour or two in order to flash their jewels; but on the outlying boulevards were the houses they preferred. There, for a nominal sum, they could get their thrice-weekly ration of catastrophe, fire, and carnage." As under the monarchy, fairground actors earned a livelihood staging *parades* in town houses and country villas, so, round about 1805, it became fashionable to throw parties at which an author of popular repute would divert the company by reading fresh off the page his latest melodrama.

Despite a pre-Revolutionary career as the Vicomtesse de Beauharnais, Josephine, who once owned a town house on the Chaussée d'Antin, may be said to have stood foremost among these "ladies of new France," her penchant for vulgar entertainment defeating, like a Russian winter, the various and relentless campaigns Napoleon mounted against it. Whenever he left Malmaison to wage war in the outlying regions of Europe, she, as police memoranda and newspaper articles informed him, would leave it to seek pleasure on the outlying boulevards of Paris. "Yesterday there was an immense crowd at the Théâtre de la

Cité," the *Journal de Paris* reported in February 1807, a fortnight after the battle of Eylau. "Cries of 'Long live the Empress' and several rounds of applause interrupted the spectacle for some while. The august object of this uproar was not, unhappily, visible to *all* eyes; but all hearts divined her presence, and good cheer was everywhere in evidence." Cheer was evident everywhere but at French headquarters in Osterode, where another pair of eyes that could not see Josephine divined her presence. What caused the people to applaud caused the Emperor to frown. "My friend," he wrote, while Cossacks were tormenting the winter bivouac of his ragged army, "you must not occupy a little box in little theaters: it is not appropriate to your rank. You must attend only the big theaters and always occupy the grand loge. Live as you did when I was in Paris."

Josephine's flanking maneuver did not quite drive every other thought from his mind: in addition to Grand Army bulletins, he found time during this period to write letters ordering festivals in Paris, reprimanding newspapers, defending Mirabeau's memory against mud slung in the Académie by Cardinal Maury, exiling Madame de Staël, and detailing a regimen for the girls' school at Ecouen. But it nonetheless became a bone of contention he worried doggedly. "I note with pleasure that you have been to the Opéra and that you plan to receive every week: do go to shows from time to time, and always sit in the grand loge," he wrote, once again from the battlefront. Lest there linger in her mind even the shadow of a doubt as to what was big and what little, what primary and what secondary, a ministerial decree issued in April 1807 gave the measure of all such things. "Considered as big theaters are the Comédie-Française, the Théater de l'Impératrice, the Opéra, and the Opéra-Comique," it read. "Secondary theaters are: the Vaudeville, the Variétés-Montansier, the Porte-Saint-Martin, the Gaîté, the Variétés Etrangères. Other theaters now existing in Paris and authorized by the police are considered annexes of the secondary theaters."

Napoleon's own diminutiveness may serve to explain this contempt for the "little" which, though it extended far beyond theater per se, conferred upon all his policies, whether aesthetic or diplomatic, something in the nature of a theatrical stratagem. Thus, Fontaine, his chief architect, could observe, "The Emperor found it distasteful to seek beauty elsewhere than in size; he could not imagine that the two might be distinct. Whenever intermediate buildings were suggested to him, he

The Boulevard du Temple at night, early nineteenth century.
Bibliothèque Nationale

deplored the loss of the large open space between both wings, reiterating that 'only what is large is beautiful: size and space compensate for many mistakes.' " Napoleon was, moreover, foreign. Not only did he stand below eye level, but he came from outside France—a predicament that fortified his ambition to acquire a proper "name" and his intolerance for all traditions save the grand one. Did marriage, like martial tours de force, not provide—among other satisfactions—a shortcut to authenticity, as he himself suggests in his memoirs? * The evenings she spent in Boulevard boxes were evenings spent off that other stage where Napoleon enjoined her to disport herself like a theater queen. For him, such behavior constituted an impropriety in the Aristotelian sense, un-

---

* "Barras did me a service by advising me to wed Joséphine. He assured me that she belonged both to the old and the new Society, and that this fact . . . would bring me more support; that her house was the best in Paris, and would rid me of my Corsican name; finally that through this marriage I should become quite French."

dermining conventions that made plausible the role or the image he would never cease striving to embody. "Do you know what Napoleon said?" wrote Stendhal in *The Charterhouse of Parma*. " 'A man placed in high position, whom all the world regards, ought not permit himself violent movements.' " Napoleon's esteem for Talma, the great tragic actor whom he claims to have met when he first met the widow Beau-harnais and often, thereafter, honored with breakfast invitations (for normally, he ate by himself), was as high as his dream of stoic altitude.

Had it been tolerable in all other respects, still the Boulevard would have offended Napoleon by virtue of its exuberance alone—the raucous crowds it attracted, the theaters that proliferated without benefit of rhyme or reason, the mongrel genres that harked back to *sans-culottides* (even as they anticipated the Romantic drama). Dauntless on the battle-field, he was, and would always remain, frightened of berserk mobs. Reading this passage in his memoirs: "The more I study Voltaire the better I like him. He was a man who was always sensible; he was nei-ther a charlatan nor a fanatic. . . . Up to the age of sixteen [when he entered the army and suffered the loss of his father] I would have fought for Rousseau against all the friends of Voltaire. Today it is the opposite. Since I have seen the East, Rousseau is repugnant to me. The wild man without morals is a dog"—one surmises that the East was a quarter roomy enough to include both Cossacks and east-end sans-culottes of the Saint-Antoine quarter. They regularly queued up on the Boulevard du Temple munching apple-puffs, chewing Bologna sausage, quaffing tumblers of licorice water, and sucking oranges—the peels of which served as missiles later to be thrown from the cheap seats, or "para-dise," onto well-coiffed heads below. These were the same population he had seen in August 1792 throwing Swiss Guards out of the Tuileries windows and "committing . . . the worst kind of indecencies on their corpses." While Napoleon was, in their eyes, the melodramatic *ubique victor*, they, in his view, represented the intemperate mind whose fan-tasies could suborn that which he held dearer than life itself: order.

After Josephine's indiscretions of 1807 he resolved to master the Boulevard, and to master it as he had mastered the dangerously hetero-

Si d. la premier parole je ne vous dis pas la vérité Messieurs, l'exacte vérité entrez dans mon cercle, déchirez
mes cartes, traitez-moi de fourbe et d'imposteur à haute et intelligible voix: l'honneur me sera ravi, c'est ce que j'ai de
plus cher au monde; mais si au contraire je justifie la confiance dont vous voudrez bien m'honorer si au contraire
je vous retrace exactement les principaux événemens de votre existence jusqu'à ce jour et si au contraire je vous
avertis positivement sur les dangers qui vous menacent, sur les pièges que l'on vous tend et sur la réussite des entreprises que vous avez entreprises et qu'en un mot Messieurs j'ai rencontré juste, point d'approbation je ne les aime
pas, mais comme il est naturel que chacun vive de ses talents je ne vous demanderai que la simple bagatelle, le
simple déboursé de 2 sous.

A sample of the "little people" who watched from the cheap seats, commonly known as "paradise."

geneous provinces that stretched beyond Paris—by bureaucratizing it. In July 1807 the *Bulletin of the Laws* published a decree that read, in part:

> The *maximum* number of theaters in our good city of Paris is fixed at eight; consequently, the only theaters, aside from the big four, henceforth permitted to open, post bills, and perform plays are the following: 1. The Théâtre de la Gaíté, established in 1760; the Ambigu-Comique, established in 1772 on the Boulevard du Temple; these will stage, concurrently, plays of the same genre as designated in paragraphs 3 and 4 of article III of the ordinance issued by our Minister of Interior. 2. The Théâtre des Variétés, Boulevard Montmartre, established in 1777, and the Théâtre du Vaude-ville, established in 1792; these will stage, concurrently, plays of the same genre as designated in paragraphs 3 and 4 of the ordinance issued by our Minister of Interior.
>
> All theaters not authorized by the preceding article will be closed before August 16.
>
> Consequently, under no pretext shall plays be performed in other theaters in our good city of Paris; nor shall the public be allowed to enter, even free of charge; no bill shall be posted, no ticket, whether handwritten or printed, shall be distributed. Violations are punishable according to the laws and police ordinances.

Rights that the *menu peuple* had won sixteen years before were thus lost in what one victim, an elderly impresario who ended his days operating a magic lantern in the Marbeuf Gardens, called "Monsieur Bonaparte's second *coup d'état*." The pre-Revolutionary line dividing high from low was traced once again, but this time with a sword that would countenance no sly trespassings. Arrayed four against four, the theaters, by their very symmetry, were made to affirm the essential irreconcilability of two worlds, to sustain a battle drawn, and to reflect the absolute power vested in an even-handed ruler. Like Beckett characters who can, for some mysterious reason, sit but not stand, or stand but not sit, each embodied one and only one genre—the Ambigu melodrama, the Vaudeville plays with couplets sung to familiar airs, the Variétés village farce, the Théâtre-Français classical repertoire. Whatever lay outside these separate and distinct prefectures of the imagination had no right to speak or, in the French term, to "represent" itself—except physically.

Contriving not to disappear altogether, entrepreneurs went backward in time, and purveyed silent drama or divertissements suitable for children. Dwarfs, giants, and trained animals came to occupy the Théâtre des Délassements-Comiques. In the Théâtre de la Cité (where Josephine had enjoyed a delinquent interlude) acrobats did somersaults on horseback while clowns jollied up the crowd. Figures of wax and wood replaced actors, drama gave way to conjury, to fencing matches, and to demonstrations of ventriloquism; theaters were transformed wholesale into *cafés-concert* (popular dance halls) or parcelled into boutiques. Only one establishment dared to protest—the Porte-Saint-Martin, which had been built during Louis XVI's reign to house the Opéra. Distinguished by the sophistication of its shows and the magnificence of its proportions, it stood on the Boulevard without being of it. Napoleon's decree struck it from the theatrical map of Paris not only because it robbed the Comédie-Française of middle-class patrons but because the emperor's taxonomically rigid order could not accommodate its ambiguous nature. When the minister of interior, after lengthy deliberation, allowed it to reopen, he stipulated that it call itself not the Porte-Saint-Martin but the Jeux Gymniques and that it perform, in its new, unambiguously plebeian incarnation, only:

1. Gymnastic games: these games will consist of tightrope dances, somersaults, feats of strength and dexterity such as wrestling, boxing, gladiatorial contests, jousts.

2. Historical tableaux: of the Servandoni genre. In these tableaux, the decorations will be of the essence. Each tableau will be allowed to present one fact, one great event.

3. Military maneuvers: this spectacle will consist of marches, assaults, infantry and cavalry combats.

4. Prologues: these will feature one, or at most two, characters. It will be permissible to explain by such prologues the subjects of the historical tableaux, maneuvers and other games. The characters who figure in these, and the dotards or buffoons whom one normally employs in the feats of strength or dexterity will be the only ones allowed to speak in this spectacle.

It is noteworthy that the man who formulated this remarkable syllabus, Montalivet, otherwise commended himself to posterity by organizing great public works and championing France's industrial expansion. Any departure from the cadre of official amusement, any word exchanged in all seriousness by plausible characters would straightaway inspire him to issue a call-to-order that began, typically: "I am informed that you have, in defiance of your obligations, given performances that step outside the genre assigned to your spectacle, that you have staged, under various aliases, true dramatic plays, although this genre is reserved exclusively for the capital's eight theaters. I warn you . . ." The Boulevard was thus classified, beyond appeal, as a primitive outskirt, a suburb indifferently childish and senile, a Bedlam.

Held captive in genres, with its very irrationality rationalized, Boulevard theater had no choice but to rant and rave or else be silent, like some wild beast caged in a zoo. Outside proper society, proper society might visit this permanent exhibition of its past without falling prey to it. Juridical bars now separated fantasy from reality and reason from unreason. Behind them, on a penitentiary stage, the monsters did what monsters ought to do. Indeed, enshrined as *monstres sacrés*, they performed a ritual function, justifying Order by being incorrigibly wild, maintaining the status quo by preserving an image of the status quo ante. "This spectacle is necessary," declared the *Opinion du parterre* after the inauguration of the Théâtre des Variétés in June 1807. "In a big city where several theaters are open every day, there ought to be one specially consecrated to coarse gaiety. On other stages only spiritual gaiety is admissible, gaiety which is cold, restrained or, in a word, such as it must be to please people of good tone. The old kind ought to have asylum somewhere." Asylum it was given, on what many bourgeois came to regard as a lunatic fringe of the city, or a penal colony within it—an "underworld."

In a country where *la gloire* covers a multitude of sins, the Boulevard proved to be France's most indulgent neighborhood. Napoleon's legend was even more despotic than Napoleon himself, and the freedom won by theatrical entrepreneurs during the 1830 Revolution might have been construed as freedom of worship, for the *Courrier des Théâtres* informs us that on certain evenings, upward of thirty plays elaborated chapters from the great man's life, as if he were the Savior, Boulevard managers a Brotherhood of the Passion, and theater an epiphenomenon of Gospel. Among odd specimens on the Boulevard, none—not even Améline the giantess, who would saunter about carrying in her arms her friend Carolina-la-Laponne, a professional dwarf—caught the eye more readily than Gobert, Cazot, and Prudent. Cast in the role of Napoleon night after night, year after year, these actors would seem to have mistaken themselves for him, if not for one another, all three alike twirling Caesarean locks between nervous fingers, or walking solemnly, hands clasped behind the back, or again, pinching snuff from the leather-lined pockets of white kerseymere waistcoats. With their bent brows, cocked hats, and Olympian gazes, they were what Henry James would call, in portraying those too-perfect artist models of the aristocratic couple, Major and Mrs. Monarch, "the real thing." Political considerations aside, the fact that Napoleon had been betrayed, driven from the family of nations, and held prisoner on a barren rock made him a God-given candidate for apotheosis on the Boulevard, a *monstre* fit to redeem all others of that ilk. It is as though the genres, with Montalivet long since gone, had dared to venture outside their respective theaters. Did Guilbert de Pixérécourt's melodrama not, after all, resemble history, and the history of Napoleon Bonaparte pure melodrama?

Even before it enthroned itself in July 1830 as King Louis Philippe, the bourgeoisie that emerged from Revolutionary turmoil and Napoleon's wars made a ruling principle of thrift, of accumulation, of solidity. To be sure, it would never, for all its anticlericalism, altogether relinquish the messianic hypothesis that it was God's own representative on earth, that it had a message to deliver or a mission to perform. Thus, the liberal paper, *Le Siècle*, could proclaim that "France's mission is to protect all rights which have suffered or which have reason to fear violence. If it can deliver Poland, it will do so; if it can liberate Italy, it will do that too; if a spontaneous movement breaks out among the little states of Germany . . . it will offer its support. . . . That is what we mean when we say that France exercises, to its eternal honor and to the advantage of nations surrounding it, *this force of expansion God has placed in its breast*" (italics added).

But in fact its stomach expanded rather more conspicuously than its breast during the 1820s, 1830s, and 1840s when Stendhal had Julien Sorel give vent to his famous exclamation: "Oh, hypocritical nineteenth century!" However sluggishly, in comparison with England, France awoke to the industrial age. Where in 1815 it had fewer than twenty steam engines, by 1848 nearly four thousand were generating power. Factories multiplied, as did applications for commercial licenses. An article of the Civil Code provided that all a man's sons divide their father's estate equally, democratizing the money game. Alike capital and people became incomparably more mobile than hitherto. Immigrants from the countryside swelled the population of cities, while 5 percent government bonds doubled in value. "Enrich yourselves by work and thrift," commanded Guizot when he was minister of public instruction during the 1830s. "Ascend," cried others, with fervor no less evangelical for twisting the traditional terms of Catholic salvation. Not the meek but the enterprising would inherit the earth. To Adolphe Thiers—who rose very high indeed, first entering Paris as an obscure lawyer from Marseille, marrying into great wealth, attaining the prime ministership (1836, 1840) and, several decades later, the presidency of the republic before exiting to occupy, offstage, the largest mausoleum in Père-Lachaise—history was a dynastic progression, a *Bildungsroman* without end. "The father was a peasant, a factory worker, a merchant sailor," he wrote in *On Property*. "The son, assuming his father was diligent and frugal, will be a farmer, a manufacturer, a ship's captain. The grandson will be a banker, a notary, a doctor, a lawyer, a prime minister perhaps. Thus do the generations rise, one above the other." To Balzac it was a Dantean epic, but human rather than divine, in which men and women clamber up the golden ladder or slip from it, in which fiscality permeates life, with numbers present everywhere, dancing around the cradle of newborn infants, following lovers to bed, and stalking dead men to their grave, if not beyond. Like God, the devil, in the person of Vautrin who presides over funds amassed underground by the criminal community, is a banker.

As for liberty, fraternity, and equality, a banker—this one a real banker of colossal wealth named Lafitte—formulated what was to become the constitutional monarchy's political credo when he wrote in 1824, six years before the July Revolution: "I have always considered the material weal to be least problematical, least difficult to achieve, least infiltrated by government; I have always thought that, when all

Daumier's devastating caricature of King Louis Philippe as an insatiable Gargantua swallowing all the resources of the state. Bibliothèque Nationale

other forms of well-being were almost impossible, we had to fall back upon that one. One cannot give a land freedom: give it, instead, the fortune that will soon render it more enlightened, better, and free. Governments will always accept the bait of wealth and will soon be surprised to discover that any development in men, whatever it may be, always leads to freedom."

Far from representing a universal given of human nature, liberty belonged to those who had contrived to earn it. Though laws protected all men equally, under the *régime censitaire*, so called on account of a law that made electoral privilege contingent upon property qualifications, only free men could legislate. (The king, the ministers, the deputies, and the approximately two hundred thousand electors constituted what Guizot called *le pays légal*. The "people" was in his view a legal nonentity advertised by "pamphleteers" and "idlers.") The year 1848 would demonstrate to what degree their legislation served their own proprietary interests and reflected their fear of the mass underfoot. Even as they spoke of "delivering" Poland from the oppressive hand of Russia, of "liberating" Italy from papal tyranny, of "supporting" the little German states against a Lutheran squirearchy, otherwise liberal bourgeois ruled like Russia, Gregory XVI, and Prussia, over the disenfranchised poor, denying the right to work to those thrown out of work by machines and denying workers the right to bargain for a livelihood, stopping their ears to pleas on behalf of children who drudged in factories or mines from dawn to dusk, and tabling, decade after decade, the idea of a vocational-school system. Not that they were badly unconscionable Ubus. On the contrary, they did what they did in good conscience, invoking Wealth or Production to justify a slave class rather as Robespierre had invoked the Supreme Being to justify "the despotism of liberty."

France was business first of all and philosophical allegiances deferred to the bottom line. Except for the word "subject," this opinion—"The king's most faithful subject is he who is best able to pay his taxes"—might have issued from the mouth of almost any post-Revolutionary dignitary rather than from Baron Louis, Louis XVIII's minister of finance. The tax roll, in short, was tantamount to a patriotic register. A man could consider himself a "true" citizen when his name figured on it, as opposed to beneficiaries of the dole, wards of the State, losers in the Darwinian struggle for survival. If these losers provided eleemosynary careers for social matrons condemned to a life of pious leisure, all the more reason to regard them not as citizens but as savages morally estranged from the nation. "Workers are outside political society, outside the city: they are the barbarians of modern societies," declared the arch-conservative *Journal des Débats*. In grade schools and in free public lectures, teachers sought to inculcate homilies that would help the poor to endure a wretched life rather than skills that would help them rise above it.

Such philanthropic exertions call to mind Clausewitz's dictum that war is policy continued by other means. Now teaching the beast to lie still, now crushing it outright, the bourgeoisie might have been neither so missionary nor so callous, neither so prodigal of gifts to charitable institutions nor so mercilessly exploitative of labor had they not believed their order threatened by an alien species, a primitive horde, by a race inherently different from themselves. "Drunk," "savage," "barbaric," "criminal," "nomadic": these figured prominently among the epithets often foisted upon *le menu peuple* by men who were all the more apt to disown the lower class for having, in many cases, recently emerged from it, and who, to bolster their social position, invoked crypto-racist mystiques like Gall's phrenology, which gained widespread credence among French bourgeois. Where history failed them in having failed to give them aristocratic blood, appearances would suffice, furnishing as they did evidence that anatomy was destiny.* What could they have in common with those dark gnomes streaming into Paris from the Auvergne, or with wretches whose cranial structure exhibited not the effects of lifelong inanition and unremitting labor but a natural propensity for destructiveness ("the predatory instinct," as Gall called it)? Could nomads understand the concept of property or the sanctity of a hearth, and inebriates the life of reason?

Bound together geographically and economically, the higher and

---

* Phrenology is the theory developed by Franz Joseph Gall that mental faculties can be judged by the shape of the skull. His land of bumps and bulges was a wonderfully faithful reflection of the bourgeoisie's moral geography. It is divided into "lower sentiments" and "superior" sentiments. The "propensities" include "love of progeniture," "feeling of property," and "sense of mechanics." One might mention, in this connection, the "recognition scenes" that were the crux of so many eighteenth-century domestic dramas. In the birthmark or "strawberry," which constituted proof of a long-lost child's kinship, the bourgeoisie celebrated a myth analogous to aristocratic *naissance* or *sang*.

lower orders regarded each other from either side of a palisade, with terrified circumspection. "Workers," wrote one social commentator, Eugène Buret, in *The Wretchedness of the Laboring Classes*, "are as little duty-bound to their masters as are the latter to them; they consider them men of a different class, not only standing opposed but standing in violent opposition. Isolated from the nation, cast outside the social and political community, alone with their needs and their miseries, they struggle to get out of this frightful solitude and, who knows, may, like the barbarians to whom they have been compared, be plotting an invasion." Similarly, Eugène Sue, a ship's doctor who gave up medicine and the sea to write novels about Paris's lower depths, presents himself in one such novel, *The Mysteries of Paris* (1843), as an anthropologist recording the customs of a primitive society. "Everyone," he declared in his preface, "has read those admirable pages in which James Fenimore Cooper . . . traces the ferocious customs of savages, their picturesque, poetic language, the thousand ruses by means of which they flee or pursue their enemies. . . . The barbarians of whom we speak are in our midst; we can rub elbows with them by venturing into their lairs where they congregate to plot murder or theft, and to divvy up the spoils. These men have mores all their own, women different from others, a language incomprehensible to us; a mysterious language thick with baneful images, with metaphors dripping blood." What moral obligation did one owe to a race who spoke not French but a "mysterious" tongue, a language that translated appetites, violent impulses, and animist beliefs, as if it were the instinctual life in its purest expression? Threatened by a Stone Age neighbor radically bereft of reason, bourgeois felt compelled to defend themselves with every means at their disposal. Though they found Sue's tales utterly absorbing, few dared accept his invitation to tour savage Paris. Instead, they sequestered themselves from the feral "other" behind walls of *politesse* so elaborate as to make life at Versailles seem lax by comparison. One manual, for example, argued that on a rainy day the "truly polite" person could shelter someone caught without his or her umbrella "provided age, sex, attire did not oppose the gesture, for it would be entirely inappropriate to address oneself to people of the lowest social class."

What is more, the bourgeoisie built a capital, a separate city that transformed such propriety into stone and marble and iron and glass. Under the constitutional monarchy, during the 1840s, well-to-do people deserted central Paris for new *quartiers* at the northern and western periphery, drawing commercial establishments along with them; what they deserted became a forsaken island within the city whose labyrinthine streets and tenements were dense with humanity pressing in from rural France. It was, in part, to reverse these migrations that Napoleon III laid waste to the old neighborhoods. As a result of the upheaval wrought by Baron Haussmann's engineers, indigent people found themselves swept outward beyond the customs barriers into a pariahdom that time and suffrage would dignify with a symbolic place name, "the red belt." "The circumstances that oblige workers to live at some distance from the center of Paris are generally noted to have had maleficent effects upon their conduct and morality," the Chamber of Commerce and prefect of police stated in 1855. "As a rule, they used to inhabit the uppermost stories of houses occupied down below by families of industrial entrepreneurs and people relatively well-to-do. A kind of solidarity would form among residents of such houses. . . . Workers would find succor and assistance when they fell ill or lost their jobs; in addition, human respect would inject an element of regularity into working-class habits. By transporting themselves north of the Saint-Martin Canal or beyond the barriers, workers live where there are no bourgeois families and find themselves deprived of help and freed of the bridle that such proximity formerly imposed upon them." Though matters had come to this sorry pass only one generation after the *Trois Glorieuses,* the glorious days of July 1830 when an otherwise sedate gentleman like Barbier eulogized "the great populace and the saintly rabble" who had fought and perished at barricades, there were those who could foresee it even then. Hearing someone shout, "How beautiful to have drawn this populace out of its ghetto!" Casimir Périer, Louis Philippe's first prime minister, rejoined: "It will be far more beautiful to drive it back in!" By turns sainted and damned, the *peuple* was, in either event, an outsider.

Society exercised its values no less in play than in work. The honor bestowed upon an essentially antiquarian young dramatist like Casimir Delavigne, whose star easily outshone Hugo's or Musset's during the Restoration and the July Monarchy, constitutes one measure of the extent to which academicism supported the bourgeoisie's racist mythology. As comforting as the progressive bromides strewn throughout *The Sicilian Vespers, The School for Old Men, Marino Faliero,* and *Louis XI* was the emphatically regressive style in which Delavigne formulated them: the periphrastic turns of phrase that curled backward to the Old Regime, for example, or the embellishments that made his work seem venerable at birth. For sober, common-sensical pleasure, people had recourse to other playwrights, notably Eugène Scribe. What Delavigne gave those parvenus who, following Napoleon's example, eschewed Boulevard melodrama, was a proprietary stake in the grand tradition, a deed to French culture. That one of their own kind could fabricate alexandrine verse scanned and buffed to a fare-thee-well; that tragedy, the genre of genres, could emerge from within their own collective soul represented something tantamount to evidence of a *generic* distinction from the plebs. Hugo might protest in his preface to *Cromwell* that "the French language is not *fixed* and never will be. A language cannot be fixed. The human mind is always on the march or, if you will, in movement, and languages move with it. . . . Languages are like the sea, they undulate ceaselessly." No matter. Such words were anathema to a public of two minds about marches and movement, to *arrivistes* who diligently attended the Théâtre-Français as much to acquire a patina as to witness drama. "If you dare," wrote *Le Globe* in 1825, "go sit once a week in the orchestra of the Salle Richelieu or the Odéon, amidst that group of amateurs whose starchy features and superdignified attitudes announce a pretension to judge far more than a desire to enjoy. . . . The theater is, in their eyes, a kind of academy where pompous orators come to declaim, methodically, long speeches."

Similarly, Hugo might call for a new dramatic style in which the verse line would, "like Proteus," assume a thousand forms "without departing from character" and be beautiful or ugly but beautiful or ugly by the way, as though its content were its energetic movement and its appeal its lack of memory, its innocence of aesthetic categories, its unselfconsciousness. Here again, his manifesto was calculated to fill ladies and gentlemen with consternation, for "Protean" belonged to that family of epithets ritually convoked to poormouth the lower class: nomads who lacked a fixed place lacked a fixed shape. Without genres to distinguish high from low, there could be no foundation on which to predicate distinctions of breed, no *essential* hiatus between the orders, no structure consecrating power and property. Everything would fuse. Everything would be possible. "If the effect of democracy is generally to question the authority of all literary rules and conventions, on the stage it abolishes them altogether, and puts in their place nothing but the whim of each author and of each public," wrote Tocqueville in *Democracy in America*. "When the heroes and the manners of antiquity are frequently brought upon the stage, and dramatic authors faithfully observe the rules of antiquated precedent, that is enough to warrant a conclusion that the democratic classes have not yet got the upper hand in the theaters."

Even as Romantics laid siege to the fortress of rhetorical Beauty, rolling out Shakespeare's name like a battering ram, bourgeois took refuge behind its walls. When, in 1833, the Théâtre-Français staged *Edward's Children*, a tragedy by Casimir Delavigne, those critics who beheld themselves as interior decorators of the mind (upholding *le bon ton* or *le bon goût*) found it very much more to their taste than its model, Shakespeare's *Richard III*. Duviquet, for example, praised the author for not leading his public, like Shakespeare, "on a three-hour jaunt through a labyrinth of crimes and horrors" and for sparing "delicate" nerves the obscenity of Buckingham's execution. "Never would a low word have the nerve to show itself therein," he wrote, defending Delavigne's work as if it were a private club and he its concierge. Indeed, monitors of Order drew upon the same fund of metaphors whether commenting upon the stage in particular or upon the city at large. Thus, "a labyrinth of crimes and horrors" might serve to describe either Shakespeare's dramaturgy, the Boulevard du Temple (Nodier was fond of calling Pixérécourt "Shakespirécourt"), or infamous ghettos like "little Poland" on the Ile de la Cité.

Had the champions of this social mythology ever found themselves disposed to seek a perfect incarnation of their nightmares, they need only have visited the Boulevard du Temple where, some few months after that neo-Jacobin uprising in Lyons in 1834 whose bloody consequence was the massacre on the rue Transnonain, the actor and playwright Frédérick Lemaître created *Robert Macaire*. To allow that this play, which seldom figures in literary histories, won popular acclaim is really to understate the truth. Its titular hero became proverbial among outcasts of every stripe—among *le petit peuple* who could recognize in him certain vestiges of the traditional bandit; among aristocrats who, avenging themselves upon history for having made them its sport, had recourse to such murderous irony as constituted the very stuff of *Robert Macaire*; among intellectuals who echoed Heine's view that "the thinking men who worked indefatigably throughout the eighteenth century to prepare the French Revolution would blush if they could see personal interest busily building its wretched huts on the site of the ruined palaces, and from these huts a new aristocracy emerging, even more unpleasant than the old. . . ." The character of Macaire sprang from the bin into which capitalist society dumped its waste, like a scarecrow amalgamating nobiliary particles, Revolutionary ideals, criminal slang, and the poor man's rags. Conjured up not by a writer but by a great actor, the greatest actor of the Romantic stage, he embodied, as if natively, that histrionic remoteness, that sense of unreality, that expatriate air the *mot juste* for which was "Bohemia."

As to his origins, Macaire very nearly missed being the stock villain of a melodrama, *The Inn of Les Adrets*, written in 1824 by three Boulevard hacks. If it had not been for young Frédérick Lemaître, who found himself cast in that role, Macaire would have disappeared, along with the play itself, after several dozen performances. But Lemaître "guyed" the part—whether to make his mark by a flamboyant departure from convention or simply to keep from laughing. Thus, instead of tiptoeing onstage with his arms raised to hide his face, the way villains axiomatically did, he strode forward like a father or a lover. Attired not in the uniform of evil but in a motley assemblage that consisted of patched trousers, bedroom slippers, a dirty white vest, a green coat much the worse for wear, and a gray felt hat raffishly tilted to one side of his head, he looked every inch the scavenger. *The Inn of Les Adrets* provoked gales of laughter, bringing its authors a "tearful success," though not the success or the tears on which they had confidently banked, and it married its star to a role that shadowed him even beyond the grave.

With Macaire, who "quipped as he killed," black humor, or gallows humor, acquired a face and a demeanor. Having come into existence as ridicule of the moral scheme sustained by melodramatic formulas, as a character in quotation marks, he spoke to the feelings of profound dissociation that beset his diverse audience. Where villains and heroes upheld the Just Society from opposite poles, keeping it glued together by magnetic tension, Macaire, who combined features of both,

Frédérick Lemaître in old age posing as Robert Macaire.
Encyclopédie du Théâtre contemporain

was a kind of con artist transcending ethical distinctions, an "outsider" beholden to no common ideal, a *homo duplex* killing gratuitously or assuming aliases for the fun of it. "The people," wrote Heine, "have so lost faith in the high ideals of which our political and literary Tartuffes prate so much that they see in them nothing but empty phrases—*blague* as their saying goes. This comfortless outlook is illustrated by Robert Macaire; it is likewise illustrated by the popular dances, which may be regarded as the spirit of Robert Macaire put into mime. Anyone acquainted with the latter will be able to form some idea of these indescribable dances, which are satires not only of sex and society but of everything that is good and beautiful, of all enthusiasm, patriotism, loyalty, faith, family feeling, heroism, and religion."

Every revival of *The Inn of Les Adrets*, with which Lemaître made do until he wrote *Robert Macaire*, transforming it from a play into a vehicle for topical extemporizations, had blazing success. That he could pack the house simply by announcing as he did on one occasion— "Ladies and gentlemen, we regret that we are unable to murder a gendarme this evening, as the actor who plays that part is indisposed. But tomorrow we shall kill two"—suffices to evoke the desert of mutual hatred separating haves and have-nots.

In 1832, when cholera swept Paris, there arose among the poor a suspicion (fueled by radical journalists) that the disease was not at all a disease but one more lie propagated by authorities intent on poisoning them *en masse.* So firmly did this idea take hold that the mob lynched innocents unfortunate enough to have been caught bending over wells or lingering outside wineshops. "To the lamppost with poisoners!" became a cry commonly heard. Nomads in a land of property, drunks in a sober nation, and trash in a republic of avid collectors, the "little people" had reason to expect that they could be expunged summarily, liv-

---

* The cholera pandemic of 1831–32 had begun in Bengal and spread throughout the world. The toll taken by the disease in European cities was nothing like as severe as it was in, say, Cairo, where 13 percent of the population succumbed, but everywhere it struck, cholera sent great shock waves through the population. "[It] seemed capable of penetrating any quarantine, of bypassing any manmade obstacle: it chose its victims erratically, mainly but not exclusively from the lower classes in European towns," wrote William McNeil in *Plagues and Peoples*. "It was, in short, both uniquely dreadful in itself and unparalleled in recent European experience. Reaction was correspondingly frantic and far-reaching."

ing, as they felt they did, on sufferance. Men in high position were, on the whole, more inclined to exculpate themselves by mobilizing racist clichés than to admit the possibility of social explanations for the myth that had gained credence among the downtrodden. The "nation's moral illness"? Rather, mob violence was endemic to the barbarian, and the barbarian was someone outside the nation. "Civilization is sleeping on an immense mine of barbarism," declared Guizot, exhorting civilized Frenchmen to meet violence with violence, to destroy an inherently destructive force or, at the very least, to remain eternally vigilant. "It is not the thought of a civilized people, but the cry of a savage people," Prime Minister Casimir Périer ventured to say when told of rumors about poison, wrapping up the situation with a fine rhetorical flourish just before cholera made him its most distinguished victim.

Rich and poor were each the other's plague. If bourgeois did not, like the plebs, embrace an arrantly melodramatic thesis, if they had olfactory grounds for associating cholera with eastern Paris, whose streets stank to high heaven whenever the wind blew westerly carrying odors from the ancient sump of Montfaucon, terror made them animists in their own peculiar way. Refuse became indistinguishable from people, and germs tantamount to barbarians. In blaming the "local deterioration" of society's organism on "the invasion of foreign women, the daily cargo of exotic mores brought by railroad," Dumas *fils* may be said to have fished his metaphor from the bourgeois deep where physical disease and violence done to the moral Order, where foreigners and plague lay together in ambush.

For generations, Paris had been ritually invaded twice a year, on Palm Sunday, when Christ would enter it to the chanting of "Qui est iste Rex?" (Who is this King?), and at Carnival time, on Ash Wednesday, when the plebs would descend upon the Temple district, crowding down the outlying bluffs pell-mell in a human avalanche known as "the descent from la Courtille." By the nineteenth century, Catholicism's perimeter having retreated from the city gates to the cathedral porch, liturgy fixed the Palm Sunday entrance ritual at the doorstep to Notre-Dame. The descent from la Courtille continued in full force, however, growing if anything wilder than hitherto and attracting not only the

A painting of the "descent from la Courtille" which traditionally inaugurated Mardi Gras festivities. Bibliothèque Nationale

lowest elements but playboys of the sort Baudelaire was to glorify in "The Dandy" as "men declassed, disgusted, unemployed, but rich in native vigor." For four or five hours everyone milled together in taverns uphill from the Boulevard du Temple until, when morning came, the motley assortment of revelers would rush toward Paris in a motley assortment of vehicles, throwing sugared almonds, bouquets, eggs, and flour on spectators who had meanwhile lined the road. What had always been a universally sanctioned hiatus in the workaday year, a therapeutic reprieve from labor and rules and otherwise inescapable identities, acquired a belligerent spirit during the 1830s: war came into play, as if those diverse elements which the middle of the road of bourgeois society could not accommodate banded together, demanding their due, and more. Heine was by no means the only observer to remark upon this ludic frenzy and to find its ultimate expression in the cancan. Like Jansenist convulsionaries dancing amid the tombstones of Saint-Médard Cemetery, people convulsed, but, destitute as they were of a God and of a future, convulsed for convulsion's sake. "When one sees," wrote L. Rellstab, "with what gestures and movements of the body the masked men approach the masked women, press close to them, and actually throw them backward and forward between themselves to the accompaniment of continual cries and laughter and ribald jokes, one can only be filled with disgust, nay more—with horror and revulsion at this mass depravity, this flouting of all morality and shame."

At the Théâtre des Variétés, whose musical director, Napoléon Musard, was a kind of nineteenth-century Mick Jagger, pockmarked, spastic, and clad in black, pandemonium reigned with, as one appalled gentleman put it, "masked women, like ecstatic maenads, their cheeks flushed, breasts heaving breathlessly, lips parched, hair undone, careering round the room, less on their feet than being dragged along bodily until with the last chord they collapsed on the nearest seat." Another contemporary observed that Musard's orchestra was equipped with pistols which, when discharged during the quadrille, "produced a remarkable effect on the hips of the dancers." While the French army was forcibly subduing Algeria, at home natives were demonstrating how cheap they held bourgeois law and order in wild dances of Revolutionary origin, particularly the cancan. From low suburban taverns, the cancan spread until Charles de la Battut, who cut a prominent figure among Parisian madcaps, introduced it to the smart set, with the result that tilburies were soon lining up two abreast before the Variétés and discharging yellow-gloved dandies intent on declassing themselves. Just as in September 1835—soon after a bomb thrown at Louis Philippe on the Boulevard du Temple nearly blew him to kingdom come—the government restored censorship "for dramatic works, drawings, engravings, lithographs, emblems, and songs," thus outlawing not only Lemaître's role but Daumier's brilliant images of Macaire, so did it try to shackle the cancan by passing a law that made it illegal for dancers to kick their legs higher than a specified number of centimeters.

Although the censorship laws, otherwise known as the "September Laws," successfully constrained those who spoke for the populace to bide their tongues, they were ineffectual against the language of the dumb. How, after all, did one go about silencing a mute? Flaubert, after visiting the original inn of Les Adrets, wrote in 1845: "I looked at it with religious awe, thinking it was here the great Robert Macaire had taken wing for the future, here that the greatest symbol of the age, the epitome of our times, had originated. Types like Macaire are not created every day; indeed, I cannot think of a greater one since Don Juan." But to the illiterate who communicated by gestures, by signs, and by words that had come to form a quasi-hermetic code, Pierrot or Gilles was as much a symbol as was Macaire, and the great name Jean Gaspard Deburau as much a culture hero as Frédérick Lemaître.

Born to a Silesian peasant woman and a French tumbler who had (like Pixérécourt) emigrated during the Revolution, reared in a showman's caravan that crisscrossed Central Europe for fifteen years, pushing east as far as Constantinople, and unacquainted with France until his eighteenth year, when Napoleon fell, Deburau spoke every language as a foreigner. Between the two revolutions of 1830 and 1848, this consummate exile reigned in silence over the Boulevard and would, no doubt, have remained forever unknown outside its boundaries if not for Jules Janin, a critic whose respect for mime earned him no end of abuse from the critical fraternity. "My hero is gracious and witty throughout all the vicissitudes of life," he wrote of Deburau as Pierrot: "Beat him and he laughs; beating others, he goes on laughing. He hasn't a single word to speak but I defy you to present yourself before him, to go study my admirable buffoon—you useless men! It's obvious that he's mocking you, but with nary a word; his sarcastic assaults on the vicious and the mighty consist in a grimace, but one so piquant that all of Beaumarchais's wit cannot match it. . . . *He is the instinct of the people,* the spirit of the people, the life of the people."

In Deburau's humor there was, one gathers from Janin, an edge of disaffection that cut like Macaire's quips. Gaunt and dour, he distinguished himself not as a lyric presence but as an outsider bleached of tender spots, as a neuter clad in innocence and immune to appeals of conscience. White from head to toe except for a black skullcap that made his anemia all the more emphatic, without blood to let, his was a figure silhouetted against the dark broadcloth of middle-class respectability and power. "He sired a new species of clown," Janin asserted. "He replaces petulance with sang-froid, enthusiasm with premeditation; no longer the clown who scurries hither and yon to no purpose, he is an impervious stoic who gives way, mechanically, to all the impressions of the moment, an actor without passion, without speech, and almost without face; who says everything, expresses everything, mocks every-

Robert Macaire with his accomplice Bertrand, from Daumier's series
"The Hundred and One Robert Macaires." The confidence man has established
an Enema Society. His advertisement reads: "In health: beefsteak.
In sickness: warm water." Bibliothèque Nationale

CE BLANC PIERROT QUI, DU BOUT DE SES MANCHES
EN SOURIANT, SEMBLE APPELER LES GENS
C'EST DEBUREAU, SEMAINES ET DIMANCHES
À SON THÉÂTRE. IL CHARMAIT LES ENFANTS.
MIME EXCELLENT, NAÏF, BRUTAL OU TENDRE
OBJET SURTOUT D'UN ÉCRIT JUSTE ET FIN
PIERROT FUT GRAND. ARLEQUIN ET CASSANDRE
ET LEURS VIEUX DOS, S'EN SOUVIENNENT TRÈS BIEN.

thing; . . . who is equal to all the idiocies of our age and who truly brings them alive."

In the eighteenth century fairground scatology appealed to aristocrats who could no longer observe the decorum that befitted their class. By the mid-nineteenth century, it had become organic food for bourgeois mavericks like Janin, who fancied, if not nature in the raw, then the detritus of a consumer society. Janin's digressions on Boulevard theater anticipate the excursions that Surrealists would make after World War I to the Saint-Ouen Flea Market searching for *objets trouvés*, objects divorced from the purpose they had served during a former life. "The ignoble theater is the only one possible today," he declared while inveighing against "noble" theater. "All that is old, flawed, toothless, unkempt, and unhealthy in the theater is salvage for ignoble theater. . . . Ignoble theater is the bilge into which art's impurities are channeled; it is the Montfaucon of provincial theaters, the city dump of Paris. . . . Go to the ignoble theater if you want to find relics of old drama and comedy. What a book could be made with this world, this naked and peeled art destitute of everything, everything including its rouge, which won't stick!"

This passion for discarded and outmoded things manifested itself most conspicuously in apparel. Robert Macaire's epiphany in second-hand clothes took place only three years after the premiere performance of *Hernani*, when the young Romantics who formed a militant claque came to the Comédie-Française "bearded [in Hugo's description], long-haired, dressed in every fashion save the reigning one, in sailor-jackets, in Spanish cloaks, in waistcoats à la Robespierre, in Henry III bonnets, carrying on their heads and backs articles of costume from every century and clime, and this in the middle of Paris and in broad daylight." To wear costumes that proclaimed their anachronism was to create havoc by dumping on the established order the jetsam of centuries past or to resurrect a history buried alive. (Did Hugo not trumpet his intention to "put a red bonnet on the French dictionary"? Henry III and Robespierre personified distasteful eras, the one preclassical France, the

The celebrated nineteenth-century mime Jean-Baptiste Deburau in 1840, depicted here as towering over the stage of the Théâtre des Funambules. Bibliothèque Nationale

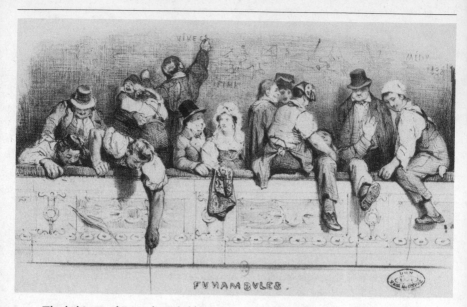

The habitués of "paradise" led an active social life. Bibliothèque Nationale

other postbourgeois.) "We shall be whatever we please," declared middle-class rebels who extemporized themselves on nineteenth-century Paris's equivalent of Carnaby Street, suborning the authority that sought to govern their lives, defrauding power's image of itself by characterizing it as an image rather than a material datum while arguing the substantive reality of the personae they themselves wrote and drew. The demiurgic role bestowed upon the artist was something akin to the mystique of the outlaw who may assume any guise, but particularly guises that terrify, who leaps from the sump of time like a fallen angel or a human rag doll avenging wrongs done by *les grands* to *les petits*. Here, Victor Hugo joined battle as Trimalchio or Quasimodo and Stendhal as Fabrice del Dongo—that militant actor who assumes alias after alias, always playing the dangerous man. There, on the Boulevard du Temple, in a macabre pantomime devised by Cot d'Ordan, Pierrot kills a used-clothes man while stealing the uniform he must have in order to attend a fancy-dress ball where he will meet the duchess of his dreams.

As for the truly destitute, who could not articulate their homage to

Deburau except by laughing or sobbing as a crowd, they lined the streets for him when the mime passed away in 1846. His funeral cortege from the rue du Faubourg du Temple up the heights of Belleville to Père-Lachaise Cemetery was for them what the translation of Hugo's remains to the Panthéon would be for bourgeois republicans forty years later. Borne aloft not by professional pallbearers but by stagehands from the Funambules, the Mute was apotheosized with a rictus on his face. "From the foot of Belleville as far as the church, windows and sidewalks were thronged with people who sought once more to greet him on the street he had crossed so often," wrote Champfleury. "They were murmuring: Deburau! and following the procession of the mime whom they would never see again."

Exactly two years later, during the 1848 Revolution, the streets traveled by Deburau's funeral coach would be splattered with the blood of his mourners and the Temple district barricaded from Paris as the potter's field in Père-Lachaise was walled off from the bourgeoisie's mansion-like sepulchers. For four days in June—the twenty-third through the twenty-sixth—Temple residents would repulse French soldiers with every weapon at their disposal, including swords and halberds taken from the prop stores of Boulevard theaters. Cannonballs would rent the air, and accusations of espionage, and, once again, rumors of poisoned wellwater. While Balzac, after venturing abroad one day, exclaimed to a friend: "Mais, on se tutoie!" ("It's extraordinary, people are addressing one another in the familiar!"), Louis Caussidière, implying in his memoirs that *tu* can voice scorn as well as fraternity, concluded that "left to their own devices, half of Paris will imprison the other."

They did worse. (And of course, the barricade did not prevent each half from dividing into murderous factions, for laborers and bourgeois fought on either side of it.) Incidents like the following, reported by a general commanding the place de Paris—"At 8:30 a.m. two men tried to escape as the cells were being reallocated. They were killed and immediately thrown into the Seine. . . . Today at 5:00 a.m. two detainees who were attempting to escape after forcing a lock were immediately killed"—occurred so monotonously as to suggest that prisons were not definitive enough to contain the fury of internecine combatants, that nothing less than a hecatomb would allay fears of total extinction besetting each side. "The struggle these last few days . . . has been clearly and forcefully delineated," declared a moderate republican paper, *Le National.* "Yes, on one side there stood order, liberty, civilization, the decent republic, France; and on the other, barbarians, desperadoes emerging from their lairs for massacre and looting, and odious partisans of those wild doctrines that the family is only a word and property naught but theft." In addition to the thousands who died, thousands more were arrested and deported to Algeria, where, as Proudhon put it, "they would fatten the soil of Africa for future owners with their own bodies."

Insurgents who tore up the paving stones of the Boulevard to construct barricades ten and twelve feet high may be said to have paved the way for Napoleon III's urban engineers, who, fourteen years later, flattened the neighborhood without a fight. In July 1862 bills were posted announcing auctions of theatrical equipment, everything from costumes and properties to benches and statues. On the fifteenth, the theaters marked for demolition gave their last performance. People crowded into the Folies-Dramatiques for an impromptu entitled *The Boulevard du Temple's Farewell* much as they had thronged to the Saint-Germain fairground for *The Funeral of the Fair.* And the Funambules delivered a silent valedictory, *Pierrot's Memories*, in which Deburau's son played Pierrot dressed in black. A fortnight before Christmas Napoleon III and Empress Eugénie drove in state over level ground where the Petit-Lazari, the Délassements-Comiques, the Funambules, the Gaîté, the Folies-Dramatiques, the Cirque-Olympique, and the Théâtre Lyrique had stood side by side, and inaugurated a new boulevard named after their young son: the boulevard du Prince Eugène. As if this effrontery angered the savage gods enough to bring their wrath crashing down upon an innocent head, poor Eugène would die at age twenty-four while fighting with British troops in South Africa, impaled by a Zulu spear.

In his memoirs, Jean-Louis Barrault describes a grandfather who, notwithstanding the fact that he was Parisian-born and bred, always felt obliged to deny that his mother had come from the Auvergne, the Auvergne representing the Boetia of provinces, or provinciality in the utmost degree. This embarrassment was commonplace among immigrants bent on acculturating themselves. For them, as for the *noblesse de robe* who had risen above their born estate and won the consecration of a title, the will to transcend presupposed a willingness to disown the past, to flee the confining definition of regions and dialects. "The parvenus who emigrated from the countryside and managed to find purchase in the Parisian middle class seldom kept in touch with their native land," writes one French historian, Adeline Daumard. "The bourgeois of Paris were urbanites camped in the midst of the countryside whose resources and amenities they availed themselves of without caring a whit about its inhabitants. . . . To segregate the provinces and rural life from the domain of their concerns was for them to disavow what el-

The razing of theaters and the Circus on the Boulevard du Temple in 1862.
Bibliothèque Nationale

ements of the primitive, of the irrational subsisted in the civilization of their age." Louis Napoleon and the Third Republic staged World Fairs to enhance the myth of the city's universality, but Parisians regarded non-Paris as an exotic circumambience reducible to pavilion displays, as a backcountry, an offstage. In *The Last Time I Saw Paris* Elliot Paul summed it up neatly when he wrote of his neighbors on the rue de la Huchette that they, "like other middle-class Parisians and Frenchmen, thought of the world as if it were a sort of dish, the bottom being France and all lands and peoples being grouped together around the narrow, slanting rim so that stray objects and personalities slid down into their ken now and then."

Inevitably, the disaffected offspring of this middle class, from Rimbaud to the Surrealists, would identify with the primitive, now fancying themselves marauders aflame with passion, now disappearing beyond the rim or "dropping out." "My day is done, I am leaving Europe," declared Rimbaud in *A Season in Hell*. "The sea air will burn my lungs; lost climes will tan my hide. To swim, to chew grass, to hunt, above all, to smoke; to drink liqueurs as strong as molten metal—like those dear ancestors who'd camp around the fire." Surrealist narratives of any length sooner or later gravitate to the *banlieues* or to culs-de-sac where civilization has left no imprint. In *The Peasant of Paris*, for example, Louis Aragon, who wrote it in 1924, leads the reader down an arcaded street marked for demolition by Haussmann's twentieth-century successors, moving with infinite loquacity from barbershop to brothel to workers' bistro to bathhouse to porno theater, as if his purpose were as much to foul as to flaunt his verbal resources, to immolate in low establishments the language of a virtuoso monologist. One paragraph will suffice:

Number 29a is the Théâtre Moderne. This theater, whose only purpose and means of subsistence is passion, is unique in presenting us a show free of gimmicks and truly modern in spirit. Just wait; it won't be long before the snobs, wearying of the music hall and circus, descend like locusts on these spurned theaters where the necessity of providing a few girls and

A composite portrait of Boulevard du Temple fauna, in and out of roles, after their eviction in 1862. Bibliothèque Nationale

pimps with a livelihood has given rise to an art form the equal of medieval
mystery plays, possessing its own conventions and audacities, its discipline
and conflicts. The great devices of ancient comedy—mistaken identity,
travesties, amorous spite, and even Menaechmianism—are current coin
here. The very method of primitive theater is sustained by the natural communion between audience and stage, which the actresses' provocations or
desire or private chats foster; the audience's commentaries, its belly laughs,
the epithets hurled by dancers at their uncouth public, assignations arranged on the spot: all add spontaneous charm to a script delivered by
rote, brayed, stammered, whispered, or read on the spur of the moment,
without makeup.

Like the nineteenth-century *déclassés* who venerated the image of
Robert Macaire, many young intellectuals among those who survived
World War I stripped themselves with a vengeance and glorified the
junk pile, the whorehouse, the "primitive" landscape, the Wild West.
They embraced, in its various guises, a melodramatic world view that
made passion the infallible measure of right, thereby reprieving themselves from mortal ambiguity, from the strategies and constraints of
civil discourse, from goals upheld as worthy and objects reckoned valuable by their grandfathers.

As for melodrama itself, it migrated to the *banlieue* along with its
public, enduring not only in the sado-masochistic spectacles of Grand
Guignol, but in dramas that could quite plausibly have been written by
Guilbert de Pixérécourt. On the periphery of Paris, all around the city,
during the late nineteenth century there sprang up neighborhood theaters or *théâtres de quartier* that constituted a far-flung Boulevard du
Temple, a "circuit" whose veterans wandered from Montparnasse to
Les Gobelins to Saint-Denis and Montmartre. Half-urban, half-rural,
this twilight zone kept alive conventions that had long since come to be
regarded by bourgeois as childish or "green." What with plays like *The
Hunchback, The Son of Night, Mysteries of the Inquisition, Mysteries
of Paris, Douglas the Vampire*, and the rapt credulity of surburban
spectators, an historically minded visitor in 1910 might have thought
himself privileged to witness some archaic event. Not for a moment
would he have suspected that this early-nineteenth-century slice-of-life
contained germ cells of the future, that a theatrical avant-garde would
soon emerge from the outskirts of Paris and from the back streets of the
Left Bank. But emerge they did. Jacques Copeau would transform a

little music hall into the Théâtre du Vieux-Colombier. Gaston Baty would convert the Théâtre Montparnasse into an experimental stage. The Théâtre Montmartre would become the Théâtre de l'Atelier, where Antonin Artaud, Etienne Decroux, Jean-Louis Barrault, and Marcel Marceau, among others, pursued their stage careers under the aegis of a country boy named Charles Dullin. What was past would prove once again to be prologue.

CHAPTER IV

✦ ✦ ✦ ✦

A SAVOYARD
BOYHOOD

"My vocation," wrote Charles Dullin, "got pieced together from all the fantasies that filled my childhood. It grew up outside me. I owe it to the poets I read, to my old uncle . . . to the pedlars who bivouacked near our house, to the countryside, to a thousand things that have no direct bearing on theater." He owed it as well to the biblical predicament of having been born last to a couple who sired eighteen children, several of whom he would never meet. If that were not sufficiently bewildering, his boyhood domicile, a Savoyard mountain fortress partly demolished during the Hundred Years War, further laid waste under Henry IV's reign, and pillaged by serfs in a Revolutionary Jacquerie, resembled free-form sculpture. Le Châtelard, as it was called, had survived history's gauntlet with nothing of its original structure intact but four rough-hewn towers. These, and the bell turrets, the outbuildings, the chimneys, the weathercocks, the hundred barred windows, the maze of walls crumbling or patched with stone of various texture, gave it the appearance of a village. Having inherited it from a childless relative, the Dullin family spawned inside this ruin high above Yenne, between the Rhône Valley and the Lac du Bourget, like marine life inside the tiara of a dead crustacean. Their land, lying below a peak called the Cat's Tooth, by whose shadow the locals could reckon time to the quarter-hour, was sufficient unto itself. Four tenant farmers provided food, and a vineyard wine. Upon the face of the visible world a dial five thousand feet high marked the sun's rotation. "Far from everything, we lived there like savages," reminisced Dullin's sister Pauline, who wrote a remarkable evocation of that life. "The noises of the century were echoed by the postman and by gendarmes when they reported to my father, Yenne's justice of the peace."

What Esmé Wingfield-Stratford observed of Victorian England's squirearchy—"One attribute it shared with the bourgeoisie consisted of an almost demonic energy; if we may compare men with machines, we should say that the squire, like the businessman, registered an enormous horsepower"—would describe Charles's father, Jacques, a man of such temper that he could as easily have hoist himself on his own petard early in life as lived to eighty-one swearing like a trouper, riding harum-scarum up and down the slopes of his bailiwick, and irrepressibly mounting the nubile girl, Camille Vouthier, he snatched out of convent school; a Tolstoyan figure whose contradictions, far from withering the personality, kept it forever green. During the early 1840s, when Savoy belonged to the Kingdom of Sardinia, Jacques Dullin studied law in Turin. There, Risorgimento was the cry on everybody's tongue, and Jacques apparently lost no time harking to it. The unruly young man who had left home (home being Yenne) at odds with his pious, well-heeled parents returned a republican and a militant republican, given at every opportunity to proclaiming anticlerical slogans like "Laissons le prêtre à l'autel!" ("Let's leave the priest at the altar!"). To his parents' dismay, Jacques became the leader of a local radical movement that called itself Les Voraces (the Voracious Ones). Little did they suspect that forty years later—Savoy having meanwhile been absorbed by France and the republican assembly having passed the Law of Congregations—their son, whose duty it was as justice of the peace to evict local Capuchin friars, would refuse to do so.

But time had not made him any the less red in tooth and claw. Camille, who sought refuge in her convent-school missal whenever Jacques let loose a blasphemous thunderbolt, could vouch for that. What he hated above all was not the Church but authority, all except his own. *Ignorants! Ignares!*—such expletives laid low all opposition, and answered questions that found him unprepared. "He always wanted to command," his daughter recalls, "but had no practical experience. Whatever he knew about agriculture had come from books. His most lucrative product, wine, often remained too long in the cask and, turning to vinegar, could not be sold."

Rather like the hero of Montesquieu's *Persian Letters*, Usbeck, who regards Europe through the eyes of a *philosophe* while exhorting his eunuch back home to rule the seraglio with an inflexible hand, Jacques Dullin upheld freedom outside the family, even sheltering the occasional fugitive from justice, as staunchly as he deplored it within. Thus, some years before Châtelard became his, it had served as refuge for an uncle who abandoned his parish sooner than pledge fealty to Rome when the French Church lost certain privileges called Gallican Liberties. One of Jacques Dullin's first acts of proprietorship was to demolish the renegade priest's tower and burn his cassocks. "My father would not tolerate the forswearing of oaths—according to him, one either remained a priest or did not take the cloth to begin with," his daughter relates. An object lesson worthy of Robespierre, this was no doubt addressed to the miniature nation Jacques had gotten upon his pious Camille: living in Châtelard meant recognizing the infallibility of its pontiff. One stroke demolished the Church and preserved the ideal of Holy Orders. That Camille had—many years before, when they still lived in the valley— surprised Jacques in bed with a barmaid did not derogate from his authority; virtue swore by its embodiment, not he by it.

Making Châtelard home had not been his idea—it was Camille who first moved there, after the scandalous event, intending to shun him—but Jacques embraced it as though it were. He sold for a pittance his rich practice in Novalaise, some ten miles distant from Yenne, and renounced polite society to live on this mountain which the peasants climbed with their neolithic grievances. As intolerant as he was of the foibles of civilized people, among the hillfolk who solicited his judgment and paid him for it in pullets and doves, he was Solomonic. What his eavesdropping children heard in court (the dining room served as courtroom) was not the despot whose frequent outbursts they nicknamed *le foutro* but a supple, humane gentleman who answered patois in patois. To a farmer upon whom the local witch had cast a hex so powerful that the usual antidote, which was to boil seven rusty nails for one hour, proved ineffective (first his pregnant cow had dropped dead, then he could no longer urinate), Judge Dullin, looking dourly continent in wing collar and black tie, might say: "Well, you know, *mon pauvre vieux,* I pity you, but I'm going to give you the remedy. Have your wife, La Sacon, prepare an infusion of couch grass, not with the grass itself, mind you—that's for dogs and cats, it purges them—but with the root. Drink it during the day instead of wine; you'll see, before long you'll be peeing with facility and pleasure. . . . Then, cut down the walnut trees around your house, enlarge and open your doors and windows, drain off the water in your house and stable. Let the sun enter, let light in, and La Tambourine will have lost her power to harm you." To a spinster who charged that a neighbor—the unobliging object of her matrimonial ambitions—had taken her virtue by force, Judge Dullin said: "See here, I'll give you this candle, you stick it in the holder, which I shall grasp with one hand." When she complained that he was jiggling it—"Hold still, Monsieur le Juge! How can I put it in?"—he made short shrift of her accusation: "You understand now that if you had wished, you could have defended yourself."

Having razed a tower, he would, almost every year, make equally quixotic revisions in the landscape, as if to prove that Châtelard was not merely a piece of property but an epiphenomenon of his will. Did the children like to play blindman's buff on a certain patch of greensward? Directly it became "theirs"—a playground, a colony, a terrain of private conventions—he abolished it, planting grape vines. On one occasion, the local hand hired by Camille to dig her a vegetable garden had no sooner traced its border, casting seed and planting onions, than Jacques Dullin's pet crow, Portos (who flew around the château uninhibitedly), despoiled it. "What an intelligent bird!" the justice of the peace was heard to exclaim gleefully while watching his virtuoso thief purloin the buried treasure. "I wouldn't exchange him for a cannonball!" His progeny must often have wished themselves winged and black so as to enjoy the bird's freedom and delight in the praise it won. Since they were not pets, they were, perforce, servants. Indeed, their bondage could not have been more complete had Father been a helpless tyke. " 'Give me my handkerchief. Fill my pipe.' He would take pleasure disturbing us to fetch things within his own arm's reach," Pauline recalls. "He never found the cooking as good as his mother's. He never had soup because lifting the spoon time and time again exasperated him."

Where at Versailles, absolutism may be said to have found perfect expression in the *lever du roi*, the quasi-liturgical gestures that attended Louis's Alighting from Bed, at Châtelard it consummated itself after nightfall, in the *coucher de Jacques*. Exactly like chamberlains and ladies-in-waiting, his sons and daughters took turns helping him undress:

Father lent himself to his divestiture prudishly. His greatcoat slung over the chair, he would sit down while we, on our knees, strained to free him of his heavy boots. . . . Next came the socks, the trousers which he had unbuttoned himself, and the long underwear. We would present him first his nightshirt, then his nightcap. . . . . Even after he climbed into bed, our task was not yet done, for we had still to tamp his pipe and strike a match (making certain never to light the tobacco before all the sulfur had burned). We would open his newspaper, tuck him in, and, very timidly, kiss him, one lip on the brow, the other on his nightcap, saying: "Good night, Papa." He would answer, perfunctorily, "Good night, my child," adding, if he happened to be in good humor, "Tomorrow morning you will come drink the drop." This "drop" was what remained of his morning coffee, a siropy residue we didn't relish but couldn't refuse.

Nor could they refuse the sobriquets he gave them, for whatsoever Jacques Dullin called every living creature, that was its name. Once given, a name stuck, like a frozen grimace or a childhood pose consecrated for all time. Though it required some effort on his part to distinguish his *baptized* offspring from one another, he would instantly recognize Three-Quarter Moon, Nibbled Cheese, The Sacristan, The Peddler, Persephone, d'Artagnan, Countess Blueblood, Vinegar Piss, The Madonna, Queen Margot, The Catastrophe of Saint-Gervais, and, in Charles's case, "Lolo." Over this brood he watched with ursine solicitude, sometimes cuffing it (particularly the boys), sometimes pawing it. Every aspect of its life was a reflection of his taste, his will, and his measure. Not even the garments it wore were left to chance or fancy. At the beginning of each season, when a seamstress from Yenne would spend one week in Châtelard and make clothes, it was he who chose the style, the cloth, the colors. "He attended the fittings," wrote Pauline. "Everything had to be ample and sturdy, and when he ordered a garment through the Louvre-department-store catalogue, he himself took our measurements. I see myself as a little girl rigged out in a fur coat whose back sagged down to my heels and whose sleeves extended to my fingertips. Mother, being large and strong, could easily carry this extravagance of amplitude and length, but we little ones were lost in such advantages."

The girls made proper marriages for the most part and settled nearby, in the Rhône Valley, where an ennobled branch of the Dullin family—the Dullin de Commène—had taken root. The boys ended up in Guadeloupe, in Algeria, in Paris, in Russia, like pollen blown far and wide by Jacques's furious puffs. One joined the French foreign legion. Another became a professional gambler. "I have more luck with my daughters than with their blackguard brothers," Jacques would lament. And yet, did it not, inadmissibly, please him to have sired a Diaspora of Dullins? To have broadcast germ cells of himself all over the globe? Once his anger was spent, he would open an atlas and with the frame of his spectacles measure the distance from Savoy to his fugitive sons, as if envying them or admiring them for the first time. He would study the atlas for hours on end. It became his favorite book. As reclusive as he was, life outside the absolute domain he had made of his one hundred hectares filled him with wonder.

To another resident of Châtelard, Jacques's older brother Joseph-Elisabeth, whom Charles Dullin always held in the highest esteem, the outside world was a dead letter. No one knew quite why he had gone into retreat many decades before, at twenty-five, sequestering himself in a tower opposite the renegade priest's, or, rather, why some subsequent impulse of the heart or the mind had not lured him back to civilization. His reasons were one more household enigma with which the children grew up, something opaque in their midst curtaining the edge of perception. That the old hermit, whom they could not imagine otherwise than draped in rags had, once upon a time, loved clothing so immoderately that his brothers and the villagers called him "le Dandy," that this would-be Diogenes used to strut though Yenne like a peacock gave them some further inkling of hidden selves, of the ghosts in people. While outside Châtelard there was a world populated with unrecognizable brothers and sisters, inside it there was a consanguineous stranger.

The children knew that Uncle Joseph, after he finished humanities at a Catholic school, the Collège de Rumilly, had come home with every intention of staying home for good. Unlike his brothers, who had begun careers in commerce and law, he, a strapping, blond youth, read literature all day long, or else preened, doting over his sartorial image as though ministering to his soul. For several years, parental nagging made no impression on him, or so it seemed until the day he announced that he would follow a younger brother to India and set up in business there. Bewildered by this boy, who could not bring himself to leave the village except to circle the earth, Monsieur Dullin gave him his blessings. One week in Marseille, waiting for the ship to embark, convinced Joseph

that he ought never have ventured forth in the first place. "I am returning to Yenne as soon as possible; I have decided it irrevocably," he
wrote to his parents. "I shall not continue my voyage. To stay here any
longer would be to risk my soul. Whatever lies beyond, Marseille is a
city of perdition. I have seen abominable things . . . incredible! The
women are provoking, the girls devoid of shame, lost; sluts one and
all." The taunts at home soon proved to be as unendurable as the provocations abroad, however. Temperamentally a cenobite and intellectually a *littérateur*, this Christian without Christ could live nowhere but
in a profane cell, and so, some months after returning from Marseille,
he betook himself to Châtelard, swearing as he climbed the hill that he
would never climb it again. Joseph made a faithful wife of solitude.
During the next sixty-one years, until an oxcart transported his remains
down to the cemetery, he did not once set foot outside the perimeter of
Châtelard.

Had he kept a diary, his survivors might have acquainted themselves with him posthumously, but they knew better than to search for
one. The letter written from Marseille represented a last will and testament, a renunciation of the worldly self. "My little pen doesn't work
anymore," he told the children. Living more at night than in daytime,
his life articulated only by the evening Angelus when he would solemnly
cross himself, and by the crowing of the cock when he would go to bed,
Joseph idled or read. No clocks, no mirrors. "The only laws he knew
were those of his conscience," Pauline contended. "Never did he utter a
vulgar word or blaspheme, like his brother Jacques."

In every respect the brothers played each other's foil, sharing what
made sharing itself difficult—an aversion to the diplomatic protocol of
everyday life. Where Jacques found it a pleasure to engender children
and a nuisance to father them (shortly before her death Camille told
Pauline that she could no longer bear up under the amorous assaults of
her seventy-eight-year-old husband, and had implored him to take a
mistress), quite the reverse was true of Joseph. In the summer, when he
would venture out-of-doors and dare to spend several midafternoon
hours in a grape arbor so thickly matted with the flowers and fruit of
wild Chasselas vine that it afforded him almost as much privacy as his
tower cell, Jacques's children came around begging for instruction. The
man who otherwise hoarded himself set them a banquet on which they
feasted for the rest of their lives—talking helter-skelter about Plato,

Socrates, Diogenes, and kings, about Bossuet, Voltaire, and Rousseau, about the gods of antiquity, the pharaohs, the stars and their legends, showing them the world from the viewpoint of migratory birds, inventing dramatic dialogues between the weathervanes of Châtelard to make the wind palpable, enacting La Fontaine's fables for their moral edification, and naming all the plants within pointing range of his cane. French classical drama figured prominently in their studies. Naked to the waist, his shirt airing in the breeze and his hair standing on end because of the heat and the exertion, Joseph would declaim the messenger's account of Hippolytus' death with broad gestures, gestures as broad as his arbor, and a look that transfigured him. "One day," his niece recalls, "he made me burst into tears reading *The Death of Madame* by Bossuet, the great Bossuet who, he would say, fearlessly stood his ground before the Powers-that-Were and told them the truth."

Whatever the subject on which he chose to expatiate, by means of it Joseph preached resistance to the high and the mighty. "What are the little ones doing out there?" Jacques would ask Camille. "What can that madman be telling them?" He could be telling them that animals were happy until men, in domesticating them, made them as fatuous as they themselves (witness Portos, the crow, guzzling wine at the dinner table and flopping over in a state of inebriation); or that La Fontaine, whose mind had no room for "trifling matters," forgot all about his wife until reminded of her existence by a friend one day. As Uncle Joseph considered men of authority indiscriminately knavish—the power vested in them being that to which they all sacrificed their souls—his history lessons made a hecatomb of Great Names. Slashing both right and left, he spared only one figure, Louis Mandrin, the Savoyard Robin Hood (popularized in rural pulp magazines such as the *Bibliothèque bleue*) whose private army terrorized that region in the mid-eighteenth century. "He did the poor no harm and stole from the rich. . . . Uncle Joseph, wishing to keep our minds unsullied, glided over his dubious exploits and related only the chivalrous ones."

No sooner indoors than Joseph became the stranger once again. Following an invariable routine, he would emerge after everyone retired at 9:00 p.m., carefully lock his door, put the key in his "canteen"—a wicker basket that contained a handkerchief, a vial of eau-de-vie, a wooden rasp for filing corns, and books—and steal into the kitchen, where he kept vigil until daybreak, convinced that Châtelard, if not for his nightwatch, might be taken unawares by fire. Only the fear of fire, and the need for it on especially cold winter days when everyone gathered round the hearth, could make him interrupt his self-imposed exile. Seeing lightning flash overhead, he would straightaway don a gray bowler which served as a magical helmet—perhaps a voucher of propriety—rush downstairs wild-eyed, leaving his door open, and join the family circle, or rather, sit at a tangent to it, aquiver like a turtle driven from its shell. "Joséphine, you're in your trance!" Jacques would scoff. The children, who used every subterfuge to explore their uncle's cell when he was there to barricade himself, never satisfied their curiosity when the door stood ajar and unguarded. What forbade it? Pity? Contrition for having wantonly played upon his fears? The rules of the game? Or was it also a certain reluctance to lay bare his secret once and for all? Might that secret prove horrifying? And if banal, might the discovery have cost life something of its depth, its inwardness?

Stolen glances told them this: Uncle Joseph, instead of burying his past, had buried himself in it. Though lacking a Proustian pen, he had created a kind of Proustian nest. Infolio volumes of Latin, Greek, and Old French literature lay piled on the floor, gathering dust. Strewn everywhere were ordinary objects—nails, glass beads—which a scavenging instinct had compelled him to bring home. From a coatrack there hung old jackets and quaintly styled capes. His closet bulged with garments that fashionable young gentlemen had worn in the 1840s, during Louis Philippe's regime: high hats, gaitered pants, pinked waistcoats sewn with pearl buttons, frock coats disgorging lace ruffle, silver-knobbed malacca canes. If each object uncovered by inquisitive eyes left some hope that the next might hold Joseph's secret, their mystifying sum gave rise to suspicions that it must lie not *in* the room but *behind* it. Why else would he have sealed the fireplace with a marble slab? Nothing daunted, the Dullins, who were as mystified by this space as was its tenant by the world outside it, resolved to make the excavation of excavations. "Father . . . decided one day to satisfy his curiosity. He pierced the outside of the tower at what he judged to be the level of the fireplace. We all stood at the foot of the ladder with baited breath. . . . Lolo, the littlest one, wedged himself through the hole, but, suddenly panic-stricken, called for help and was pulled out. My brother Jacques and I . . . entered forthrightly." They found nothing but nutshells left by the field rats.

In 1904, at the age of eight-six, Joseph-Elisabeth died. "While taking care of him," Pauline recalls, euphemistically, as if to leave a respectful shroud over her beloved uncle's memory, "I saw his sex and realized that it did not have the shape of a man's."

Although infants arrived in the Dullin family with calendrical punctuality, causing excitement to be sure, but not very much more than did the Italian chimney sweeps who descended from Saint-Rémy-en-Maurienne every autumn or the laundresses who marched up from Yenne six or seven strong to boil the linen every other season, Charles came unexpectedly, in 1885, disproving Camille's assumption that she was past bearing children. Who knows if the effort it required to wrest life from a putative grave did not somehow account for Dullin's intensity, his singlemindedness, the pride he would take forever after in surviving by expedients and in conjuring spectacles out of makeshift material? All his friends remarked upon it. "Frail in appearance," wrote Alexandre Arnoux, "he possessed a kind of physical voltage that nothing could exhaust, a stubborn streak bordering on the manic."

Charles had every reason to consider himself not the latest edition in a long series, but his parents' only child, begotten miraculously so to speak. Camille vowed that she would repay heaven by making him enter the priesthood. As for Jacques, he found through his benjamin a grandpaternal vocation and treated him with such tenderness, such unprecedented clemency, that the other children lost no time naming him *le dauphin*. When Camille rocked the infant to sleep humming: "En attendant, sur mes genoux,/Mon beau Prélat, endormez-vous" ("While you wait upon my lap,/My handsome prelate, take a nap"), Jacques, who normally shunned cradles, would declare that she sang abysmally out of tune and, having thus silenced her, deliver a peroration calculated, one would have thought, to rouse rather than to soothe:

> Tyrans, descendez au cercueil,
> La République nous appelle,
> Sachons vaincre et sachons périr!*

✦   ✦   ✦

----

* "Tyrans, down into your coffins, / The republic summons us, / Let us prove that we can conquer and die like men!"

By day, however, their dream child whom they dressed, the one in clerical black, the other in madder red, had only to sneeze—but then, he was forever sneezing and sniffling—and greasy wool blankets would immediately envelop him. Did Joseph sit upstairs his bowler at the ready? Downstairs, Jacques kept an enema bottle beside his tobacco pouch, believing, as he firmly did, in the efficacy of purges. Throughout childhood, Charles breathed the atmosphere of parental consternation. It stuck to him like croton-oil compresses and mustard plasters, leaving a ubiquitous scent. Not for Lolo the escapades of his siblings, who would sometimes arrange to have a ladder placed against their windowsill after dark and go fishing by lanternlight, since Lolo slept in his parents' bedroom. Nor could he taste the fruit of their delinquency—the crayfish they had caught and given Jacques the next day, telling fibs as to its origin: his diet was an invalid's. "Poor little chap! It's poison for him! If he eats any, he'll get convulsions," Jacques would protest. Although Lolo learned to use his frailty, to exaggerate it for all its worth, every prerogative won isolated him the more. Had Jacques ever scolded him, Lolo could then have made common cause with the other victims of *le foutro*, after whom he would traipse, a forlorn cynosure, his nose mucus-wet and his eyes fever-bright, looking for mischief. Apart from several seasons in the grade school of Saint-Paul, two miles downhill, he had no teachers but his sister Pauline and his uncle Joseph—none, that is, until it came time to fulfill Camille's bargain with God. Thrust upon himself, he would often spend the whole day reciting poems of La Fontaine, Hugo, Déroulède, Lamartine, and Musset, which Joseph had made him copy, interrupting his monologue whenever he pleased to observe nature stirring round about or to seek the company of lumbermen in the Rôtet Forest. On the face of it a dilatory child, he was what the French call (more often than not admiringly) *sauvage*—intransigent, wary, high-strung, "asocial." "During lessons," Pauline observed, "he heard only what he wanted to hear." Like Joseph and Jacques, Charles Dullin, for all his bashful elegance, would always resist laws other than those of his own devising.

If one did not lord it over a domain absolutely, one might just as well live footloose. There were no alternatives, it seemed, but Châtelard and vagabondage. Indeed, the open road exercised as much fascination upon Charles Dullin as the inner sanctum. Like that ladder set against Joseph's tower, it stretched not horizontally but vertically, promising a

kind of geographical transcendence, or admission to some exotic netherworld. Clambering up it came Piedmontese peddlers dressed in shiny
cloth (called devilskin) and red neckerchiefs and shouldering bags that
held something for everyone—wooden whistles, mint pastilles, yarn,
hair pomade, chromo-lithographs, religious medals, saint dolls, pulp
romances. Up it came wayfarers from every quarter, one of whom
earned his night's bed and board by whittling a toy Charles was never
to forget: "It was my joy for several years. The hulking man, a Pole
who spoke almost no French, sat at the kitchen hearth with blocks of
wood and a knife. . . . My eyes were riveted to his handiwork. Now
and again he would smile at me benignly. To my sorrow, bedtime arrived before he had finished, but in the morning there it stood, on the
table, a windmill perfect in every detail. . . . My benefactor had already left."

When, years later, Dullin, hoping to revive popular traditions,
founded a *théâtre de foire,* a fairground theater, it is altogether possible that he had in mind not only the *jongleurs* of old but the magi who
would saunter over the horizon with their cornucopiae and their tricks.

As soon as her God-given child reached the age of ten, Camille
decreed that he must prepare himself for the celibate life and, somehow
overruling Jacques, sent him to a seminary in the town of Pont du
Beauvoisin. There he remained for five years. "It has left me with nothing but sordid memories." At first he consoled himself by writing elegies
about Châtelard, or suicidal farewells in the style of Nicolas Gilbert,
reciting his work aloud beside a stream that ran near the *collège;* he
filled one thick notebook, then, when the priests confiscated it, a second
of equal girth and moroseness. Before long, however, Charles, much to
his mother's delight, transformed himself into the model student, winning prizes in Latin and French composition. While during the first year
he tried repeatedly to escape, during the years that followed he became
his own most rigorous warder, as though—still a fugitive but a fugitive
from the outside now—seeking freedom in sequestration and selfhood
in the image Camille proposed for him. Pauline wrote that he took his
first communion in May 1897 "with much piety and conviction" and
that his mother accepted this as proof that he would indeed enter the
service of God one day. "I myself gave him a missal and a medal of the
Virgin which he would carry on his watch chain for quite some time."

It could be said that Dullin had given his first great performance. In all innocence he had made a kind of Pascalian wager, feigning pious manners and doing it with such success that he trapped himself inside the semblance. People actually believed him. Between him and Camille, indeed between him and himself, there now stood a double, an impostor whom he could neither own nor disown, his creature having become his tyrant. Since it had no *raison d'être* but its own perfection, this paragon imposed upon him a norm of sublimity, demanding proof after proof. His game, rather than make him feel less lonely, made exile a fate. "As to my 'religious vocation,' all it did was entangle me in coils of remorse. What would my mother say? How was I to find my way out of this tragic impasse?" Though Dullin eventually turned his sham conversion to artistic account—staging the first French production of Pirandello's theater, for example—in adolescence it seemed to him uncatalogued and abhorrent, something so far removed from the order of human experience that Providence alone could save him, or reincarnation beyond some Romantic frontier. What independence and self-esteem he found, he found (as had his father) on horseback. Without Jacques's stallion "Black," he would have languished at Châtelard. In mounting the animal, it was as if he hoist himself above earthly entanglements, above eye level, above a weakling child, and might as easily have spent life riding as acting. (In a sense he did precisely that, for the Atelier, the theater with which his name has become synonymous—today it stands on the place Charles-Dullin—was no less his stable than his stage. Long after automobiles had evicted horses and carriages from Paris, Charles Dullin riding Mandrin was a familiar sight in Montmartre.)

When the priests of Pont du Beauvoisin made a pilgrimage to Notre-Dame-de-Myan, Charles, hopeful that miraculous intercession by the Virgin might solve his dilemma, joined it, carrying a purse which some elderly folk from Yenne had given him to buy and burn liturgical candles in their name. His orisons were indeed heard, though, as it happened, not by Mary, and answered, though not in church. When Charles, who was fifteen years old, reached the provincial capital, Chambéry, a former classmate of his waylaid him from his devout purpose. Enflamed by women of easy virtue at the Brasserie Lyrique, opposite Chambéry's theater, he bought their favors with the candle money and spent the Holy Days of 1900 repeatedly losing his virginity. Several months earlier, in February, Jacques Dullin had written to the

Father Superior: "I have just now received my son's report card, which furnishes us immense satisfaction." By July, however, Charles was an ex-seminarian. Through the good offices of his brother the foreign legionnaire, who interceded with Camille on his behalf, he was withdrawn from the seminary.

Thus did one vocation end and another begin. In what ways the two were related, by what indirection an apostate heading toward the theater could have backed into a church, would become somewhat clearer four years after his fateful pilgrimage. Camille had meanwhile died, the tumor that took her life announcing itself, as though on purpose, soon after Charles returned from Chambéry. "On the night of her death," wrote Pauline, "she had the priest brought to her, answered the prayers herself, extended her hands for the unction of holy oils, invoked her brother Charles the monk, and began to sing a canticle to the Virgin which she remembered from convent school: 'Emmène-moi, Marie/Au ciel, ma Patrie.' It had been a long time since my father heard the voice of his beloved Camille sound so pure, so resonant. He fell to his knees, he the skeptic, and prayed upon the missal of his young bride." Stricken with grief, Jacques followed her to the grave one year later (not before dismissing the Capuchin monk who sought to administer extreme unction), and then Joseph, whereupon the firstborn, the Novalaise children, flew up to Châtelard like crows, ransacking it for their bourgeois nests in the valley. What they could not use they auctioned. What they could not auction they burned, making of Uncle Joseph's secret wardrobe, of his gazettes, of his books, of his letters, and of his gray bowler a bonfire that lasted three days. The younger children, for whom this paraphernalia represented the *prima materia* of life, were ignored. French law allowing them no other recourse, they lodged purely symbolic protests, so that when the enemy put Châtelard itself up for sale, whoever bought the château found scrawled upon its walls graffiti like "Death to the bourgeois, to justice, to attorneydom, to pillagers of orphans!" The stone bearing its coat of arms lay in the clover, where it had come to rest after Charles rolled it down the mountainside.

It was still lying there several years later when, during the vintage season, he and Pauline vacationed nearby, in Théou, a village from which they could contemplate Châtelard. Never had the walls looked quite so formidable or the chimneys so numerous, now that home for them was a flat of rooms in Lyons, fifty miles west. "Despite all our sorrows and the upheaval of our existences, we danced through the fields and underbrush," recalled Pauline, to whom Camille on her deathbed had commended Charles, requesting that she assume the mother's role. "Ibsen, whom Charles had recently discovered, was haunting him; he wanted to play Peer Gynt. He 'felt' this character profoundly. . . . In the evening, when I lay in bed, he sat astride the bolster and managed to convince me [as Peer convinced his mother Ase] that we were departing on horseback even as death was clouding my eyes. This made so forceful an impression on me that I burst into tears."

Peer Gynt, ne'er-do-well, poet, fantasist whose debauches bring shame upon Ase, returns from troll-country to find her dying. He sits at her feet, pretending that the deathbed is a sleigh, and improvises a lullaby of salvation. Across the moor they fly, drawn by Grane and Blackie, then across the fjord to Soria Moria Castle, where a table has been laid for privileged guests. At its gate stands Saint Peter—the soul of dubiety, the ultimate butler—whom Peer sweeps aside, interceding with God Himself on Ase's behalf, like a priest. An equestrian priest, be it noted.

This scene from *Peer Gynt* calls to mind another ghost with whom Charles Dullin conducted private dialogues throughout his life, the ghost of his maternal uncle and namesake, Charles Vouthier. What Pauline says about Charles Vouthier, who as a young man had practiced law in Turin and published a thesis on capital punishment, is perhaps the strangest anecdote that emerges from her chronicle:

A freethinker and *Carbonari* leader, a poet and reader at the Sardinian Court in Turin, he was, like his sister, handsome, large, elegant, and aristocratic. He moved in lofty circles and fell madly in love with the Princesse de Solms, Lucien Bonaparte's granddaughter. Married to an old man, she led a loose life, always in quest of new adventures. This one had tragic consequences. Driven to despair by her infidelity, he slit his throat. After wavering at death's door, he survived the ordeal, though in a weakened state that lasted for quite some time, despite the ministrations of his frivolous innamorata. He then made a complete about-face, returned to his original beliefs, forswore the temporal world, deserted theater, poetry, the Turin bar, politics, and embraced God with passionate conviction. On the main square of Saint-Jean-de-Maurienne, he delivered a public retraction, donated all his money to found an orphanage, burned his poems, along with his writings on the secret society of the Carbonari, and entered the monastery of Sénanque.

After marrying off his sister Camille, whom he never saw again, he did his theology, and died suddenly in 1866, at the age of thirty-one.

Had it been possible to clutch forever the hand that offered her up, Camille might not have left Charles Vouthier, for on being told in a confessional booth of the Convent of the Visitation that God had sent her a husband more than twice her age (she was fifteen, Jacques thirty-five), she fainted dead away and entered marriage like a sleepwalker guided by her Capuchin director. While Jacques Dullin never mentioned Charles Vouthier without declaring him insane, in Camille's heart he occupied an inviolate place. During the delirium of fever and the labor of childbirth, it was her brother she would invoke with cries of "Charles, viens à mon secours!" ("Charles, come help me!"). She named her God-given child after him and *in articulo mortis* confused son with brother. "The night my mother died, I sat vigil alone at the head of her bed," wrote Charles. "Suddenly she turned to me and said: 'You are my brother Charles, are you not? Why have you been so long in sending me word of yourself?' "

Under Pauline's care, Charles lived in the Croix-Rousse quarter of Lyons, a hillside ghetto inhabited by textile workers many of whom had, like himself, come down from the mountains to settle on yet another height. He found work first in a millinery store, then in a bailiff's office, and finally at a fabric house—Maison R. et B.— whose proprietor kept him on mainly out of consideration for Pauline. "He's a sweet chap, your brother. He never says no. Polite? I've never seen his like. But he doesn't have a head for business. Do you know, he writes poetry on our labels. Talks to himself, gesticulates." This revelation did not take Pauline by surprise. "Charles was famous up and down the Grand'Rue for his strange demeanor. He was absent-minded and would bump into people while muttering verse." Nor could she have found much comfort in the draper's optimistic assurance that "we'll make a salesman of him yet—ça viendra, ça viendra"—for knowing Charles as she did, she knew that never saying no was just another, rather more as-

tute way of never saying yes, that politeness camouflaged a stone wall
behind which the child in him, or the lord, withstood every attempt to
evict him from his inner Châtelard. Filled with nostalgia, he wrote dark
elegies like this one:

>   . . . Enfant de la montagne
> La solitude fut ma soeur et ma compagne . . .
> Je n'eus que ce dont Dieu m'a bien voulu parer! . . .
> Oh! peu de chose, hélas! . . . mais un amour sacré
> De la nature. . . . En la voyant immense et belle
> Amant de l'Idéal, je m'étais épris d'Elle.
> Et lorsque avril venait tout inonder de fleurs,
> Je sentais dans mon coeur . . . vibrer d'amour: des coeurs. . . .
> Depuis que j'ai du fuir le pays de mes rêves,
> Les heures de bonheur se font toujours plus brèves;
> Je n'ai plus maintenant ce besoin d'infini!
> Chez vous c'est le néant qui dévore et finit. . . .
> Rien n'est beau . . . rien n'est vrai dans votre grande ville.*

And he recited these to friends who visited him in his garret overlooking
the city. "He occupied an old silkworkers' atelier, a high-ceilinged,
sonorous mansard, where our madness must still be echoing faintly,"
wrote one such friend, Henri Béraud.

To get there, one had to climb that near-perpendicular slope we call the
Grand'Côte. But at the summit, what a reward! The whole city lying at
anchor between its rivers like a naval squadron and, in the immense hub-
bub of work, a thousand plumes of smoke twisted by the rain and evaporating in a pearl-gray sky. How many ardent days, how many hopeful
nights we spent there, in this poor room! I can still see a little iron bed, a
white wooden table, a narrow window that looked out over roofs. I can
still hear the bitter muffled sound—of "Chante, ô barde! Ce soir, mes
pensives cohortes/Ont peuplé ton espirit hanté d'un mal ron-

---

* Child of the mountain / Solitude was my companion and sister / I had only that
which God saw fit to adorn me with / Oh! not very much, alas! but a sacred love / Of
nature. . . . Seeing her immense and beautiful / Lover of the Ideal, I fell in love with
Her / And when April came inundating everything with flowers, / I felt in my heart,
hearts vibrating with love. / Since I had to flee the land of my dreams / The hours of
happiness have become ever more brief; / Now I no longer have that need for
timelessness! / Here, nothingness is triumphant. / Nothing is beautiful, nothing is real in
your big city.

geur. . . ."*—and see Charles brandishing his fist at the clouds above while hurling his juvenile verse at the doleful city below. He lived for poetry and theater. It was as if they burned him.

One can readily imagine what the good draper would have done had he encountered his apprentice on native grounds, or known that the gnawing pain Charles celebrated in verse was symptomatic not only of "spleen"—that disease endemic to *poètes maudits*—but of syphilis as well.

In turn-of-the-century Lyons, which Béraud described as the one place on earth where even laughter was disciplinary, young men spoiling to shock the bourgeoisie wore their hair long and championed the music of Richard Wagner. So it came about that Charles and his companions were dubbed "the Wagnerian mopheads." Parading through town in loosely tied bows, threadbare capes, and old-fashioned jerkins, they went out of their way to engineer hoaxes, to pick fights, to flaunt ragdom in a city that lived by cloth, to create diversions from the *banal quotidien* which would otherwise have made life unbearably dismal. Béraud, who later became a literary journalist noted for his pugnacity, evokes this period with mixed feelings of anger, compassion, and self-contempt:

> Our farces deceived no one but ourselves. Or, to put it differently, we sought in them a substitute for boredom. As we pseudo-bohemians were wandering through the side streets of the city we were confusedly yearning for a key to our dreams, a congenial voice, a rift in the leaden sky which hung overhead like our enigmas. But we were alone, unbelievably so. Not a guide, not a master, not an elder. The only examples of our kind amidst half a million serious people. Trapped between walls that sweated commerce and beneath a sky as bleak as if it had been minted, we went groping after our ideal.

Those half million serious people were all the more intolerant of their scintillation for harboring fears that one stray spark might be enough to ignite a powderkeg. Since the Terror, Lyons had known periodic outbursts of violence. In 1831, 1834, 1849, 1870, and 1871, the *canuts*, or

---

* "Sing, o bard! This evening my pensive cohorts crowd your mind haunted by a gnawing pain."

silkworkers, had risen against their masters to suicidal effect. Then, in 1894, there took place an incident that traumatized not only Lyons but all of France, On July twenty-fourth of that year, President Sadi Carnot, while driving through crowds in an open carriage en route to the Lyons Exhibition, was set upon by a young Italian laborer, who cried, as he thrust a dagger six inches into the president's stomach: "Vive la révolution! Vive l'anarchie!" Carnot died three hours later. The next day, his wife received a letter that the assassin, Caserio, had posted before the attack. Addressed to "the widow Carnot," it contained a photograph of Ravachol, an anarchist bomber guillotined in 1892, with the inscription: "He will be avenged."

By 1902 or 1903, when Dullin's gang came of age, the constabulary held under surveillance every Lyonnais known to sympathize with anarchism, as though the poor wretches who fulminated in café basements and back rooms on the Grand'Côte were so many sappers mining the Crédit Lyonnais. Here was another lost cause available to angry youths intent on making their presence felt. As Béraud describes it, they found in the romance of clandestinity a reprieve from the bleak future. And if, to feel dangerous, they had only to recite violent imprecations somewhere underground, then so much the better. "We listened to the orators," he wrote. "Their doctrine was excessively simple. They would begin with '*Ni Dieu ni maître!*' ['Neither God nor master'] and end with '*Crève donc, société!*' ['Drop dead, society']. These potent ideas were expressed in language inspired by Kropotkin's pamphlets, which someone named Libertad, a cripple with the mane of a Greek Orthodox pope, peddled on the sly. He, like everyone else, invoked the Russian prince. . . . All in all, this scene, with its perorators, leaders, provocateurs, and simpletons had a melodramatic picturesqueness well suited to the driftless lives we working-class boys led."

Never for an instant did Charles forget that half a century before, Jacques Dullin had gone against family and Church by joining Les Voraces. To mouth antibourgeois curses was to keep alive the echo of his father's voice. "Dullin would stop his usual scoffing and assume a ferocious air when he recited the Solness Ballad of Ibsen."

Where theater per se was concerned, the only account Dullin ever gave of his first efforts to learn stagecraft confirms Béraud's observation that in Lyons an aspiring young artist found no guide, no master, no elder. What passed for conservatory training was the wrists-up school of acting as taught by a middle-aged gentleman who wore Russian boots all year round, his great role having been that of Michael Strogoff, and whose recalcitrant wig would go askew whenever, with ticlike automatism, he brought the back of his hand over his forehead to wipe away imaginary beads of sweat. This definitive gesture, along with a leaning on his right leg and a crossing of his hands over his breast, constituted, according to Dullin, "the sum total of his technical baggage." Now and again, some actor from Paris would set up a school outside the conservatory, sending ripples of excitement through the provincial slough. Such was Georges D., whose association with the Comédie-Française, brief and inglorious though it appears to have been, guaranteed him a clientele in the hinterland. When word got around that he taught diction, Dullin, who had a nasal whine for a voice, presented himself straightaway:

> The course took place every Sunday morning on the stage of a little café-concert called L'Horloge. I decided to go see him. He lived in a furnished flat of bourgeois stolidity where I was greeted by an ill-humored, unkempt lady wearing a flowery peignoir. She ushered me into the living-room, then shuffled away, after bellowing "Georges!" Georges, who was enormous, had, to his credit, an admirable basso profundo. He sat down and with a sweeping gesture indicated that I could begin. I threw myself into Hernani's tirade: *"Monts d'Aragon, Galice, Estrémadoure!"* Though nature had not given me much voice, my ardor doubtless compensated for this deficiency, which was to cause me such grief in the years ahead. Georges listened, his eyes half-closed, reckoning, I should think, not only my prospects but the extent of my resources. He got up and summoned his wife, who was none other than the lady in the peignoir. When she reappeared, he said, "Begin again, *mon petit.*" I was out of breath, hoarse, distraught. I began again. Georges underlined with a gesture addressed to his wife those passages that revealed a theatrical gift. *"Mon petit,"* he concluded in a solemn voice, "I predict a great future for you. Private lessons cost six francs an hour . . . and my larger course twenty francs a month. In two years' time I shall launch you!" Georges invited me to come watch him play Papa Mulot in *Two Kids* at the Eldorado.

The stage on which Georges gave lessons in diction was in a café named all too aptly The Clock, alas, for after several months of flexing his basso profundo, denouncing the cabal that had driven him from the Comédie-Française, and generally touting his custom, time ran out on poor Georges D. "He fell gravely ill and was rushed to the hospital," Dullin continues.

> One day, when we were visiting him there, he brought his hands up to his chin with a theatrical gesture, seized his enormous jowls, which now sagged like dried-up breasts, and stretched them over his mouth while making a horrible grimace. "I've had it, *mon petit.*" Several days later he died. Half a dozen of us followed his coffin. Coming back from the cemetery we gave vent to generalities on the grandeur and wretchedness of the theatrical life, which shone in our eyes with a nimbus of martyrs.

What sustained Charles Dullin was the knowledge that, impresario or no impresario, he would eventually escape Lyons and fly up the Rhône to the artistic Jerusalem of Paris. From his mansard studio on the Grand'Côte, he and his friends aimed their dreams like homing pigeons at roosts on the "sacred Butte." Everything God promised His children awaited them to the north, where they imagined poets improvising symposia, people dancing for joy, and girls all imitating Louise, the dressmaker heroine of Charpentier's opera who, despite her family, goes to live with an artist in Montmartre. "At the heart, at the very heart of our dream there was a blown-up image of eddying crowds, of festival lights, and, overhead, of windmills turning in the twilight on the summit of the Butte-Sacrée," wrote Béraud during the Nazi occupation, when Frenchmen found solace in the recollection of past adversity. "The Paris that haunted us day and night, the Paris of our eighteen years was the fairytale bohemia of *Louise*. We harked to its call with fervor. The morning cries of Montmartre and the fanfares of the coronation of the Muse filled our heads."

It was summertime in 1904 when they finally made their break, one of them, Albert Londres (who was also to become a well-known journalist), having preceded the others and sent letters of encouragement from the capital. To spare himself a scene, or avoid the risk of letting conscience veto his resolution, Charles left without telling Pauline, who was thunderstruck. Years later, in 1910, he assured her: "I have not changed since our mother's death, despite the struggle, the poverty, the evil deeds. I have remained Lolo in the depths of my soul." And seven years after that he again pledged fealty to the family romance, declaring: "I am destined to live like a savage, apart from others. . . . You will find me as you left me, unchanged. . . . You, Châtelard, our shared memories—that is what consoles me for the ugliness of all the rest." But for the moment, Paris beckoned him with prospects of some altogether new life, and with the image of enormous windmills. Like a Stendhalian adventurer, half-red half-black, he fled the province he would always miss. "We spent the night traveling north in a fever of anticipation," wrote Béraud, recalling, in the yellow of his life, what it had felt like to be green. "We couldn't keep still. Somewhere between Tonnerre and Joigny, the wind carried off Dullin's hat, so that he arrived bareheaded in Paris, which seemed unmoved by this splendid gesture of salutation."

CHAPTER V

✦ ✦ ✦ ✦

THE BOHEMIAN
FRINGE

Bohemia," wrote a journalist in 1849, when Henry Murger's *Scenes from Bohemia* was making that term widely familiar, "is a district in the department of the Seine bordered on the north by cold, on the west by hunger, on the south by love, and on the east by hope." He might have added that to escape the cold, stay their hunger, discuss their love, and kindle their hope its citizen-expatriates would gather in cafés, or rather (since necessity fosters communality and dire need strange bedfellowships) in some *one* café. During the 1840s and 1850s, for example, they flocked to the Momus, a formerly quiet establishment very near the Pont-Neuf, which had little to recommend it but the nickel cup of coffee and a proprietor, Monsieur Louvet, who held no brief against down-at-heel artists inasmuch as he entertained literary ambitions of his own. Here, for the minimal price of admission, they would linger all day long despite Louvet's meek protests, with authors scribbling articles, lithographers scratching stones, painters stabbing at easels, and all raising a din sufficient to drive away not only the domino players who had been the Momus's original clientele but the dull ache of failure that awaited them like a consumptive wife in garrets round about the Latin Quarter.

Charles Baudelaire was not yet Baudelaire; nor was Gustave Courbet Courbet, Gérard de Nerval Nerval or Félix Tournachon the pseudonymous Nadar. To an unprophetic eye, they were all doing time one flight up, where the pipe smoke always hung heavy, shabby figures in-

Shacks on the Montmartre heath—the maquis—*as photographed in 1905.*
Bettmann Archive

distinguishable from those others who evaporated in talk. Murger's
elegy made short shrift of the white knuckles and threadbare trousers
that were all that shone through the murk. When fame dignified their
misery, when, that is, bohemia evolved into an operatic never-never
land, the bourgeois who converged on the Momus looking for the romance of it saw themselves looking at one another. It is unwritten history what finally became of, say, Jean Wallon, a theological student
from Laon who would regularly materialize at the Momus and renew
his pledge to reconcile modern society with the Primitive Church; his
obsession might have led him to a monastic retreat, a barricade, or a lunatic asylum. We know, however, that Nerval, who occasionally slept
in the gypsum pits of Montmartre, hanged himself from a lamppost;
that Baudelaire, in the tertiary stage of syphilis, lost all speech but the
two words *sacré nom* and nodded politely whenever introduced to his
image in the mirror; that Courbet died a penniless exile in Switzerland
where he, too, must at times have had difficulty recognizing himself. The
poet Francis Carco wrote of his young manhood in Montmartre during

the decade that preceded World War I: "I couldn't do better than compare the bohemian existence to a half-submerged raft around which a handful of unknowns flounder while screaming for help with all the might of their anguished souls. There were evenings when we had the feeling that no one in the world could hear our distress signals." This could have been said even more poignantly fifty years before when those who found themselves living on the fringe did not have purchase in a convention of unorthodox life or in legends of le poète maudit, when their predicament still lacked a name and cabaret-owners were yet to become speculators dishing out meals in exchange for pictures that might, with some luck, assure them a comfortable independence.

The artists and writers incorporated under Carco's "we" were residents of upper Montmartre, of the so-called "Butte," whose streets formed a dingy maze, crisscrossing at peculiar angles, like lines graven on an old face, and stopping dead—here at quarries, there at a heath known locally as le maquis, or elsewhere at the roughcast walls of cemeteries and convent schools. Measured by people who could not always afford the horse-drawn omnibus, let alone a flat in the valley below, where urban engineers were still in 1905 and 1910 accomplishing Baron Haussmann's blueprint, Paris lay quite some distance away. To be sure, it crept nearer year after year. Seeding the lower slope with beer gardens and, higher up, planting the monstrous white onions of the basilica of Sacré-Coeur, it was as though this invader used the bottle and the cross to soften terrain it meant to absorb. Windmills that had once, within living memory, ground wheat from the Saint-Denis Plain (the Saint-Denis Plain having meanwhile become an expanse of cobblestone) now ground out popular tunes for the working class. Eight-story tenements built during Napoleon III's reign lined the rue Berthe, which looked rather like Naples, or so it seemed to Picasso, with mattresses slung over windowsills and sheets catching the breeze.

But upper Montmartre otherwise remained to all appearances a poor mountain village or a provincial shrine-town, whose chief industry was the sale of liturgical objects to pilgrims drawn from every quarter by the Sacré-Coeur. In the spring, it smelled of leaves and flowers. Communal life found its bearings on the place du Tertre, the marketplace where acacia trees as green as acid rose higher than the yellowish, reddish houses round about, where gossip collected from the little streets that flowed into it like so many tributaries, and where Saint-Pierre-de-

Montmartre, the vestige of a great Benedictine abbey demolished during the Terror, held fast to ground it had occupied since 1134, welcoming parishioners intimidated by the new basilica that loomed behind.

In upper Montmartre the mania for civil apotheosis had not cluttered up the squares (though Louis XVI came very near to establishing on these heights a royal necropolis and Napoleon to building a monumental Temple of Janus that would have housed still another replica of himself). One encountered few commemorative statues here—only people, little people performing their daily errands, coping, and, as a rule, tolerating one another's persuasions, which they wore quite literally as caps—some the mitered *bigouden,* some the felt slouch hat symbolic of bohemia, or kepis that dated to the Commune. Seedy things quietly grew seedier, as they were not entitled to do down below, making their last legs endure and acquiring in their dotage a picturesque beauty that distinguished them from the city slum. "All that sustains these old houses is their old soul, for there can be no question of imposing on

The Lapin Agile in 1903, with the Saint-Vincent Cemetery on the right.
Bibliothèque Nationale

them a decorative style," wrote Pierre Mac Orlan, who must have had in mind, among other houses, the ramshackle Bateau Lavoir, or Laundry Barge, where Picasso painted his early harlequins and saltim-banques.* "The most endearing are those that are all askew and in a state of imminent mortification. Vines hold in place the hinges of a worm-eaten door, a pot of geraniums rouges some weathered façade. The one thing to be said about these ancient little hovels on the rue Saint-Rustique, the rue Norvins, or the Impasse Trainée is that they shelter men and girls whose names we know." As death swept through these alleys, its course unimpeded by municipal effigies, so night fell with a thud each time it fell on the Butte of 1905, enveloping it in dreamless quiet. After ten o'clock or so, only strays were to be found awake—dogs, drunks, gangs, and, among the latter, the gang of artists who gathered by paraffin lamps in one another's ateliers, or in a few cafés that would accommodate them, particularly in the Lapin Agile.

Were it not for its motley clientele, the Lapin Agile, which nestled beside the steep grade of the rue des Saules, in a trough half-hidden from view by beeches and a spreading acacia tree, could have passed for some country posthouse. A stream meandered in front of it. During the 1880s and 1890s it was known as Le Cabaret des Assassins, a name which its proprietor, one Père Salz, found by no great stretch of the imagination, as directly across the street, against a wall of the Saint-Vincent Cemetery, cutthroats and pimps who conducted business nearer the city liked to settle delinquent accounts. After the popular balladeer Aristide Bruant bought it in 1900, it grew more convivial, both in name and atmosphere, if subject still to sporadic outbursts that traumatized the village and sent curiosity-seekers fleeing for dear life. This transfor-mation was the work of Bruant's tenant, Frédéric Gérard, better known as Frédé, who cut a locally famous figure in his wide, velvet trousers, big sabots, and fur cap, not to forget a mustache that drooped menac-ingly around his mouth like a Mexican desperado's. Far from being Mexican, he had emigrated from the farm country outside Paris, whence his mother, a midwife, would come and pay him visits, ascend-ing the Butte on a donkey. Montmartre swarmed with such refugees— young men of humble birth who assumed the guise of freedom though

---

* "To Picasso, 'good taste' and interior decoration are obstacles to his imagination, a stagnation of the spirit," wrote Roland Penrose.

their artistic endowments did not often match their desire for an existence other than the one in which they were jailed below as a tailor's apprentice, farmhand, or a printer's devil; they would let their hair grow long, they would puff long-stemmed clay pipes, they would wear hussar tunics, bandannas, medieval pelerines, Spanish capes, dolmans, and whatever other costume served to proclaim their social incongruity. Unlike most, Frédé could wrest a livelihood from his small talents for having in him as well the stuff of an impresario. Where he failed to write memorable ballads or to paint distinguished paintings, he succeeded in creating a remarkable room. The jackdaw suspended in a wicker cage, a huge plaster Christ by Wasly that stood in lieu of a coatrack, and a gaunt harlequin by Picasso (who generally sat facing his work) became household spirits for habitués who pictured themselves, when they were up to picturing themselves at all, as martyrs to bourgeois convention, as playboys of the Western World, as cowboys and Indians on a suburban frontier, or as circus hands. "This need of mine to break faith with the most tender loves, this impulse to undo ties, be it at the risk of finding myself desolately alone, have always been so strong in me, that people would say that Negro blood flowed through my veins. . . . With its heath, its white nights, its ineradicable grudges, and Père Frédé's bandit garb, the Butte offered me a certain wildness of decor and manners," wrote Francis Carco who, on the first evening he spent at the Lapin Agile, firmly established his credentials there by singing songs from the repertoire of the African Batallion, a convict corps (which looked to Montmartre's lowlife for fresh recruits and could, moreover, boast genuine alumni representing it at Frédé's cabaret).

If the artists and writers who foraged together in what were known as *bandes—la bande à Picasso* for one—liked this metaphorical liaison with the hooligan community, the Lapin Agile's gloomy common room would have brought to mind a den where newcomers were not suffered gladly until they gave proof of kinship by exhibiting their tattoo, their stigmata. "Sitting before a fire in the big hearth or, during warm weather, beneath shade trees on the terrace, we felt good and did not even have to close our eyes in order not to see the imbeciles who surrounded us," was the way André Salmon, a poet with rooms that overlooked the graveyard, remembered it. When, on one occasion, three young German scholars who had just examined the blue harlequin began to dun Picasso for a theory of aesthetics, Picasso drew a pistol in response and fired it several times skyward. Not that ideas weren't in the air of Montmartre, only that they flew like bullets aimed at the custodians of perception, rather than like little dappled things easily brought down, cooked to middle-class taste, and digested accordingly. What Picasso said in one way, André Breton would say in another some years later, promulgating that "Beauty shall be convulsive or it shall not be." Lip service to violence was the aristocratic fashion. As for ordinary folk who rose early and trudged downhill to factories in Saint-Ouen, miles away, it was all one whether the pistols that kept them awake preached beauty, anarchy, or nothing at all. Despite Montmartre's libertarian tradition (Saint-Vincent contained the bodies of three hundred Communards massacred in 1871), feelings sometimes ran high.

On Saturday and Sunday, when a pianist played at the Lapin Agile, evenings were given over to song. Aristide Bruant, who had grown moderately rich composing proletarian laments, would appear now and again, dressed just as Toulouse-Lautrec painted him. Sixteen-year-olds named Fernande or Marcelle or Henriette—the Butte was a haven for runaways—would sing renditions of "The Swallow of the Slums," then pass the hat. Frédé, hugging his guitar like a grizzly bear with a fondness for sixteenth-century verse, would murmur Ronsard's "Stances" or, in another mood, invite the company to sing bawdry. Anybody could hold forth and, indeed, most anybody did.

One youth, who wore sackcloth on such occasions, emerged in 1905 as a regular, a voice peculiarly well tuned to the grievances held by this audience, as a petitioner for the down-and-out, the exiled, the angry. After bivouacking with fellow expatriates from Lyons in a sleazy hotel just off the boulevard Poissonnière for several months, Charles Dullin gravitated uphill to Montmartre and, no sooner there, made his presence felt at the Lapin Agile, whose reputation had spread far beyond the Butte. "He was unknown except on the Butte, but we admired him," wrote Roland Dorgelès. "When he'd recite verse, his mouth would curl, his eyes would flash, his long locks would sweep his forehead. He didn't merely declaim: he'd live the poems, he'd embody in turn Baudelaire, Verlaine, Laforgue, Rollinat. Then his lips would tense even more and he'd moan Villon's 'Regrets de la belle Hëaulmière' ":

> Quand me regarde toute nue,
> Et je me voy si très changiée,

Povre, seiche, mègre, menue,
Je suis presque toute enragiée.*

To his sister, whom he had left in the lurch the year before, Charles wrote, half-penitently, half-triumphantly, making of his penitence a tearful triumph:

When I can afford to bring you here, I'll take you to the Lapin Agile; you'll nibble cherries in eau-de-vie. In the common room there's a large smoke-blackened crucifix which seems to extend its arms to everyone, young and old alike, consoling them for the disappointments of the day. . . . I've made my mark, you know, in this world of artists, some established, some rising, some wrecked. One evening, I saw a little woman, tucked away in a corner, sob as she listened to me recite Villon's "Ballade des pendus" [Ballad of the Hanged Men]. I felt glad for having been understood.

Dullin's letters home relate all the imbroglios, miseries, and paradoxes that characterized the bohemian scenario of *fin-de-siècle* Montmartre. To begin with, an artist-waif, finding himself pitted against a stock villain, the callous landlady, would dodge hither and yon in a landscape especially well suited to desperate games of hide-and-seek. "I've found a little room," he announced in 1906 after eighteen months adrift (and when all else failed, the Didis and Estragons of the Butte would bed down on the heath). "I'd like to be able to keep it, to be alone in my own place. My landlady doesn't seem all that confident and on the fifteenth, at the crack of dawn, will rap at my door. I'm already quaking, I don't yet have enough to pay the month's rent and should like to do a moonlight flit." The sequel proved to be as familiar as the circumstance. Evicting him, the landlady, like the false Dullins who looted Châtelard, seized mementos that were his if not by law, then by reason of nature. The "pitiless bitch," as he took to calling her, demanded that he give her a little Picasso in forfeit. "I did, all right, but with a heavy heart, believe me. I've pawned everything that's worth something: my father's signet ring, the lovely silver coffee pot. My Paulin [Charles habitually dropped the "e"], you're going to tremble

---

* "When I see myself naked / And see how much I've changed, / Poor, dried-up, skinny, small, / I am almost beside myself with rage."

and think me heartless for having separated myself from my parents' precious heirlooms, but what would you have me do? One must survive and eat."

How to eat and where to sleep were questions that arose every morning, unfailingly, like the sun, and sometimes remained unanswered after nightfall, exhausting the Butte's keenest wits. Charles lived for days on nothing but cod-liver oil and Scott Emulsion. When, as was often the case with people in his world, they required even more urgently than food a daily ration of absinthe, hashish, cocaine, or ether (which could be bought in liter bottles at the corner drugstore), their perplexity often led them around corners they would never see again. "A rollcall of those among us who really led this existence, with all the humiliations and grotesque peripeteias it entailed, would demonstrate that eight in ten did not survive it," wrote Pierre Mac Orlan, who knew whereof he spoke, having had several narrow escapes himself. Just beyond the pawnbroker's lay the shady world of the Milieu, whose proselytes beckoned girls with nothing left to sell but themselves, and boys with nothing more to lose but their citizenship in what Guizot had called "the legal nation." Some became converts and spent life, a good part of it anyway, in the brothel, in the Santé Prison, or in garrison towns across the seas, if they did not meet violent ends straightaway. Some flirted with the line, however, stepping over, though in their minds innocently, and hurrying back to the literature, music, and theater of banditry when officialdom held them accountable for actual crimes. Did Mac Orlan really convince himself that the barfly who commissioned him to fill his sketchbook with drawings of artifacts in remote Breton churches planned a pious excursion to the countryside? When the police caught the thieves, Mac Orlan was arraigned as their tout and his graphic inventory used in evidence against him.

Some such near-catastrophe seems to have befallen Dullin, for in 1906 he sent his sister this cryptic message:

I have a good friend, a companion from the Lapin Agile, who has just done me a great service. I can tell you now that it's all over, he got me out of a jam. You know how it is, one is young, one gets carried away by certain friendships and realizes only afterward that one has taken a wrong turn. I won't go into it, the matter has been settled and I feel as light as a feather. Guillaume, thanks to an influential friend, was able to extricate me from the dead-end into which I had wandered with the unconsciousness of a foal.

If the Guillaume was Guillaume Apollinaire, and so it seems he was, five years later Dullin's benefactor would need all the influence he could muster to defend himself against accusations that he helped steal the Mona Lisa from the Louvre. Police following the trail left by a drifter named Géry-Pieret, who had stolen Phoenecian statuettes from the antiquities collection, found his loot in the possession of Apollinaire (or Wilhelm Apollinaris de Kostrowitsky, to call him by his real name) and Picasso. Foreign names did not stand them in good stead, of course. That Apollinaire had been heard at the Closerie des Lilas to favor "the destruction of all museums because the past paralyzes the imagination" compromised him still further. But his pornographic works, among them *Mirely, or The Affordable Little Hole*, constituted proof positive that he was at the very least quite capable of hoodwinking her guards and ravishing that national virgin, the Joconda.

What drove Apollinaire to write erotica drove Van Dongen to hawk newspapers on the street, Bottini to warm gruel over his paraffin lamp, Vlaminck to walk ten miles rather than take the bus (which in all events serviced the periphery at infrequent intervals), Max Jacob to cast horoscopes for rich people of his acquaintance, and Dullin to work as a hired hand at farms outside Paris or recite verse in the lion's cage of a traveling circus. On the social precipice he called home, the bohemian artist could as easily move up as down and on any given day traffic with vultures from the Milieu or with birds of paradise who liked, on occasion, to dirty their feathers outside the "world." Self-abasement had become very much an aristocratic mode in turn-of-the-century Paris.

Among aristocrats who set fashion and bourgeois who followed them, to be "primitive," or loudly to profess a love of whatever went by that name, was to establish one's class credentials, for it testified to blood so blue, to a palate so jaded, to a mind so refined that only nature in the raw could provide a restorative jolt, a "new shiver." Like eighteenth-century nobles who relished the "fishmonger style," dandies of Proust's generation would affect *le parler rosse*, "tough talk," which required that they slur their speech and punctuate their conversation with underworld slang and expressions lifted from Aristide Bruant (*bruandailles*). "Snobbism has it that one must talk tough if one wants the reputation of being in the swim," declared a social chronicler, reviewing Talmeyr's play *Among Low Breeds*.

When such plays did not seem real enough, the audience staged its own, venturing into the jungle itself. Thus, for example, "The Hoodlum's Ball" on rue Charras. Turning upside down that old pantomime *Old-Clothesman*, where Pierrot steals a proper uniform in order to meet a duchess, scions of distinguished families and their demi-worldly companions would come travestied as characters from Zola's *L'Assommoir* (*The Bludgeon*) in order to mingle with choice specimens of the native population. "At these balls, where one descends to the level of Nanas who have become Gervaises once again, one hides one's coat-of-arms beneath Alphonse's overalls; these are deliberate falls," complained the society paper, *Le Gaulois*. Another calculated fall was the "Grand Duke's grand tour," an excursion named for Russian nobles who made it whenever the opportunity to visit Paris presented itself. After congregating at some artist's studio, gentlemen-tourists would visit stews like the Château-Rouge on rue Galande, where bullwhips hung very much in evidence, or Le Père Lunette, near place Maubert, where they ate cherries spiked with eau-de-vie while studying whores so ravaged by life that only aristocratic perversion made it possible for them to go on plying their trade. This tour would lead next into neighborhoods where there lurked the danger of being set upon by thugs—"apache territory"—and conclude on an appropriately blasphemous note in a low dive called L'Ange Gabriel.

Not everyone who hungered for the slice of life (some people called it a "supplement of being") could bring himself to hunt it on its native grounds, however, much less digest it without a literary palliative. Rich aesthetes staged their fantasies at home (like Des Esseintes in *Against Nature* or Henri Dufferein-Chautel in Colette's *The Vagabond*, at whose party Renée impersonates Salomé with veils inspired by Loie Fuller), hiring actors through an artist-procurer.* So it was that Charles wrote to his sister:

Yesterday evening, I recited verse for Monsieur the Count de N.—until the wee hours. There was a big gathering of his friends on the illuminated ter-

---

* In return for these private performances, which put one in mind of those organized by Marie Guimard in the eighteenth century, *artistes* received a *cachet en ville* (town fee). "Stretching his limbs before a mirror, Brague in Pierrot's white face and loose smock looks immaterially thin," wrote Colette. "He doesn't like the *cachet en ville* either. Not that the absence of a footlight barrier between him and them bothers him as much as it does me, but he has little use for what he calls the 'salon client' and shows upper-class spectators something of the same malevolent indifference with which they regard us."

race of his mansion, which commands a view of Paris. Electric lamps were
hidden in shrubs and between flowers to soften the glare. There wasn't a
single woman there. Rather mysterious assemblage, I must say! I was a bit
intimidated by these swells, but Max Jacob reassured me. What made me
squirm the most was my shabby appearance. Dear Paulin, you would do
me a great favor by sending along one or two pairs of socks. I don't have
any left, and for this soirée wore my shoes *à la russe* [stuffed with newspa-
pers], using remnants of a sock to cover my ankles. I was thinking of my
brother Villon whose poetry they wanted me to recite. I pictured him
naked and poor like myself and thereby salvaged a little pride. I am in
demand at other upper-crust salons, but I assure you, my Paulin, that I'll
feel even less at ease there. What forces me to go is necessity of collecting a
fee.

Through the good offices of Max Jacob—a Jew, a homosexual,
and a Breton, who could commute between such apparently disparate
milieux as the one described above and the Lapin Agile for being a
threefold pariah in bourgeois Paris—Charles may very well have found
his way, still sockless, to the faubourg Saint-Honoré, where Paris's eminent couturier, Paul Poiret, held court in an immense eighteenth-century
town house. On weekends, Poiret would stage fêtes for the delectation
of the city's High Society, deploying his fortune and ingenuity to create
an "oasis" (as he called it) in the bourgeois desert, a magic world outside quotidian banality, a theater that resembled nothing so much as the
théâtres de société of Louis XVI's era. Guests had no obligation or
choice but to be mannequins—the master provided apparel befitting the
theme, whichever one he had devised that week. When his garden was
transformed into a *café-concert*, for example, they wore cheap finery
and heard "tough talk" as spoken by Bruant himself. At The Moonlight
Fête, gentlemen became little Pierrots in raffish white berets gamboling
with Colombines in feathery boas. At The Thousand and Second Night,
three hundred people spent the evening dressed as fairy-tale Persians while
monkeys screeched from the trees and pink ibises strutted around the
fountain.

The Stomach of Paris, a fête whose title had been chosen with
Zola's novel in mind, of course, demonstrated how firmly Poiret held
fashion by the scruff, how well he knew a clientele that often made no
distinction between spirituality and animality, that would have situated
the soul, if asked where it was, in the lower regions of France's anat-

omy, or else outside France altogether, in Europe's wide suburbs (there was a "Russian soul," a "Nordic soul," a "primitive soul"). On this occasion, Poiret arranged to have his garden look like a village marketplace. Farmers in carts laden with fresh produce bound for Les Halles made a detour from the route they normally took, arriving at Poiret's mansion after midnight, whereupon gentlemen disguised as market porters did what porters do and distributed the vegetables among ladies who had come equipped with their maids' net bags. "Everyone left with ingredients for his stew," chuckled Poiret, whose bucolic fantasies induced him to purchase and restore Butard, a formerly elegant lodge near Versailles, built by Ange-Marie Gabriel for Louis XV. No doubt Marie Antoinette's model farm was the estate on which he had really had his heart set.

Where Max Jacob, after losing faith in remedies like ether and the puns he made obsessively (as if to buoy himself, to subvert the weight of words), finally cured himself of Max Jacob by getting reborn a devout Catholic and repudiating Society, Charles Dullin, on the contrary, embraced his past, or a mythic version of it. The benjamin who stood apart, the sinner tethered to a premise of sainthood, the bandit who administered justice, the lord orphaned of his birthright—from whichever angle he saw himself, he cut in his own mind the figure of an outsider, but a militant one who thrived on contention, exile, and martyrdom. "You know that the bourgeoisie and titles of nobility are far from enchanting to me!" he reassured Pauline. "In fact, I'd prefer any day to eat a bowl of soup offered by Père Frédé at the Lapin Agile and always be certain to find there my companions in poverty. They're almost all as bereft as I am, yet they nurture the hope of better tomorrows. We'll arrive, we'll triumph, and the bourgeois in my family, who disown me right now, will smile wan smiles some day."

No doubt his words echo the anarchist cant in which anyone who considered himself a freethinker had obligatorily to prate during those years. Anarchism imbued Paris like the Holy Spirit. It was manifest in the air one breathed, in the soup one ate, in the graffiti chalked on bourgeois walls, in the veneration for every broadside let loose by Elisée Reclus, in cult novels like Gide's *Fruits of the Earth* and Maurice Barrès's *Enemy of the Laws,* in literary reviews entitled *Revolt* and *The Outside,* in the dandy's perfect cravat and in the bohemian's pelt. Bourgeois pieties having become unfashionable, execrating the family or the language or the Bourse had become ritual theater. When they did not actually hurl bombs, it behooved artists or intellectuals to praise those who did. "A saint is born to us," exclaimed Paul Adam, alluding to the terrorist Koenigstein, alias Ravachol, whom he glorified, during his trial for murder, as "a renovator of the essential act." Laurent Tailhade, an actor who enjoyed some notoriety offstage as a satirist and dandy-about-town, hastened to declare, in December 1893, when told about a poor wretch named Auguste Vaillant hurling a homemade bomb at legislators in the Chamber of Deputies: "What does it matter, the death of a few vague human beings if the individual affirms himself thereby? Of what importance are the victims if the gesture is a splendid one?" And apparently he held fast to his belief in beaux gestes even when another bomb cost him one eye, for several years later he would use such abusive language to protest against the hoopla surrounding Tsar Nicholas II's state visit that the government, one of whose magistrates was Tailhade's own father, had him locked up for a year in the Santé Prison, where Charles Dullin paid him visits. "Steal from the wretched poor, steal the wealth that might make cold and hunger less intolerable for them during a long winter. Burn Chinese lanterns for sovereigns!" Tailhade vituperated. "Trot out your dancers, your bishops, your officers, yourselves, all the saltimbanques, the whores, in order to entertain with the spectacle of your scurrility guests who deign to bring you their crown, their scorn, and their commandments. What a joy it would be if, before these pigs fattened on flesh and gold . . . there appeared, in one cataclysmic flash, the redoubtable face of the Poor."

Whatever this creed may have been that men invoked now on behalf of the Great Individual, now on behalf of the anonymous poor, this *cri de guerre* that licensed at either extreme "the fauve animality of aristocratic eras" and proletarian reprisals, anarchism served to accommodate Charles Dullin's divided allegiances, to harness, if not indeed to glamorize, contradictions that might otherwise have torn him asunder. "You know, I am taken for an anarchist because I've met Tailhade and hang out with him a bit," he wrote to his sister. "Now don't fret over my associations, Paulin. You'll soon be persuading yourself that I am lost to the world and double your Hail Marys! Don't worry; I keep just this side of the boundary line, I have my father in mind and shouldn't want to do anything that would make him blush." Given a father whose idea of a lullaby was "Tyrants, down into your coffins," one might think that the paternal blush would have allowed him more latitude in his social comportment than the legal code did. Wasn't being an anarchist, or at least a fellow traveler to that cause, one way of keeping faith with Jacques Dullin, justice of the peace? The thought that his pirouettes on the brink would compel Pauline to tell her beads must not have been very far distant from the memory of father uttering terrible blasphemies and mother seeking refuge in her convent-school missal. Jacques had bequeathed an image of strength, of virility, of Zeus-like intemperance that made it possible for Charles not only to join battle with an impregnably smug establishment, to challenge it from above after the fashion of Balzac's Rastignac, but to disobey signals of defeat emitted by his own treasonous body. Among other enemies he carried inside himself, rheumatoid arthritis was perhaps the most redoubtable.* "It's bloody cold in Paris and that doesn't do my rheumatism any good! Happily, I am not a milksop and on the stage, in the heat of action, it doesn't bother me," he wrote, putting a brave face on things and acting the more passionately for acting in defiance of nature. "This damned shoulder doesn't seem about to move as it should. But I have a good doctor who's treating me free of charge. He'd like to avoid the cast which would paralyze my shoulder. Then the jig would really be up! I'd be like Perrette and the bowl of milk. But let's not darken our beautiful days!"

And yet, even this intimation of something stronger than his will, or the prospect of having a rack for a body and living on it in pain, furnished moral advantages. When Father did not sustain him, he could appeal to his patron saint, Uncle Joseph, whose secret world, like the hunchback that brings good fortune to those who touch it, became a storehouse of wisdom. "Uncle Joseph was right in telling me: 'Beware of women. They give us life, but they poison it for us as well!' He who had no experience of them knew them better than we do," Charles declared after reporting the murder of Frédé's son in the Lapin Agile and surmising that jealousy over a woman must have provoked it.

---

* It has also been said that his orthopedic disorders stemmed from inept treatment of syphilis.

Inclined as he was to sympathize with men like Max Jacob and Laurent Tailhade, who shared little but their stratagems of incalculability, their dandyism of wit, manner, dress—did they perhaps revivify the ghost long hidden in Joseph's clothes closet? And did the sackcloth Charles wore when he recited poetry at the Lapin Agile evoke for him memories of his uncle addressing the wilderness from his grape arbor? By turns the justiciar who ruled Châtelard and the saint who observed therein a vow of silence toward the world, Charles, though he may never have read Barrès's *Enemy of the Laws*, formulated for himself something rather like its hero's credo: "A man and a free man, I shall accomplish my destiny, respect and favor my deepest impulses without consulting anything from the outside." To live outside codes upheld by bourgeois society was to obey orders from no authority but one's "soul." As young Dullin grafted the mythology of his childhood onto anarchism, so he brought to theater naïve images that all came together in the apostolic view he maintained of himself. But naïveté took its toll. "This afternoon, it was so cold that I had to subtract four sous from my already meager repast to buy some wood," he noted one night, during his first winter in Paris. "And in front of my fire, I dreamed. I saw once again the valleys from Châtelard at different moments of my youth. My métier requires an expenditure of strength that exhausts me, what with all the other privations I endure. My candle is guttering; no more light."

When he arrived in Paris, Charles auditioned for the Conservatoire and, like many distinguished actors before him, found himself sentenced by a State-subsidized jury to learn his trade as best he could from teachers other than those associated with the Comédie-Française. Not that his talent was easily discernible, but even if it had already been what it eventually became, the figure he cut with his hoarse voice, his ungainly air, his felt hat, his hollow cheeks, his lips always verging on a curl, and his squint of bright little peasant eyes sufficed to dismay any jury recruiting youths to staff the bureaucracy of an urbane tradition. Like chooses like. If Charles would have agreed with another Montmartrois, Victor Serge, that "the luxurious Paris of Passy and the Champs-Elysées, and even of the great boulevards of commerce, were for us like a foreign or enemy city," so would he have acknowledged that enemies may recognize one another at first sight, in signs more reliable than words. Officialdom having made short shrift of him, he introduced himself to a certain Monsieur Larochelle, who presided like a ringmaster over several *théâtres de quartier* or *théâtres excentriques*—theaters that stood off Paris's center, in the peripheral neighborhoods of Montparnasse, Gobelins, Grenelle, and Saint-Denis.

The realm of melodrama, or simply "drama," was coextensive with the great working-class town that surrounded bourgeois Paris on three sides, coupling with it in shady border districts like Clichy, but climbing the Belleville heights northeast of the place de la République to form thereupon a distinct, plebeian capital before trailing outward into a no-man's-land of canals, waste plots, factories, and bastioned scarps called "the zone." This wraparound city improvised its stage life, as indeed it improvised life offstage, from whatever material lay near to hand. Cloak-and-dagger plots, which had long since become the laughing-stock in Paris proper, still circulated in these outskirts like old coins used as play money by *les petits* when they were no longer recognized as legal tender by the grown-ups. Costumes too worn and dated for the fashionable stage would retire to the suburbs after being snatched from oblivion at end-of-season auctions. The actors were themselves castoffs, many of them—relics of another age, decrepit shades eternally rehearsing neither here nor there, in a limbo situated between Paris and its rural apron.

Limbo did not of course necessarily consider itself such, which is to say that its shades, though they might lack scope, did not for all that lack passion or vanity. On the contrary, they who buried themselves there buried themselves very much alive, in a community as hectic and hierarchical as an anthill. Struggling upward from rank to rank, a young actor might be induced to forget his childhood designs upon the great world outside and ascend ever deeper into a hole. When nature endowed him with good looks, he would begin as a *premier amoureux des seconds* or a *second jeune premier* (for each story of this underground tenement had several mezzanines), graduating in due course to *premier jeune premier des jeunes,* then *jeune premier rôle,* from which eminence he could decry the *premier rôle des seconds* and, highest of all, the *grand premier rôle en tous genres.* Beginning as a *grande utilité* (utility actor), he would play first or second dotard (or "second of first"), "cloaks" (old men), "financiers," "jovials" (literally *ron-*

deurs, or roly-polies); in the best of circumstances, he would reach a pinnacle second only to the hero's, namely, *grand premier comique en tous genres.* When, finally, some physical disgrace condemned him to play *couteau* (dagger) or *troisième rôle* (third role) for the rest of his life, he would find a ladder of success even in this cul-de-sac and become first dagger after growing bald as second or third.

To be sure, melodrama made terrible demands upon its indentured servants. Every Friday, plays rotated around the faubourgs, moving lock, stock, and barrel from epicenter to epicenter like horses on a merry-go-round. The cast had no sooner dismounted one than it would find itself obliged to mount another, and joust with spectators as indecorous as any on God's earth. An actor needed a gladiator's stamina, not only to last the season but to last a single performance—a single performance meaning five hours of sound and fury interrupted by half-hour truces during which the audience would restore itself at neighborhood bistros or at the theater's bar. And when the season closed in May, still harder times ensued, for his wages were so meager that the *cabot,* the "trouper," could barely live on them, much less save. Men would then make the round of fashionable cafés selling dolls and artificial flowers (known as *articles de Paris*) or else spread a rug on the pavement and declaim, unless they managed to join up with an "ambulatory theater," of which there were several always circulating through the hinterland. Women had recourse to embroidery and domestic work.

But however great the sacrifices, these did not seem unbearable when calculated by other measures than gold or art or Paris. In his neighborhood, even a supernumerary was "somebody," and tradesmen who the night before had all but leaped onstage to arrest the second dagger would, in the morning, sell him necessities cut-rate, at "the artist's price." What would such people not have done for *grands premiers rôles en tous genres* like Gaston Fontaine, whose fame swept beyond one neighborhood, across three or four, in a narrow crescent of the Left Bank! Quite unknown to bourgeois Parisians, in Montparnasse and east as far as the avenue des Gobelins, where he would take conspicuous strolls, Fontaine was the King, the Romantic hero who fairly radiated charisma. Like most melodramatic prodigies, he had no literary culture to speak of; indeed, he wanted none, and made himself ridiculous a hundred times over mispronouncing "Harpagon" "Harpajon" (the latter being the name of a town near Paris, the former being the name of

Molière's miser) sooner than stand corrected. But he possessed *le don* (the gift)—the power to make his plebeian audience dissolve in tears or obey a call to arms. Had he been born earlier or later in what he called "this century of cows," his style might have found employment on the Romantic stage or on the silent screen. As it was, only the periphery gave the raw "gift" its due. One elderly *premier rôle* articulated this due when he said to Charles Dullin:

A king of tragedy is immutable. There he stands decked out in titles of nobility, even when he doesn't play his part all that well; an author of genius wrote his speeches, an old tradition enforces protocol, he always finds himself in decent situations. But a king of melodrama? They plunk a dented old crown on your head. They give you a broom for a scepter. You step into an arbitrary situation and expose yourself to the jeers of a public thirsting for blood. . . . Here's where you play *mélo*, with the heart (thumping his chest). In tragedy, talent suffices; to perform melodrama, you need genius. I know that to be the case, my boy, I know it because I've never had any.

Long after he had made his mark in the theatrical avant-garde, shortly before his death in fact, Dullin declared that he had learned all he knew from "the school of melodrama." In truth, old troupers, however deficient they were in every other respect, could scarcely have grown old in melodrama had they not mastered the tricks of the trade. Theirs was an artisanal tradition that Dullin commemorated in the name he would give his own house, the Atelier. Unequipped to formulate the dramatic enterprise in abstract terms, to justify what they did aesthetically, they spoke as sawyers and masons of theater, dropping hints that a prospective architect might find eminently useful. Fontaine's disclosure, for example, that he never grew tired while acting because "I breathe on the vowels and chew the consonants" helped Charles cultivate acceptable diction and project, or "place," a voice whose native tendency was to die onstage. Admonished by another *cabot* to "build lighter bridges," to end one idea and begin another without braying his transition, he became grudgingly aware that the actor shapes a role as much from without as from within himself, that in theater, where artifice commands nature, even the heart must wear some bister and rouge to convince the public of its authenticity.

If Dullin did not absorb such lessons straightaway, an observation once made by Louis Jouvet—"One practices theater because one feels that one has never been oneself, that one is incapable of being oneself, and that, at long last, one will be able to be oneself"—may explain his predicament. Wanting above all to inhabit an emotional plenum, how could the apprentice square this desire with the presence of spectators? How could he clasp himself (or his part) utterly, yet afford the inner distance that corresponded to his audience's vantage point? An awesome director standing *in locus parentis* might have silenced his questions by issuing orders or expounding theories, but the melodramatic stage did not provide any such surrogate. Nor was the crude language in which it couched its wisdom apt to seduce an idealistic youth. When Charles made good his escape from melodrama, when, after trying and rejecting other theatrical schools, particularly naturalism, he considered it from afar, only then could he judiciously frame his experience of it:

> I used to smile at the "third role" who would stamp his feet before he appeared onstage and open the door with a swift, conspicuous flourish, marking time before he'd speak. I smiled because I had seen performances at the Théâtre Antoine, where everything came off as in life, where this kind of theatrical expedient was ruthlessly suppressed. The public didn't laugh, however. It felt a definite shock. Often it applauded. When I myself began to play third role and, out of concern for the truth made a normal exit, I felt that something was lacking, that I would need, if not the foot signal, some theatrical equivalent of it. . . . Later, when I discovered Japanese theater and heard a "clapper" sound at the climactic moment, I couldn't help drawing a parallel between it and the footcall of my third role. However ridiculous this foot signal, however hammy its intent, still, it contained the spirit of theater.

This spirit found expression not in trompe-l'oeil mock-ups of reality but in a dream world where masks were more plausible than faces and where symbolic or ritualistic gestures constituted a natural form of deportment.

For Dullin, who would always remain his mother's faithful renegade, the word "spirit" signified something that dwelt in the breast more than in the mind, like the divine afflatus. So, theater for him was not merely a sum of techniques but the praxis of a religious enterprise he had undertaken in order to recover and consecrate a childhood whose very landmarks had been stolen from him. His acting was a "calling," he declared—a *vocation*. All the elements that stirred the spirit in him—"the poets, my old uncle . . . the chimney sweeps, the lay of the land"—these "and a thousand other things foreign to theater" had their place reserved in a mythology altogether congenial with melodrama. Like Châtelard, the *théâtre de quartier* stood outside bourgeois culture, providing shelter for nomads, asylum for the outcast, and justice for those who could not have their grievances litigated anywhere else. Like the world-view whose central image was of a Dullin tribe split into antagonistic moieties, one living by the imagination and one by bread alone, one consisting of children of nature and one of imperialistic city folk, melodrama recognized no neutral ground, no moral ambiguity but the unalloyed courage, lust, greed, cowardice, goodness, orphanhood, and proprietorship that emerged from the mold as *rôles* in a perfectly legible universe.

Cast as "third role" by his employer, Charles had played that role long before setting forth on a theatrical career, and would continue to do so after leaving the suburban circuit, in characters with whom his name became virtually synonymous. Third role amalgamated Mandrin and Villon and Uncle Joseph and the lastborn who sprang from a withered source. To be sure, Dullin's pain-racked body would endorse any claims he ever made that the part had not been one of his devising, that fate had thrust it upon him. "The drama of my life lies in my round back," he confided to a friend. "I cannot play roles in which one looks up at heaven." But if contents shape the container, this hump of flesh might as well have been the visible and concrete child of a mind acquainted from earliest memory with the power held by invalids, with the authority exercised by nature's sports. To play third role was to uphold the sanctity of first, to restore a world in which he starred as the prodigy.

However obvious the mediocrity of *cabots*, Dullin felt the same affinity to them as he would presently feel to Pirandello's characters searching for an author and to Henry IV finding refuge from death in a theatrical persona. "Though it made me laugh at first, I have often given thought to this sketch," he said of a picture by Forain that shows a middle-aged *premier rôle* sitting plunged in Napoleonic gloom, his hand in his waistcoat, while a shrewish wife explains to a neighbor that he had been divested of his imperial career. "After all," Dullin went on to say, "if we no longer encounter such absurdity . . . we have also lost irremediably an epic sense which was at the source of it. This actor was perhaps a bad one, stupefied by vanity, but he had a smell of theater about him, a taste of characters born to live onstage; there was in him, as in every caricature, a touch of the hero." Had Jacques Dullin ever extended his hospitality to a wayfarer with Forain's wit and pen—the justice lecturing medieval peasants, the king having himself disrobed by his offspring, Jupiter Fulminator thundering from atop a little French Alp, the hermit stealing from his cell in the dead of night, the wild man who erupted from the woods (and there was such a man: he later gave up his lair near Châtelard to become a spiritual adviser in Lyons, whence his reputation spread abroad as far as Tsarkoe Selo, or so it seems, for he visited the Tsarevitch at the Tsarina's behest)—all these would have provided material for an extraordinary album. Did that little tract of mountainside not, indeed, resemble a stage curtained off by some special Providence, from which leave-taking was tantamount to a Fall? And did the youngest of its inhabitants not view his kith and kin as "characters born to live onstage," as roles without a history enacting themselves in a play without a text? Like the "mysterious domain" lost then rediscovered by the bohemian hero of Alain Fournier's novel *Le Grand Meaulnes* (*The Great Meaulnes*), Châtelard became the exile's Promised Land, the actor's sacred theater, the manchild's utopian redoubt. Before separation from the Gods, there had been Châtelard.

In the Romantic tradition, Charles situated his heroic dream outside "the legal nation," in a Wild West which he projected against real life as though it were a magic-lantern slide capable of dissolving the squalid walls that imprisoned him. "When I was with the Théâtre Montparnasse," he reminisced many years later, "every Friday morning a two-horse omnibus would pick us up at the Montparnasse station and take us to Saint-Denis. The *premiers rôles* sat inside while we, the 'little ones,' huddled beneath a canvas that covered the vehicle. . . . I can remember the departure, with Fontaine, alias d'Artagnan, mounting the footboard last and a whip cracking in the wind. I hear the bells of melodrama and, despite everything, this life still seems to me infinitely seductive."

Although Dullin, in "third role" parts, soon earned a reputation such that the young swells of Belleville, the *titis*, would wait for him backstage when the curtain rang down on *Les Misérables, The Two Orphan Girls, Don César de Bazan, Biribi,* or *The Adventures of Cap-*

tain Corcoran, he could scarcely bring himself to believe that this career might ever lead him anywhere but round about, or that a script worth waiting for might ever visit this circle of neighborhood theaters, and kept one eye fixed on the main chance.* "I see the flaws of the old troupers who want to give me lessons: I take some, I leave others, and remain what I am." After two years of centrifugation that all but separated his soul from his body, the main chance seemed finally to present itself when André Antoine took notice of him one evening at the Lapin Agile. "Yesterday, I had fire in my guts reciting Baudelaire, Laforgue, Poe, Rimbaud, Villon, Verlaine long past midnight," he reported to Pauline. "Antoine, who happened to be present, came up afterward and said: 'My boy, you've got the stuff, I'm sure you'll go places. Come see me!' His words left me speechless. When he departed, he waved goodbye. This is all very reassuring to me. Antoine is somebody, you understand, and somebody I can trust. . . . I plan to see him and shall write about it straightaway. Should the Odéon pan out, I believe that we'd be spared all these cares that dampen our joy and our youth."

Charles hastened across the Seine to the Latin Quarter where, at Aristide Briand's urging, Antoine had recently installed himself as director of France's junior state theater, and he came away with a small role on which he lost no time predicating immense hopes. "My Paulin! Victory! I've been hired by Antoine and am playing a role in *Julius Caesar,* that of Cinna the poet. . . . This springs me free from *mélo;* I'm in the midst of good actors and have learned many things. De Max [a famous tragedian of the day, who had been cast as Caesar] is very nice to me; everyone calls me *le petit* and makes me feel like the company's pro-

---

* Of Dullin's theatrical debut as third role in *The Adventures of Captain Corcoran* at the Grenelle, Henri Béraud wrote: "The Théâtre de Grenelle had survived from the Boulevard of Crime. A smelly audience throbbed in its shadows and became passionately involved with the dramatic action. . . . The action took place in India. There were snakes and Englishmen, rifleshots in the moonlight, and *bayadères* executing belly dances. I could understand nothing of the plot except that an old Brahmin, a kind of worm-eaten Gandhi, was the father of the traitor, in other words, of the Anglophile. In the end this false heart assassinated the author of his days, and the old Brahmin expired while hollering, 'Traitor and parricide, I curse you!' The old Brahmin was none other than Dullin. He looked a greenish fakir, raised from the sepulcher after three years of fasting. . . . This apparition stunned Grenelle and when Dullin, on delivering his unworthy son to the wrath of the gods, dropped dead, stiff as a board, there rose from the orchestra deafening applause and from the stage a cloud of dust."

A *crowd scene from André Antoine's production of* Julius Caesar *at the Odéon in 1906. Dullin is left of center, leaning forward on his left arm.*
Encyclopédie du Théâtre contemporain

tégé." His enthusiasm proved to be as shortlived as his role, however. Once *Julius Caesar* ran its course and Dullin found himself playing second customs agents, first messengers, and Moorish valets, he could afford to detest the lowly state he had bargained for: Charles *le grand* would habitually take umbrage at the patronizing endearments solicited from on high by Charles *le petit.*

There were other grounds than temperament for the clash that occurred between him and his director. Antoine, though he had risen very high since 1886 when, in Montmartre, he first assembled Sunday actors like himself with a view to performing plays adapted from Zola's *Rougon-Macquart,* had borne aloft that cornerstone of naturalist aesthetics, the "milieu." * Whereas Dullin demanded room for his imagination on the stage, Antoine cluttered it with fixtures and, to sanction his own prosaism, quoted Ibsen's remark, "I knock down the wall of an apartment, then observe what's taking place inside." Each actor made the theater his home, each seeking therein a heightened sense of himself, but one felt at home in an ontological netherworld of archetypes, while

---

* Not to be confused with the criminal "Milieu."

The naturalist stage set of a laundry, circa 1903. From Le Théâtre

the other could never inhabit the here-and-now precisely enough or pin
down sociohistorical circumstance with sufficient detail.

Antoine was a materialist and determinist by persuasion. "The intimate, irreplaceable necessity of the milieu," as he put it, reflected a
belief that the "secret" life had to divulge itself through its physical context inasmuch as the medium shaped the man, that to situate someone
correctly was to know him absolutely. Provided a director set the scene
right or built the appropriate frame, an image would necessarily unfold
of itself, "like a ball of wool unraveling." Antoine's scrupulously realistic sets (in *The Butcher*, for example, sides of beef hung onstage) were
therefore designed as cognitive portraits of the dramatis personae, as
objectifications of the psyche. It is obvious that he responded at some
profound level to what he called "the incessant mobility, the fleeting
splendor of life"—and yet his every dramatic move was calculated not

to evoke "glimmers, shadows, deliquescences" but to still the moment, to make *tableaux vivants* of thought, to reify human nature. In 1906 and 1907, Dullin had not yet spoken about "retheatricalizing the theater." When, some years later, he thus formulated his aesthetic strategy, he prosecuted Antoine for having dealt a fatal blow to the Romantic actor and constructed "real houses in a garden that Harlequin's fantasy has made as artificial as can be." That they both upheld, from radically opposite ends, an ideal of life governed, if not indeed consecrated, by an objective text occurred to neither, and in the event it had, they would doubtless still have been at daggers drawn.

Set free from melodrama, Dullin found himself nonetheless obsessed by "naïve" forms traditionally associated with the plebs. On leaving Antoine's company, in 1908, he induced several friends—among them Alexandre Arnoux, who wrote for him a skit, or *parade*, entitled *Noël des Fantoches*—to help him launch a *théâtre de foire* at the Neuilly Fair.* Since 1890 or thereabouts, various young men had endeavored to set up outposts of culture in the hinterland and in proletarian backwaters such as the Saint-Antoine district. Along with people's universities, little theaters—the Théâtre Civique, the Théâtre du Peuple, the Théâtre Populaire de Belleville, the Théâtre Populaire de la rue de Tocqueville, and the Théâtre d'Avant-Garde de Ménilmontant, to name but five—bore witness to a socialist faith whose zealots were propelled beyond civilization into the wilderness. "During the past ten years, a curious phenomenon has occurred. French art, the most aristocratic of all arts, has come to realize that there exists a plebs. . . . Socialism's progress has attracted the attention of artists to this new sovereign whose sole interpreters have hitherto been the politicians," said Romain Rolland in *The Theatre of the People*, a book written to illuminate the obscure work being done without any government support and independently of one another by cultural missionaries like Louis Lumet and Henri Dargel.

Dullin's enterprise differed from theirs in one essential respect. He might have seconded Lumet's declaration of war against Boulevard theater: "The theater is marked by the coarseness of its stimulants, by its

---

* Dullin had apparently read a book on the fairground theater while undergoing treatment for his ailments at the Cochin Hospital, where he spent two months in 1906, or else afterward, at Pauline's home in Lyons, where he spent some weeks convalescing.

pretentiousness, by its absurd and predictable stupidity. The time of
ariettas and *aubades* has passed. We want to act and our ambitions are
unlimited. A new age must dawn. And, to accomplish this work, we
want to make direct contact with beings to whom we shall give a soul, a
life. As a testing ground for our strength, we have chosen the theater."
But he made it his goal to revive a lower-class tradition rather than to
propagate a classical repertoire, to acquaint the common people with its
own forms rather than to visit something "foreign" upon it.

Just how true this was would emerge quite explicitly some seven
years after his fairground theater folded (and it folded almost as soon as
it opened), in letters he sent from the battlefront. "The people is instinct," he informed Elise Toulemon, a young dancer who had become
his mistress, exhorting her to "beware of the culture that has left its
mark on you lest it domesticate you and drain you of energy." Not only
was the people instinct, but other remarks seem to argue a conviction
that this collective entity was "objective" and its instinct oracular:

> I have discovered a genuine actor and three improvisers, two of whom
> must descend in a direct line from fairground performers [the reference is
> to soldiers who staged a variety show under his direction]. I gave them a
> scenario and they improvise anything I like. They sing, clown, do Japa-
> nese, Spanish, and Italian dances, speak gibberish that sounds just like
> foreign languages! Evoke for them in one word some foreign civilization
> about which they know nothing and it's enough to trigger the most un-
> foreseen and droll fantasies. The eighteenth century and fairground theater
> survives in these blokes intact! One is a jack-of-all-trades from the fau-
> bourg Saint-Antoine. Galvani is a woodcarver from the faubourg Saint-
> Antoine, and another a carpenter, also from the faubourg. . . . It comes
> from instinct, all this, from the *génie de la race*. I have always had a predi-
> lection for the common people, but now more than ever am I determined
> to move in its direction. No one but the *peuple* possesses the secret of great
> revolutions in every sphere.

By following the same circuitous logic that joined the dandy to the
red Indian in Baudelaire's poetic universe, the verbal wizard to the
primitive Gaul in Rimbaud's, and the unattainable nymph to the una-
chievable Book in Mallarmé's, Dullin could readily declare the consummate actor a noble savage and the mimetic gift a force of nature. Like
"characters born to live onstage," the Artisan, who filled a role at birth,

who derived his identity not from the experience of life but from his own hermetic archetype, had only to clasp himself in a total embrace to monopolize virtue. Transcending profane time and space (what Pauline would have called, in biblical language, *le siècle*), this "born" actor embodied the principle of Birth or Blood by which a former age had striven to exempt the aristocracy from historical vicissitudes and social process. At once nature's child and art's prodigy, a tabula rasa and a sacred image, he could not change except to become, like Poe as eulogized by Mallarmé, "Himself"; for his was a state of Grace manifest even in the gibberish he uttered. If *le génie de la race* that filled the space left vacant by God bore a family resemblance to God, its elect inherited the gift of primitive Christians who spoke "with tongues." Surely Charles had "speaking with tongues" in mind (as well as "harlequinery") when he noted that "they utter gibberish that sounds just like foreign languages." And surely the secret of great revolutions signified the New Life reserved for true believers. Reiterating a view to which Jean-Jacques Rousseau had given classically pious formulations, Dullin bestowed universality on a hermit. Saint-Antoine and Châtelard, the Butte and the fairground stage, the Far West and the war front were so many paradigms of a virgin interior exempt from bourgeois law, of a "Self spread to the limits of Creation."

Dullin spoke perfectly in character, then, when he confessed that "I would certainly have been a monk had I not become an artist," and all the more in character for making a love letter to Elise Toulemon the vehicle of this confession. Elise found herself caught between two Dullins, one of them forever striving to betray her and the other constantly trying to convert her. As she describes it, they surrounded her even in bed where he would lie side by side with himself, half-naked, half-frocked:

One day, my heart torn by doubts, I entered a dismal hotel on the rue Fontaine [in Montmartre], wondering, as I tiptoed up the staircase, whether it wasn't a brothel or a hangout for pimps. Above me I heard a muted voice like a priest's in the confessional. What was my surprise to find Dullin on the fourth-floor landing seated at a little table opposite the *Brothers Karamazov* poster, which he kept like some sort of icon. His cheeks looked horribly puffed: in fact he was practicing diction with two balls in his mouth. On seeing me he spat them out, and stuffed them in his pocket as deftly as a sleight-of-hand artist. In a faint voice he invited me to enter his room. I had no sooner taken in the squalor than he locked the door and chucked the key out the window. Confronting me, he spoke in the manner that hoodlums assume when they mean to seize an object they covet. He threw me onto his dirty creaking bed. "I'm going to make you my girl for good!" he said.

Hours passed. Dullin recharged himself with a bottle of Porto Flip which stood next to his cod-liver oil, swigging it while his legs remained entwined about me. The first thing I saw at sunrise were dubious cracks in the ceiling. Grandeur and poverty presided together in the room of my lover, who was at once youthful and old. He lay there reflecting with his eyes closed. He guessed that his captive was impatient to find more comfortable quarters and, without even stirring, in a voice as deep as a shade's, said, "I'll find a way to shut out everything wily in you, I'll carve human wrinkles into that brassy face of yours and give you, in exchange, a key to the earth's genuine treasures."

Besides reflecting Dullin's dire circumstances, the bottle of cod-liver oil would seem to vouch for the authenticity of a scene which had as much to do with moral fortitude as with carnal love. It was another legacy salvaged from Châtelard, where the enema sat beside the tobacco pouch, uniting a powerful old man to a decrepit child. Tormented by his frailties, Charles disowned them with bravado, wearing the anarchist's red shirt, the apache's bandanna, and the laborer's brown velvet trousers like a composite clean bill of health. Male pride led him to play now the brute disdainful of social amenities, now the guide whose vocation was to redeem and to suffer. So it happened that when he won Elise by main force, he rose up against her profane impulses—her "wiliness" or "underhandedness"—and translated a sexual conquest into a spiritual initiation. Did their first night begin with the disposal of a key and end with the promise of a shibboleth? Having ravished her in a bedroom locked inside and out, he offered to absolve her of her sinful nature. Not for nothing had he become famous on the periphery as a *grand guignol* terrifying audiences with his impersonations of madmen, morphine addicts, and abominable bandits.

Yet this *grand guignol* yearned for legitimacy. Irresistible though he found painted dolls like Elise (who later married Marcel Jouhandeau, a homosexual writer, and figured as the star, or sacred monster, in his literary oeuvre), it would seem that he dreamed of initiating a fifteen-year-

Charles Dullin as Smerdiakov in Jacques Copeau's adaptation of
The Brothers Karamazov, *produced at the Théâtre des Arts in 1911. The stage set was designed by Maxine Dethomas.* Encyclopédie du Théâtre contemporain

old convent girl who had had no experience of life. "My anarchist, all reserve and shyness on the surface, was a force of nature," wrote Elise. "His amalgam of cruelty, perfidious sensuality, and bourgeois rectitude made me recoil from his marriage proposal, for he insisted upon the traditional benediction, the solemn engagement of our two wills before a tricolor sash."

One more object noted above spoke of Charles's sympathy for the uncouth, of the conviction he held that Nature was the great outsider and virtue an appanage of "naturals" disinherited by society. Dullin first made Paris take notice of him when he played Smerdiakov in Jacques Copeau's adaptation of *The Brothers Karamazov* at the Théâtre des Arts. How he had met the rich and cultivated amateur, Jacques Rouché—who used this theater to illustrate certain principles formulated in *Modern Theatrical Art,* a book he had written after acquainting himself at first hand with the revolutionary work of Georg Fuchs, Max Reinhardt, Fritz Erler, Meyerhold, Stanislavski, Gordon Craig, and Adolphe Appia—need not concern us here. Suffice it to say that in a capital whose theaters were as firmly buttressed against the new ideas swirling round about France as was its social establishment, he found the one most notable exception, and that this stage helped lift him from nowhere by providing a role lopsided enough to accommodate all his incongruities. Luck did not, of course, "provide" the role, but only the material, which Dullin cut to measure. Whatever Dostoevski may have meant by Smerdiakov, Dullin discovered a Smerdiakov deep within himself; though in the account he gives, the character took shape outside him, like an hallucinatory image projected before his eyes by an impersonal force:

On April 5, 1911, the day of the opening, I was all at sixes and sevens. The night before, Durec, my director, had said to me: "Everything will turn out perfectly when you make contact with the public." That word "perfectly" disabled me. If perfect was all it was going to be, then I might just as well throw myself into the Seine right away. Several hours before the performance, I was wandering aimlessly near the Parc Monceau, my head on fire. It seemed to me that the way I had been playing my last scene was pitiful; I rehearsed it to myself. Then, suddenly, when I came to the point at which I ask Ivan to show me the *famous rubles* one last time and shout "Farewell, Ivan Feodorovitch!" I felt an irresistible need to run, which I did, despite myself, skirting the Parc Monceau's iron gate as if I wanted to lay hold of my character whom I could glimpse on the other side climbing the staircase to go hang himself. That evening, during the performance, I climbed those steps like a somnambulist . . . imitating the phantom whom I had seen in a strange flash of lucidity . . .

This manifestation at once animal and spiritual, in which body and soul experience the need to melt so as to externalize a character, gave me possession of the character while dictating to me, in a more general way, one of the central laws of the actor's art. Until then I had had an unfortunate tendency to bridle instinct in favor of composition; I attached such weight to the text's intelligence, to its verbal power, to its literary nuances, that my playing had no guts. . . . The need to scour my mind clean . . . had led me toward a kind of poetic recitation; in my neophytic ardor, I'd formulate the problem from the outside and say, "Dullin . . . yes . . . an intelligent actor," damning myself, though quite unwittingly, with faint praise. Smerdiakov taught me to use my true resources. . . . Since then I have always tried never to let my intelligence and critical faculty get the upper hand of instinct.

This remarkable memoir calls to mind the place in which Dullin had elaborated his first persona, the seminary of Pont du Beauvoisin, where, pent up by Camille's vow, he had written suicidal farewells before assuming a pious demeanor. It may be that to escape from prison with moral impunity, to violate the pact made at birth between his mother and God (or Charles Vouthier) yet preserve his innocence, he had seen no way out but to divinize nature and beget himself anew as the wunderkind of holy instinct, to become his own mother sanctioning calls from the lower self. Not only did he "melt" in order to "externalize" Smerdiakov but his offspring appears on the far side of prison bars. And not only does Dullin's language suggest an act of self-parturition but one may venture to infer from this birth, always keeping in mind *which* character emerged, that it abolishes the past, or the God and moral authority of an old regime, for Smerdiakov is a parricide. Dullin knew by heart the "Third Interview" in which Fyodor's bastard son explains himself as follows to Ivan Karamazov:

> "I don't want it at all," Smerdiakov said in a shaking voice, with a wave of the hand. "I did have an idea of starting a new life in Moscow or, better still, abroad with that money, but that was just a dream, sir, and mostly because 'everything is permitted.' This you did teach me, sir, for you talked to me a lot about such things: for if there's no everlasting God, there's no such thing as virtue, and there's no need of it at all. Yes, sir, you were right about that. That's the way I reasoned."

Virtue did not die easily, however, if at all. It lay embedded in the mythic prestige with which Dullin surrounded "instinct," in the *vocation* he embraced, in the martyrdom that was for him a sine qua non of artistic distinction. Fornicating and evangelizing in turn, he could readily identify with a character who assaults first his father, then himself; who kills the king, the mounts the scaffold; who sets himself free from God to begin a life where everything would be permitted him, then makes of that infant life a sacrificial offering. "The evening of the performance I stumbled on a step of the tragic staircase, the very staircase on which I had had my conversation with Ivan just before committing the murder." Insofar as stumbling may be said to resemble a slip of the tongue, then perhaps he stumbled not so much on the step of a staircase as on the ambiguity of his ascent. Where, upstairs, did Heaven lie—in a lover's bedroom, or in a penitent's cell? How did he witness that hallucinatory image beyond the bars—as a captive yearning for release from bondage to a vow of celibacy pledged by his mother on his behalf, or as a free man yearning for imprisonment in a state of grace?

The Brothers Karamazov gave a doubly decisive twist to Dullin's life; for besides introducing him to a congenial role, it introduced him to a man who would form the gifted director he eventually became. Until his adaptation of Dostoevski's novel met with success, Jacques Copeau had always stood at arm's length from the stage. As editor-in-chief of the Nouvelle Revue Française, a journal imbued with the passion for classical astringency and the sense of high purpose that characterized its founders (among them, André Gide), it behooved him to throw an occasional stone at the Boulevard, but otherwise to consider the Seine a moat between the heathen spectacles bourgeois Paris offered itself on the Right Bank and his literary emplacement on the Left. In 1911 no one among his confreres could have foreseen him organizing a theatrical company, much less dedicating his entire life to the theater. And yet that is precisely what the future held in store. When, ten months before the Great War broke out, the Théâtre des Arts closed, several members of the troupe, including Charles Dullin and Louis Jouvet, had already begun life anew on the rue du Vieux-Colombier, in a former théâtre de quartier renovated to suit Copeau's vision of the ideal dramatic rite.

CHAPTER VI

✦ ✦ ✦ ✦

JACQUES COPEAU'S NAKED STAGE

Jacques Copeau inherited his enterprising spirit from his father, a man, the sort glorified by nineteenth-century bourgeois, who had risen above humble circumstances to become the owner of a foundry. Born in 1879 and raised in the faubourg Saint-Denis, a predominantly lower-class neighborhood, Copeau enjoyed privileges that money alone could buy, perhaps foremost among them a classical education at the Lycée Condorcet. By his own account, family life was as dour as it was solid and would have been unrelievedly so if not for his paternal grandfather who acquainted him with a make-believe world in which his imagination thrived. Where Copeau *père* went early to bed and early to work, Copeau *grandpère* had joined the official claque of the Comédie-Française in order to satisfy gratis a large appetite for theater. Where father upheld the industrial present, grandfather was wont to evoke, interminably, an heroic past in the person of Frédérick Lemaître, with whom he had, on occasion, played dominoes in a café near the Porte Saint-Martin.

That this antithesis may have been less sharply drawn in reality than Copeau's laconic memoirs lead one to believe hardly compromises its significance as a myth. Myths, after all, do with reality what they will, now dwarfing the big, now magnifying the little. Consider, for example, a *guignol*, or puppet, that grandfather Copeau gave to Jacques when he was five years old. However disproportionate the value he would always attach to this object, everything else we know about him suggests that it matched the proportions of a desire—a desire he could never educate—which was to manipulate himself and others, to exist as a totally autonomous being. Did he erect this fetish *au commencement*, as if to argue that his grandfather rather than his father planted the seed from which his "real" self had sprung? Perhaps. What is certain is this: that throughout childhood and adolescence the theater constituted a spiritual underground where he held out against the career for which his father, who had him tag along on business trips to England every year, was grooming him. Jacques would attend plays on the sly and, like Victor Hugo swearing at age fourteen to be "Chateaubriand or nothing," nurtured fantasies of becoming France's new Lemaître.

Shortly before graduation from Condorcet, where Mallarmé had taught for many years, he wrote a play that suddenly made the underground life something real and public, for his play was not only performed at a legitimate theater (to an audience consisting of fellow students) but given favorable notice by Francisque Sarcey, the foremost theater critic in Paris. As a result of this quasi-official accolade, and of his brilliant work in school, Jacques seems to have won a reprieve from the fate his father had originally proposed. It was with his father's blessings, in fact, that he set about preparing himself for France's elite academy, the Ecole Normale Supérieure. Several years later he was still preparing himself, ever more desultorily, as if any institution approved by Copeau *père* stood for business—even the Ecole Normale—and business for a sentence of execution. Following literature and philosophy courses but playing truant nearly every night, whether in André Antoine's Théâtre Libre or in Lugné-Poe's Théâtre de l'Oeuvre, he clung to the life he had led at Condorcet, which, like a Jesuit *collège*, made certain of its students its children for life, inviting those already estranged from home and society to lay down roots in an abstract soil. Jacques postponed the future as long as his father was alive. Then in 1901, when his father died, he fled, going north, as befit a young man of his Hamletian disposition, to Denmark.

Flight from one thing often masquerades as pursuit of another. Copeau expatriated himself, dropping his *curriculum vitae* like a lead weight, in order to marry a Danish woman seven years older than he, Agnes Thomsen, whom he had known, intermittently, since 1893. (At the age of sixteen he had become her mathematics tutor, which brings to mind Ionesco's celebrated observation that "arithmetic leads to philology and philology to crime"; though nature is not bound to run this criminal course, in France most particularly passions have had an odd way of slumbering behind numbers.) At his mother's behest, the marriage was celebrated according to Catholic rite, and the child subsequently born of it was baptized; Copeau himself felt all the more free of past and future for having found asylum in a country whose people spoke a language foreign to his ears and observed a faith other than his family's. Here he could live in secret. The vow recited by the hero of Gide's *The Immoralist*—"I would like to begin life anew, from scratch. I would like to jettison what remains of my legacy"—might have come from him. He had, indeed, been an ardent admirer of Gide ever since reading *Fruits of the Earth* at Condorcet. "Along with Rimbaud, nothing marked my adolescence more indelibly," he declared. *The Immoralist* left an equally indelible mark on him. While one novel prompted him to make Gide the confidant of his pubescent adventure (he would hold familiar conversations with him in a journal he kept), the other sanctioned his elopement, inspiring him to write a review for *L'Ermitage* that earned him Gide's gratitude, encouragement, and—in due course—friendship.

In Copenhagen, Copeau earned his livelihood teaching French. When finances permitted, he would visit Paris and during his brief sojourns there see as many plays as possible. Then, from abroad, he would dispatch articles exposing with a keen critical knife the flim-flam that passed for art in works by fashionable playwrights like Paul Hervieu and Henri Bataille. Distance serves those who want their voice to resound with a kind of prophetic amplitude. It also dampens the sound of rejoinders. Copeau was not yet ready to risk having his image defined on native ground, or to discover his limits in the rough-and-tumble of professional reality. He lived abroad until 1903.

What Copeau senior could not accomplish during his lifetime came to pass in consequence of his death. Jacques grudgingly assumed direction of the foundry, which was situated in northeastern France, quite near Charleville—an industrial region whose dismal countenance Rimbaud had fled for the Arabian desert some twenty-five years earlier. If Copeau junior found it impossible to flout his father's posthumous wishes, his father, in turn, was past being able to save the enterprise he had so arduously built from falling into bankruptcy. Less than two years after he became its director, Jacques presided over its ruin. Nothing more stood between him and Paris, to which he now returned, towing the family he had meanwhile brought upon himself. Through a painter friend named Albert Besnard, he found employment at the Georges Petit Art Gallery, first as an assistant, then as director of exhibitions.

Gide, who welcomed him to Paris, drew this telling portrait of Copeau in 1905:

> At twenty-seven, he seems ten years older than his age; his overly expressive face is already weary from suffering. His shoulders are high and hard, like those of a man who bears a heavy burden. At times, the softness of his voice is almost disquieting; he would seduce people naturally if he did not, now and again, work too hard at it. He expresses himself so well that one feels wary; his voice obeys every inflection he wishes to give it. I admit that it took me a while to realize that all this could sit on a man of sterling quality. One tends to doubt the sincerity of expressions that are too flawless. Everything about him gains in being known, explained, even when the explanations come from him.

There is something here of the puppet whose least gesture entails a calculation upon its unseen master, or of the self-made man working his surrogate from behind the scenes as though reluctant to venture forth, to let slip even one word that might subject him to other minds, to show a flawed face. However difficult life may have been, what aged Copeau prematurely, one feels, was not exile or unsuccess but the constant labor of pulling strings fastened to himself. His pride had condemned him to fashion small perfections.

Where did he come from? Though he looked older than his years, there were few traces of a past, save the lines on his face. Who was he, apart from the lapidary phrases he uttered extemporaneously? Gide took him for a Jew. "Copeau, supple mind like a Jew's (I thought he was one at first): 'I have no great worries on your account,' I said to him. 'I feel that you are well armed.' He smiled. 'Yes, I believe I am, too,' he answered. 'And yet I accomplish nothing. Do you know what I'm lacking? A milieu. *Yes, I have no milieu.*'" To be sure, Copeau did himself a serious injustice in feeling that he had accomplished nothing. He had read widely and thought intensely. Yet the creative urge that might have brought forth a work of art had shaped, instead, a persona devoid of context, an exile, a role awaiting consecration from outside.

Jacques Copeau photographed in the Georges Petit art gallery, where he worked for some years after his return to Paris in 1905. From Le Théâtre

The man without a milieu was not only a man who yearned for membership in an artistic family, but Lemaître without an audience. His very injustice to himself bore, inversely, the stamp of his radical ambitions: behind "nothing" there lay a *chef d'oeuvre inconnu.* Unknown this masterwork would always remain.

From scattered remarks in Gide's *Journal* one may form an idea of the ascendancy Copeau soon gained over him and his intellectual confreres. "Yesterday evening, went to Copeau's and read all I've already written of *Strait Is the Gate....* What work lies ahead! Must take it all in hand from the beginning. A most profitable evening. Copeau a good doctor, not cruel, if anything too indulgent, yet reinforcing my impression with his own; and I already know him too well to feel particularly bashful about showing myself to him ungroomed," Gide noted in 1906. A year later he resolved never to "temper my harshness toward myself or go backward or make palinodes, but plunge ahead on my own path austerely, fiercely," then, as if taxed beyond endurance by his thought, rewarded himself with the prospect of "resting for a bit at Copeau's out of need to see my image again in a somewhat flattering mirror." In time Gide came to feel smaller and to see Copeau loom larger, so that by 1912 the former was basking in the latter's presence. "Copeau came yesterday.... What good it does me, the feeling of his worth! He read his chronicle on Louis Bertrand," or again, "Copeau's serene assurance and exaltation braced me." Now priest, now doctor, now mirror, Copeau became a master to the men he served in deserting his own literary endeavor and taking shelter under theirs.

If Gide ever harbored suspicions that Copeau was unequal to the blank page, beset with doubts, or mortified by criticism, certainly the *Journal* hints at none of it. From his own doubts he extrapolated a figure as self-assured as he was not, a paragon who was beyond feeling driven to prove or complete himself in books, a saint whose editorial ministrations could help Gide become Gide. What did it matter that Copeau had never written fiction or theater (apart from the high-school play praised by Sarcey as being "well made," in the tradition of Dumas *fils*)? His very silence was perceived as a virile act consummating his "worth." Studentlike, Gide would deliver the rough-hewn stuff of himself in order to learn its true design from this frocked intercessor. Others held him in equally high regard. Roger Martin du Gard, a writer not given to making hyperbolic estimates of men, nor to having love af-

fairs with them, who understood Copeau better than most, stated in a
letter that "he is one of our great modern writers, one of the few powerful geniuses of the present day. He bears within himself plays and
novels of unsuspected value, which none of us equals, and which will
perhaps never see the light of day."

Believing that their intimate friend carried the unborn novel of
novels or play of plays, that they stood in close proximity to a classical
accomplishment, must have given them a terrific boost. Copeau's genius
redounded upon them. The works they published under his aegis were
beneficiaries of the Absolute gestating in their midst. But their faith,
however inventive and self-serving it may have been at times, would
have collapsed without evidence of some kind to sustain it. Copeau had
very real analytic gifts. Soon after meeting him, Martin du Gard noted
in his diary:

> From the first, the range and quality of his literary culture struck me. . . .
> He was as well acquainted with the great English, Russian, and Scan-
> dinavian novelists as with Balzac, Stendhal, and Flaubert. . . . He had
> done far more than acquaint himself with them: he had striven to under-
> stand the secrets of their art, he had studied the fabrication of every book
> he loved, he had labored to discover and compare the technical skills
> peculiar to each author. All the subtle devices to which one may have
> recourse in the composition of a novel had become familiar to him; and he
> had derived certain general laws on which he would often insist, and insist
> the more cogently for having pertinent examples at his fingertips.

Defeated by the task of creating live characters, Copeau was triumphantly successful at drafting laws that seemed to govern creation itself.
Therein lay a predicament whose ramifications would grow ever more
tangled and finally inescapable. How could he be at once storyteller and
seer? How could he construct imaginative works while devoting his
energy to the fabrication of a persona that made his history prehistoric
and his deepest emotions a Devil's Island? It was not, to quote Martin
du Gard, "laziness in the face of the artist's slow, solitary work" that
traduced him, or not laziness as such (for he was capable in other respects of driving himself beyond exhaustion), but a desire to escape
Jacques Copeau and inhabit some other, "objective" self. When all he
derived from the study he made of literature were "laws" that had no
individual taste or smell or texture, is it any wonder that he himself

could not portray a human figure without drawing a skeleton instead? Much as he admired Dostoevski, the book he may have wished to write even more than *The Brothers Karamazov* was the one of which Flaubert dreamed, a book "about nothing, a book without any external support, which would be held together only by the inner strength of its style, the way the earth hangs suspended in space, a book that would have almost no subject, or at least in which the subject would be almost invisible, if that is possible, for the most beautiful works are those in which there is the least matter."

Though several years would elapse before the "pure structure" got translated into a theatrical strategy, Copeau's critical assaults on Boulevard theater between 1905 and 1913 already reveal the grammarian burning every piece of furniture on stage, smashing every device of the well-made plot, inveighing against appeals to the public's interest in violence and sex. He who had found home life "asphyxiating" wanted to make this house clean and clear. "We cannot repeat it too often and too vehemently: all of that is worthless," he wrote in reviewing a play by a fashionable hack named Brieux. "All these material methods, these crude precautions, these cheap gimmicks constitute a false métier, a bad métier." The character, which counted for nought in the land George Bernard Shaw called Sardoudledom, had to be sprung from situational imbroglios, domestic clutter, and bourgeois prose. What Copeau understood as "the human truth" would, he felt, lay itself bare nowhere but on a platform stripped of place-names, in a milieu subject to rules as self-referential as a cenobitic community's. Middle-class theater was by definition "inhuman" and "untruthful"—not at all because it censored licentious fantasies but because it was middle class, meaning that it manufactured a product for gain, like any commercial enterprise or industry. While the "true" dramatist makes us "forget material imitations," the "false" offers his corpulent audience a trompe-l'oeil image of itself, declared Copeau, whose repugnance for the senses was Savonarolesque. It would appear that by humanity he had some other species in mind than the French bourgeoisie.

As Copeau *père*'s son perceived human affairs, to become human was to divorce oneself from a physical matrix, to combine one's substance with an axiomatic form, to join, if not to found, an impersonal brotherhood. Eventually this perception would see him embrace Catholicism with great fervor, but for the time being he sought redemption, or something very like it, where he had been taught to find it: in the grammar of classical art. "The classical form," he wrote in 1909, "even if it wounds our fantasy at times, even if it rubs against the grain of our modern sensibility and constricts the imagination, must remain, in spite of everything, the immutable model on which it behooves us to shape our thoughts. For we possess nothing more solid, more beautiful, more evident." Scaffolding a virgin order on immutable models, invoking pure form ("Reason," "Beauty") to legitimate outrage against parental authority, classicizing the self—all this was not without precedent in France, where the intelligentsia had traditionally rallied in greater force to a messianic ideal than to bodies of evidence. If France nurtured Robespierre and Saint-Just, men who nearly transformed the nation's civil life into a closed system, vilifying any threat to it from the world outside as "inhuman," so did it breed terrorists who would have made the French language itself the instrument of a utopian design. Rimbaud and Mallarmé, the one endeavoring to create an hermetic science of language and the other to banish from mind words of common barter, obeyed much the same totalistic impulse that had brought into existence the Académie française.

However considerable his wit and erudition, it was not these that earned Copeau his singular prestige but the impression he conveyed of having it in him to lift people above happenstance and opacity, to save them from their random lives and marshal them around a sacred cause. "I felt that I had to begin everything from the beginning and follow the teachings of this master," declared Blanche Albane, an actress married to the novelist Georges Duhamel. "At an age when I needed to believe in what I had undertaken," wrote Charles Dullin, "Copeau brought me what I was looking for, that elevation of thought, that faith and enthusiasm without which we actors would be nothing but commercial travelers." Far from giving them pause, the fact that Copeau had not done any work in the theater (aside from his adaptation of *The Brothers Karamazov*) induced such actors to flock after him even more enthusiastically when he decided to organize a troupe; for what they sought was an epiphany rather than a career, a master who would deliver them from the bondage of métiers rather than a worldly-wise director. Copeau winnowed the chaff from the wheat accordingly. "If I could not bring to bear very much technical knowledge, I followed an instinct which had never led me astray," he wrote, referring to auditions he held in Dullin's Montmartre flat in 1913. "What I tried to discern in each one was not so much the appearances of talent or savoir-faire but the natural core." Just as he made a mental erasure of all marks left upon them by other teachers, of characters imprinted by the past, of skills acquired along the way, of everything that put them beyond his reach ("savoir-faire" constituted a delusory surface or appearance and untutored nature the "core"), so he covered his own tracks, according himself the infallibility of instinct. Where knowledge pays tribute to history, instinct starts the world from scratch. Where time and space set limits to the one, the other speaks as a seer, and it was a seer around whom the faithful saw themselves gathering in July 1913. "We were pure spirits, everyone of us. Whence the enormous consequences of this tiny little affair," Dullin was to say years later.

Following the example set by Stanislavski, whose art theater had been welded together one summer in a barn thirty versts from Moscow, Copeau had the actors congregate east of Paris, near la Ferté-sous-Jouarre, where his mother owned a country house. During July, August, and September, nothing foreign to their enterprise impinged upon their lives that did not have to reckon with him first. Copeau delivered daily *explications de texte*, or textual analyses in the French classroom tradition, so that a play would have been drenched to its last indefinite article with *his* thought before rehearsals even began. And when he left the dais, it was to hover about them ubiquitously, choreographing gestures from every angle. "We shall propose that the classics be our constant example, as an antidote to false taste and aesthetic crazes. . . . What in truth could be more frivolous than to rejuvenate from the outside (sets, decor) what is eternal in its core?" he wrote in a manifesto declaring it his mission to find the "essence of theater" hidden beneath temporal accretions, to discover a "grammar of dramatic invention" that lay, spare and selfsame, inside a worldly carcass. There would be no milieu but the text itself, no furniture to give the actor his bearings in social time and space, no "outside" but the "timeless core" explicated by Copeau, who cut a figure so gaunt that it seemed his aesthetics had cost him his flesh.

Though Paris lay only fifty miles away, it became increasingly remote as the walled garden of this country villa became increasingly a structuralist's Eden wherein nothing, not even freedom, was left to chance. After rehearsals, the troupe did one hour of physical exercise. Then, for two hours more, they would sight-read poems, plays, and excerpts of classical prose in order to perfect their speech, to unlearn their idiomatic voices, to become sound chambers echoing, as if naturally, an impersonal music. When day was done, Copeau had them improvise *commedia dell'arte* scenarios of his own devising. He did not surrender them to the neighboring farmhouses where they lodged until past midnight. "I sought by every means and in particular by a constant solicitude to raise the actor to a certain dignity, to give him an elevated idea of his function, to develop and enrich his awareness, to redeem him from the out-and-out specialization that mechanizes him. . . . While I cannot boast of having transformed the actor's nature, I disciplined him. I was the master of my troupe." If he did not ultimately transform human nature, it was not for lack of desire.

Defining the project on which he embarked as an "essay in dramatic renovation"—an essay rather than a theater—Copeau held sway over journeymen who labored day and night to create spiritual goods they could never sufficiently perfect or *finish*, much less market. The filial piety that compelled him to give his father a good account of himself ("I was the master of my troupe," that is, director of his company) was fraught with filial hatred of the dehumanizing machine-world from which he had fled, shepherding his flock like a modern-day Bernard de Clairvaux. "To detested realities, we place in opposition a desire, an aspiration, a will . . . and if we were to name more explicitly the feeling that animates us, the passion that spurs us on . . . it is *indignation*," he declared. The enterprise that first took shape in this village of Limon glorified toil to no end except unworldliness, Copeau making conversion his business, as had Copeau *père*, but converting human substance into aesthetic tools rather than iron into implements. A parodic replica of the foundry, the essay in art for art's sake was also a classical lyceum dedicated to refining alike its masters and pupils, a Condorcet without diploma from which no one ever graduated. The facetious observation made by *Le Figaro*'s theater chronicler Régis Gignoux that a "monastery of actors" had established itself at Limon would prove, in time, to have been very nearly prophetic. Leaving his garden for Paris, admitting to consciousness the expectations, scrutiny, and material bother that at-

Jacques Copeau with the original Vieux-Colombier troupe assembled during the summer of 1913 at his mother's country house in Limon. Dullin is seated at the far left and Suzanne Bing opposite Copeau. Louis Jouvet is the middle one of the three standing figures. From Le Théâtre

The Vieux-Colombier doing ensemble gymnastics in preparation for its first season. From Le Théâtre

tend public performance cost Copeau a dream—a dream that quietly sabotaged what had not even officially begun. His Théâtre du Vieux-Colombier on the Left Bank, near the Saint-Sulpice Church, was to be for him a halfway house between two rural hermitages.

Had a modern-art cinema suddenly mushroomed up among pre-World War II movie houses it would not have seemed more aberrant to the public of 1939 than did the Théâtre du Vieux-Colombier to Parisian theater audiences of 1913. Copeau rented a derelict *théâtre de quartier* known as the Athénée Saint-Germain and had it stripped clean. Lyres, garlands, cherubs, mirrors, gilt, chandeliers—all the gingerbread that the nineteenth-century theater shared in common with the nineteenth-century brothel were carted away, leaving behind a bone-bare interior. Swathed in some neutral tint, the hall's structural lines offered no distraction from a stage now almost half again as large as it had been. Framing this stage, which had devoured seventy-five seats and seemed

jealous of those it spared, was a proscenium arch painted black, like the
border of a condolence card. Indeed, critics ill-disposed to such auster-
ity vied with one another in making morbid puns ("Columbarium near
the rue du Four," for example—the Columbarium being a place where
funerary urns are stored, and the rue du Four, or "Oven Street," a thoroughfare transecting the rue du Vieux-Colombier, on which the theater
stood) when they did not suggest that Germany was to blame for it all,
that Copeau represented an alien spirit. "There is a puritanical pall
hanging over this Théâtre du Vieux-Colombier, something of Germany
and Munich," wrote the curmudgeonly Paul Souday in October. "The
organizers seem importunate in wanting to let us know that we have
not come there to have a good time."

Alien, too, was the rule eventually adopted by Copeau of forbidding latecomers to take their seats until the first break in action. Had he
hired a beadle and expelled from services women too conspicuously
gussied-up, the illusion of a Huguenot chapel would then have been
complete. Its geometrical rigor, its virtually naked stage, its blandness of
color, its want of ornaments or details to greet a roving eye proclaimed
that here the director would tolerate no nonsense. What Copeau found
praiseworthy in art—"a detachment from contingencies, a stripped-
down quality, a certain coldness which is characteristic of durable productions," as he put it—imbued the house he built, the milieu of which
he had long since felt bereft. Those who preferred plush to pews began
calling it "the Calvin Follies."

Like its physical interior and its situation on the Left Bank at a belligerent remove from the Boulevard, the Vieux-Colombier's repertoire,
was not devised with the public's convenience in mind. One might even
have taken it for a suicidal strategem. Of seventeen plays staged between October 1913 and May 1914, no more than two or three offered
theatergoers the solace of old acquaintance. Reeling across five centuries, from Adam de la Halle's medieval pastoral *The Play of Robin
and Maid Marian*, and an anonymous *Farce of the Furious Cobbler*, to
Paul Claudel's *The Exchange*, the cast seemed drunk on its virtuosity,
yet sober enough to sidestep every repertorial landmark but one, Molière's *L'Avare (The Miser)*. Copeau threw caution aside. Not only did
he reach abroad, inaugurating the season with one Elizabethan comedy,
Heywood's *A Woman Killed with Kindness* (adapted by Copeau, who
knew English well), and concluding it with another, *Twelfth Night*, he

(ABOVE) *The Athénée Saint-Germain before Copeau had it converted into the Vieux-Colombier.* (BELOW) *The stage of the remodeled Vieux-Colombier in 1913; the proscenium arch has been abolished and steps (barely visible) lead down to the orchestra.* Bibliothèque Nationale

dug deep for obscure works by famous Frenchmen (Molière's comedy-ballet, *The Doctor Lover*, and his Italianate farce, *The Clown's Jealousy*; Musset's *Barberine*) as if to gainsay the public its favorite cultural arias, or to make it feel dumb and expatriate within its own tradition. There were, no doubt, multiple purposes at work behind this choice of repertoire. Its hotch-potch nature kept actors perpetually uprooted lest they go stale or perform by rote, dispatching them from farce to tragedy to pastoral rather as the Society of Jesus dispatches priests from backwaters to capitals. Its predilection for *Nouvelle Revue Française* authors like Henri Ghéon, Jean Schlumberger, and Roger Martin du Gard affirmed an intellectual kinship between theater and publisher. Its esoterism, even as it called attention to the Vieux-Colombier, denied critics a platform on which to stage odious comparisons, thus affording Copeau the blessings of fame and of obscurity. If *alternance*, or rotation, justified itself on practical grounds, was the hectic pace it set also a means of distracting with constant novelty judges who might otherwise have dwelled too closely on any one production? And if the small works of great men demanded notice, did they not demand lenience as well, or at least guarantee the Vieux-Colombier amateur status? Whatever private thoughts he may have had, Copeau declared one goal the ultimate arbiter of his mind: that being to "tear people from their habits," to "marshal, enflame, and create" a following distinct from the bourgeois community. He beheld himself, above all, as a teacher, not an entrepreneur. His Vieux-Colombier was his school and the repertoire his curriculum.

Indeed, the theater was a shadow to the idea of a school that had long burned brightly in Copeau's imagination. Although war would delay its advent, he heralded a School of the Vieux-Colombier as early as September 1913, during rehearsals at Limon. "It would charge no tuition," he wrote in the *N.R.F.* "We would call to it very young people or even children on the one hand, and, on the other, men and women possessed of a love and instinct for theater, who have not yet compromised this instinct with defective methods and vocational habits. Such a contingent of new forces would eventually certify the grandeur of our enterprise." And what did he propose to do? "We would strive to renormalize these men and women whose vocation is to feign all emotions and human gestures. Insofar as we can, we shall call them away from theater and put them in contact with nature." Candidates "possessed of a love and instinct for theater" were people of a kind most likely to heed a "call" to flee workaday society, to sever ties with their past and be incorporated as a phalanstery led by a Master. Copeau's project answered the dream of rebirth-through-art that had, in one form or another, been stirring Frenchmen ever since the Revolutionary era when David's pupils, those who styled themselves "Primitives" or "Meditators," forgathered in a ruined monastery outside Paris, read poetry "untainted" by civilization (Ossian, Homer, but particularly the New Testament), and echoed the pronouncements of their bearded leader, Maurice Quai. Just as Romanticism made art stand proxy for religion, so did it confer divinity on artist-heroes like Werther, whose achievement resides in their charisma rather than in palpable works, whose nature transcends the personal, evoking a primal integrity or wholeness undone by conventions that have "mechanized" man.* Born to live onstage, born as laws unto themselves, they are heroes of nativity, their "theatrical instinct" adumbrating that "moral instinct" which had set *le Peuple* of year I essentially apart from the nations outside.

The school Copeau had in mind sprang from this tradition. It would endeavor not so much to acquaint its pupils with reality as to restore them their innocence, not to inculcate knowledge but to mend an ontological flaw apparent in the seam of years, in ties of blood, in the darkness that conceals audience from actor. What sustained Copeau, who could not brook limits imposed upon his perception or bolts from the blue, was the idea of life lived according to some grammatically unexceptionable decorum. In his theater *cum* academy, he set forth a universe where there would be no "I" and "other," no illegible crannies and unforeseeable events, no inside harboring the past or outside designing the future. He sought, at all costs, to scripturalize existence, burying alike his novel and his self under the lines of holy writ. Now tiny in his own estimation, now colossal, Copeau could no more size himself up than comprehend some middle term between all and nothing. This extremism fomented an atmosphere that Roger Martin du Gard described as follows:

---

* "But a man is a god when he resembles you," says the devil, Vautrin, to the young hero, Rastignac, in Balzac's *Father Goriot*. "He is no longer a machine wrapped in skin, but a theater wherein the most beautiful feelings stir, and feelings alone are what I live by."

So imbued was he with the grandeur of his role, so intoxicated by the ab-
negation with which he gave himself to his task, that it did not occur to
him that one might have something better or more urgent to do than to
gravitate around him, to second him, to approve him, to encourage him, if
only by one's continual presence. To work zestfully, he needed a circle of
assistants ever available and fanaticized, ready to perform any task or give
any proof of devotion; very often he employed them at nothing, but their
nearness was a stimulant to which he had become addicted.

The author of *Jean Barois* and *Les Thibaults* spoke from experience, having for several years postponed his own creative work, as
though it were relatively inconsequential, in order to become one such
zealous steward. If Copeau was an addict, it must be said at least that
(until paranoid fantasies got the better of him) his addiction fed upon
substantial presences. Not only did he recruit Léon-Paul Fargue to
address publicity notices, Roger Martin du Gard to man the cloakroom,
and Georges Duhamel to whisper cues from the prompter's box, but he
induced other literati—among them, Gide, Verhaeren, Viélé-Griffin,
Thibaudet, André Suarès, and Jacques Rivière—to conduct *matinées
poétiques* of which twenty-four took place during 1913–14. While
actors held forth in the evening, in the morning these gentlemen rotated
onstage, some reading poetry or providing a historical account of
French verse, some dissecting plays and otherwise subjecting modern literature to critical scrutiny, so that the Vieux-Colombier was never altogether vacant, except at night. One is reminded of an unpublished
note Copeau made many years later, in 1940: "Stripping the stage bare.
This purgation corresponds to the Cartesianism of our age, to its need
for a tabula rasa. But the stage's climate is tropical. Plant a seed and it
will soon choke all the space. Difficult to limit the vegetation." Much as
he resembled Flaubert and Rimbaud in preferring landscapes where
matter does not challenge the mind's taxonomic imperatives and life
pullulate at random, Copeau had to fill the desert with voices. His
abhorrence of scenic clutter was oddly underscored by his abhorrence
of the very voids he created—of the blank page that always awaited
him. Like a compulsive talker who cannot be quiet for fear of losing
face or of being infiltrated by unwanted thoughts, who shies from the
margin of silence that surrounds and enters ordinary conversation, he
made his theatrical milieu his Day, allowing chance no opportunity to

puncture it. "One must encumber the precincts of a theater with so much humanity that one will always feel cramped. Where there is a bare wall that cannot be 'humanized,' death straightaway creeps in, sticks to the spot, and freezes." Jean-Louis Barrault wrote these words by way of explaining the three-theaters-in-one he devised during his tenure at the Odéon, but they could sit comfortably enough over Copeau's signature.

It was the Vieux-Colombier that came to exemplify the ideal of the theater as a pastoral mission, or as a house glutted with Spirit, where parishioner-like subscribers could seek refuge from emptiness. However flagrant his shortcomings—more often than not, Copeau himself gave overblown performances in the roles he played and, at times, when his need for just the right gesture or choreographic image verged on delirium, would badger his actors to distraction—Copeau had the genius of an *animateur*. Staging play after play and lecture after lecture, he maintained a constant hub-bub, an intellectual agitation, that enabled his theater to survive periodic flops.

The few triumphs made a more durable impression than the flops, however, in particular upon custodians of the Left Bank's cultural memory. "Last week at the Théâtre du Vieux-Colombier I saw Becque's *The Merry-Go-Round* for the first time. A marvel, both in itself and in the performance of it. This is theater," Paul Léautaud noted in his *Literary Journal*. "Oddly enough, I felt for the first time in my life that theater can be an interesting art." When, at season's close, *Twelfth Night* filled the Vieux-Colombier to overflowing, Gide observed in his own *Journal* that "this triumphant success makes me almost uncomfortable, so accustomed have I become to predicting nonsuccess as the fate that awaits works of merit." That a subscription form distributed by the *Nouvelle Revue Française* netted four thousand pledges for the 1914–15 season bears witness to Copeau's feat of having "marshaled, enflamed, and created" a theatrical sect within one year. The agitation on rue du Vieux-Colombier sent ripples even beyond the borders of France. In Switzerland, the *Journal de Genève* dismissed as second-rate all Parisian theaters save the Comédie-Française and Copeau's. Invitations arrived pell-mell from Italy, England, Belgium, and Germany. Cologne chose the Vieux-Colombier to inaugurate its recently completed Neues Theater, informing Copeau of this signal honor several weeks before Archduke Francis Ferdinand's assassination in Sarajevo.

Being of two minds about almost everything in life, including life itself, Copeau did not regard the widespread acclaim of his enterprise unambivalently. While he felt elated and lost no time making ready for the season to come, he also felt trapped by public expectations. It was as though "promise" sufficed to materialize the specter of promise unfulfilled, or auspicious beginnings to stir in him a dread of maturity. Against this dread he defended himself with the esoteric strategies that came increasingly to mark his artistic career:

> Work is my companion. It lives with me. I almost always experience success as something working against me. It's a stranger. Not that I spurn it, but it does not fulfill me. And if it eludes my grasp, I do not feel the poorer for that. We don't understand each other. I have known, like everybody else, the emotion of bringing off a part or of muffing it, but it has never changed me deep down. In no way is it comparable to the feeling that rewards an artisan who beholds some perfect detail of his handiwork, a detail of which no one else, perhaps, has taken notice, but into which his heart has secretly entered.

Like the perpetual experiment, work for work's sake girded him, though never very effectively to be sure, against considerations of success and failure.* Damned if he did and damned if he didn't, he could no more suffer an "anonymous" life than tolerate for any length of time the gimlet eye trained upon his visible self. Was it wiser perhaps to retire from view with one's Idea uncompromised than to let exposure damage it beyond repair? No one could impugn the perfection of a secret detail, of a *chef d'oeuvre inconnu*. Martin du Gard wrote to Copeau in July 1914: "We are all counting on your play, dear Copeau, we are counting on it as on a kind of revenge. [Copeau had been working for some time on a play entitled "The Birthplace."] The leader of the Colombier must be something more than a director of genius or an intelligent actor. . . . Think about it, old man. No bankruptcies. Don't

---

* Jules Romains, who later became director of the Vieux-Colombier's school, attests to the fact that Copeau's self-deprecation was as contagious as his zeal: "We were all unjust to the Vieux-Colombier during its hey-day, including Copeau himself, who, out of noble perfectionism and a kind of messianic tendency . . . to seek his certitude and delectation in the future, liked to regard his house as a temporary construction site and everything that took place therein as a series of sketches, as feeble allusions to some future work."

disperse yourself in a thousand glittering projects. *Age quod agis,* sir!"
"Good God, man, do you think I'm training flies here in the country?" answered Copeau. "When I tell you that I'm working, I mean by
that 'The Birthplace.' And I had best contrive to finish it, if only to get
you off my back! . . . In all seriousness, I am working doggedly,
though not without perturbation."

Such conflicts as beset him in July were resolved in August when
France mobilized her population against Germany. Quite suddenly
events burst open the Vieux-Colombier, scattering its company hither
and yon. There would be no Paris season, not again until 1919. Copeau's right hand, Louis Jouvet, who had originally quit pharmacy
school to become an actor, was drafted as a medical aide. Charles
Dullin, though exempt from the military, volunteered his services and,
accompanied by Elise Toulemon, departed for Tours to do basic training as a dragoon. "I would sometimes plant myself in front of the barracks to watch Charles tend the horses. It seemed that his skill was
being put to the test. One day, a mare wounded herself through his
negligence and they locked him up for a week. I spent days and evenings at the window of my hotel room, waiting," wrote Elise (whom we
shall leave waiting until we resume with Dullin in a subsequent chapter). As for Copeau, the master found himself clerking in the Quarter-
master Corps' division of parks and slaughterhouses on rue Oudinot, a
short walk from the Vieux-Colombier, which the government converted
into a refugee center.*

Early in 1915 Copeau was remanded to civil life when a radiograph
showed signs of what physicians diagnosed as *infiltration bacillaire,* or
tuberculosis. He wrote to Martin du Gard, who had meanwhile fought
with the Army of the East, that "it will always be a source of chagrin
for me not to have participated in this great war. . . . It's not a matter
of patriotic exaltation but I am obsessed by the thought that our national defense, however admirable it has been, has not made full use of
its resources or has, in large part, squandered it. I am humiliated, sad-
dened not to have done anything." (A bourgeois sentiment, this hatred
of squander!) Yet the man whom Gide met in wartime Paris seemed on
the verge of levitating: "He appears younger than before, more Diderot

---

* Afterward, Copeau rented the theater to a singer, Jane Bathori, who organized
chamber-music recitals there throughout the war.

than ever, embracing every new project wholeheartedly and whole-mouthedly. He speaks of reopening the Vieux-Colombier with plays and readings improvised for the occasion, or of traveling abroad, since he's not doing anything in Paris—he would like to see more."

In fact Copeau, notwithstanding his sickness and impecunity, prospered during chaotic times. The "commercial" world—which meant for him an inexorable waxing of years, an accumulation of matter (words? pages?), an elaboration of private designs—had given way to heroic imperatives. It behooved Frenchmen not to profit as individuals but to sacrifice themselves as one: war provided the fillip for a movement of national self-purification, the Arch-enemy exorcised the foe within, and danger obviated the moral riddles that necessarily haunt civilized existence. In this apocalyptic atmosphere, where every breath he drew brought home thoughts of death, Copeau felt once again, as at Limon, unencumbered by time and space. "It's barbarism! The Middle Ages! What was all our work for?" someone heard him exclaim on August 4, 1914. But the Middle Ages held much more appeal than the age it interrupted. Was it not for *this*, his work? A sense of pious communality, of the human enterprise radically simplified by a struggle for salvation, of history brought to heel at Armageddon, and of Paris stripped clean filled him with beatitude. (Twenty-five years later, many Parisians would similarly rejoice, despite the Nazi overlord, in the city's archaic quiet, in the sensation of having dropped out of an historical grind.) If wartime would lend an odor of sanctity to the demons that exercised him, impersonalizing his anger, it would, by the same token, abolish realities that had hitherto curbed his penchant for messianic self-aggrandizement. "We are giants if we don't give a damn about anything except pursuing our work to its absolute limit," he wrote to Louis Jouvet. "There is no common denominator between us and all those blokes who talk about art." The word "egoism" having become, as during the Terror, synonymous with treason, Copeau felt very much in his milieu.

Foremost among the burdens lifted by war was the *material* Vieux-Colombier, which seemed, in retrospect, an infant prodigy. Without live actors and audiences to encumber him, without budgets, programs, and calendars to stand between his work and its "absolute limit," Copeau dismissed from mind almost all questions save those that bore upon the theater's formal vocabulary. When Martin du Gard lamented that he had not read a book in three months and felt himself to be in imminent danger of becoming a vegetable, Copeau responded: "But, dear old chap, I haven't even glimpsed a book in much longer than that. Do you really find books so indispensable? I myself have never done without them so contentedly as now. I look at them, but I don't like to read them. Either—as is usually the case—they bore me to death and I throw them aside, or else they interest me from the outset and put my mind in a state of excitation such that I close them straightaway in order to imagine new things."

The "new things" that stimulated him were indeed *things*, and things all of the same description. His mind vacated by literature, Copeau became obsessed with cubes. Cubes, as he saw it now, represented the basic unit of a grammar appropriate to any dramaturgical circumstance. The cube would make furniture superfluous. It would be the absolute building block of a world oriented around its own, hermetic reality. It would emancipate him from local color and mundane styles. In collaboration with the painter Théo van Rysselberghe, he spent months elaborating what one might call a proto-minimalist vision of the "objective" stage and excitedly communicated his thoughts to Louis Jouvet, who must have found them something less than relevant (or perhaps a welcome relief) in the blood and mire of trench life:

> For solidity, cubes of varying resistance would be difficult to achieve. If they are to be indefinitely practical, they must be indefinitely interchangeable. As for the problem of assemblage, besides inventing a means of getting them to stick together, we must find the *common denominator*. The first size would be half that of our present cubes, which were calculated in relationship to the thickness of the proscenium arch. We would thus have two units: 1) Cubes capable of suggesting slender shapes like window stiles, colonettes, staircases, balustrades, et cetera; 2) Cubes suggesting bulky mass even as large as the perfect wall—battlements, towers, high porticoes, or indeed any arrangement imitating nothing precise but suggesting *by simple proportion* the impression one wishes to convey.

Copeau wrote letter after letter, always coming back to this same subject.

Just as cubes and the few noncubic figures he would condone (templates, ogives, cornices, capitals) had to emerge from artisanal hands as objects beautiful in themselves, so the structural vocabulary they

formed redounded upon itself like an abstract canvas, fascinating Copeau much more than the dramatic occasions for which he presumably
devised it. "We must not predicate the construction about which we are
dreaming on that which we shall have to construct. We must seek those
architectural elements . . . with which anything and everything can be
constructed." The veneration formerly reserved for texts, of which he
had made himself the absolute exegete within his company, now devolved upon a holy erector set. In this rigorously autonomous milieu, he
would preside not as a faithful surrogate of writers but as a priestlike
figure excogitating a new reality. "I would like to put all your books
under lock and key, forbid you access to them," he told Jouvet, the
"you" embracing everyone associated with the Vieux-Colombier. "You
would have nothing but graphic documents to look at. The ac-
cumulated learning of mankind, it is *I* who shall absorb it, digest it,
clarify it, and transmit it to you little by little completely fresh, completely new, together with elements culled from my own original
science. No reconstitutions but instead, creation. Life."

Anticipating Artaud's call for exorcistic rituals, but drawing upon
an idea of theater clearly set forth one hundred and fifty years earlier by
Jean-Jacques Rousseau, Copeau, who found it very difficult to write
about his real past in "The Birthplace," sought to create an impersonal
womb in which all would be One. Behind the spinach-green sweater,
the broad-brimmed felt hat, and long muffler that constituted his bohemian uniform, he seemed to see himself as the Logos directing virginal
minds in a desert of cubes where his voice would be gospel. "I have in
mind not only the actors, whose ranks I plan to fill by means of my
school, but the mechanics, prop men, electricians. . . . We must school
them as well; a real rapport must establish itself between them and us
so that they sit *in our hand* and our word really enters their hearts—
really, not fictionally," he wrote to Jouvet, his confidant. Nothing less
than pure geometry on the one hand and pure feeling on the other could
allay the doubts he entertained as to his own reality. When he had
located everyone belonging to the Vieux-Colombier in a three-dimen-
sional grid or else reduced them to a sentient collectivity, only then
could he be Jacques Copeau. "Our action will have no force, our art
will have no soul if all of you do not melt into one Being aflame with a
single passion, if you do not understand, obey, aspire in a common
upward thrust."

✦ ✦ ✦

The ideas Copeau imparted to Louis Jouvet were not begotten in a total vacuum. They reveal, on the contrary, the extent of his debt to various scenic designers working outside France, particularly to Edward Gordon Craig whom he knew as the author of a highly controversial book of essays entitled *The Art of the Theatre* and as the publisher of a magazine, *The Mask*, which had won for itself a small but zealous readership among cognoscenti (including Strindberg and Yeats) exasperated with theatrical realism. In September 1915, with Europe embroiled in trench warfare, Copeau set out on what might be called a tour of his elective affinities, a tour that took him first to Florence, where Gordon Craig had settled after years spent wandering, then to Geneva where he met Emile Jaques-Dalcroze, who had recently established the Eurythmics Institute, and Adolphe Appia, a Swiss theorist who, in attempting to resolve the *mise en scène* for Wagnerian opera, had propounded revolutionary principles of stage design.

Unlike Copeau, Gordon Craig came by his interest in theater natively, for he was the bastard son of England's greatest actress, Ellen Terry, and of an architect noted for his scenic designs, E. W. Godwin. From earliest childhood, the real center of his life had been the Lyceum Theatre where his mother reigned over *fin-de-siècle* London alongside Henry Irving, who became Craig's idol and—with Godwin's departure—his adopted father. Ellen Terry arranged to have him play walkon roles in *Hamlet, Twelfth Night*, and *Much Ado about Nothing* when he was a small boy home from one or another of the boarding schools through which he drifted somnambulistically. But he made his official debut with the Lyceum at the age of sixteen. "In 1889, Lyceum Theatre and Henry Irving—my real school and my real master. . . . I became an actor. And now the mere physical state of being in a theatre—in the best in England with the greatest actor in Europe and with my motheractress—that was enough. . . . It was a beginning."

Craig's career lasted only until 1896. Having reached an impasse where it seemed that he was to become "a feeble imitation" of Irving, whose personality overwhelmed him, unless he found out "who I was," he quit the stage and during three years lived in studious retreat. This sabbatical saw him undergo a profound change. He spent days at the National Gallery observing, with pen in hand, the works of Renaissance masters. He read Ruskin, Nietzsche, Wagner, Goethe, Tolstoi,

Coleridge. Above all, he found release for his creative energies in a different medium when his friends James Pryde and William Nicholson, who had helped launch the New English Art Movement, taught him how to engrave woodblocks. Representing as it did a protest against the fussy historicism that marked Victorian scenic design and academic painting, the New English Art Movement, through these two members of it, enabled Craig to wean himself from aesthetic pieties on which everything in his past had nurtured him. At little woodblocks, which imposed upon him the discipline of building decorative compositions from simple dramatic elements, he served a second theatrical apprenticeship.

When Craig emerged from seclusion in 1899 to stage operas for The Purcell Operatic Society, he emerged strong in the belief that a dramatic spectacle should be a unity, or pattern, where light, color, movement, and sound reinforce one another synaesthetically. His production of Purcell's *Dido and Aeneas* at the Hampstead Conservatoire in 1899 took place on a stage as far removed from the Lyceum as the Vieux-Colombier's was to be from the Boulevard. No perspective views of Carthage but, instead, a purple-blue sky-cloth lit by lamps suspended from a bridge overhead and by projectors behind the audience. No ponderous furniture to emphasize the antiquity of the scene but a green trellis running across the stage, with an aperture in it for Dido's throne, which stood heaped with red cushions and surmounted by a delicate canopy. No greaves and breastplates but draped robes and tunics swirling in color combinations reminiscent of Loie Fuller's veil dance. When, soon afterward, the Purcell Operatic Society produced *The Masque of Love* from Purcell's opera *Dioclesian*, Craig made a set even more radically devoid of historical clues, for he wrapped the stage in three large cloths, all painted gray, a flat tone that would not distract from the light playing over green and white costumes. By 1902 and Handel's pastoral opera *Acis and Galatea*, for which Craig designed a white tent made of long white ribbons that hung down from the flies against a pale-yellow backdrop, there was no mistaking the direction he felt compelled to follow. Of *Acis and Galatea*, Arthur Symons (who, along with William Butler Yeats, belonged to the small circle of Craig enthusiasts) has left a graphic account in an article entitled "A New Art of the Stage":

> Mr. Craig, it is certain, has a genius for line, for novel effects of line. His
> line is entirely his own; he works in squares and straight lines, hardly ever

in curves. He drapes the stage into a square with cloths; he divides these cloths by vertical lines, carrying the eye straight up to an immense height, fixing it into a rigid attention. He sets squares of pattern and structure on the stage; he forms his groups into irregular squares, and sets them moving in straight lines, which double on themselves like the two arms of a compass; he puts square patterns on the dresses, and drapes the arms with ribbons that hang to the ground, and make almost a square of the body when the arms are held out at right angles. He prefers gestures that have no curves in them; the arms held straight up, or straight forward, or straight out sideways. He likes the act of kneeling in which the body is bent into a sharp angle; he likes a sudden spring to the feet, with the arms held straight up. He links his groups by an arrangement of poles and ribbons, something in the manner of maypole; each figure is held to the centre by a tightly stretched line like the spoke of a wheel. Even when, as in this case, the pattern forms into a circle, the circle is segmented by straight lines. This severe treatment of line gives breadth and dignity to what might otherwise be merely fantastic. Mr. Craig is happiest when he can play at children's games with his figures, as in almost the whole of *The Masque of Love*. When he is entirely his own master, not dependent on any kind of reality, he invents really like a child, and his fairytale comes right, because it is not tied by any grown-up logic.

The problem of trying to reconcile this abstract, hieratic vision with the world in which he lived saw Craig grow increasingly isolated, increasingly impatient of any situation that did not let him impose his will just as he wished. In 1904 he left England to design a production of Otway's *Venice Preserved* at the Lessing Theatre in Berlin, and never again made England his home, except for brief sojourns. He became a wanderer, a venerable *Luftmensch* whose rare and quarrelsome collaborations, as with Eleanora Duse at the Teatro della Pergola and Stanislavski at the Moscow Art Theater, confirmed him in his solitude while redounding to the credit of his books and woodcuts, which circulated through Europe like messages from another world.

Once his roots had been cut, Craig's interest in movement gradually detached itself from actors and literary drama, leading him to picture the stage as a self-referential construction, a cube whose interior would, at his command, transmute itself into different patterns. Captivated by Sebastiano Serlio's sixteenth-century treatise *Five Books of Architecture*, and by two illustrations in particular, one showing a chessboard pattern drawn on the ground, the other this same pattern

with several squares thrust upward to form complex parallelepipeds (a cubed cross, a ziggurat wall), he came, round about 1905, to envision what he called "Scene." The stage would be so constructed that cubes could descend from its ceiling and rise from its floor, as in Serlio's plates. An organlike apparatus would enable him at once to manipulate these digits (making them grow longer or shorter at various speeds) and control lights overhead, to shape the scenic void in accordance with principles as exact as those that regulate musical composition.

What his numerous woodcuts of "Scene" reveal is a forest of vertical slabs, a kind of Fingal's Cave bristling with stalagmites. When, as is sometimes the case, people dot this inhumanly beautiful wasteland, their very diminutiveness proclaims their irrelevance.* Wraiths or spec-

---

* In 1905 he did a series of sketches entitled "The Steps," in which vague little figures stand on monumental flights of stairs. Of one such sketch he wrote some years later, in *Towards a New Theatre:* "But although the man and woman interest me to some extent, it is the steps on which they move which move me. The figures dominate the steps for a time, but the steps are for all time."

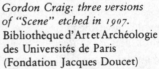

*Gordon Craig: three versions
of "Scene" etched in 1907.*
Bibliothèque d'Art et Archéologie
des Universités de Paris
(Fondation Jacques Doucet)

ters, they might bear comparison to the wee derelicts in Piranesi's engravings (Craig had discovered Piranesi and Jacques Callot through his
new English Art Movement friends), except that Piranesi's figures are
overwhelmed by ruins that evoke a glorious past, while Craig's are
dwarfed by monoliths that celebrate a region of the mind in which
nothing waxes and wanes but ahistorical form, in which thought itself
is something impersonal, unfolding "lawfully," like patterns seen in a
kaleidoscope. "The most important thing is that movement which is at
the root of this art of revelation, must be translated through inanimate
forms," declared Craig:

I speak here of movement in an actual, not in an imaginary sense. Impersonal movement in an actual sense exists in no modern art. I have constructed an instrument. By means of this instrument the artist is enabled to
bring before the beholder a sense of the law which controls our system—
the law of Change. Movement will be for the sake of Movement—ever attempting to create the perfect Balance, even as in Music Sound is for the
sake of Sound, ever attempting to create the perfect Harmony. The Imita-

tion of Nature has no part in this art. The mind and the thought of the artist passing through this instrument shall raise by it one mutable form after
another, living only a moment; ceaselessly, if imperceptibly changing; arriving at last at its final and definite state—only to fade—to re-form itself
once again—an infinite progression.

Long before Copeau set out to discover those architectural elements
that would constitute a grammar suitable for every occasion, Craig had
devised an abstract *perpetuum mobile* that was for him the play of
plays. "I want to remove the pictorial scene but to leave in its place the
architectonic scene," wrote this orphaned son of an architect.

Tortured by an imagination that could paint brilliant scenes in a
flash (as it did for Stanislavski's production of *Hamlet* in 1911, when
Craig dressed the enthroned Claudius in a cloak of gold cloth that covered almost the entire stage, with slits in it through which the heads and
shoulders of squatting courtiers protruded like tombstones littered over
a golden graveyard), he made pure dimensionality his god, sacrificing at
the altar all his visual wealth, his whole unconscious picture collection,
as if to cleanse or objectify himself, to become the agent of a divine instrument. Comments he made about Hamlet, with whom he strongly
identified, explain in part the movement toward abstraction that may
have saved him from literal suicide: "He set out to cleanse social and
official life of its moral grime and its degeneracy. He set about his task
with direct purpose, and with the full enthusiasm of a young, virile, and
cruelly wronged man. His ideas were logical, and he reasoned and
thought out every movement and act during that brief time of storm
and stress that ended in tragedy. That is my idea of Hamlet." * Here
there is no choice, no conflict, no fury and mire of human veins. The
aesthetics of abstract movement had a moral correlative in the kingdom
virtuous to its core, and the impersonal Manager of Forms an alter ego
in the virtuous logician directed from beyond by his father's ghost.
When at last mankind transcended nature—and being Ellen Terry's bastard was, according to his own bastard son, something Craig experi-

---

* In *My Life in Art,* Stanislavski quotes him as saying: "In order to lighten the suf-
ferings of his father it was necessary for Hamlet to cleanse the entire court of evil; it was
necessary to carry fire and the sword throughout the kingdom, to destroy the harmful, to
repulse old friends with rotten souls . . . to save the pure of soul like Ophelia from
earthly ruin and immure her, safe at last, in a monastery."

enced as a caste mark—the stage would transcend plots and people, beginnings and ends. When his topological machine became a sequel to human theater, in the wordless aftermath to desires and strivings, Craig would then become a self-created Creator:

> The Beginning . . . the Birth . . . There are no definite forms. Nothing seems to bound the horizon, the ground is invisible, overhead is a void. Soon, in the centre, a single form stirs and slowly rises, like the beginning of a dream; and then a second, a third. And now, on the right, something is unfolding, without haste. Forms descend mysteriously. *The whole space is in motion.* . . . In a few minutes I shall have given birth to that which has for a long while been preparing, far back before I was born, and all during my life and now I am the one selected to this honour and am among the Creators.

Under this new Order, there would be no need for speech and no ontological basis for spectacles other than the one whose content lay in its formal structure. If *Hamlet* represented the end-game of depraved mankind, "Scene" would inaugurate a reality predicated on abstraction and celebrated on the stage of a theatrical temple.

By 1909 Craig had gone so far as to design screens with four, six, eight, ten, or twelve monumental leaves that could bend backward or forward and thus approximate the original vision of maze-like parallelepipeds continuously in motion. What excited him most about Stanislavski's production of *Hamlet* was not Shakespeare's tragedy but his own screens, which he saw as a play within the play, or rather, as a drama above and beyond the wretched mortals onstage, unfolding on double hinges like angel wings beating the ether. Wherever he set up house, one room became his model stage and a clientele of potential believers was invited in for a demonstration. As his son, Edward Craig, describes it:

> He took rooms on the top floor of 226 rue de Rivoli, next to the Hôtel Meurice. This apartment had once been done up by a very important dignitary in government circles to accommodate a little lady friend, and the walls were covered with laurel-green silk embroidered with golden wreathes. . . . He moved in and set up his model stage in the silk-covered room, and important people like Jacques Rouché, Antoine, Gabriel Astruc, and Edward Steichen all came to watch his moving screens.

And later:

> Craig took a house, no. 7 Smith Square, Westminister, and did a lot of en-
> tertaining. Bringing over his large model stage from Paris, he had it erected
> in a special room there, and demonstrated how his screens worked, hoping
> that this would awaken interest amongst actors and theatre managers.
> Among those who came were Nijinsky, Diaghilev, and Kessler—but when
> Diaghilev started chatting during a demonstration, Craig switched out the
> lights and refused to go on with the show!

Such episodes bring to mind Arthur Symons' observation that
Craig was happiest when playing children's games with his figures. This
one-man show took him all over Europe, from London to Paris to
Florence to Moscow, converting some few but giving bourgeois society
a very wide berth. Always the outsider, estranged from England and
from himself, he withdrew into his model stage, which he toted around
with him as though it were a carapace of virtue and legitimacy. Like
William Butler Yeats, who had written in "Byzantium," "Once out of
nature I shall never take/My bodily form from any natural thing," he
hailed the Superman and, like Yeats, called it "life-in-death" or "death-
in-life."

From his belief—a belief stated and restated after 1907—that "art
can admit of no accidents," it followed that for theater to become an
artistic medium the actor had either to disappear or else die and be
reborn an instrument capable of executing flawlessly the designs of a
mastermind. Craig was by no means alone in his struggle against the
"star system," but ensemble theater as he championed it fell foul of its
traditional piety toward the literary text and its finite ideal of interpretative craftsmanship; discipline became part and parcel of something
else, of a totalistic scheme in which the stage, or "Scene," featured a
dream of reality abiding by his will. Hence the "Über-Marionette," a
term Craig coined in 1905 in *The Art of the Theatre.* "If you could
make your body into a machine, or into a dead piece of material such as
clay; and if it could obey you in every movement . . . you would be
able to make a work of art out of that which is in you," he wrote. "This
flesh-and-blood life . . . is for me not a thing made to search into, or to
give out again to the world, even conventionalized. . . . I think my aim

shall rather be to catch some far-off glimpse of that spirit which we call death." Puppets, with their "beautiful and remote expression," evoked for Craig not only an idea of life after death but a primeval state, an impersonal condition mankind relinquished in leaving the lap of God to become the body's slave. "Form," as he put it, "broke into panic"; the "calm and cool whisper of life in trance" had given way to the pandemonium of realism, when "up sprang portraits with flushed faces, eyes that bulged, mouths that leered, fingers itching to come out of their frames, wrists that exposed the pulse; all the colours higgledy-piggledy; all the lines in hubbub, like the ravings of lunacy."

Pure style or pure automatism was a consummation that defined the Apocalypse. Should human feelings ever dwindle to puppet size, art would see puppets restored to their original stature. And in *The Art of the Theatre* Craig contended that once upon a time puppets had indeed been monumental, that Punch descended from a huge archetype brought low by "jealous actresses." According to this fairytale, the Adamic puppet inhabited an Edenic kingdom: "In Asia lay his first kingdom. On the banks of the Ganges they built him his home, a vast palace springing from column to column into the air and pouring from column to column down again into the water. Surrounded by gardens spread warm and rich with flowers and cooled by fountains; gardens into which no sounds entered, in which hardly anything stirred." Homologous with the idea of scriptural birth outside history was that of a holy cradle outside Europe. True civilization lay not in the West, where heathens driven mad by material progress had martyrized the puppet, reducing it to a plaything, but in Asia and in Africa. "There the great masters dwelt, not individuals obsessed with the idea of each asserting his personality as if it were a valuable and mighty thing, but content because of a kind of holy patience to move their brains and their fingers only in that direction permitted by the law."

That Craig fashioned his myth for a child subject to manipulative adults, that this myth was made to accommodate emotions he could neither control nor satisfy in his own name would seem obvious enough. Persuaded of an inherent disproportion between big people and little, it is as if he played Chinese shadows with his dwarfish figure in projecting it against a primeval backdrop (not unlike the Revolutionary terrorists who spoke through classical oracles, invoking the giants of antiquity to confer upon their deeds the sanction of a moral order *ab* *origine).* * Unable to comprehend growth, he foresaw a miraculous aggrandizement, whose obverse was the catastrophic event that belittled him. Had human history, which marked him illegitimate at birth, brought him humiliation? At the end of time he would loom impassively overhead, becoming once again the giant he was before time began. Did people jerk him every which way and read his mind? He looked forward to the day when man's puppet would get transformed into God's marionette. Born good but "alienated," born transcendent but reduced to a toy and a mockery, born the cynosure but evicted from center stage, he would recoup his losses after his epiphany.

But if this myth reflected his personal experience, it also had roots in the Romantic tradition, a fact borne home by the many fantasies of automation that obsessed nineteenth-century artists and writers. Indeed, Craig was given to quoting Flaubert's famous manifesto that "the artist should be in his work like God in creation, invisible and all-powerful; he should be felt everywhere and seen nowhere. Art should be raised above personal affection and nervous susceptibility. It is time to give it the perfection of the physical sciences by means of a pitiless method. . . . I have always tried not to belittle Art for the satisfaction of an isolated personality." The stage as Craig envisioned it in "Scene," where an invisible director would "play" geometric forms calls to mind another music box, the violin, and another soloist, Paganini, whose virtuosity inspired legends that a preternatural force was operating in him, that he was not human but a *Hexenmeister* (master magician) or a *Hexensohn* (a witch's son).

Among Romantic writers such virtuosity seemed proof of a constitution radically unlike other men's; miraculous, it bespoke a phenomenon outside nature, yet born of its occult essence. "From the point of view of pleasure, which for me always hovers in a sphere midway between the senses and the intellect, I can find no base to this column of flame and cloud," wrote Goethe. "I can only say that I heard some meteoric sounds for which I have not yet found an interpretation." Balzac

---

* On the subject of dwarfs, Craig's son wrote that his father had been greatly impressed as a boy when, during a family excursion, Henry Irving dispersed a pack of hooligans by assuming the most fearsome posture from his catalogue of grotesque attitudes and thus advancing upon them. "Forty years later he remembered this and scattered a crowd in Italy by advancing on them in the same way, but with his stick held high and shouting: 'I am the demon dwarf of blood'—a line he had once heard in a pantomime."

was likewise struck by a prodigy that could not be accounted for in human terms, that seemingly had no "base" or history. "I am at present marveling at the astonishing miracles performed by Paganini in Paris. Do not imagine that it is merely a question of his bowing, his fingering, or the fantastic sounds he draws from his violin. . . . There is, beyond all doubt, something mysterious about this man. . . . He seems to me the Napoleon of his profession," he declared. In *Cousin Bette* he took up Paganini once again, having meanwhile found an explanation that is prophetic of Craig's *Über-Marionette:*

> If Paganini, who made the strings of his violin tell his whole soul, had let three days pass without practicing, he would have lost, together with his power of expression, what he called the *register* of his instrument, by which he meant the close union existing between the wood, bow, strings, and himself. If this accord were broken, he would at once become no more than an ordinary violinist. *Constant labor is the law of art as well as the law of life.*

Who is this creature so perfectly self-attuned that its perfect pitch becomes its soul, this Stoic Nature, this innocent sentenced to an eternity of hard labor, neither delighting in its power nor suffering from its confinement—who if not the automaton? Repugnance for an industrial society that threatened to mechanize human affairs, to destroy the artist's soul and render his creation infantile, went hand in hand with machine worship. By incessantly practicing, Paganini makes himself the artifact he embraces, according to Balzac; its acoustical properties and physical laws are the properties and laws that govern him, its chamber is his diaphragm, its register his voice. Having been at one with this harmonious instrument (which is also a *moral* body) and soared above the contingencies that afflict humankind, he would fall from Grace. Strings would change into nerves, emotions would untune him, the subjective inwardness that is human would fill the acoustical chamber, garbling his voice.

Both Balzac, who dreamed in 1835 of a national soul roused by a thaumaturge, and Craig, whose twentieth-century fantasy was of an *Über-Marionette* saving humanity from itself, looked to Napoleon for support. Where Balzac likened Paganini to the Emperor, Craig wrote, in "The Artist and the *Über-Marionette*," that "Napoleon is reported to have said: 'In life there is much that is unworthy which in art should be omitted; much of doubt and vacillation; and all should disappear in the representation of the hero. We should see him as a statue in which the weakness and the tremors of the flesh are no longer perceptible.' " What defined the hero and the artwork was not their human intensity but their mechanical impersonality. Another leap in time and this contention reasserted itself after World War I in the Surrealist movement, which made automatism a radical orthodoxy with *écriture automatique*, revealing the bedfellowship of totalitarian ideologues and aesthetes banded against the rational mind. He who wrote "automatically," that is, without regard for the censor, proclaimed himself to be a "moral nature" and an objective machine.

When Craig first entered Italy in 1906 aboard the Nord-Sud Express reciting Goethe's "*Kennst du das Land, wo die Zitronen blühn*" and seeing pictures in the National Gallery spring to life outside his window, he felt that he had "come home after a long period at school." When he came home again to Italy seven years later, this time for good, he hoped, and with a large sum of money donated by his friend Lord Howard de Walden, it was to establish a school—a laboratory where pupils would help him to discover the basic principle of an art whose counterfeits had become the common coin of European theater. "I want to study the theatre—I do not want to waste time producing plays—for that is vanity—expensive—unsatisfying—*comic*," he wrote in his Day-Book. "I know something about my art after twenty years' study. I want to know more. I want to know enough to be of use to those who can *do* more. I want to leave behind me the seeds of the art—for it does not yet exist, and such seeds are not to be discovered in a moment."

Having settled his dreams on Florence, there he rented an old, open-air theater, the Arena Goldoni, which delighted him the more for its having stood so long in such neglect that weeds grew in every corner of the auditorium and stout trees from between cracks in the wall. Since none but men could hope to grasp the arcana of this new form, and among men, none but innocents lacking any previous experience of theater, the half-dozen applicants he chose from among the many who responded to his advertisement in *The Times* formed a student body as scruffy as the Arena Goldoni itself. They were an electrical engineer, a musician, a medical-school casualty, an artist, a jack-of-all-trades. Drifters, or would-be cenobites, they wanted not only to escape England but to become stage directors.

They became, instead, the curatorial staff of a small Continental museum. Craig's son Edward has summarized the program of studies as follows:

> First and foremost came MOVEMENT: "The movements of the Elements and Man." To help with this, he even thought to make use of films, because he had seen motion pictures showing the growth of plants and the formation of clouds which he had thought most beautiful. Connected with movement would be DANCE—ceremonials—posture, etc. Connected with dance would be MIME. Next on his list came LIGHT—the lighting of static objects with moving light such as reflections from moving waters, projected colours, and so on; then the effect of light on moving objects, as when figures emerge from shadows, exist briefly in the light, and disappear again into the darkness.
>
> Connected with the above, would be experimental work with his SCREENS. The use of gauzes, scene-painting, the study of optical mixtures as demonstrated by Seurat in order to get great depth of colour and three-dimensional effects. Then there would be experiments with marionettes of all kinds and sizes, in his ever-lasting quest for animated figures which could be controlled by an artist; connected with this there would also be experiments with MASKS.

But this curriculum was never to become a real curriculum, any more than "Scene" was ever to materialize on a real stage, or the school-master to emerge as a real teacher. Craig, far from sharing himself, was of a mind to collect or to hoard rather than to teach, and hoarded, among other things, his students whom he could not completely trust, even when they had taken an oath that read, in part:

> No member of the School is to write to anyone outside the School news concerning it, or express his or her "opinion" of the work being done, or of other members. "Opinions" are wanted neither inside nor outside the School.
>
> Discretion, silence, and attention to work are expected.
>
> When outside the School, rather than talk of its work, methods, personalities, and results, the student should wear a mask of ignorance. "I do not know" is the one reply to make to the inquisitive.

While he sought to conceal his theatrical monastery from prying eyes, there was the fear that some "opinion" born among his novitiates might sow discord in his very midst. Having contrived to live in a world where, by law, his mind was the sole text, even there he could not but feel that those who "read" him would inevitably plagiarize him. "There was one subject that was never mentioned in the School—his vision of a moving 'Scene,' " wrote his son. "He had given the public a glimpse of its conception in his etchings made six years earlier, at the most inspired period of his life; now, he dared not take the risk of anyone shaking his belief in its realization, so he had to believe in it secretly."

Only puppets would do, puppets of the wooden variety, that is, and Craig recruited them from everywhere. In the attic of an ancient palace on the Grand Canal in Venice he discovered an extraordinary collection of Javanese shadow-puppets. At a London sale he bought an equally remarkable collection of Burmese puppets, and he found others in Florence. They became so numerous that Craig annexed a disused church behind the Arena Goldoni and made it a regular glory-hole, storing therein not only his cast of all nations but his masks of all tribes, his collection of treatises on perspective, his library of monographs on marionette theater and *commedia dell'arte*. Craig's special pride, however, was a puppet fashioned for him by Florentine woodcarvers who, on the day they presented it, had it bow and say slowly, as if reciting a lesson learned after the most diligent application, "Good luck to you in all your undertakings." Though this cretin did not quite answer his dream of an oracular archetype that lived beside the Ganges, it was, for all its manifest shortcomings, eight feet tall. And eight feet tall, it presided over the school.

With the outbreak of war, in August 1914, the year-old school became an altogether ideal phenomenon, its "pupils" returning to England or drifting elsewhere. When Jacques Copeau arrived in Florence about one year later, Craig had him tour the clutter of uncatalogued books, masks, marionettes, and model stages as he expatiated on plans for a colony where theatrical artisans would perfect themselves under his aegis. If he thought that in Copeau a congenial spirit had descended upon him, a man of apostolic temperament, a worthy vehicle, in short, for the propagation of his screens, the facts of the matter were rather more complicated. As a rival seer yet to make his mark in Europe at large and envious of this Englishman with whom he had so much in common, Copeau judged him harshly. Precisely because he had so much in common with him, he may also have wished to distinguish himself from Craig, whose isolation undoubtedly worried him. Copeau noted in his journal:

He speaks about nothing but colossal enterprises and the millions needed
to accomplish them. "My interests," he says, "are neither in London, nor
in Paris, nor in Berlin, but here in Florence and in America." The truth is, I
believe, that they are nowhere. G.C. is attached to no country, no public.
His action has no soul. It is effectively endorsed by no one. His friends are
scattered over the four quarters of the globe. I am convinced that my little
theater, for all its poverty and imperfections, has infinitely more soul, that
it is infinitely more fertile than all the musings of this megalomaniac.
Which doesn't detract from his importance as an inventor, an initiator.

But to Louis Jouvet, Copeau wrote letters that convey an excitement and awe belied by his journal. Craig's geometrical stage sets made
the most forceful impression on him:

It answers to a tee the needs of our stage. It's altogether beautiful, marve-
lously limpid and "made for us." Completely along our lines. . . . To be
brief, Gordon Craig *has offered me*, out of friendship, the benefit of his
French patent for the "Screens" (and I become the representative of his
ideas in France). Furthermore, he showed me a lighting system that produces admirable results and seems wonderfully simple and practical in
scale model. . . . It involves the complete abolition of ramps and battens.

So far as one can gather, the war was conspicuous largely by its absence from their conversation. Or is it that in some unspoken way
they regarded the monstrous upheaval as a wiping-clean-of-the-slate, a
prolegomenon to the naked stage? While "out there" Europe brought
wrack and ruin upon itself, these two sauntered through the Elysian
Fields, with Craig guiding his fellow director down alleyways from
atelier to atelier. "There is something to be written about the influence
of a milieu like Florence on Gordon Craig's work," Copeau noted in
his journal. "The monumental sense. The solidity of the stone. The
mass. The order and symmetry, all the geometrical resources enflamed
by passion, softened by grace. . . . Nothing picturesque. Stendhal said:
'somber Italy.' Craig's inspiration is no less severe." They visited pot-
ters, bookbinders, weavers, dyers. They fondled incunabula at the Mar-
celliana and Mediceo-Laurenziana. They spent hours in museums and
monasteries delighting in the wealth of a Renaissance whose stage picture they were out to destroy. One day Copeau played scenes from
Marivaux, by himself and for himself, in the Boboli Gardens overlooking Florence, and dispatched euphoric postcards to friends back home.

"Carte de Copeau hier soir, étrangement 'out of time'; il parle de Florence, de l'Angelico. . . . Tout cela existe donc encore?"* Gide asked himself on September 27, 1915, two days after the launching of an Anglo-French offensive in Artois that was to cost several hundred thousand men their lives.

After one month with Craig, who proposed that they collaborate on an American production of the Saint Matthew Passion, Copeau visited Geneva, where it came as a welcome relief to observe a real teacher, Emile Jaques-Dalcroze, teach real students in a real school.

Dalcroze had been a professor of harmony at the Geneva Conservatory for some years when he began formulating the theory and method he called eurythmics. His experience taught him that a musician's technical progress seldom went hand in hand with the development of his musical faculties, that instrumental specialization from early childhood created technicians whose "inner consciousness" of tone and rhythm lay asleep. To awaken such consciousness, he had students practice solfège, and then, remarking how they found vocal work more real when they beat time to their singing, he wrote a series of "gesture songs," which met with great success. These songs led him to devise a system whose basic premise was that physical movement should be not merely the accompaniment of music but the means of expressing it. By 1910 or so eurythmics had evolved into a full-fledged pedagogy which one practitioner has described as follows:

> It consists of three parts: a.) rhythmic movement, b.) ear training and c.) improvisation (practical harmony). Of these the first is the essence of the Dalcroze method and is fundamentally new. . . . In the system of exercises upon which the method is based, *time* is shown by movements of the arms, and *time-duration,* i.e., note values, by movements of the feet and body. In the early stages of the training this principle is clearly observed; later it may be varied in many ingenious ways—for instance, in what is known as plastic counterpoint the actual notes may be represented by movements of the arms, while the counterpoint in crotchets, quavers or semiquavers is

---

* "Got a card from Copeau yesterday evening, oddly 'out of time'; he speaks of Florence, of Fra Angelico. . . . You mean, all that still exists?"

given by the feet. . . . The whole training aims at developing the power of rapid physical reaction to mental impressions.

Going beyond the Conservatory with a view to training young children and campaigning for the adoption of his method in elementary schools, Jaques-Dalcroze, who believed that eurythmics might help to create a new folk culture, founded an institute at Hellerau, in Bavaria. When war erupted, the institute was moved to Geneva.

Two demonstrations of the Dalcroze method sufficed to convert Copeau, who wrote in his diary: "There is a definite affinity between Dalcroze's methods and those I have been pondering: I am convinced that there is virtue in a general rhythmic education as a basis for the actor's professional training." As soon as he reached Paris in November 1915, after an absence of six or seven weeks, he began to train a chorus with twelve adolescent boys and girls. "First we would render bodies obedient, then rise progressively from gymnastics to the idea of interior rhythm, to music, to dance, to masked mime, to the word," he noted. The re-creation of theater presupposed the re-creation of actors in accordance with a discipline that would purify their sensibilities and make them more exact physical instruments. Not until an apprentice had become "depersonalized" by rhythmic dances enabling his body to suggest "nuances that elude logical formulation" or by the mimicry of nonhuman objects could he execute human gestures. Likewise, he had to convey emotion onomatopoeically, to imitate animal cries, for example, or the sound of wind, of rain, of torrents, his master denying him speech until such time as words sprang from him "naturally," without rational guidance, social direction, or historical consciousness. Where André Antoine believed that a play should unfold "of itself" once the material stage had been furnished right in every detail, Copeau held that a character's words should issue ventriloquistically from an actor's mouth once the inner stage had been laid bare. Rather than lend himself to his character, the actor would evacuate himself for it. Rather than bring a dowry of personal experience, he would marry the part in all innocence. Even before it came to words, he would have "felt" an author's purpose, a character's soul, or a director's direction, with music arranging this symbiotic union. There is no "ego" here, only instinct and absolute authority, which are so mutually implicated that orders from outside come from an internal source.

Copeau's curriculum would have had his young apprentices follow a hermetic path that led from musical gymnastics to speech, from an "obedient" body to a "natural" language, bypassing the mind and ignoring all the tools of reason. It was designed to train noble savages, infallible puppets, flawless aesthetes. Properly schooled, they would have no faces but the masks they wore, no voices but the characters' (i.e., director's), no desire to move but in unison with their brethren and according to a prescribed cadence. "The mask," wrote Copeau, "is a perfect symbol of the interpreter's position without regard to the persona, and shows in what way there takes place a fusion between one and the other." And elsewhere: "The actor received from this cardboard object the reality of his persona. He is commanded by it. He obeys it irresistibly." This totemistic idea—for such it appears to have been—found its consummate method not in Jaques-Dalcroze's eurythmics but in Vsevolod Meyerhold's "biomechanics." That the "natural" actor could also be the perfect technician was a paradox characteristic of neo-Romantics given as much to longing for machinelike impersonality as to nostalgia for a "primitive" or "organic" community.

What justified Copeau's pedagogical agenda was his vision of some such community. Though he professed a commitment to literature, literature or repertoire became more and more a pretense as his vision became increasingly despotic. His memoirs suggest that the chorus's ultimate *raison d'être* lay in itself, that it represented for him a utopian body or a religious order unified by faith. "We liked to believe that when the group had evolved into itself, its members—all having issued from the same general culture, imbibed the same spirit, absorbed the same sap—would gather, as it were, the fruit of one and the same tree: the poet, the musician, the dancer, the mime, the protagonists, and the chorus, all the artisans, all the stewards of drama, not artificially regrouped and styled but inspired from within, associated organically."

Copeau, like Craig, invoked a tree to describe the rootedness and corporate identity that would attend life under the new dispensation, and he also shared Craig's desire to carve from the tree a puppet society whose constituents would transcend literature as immutable "types" or born characters improvising themselves ad infinitum.* "I would like

* The tree as a symbol of kindred yearnings appears in the works of Martin Heidegger and Jean-Paul Sartre.

to form, in the Vieux-Colombier, a troupe (six or eight persons) of
zanni, of *improvisors* who would stand absolutely apart from the other
actors but would constitute an orginal core from which I believe a New
Comedy will be born," he confided to Martin du Gard in February
1916. "Dream about it, my friend. The idea is to break away from all
more or less *literary genres*. Do you understand? It would be for each to
pull gratuitous stunts and seek his own character. I have already put in
quite a lot of work on this. It begins teeming immediately you touch it."
The six or eight soon became ten, and their scope broader than originally conceived:

> I foresee ten *modern* personae—synthetic, expandable, representing preva-
> lent traits, quirks, passions, foibles, moral, social, and individual. The ten
> personae of an *autonomous* theater encompassing all genres from pan-
> tomime to drama would be entrusted to ten actors. Each would make his
> persona his *property*. It would become himself, he would nourish it with
> himself. . . . There's the great discovery, the great revolution or rather the
> great and majestic return to the oldest tradition.

The oldest tradition put Copeau quite naturally in mind of old names,
names that had lapsed along with the faith they bespoke. "A confrerie
of farce-actors always playing together, improvising together, authors,
and actors, singers, musicians, acrobats (our clowns are only the vestige
of all that). . . . These ten personae run through all possible permuta-
tions. It would be the infinite meeting-anew, a constant renewal. . . .
Always the same accessories, immutable, like the physiognomy of the
actors."

Immemorially familiar but meeting one another always for the first
time, these personae constituted Copeau's ideal milieu, and this milieu
the novel he could not otherwise produce. Its infinite episodes would
unfold in a perpetual present, starting nowhere and leading nowhere,
featuring characters known a priori who are whichever mask they wear.
Paradoxical though it may seem that he, the supreme formalist, should
have loved nothing more than compact works, long and tufted novels
"where," as he put it to Martin du Gard, "you lose yourself, where you
forget everything, where you plunge, as though it were the heart of a
forest, into a dense, closely-woven prose, *without paragraphs*," the
paradox makes sense. Verbal mass and abstract movement, the space-
less interior and the facial conceit were equally plausible alternatives

to the elaboration of character *in time*, to the disclosure of a self best kept hidden, or to the acknowledgment of a world that steals faces and invades minds. Many years later, during World War II, he exclaimed, in a letter to Martin du Gard: "I must record it, later, when things calm down [he had just related a youthful escapade]. . . . I have so much to say! . . . Just one book, but enormous: all my memories. . . . My life! . . . And you'll see, Roger, it will be a beautiful book!" But like the ancient couple in Ionesco's *The Chairs,* drawing up chair after chair for imaginary guests invited to hear an Orator deliver their life message, or like the Orator himself, Copeau could not find his tongue. As keen as he was to fill a theater with revelations, to give therein a full account of Jacques Copeau and hold the audience perpetually in thrall, what emerged from him instead was this vision of ten nonstop jokers wearing emblematic dress, of numbers dancing through mathematical space. "I" needed an oracular ventriloquist.

The idea that theater had followed an aberrant course since the Middle Ages, that its psychological *raffinement* and estrangement from the Folk had cost it its soul, took root in avant-garde circles throughout Europe, giving rise to forms more or less militant intended for publics more or less disenchanted with urbane conventions. Nearly every issue of Craig's magazine *The Mask* featured articles on *commedia dell'arte* and marionette theater. In Russia, the Constructivist movement found one of its earliest champions in Meyerhold who, while ridiculing Stanislavski's allegiance to "the inner experience" or "authentic emotion," declared that actors should model themselves on the puppet. "Words in the theater are only embellishments on the design of movement"; and "Only via the sports arena can we approach the theatrical arena," were two precepts of an intellectual manifesto driven home with his productions of Blok's *The Fairground Booth,* Solovyov's *Harlequin, The Marriage Broker,* and *Colombine's Scarf* (an unsentimental version of Schnitzler's pantomime *The Veil of Pierrette*). During World War I, in Paris, that émigré-soon-to-be Serge Diaghilev, whose audiences both home and abroad liked folk art sublimated through the gorgeous prism of the Ballets Russes, staged *Parade,* a spectacle where fairground puppets come alive as in *Petrouchka.* Copeau's ideas therefore echoed a

Zeitgeist that amplified them enormously and made his project seem altogether cogent to friends like Gide:

> Morning session at the *N.R.F.* with Copeau [Gide noted in January 1916].
> We chat at length about the possibility of forming a little group of actors,
> sufficiently intelligent, skilled, and well trained to improvise on any given
> scenario and capable of reviving *commedia dell'arte*, in the Italian manner
> but with new types: the bourgeois, the nobleman, the wine merchant, the
> suffragette would replace Harlequin, Pierrot, and Colombine. . . . If this
> project comes to fruition, I predict and hope for a public that would
> become an accessory to the action, goading and exalting the actors.

As for Martin du Gard, whose mind was at the beck and call of Copeau's, the latter had only to say "Dream about it, old man" to set him dreaming for months. "I dream of a spectacle as spontaneous as an improvisation but wrought as finely as a fable, where a public hot and bothered by current events would come to relax and laugh without any ulterior thoughts at the irresistible shenanigans of *live marionettes* who would be their old acquaintances," he wrote, having all but persuaded himself that the idea for a fairground theater, or *Comédie des Tréteaux*, as he called it, had originally been his. "I carried the idea with me throughout the war, from billet to billet, like a viaticum," he recalled years later. "I would plunge into it nostalgically before falling asleep." What he saw in his mind's eye were a thousand extravagant and dexterous stunts executed by a "new breed" of actor trained at the Vieux-Colombier, an actor "full of verve and authority, supple as an acrobat, excelling like English mummers, in gestures, attitudes, walks, curtseys, mimicry, leaps."

But there was more to this fantasy than circus shenanigans distracting Martin du Gard from his dangerous and dismal occupation. It resembled a grudge fondly nursed night after night, a war—fought in a theater built for the purpose of enshrining it—between type and type, essence and essence. Against eight or nine such types representing "bourgeois society" there would be an equal number of opponents—"all those whose eye has been sharpened by constraint, injustice, and poverty, who condemn without appeal the civilization we have and openly rebel against its rules." Bearing out Eric Bentley's formulation that "melodrama is the naturalism of the dream life," Martin du Gard lulled himself to sleep with dreams of class warfare ritualized by "live marionettes." That dream would unfold, and much as he imagined it, though not at the Vieux-Colombier or even in France. When Meyerhold (who had meanwhile acquired the title "People's Artist of the Republic") produced Ostrovsky's *Forest* in 1924, he made every principal wear costumes revealing his "essential nature." In accordance with the ponderous dictum that "a play is simply the excuse for the revelation of its theme on the level at which that revelation may appear vital today" (meaning propaganda), character development, or, indeed, the character itself as understood by "bourgeois" gave way to "social masks," to the instantly legible embodiments of a Manichaean universe.

CHAPTER VII

✦ ✦ ✦ ✦

FROM ABSTRACTION
TO RELIGION

While Roger Martin du Gard excogitated a puppet theater with the persistence and loyalty characteristic of one who wrote long, tufted novels, the ever-restless Copeau deserted his project when, in August 1916, Philippe Berthelot of the French Ministry of Foreign Affairs proposed that he help kindle American enthusiasm for the Allied cause by reassembling the Vieux-Colombier troupe and touring the United States with it. Germany, it was felt, had had much the better of it exporting its cultural resources. German conductors fashioned American musical taste, German philosophy and historiography held sway at American universities, and German theater put the French to shame, what with the exertions of Max Reinhardt, who had set up annexes of his Deutsches Theater in major American cities. Were Copeau to do nothing more than quickly revive New York's moribund Théâtre-Français, he would have done his bit to convince influential patrons that the Grand Army had not yet lost its élan. Then again, French authorities believed in the inherent seductiveness, the almost evangelical presence of the French language. ("For France above all, language is the necessary instrument of colonization. . . . How could our schools be otherwise than loved by the native populations! There most especially does civilization display itself to them in its gentle guises: they learn the language of their conquerors and feel nearer them by intelligence," Jean Jaurès told the Alliance Française in 1884.) At first Copeau was most reluctant to uproot himself and his family, which now numbered four, but he weighed the advantages, as in this letter:

> If I heeded nothing but my personal inclination, I would continue preparing for future seasons in all serenity. But there are other considerations, notably this one: I would get my actors back, in other words Dullin, Jouvet, and the others would be *saved*. The troupe would thus be reconstituted for a common labor which would prepare it for the reopening in Paris. I would doubtless return from abroad with money sufficient to launch me again here without my having to raise additional capital. And finally, I may perhaps be able to get financial backing for the future from Americans.

Before long, the qualms that beset him had been defeated by hyperboles he mobilized from his private romance of giants and dwarfs. "This tour in America will be *magnificent*, assuming I am given the means to do it," he prophesied to Martin du Gard in September 1916.

When the War Ministry balked at releasing Jouvet, Dullin, and others from active duty, Copeau, nothing daunted, set sail for America all alone, with a view to reconnoitering the terrain and making himself known there while bureaucratic skirmishes took their course. His individual tour was a successful one. Not only did he generate interest in the Vieux-Colombier at universities throughout the Northeast but, more to the point, he thoroughly ingratiated himself with the cultural powers-that-were. Otto Kahn, a rich banker who counted the Metropolitan Opera and the Théâtre-Français of New York among his fiefdoms, offered Copeau absolute control of the latter, pledging to raise $100,000 should he deliver the Vieux-Colombier to America. Mmes. Philip Lydig and W. K. Vanderbilt made him their special protégé, mothering every step he took in High Society.* At home life resembled an obstacle course, while in New York it unfolded as an endless donation: being Jacques Copeau was rather like being a beautiful woman

---

* In particular Mrs. Lydig, an energetic Francophile, of whom Copeau wrote: "Her activity is fantastic, even though she can't eat or sleep. She has little to do with High Society, which she detests and which suffers her, but she often receives at home, concerns herself with artists and poor people, visits the sick and prisoners, is in touch with political agitators, writes for the papers and speaks at meetings. She's already evolved a whole strategy for me."

who need only appear for an adulatory public to offer her valentines. Did he want a theater? He could have his choice of two or three. And an endowment for the future school of the Vieux-Colombier? Mrs. Lydig prevailed upon the Women's Commitee to solicit funds in its name.

It is hardly surprising, then, that prospects of a "magnificent tour" should soon have ballooned into a vision of colonial conquest. He wrote to Gaston Gallimard:

> My personal impressions, which have been confirmed unanimously by the many Americans with whom I have talked, lead me to believe that beyond all doubt times have never been more propitious than now for the organization in America of a large enterprise fostering French influence.
>
> Since the war, and especially in recent months, French enterprises initiated by individuals or groups have cropped up everywhere, but I believe that the Théâtre-Français can stand foremost among them and constitute, *for the first time in America*, an absolutely unique sphere of influence. . . . In its vestibule I would set up a display of *Nouvelle Revue Française* editions. Besides this, we ought to found a library of French authors, classical and especially modern, with whom a cultivated person in American society ought to acquaint himself. If we acquire the habit of directing these people who ask only to be directed . . . I have no doubt that we shall swiftly extend our influence and that of our authors.

The publishing empire had much the same effect upon Gallimard that the puppet theater had had upon Martin du Gard. With every such notion, Copeau, like a virtuoso juggler, set heads spinning in his orbit.

The influence he hoped to exert was as absolute as the stage he sought to direct. Whether it made itself felt in some walled country garden or ubiquitously (for Copeau, like Dullin, moved between cells and boundless space), its psychological underpinning was a rage for uniqueness, an intolerance of rules imposed by others, of limits suggested by experience, of arbiters other than impulse or feeling. "You see, my dear Gaston, when I have in hand the troupe I wish to have, with a suitable organization and the money I need—no more—after the war *I shall be able to travel the length and breadth of the world with my actors* [italics added], and I am quite certain that wherever we go we shall be admirably received." Where there was no avowable center, there could be no personal circumference. Denying his own motives and history, hiding from himself, Copeau felt at home in the ideally "self-less" ambience he projected, in the space of moral generalization and abstract ideology, in a theatrical *Umwelt* whose inhabitants would be reified as ceremonial objects and oriented by axiomatic forms (the cubic stage) or else absolved of all definition. While power excited him (he was, like Rousseau, much taken with the Pygmalion myth), moral indignation invariably sanctified the color it brought to his cheeks. And though he harbored unlimited ambitions, he saw himself opening a market not for goods or profit but for blessed poverty. What was originally undertaken with practical reasons in mind soon evolved into a soteriological journey. "Our friends will say that the Vieux-Colombier is growing too quickly, that it has one foot on the Old Continent and one on the New. I shall respond that if I were not certain of maintaining the moral integrity, and the very soul and spirit of the Théâtre du Vieux-Colombier such as it was at the beginning, *and of thereby saving France with our spirit* [italics added] . . . I would not launch myself into such a venture," he declared. By transplanting itself in virgin soil abroad, the Vieux-Colombier troupe would once and for all lose its separate and individual histories. It would become the "organic community."

When, in the early spring of 1917, word arrived that the War Ministry had at last consented to release his actors, Copeau straightaway selected a theater of appropriately modest proportions, the Garrick, on West Thirty-Fifth Street between Fifth and Sixth avenues, and engaged Antonin Raymond, a French architect, to renovate its interior. As with the Athénée Saint-Germain, so here all the gimcrack would disappear—to the bewilderment of Copeau's sponsors, who belatedly understood that they had in their midst something other than a brilliant parlor wit, or even a winner. Sacrificing the pecuniary advantages that were supposed to justify this venture, Copeau did away with lateral loges and the second balcony—nearly half the Garrick's total seating capacity of nine hundred—in order to construct upstairs a hall where plays other than the main bill could be rehearsed. Its new stage departed from convention even more radically than had the Vieux-Colombier's, for in addition to jutting well beyond the curtain (here again, invading revenue) it abolished that venerable margin between actor and spectator, the footlight barrier. Where the barrier had stood there were now steps—an arrangement repeated at center stage in ziggurats that formed little staircases leading up to a cubic dais, all very Mayan-like

The stage of the Garrick Theatre in New York City as renovated by Copeau in 1917. Bibliothèque de l'Arsenal

but inspired by Sebastiano Serlio (via Craig). Six doors—two squat ellipses, two slender ones, and two oblongs symmetrically disposed—left no expanse of wall sufficient for background scenery. Above them and extending all around the stage was a clerestory of windows and windowlike grids that bore a startling resemblance to the geometrical compositions Piet Mondrian had begun to paint in the same year.*

"Blueprints of the Garrick are staggering," wrote Martin du Gard during the summer, Copeau having meanwhile gone back to France to make preparations for the company's trip. "On the basis of his plans, they're doing 250,000-francs' worth of construction on a stage that will allow him at last to put his ideas into effect. It's mad. Really, his platform is a stroke of genius, unimaginably simple and clever. . . . He is more and more *alone, central,* sweeping everybody into the background, holding personal views on everything—costumes, decor, etc. . . . Less and less is he able to accept collaborators; he can tolerate only laborers, employees, docile workers."

The thought voiced by Martin du Gard that this stage might seem

---

* The false windows were divided into little panes, some "lit" and the others dark.

pauvre (impoverished) in American eyes provoked an outburst that allowed him to gauge the proportions of Copeau's aesthetic imperialism and the intensity of his anger. *"Je m'en fous!"* he exclaimed. "In fact I insist on doing exactly the opposite of what most people do who go to America. They make concessions to American taste, I shall impose my taste on America. I am no more prepared to alter the fabric of my costumes for a public of millionaires than to alter the acting style of my troupe and my conception of characters." He would remain poor at all costs, in defiance of those who proposed to feather his nest. He would defeat them, come what may, though it meant penalizing himself. Aesthetically as well as financially, to be poor was to be impenetrable, to be impenetrable to be chaste, and to be chaste was to transcend the "childish" emotions that made him view himself as a dwarf among gods. Intent on leaving his mark, what Copeau sought in pure style was a refuge from all judgment, a thinglike impeccability that calls to mind Baudelaire's dandy.

Like other hermetic ideas that crossed the ocean and found material embodiment in America (Fourierist phalansteries, for example), the Vieux-Colombier de New York as envisioned by Copeau was to be a little world sufficient unto itself rather than an integral part of urban life, a commune occupying its own ideological space. "City" is the word that struck Martin du Gard during his conversations with Copeau. "And his thought is expanding, stretching to encompass a whole bundle of enterprises of which the theater is but the kernel, the kernel of an assortment of French arts, a veritable city including library as well as restaurant, school, swimming pool, theater review, literary meetings. A whole world," he noted in his journal. And again: "It's a kind of new city which he is creating for actors and their audiences."

It would seem that to accommodate the secrets he kept even from himself, what Copeau required was a deracinated settlement, a closet community, a hermitage exempt from norms and discriminations that obtained outside. In fact he led two quite distinct lives, one revolving around his legitimate family, and the other around his principal actress, Suzanne Bing, who, unknown to everyone but Martin du Gard, bore him a son in March 1917. Where his wife, Agnes, for all her meekness, held sway over him by virtue of being seven years older and having a Lutheran spine around which she organized domestic life, he found in Suzanne Bing a perfect Galatea, a female alter ego with whom he eloped every day to his own ludic kingdom, a worshipful servant who always called him *le Patron*. Except for the existence of children, this schizoid arrangement resembled Gide's with Madeleine (indeed, Gide once described himself as a combination Protestant pastor and mischievous little boy, each exasperating the other), but children made all the difference. Where Agnes could be relied upon to temper justice with mercy, or to rationalize on his behalf and on her own, Copeau saw that his children—*les purs*—delivered unappealable verdicts. As the Incorruptible condemned, so he fancied himself condemned. "In the cab that brought us back, Copeau suddenly began to tell me about the frightful complication of his life," wrote Martin du Gard several months after the American experiment had drawn to a close in 1919:

> He said: "I know what I'm risking. I think about it, alas. . . . I'm risking the happiness and coherence of my home, the affection and respect of my children. For quite some time Agnes has had a feeling of respect for me, of profound esteem that mitigates to some extent the pain of realizing that I can love another. But she believes herself to be the only mother, she believes that that is her unique claim, and I'm not sure what will happen the day she learns the truth. . . . And my children! . . . I have no idea what they will think, what they will do. . . . Maïène sometimes has a face drawn shut in the presence of people and actors of whom she *disapproves,* which makes me quake for myself. . . . And she's so quick to detect resemblances that she won't be long in guessing. . . . But Pascal scares me even more. He is horrified by anything that isn't clear and straightforward. . . . He is terrible in his judgments. It's a good thing the little shaver is exceedingly kind. I shall appeal to his tenderness. . . . All this makes me sick. I could not witness a civil war.*

Condemning himself before this jury of children made Copeau all the more anxious to have a school where he could rule boys and girls devoid of any basis for scrupling. If he was defenseless outside his theatrical microcosm, inside it nothing and no one would challenge reality as he decreed it. The abstract ground on which actors performed quasi-

---

* His appraisal of Pascal's character was borne out twenty-one years later, under circumstances graver than this one. During the Nazi occupation, Copeau, who had been lured from retirement to direct the Comédie-Française, was asked for a list of its Jewish actors. After stalling, he capitulated. Meanwhile, Pascal, who had joined the Resistance movement, was broadcasting patriotic messages via Free French radio.

liturgical figures eight, the geometrical stage which arrogated to itself an impersonal or objective truth, stood directly over chaos. It declared the actor-director innocent of wrongdoing, innocent of ulterior motives.

America proved invincible. Copeau came to it as a conqueror and retreated after two theatrical seasons with his spirit and his company in disarray. Though there were the few who admired him greatly, on the whole New Yorkers did not like what he had to offer—neither the stage, which they thought faddish, nor the repertorial rotation, which they found confusing, nor the "laborious jugglery" of his *mise en scènes,* nor the esoteric repertoire. Sooner than play to a half-vacant hall in a foreign land with actors some of whom were raw recruits, Copeau betrayed every value hitherto upheld against the enemy. He could not readily desert his new stage, but he threw out the better part of his repertoire and improvised another that would have stood him in good stead on the Boulevard, including as it did plays by clever craftsmen like Henri Bernstein, Georges de Porto-Riche, Henri Meilhac and Ludovic Halévy, Maurice Donnay, Edmond Rostand, Anatole France, Erckmann-Chatrian, and Clemenceau (who had been instrumental in sending him overseas). This feat of self-betrayal brought him meager rewards. People attended, but tentatively and in smaller numbers than at first, while the troupe, which found itself obliged to mount a new production every eighth day, like Sisyphus never quite reaching the top, grew desperately tired and finally mutinous. If one studied the years 1917–18 with no other historical source material at hand than letters written by Copeau, one would not guess that, say, a revolution had taken place in Russia. The days that shook the world were a distant rumble on West Thirty-fifth Street, where its own quarrels deafened the Vieux-Colombier to life outside.

The dissension rife among younger actors would not have created such havoc had the old boys—Dullin, Jouvet—made common cause with Copeau, but here, too, a rift had opened, a rift for which the war was partly responsible. As Martin du Gard said, by way of explaining in the summer of 1917 why he could not accompany Copeau to America:

I became increasingly aware of a deep division between those who have seen battle [*ceux qui en sont*] and those who have not; with each successive furlough I can measure more accurately the extent to which the war transforms *me,* rids me of the past, orients me toward some as yet undefined but nonetheless fundamental, irreplaceable evolution. I'm certain that at war's end, those who fought in it will be the ones to form the enormous assault force of Thought Renewed. I have done too much, endured too much, not to fight this out to a finish, not to resist activities that solicit my attention but seem marginal to my path.

To be sure, he would express different sentiments fourteen months later, when armistice lay in the offing ("In my musings about the future I bump into you at every step. . . . This war will have separated us terribly—for an instant. We no longer had the same eyes or the same tongue. All that is over now"), but his original view, which had cost him a reprieve from mortal danger, was the more realistic one. There did indeed exist two Frances now, or two populations—civilians on the one hand and on the other a soldierly mass bereft of any place in the world, an unassimilable gang formed by trench warfare that referred to itself as *ceux qui en sont,* "those who are *of it.*" When Marshal Joffre, who adopted the Japanese principle that war should be waged "silently and anonymously," sealed off the "Zone of the Armies" from the "Zone of the Rear," lest useful information go astray, he thereby helped to create a no-man's-land even more hostile than the one between trenches, a gap across which the Franco-German civilian population and the Franco-German warrior tribe beheld each other as across a distance of centuries. Martin du Gard's word for the spiritual divide he could not imagine himself crossing—*fosse*—is in fact a word for trench.

That Dullin and Jouvet might have changed during their absence at the front, that the three years they had spent apart from him before coming to America were not a blank vigil or a dreamless sleep but time filled with pictures and words to which he was not privy drove Copeau half mad. Rather than treat with experience, he became more intolerant of it. Instead of recognizing that his former pupils had come into their own, that they could no longer bend quite so promptly, or that the battles they had fought elsewhere in common with others subtracted from his authority, he sought to restore the status quo ante.

Even those who stood by him after one lackluster season lost heart

during July and August of 1918, when the entire troupe congregated on
Otto Kahn's estate near Morristown, New Jersey, for Copeau would
not allow that 1913 lay beyond recall. Morristown was La Ferté-sous-
Jouarre reincarnate, Kahn's estate was Limon, the summer was that
same idyllic summer of initiation, and the text was the text still read according to him. But no one listened now except Suzanne Bing, of whom
he said that "she alone stayed afloat in this shipwreck; she belongs to
the race of those who sacrifice their life for a faith, for an ideal." The
faithless made merry as best they could in north central New Jersey,
availing themselves of every opportunity to visit Morristown, whose
diversions did not extend much beyond a movie house and an ice-cream
parlor, or—in Dullin's case—riding horses at a nearby manege, while
Copeau inveighed against "plotters" in his midst. He who declared that
he could not witness a civil war, witnessed one. As the summer wore
on, nerves wore increasingly thin until a queer look sufficed to make
tempers flare. Incapable of solving this dilemma by any diplomatic
strategy, Copeau did what he had always done in circumstances that
required self-scrutiny and compromise with a will other than his own.
He fled, betaking himself in poor health to the Adirondack Mountains
where, one night, something like a mystical vision showed him—
without his being able to describe it—"the future stage." As he later
wrote in a letter to Martin du Gard:

> What I call my ideal has not merely survived but been purified, fortified,
> exalted in adversity. Adversity is the word. Alone, against all the adverse
> forces. Everything I had conceived, discovered, affirmed or simply sketched
> during three years of solitude and meditation has become more precise,
> more evident, more transparent. . . . I know where I'm headed, I see what
> must be done and how to do it. There, displayed before my eyes like a
> whole or a block, is *the entire problem* of the theater. And my way of en-
> visaging it will, I believe, give the Vieux-Colombier a unique place in the
> world. We are, I assure you, far from the distinguished gropings of
> 1913–14. And I've just begun. I shall relate at length, in a book, what path
> brought me here, and this history of an idea will touch upon all the prob-
> lems of the theater and encompass the history of all the conceptions which
> have, during these past twenty-five years, incited and nourished "the new
> movement."

Here was one more book never to see the light of day. A vision, and
particularly an incommunicable vision, confers upon the Seer such im-
munity to judgment as no book can provide its author. Books emerge

from within; visions descend from above. Where authors are finite beings, visionaries embrace the Whole. Yearning for a *deus ex machina* that would rescue him from his tangled plot, for a bit of Revealed Truth to quiet his obstreperous company, he found God and Writ atop a mountain. Who could imagine, much less deny, the transcendent *evidence* he found on high? If their absence had given Jouvet and Dullin pictures forever invisible to him, his had begotten a vision for which words were inadequate. The Vieux-Colombier he left behind was an impostor, a shadow of itself, a fallen idea. The *real* troupe lay safely tucked away in the future, flawless and all-encompassing, like his unwritten masterpiece. "All the evil came of their not believing me enough," he declared.

Halfway through the 1918–19 season in New York, Dullin, whose brilliant performances of Harpagon the Miser had been a beaconlight in the storm, suddenly quit and returned to Paris, with Copeau's imprecations speeding him home. Though Jouvet did not follow suit, he lingered as much for the sake of argument as of art, it would seem, and when he parted three years later did so in equally bad odor. Gaston Gallimard, who had spent one year abroad with the Vieux-Colombier, could not endure a second. Shaken by these defections, Copeau nonetheless made plans that revealed the forger of souls girding himself for yet another crusade—a children's crusade, as one might describe it. "In Paris, I shall definitively give up acting," he told Martin du Gard. "I shall reorganize everything so as to be certain of holding everything in my hands. I shall recruit some fresh collaborators. I shall live by the precepts of absolute intransigeance, discipline, originality. Maïène will already be old enough to work at my side. AND I DREAM OF INAUGURATING A LITTLE SOCIETY OF CHOSEN CHILDREN WHO WILL BE THE SOURCE OF OUR RENEWAL AND OUR PROMISE." Copeau repeated himself several months later, confiding to Martin du Gard that "one of my pet projects is to reunite our children, to have them work together, to assemble around this core carefully chosen children who will begin a tradition of art and thought."

And when, back in France, questions flew thick and fast as to the misfortune that had befallen him in America, his response was that of a child disclaiming all responsibility for it:

If someone told you that a small child born in the valley of the Seine found itself suddenly torn from its mother's breast and trotted to the North Pole or to the tropics for two years, you wouldn't dream of reckoning these years as years of growth. You would be amazed that it didn't perish. It is therefore correct to say that the Vieux-Colombier *did not exist*, did not materially develop, did not act upon its public in any direct way for over one and one-half years.

The mind that understood life in dualistic terms obeyed its nature in formulating this melodramatic plot, complete with recognition scene, to protest its innocence. What had taken place in the largely hostile climate of New York *had not taken place*, since the Vieux-Colombier had ceased to be itself when torn from the motherland. Inherently virtuous, it became something else outside France—a nonentity, a self-divided alien whose words, gestures, and appearance cast no reflection upon its soul.

By playing a second year at the former Garrick, Copeau had lost whatever remained after one season of the endowment initially raised for him by New York's rich subscribers. That this loss was accomplished willfully, that he drew dividends from it despite himself, touting his penury even as he laid claim to an ideal purer and cleaner than before, is evident in the correspondence. "Right now," he wrote to Martin du Gard in December 1918, "it can be said that initial prospects of material success have given way to omens of a real crash. Once again I shall have skirted advantages offered me. In other words, I refused them. I counted on returning to France with some money. I shall return poorer than when I left." He had boasted that he would impose his poor stage on American millionaires. So he did. Squandering father's legacy was itself an entrepreneurial triumph of sorts.*

Copeau left New York nonetheless innocent of the ordeal he had survived. His compulsion to delete episodes that spoke ill of him, to purge burdensome thoughts, ambiguous facts, and captious friends gave him amazing resilience, however cruelly it narrowed the circle in which he could operate. Like Rousseau, whose *Confessions* open with the bald assertion that "I have conceived an enterprise which has no precedent and shall have no imitator," he was always creating the world anew.

That nothing merely human would command his aesthetic recogni-

---

* Like Martin du Gard, whose father had been a lawyer, Copeau enjoyed independent means, though nothing like what was required to run a theater.

tion or prevail upon him to negotiate with "the other" became clear once the stage he built for his theater on the rue du Vieux-Colombier had been unveiled in February 1920 with a performance of *The Winter's Tale*. It was Thirty-fifth Street all over again but *en beau*—a wide staircase replacing the orchestral barrier, steps providing access to a cubic platform at center stage and, in the background, more steps coiling around from either side, then rising ziggurat-like to form a bridge that spanned the whole. This fixed, architectonic landscape left room for only three hundred sixty seats, or one-third fewer than before. Copeau did not stop there, however. A further innovation, one by which he set great store, suggests that the thrust-stage was devised as much to nullify as to embrace the audience, that it embodied a refusal to vouchsafe spectators their own inalienable space and thus to acknowledge their judgmental function. Copeau had workmen rip out the stage boards and lay a concrete floor, which gave his cast no acoustical support whatever, serving, on the contrary, to muffle sound, to keep it "inside," as though it were another dead secret. "The constraints of the stage and its broad artifice will be unto us as a discipline, forcing us to concretize all truth in the feelings and actions of our personae," he had written in 1913. "Let us abolish its magical conceits and, for the new era, make do with a bare stage [*tréteau nu*]!" Many who reread this manifesto after the war understood in light of subsequent evidence that words like "discipline," "new era," and "bare" had constituted a theological gloss. Vieux-Colombier actors would, if Copeau had his way, view themselves as disciples performing ritual drama not for the benefit of an audience but ad majorem artis gloriam, and doing so inside the main square, the scene-cloister as it were, of a conventual village that came to include seamstresses, carpenters, and electricians.

With the Arena Goldoni vividly in mind, Copeau built ateliers whose personnel made the Vieux-Colombier all but independent of services offered by the world outside. And like Gordon Craig, he launched a periodical, *Les Cahiers du Vieux-Colombier*, upon which he had begun to reflect five years earlier in the following terms: "We must create the book of good artisans. . . . Everything being done abroad will find its place in it. I have begun to marshal correspondents in every country. I want people to talk about this publication from the outset, much as they talked about the theater itself. . . . It will allow us to do some serious meddling with reality. . . . We must be in the first rank,

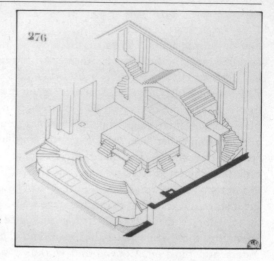

A perspective view of the Vieux-Colombier's stage in 1924. Bibliothèque de l'Arsenal

superior to all others; we must demonstrate this. . . . A platform and a journal." Paradoxical though it may have been, his stratagem of inaudibility accommodated a desire to be heard everywhere, to rise triumphant above all other voices. Reasons akin to Copeau's would see intellectuals of a different stripe—Surrealists and Marxist-Leninists among them—also speak from concrete platforms, "concrete" being destined to emerge as a key metaphor in postwar ideological cant. It went together with the visionary's "evidence."

A man violently at odds with himself may generate vast amounts of energy for nought, or embark upon voyages of world exploration in a boat designed to sink, his otherwise superb intelligence dissimulating holes beneath the water line, ignoring reefs dead ahead, plotting abstract courses, evoking heavenly ports of call and, withal, playing the fool to a self-destructive will. Had they been filled night after night by an eager public, even so three hundred and sixty seats could not finance the artisanal corporation that Copeau organized during the 1920 season. Arithmetic soon made this inescapably clear to everyone except Copeau, who had much the same contempt for his box office that bearded stoics of antiquity had for their mouths, regarding it as an ontological defect in the theater, a tare best hidden from view. What difference did arithmetic make when virtue was at stake? And virtue demanded that he be the forlorn infant torn from its mother, that he starve in public, like Kafka's hunger artist, or (however staunchly he would have denied this) bankrupt a hubristic enterprise. If the Vieux-Colombier was "a little thing," its diminutiveness made him proud, he told an American journalist in 1917. "Because it is little, it is pure. Because it is little, it is spirit alone, and pure it must remain. Being only spirit, it has not been defeated by the commercial difficulties that exist during times of war."

In rewinding the clock after a four-year hiatus, in opening a future that challenged him to grow, the armistice marked the resumption of Copeau's war with his patriarchal nemesis. When the government, whose sponsorship had been acceptable three or four years earlier, during wartime, offered him a regular subvention, he would hear nothing of it despite pressure brought upon him by well-intentioned friends. Those who dared to suggest that he do what Antoine had done at the Odéon with (as they saw it) artistic impunity ran the risk of provoking his wrath. "I want no money from financiers; it would bind me," he declared. "I want no state subsidy, it would stifle me." Even if gifts had been given him carte blanche, merely to receive a gift was to entail upon himself crushing expectations, to feel that he owed an account of himself, to recognize a power that would necessarily enslave him. What choice did he have, then, but to find larger premises and earn his independence? Benefactors who offered to finance the construction of a new theater in accordance with his design found themselves treated as sworn enemies:

> The Vieux-Colombier would no longer be for me the living work to which I have devoted my life. . . . I would let it enjoy, under someone else's aegis, a prosperity in which I refuse to participate. It is to real death that you [friends of the Vieux-Colombier] sentence us if you would have us live a factitious life, if you do not respect our thought above all else, if you are unable to see anything but a material resource in that which owes its existence to the spirit, if you want to *exploit the idea of the Vieux-Colombier* before it has reached its maturity, before the *fact* of the Vieux-Colombier has been accomplished.

It became increasingly apparent, however, that the Vieux-Colombier was born never to mature, that the material imperfections of a real stage, the velleities of real actors, and the expedients of public performance filled Copeau with contempt even for his successes, that he felt safe only at a certain inner distance from himself, in the limbo of non-factuality where he stored his Platonic idea of theater and his would-be novel. What frightened him far more than economic ruin was the obligation, the obligation "imposed" by donors, to survive as an entrepreneur.

Copeau met with considerable success. Between 1920 and 1923 tickets for performances at the Vieux-Colombier were so hard to secure that provincials demanded he create a touring company.* Major critics gave him serious attention in the major dailies. His idea found disciples abroad, with Lensvelt in Holland, Pirchau in Germany, and Hume in America all adopting versions of the architectural stage. It was he who represented France at a World's Fair of Theater held in Amsterdam in 1922.

But the judgments passed by those nearest to him tell another story. Whatever Martin du Gard said or left unsaid in person, he wrote the most savage observations in his journal: "Copeau allows himself to be ruled by his taste for the excessive, the theatrical. He has the reputation of being an admirable reader, and no one will ever make him understand that listening to him is more painful than it is agreeable; he brings to mind Diderot's man-orchestra, sweating, puffing, flinging himself about, imitating all the instruments with his nose, his mouth, his fingers. There is charlatanism in Copeau's dramatic taste. An irremediable bad taste."

Martin du Gard likened the actors to elderly whores rehearsing come-ons before a mirror. So meretricious was their speech and predictable their gestural vocabulary that they might have risen mummified from the nineteenth-century melodramatic stage. "Everything, everything," he exclaimed, "reeks of the work of art coldly conceived, coldly executed, of emotion learned and studied." Copeau seemed to him no longer the splendid furioso of 1913 but a despot hectoring people mercilessly while working at cross-purposes with himself. After five months of collaboration as Copeau's amanuensis, confessor, therapist, and script editor, he wrote, in 1920:

---

* The most popular performances were of plays in the classical repertoire: Molière's *Le Misanthrope, L'Avare, Le Médecin malgré lui, Les Fourberies de Scapin, Sganarelle,* Shakespeare's *Twelfth Night,* Carlo Gozzi's *The Princess Turandot,* Carlo Goldoni's *La Locandiera,* Marivaux's *La Surprise de l'amour,* Beaumarchais's *Le Mariage de Figaro.* In addition, Copeau staged with considerable success Chekhov's *Uncle Vanya,* Charles Vildrac's *Le Paquebot Ténacité,* and Roger Martin du Gard's *Le Testament du Père Leleu.*

Everything he organizes is incomplete, improvised, ephemeral. He often has no sense of realities. He deceives himself about people. He often makes a bad choice of collaborators. He is incapable of establishing rules and abiding by them. . . . He commands badly, leaving the impression with his subordinates that he is a capricious, fantastical, imprecise being. He tires those who work with him, demanding suicidal exertions of them when he is himself in full swing, then abandoning them to their own devices; he does not take into consideration the individual's character, his natural weaknesses, his ordinary tastes. He wounds people, lacking the appropriate word and failing to give encouragement when it is due. I hold no brief against him for this, moreover. In his capacity as Director, he is, as in everything else, a *genius* who creates freely, in a dream state, and the apparent capriciousness of his work is the very rhythm of his genius. . . . He is made to invent *mise en scènes*. The theater will function only when it falls into the hands of qualified administrators, enlightened businessmen *who will exploit Copeau's genius.*

In weighing these remarks one must of course give due consideration to the writer's own predicament. Did Martin du Gard, who had hitherto always taken Copeau at his word, anticipate a phenomenon so gloriously original, a theatrical visage so altogether novel that recognizable features made him feel the dupe? Having recently embarked upon what was to be a four-volume saga, *Les Thibaults*, did he perhaps exaggerate Copeau's defects the better to gain distance from someone who otherwise held him in thrall and thereby affirm his own vocation? No doubt self-righteous anger browbeat feelings of guilt with which he could not easily reason. But what he wrote cannot be dismissed out of hand. His caricature—if caricature it was—prefigured bumps and wens not yet visible to a casual eye, for as the life Copeau led became ever more chaotic, the stylistic protocol he enforced onstage became more byzantine. Wrecking friendships with imputations of disloyalty, spurning authors, letting manuscripts pile up unread and unacknowledged, isolating himself in every conceivable way from the outside world, he clung tenaciously to his puppets. "We were witness to something very like the birth and flowering of a dictatorial will," wrote one young actor, Jean Villard, who had no idea that this drama was a consummation rather than an epiphany. After patching up his differences with Copeau early in 1924, Jouvet—another "defector"—reported that "he confided in me that he was fed up, that it all meant nothing, and that all plays were the same."

When Copeau had returned from America, he had straightaway made all necessary arrangements to found a school and educate a "chorus of twelve." This *idée fixe* gradually dislodged every other object and concern, rather like the "white angels" that obsess Balzac's ill-starred genius Louis Lambert (who also couldn't give birth to the masterpiece in him). In September 1920 the Ecole du Vieux-Colombier came true at last, with its brochure designating it a "technical" school. While certain courses like "Theory of Theater" and "Theory of Theatrical Architecture" were open to the adult public, for regular students there was a "closed" curriculum that embodied those very principles Copeau had set forth in 1916 after his mid-war pilgrimage. Now as then, gymnastics and Dalcrozian exercises constituted an initiatory discipline whose purpose was to "tone" bodies, to purge minds, to form sonorous instruments. During three years, apprentices would have no audience. Not until they had become wholly immersed in the *milieu* could they risk exposure to an outside world that lived by values they were taught to hold in contempt. Although they might attend performances given at the parent theater, backstage was off-limits. And although they made periodic excursions to museums, the living streets in between figured as unconsecrated ground. Whatever they did, they did together. Wherever they went, they went en masse, it being Copeau's stated hope that such cohesion would produce a body as well-knit, as mutually responsive, and as disdainful of earthbound life as a family of trapeze artists. In return for the education given him tuition-free, each student pledged to follow courses nowhere else, to act on no other stage, and—should the Vieux-Colombier offer him an engagement—to accept it.

The *acteur total*, that technical masterpiece of Copeau's dreams, came to grief on the conviction he held that success and he were born strangers, that a "finished product" necessarily represented a spiritual calamity. "Journalists expected to see all the features of our original nature drawn clearly on our signboard, like an advertisement," he had written of the first performance ever given by the Vieux-Colombier. "And I laughed at their discomfiture, knowing that we kept our real strength secret, that would discover our originality—if such was our lot—only after prolonged torment, at the end of our labors, like a reward." So, in the late 1920s, when recalling the *Kanton,* the hieratic Japanese drama that was to have allowed the public its first glimpse of his students and to have demonstrated the validity of his pedagogical

theories, he would say: "This *No* play, as I saw it unfold at dress rehearsal, remains for me one of the gems, one of the secret treasures
produced by the Vieux-Colombier, so profound was its scenic understanding, its measure, its style, the quality of its emotion." No one
could disagree, since the dress rehearsal turned out to have been a finale.*

Soon afterward Copeau boarded shut the theater and the school,
declaring that he would not "peddle" his existence from day to day or
lend himself to "suspect dealings." His class had, in effect, toiled three
years to produce an aristocratic entertainment for him alone, a secret
chef-d'oeuvre. If the *Kanton* accomplished his "vision of the future
stage," like his vision (and Craig's "Scene") it was an event that took
place out of time and behind palace walls, a solipsistic image upon
which the vulgar would never lay eyes, a mystery to which money could
not buy admission. The ideal of *poésie pure* landed Copeau right beside
its most illustrious exponent, Stéphane Mallarmé. Directing puppets
through liturgical maneuvers in an empty hall, he created something
equivalent to Mallarmé's blank page. And this blank page was all that
his students would ever receive by way of certification or diploma, for
as the ideal theater had no box office, the ideal school had no exit.
When the *infantes* matriculated, they had done so, unwittingly, for
good. "I left my theater in much the same way that I left my family at
the age of twenty. And the way a man in love leaves his beloved to answer a call more urgent than love. Where that call came from I did not
yet know."

What suggested a connection between his family and his theater
was the play that had cost him more than ten years of intermittent
labor. Copeau finally completed "The Birthplace" in 1923. In December
1923 it had been unveiled by the Vieux-Colombier and found wanting
by the public. " 'The Birthplace'—flop, flop, flop," he wrote to Martin

---

* Several intimates were allowed to witness this performance, among them Gide
who, several years after the fact, noted in his journal: "He appalls me when he declares
that he has never been closer to attaining his goal than in the *No* he has staged . . . and
whose final rehearsals I saw. . . . A play without any bearing on our traditions, our customs, our beliefs in which, factitiously, he brought off a 'stylization' whose fidelity to the
original could not be verified. The whole thing was artificial, made up of slownesses, of
stops, of a straining toward the supernatural in the tone of voices, in the gestures and in
the expression of the actors."

du Gard. "Very weary. But I'm escaping. Soon, I hope, I shall be reborn, I shall grow younger."

A mischievous bon mot that Erik Satie slung at Ravel's music—"Although he has refused the Legion of Honor, all his music accepts it"—might apply to Copeau's professions of irreligion. However much he prided himself in never attending church, his theater was scaffolded on a divine imperative, on a cenobitic model with which his life had always been painfully (though in some ways mercifully) at odds. Unable to produce The Book, he built a Space or a Void that was a monument commemorating his impotence. Endowed with the gifts of a middleman, he would be a middleman to none but God and stripped things bare as if to achieve fulfillment through barrenness, to make a desert his garden and live in it alone. Had he been Adam fallen from Grace, he could not have remembered Eden more vividly or longed for it more stubbornly. Indeed, his *tréteau nu*, above and beyond the justice it did in an aesthetic cause, expressed a hunger no literature could appease, a feeling of loss or of exile so great that it demanded perfect union with his audience. "You have rightly sensed what fascination the idea of saintliness holds for me," Copeau told Alain Fournier's sister, Isabelle Rivière. Wanting to be unique in order to be, he meant to regain Paradise one way or the other, and if not by dint of a prodigious *oeuvre*, then by virtue of a saintly career. These were parallel dead ends, however. As he discovered, a saint without a God had no more claim to transcendence than a writer without a masterpiece. The abstract stage became his prison house.

It took the death of his mother to "awaken" Copeau. Under any circumstances this event would have dealt him a staggering blow but in September 1924, when he was destitute of a theater and a future, it found him especially vulnerable. "I try to spread, round about myself and in secret, the field of the good word. I have had no other ambition since I learned how to pray again at the bedside of my dying mother," he wrote, years later, to Isabelle Rivière. Perhaps it was, in part, the desire for her posthumous companionship that made him a pious man. The "field of the good word" which he "spread round about" himself echoes the deathbed scene in Benjamin Constant's *Adolphe* (a novel he knew very well) where the hero says of Elléonore that "she was still breathing, but already I could no longer confide my thoughts to her; I was already alone on the earth; no longer did I live in that atmosphere of love which she spread all around me."

If he found his mother's faith in mourning his mother's loss, he did not find it right away, for at first his grief fed upon itself hungrily, eliminating palliatives. And furthermore, the part of scapegrace was not to be relinquished without silencing a family quarrel that kept the family alive for him. When, on Christmas Day, Suzanne Bing proposed that they attend midnight mass, Copeau had a temper tantrum. "What was perishing in me was the faculty of loving one's own creation, of believing in oneself, of according one's confidence to others." For the moment he could no longer declare the past null and void, or emerge newborn from the ruins of a ruined enterprise, or summon belief in his ultimate mission. Like previous fresh starts, conversion required a sense of gravitating to an absolute center where he would find his lost identity again, of heeding a Voice that called the orphan home. But that voice was ghostly faint. "I had only myself to call, and I did not answer my call." He who built acoustical chambers had himself fallen out of earshot.

Bereft of self-esteem and melancholy to the point of suicide, Copeau sought guidance from the one author most likely to provide him a role consonant with his lifelong scenario, Paul Claudel, who, since his mystical conversion in 1886, had been evangelizing France through poems and plays while serving the temporal powers as a foreign-service officer with ambassadorial portfolio. Claudel's play The Exchange had, indeed, figured in the Vieux-Colombier's repertoire. "Write to me, I implore you, it does me infinite good, my dear Claudel. I understand now that for a very long time I have been profoundly in agreement with you. The only thing I couldn't do was love you," he wrote in 1925. Loving Paul Claudel was a feat attempted by few and accomplished by fewer still. Stage directors in particular rarely survived collaboration with him unmaimed. Though several years earlier Copeau would have found something akin to his own experience reflected in Gide's confession—"with Claudel I feel utterly deficient; he dominates me; he beetles over me; he has more base and surface than I, more health, money, genius, power, children, faith, et cetera—I think about nothing but tiptoeing away when I'm with him"—what he needed now was to have commands given him by a bully anchored in the conviction that his intelligence came from above. Of course no one could better understand this petitioner than Claudel, whose heroes long to inhabit a musical plenum, to be "legible" or, as one such hero puts it, "pronounced like a word supported by the voice and by the intonation of its speech." * But Copeau did not love his likeness. Rather, he loved a doubt-proof mind that would save him from the wilderness, a puppeteer who would manipulate him as he himself had manipulated others.

What did Claudel, in turn, stand to gain? Ever more substance, ever more bulk. Manipulation on behalf of the Logos was his stock-in-trade, and if his hands had been itching twenty-five years to seize his arch-rival, André Gide, who made a sport of coming within reach then darting free, he eagerly grabbed consolation prizes from the N.R.F.'s inner circle—first Jacques Rivière, and now Copeau. "Yes, one must become Christian, one must stop living apart, one must convert to the universal, one must rediscover the Father, as Philip the Apostle used to say," he admonished Copeau in May 1925. Three weeks later he cast his line once again: "I've just returned from Rome, where I spent much time praying for you in this Jubilee Year when all the doors of Grace are unlocked. . . . Why postpone any longer a thing which you have set your mind to do?" He had clearly taken the measure of this self-hooked fish and gave him no play.

Copeau's tergiversations, rather than indicating a desire to escape, let Claudel know which words would best haul him in. "Conversion is not a matter of splitting hairs, it is above all a necessary thing. Why wait when we are awaited? And everywhere I go I hear about nothing but conversions. All the rest is shadows, confusion, and asphyxia," Claudel proclaimed in midsummer, furnishing the neophyte a syllabus of religious texts to help him recuperate from the depredation of the intellect and from a lifetime spent underwater, without light or air.

Soon afterward, Copeau resolved to do what Claudel once did at a crucial juncture and visit the Benedictine monastery of Solesmes. Claudel bade him go, exclaiming: "What happiness! Thanks be to the Holy Virgin! If you only knew what you have escaped from!" But qualms survived this pilgrimage, the first of two he made in 1925. "Yesterday I saw Isabelle Rivière, who told me about the attack of sorrow and dis-

---

* Mésa in *Break of Noon*.

couragement that you are experiencing right now," wrote Claudel in October. "It doesn't surprise me; all converts have known it and it is inevitable that death throes should precede a new birth. . . . It is absolutely necessary that you respond to the convocation of the life and the light which lies ahead, only one meter away." Copeau's response was not long in coming. "My friend, do not misconstrue my slowness, I beg you," he wrote.

> In my heart there is not the least hesitation, not the least change of feeling. Even the hours of dryness and abandonment do not discourage me. My eye is constantly fixed on a point of light that doesn't vacillate. I give you my word that if, in the very near future, I cannot visit Solesmes again, I shall simply make confession to the country vicar, who is my neighbor and whom I often see. He is a saintly priest. In that case I would go to Solesmes later, with you I hope. Keep praying for me. But have no fears. Suzanne Bing will receive baptism before Christmas, and I hope that several souls will follow suit. I feel the responsibility that God has placed upon my shoulders; I shall not fail Him. . . . I cannot tell you how *happy* I am made by your caring about me. . . . It is appallingly hard not to answer your call straightaway, not to visit Solesmes, Chartres, and Mans with you . . . but you will not punish me by refusing to accompany me later on, will you?

A proselytizer even before he became a proselyte, Copeau finally dragged himself the "last meter" in December at Solesmes, where the Gregorian choir sang praise to God for his conversion. Had God quoted Pascal on that occasion and said "You would not have sought Me if you had not already found Me," Claudel might justifiably have felt cheated of a hard-earned finder's fee, though Copeau's journey had indeed been parabolic, leading him as it did from cloister to cloister, from *milieu* to *milieu*. "Give thanks to God along with me, and let me offer you a handsome place . . . in this heart to whose joy you have contributed," Copeau wrote to Claudel on December 6. "It is rejoicing quietly, deeply, humbly. It is spelling the first word of a sentence which . . . it knows will unfold completely and which will deliver unto it the secret of the universe's logic."

When logic had failed, life had run wild. With faith came the restoration of syntax. What was faith but a phrase assigning everything in creation its name and place, a masterwork to end all masterworks? And

which was the heart that enshrined it if not that of a student at Condorcet, still aspiring to demiurgic eloquence? "A platform and five or six
actors would suffice to relate the Universe," Copeau declaimed on the
threshold of the New Year. His salutation sounds as if it had been
translated from Descartes's Latin: *Mundus est fabula*—"The world is
our story [or play]."

These months of spiritual waffling had been months of physical
wandering, too, for soon after his mother's death, Copeau fled Paris
along with his family, Suzanne Bing, several veteran actors, and thirty
young disciples. Convinced that the capital would "robotize" him, he
made numerous inquiries as to a rural site for his commune before finding one in the Burgundian countryside:

> I settled in Morteuil temporarily, having chosen it for its geographical situ-
> ation and with the idea of wheeling through the hinterland. In those days
> my calling card bore the address "Château de Morteuil" which was noth-
> ing like as fancy as it sounds, the "château" being an old ramshackle af-
> fair. I had taken refuge there with several of the tried and true. . . . My
> withdrawal was not that of a director who lacks money—I was offered
> some—nor that of a man with nothing more to say. It was done instinc-
> tively, out of self-preservation. To live, we had to stage shows in villages,
> on public squares, in markets transformed into banquet halls. What lovely
> memories I have of that experience!

Years later, there emerged a far more lugubrious image of the figure he
cut: "Instead of a good rest home," he wrote, and a rest home is what
he needed, "what devolved upon me was the direction of an abbey that
had no benefice or provisions, no abbot and no God. The sight of all
those faces seeking guidance from mine made me tremble for the first
time." A great one for departures, he was altogether useless at settle-
ments. Like Sir Walter Raleigh sailing across the Atlantic after reading
tall tales he himself had spun in *Discovery,* Copeau, who loathed being
taken unawares, proved to be his own most gullible listener. As the
New World refused to cooperate with Raleigh's Arcadian description of
it, so here in Burgundy nature refused to play providence and succor
free of charge those who nestled in her bosom. Though at first Copeau
taught them history, French literature, and language, it soon became evident that for all his ability to evoke faraway utopias, this mystical
conquistador could neither navigate nor fend, that the flesh-and-blood
colony born of his winged vision was an incubus weighing him down.

Copeau took flight once again, but this time into sickness. "A mixture of fatigue, anxiety, despair, illuminations . . . the toll taken by insomnia, by the utter absence of self-management . . . and anger grumbling in me constantly." If the Château de Morteuil failed to qualify as a sanatorium, it was not for lack of an inmate bent on wishing away the importunate world outside. Urgently summoned by "great future projects" (this, too, a refrain), he let it be known that any demands made of him would go unheard and, after three months, he scuttled the company. ". . . frenetic attachment to ideas, things, customs which those around me judged unimportant. My passion made me ridiculous in their eyes."

Matters did not rest there, surprisingly. Rather than go their separate ways without further ado, six of the student-actors decided to form an itinerant troupe and called upon their sullen master to sanction the venture and lend them whatever costumes they might need. Before long, these "Copiaus," as locals dubbed them, were known throughout the wine region—in Dijon, in Beaune, in Chalon, in Mâcon, in Louhans, but especially in backcountry villages where they would materialize on squares and under marketplace arcades. Doing improvisations on *commedia dell'arte* scenarios adapted by Copeau, miming, singing, executing choral dances, performing eighteenth-century *parades*, they scoured eastern Burgundy like six zanni in search of a context for the ritual maneuvers bred into them. To awaken a primitive "soul," to restore drama to its origins and the cultic mantle that bourgeois had torn from her to nature was their larger purpose. During harvest festivities in the municipality of Nuits-Saint-Georges, for example, they staged a "Celebration of Wine and the Vine," the first of many such "Dionysiae" that would earn them some notoriety (and, forty-five years later, after the events of 1968, inspire Jean-Louis Barrault's *Rabelais*). On this occasion so many people arrived from the neighboring townships that four performances a day could not accommodate them all.

Whether those who came hoped to participate in a primitive revival or to witness a superior freak show is moot, but unquestionably the acclaim given the Copiaus everywhere they went revived Copeau himself from his fitful trance. That creatures of his mind had prospered while he was absent, that the company bearing his name and exploiting his precepts had become happily self-sufficient was a shock to the entrepreneur he could never quite be nor ever quite cease to be. Suddenly galvanized, he wrote brief *divertissements*, one after another, in the spirit of a man eager to prove himself alive by laughing with all his might. But the guffaws—*The Widow*, *The Object*, *The Tax*, *Harlequin the Magician*—were a mirthless noise. They rang hollow, like raps of the chairman's gavel, or so one gathers from Jean Villard, a young actor who felt oppressed as much by Copeau's return as by his desertion. "Everything he wrote was dry, without warmth, demonstrative. . . . He was a theoretician who couldn't give his theories embodiment." When Copeau did not attempt humor, he did worse. He wrote about a suicide that had recently shaken the district and, what is more, acted the part himself with terrible conviction.

Nothing could finally distract this *écorché* from the absolute he sought and had always sought. Conversion did not make him "turn about"; it only straightened the course he set himself early in life. What had been an aesthetic ideal pursued over and against bourgeois society became a doctrinal *summum bonum,* as his followers were soon to discover. After the conversion at Solesmes, Copeau and Copiaus made common cause once again. Having bid good riddance to the dank farmhouse of Morteuil, they transplanted themselves farther north, near Pernand Vergelesses, on a hillside that had formerly been the property of a vintner. "When you return, I shall show you . . . something beautiful on my little Pernand knoll, which is a heavenly place [*lieu d'élection*]," Copeau wrote to Paul Claudel, France's new ambassador to Japan. "A simple house, situated at the apogee, three terraced gardens, a big meadow and . . . a vat house within whose four walls I shall establish my platform." *

Copeau's first proprietary gesture in Pernand was to have geometrical guidelines tattooed on the concrete floor of the vat-house-cum-theater, to consecrate a pattern that would govern movement even in his absence and give holy ground a liturgical center. "The Space," as one might call this enclave, had its counterpart in "The Day," and before long, life under Copeau became monotony itself, with gymnastics, diction, and choral chanting forming an invariable routine, an agenda by which the Master could tell time. Copeau would declare some years later that Paris was a machine, but the pastoral utopia he wrought was in essence mechanical. Abolishing seasons, it let nothing interfere with

---

* "Apogee" is the translation of *en plein midi*, an obvious reference to Claudel's play *Partage de Midi* (*Break of Noon*).

its own fixed cadence. Ignoring repertoire, it upheld an ideal of technical perfection that constrained its virtuoso puppets to practice scales ad infinitum. Canceling all future rendezvous with the outside, it disqualified benefits that only exchange with an audience can provide. "Trade" and "vocation" stood in the same relationship as toil for profit and toil for toil's sake, or "the spectacle-producing machine" and this apparatus which constituted his astringent brainchild. Where "trade" made him feel the ever-hapless, ever-wrathful son, to pursue a vocation was to enjoy the sameness, the inherently objective nature, the dictatorial power of a timepiece. Absolutists thrive on redundancy. Had he been *né* instead of commonly born, Copeau might have found refuge from a usurpative world at Versailles and taken comfort there in Le Nôtre's topiary landscape, in the fountains that pulsed around the clock, in the diurnal rites that Saint-Simon likened to "a machine." Had nature provided him with Pirandello's dramatic genius, he would have begotten a character like Henry IV, who foils time and tide by ducking behind the mirror into a royal persona. Such as he was, doubly disinherited, he made himself a master of ceremonies presiding over abstract space, or the abbot of a puppet theater. "Already in Limon we felt that Copeau had in mind the image of a monastic assembly. He conducted his young troupe, regimented it, like an abbot," wrote Jean Croué, an actor at the Comédie-Française and a childhood friend of Copeau, who had helped him adapt *The Brothers Karamazov*. The entrepreneurial vicissitudes he had experienced since 1913 were like the trade streets that dared not impinge on the visual field of Vieux-Colombier students en route to a museum. If Limon foreshadowed Pernand, Pernand brought Copeau full circle. "Pernand is beautiful," he told Claudel. "There is a beam of God's light on this hill. May it touch all the hearts that surround me. That is my chief concern." On Christmas Eve 1925 he led as many as would follow him to midnight mass at Pernand's medieval church.

After several months, Copeau rarely descended the hill. While his mechanical show unwound down below, up above he became increasingly embroiled in the conflict between ambitions that refused to die and the self-effacement urged upon him by his confessor, between a desire to make himself renowned and a will to achieve silence without tears. No longer did he concentrate on dramatic literature, much less formulate textual analyses of the kind that riveted his original company.

Actors had to petition him now, and when they did so they often found him studying theological works like *The Catechism of the Holy Council of Trent* and Dom Paul Delatte's *The Gospel of Our Lord* or especially Thomas à Kempis's *The Imitation of Christ* which, as he said, "speaks to me like a voice." In 1916, during the midwar holiday from professional life which he described as the happiest years he had ever known, he had told Jouvet: "I would like to put all your books under lock and key, and forbid you the use of them." It is fitting that so perverse a wish should have come home to roost upside down, as it did one decade later, in Pernand, where there were, to all intents and purposes, no books but one (and its commentaries). Wanting more than ever to *be* gospel, Copeau embraced a life of functional illiteracy.* "Imagine the drama of this loner forever pursuing something that kept eluding him," wrote Jean Villard, who took advantage of Copeau's occasional absences from Pernand to join the other Copiaus and improvise *parades* in the neighborhood.

The ignis fatuus that guided Copeau was a prize that he could never, in his own estimation, be either man enough or saint enough to win. "It is true my life has been hard," he wrote to Claudel in March 1926.

> This uprooting and transplantation of what used to be my existence, then this effort to reestablish myself little by little in the face of weariness, poverty, the many discouragements and losses that accumulate in life, and at last this solitude without which I would not have understood that God is there. Ah, dear friend! I have not yet possessed myself of Him! I am very weak indeed, miserable, easily tempted by pride, by frivolity, by the flesh. How many falls I have taken, and to what darkness have I not returned! All the same, my friend, I am no longer spoilt. . . . I am no longer the hell-bent wild man I was. It is no longer sin to which I aspire. I stand up uncertainly, but stand all the same. . . . I am still very ignorant but try to instruct myself.

Beset with a feeling of unreality that would perhaps have vanished long before if not for the protection it gave an angry, terror-stricken child in

---

* After a visit to Copeau, Gide noted in his journal: "I would like so much to see him stop struggling against the Chimera, which now inhabits him, and concern himself with bringing to fruition the literary work about which he spoke to me in Pernand. That, at least, will survive."

him, he combated his illness as only an actor could—by denying himself.

But imitations, even of Christ, were imitations nonetheless, and prayers to Superman were a child's artifice. The role could not be made something other than theatrical, any more than the player could transcend human nature, though Copeau yearned to do both, to induce hallucinations that would make him "whole." Just as he heard Thomas à Kempis preternaturally, "like a voice," so he would visit Assisi in hopes of receiving new eyes from Saint Francis. "A week from now I leave for Rome which I shall be visiting for the first time and where I hope to receive the benediction from our Holy Father. I shall remain there for a week, then spend another—Easter Week—in Assisi," he wrote to Claudel on March 10, 1926. "I expect a great deal from Saint Francis, who has already done so much for me. Everything in me that wanted to be dragged toward God fastened onto Him, to His person. It seems to me that over there I am going *to see Him.*" Leaving his troupe to seek vision on a mountaintop had already become a ritual drama of its own, a rite of passage that led him round and round in ever-narrowing circles.

His loftier exertions did not always distract Copeau from the business at hand. However anorexic he was in the usual conduct of his life, he could still bestir himself to act when not to act would have meant actual starvation. During the 1925–26 season he gave dramatic readings that filled Paris's Salle Gaveau with people many of whom had come as much to gawk at The Martyr as to hear him read Aeschylus, Racine, Shakespeare, and Claudel. One year later he went back to New York City, having been invited to direct Alfred Lunt, Lynn Fontanne, Edward G. Robinson, and Morris Carnovsky in the Theatre Guild's production of *The Brothers Karamazov.** Though having crossed the ocean for a handsome fee proved easier than descending his native hill to lead actors and apprentices (for apprentices had come from all over Europe) who represented a half-loved half-loathed part of himself, even at home the pall that hung over him would occasionally lift. With the Copiaus,

---

* The Theatre Guild made its first public appearance in 1919 at the Garrick Theater, which it took over when Copeau left for Paris. It remained there until 1925 and the opening of The Guild Theatre. Despite its contretemps in New York, the Vieux-Colombier had been a direct source of inspiration to this subscription society for the presentation of uncommercial American and foreign plays.

he toured Burgundy playing Molière's *Le Médecin malgré lui* (*The Doctor Despite Himself*) and took them farther afield, to Italy, Belgium, Holland, Switzerland, and England. A brief spurt of literary activity saw him conflate Fernando de Rojas's *Celestina* and Corneille's *Illusion Comique* into a play entitled *The Illusion,* whose protagonist, a sterile actor jollied up by self-confident young people, spoke to the circumstances of his own life. But there was no jollying up someone so amorously fastened upon the *memento mori* he held before his eyes; movement itself became onerous and the least gesture of self-preservation or social intercourse was an act halfheartedly "performed." He wrote, in reference to the tour with *Le Médecin malgré lui,* that "I felt intimate contact with the joyous crowd of country folk; I served Molière in his own backyard," but the romance of folk culture may have blurred the history of his own melancholia. A letter written from New York in December 1926 portrays him as taxed almost beyond endurance by the necessity to do what "bourgeois" do. "Once more I am a victim of the terrible strain to which I am subjected as a result of having to earn my livelihood," he wrote to Pierre Varillon.

Despite its air of philosophical skepticism, our age offers abundant proof that holiness is still a surer road to artistic and intellectual recognition than self-knowledge, and a moral legend more generally honored than an ambiguous truth. In France, bourgeois society gives highest marks not to its humanists but to its ruthless saints, not to those who stand by it, albeit crankily, but to those who assail it for its appetites, for its enterprise, for its restrictions and freedoms, for its language. The dream of a commune that will merge individual destinies, of a Great Outside where salvation waits in the form of pristine nature or of the Thing-in-Itself is as equally distributed among Frenchmen as Descartes's "common sense." Allowing them the honor of virtue without having them forfeit the pleasures of vice, it explains the official halos that crown *poètes maudits* like Rimbaud, the Surrealists' theology of childhood, the accolades paid to Mao Tse-tung by residents of Paris's fashionable west end, and even the Club Méditerranée, whose founder was genius enough to devise a holiday replete with Rousseauian ornaments.* It has its martyrs, its prelates, its entrepreneurs (publishers

---

* In *The New French Revolution,* John Ardagh writes: "In all the Mediterranean villages you sleep down by the beach in little round Tahitian thatched huts, two or three

most notably). And in Copeau it found an *homme de théâtre* who was all three. "What interests us is what Copeau did by virtue of intransigence," wrote Albert Camus in the 1950s. "It can be summed up succinctly. In the history of French theater, there are two periods, before Copeau and after Copeau. It is for us to remember this and always to make a mental bow to the severe judgment of the only master eligible for the threefold recognition of authors, actors, and impresarios." After death, he became the fulcral moment, the New Dispensation he had always wanted to embody. Springing him free from his enormously complex inner life and producing an hagiological likeness, his survivors did for Copeau what he could never quite do for himself.

The process of consecration began long before his burial, however. As early as February 1926 Antoine proposed that the Fine Arts Ministry name him director of the Odéon, France's junior state theater. Copeau made himself unavailable. Nothing could interest him less, he said, than to follow the "inexorable itinerary" whose point of departure is the avant-garde, whose point of no return is the Odéon, and whose ultimate destination is Père-Lachaise. Three years later his name arose once again, but this time in the Comédie-Française itself, where several actors, unhappy with Emile Fabre's meek custodianship, demanded a general administrator capable of breathing life into the moribund house. Copeau was not deaf to their overtures:

> Lunch with Pierre Fresnay at Igny. He urges me to accept, to consider the question of the Comédie-Française. He knows the latter by heart and offers to enlighten me. His fervor and his straightforwardness shake me. Back in Pernand, I write him that I wish to give the matter due consideration. He answers that this simple acquiescence is enough to make him feel confident of success for in his eyes I am the only one who can save the house from decadence, and that it, in turn, is the only place in which I can bring to fruition what I have begun. The ardor and confidence of this young man awaken me.

to a hut; and many of the more dedicated Club members go around all day in next-to-nothing but a *pareo* (gaudy Tahitian sarong), uniform of the new utopia. In some villages you can also wear flower-garlands. . . . Virtually no money changes hands within the village, save in the form of pop-art beads, worn like a necklace. . . . Everyone, staff and members, calls everyone else *tu* and by first-names (astonishing, for France); and the staff, known as *Gentils Organisateurs* (GOs), help discreetly to imbue the *Gentils Membres* (GMs) with *le mystique du Club* in which many of them apostolically believe."

To awaken, as he did in the following days and weeks, was to entertain a dream much like the one that propelled him to America in 1917. Instead of conquering the New World, he would rejuvenate the Old. Instead of propagating French culture outside France, he would work miracles bound to assure him the ultimate recognition he had always wanted, *malgré lui,* from bourgeois Paris. If Copeau declared it his purpose to serve Molière in the house Molière built, to rid the Comédie-Française of its patina and make it *what it originally was,* this latest rebirth bespoke a yearning for classical honors that the world could never appease.

With the intuitive brilliance he often brought to bear upon Copeau, Roger Martin du Gard warned him:

> I fear for you the influence of this house. . . . I have often sensed in your acting and even more so in your readings, faults which you have valiantly sought to combat and which the tradition of this house generally symbolizes. I have often thought that somewhere inside you you must always have been muttering to your students: "Do what I tell you, for I see clearly; but don't do what I do, for I date back to 1880, I have been nourished in the orchestra of the Comédie, and idiosyncrasies of this rotten theater entered my blood, despite myself, at the most receptive age." Is that totally inaccurate?

Martin du Gard guessed right, though he may not have known of Copeau's first puppet given him by a grandfather who belonged to the Comédie's nineteenth-century claque, or of the ideal paternity this little object had come to symbolize. Always dying and beginning anew, forever creating puppet theaters then deserting them, Copeau was something of the venerable old man and the young child bound up in one mind.

Against Fabre and those "holy monsters" who dreaded the prospects of a regime that promised to crimp their style, Copeau deployed as many big guns as he could mobilize from the literary establishment. "I am immediately writing to Berthelot along the lines you have suggested," Claudel replied to a request he made. "I am telling him all that you did in America and what Otto Kahn has often repeated to me. . . . You are the only French man of theater who enjoys a worldwide reputation. *If it is possible* to extricate the Comédie-Française from the shameful state into which it has been plunged by sorry cretins who uphold the traditions dear to René Doumic, you alone can do it."

In September 1929 the *Nouvelles Littéraires* published a petition to the minister of public instruction and the under-secretary of state for fine arts signed by such luminaries as Gide, Martin du Gard. Mauriac, Giraudoux, Montherlant, Claudel, Cocteau, and Léautaud. Other articles appeared during the fall, including one by Copeau himself entitled "On the Comédie-Française" in which he gave notice of his intention to form a "team." These appeals to the public's sense of aesthetic justice were countered on the one hand by public apathy and on the other by the exertions, in private, of actresses who knew from long experience when best to collect a favor for favors bestowed. The rule has it that most such campaigns are decided below the belt, and this one was apparently no exception. At any rate, Copeau lost not only his bid but his troupe as well, for in June 1929 he bade farewell to the Copiaus, having told himself beforehand and against formidable odds that his "cause" would prevail. Is it mere coincidence that this rural commune lasted only as many seasons as its urban predecessor? Or did a quinquennial cycle represent a lifespan for Copeau? Martin du Gard scolded him in a letter never posted but never destroyed:

> I was upset to learn, quite by accident . . . that what you started in a spirit of self-consecration has once again gone bankrupt. . . . Things can be presented twenty different ways and I know that one can substitute "evolution," a "necessary" or even "beneficial" evolution to what I've termed, too harshly no doubt, bankruptcy. But I who view matters through the coarse eyes of common sense see for the second time a group of beings whom you've taken under your charge abandoned, surrendered to chance and trials, and unhappy with you, despite all that you've done on their behalf and all the sacrifices you've made; but unhappy nonetheless because you had them glimpse the future in a very different light. And in recent days I've been thinking about the cruel misdeeds that have come of your magician's gifts, and of the many victims you've left strewn along the way.

Intentionally or otherwise, Martin du Gard spared his friend in the present and flogged him before posterity.

Among other victims strewn along the road, Copeau left behind a life—his own—harrowed by the god he could never quite embody. Alone amid the relics of a theater school, he was to live in Pernand

Vergelesses for years, feeling half at home there, but half-exiled from Paris, whose ins and outs he registered with mixed emotions. Several alumni prospered in due course—Etienne Decroux, for example; others fell by the wayside. Of Copeau's ability to imprint himself upon them, to have young minds marry the visions he conjured up, none, however, gave more eloquent proof than his own daughter, Edwige, who became a Benedictine missionary, assuming the name Mother Francis. Five years after the Copiaus left Pernand, she was made director of novitiates at the convent of Ambositra near Tananarive in Madagascar, and fulfilled her charge steadfastly.

Copeau had not seen Florence since the days of Gordon Craig. In 1933 he returned for the Florentine May Festival, emerging from semiretirement to direct a fifteenth-century miracle play, *The Mystery of Saint Uliva*. While high above him in the Boboli Gardens Max Reinhardt staged *A Midsummer Night's Dream* with all the material resources at his command, Copeau deployed one hundred fifty actors in a landscape as symbolic and austere as the text he chose—the cloister of the Santa Croce monastery. At the center, surrounding the well, he built a central stage with apron, two lateral stages on either side but pushed forward, and two footbridges joining the central stage in the middle. Actors mingled with spectators underneath the cloister's arcade and, it being a miracle play, strolled all over the earth, changing time and place as they went. "The methods were very simple: when a king presented himself, he was accompanied by two standard-bearers, which sufficed to evoke settings," wrote Copeau's collaborator, André Barsacq. "There was no need to make scenes more precise by means of decor. For a brief episode that took place in a tavern, a stool and innkeeper were enough to convey the illusion perfectly." Situated in a gallery above the cloister, where paradise had been installed, an orchestra and choirs cadenced the action, which unfolded uninterruptedly.

The poor stage had at last found its ideal site, out-of-doors, and indeed, Copeau told Suzanne Bing that "henceforth I cannot see myself working within three walls." No longer restrained by a proscenium arch, the stage filled the entire space, with bridges linking a platform reminiscent of the cubic dais on the rue du Vieux-Colombier to arcades that constituted not backstage entrances and exits but the theater's very boundaries. Ubiquitous, it erased the conventional line that divided spectators from actors who now commingled indiscriminately, all alike having become supernumeraries of the ritual drama unfolding in their midst. To erase this line was to step far beyond it, however, and assault every other line drawn by those Renaissance aestheticians responsible for our "unified stage picture." Staunch in his conviction that theater lost its primitive soul when it deserted the cathedral porch, that it succumbed, indoors, to a rational view of time and space (*les unités*) whose champions set the mind against itself, that it was a "natural" alienated by a bourgeois education, Copeau beheld himself as the apostle chosen to free mankind from a perceptual straitjacket. With actors strolling all over the earth, changing place and time as they went, no barriers remained. Its circularity aside, the universal "stroll" alone suggests how modern this *mise en scène* was in form and purpose, how congenial with, say, Apollinaire's *Zone*, much of Breton's poetry or *Nadja*, and Louis Aragon's *The Peasant of Paris*. Surrealist narratives often seem to take their cue from the miraculous travel literature of medieval saints. Unfolding as the author walks, they are an asyndetic excursion beyond the visible world, or a log of the truant who hallucinates *en passant*, without regard for connectives. "New myths are born beneath each of our steps," declared Aragon. "A mythology takes shape and comes undone. It is a science of life that belongs only to the innocent." There is nothing more characteristic of the virgin traveler than his propensity for erecting a wall between himself and the world while denouncing barriers, for excommunicating infidels while upholding the cause of unrestricted freedom. As Surrealists were governed—wherever their flights of fancy took them—by an essentially hermetic doctrine, so the stage on which actors strolled all over the earth like God's spies was codimensional with a cloister.

In the middle of the eighteenth century another hermit had assailed places where corruption breeds and men hide from one another. It may be appropriate to recall Rousseau's idea that orators of antiquity could make themselves heard by an entire city-state massed out-of-doors, that human history records the gradual diminution or atomization of a single voice. According to this version of the Fall, innocence vanished when a public giant who spoke for all mankind was brought low by dwarfs, each entertaining "hidden" designs and whispering words

Copeau's production of Alessi's play Savonarola *on the Piazza della Signoria in Florence, 1935.* Bibliothèque Nationale

scaled to the bordello and the theater, or when a Whole devolved into a society split between actors and spectators, subjects and objects, surfaces and depths. The civic rites, the Spartan contests which were to replace profane drama and see *le Peuple* affirm itself as a single, indivisible body would mend humankind in abolishing separate pasts. Along with linear time, "growth" and "character" would become obsolete notions, for a corporate identity required an archetypal cast whose scenario would constitute the inner life (the "racial Unconscious" in Jung's terminology) of those reenacting it at liturgical intervals. Just so did Copeau envision a "popular theater." That Rousseau invoked classical antiquity and Copeau the Middle Ages, that one summoned men to celebrate heroes while the other would have had them worship saints were differences less significant than the ontological suit they pleaded in common. Alienated from itself, humankind would regain its original in-

nocence by heeding a Voice—here the *vox populi*, there The Word—
that called upon it to flee cities, to repudiate its cultural legacy, to shed
patronymics, to merge into a choral body. Carried out of time, it would
transcend the personae in which it feigns life and achieve reality as a
divine instrument executing *necessary* gestures.

Copeau did himself one better during the May Festival of 1935
when a production of Rino Alessi's play *Savonarola* sent the chorus
master into full swing. His cubic dais reappeared as a huge cruciform
stage erected on the Piazza della Signoria between the Palazzo Vecchio
and the Loggia dei Lanzi, where Savonarola burned "the vanities" before suffering their fate. Crowds dressed in yellow, green, red, and blue
tunics swarmed round about it. Trumpeters mounted it to sound a
call to arms. Spotlights illuminated now one architectural detail, now
another as the action shifted from a balcony to a window to the stage
itself. Musicians and choruses were in evidence throughout, providing
not only commentary but a beat or tempo that governed every movement. In *son et lumière* Copeau thus paid homage to the friar under
whose ascetically logical regime Florence became the very model of a
Christian city, with promotion of the public welfare a rule of government second only to the fear of God. And he did so, moreover, under a
regime whose leader had stated one year earlier that "Fascism respects
the God of ascetics, saints, and heroes, and it also respects God as conceived by the ingenuous and primitive heart of the people."

The aesthete provided the demagogue a platform on which to bray
melodramatic arias on the New Order, and in turn the demagogue gave
formalist aesthetics a national stage. What Copeau saw in 1915 when
Gordon Craig showed him woodcuts of "Scene" with its monumental
slabs dwarfing human beings was a veritable blueprint of the railroad
stations, the stadia, the government buildings, the tenements that
forested Fascist Italy in 1935.

CHAPTER VIII

✦ ✦ ✦ ✦

ACTORS AT WAR

W̶e are living in heroic times. One must acquire a different soul," Charles Dullin wrote to Elise Toulemon in August 1914, just before he joined a regiment of Dragoons and vanished from civilian life for three years. He was convinced that at last he was participating in what was felt almost universally to be a crusade against the infidel. As theater had "called" him, so did war, now that melodrama spilled out of *théâtres de quartier* and become a national scenario. "I'm fed up, fed up! Fortunately I shall soon put myself in tune with my destiny," he exclaimed, prompting Elise to observe, "The Anarchist turned into a crusader; it's as if, all at once, humanity stopped at the borders of France and England."

Though such conversions were epidemic in August 1914, the one that speaks most eloquently to our subject had taken place several years before and involved Charles Péguy, a Catholic poet greatly admired by Jacques Copeau and Dullin. The French intelligentsia of 1900 had had no more outspoken pacifist than he. During the Dreyfus affair, Péguy had seized every opportunity to admonish France's military establishment and those political leaders who were spoiling for "Revenge." When avant-garde periodicals begrudged him all the space he required or squirmed at the extremes to which his pseudo-incantatory rhetoric sometimes carried him, he founded *Les Cahiers de la quinzaine* and wrote regular jeremiads against the "eternal adultery of soul, of body, of art, and philosophy" committed by a decadent society. From atop his own masthead, he heralded a socialist future that would rid France of "bourgeois vice." This was the position he held until 1905, when Kaiser Wilhelm set foot on Moroccan soil and precipitated the so-called Tangiers Crisis that brought Europe to the brink of war. Péguy thereupon executed a remarkable somersault. France suddenly became virtue incarnate and Germany the evil power that threatened to dishonor it. As vigorously as he had ever assaulted warmongers, Péguy now rounded on pacifists and, accordingly, poured all his messianic energy from the receptacle of socialism into the idea of a purgative struggle, an Armageddon that would settle moral accounts once for all time. The war scare made him realize, as he said, "that a new period had begun in the history of my life, in the history of this country, and assuredly in the history of the world." With one step, mankind reeled from history into metaphysics. Overnight, the temporal continuum was an *ancien régime*, Germany's belligerent maneuver having set the stage for a Final Judgment:

> Every last one of us knew *at the same time* that the threat of a German invasion was present, that it was there, that the imminence of it was real [wrote Péguy in *Our Fatherland*]. It was not news communicated from mouth to mouth, news communicated laterally like ordinary news—it was only the confirmation for each person of news that came from within; the knowledge of this reality spread by degrees, but it spread from one to another like a contagion of inner life, of inner knowledge, of recognition, almost of platonic remembrance, of anterior certitude. . . . The knowledge was total, immediate, secret, immobile, and ready-made.

Responsible for the dissemination of this "deep and secret" knowledge, he went on to say, was an inner voice—the "voice of memory submerged and banked up since heaven knows when." Throughout France there echoed, from within, "an identical sound."

France emerges as an echo chamber of The Word, a community defined by its being within earshot of the parish bells. Though people converse, they do so only to enunciate truths known a priori. Péguy would have it that Kaiser Wilhelm's threat, in stirring "the voice of memory," brought alive the saints, martyrs, and heroes who constitute a family bred into every Frenchman at conception. This family is his "depth." Insofar as civilian life encourages individuality, or divorces the individual it creates from his *born models* by substituting experience for instinctual knowledge, parental authority for natural law, and social discourse for the impersonal Voice, it alienates us. As we "grow up," we each become a *personnage*, a character whose anecdotes are the stuff of bourgeois fiction and whose patronymic is an alias. When compatriots follow not the dictates of conscience but the orders of an inborn faith that transcend moral codes, then they will have retrieved their depth. Bourgeois society fashions self-estranged actors who may win their birthright in the holy war that opposes an hieratic interior to the aimless reaches of outer space and immortal archetypes to generational time.

"One doesn't give a damn about virtues. What one requires of the warrior is not virtue. And what Joan of Arc required of her men was not virtue but something incomparably different—the Christian life. Ethics were invented by the puny and the Christian life was invented by Jesus Christ," Péguy wrote one year before World War I in *Money: Sequel,* a collection of diatribes directed against the intelligentsia and "the reign of money." Calling men away from the trades they ply and the professions they exercise, war is a vocation in the religious sense, one that induces all to merge with the sacred motherland as embodied by a female warrior:

> France is not only the Church's elder daughter . . . she has, in the lay realm, a parallel vocation, she is undeniably a kind of patroness and witness (and often a martyr) of liberty in the world. In the Christian realm, in the sacred, she is keeper of the faith. . . . But in the lay realm (I do not say profane, mind you), in the lay and perhaps in another kind of sacred realm, the civic . . . she is undeniably keeper of that freedom which is the very condition of grace, which is bound to grace by singular and obstinately mysterious ties.

Joan of Arc's campaign and the Revolutionary battle of Valmy amount to coefficient episodes in this melodrama of embezzlement and sacred trust that illustrates France's uniqueness. They are a single idea repeated paradigmatically, a scenario whose roles never change but whose revolving cast simulates linear movement and temporal expanse. Try as the bourgeoisie may to objectify growth, accumulation, and progress, God reveals his hand at certain moments when the social fabric is suddenly rent, when timepieces go haywire and human affairs come full round in an *Ur*-play that shows Caesar's descendants still conspiring against the divine prodigy, or temporal powers still laying siege to a fortress of innocence. Inside one historical narrative, the "profane," there is another, the "real," which moves from battle to battle, each chapter reiterating a virgin birth that emancipates humankind from the tyranny of years. Truth emerges only at beginnings and ends; woven in between is a tissue of lies.

Péguy spoke for the *grand premier rôle* screaming to be let out of society's countless supernumeraries. Alsace and Lorraine, which Germany had annexed forty-three years earlier, became a universal *casus belli* not only because they were political and economic trophies but because they represented the stature of which men felt bereft, the destiny absent from days that did not add up to something more than existence. In this respect time had stood still since 1870, when Henry Adams, who was in Paris during the first days of the Franco-Prussian War, observed that "patriotism seemed to have been brought out of the Government stores, and distributed by grammes *per capita.*" A war fought on behalf of dishonored France fulfilled the longing for a heroic imperative and for physical magnitude. "We do not know whether we shall be happy, but we know that we shall not be small," declared Péguy. Besides inflating men overnight, the call-to-arms sprang them free from the coils of the past. Though many held no brief against Germany, how many others rushed eastward with white carnations protruding from their gun barrels, like the mob descending from La Courtille on Mardi Gras with flowers in their lapels, or celebrating Year I in a procession toward the Sublime Mountain! For such as these, to be collectively gigantic was to rejoice in the power of trampling history underfoot and beginning life anew, unencumbered by civilization's accoutrements. "Familiarity with danger and a genuine contempt for death place us well above the average lot that once sufficed for us. Let us therefore kill 'the old man' and 'the old woman' definitively," Charles Dullin wrote to Elise in 1915, proposing a kind of suicide pact fraught with Platonic intimations. "I know that my place is here, that I love you more being here than heeding my heart and senses."

In Dullin, whose theatrical initiation had taken place at an early age when he saw his sister Pauline impersonate Saint Joan in a school play, Péguy would have found a kindred spirit, had he survived the Battle of the Marne. Time, it would seem, had left intact the horrible picture of Pauline surrounded by flames, for no less irresistible than the passion Dullin felt was his need to chasten it, to give the *odor femina* an odor of sanctity and make his mistresses martial virgins. With Dullin, patriotic ardor fed on self-denial as fire on flesh. "There was something ugly in our lives, something evil. . . . Now the sacrifice has purified everything," he wrote to Elise from the front, adding, several months later: "For five months I have searched in vain the realm of my old ideas for something stable, durable, true. After encountering every imaginable mirage and discrediting every one of my speculations, I return soberly to the basic instincts, *to that which speaks in us through senses we know nothing of* [italics added]—love of country, love of my race, of French soil, love pushed to the ultimate sacrifice. It is in this very love that I have reserved a special place for you." Just as the artisans he met at the front were, in his description, "born" actors endowed with knacks, gestures, and information passed down from the medieval fairground, so here he contends that Frenchmen owe their identity to a voice speaking from a hidden place inside them. They love and hate, kill and sacrifice their lives for "impersonal" reasons, each one playing a role in the collective drama written by nature or God. Where his conscious mind produced mirages, "senses we know nothing of" told him the gospel truth. As unacquainted with him as he was with it, this hermit instinct—blind yet infallible—bore an unmistakable resemblance to the pyrophobic uncle Joseph by whose maxims he set store.

Another voice from his childhood home in Châtelard enjoined him to meet his destiny at the front. Jacques Dullin's nocturnal *ceterum censeo*—"The Republic summons us/Let us prove that we can conquer and die like men"—had not been lost upon him; that this stoic lullaby still contradicted the impulse to embrace a more lenient fate even as it conjured up images of the Outlaw Justice or the powerful Avenger is borne home by Charles's correspondence. "I would like to have you share my courage that our separate wills be but one. How much stronger I would be if I knew that you were above frailty. . . . The moment is near when we shall all have our reward. . . . Soon Germany will be obliged to yield before our implacable decision to conquer or to die," he wrote to Elise in 1915. "The war has above all stripped me of the artificiality that, willy-nilly, encumbered my spirit." However unendurable trench-life often was, danger did not bother Charles so much as the war's monotonous truces—or not during the early going—for

danger gave him an emotional fillip without which he was apt to feel insubstantial. Where life hung constantly in the balance, there were no
tenses to accommodate self-doubt or reflection, only moments, each one
isolate and sufficient, each one a beginning and an end. On this battle-
line that cut a savage swath across old Europe, instinct exercised
supreme rule, as on the melodramatic frontier. What men did outside
time they did *necessarily,* in the manner of puppets. "It's a rough
school, don't you see, and pity those who will not have profited from
it," he wrote. "Aside from . . . beautiful movements dictated by instinct, from spontaneous gestures that lift men well above his condition
and his state, I no longer believe in anything. Morality! Duty! Religion!
Bah!"

The semblance of peace readmitted time, and time the hum-drum
world. "Our life is as flat here two hundred meters from the Boches as
the life of a salesman in the Galeries Lafayette," Dullin complained during one quiet stretch. "I am filled with greed for life." Similar feelings
had assaulted him years before when he stood behind a counter in
Lyons pretending to sell woolen goods while feeling inwardly squashed
by his fall from Châtelard. The plateaus and slopes that mark his ideological terrain—with noble savages organized round a vertical axis and
bourgeois pinioned to a horizontal—portray his abiding nostalgia for
home, or rather, for that which had come to represent a heroic age
undone by the merchants, teachers, notaries, and lawyers who dwelt
below, in cities of the plain. "What would we have done without our
childhood?" he asked Pauline. Other poilus sought consolation from
priests, but Charles read and reread *The Charterhouse of Parma* whose
would-be hero he regarded as his spiritual twin.* Fabrice del Dongo
reaching young manhood just in time to join Napoleon's army at Waterloo, Fabrice borrowing identities and playing bandit, seeking danger
or flying from it, dodging across boundary lines and retreating to a
tower cell from which he communicates with his inamorata in sign
language—these were all modes of himself, who felt that he had likewise been born too late.

Born "too late," the temporal outsider cannot find purchase on the
God-forsaken ground where beliefs prove mortal and knowledge is

---

* Stendhal's novel enjoyed a considerable vogue during the war.

bought piecemeal, where appearances belie reality and where what is yet to befall him looms overhead like a threat of expropriation. Holding himself aloof, he proclaims his sacred origin in lamenting his belated arrival, for to have no other life than some life already lived is to have a "destiny," albeit one whose line extends backward from the grave. The history he invokes furnishes him a script at birth. As it starts with paragons, so it ends with them; distributing roles, it constantly rehearses a teleological itinerary, and, like its actors, progresses toward a beginning. (Were not the Revolutionaries who laid claim to the essence of Plutarchian hero-saints while declaring 1792 Year I *déjà vécus*?) Over against the historical continuum perpetuated by laymen—by bourgeois—there endures the tradition of a scriptural birth that disqualifies plurality and, like some force of nature, works havoc on all preexistent values, laws, customs, bonds.

It is in this tradition that the actor seeks redress for the sense of unreality that torments him. "I form an enterprise that has had no precedent and shall have no imitator," proclaimed Jean-Jacques Rousseau at the outset of his *Confessions*. "A new period had begun in the history of my life, in the history of this country, and in the history of the world," wrote Péguy after the Tangiers Crisis. "I shut books [that interest me] in order to imagine new things," Copeau told Martin du Gard. So with Dullin. Despite the peasant cunning that would serve him very well indeed, he was inclined to fancy himself a law unto himself—when he did not behold himself as a forgettable afterthought. "I am disorder," he declared to Elise by way of reproaching her her desire for material security:

> I am a bohemian, and not a Murger bohemian, but a real one, who follows the highroad. I cannot give any positive thought to the future. For me money is just metal that must straightaway be bartered for pleasure. Since I am not a fool, I have given some thought to ridding myself of this taste for disorder (and I *am* disorder), but I have not succeeded. These two years of war which have altered me in so many respects have not changed me in this one. I am, if anything, more bohemian than ever, for fate, to which we must constantly entrust ourselves, has obliged me to live with the idea that everything is unstable and that one must not attach overly much importance to possessions from which one can be separated at any moment.

To his sister he wrote, "I would like to remain young and never know the sluggishness of heart and mind called maturity." Though his remarks should dispel any doubt that the crusader and bohemian were congenial bedfellows after all, what they also imply is a dream of omnipotence that thrived on warfare. Telling time and counting money would not have been so abhorrent if such acts did not oblige him to acknowledge his place in a finite world. Maturity would not have made him so despondent if the sluggishness attending it did not forebode death. Where "bourgeois" reckoned, Dullin clasped "fate." They lived by the social calendar; he, on the other hand, extemporized himself, denying growth, change, experience, and loss as if this retinue of prospects might evict him from the stronghold of his self. Like Rimbaud's systematic befuddlement (le dérèglement systématique de tous les sens), the "disorder" to which Charles laid claim went far beyond disorderliness; at issue was not merely a way of life but a beatific state that would abolish grammar, repeal civil law, and overturn the world created by middle-class rationalists. As naked as faceless clocks men would recover their prelapsarian nature under this new Dispensation. "I can no longer bear constraints, I know that I have become violent . . . that I am destined to live like a savage, apart, but I have the courage and will to assume the terrible consequences of my predicament." Timeless, a savage has no contemporaries.

After twenty-five months of grooming cavalry horses, slogging through mud, and entertaining troops, Dullin grew weary of fighting the good fight. For one thing, Elise, whom he once admonished to divorce herself from "the culture that has left its mark on you lest it drain your energy and domesticate you" had taken him at his word; instead of knitting him sweaters, she was, as he learned during an impromptu visit to Paris, making love with the Viscount lieutenant B. (among others). But the loss of his would-be Muse proved less disheartening—and certainly less irremediable—than the fate reserved for Bonnat, Galvani, and Levinson, those comrades from the Saint-Antoine quarter of whom he wrote that "they were remarkable at improvising *commedia dell'arte* scenarios. . . . Our life consisted of nothing but games and slapstick routines. The most tragic situations, the misery of the trenches, the mud, the cold, the snow, death itself were food for farce." By 1917 Galvani had become a civilian, Bonnat a drunkard, and Levinson a corpse. The disintegration of his little "pirate band" left Charles alone and vulnerable, more vulnerable, indeed, than he had ever felt.

When, late in 1916, Copeau first told Dullin about plans afoot to cross the ocean, America sounded like a shibboleth. "I am proud of the Vieux-Colombier, proud to have been one of the first, and all my projects are inseparable from yours," he wrote. "You need not entertain any doubts whatever on that score. I would lay down my life for you." Copeau, who understood full well that this vassal oath couched a demand for protection, used what influence he had on Dullin's behalf, but to no avail. Neither service rendered nor an orthopedic disorder working invisible hardships upon him nor, finally, the endorsement of Philippe Berthelot at the Propaganda Bureau could mollify the powers that were. Thrown upon his own resources, Charles devised a scheme that saw him bring to bear all the experience he had gained onstage and off in a variety of *grand guignol* roles. Just as he had outwitted his ecclesiastical jailer at the seminary of Pont du Beauvoisin by feigning piety, so now, twenty years later, he earned a discharge from the Army of the East by simulating madness. "Je fais le dingo," he told a fellow actor who met him in Paris, where he had been sent to undergo observation at the Salpetrière Hospital—"I'm playing daft." Ironical though it may seem, no irony was intended in a letter he dispatched to Pauline while rehearsing his war-traumatized persona. "Those who think, who see, who cannot blindfold themselves or get drunk have recourse to Reason, and with fatal results, for directly they reason, they are sunk. War is a matter of feeling and instinct. Heroism is a sublime madness, but it is a madness," he wrote. Those "senses we know nothing of" could be a patriotic oracle justifying utter self-sacrifice or a lawyer pleading innocence by reason of insanity.

Before long, when the memory of its stench and gore had faded, heroism reemerged in all its sublime disembodiment. If Dullin had his wits to thank for assuring him a future that would provide him madman roles such as Sigismundo, Richard III, and Lear without having him risk death, he concealed this fact even from himself, lest he jeopardize his dearest belief that the stage and the battlefield were cognate domains ruled by Instinct, by Nature—by *la folie sacrée*. "Acting is not always a function of the actor's intelligence but of his instinct. Indeed, an actor who exercises his critical faculty while acting is sunk," he asserted some years later, repeating almost verbatim the language of his wartime note to Pauline. What distinguishes the hero distinguishes the great actor. Where average men calculate and maneuver with the hearth in mind, heroes are as incapable of domesticity as the fire that burns

Achilles. Where common men have "motives," heroes—those divine *guignols*—immolate their personalities the better to attain a sublime sphere, to embody a god, and thus become themselves. "The actor-hero is the very basis of theater and of all theaters. . . . Melodrama was a proving ground for actors who could play representative types of humanity, who preserved heroic models." By playing the madman, Charles may have saved his life. By claiming forever after to have been wounded in battle, he saved himself not only from public disgrace but from invidious comparisons with the namesake who set him an example of utter self-sacrifice and from those yeomen-soldiers who knew better than he how to conquer and die.

Then again, the red and the black could ill afford a front like Flanders, where war itself had become *le banal quotidien* after three gruesome years and death one more commodity mass-produced by bourgeois machines. It would not be surprising to discover that Charles's copy of *The Charterhouse of Parma* was dog-eared at this passage:

> Ah! Here I am at last, in the line of fire! Fabrice said to himself. I have seen fire! he kept repeating to himself with satisfaction. Here I am, a real soldier. At that moment, the military escort was advancing on its stomach and our hero realized that what was making the earth fly every which way were bullets. In vain did he look in the direction from which the bullets were coming, he saw white smoke rising from an emplacement far off in the distance and, amid the steady, continuous roar of cannon, he seemed to hear discharges nearby. He understood nothing at all.

For like Fabrice, whose Epinal images always clash with reality at Waterloos of one kind or another, Dullin would sooner flee than forswear the world as he had known it in childhood. And, like Fabrice, Charles was by turns actor and voyeur, the Bandit-Hero foraging abroad and the One-and-Only's One-and-Only hanging on a glance. Inhabited by a model of which he himself was the misshapen reflection, Charles did not speak lightly when he said, as he once did, that the actor's vocation is "to embody ghosts." Nor did he fashion an idle metaphor in writing that "the stage is a world outside the world, a sordid and wondrous hayloft; the intersection of corridors and boxes, never will it be the reproduction of a bourgeois interior." His strongest dramatic affinities were invariably for some play that involves a siege and some character reborn without those inner barriers separating function from function or person from person, as in a city flat. He favored Ibsen, Pirandello, Claudel, and Sartre, writers who, however idiosyncratic each in his own right, all celebrate epiphanies that set theater against home, that do violence to the established order of things, arrest time, and, withal, make men strangers to themselves.

So it was that while Copeau beheld himself as a missionary propagating the aesthetic faith overseas, Dullin, who arrived five months after everyone else, in March 1918, came to the New World as its native son and hastened to dress *comme il faut*, assembling a wardrobe that included chaps, a bandanna, a cowboy hat, boots, and a red checkered shirt. Internal strife, the labor of fifteen plays staged in as many weeks, a largely unappreciative public, material woes, the bustle of New York, and the strain of commuting between two separate ménages—all these had already ravaged Copeau, whose letters home narrated his despair in phrases like "It's hard being here. Don't envy us too much. It's hard" and "There is no public here. It's the desert. . . . We work like convicts sentenced to hard labor." * Not Dullin but he, Copeau, looked the warweary veteran, a paradox accompanied by other, even larger ones that would, as we have seen, play havoc with their friendship.

Having backed himself into a corner, Copeau took considerable pains to thwart prospective liberators. He found Dullin's presence unexpectedly irksome. No doubt *le maître* embraced in Charles a crowd of brilliant impersonations that he hoped would seduce hard-nosed critics like John Corbin of *The New York Times*, who wrote: "During the season not one feminine performance has made a really memorable impression. . . . The company is distinguished on the male side, yet it

---

* On February 8, 1918, Agnes Copeau wrote to Hélène Martin du Gard: "If life in New York can seem hard and charmless, at least this desert of stone is inundated with sunlight. Never have I seen so bright a city. . . . I can't imagine ever again living in a dark and airless little Parisian apartment. The children are doing admirably well, thanks, I believe, to this climate, which is rigorous (the temperature went down to twenty-seven degrees below zero) but dry and fortifying. . . . If Jacques consents to remain through next winter, he will have to work in better material conditions. He has been obliged by the system of weekly subscriptions to mount a new spectacle every fortnight and often every week! You understand that for someone with his conscience and lofty ideal of dramatic perfection, this has been abominable. I have never seen him so depressed as on certain days preceding a first performance. . . . We have known some bad hours in this impassive New York."

seems no one is capable of sustaining capital parts. This was virtually
admitted by M. Copeau . . . when he said he is expecting the arrival of
an actor who will play Harpagon." In appeals to the public, which
bought subscriptions by the week rather than by the year and whose
favor therefore required constant currying, Copeau waxed hyperbolic as
he called Dullin "the greatest actor in the world." But the master's
embrace could no longer contain his protégé's high spirits. If Dullin in
Molière's *L'Avare* (*The Miser*), Ibsen's *Rosmersholm,* and Dostoevski's
Brothers Karamazov suffered orders given him by a director, Dullin in
the offstage cowboy role he prized above all others was proof against
direction. "I can no longer bear constraints, I know that I have become
violent and pessimistic; that I am destined to live like a savage," he
declared, addressing himself as much to Copeau as to his sister.

Did Copeau shrink from this enthusiast who had burst upon him
like an errant bombshell? The sight of him shrinking may well have inspired Charles to expand with a vengeance. "Oh, how I should love to
show you this country!" he exclaimed to Pauline soon after his arrival
and his triumphant debut in *L'Avare:*

> How wide you would open your eyes and feel, as I do, that men are crazy
> to settle in any one place. All the tales that filled us with wonder when we
> were children, all our greatest dreams of adventure are possible after all.
> But we root ourselves in a corner and end up believing that that corner is a
> world. Whereas the world! . . . Men complain that they aren't happy.
> They don't admit that they usually have only themselves to blame. Lacking
> imagination and daring, they fail to recognize their potential until caught
> in a mesh of circumstance. Among the thousands of heroes who died for
> their country, how many suspected themselves capable of such a great
> thing? The same is true of voyages, of life. . . . This country exalts me
> tremendously and I admire it. Copeau does not share my view, but he is, at
> heart, less alive than I am. He is a literary type who prefers books to
> reality.

Underneath the reverence he had always had for the erudite
Copeau lay feelings of resentment that surfaced abroad where he, unlike
his director, who spoke English fluently, was incommunicado. While
Copeau's literary culture enabled him to form bonds in the avant-garde
community, as with the Washington Square Players and the Neighborhood Playhouse, Dullin found himself reduced to childish blather and
complete dependence.

Pedestrians who encountered Charles on Thirty-fifth Street in full cowboy regalia would have been hard put to believe that before them stood a champion of reality; but then, Charles had small regard for people on foot. From his viewpoint, America transcended its two-legged inhabitants, its cities, its business, its language. It was a picture show, a silent Western of epic duration. The real front, the front that did not materialize in eastern France, where industrial warfare made *cran* (pluck) an obsolete virtue and cavalry charges a suicidal tactic, had receded to the never-never land conjured up in cowboy films by William S. Hart, alias Rio Jim, whom Charles found positively exalting. Bred on popular folklore, Charles modeled himself after the virtuous brigand, the fugitive bound to flight as Mazeppa to his horse. He learned no English abroad—did Rio Jim ever speak? was Mandrin known for his proverbs?—but taught himself, instead, to throw the lariat.

With the same persistence that saw him tame his father's stallion, then, somewhat later, learn to project his feeble voice well beyond its range, Dullin now set about lassoing everything lassoable. "I should like to have a photograph of Papa. I often think about him. I understand him. I feel in myself the strong quality of his race. I should like to resemble him. I hope that I shall not have put to bad account the virtues he left me and that I could face him again today without blushing," he wrote to Pauline. "I am happiest when in my stable with my dog and my horse. I love silent communication with the life of animals and plants, and I believe that words spoil everything." Being told that he had William S. Hart's profile flattered him more deeply than repeated curtain calls at the Garrick and encouraged him to apply, without success, for cowboy parts at the various film studios then located in New York.

His request for Jacques Dullin's photograph was also an oblique disclosure of thoughts that do not normally visit the chaste paladin. Charles had recovered from Elise Toulemon by falling in love again, this time with Marcelle Jeanniot, a statuesque woman of upper-class breeding whom he had met, several years earlier, through her lover, the poet Léon-Paul Fargue. Odd couple though they were, this inveterate garret-dweller and the divorcée for whom he had set his cap (threatening that if she did not follow him to America, he would become a cowboy and never return), it seems that they found in each other what they urgently needed—Charles an alluring *salonnarde* six years older than he who would desert café society for love of him yet bring from it a sheen and poise he admired despite his protestations to the contrary; and Marcelle a young zealot who would seize her, along with her daughter, as she was about to drift aimlessly past forty. Their love affair had begun in Paris, with Léon-Paul Fargue cursing the day he introduced them. To Jacques Copeau's consternation, it flowered in New York. Marcelle soon learned what Elise could have told her beforehand, had they been on speaking terms, that "Copeau . . . pretended to help Dullin avoid the snares laid by women and barred them from the chapel in which Dullin, his prodigy, had to endure constant purification." But Charles would not play Tamino to Copeau's Sarastro. Convinced that Marcelle was a born actress, despite the fact that she had no practical experience of the stage, he made Copeau award her several minor roles, lording it over his director, who he felt did not appreciate him sufficiently, while serving his ladyship. And when, in due course, Copeau peremptorily dismissed Marcelle, Charles followed on her heels, like the gallant

> ". . . toujours en marche, attendu qu'on moleste
> Bien des infortunés sous la voûte céleste." *

Their marriage took place in November 1918, nine months after their mutual banishment, Marcelle having already assumed by then a different name, a stage name that Dullin must have chosen for her. Sworn to the virgin who suckles heroes, Charles wed not only Marcelle Jeanniot but "Francine Mars," and joined battle once again, arm-in-arm with a breast-plated, helmeted partner.

Coming home in February 1919, he might well have felt that four years away had sped him from youth to superannuation. Certainly Paris, which can be the most inhospitable of cities, did not greet him with fanfares. On the Butte, where Père Frédé's great white beard had become a biblical relic evoking Montmartre's Heroic Age among garish

---

* ". . . always on the march, for there are always unfortunate beings molested beneath the celestial vault."

honky-tonks, he went largely unrecognized, while down below, on the
Left Bank, or on as much of it as fell within the Vieux-Colombier's
sphere of influence, he was actively shunned. Copeau would not let
bygones be bygones, not yet anyway, and a letter like this one marshaled opinion against the renegade: "Perhaps you know, Roger, that I
had to dismiss Dullin, who conducted himself toward me like a ham
actor [cabot]. I recall that you were the first to tell me that he was one.
If you happen to meet him before my return, I would have you make
him feel that his break with me is a break with everything touching
me."

Whose support, then, could Charles enlist? As determined as he
was to do what Copeau had done at Limon, he could barely feed himself, much less organize a troupe, for the economic debacle that followed the war made works of faith more expensive than hitherto, and
pauperdom more dire. He had begun to despair of ever finding employment outside domestic drama, which meant the Boulevard, when, quite
suddenly, fortune extended him a helping hand. In 1906 the helping
hand had been André Antoine's. Now it belonged to Antoine's erstwhile
shadow, Firmin Gémier, who had long since affirmed himself as a notable director in his own right. While Copeau scorned the cabot, Gémier
befriended Dullin the more spontaneously for befriending a younger
version of himself, a latter-day product, if you will, of the uncouth
tradition that had shaped him as well. He gave Charles courses to teach
at his Syndicalist Conservatory—a conservatory for the unprivileged—
and soon thereafter engaged him to play major roles in a repertory theater called the Comédie Montaigne.

Gémier had made his theatrical debut in 1888, when he was nineteen, at the Théâtre de Belleville, which stood not far from Auber-
villiers, a working-class suburb in which he had been born to poor inn-
keepers who had hoped that he would do something more respectable
with his life than act it away. When Dullin was a mere tot Gémier was
already second dagger on the suburban circuit, infuriating spectators—
some of whom would still be there seventeen years later, in Charles's
day, hissing and spitting from the peanut gallery. Like Dullin, Gémier
failed an audition (indeed, two auditions) for the Conservatoire. And

like Dullin, he rode round and round Paris's suburbs, unable to enter the city until a fortuitous meeting in 1892 gave him the right vehicle. The Théâtre Libre, which Antoine had launched with a motley collection of amateurs, long on enthusiasm for naturalist literature and the cause of social justice but short on histrionic talent, was almost as much Gémier's creation as it was Antoine's. Between 1892 and 1895, he, more than any other actor except Antoine himself, came to embody the public image of "a slice of life." Performing major roles in works by the naturalist school, month after month, enabled him to display a virtuosity of self-metamorphosis that left agog even those who did not undertake voyages beyond the Boulevard and the Comédie-Française without trepidation, or who undertook them more to see "what strange things come out of Africa" than to witness anything that would have qualified as an artistic event. All of Paris' critical eminences—Francisque Sarcey, Edmond Rostand, Jules Lemaître—were lavish in their praise.

But none had praise for him on December 10, 1896, when it was borne home upon these conservative gentlemen that a new era was violently to desecrate the ground they occupied, that theatrical sanction given to the lower depths was to legitimate not only a lumpenproletariat but a forbidden language, and not only the *milieu* in all its circumstantiality but, worse still, the dream life in all its lawlessness. On December 10 Gémier played the title role in the first performance ever of *Ubu Roi* (*Ubu the King*), a play that unfolds, as its author told the audience beforehand, "nowhere."

For some years Gémier revolved about Antoine like a satellite within the magnetic field of a larger body. When Antoine lost the Théâtre Libre, Gémier secured engagements elsewhere, only to disengage himself soon after Antoine was appointed director of France's chronically moribund state theater, the Odéon. When Antoine quit the Odéon, Gémier improvised a separate existence until his patron reacquired the Théâtre Libre—or the Théâtre Antoine, as it was called thenceforth, When, finally, Antoine left the theater that bore his name in order to become director of the Odéon once again, on whom should direction of the Antoine have devolved if not on Gémier?

Gémier's epicyclical career between 1896 and 1906 took him farther afield, however, than so bald a résumé would suggest. In 1903, for example, the Swiss canton of Vaud invited him, at Romain Rolland's behest, to organize a pageant celebrating its hundredth year of membership in the Helvetic Confederation. This event greatly enhanced the figure he cut back home, especially as word of it coincided with the publication in France of Rolland's *Theatre of the People*, a book half-treatise half-tract, advocating theater for and by the populace. Gémier found favor not only among theatrical reformers but among Socialist intellectuals like Jean Jaurès and Aristide Briand, the co-founders of *L'Humanité*. It was, indeed, Briand who, directly he became minister of public instruction and worship, induced Antoine to make the Odéon a naturalist arena (guaranteeing him complete freedom) and to name Gémier his heir.

In January 1910 the magazine *Comoedia* reckoned that during three and a half seasons at the Antoine Gémier produced 149 plays by 103 authors of whom 79 had never before had plays produced. Such numbers did more than bear witness to Gémier's nineteenth-century appetite, or to his affinity for the uninitiated; they reflected a nature that could barely tolerate the scope of a conventional play, the apron of a proscenium stage, the walls of an indoor theater, and even the limits imposed by an urban site. It is difficult to appraise Gémier without having recourse to numbers because quantity and size, far from being extraneous considerations, lay at the very heart of his theatrical enterprise. Where Copeau, who set store by voids, contrived to grow smaller and smaller (until his Florentine *mise en scènes* made it clear what he was about), Gémier settled for nothing less than the multitude. Where Copeau sought to denude the stage of flesh, Gémier, a spirit likewise obsessed with totality, could not flesh it densely enough. Much as he loved the Théâtre Antoine, which stood on the boulevard de Strasbourg near the arch that leads to the Saint-Denis district, time spent there was a frenetic interlude between pageants past and future. His vision required space, space such as he had been able to deploy for the Vaud festival of 1903 when, outside Lausanne, in an amphitheater surrounded by lanes that bore the traffic of twenty-four hundred actors who spread out beyond an immense stage overlooking the Lake of Geneva, he retraced the canton's history since the Middle Ages in a daylong pageant. What had given him most satisfaction during this spectacle was the moment at which "the entire Vaudois population followed the cast's example and, rising, took part in the action." Soon afterward he was summoned to Geneva for a similar pageant. "It was less impressive than the one in Lausanne as it involved a cast of only sixteen hundred actors."

A crowd scene in Firmin Gémier's production of Timon of Athens
at the Théâtre Antoine, 1911. From Le Théâtre

From these ceremonies—mating elephantine cast with elephantine
audience—there sprang the idea for a theater unrestricted by season,
neighborhood, or province that could move at Gémier's command, like
la maison du roi, and enable him to make all of France his audience. Be
it noted that this idea was not his alone, nor his originally. Several years
earlier, Catulle Mendès, the poet who championed Wagner's music-
drama in France, had written that "there is not in any given location a
fervent crowd sufficiently large to nourish a low-cost theater throughout the year; but there is *everywhere* a crowd sufficient to keep such a
theater in style. Directly a theater is no longer rooted in some one place
. . . then the difficulties that arise from the need for a numberless
public will be literally effaced." It remained for Gémier to give the
vision material shape. On Bastille Day 1911, after collaborating with

288 THEATER AND REVOLUTION

two engineers for eighteen months, he unveiled the Théâtre National Ambulant, which consisted of a collapsible playhouse (not a tent but a regular playhouse) big enough to accommodate sixteen hundred spectators, trucks designed to transport it lock, stock, and barrel along with its numerous personnel, and eight steam-driven tractors capable of hauling the entire convoy across difficult terrain. That its unveiling should have taken place on the esplanade of Les Invalides, the former veterans' hospital where Bonaparte and his son lie buried, was hardly accidental, and there can be no doubt that Gémier beheld himself as the general-elect whose campaign would inspire a *levée en masse,* whose charismatic presence would unite rag-tag elements, not unlike Napoleon's on the march north from Elba. "At the very origin of our art is there not a need for the nomadic life which our age, intellectually absorbed by capitals and big cities, seems to have totally disregarded?" he wrote. "Deriving its inspiration from a millennial tradition, true theater or logical theater is that which travels, which goes in front of the crowd and noisily summons it to a spectacle, as did the first actors, our primitive forebears, those who were always on the move." In Gémier's view, "true" theater is what theater was at first, before mind got separated from nature and intellectuals came to govern the hinterland from city enclaves; and it became increasingly apparent that for him the "true" spectacle was the crowd itself rather than the repertoire, that the Théâtre National Ambulant had as its fundamental purpose national ambulation rather than cultural dissemination. Nomadism went hand in hand with an ideal of tribal oneness or of unindividuated mass for whose sake he marshaled all the technology provided by a civilization he did not suffer gladly, the movable stage recalling David's floats of 1793 while prefiguring those that would ride on the human tide of 1936.

The modern director, the *régisseur–metteur-en-scène* as we know him today, was born with a congenital interest in crowds, and this to the extent that crowds represented the quintessential "ensemble." When Antoine first saw the Meiningen Players—a troupe whose founder-director, Duke George von Saxe-Meiningen, created ensemble theater almost incidentally, by way of producing historical dramas that simulated a world in which noblemen like himself had had a place and *raison d'être*—what captivated him above all were the battle scenes and crowds. For as long as he had been going to the theater he had been dissatisfied with the way French directors handled crowd scenes, he wrote to Francisque Sarcey in 1888 from Brussels:

Indeed . . . I have never seen anything which gave me the impression of a multitude. Well, with the Meiningen I have seen it! . . . Do you know what the difference is? Their crowds are not, like ours, made up of elements thrown together at random—or people hired during the dress rehearsals, badly dressed, and quite untrained to wear bizarre or constricting costumes, especially when these demand precision. Our theaters almost always demand that the extras stand stock-still, while those of the Meiningen must act and portray their characters. Do not assume therefore that they attract attention and divert the emphasis from the principals. No, the scene is an organic whole, and wherever one looks, one is struck by a detail in situation or character. This lends an incomparable power to certain moments.

The Meiningen troupe contains about seventy artists of both sexes. Everyone who does not have a part is kept as an extra and so appears every evening. If twenty actors are needed, the fifty others—without exception, stars included—appear on the stage in crowd scenes. . . . In the crowd scenes [of Schiller's *William Tell*] the protagonist who is the center of the scene can bring about strict silence with a gesture, a cry, a movement. And if the crowd then watches the actor and listens to him, instead of watching the audience, or, as at the Comédie-Française, contemplating the leads with a mute but visible deference, their listening would seem natural and so would their silence.

Granted that one actor with his back to the audience could foster the illusion of a "real" event unfolding beyond the apron, how much more effective was an entire cast rapt in its own sound and movement, a throng that turned its corporate back on the audience, even in directing its attention to some one person within itself. "In the composition of decor, one must take care that the center of the image not coincide with the center of the stage": this Meiningen precept, which held for the deployment of crowds no less than for the composition of decor, usurped the sovereign's perspective by throwing center stage offcenter or orchestrating scenic space without external reference, as though this space were actually circular. Sovereignty thus passed from the king "out there" to the director who operated like the Flaubertian author, ubiquitous but invisible. When a crowd cluttered the stage, leaving no part of it inert, or "dead," when the director's eye resolved every nook and cranny of his domain in some design, then his authority became absolute. The crowd functioned as an ideal audience supplanting the real one, as a perfectly responsive choral instrument by means of which the director could manipulate spectators and, in manipulating them, abolish their externality.

Where George von Saxe-Meiningen, his chief collaborator Ludwig Chronegk, Antoine, and Wagner (who, as Antoine noted, split his chorus into different parts, with each set of chorus members a distinct element of the crowd) kept the audience segregated from the stage, hemming crowds inside the dramaturgical event or "crowd scene," Firmin Gémier envisioned a *literal* merger, a meta-theatrical union very like the one he had brought about during the Vaud festival when, "at the most pathetic moment," everyone rose "in a single movement." To justify this additional step Gémier had at his disposal the dramaturgical theories of Romain Rolland, which he embraced apostolically. In *July 14th,* a play Gémier produced several years before the Vaud pageant, Rolland devised a last act that called for actors to join spectators and for everyone present to celebrate the epiphany of the *peuple,* with Revolutionary songs replacing dialogue. "The object of this tableau is to accomplish a union between the public and the work, to throw a bridge between the stage and the hall," he wrote. "Though it may not be feasible today, eventually the public must be constrained to mix not only its thought but its voice in the action, this being the premise of a new popular art; the People itself must become an actor in the festival of the People." What Rolland sought to accomplish with *July 14th* was clearly a denouement that would exemplify the death of secular drama and announce the New Era. Like a self-destructive apparatus, his play consummated itself in an evangelical orgy, ending when words failed, when passion clogged intellectual space, when the *oeuvre* became the assembled mass and the assembly a self-adulatory giant or a God born on the rubble of socioartistic forms that had presupposed a distinction— the very ability to distinguish—between inside and out, subject and object, stage and audience.

Nor did this play appease the desire underlying it. It was, indeed, only one of eight plays that, taken all together, constitute *The Theater of the Revolution.* Having embarked on this cycle in 1900 with the intimation that "I feel a vast dramatic poem organizing itself; I hear the ocean rising in me, the French people's *Iliad,*" he concluded it four decades later, in 1939, with *Robespierre,* whose last act recapitulates the orgiastic finale of *July 14th.* Rolland stated that he wanted Darius Milhaud or Arthur Honegger to compose, in free and "wildly passionate"

The steam-driven tractors, and the interior and exterior of the playhouse, of Firmin Gémier's Théâtre National Ambulant, 1911. Comoedia Illustre

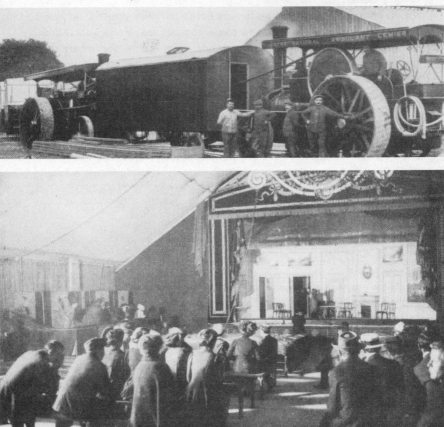

counterpoint, a powerful "Internationale" overlaying the "Marseillaise." "This conclusion must take place in an atmosphere of hallucinated exaltation which radiates from the holy battalion of the Jacobins." *

For Gémier as for Rolland, theater was theater only to the extent that it produced collective movement, emotion, com-motion. "It seems at times that the crowd is a colossal person in whom thought runs untrammeled across a thousand brains," Gémier wrote. "That is what must be translated in the theater." The Théâtre National Ambulant, the mobile theater drawn by the eight steam-driven tractors, served not merely to entertain random audiences but to mobilize crowds, or, like a peripatetic Will amassing bulk en route, to mobilize one gigantic horde. "There is perhaps nothing more captivating in reality and in art than the spiritual communion of a crowd," was the way he put it in a declaration that echoes Victor Hugo's panegyric on movement in the preface to *Cromwell*:

A single soul palpitates in a troupe of mortals. They think together, they act together, and the identity of their gestures reveals that of their feelings. There circulates among them a secret current of sympathy or of hatred whose rapidity is at times disconcerting. . . . Groups leap forward, hesitate, stop, double back, flee, disperse. Each sentence hurled by a protagonist provokes an ebb and flow. Thus do the changing dispositions of the

---

* As for Rolland's hearing the ocean rise in him, it was still rising twenty-seven years later, in December 1927, when he wrote a letter to Sigmund Freud on which Freud comments as follows at the beginning of *Civilization and Its Discontents*: "I had sent him my small book that treats religion as an illusion [*The Future of an Illusion*], and he answered that he entirely agreed with my judgment upon religion, but that he was sorry I had not properly appreciated the true source of religious sentiments. This, he says, consists in a peculiar feeling, which he himself is never without, which he finds confirmed by many others, and which he may suppose is present in millions of people. It is a feeling which he would like to call a sensation of 'eternity,' a feeling as of something limitless, unbounded—as it were, 'oceanic.' This feeling, he adds, is a purely subjective fact, not an article of faith; it brings with it no assurance of personal immortality, but it is the source of the religious energy which is seized upon by the various churches and religious systems, directed by them into particular channels, and doubtless also exhausted by them. . . . If I have understood my friend rightly, he means the same thing by [oceanic feeling] as the consolation offered by an original and somewhat eccentric dramatist to his hero who is facing a self-inflicted death. 'We cannot fall out of this world.' That is to say, it is a feeling of an indissoluble bond, of being one with the external world as a whole."

crowd express themselves. The thousand-headed hydra breathes, grumbles, knots, hisses, relaxes, bites, tears, crushes, relents, falls asleep.

Organized around a protagonist or a director consubstantial with itself, the crowd, in Gémier's conception of it, translates what its leader says into physical evidence, now heating up now cooling down, now expanding now contracting, but always responding to his message straightaway. Its identity hinges on its automatism. However brief, any lapse between idea and actor or between order and execution violates the impersonal, hermetic nature of Leviathan, for time admits an "other," legitimating scruples that must *ipso facto* prove fatal. And how does this collective being best voice its identity? Not through dialogue to be sure, but through responsive litanies, in choral chants, martial contests, national anthems, parades. During tours as director of the Théâtre National Ambulant, Gémier often improvised musico-dramatic spectacles that allowed the cast to merge with the local population. Whenever he found a municipal band and its male choir, he would produce *L'Arlésienne* (*The Girl from Arles*), a play of Provençal life by Alphonse Daudet with incidental music by Bizet. "The result," he wrote, "was always an extraordinary evening, with spirits at high pitch." *L'Arlésienne* would lead him, as we shall see, to attempt a Provençal "miracle play" staged on the grand scale.

So far as Gémier was concerned, language had no reality apart from the mobile pictures it yielded. Though he took considerable pride in his knowledge of classical repertoire, remarks he made about it bear out La Mesnardière's seventeenth-century distinction between primitives whom theater reaches through the eyes alone and cultural aristocrats capable of apprehending the beauty of dramatic verse. For him, language constituted not a possession, a cognitive tool, a means whereby one voices oneself, but something external, which is to say an instrument of repression, like the straitjacket. Rather than do what Revolutionaries had done in 1793 and proclaim classical literature foreign, he sought to establish his congeniality with it by proletarianizing dramatic genius, by characterizing great writers as would-be painters or fellow inmates of a verbal prison. Corneille thus became "Poussin's brother," Racine Lesueur's, Marivaux Watteau's. "Dramatic geniuses are the painters and sculptors of movement and life," he insisted. "Their sentences are like strongboxes that must be pried open for

their soul to go free and deploy itself in action. . . . The whole plot of
The Merchant of Venice boils down to a formidable tragic pantomime.
Well, every one of Shakespeare's masterpieces is thus conceived. They
are all a tragic or comic ballet, a series of movements. . . . *Words have
no value but to summon and second images"* (italics added). This ad-
vocacy of matter over mind saw him cast aside all aesthetic scruples
when the text seemed cumbersome, and stage, among other atrocities,
an *Oedipus Rex* rewritten for illiterates.

Language that obstructed the imagination and halted emotional
flow was intolerable to Gémier, and he found equally intolerable the
Italianate theater with its syntax of boxes and barriers. Like Jean-
Jacques Rousseau, whose authority he would often invoke, Gémier pictured utopian society as a collective singular foregathered in a house
lacking interior walls. "Present-day houses, divided as they are into a
variety of levels and compartments, isolate categories of spectators from
one another and oppose that fusion of feeling which is, in my view, the
goal of dramatic art," he wrote. It would be appropriate, he added, to
adopt the architectural layout of ancient theaters where semicircular
tiers rose with no separation and where, in consequence, "emotions
could freely propagate themselves across the entire audience." * When
he became director of the Théâtre National Populaire in 1921, he sought
and won permission from the Parisian municipality to stage summer
performances at the Arènes de Lutèce, a Gallo-Roman arena with a
stage forty-one meters wide which had been discovered in 1869, during
Baron Haussmann's excavations, and restored in 1917–18. But before
then, immediately after World War I, he rented the Cirque d'Hiver for
great Ur-spectacles, erecting in its cavernous maw tiers and staircases
that enabled the actors who formed his legionlike cast to circulate
through the audience freely. Gémier's collective ideal militated against
any architectural element that did not elide masses or serve the imperative of movement. "People have often mocked my predilection for staircases . . . but is it not logical to array a vast spectacle on tiers?" he
asked. "Nearly all the master-decorators have followed this method.
. . . In *The School of Athens* it is on marble steps that Raphael groups
all the learned men who did honor to Greece. In *The Presentation at the*

---

* Romain Rolland likewise inveighed against what he called "the stupid supremacy
of orchestra and boxes."

Temple it is on a staircase that Titian paints the priests toward whom the Virgin ascends. In *The Marriage at Cana,* it is on superimposed terraces that Veronese distributed his gorgeously costumed Venitians. I could quote twenty more examples."

Classical images carried more weight than contemporary, or Gémier might have given honorable mention here to a man he admired greatly, the Swiss theoretician Adolphe Appia, whose dictum, "Draw with your feet," was abundantly illustrated in drawings made for *mise en scènes* of Wagner's Ring which are all variations on a staircase. But even his classical gallery could not accommodate the one classical image that gripped Gémier more powerfully than any other, namely the Sublime Mountain, the man-made mountain on the Champ-de-la-Réunion (Champ-de-Mars), which the paraders of Year I ascended via a staircase that spiraled upward to the "altar of the Fatherland." Where Appia's stage sets for *Parsifal* and *The Walkyrie* evoke mysteries acted by personae situated far away in netherwordly chiaroscuro, the Revolutionary mob flowed from a horizontal plane to a vertical one, from the city to nature, from historical streets to a timeless mountain or *omphalos* on whose ledges there stood choral detachments of its body and at whose summit it worshipped a tree symbolizing its collective soul. Rely though he invariably did on the Italian school for character witnesses to plead on his behalf, Gémier's supreme model was homegrown. The director who declared that theater accomplishes its goal when "art and the people merge like the sky and the sea," when "emotions freely propagate themselves across the audience," upheld the same primitive God as Jacques-Louis David, who designed pageants with a view to exorcising from *le peuple* singular thoughts, hidden events, private allegiances.

It had always been Gémier's belief that the *milieu* determines the inner life, but in due course he took this basic tenet of naturalism far beyond stagecraft and literature by endeavoring to establish a folk religion whose anonymous celebrants would become place-names bound ontologically to the province they inhabit or to France at large. "I shall organize public rejoicings that will evoke the mores, the songs, the nostalgic dances of our provinces," he proclaimed. "Each *fête* [festival] will be tantamount to one act of an immense play that will magnify the life of the people and be enacted by the people itself in that majestic theater whose stage is the soil of France. Thus shall we establish a *culte extérieur* [outdoor cult] whose social credo requires the liturgy which is

*Two studies in Rhythmic Space by Adolphe Appia. Where Gémier required
stairs and tiers for the disposition of human masses, in Appia's theatrical
designs, the staircase evolved into the central motif of geometric
abstractions.* Property of Gabriel Jaques-Dalcroze

still missing from our civil religion." *Extérieur* bespoke not only a setting but a doctrine. Held out-of-doors, in nature, the *culte extérieur* promoted by Gémier set physical against intellectual culture, a quasi-divine mass or racial "soul" against the individual psyche, and a *raison d'être* embedded in holy soil against the otherwise fortuitous course of human affairs. Here, naturalism evolved into something rather like totemism. "Festivals are necessary," he declared, "because a people needs to externalize its ideal, which is a form of piety."

What he could hardly admit—that the externalization of this ideal was inherently belligerent, that the apotheosis of the collective body sanctioned individual violence even in rendering it impersonal—became evident in 1914. From the start, Gémier, whose tractor-driven theater curiously prefigured the tank-driven army, rallied to the tricolor. General mobilization seemed to answer his dream of a People Militant marching against infidels, for he wrote that "when, in one unanimous thrust, the citizens of 1914 left for the front, when so many sacrificed themselves so deliberately, they proved they were obeying an ideal." Although the government appointed him private secretary to the prefect of the Ardennes, this appointment was made so as to confer bureaucratic legitimacy on his freewheeling movements. In January 1915 he organized the first theatrical entertainment for front-line troops and soon thereafter reopened his Paris theater with a review entitled *The Huns and the Others*, proceeds from which went to charity. In 1916 he founded The Shakespeare Society, under whose aegis *The Merchant of Venice* and *Antony and Cleopatra* were staged as epithalamiums glorifying the Anglo-French alliance. When German air raids forced him to close the Antoine, he set up in Lyons; with subsidies from local industrialists he offered factory workers a season of classical drama. If virtue was Gémier's stock-in-trade, then war made him a prosperous man, furnishing as it did endless opportunities to labor without remuneration for a cause that put to shame all thoughts of profit. "Let our professionals who live off theater continue their commerce by making themselves valets of bourgeois vice or of the plebs's coarser appetites. We wish to edify an art accessible to everyone. . . . Nothing can be done without the people. Nothing can be done without faith." While Copeau sought converts abroad, Gémier embraced victims at home, giving benefits for the maimed, the indigent, the homeless, the widowed, the orphaned. Those who found themselves bereft of kin and limb, who had

been thrust outside bourgeois France or sundered from their past made
up the philanthropist's constituency. Determined, like Copeau, to father
a chorus, he had in mind not twelve boys and girls but multitudes born
anew. *The Clods and the Slyboots*, a patriotic allegory-play staged by
Gémier one year before the armistice, said as much as need be said of
the spirit that impelled him. In it there were scenes which had mothers
accompanying their newly conscripted sons down the aisle to "the altar
of immolation" and hammers beating rhythm on anvils for a chorus
that sang hymns to the glory of work.

From Gémier's vantage point, the Great War was Year I revisited
and its carnage the human toll taken by a God who execrated individualism. One million five hundred thousand Frenchmen had not died in
vain. Their blood enriched the virtuous earth from which an "organic"
nation would derive its sustenance. "The war and the formidable upheaval it brought about diminished the value of the individual. Or
rather, the individual has come to understand that all his strength is
drawn from the group," he wrote in 1921. With bourgeois drama having become as obsolescent as bourgeois individualism, the social muta-
tion engineered by war demanded new art forms. Progress in this regard
would manifest itself as a leap backward to the "age of faith" and faith
as an exodus from the hierarchical theater to the public square, to the
fairground, or to the open field. "Popular solemnities have become as
rare and wishy-washy as they were once frequent and picturesque," he
complained. "Among ancient Greeks, for example, the Panathenaea
united the entire city in the exercise of the faith. During the Middle
Ages, the mysteries enacted by an entire people on the porch of cathedrals and the gorgeous processions which all the guilds followed bore
witness to this same radiant flowering of the collective soul. And so,
too, did the Revolution hold impressive ceremonies, among them the
Festivals of the Federation, of Nature, of Reason, of the Supreme
Being."

Rousseau's *Letter on Spectacles* was not the only text from which
Gémier drew inspiration, but it was the subtext of every other. Lest
there be any doubt that "faith" excluded all but *le petit peuple* or that
the festivals destined to replace middle-class drama celebrated an an-
tinomical universe, a war between moral absolutes, and the vision of a
virtuous filiarchy triumphing over the bourgeois state, he would quote
(half-ironically to be sure, but only half) sentiments voiced by an eight-

year-old boy, Poupardin, at the festival of the decadi on 30 ventôse, Year II: "Oh you who are, like me, at the dawn of your life, you who are listening to me, oh my comrades, let yourselves be penetrated by the incontestable truth that man is born with love for the virtues." As Christian Europe worshipped a born God whose pascal descent upon the city each year suspended calendrical time with a long rite of death and rebirth honoring outcasts (paupers, cripples, orphans), so the child-people would all together affirm their own divinity in pageants conducted by a Leader. That Robespierre's famous pronouncement, "Slaves adore Fortune and Power; we honor Woe," should have become Gémier's guiding principle suggests other motives for his philanthropic activity than love of mankind. Peace consecrated individual success: war glorified self-sacrifice. Individuals gave and took at the marketplace; the corporate body incorporated itself in parades, liberating itself, through mass movement, from laws of exchange, from proprietors, from fathers even as it made destitution or impotence a sine qua non of citizenship in

Firmin Gémier's production of Oedipus, King of Thebes *at the Winter Circus in 1920.* Encyclopédie du Théâtre contemporain

egalitarian France. Like Robespierre before him, Gémier decried "egoism." The reign of virtue was a democracy of misfortune wherein the director would find his proper place.

Oedipus Rex, as rewritten by a playwright named Saint-George de Bouhelier in the octosyllabic verse line and naïve French of medieval mysteries, served his meta-literary purposes. Embellishing Oedipus' fall with Christ's Passion, de Bouhelier accomplished a farrago that would satisfy even the most insatiable glutton for punishment. "Here is my first step toward the goal I pursue: Collective Theater, National Theater, the Popular Festival," Gémier declared in 1919, after its premiere performance at the Cirque d'Hiver. Gémier's collaborator, Emile Bertin, designed a split-level stage with immense staircases. The multitudinous cast included two hundred athletes recruited from sports clubs throughout France who boxed, wrestled, heaved weights, shot arrows, and threw javelins—all to the accompaniment of Bach organ music. "These exercises are performed by illustrious athletes wearing almost nothing," wrote one reviewer. "The harmonious movements of ancient games have been restored to us. And then, a furious fever comes racing through the populace directly it learns of Oedipus' crimes! It's a gale of madness. Brutality knows no bounds. One hears the shrieks of women as they pursue men. . . . A drunken binge unseats the whole city. The disaster is such that everyone seeks oblivion in pleasure. . . . And it is Oedipus's Calvary. Arms extended, he seems crucified on his black cloak." While this account suggests that Gémier's taste for orgiastic denouements had grown, if anything, keener since his production of *July 14th* in 1901, it also brings to mind the policy Meyerhold formulated during the 1920s in his treatise on biomechanics: "Only via the sports arena can we approach the theatrical arena." Indeed, *Oedipus, King of Thebes* was conceived as the inaugural event of a series entitled "Olympic Games" that would have done honor to Jean-Jacques Rousseau, who had foreseen indoor theater withering away after the dissolution of kingship and kingless citizens exercising their Spartan virtue in martial jamborees.

Praise was by no means universal. In fact the spectacle prompted a bitter controversy, with several critics denouncing it as invertedly snobbish for idealizing the plebs while refusing the plebs any claim to the grand tradition. "I, who am of the people . . . understand their words and use no special language when I converse with laborers, workers, artisans," rejoined one such critic, Alfred Poizat. "I speak to them as I would to M. de Bouhelier. They are not medieval relics but inhabitants of the twentieth century. Their intellectual habits derive from the Renaissance, and all the centuries in between. You appall them when you address them in language despoiled of this acquisition. They feel mocked." Reviving the technique of old miracle plays was the vain sport of aesthetes, he went on to say, and Bouhelier's theater was a theater symptomatic of the need for false naïveté or false simplicity that manifests itself never more predictably than during the decline of civilizations. "You might as well urge upon working-class people the pleasures of laboring by candlelight or of traveling by stagecoach." *

But Gémier paid his detractors no heed. With *The Great Pastoral,* yet another spectacle of mammoth proportions—this one subtitled "Provençal Miracle Play in three acts and six tableaux: old airs and popular Christmas carols"—he demonstrated even more egregiously than in *Oedipus* that nostalgia for the Middle Ages upon which messianic ideologies would feed between the world wars and especially during the Popular Front era when Frenchmen performed Passion plays on the square of Notre-Dame Cathedral. Thrown together in the Cirque d'Hiver were singers, dancers, actors from the Antoine company, a drum corps brought up from Marseille, and animals provided by Monsieur Hachet-Souplet's School of Zoological Psychology. "Ever since regionalism began affirming itself, images from the French past have risen within us, sharply etched," declared Gémier, who spoke as a circus barker of the racial Unconscious, touting his "pastoral" in clichés prophetic of the mottoes Vichy would stamp on official coin two decades later. "The 'pickax' of regionalism seems to have laid open, in each province, a fidelity to and tenderness for our age-old customs, those born of nature, of work, of the familial or collective life. . . . Alongside one's native earth is another soil, the human soil—our people. Everything comes from the vegetal or human soil. Nothing can be done without it. So, our spectacles of old France are festivals of the earth and of the people. Today the festival is Provençal, tomorrow it

---

* Where Bouhelier medievalized Sophocles' *Oedipus,* another well-born aesthete who was given to love affairs with the lower class, Jean Cocteau, camped it up, several years later, in *The Infernal Machine,* which inspired Gide's witticism: "There's a veritable *Oedipémie.*"

will be Breton, and so forth." Although "Spectacles of Old France" ended with *The Great Pastoral* just as "Olympic Games" ended with *Oedipus*, these stammered first syllables bore witness not to Gémier's impatience but, rather, to his single-mindedness, or to the same obsession that had made him launch the Théâtre National Ambulant before 1914 and, evangelist that he was, embark upon the conquest of France. Since God was immanent in provincial earth, Frenchmen were born virtuous. The nativity festivals he envisioned would, had he had his way, have consecrated its personae as natives of a holy land.

He did get his way when in 1920 a state ripe for self-consecration had founded the Théâtre National Populaire. After considering André Antoine and Jacques Copeau, officials decided to appoint as its first director the man whose own endeavors had brought about its creation. Gémier responded in character. On the second anniversary of Armistice Day, the TNP was inaugurated with a festival, a *fête* that coincided with the translation of the corpse of the unknown soldier to his grave beneath Napoleon's Arc de Triomphe. "Next Thursday, November 11 at 3:30, we shall celebrate the Republic. . . . It is a festival in which the people play the principal role; while celebrating its heroes, on that day it must celebrate itself," he wrote in *The New Era*. Five thousand people came, or as many as could enter the Trocadero Palace, where tricolor bunting garlanded the proscenium arch.* At center stage there stood a truncated pyramid on whose level summit one group of actors imitated Rudé's famous frieze "La Marseillaise," while below them other actors milled round about in an evocation of the Revolutionary crowd hearing Rouget de Lisle's battle hymn sung for the first time and rising to it, all at once. "I am striving here to condense our national history; I am resuscitating songs that have throbbed beneath the sky of our three republics," declared Gémier, who had dutifully nurtured an ideal born at the turn of the century with *July 14th*. Nation-states, like individuals or characters, elaborate themselves in time, but Gémier's dramatic enterprise was predicated on feelings that abolish any sense of duration and selfhood, on emblematic moments, on arias sung en masse, on musical epiphanies that argue a transcendent origin. For this he

---

* The Trocadero Palace was a huge edifice with twin minarets two hundred feet high erected for the Exposition of 1878. It came down for the Exposition of 1937 and on its foundations rose the Palais de Chaillot, which from 1951 housed the TNP.

required more, far more, than five thousand seats. Indeed, the TNP would not fully earn its acronym until France itself became theater, and theater "the common echoing of an identical sound." To "condense" national history was to stage the ultimate crowd scene.

Before long, the TNP begot a satellite, a road company that circled outward from Trocadero to Paris's rim, following the path beaten by *cabots* but going well beyond it and playing, often without benefit of amenities like a stage, in working-class communes like Levallois-Perret and Suresnes. A child of melodrama, Gémier became a panjandrum of melodrama, the voyage between *Pirates of the Savannah* and *Oedipus* being tantamount to a rise from third role to *grand premier*. In 1919 he founded a Syndicalist Conservatory that commemorated his pious identification with the outcast. Two years later, he went still further in the way of shifting France's theatrical center from bourgeois Paris to the proletarian city outside its walls.

CHAPTER IX

✦ ✦ ✦ ✦

THE ATELIER

What with teaching in the Syndicalist Conservatory, doing repertorial work in the Comédie Montaigne, and playing in *The Great Pastoral*, Charles Dullin found himself swept up by Gémier. The huge impression Gémier made on him was not altogether apparent until much later, however, in 1941, when Dullin assumed the directorship of the Théâtre de la Cité—the former Théâtre Sarah-Bernhardt, whose name he changed at the behest of the Nazi Propagandastaffel. "The name I have chosen answers my desire to re-create the living community which is the deep truth of popular theater. I want strong, solid works accessible to everyone. Thus will my labor support the national effort which must help our land remain a spiritual beacon," he was to declare. "We need a theater of the Nation . . . a theater of union and regeneration." Where the Comédie-Française preserved a cultural memory, the task of his theater would be to shepherd the mass toward corporate self-enlightenment or religious cohesion by awakening what he called "the pre-memory." In Jean-Paul Sartre he would discover his Saint-Georges de Bouhelier and in *The Flies* his *Oedipus, King of Thebes.*

That metamorphosis lay beyond the horizon. When Dullin first ventured forth on his own, he cut the figure not of a generalissimo riding herd over eight steam-driven tractors but of the just man fleeing Babylon by mule or of the poilu improvising fairground scenarios at the front. It was, indeed, during a Gémier-sponsored tour of French Army bases in the occupied Rhineland that he hit upon a name for the little

band of actors and actresses he had begun to recruit in Paris, the Atelier. "Seated beside Charles Dullin in the train compartment, I saw him
write in his notebook: 'The Workbench,' 'The Anvil,' 'The Blacksmith's
Vise,' 'The Atelier.' I wondered whether he might be renouncing theater
and going into hardware," wrote a future protégé, Lucien Arnaud, who
had not yet heard Dullin pay homage to his artisanal comrades Levinson, Galvani, and Bonnat, nor yet seen him dote on horses. Several
months later, in midsummer 1921, the newborn Atelier's official bap-
tism took place, with its director issuing one of those brave new world
notices for which the French rebel has traditionally shown a peculiar
aptitude. It reads, in part:

The Atelier
A New Actor's School
Director: Charles Dullin

"Flee the precepts of those speculators
whose reasons are not confirmed by experience."
Leonardo da Vinci

The Atelier is not a theatrical enterprise but a laboratory of dramatic essays. We have chosen this title because, as we understand it, it answers the
concept we have of an ideal corporate organization in which the strongest
personalities would defer to the imperatives of collaboration, in which the
artist would master the instrument he must use as a good rider masters his
horse or a mechanic his machine.

Amateurism, dilettantism are no less dangerous than ham-acting. The
Theater bequeathed by the great masters whom we admire is a complete
art, sufficient unto itself. Its aesthetic may vary with each period, its forms
of expression must always have the appeal and freshness of novelty, especially when they are borrowed from the ancients, for the theater, like life
itself, is multiple, fluid, and mysterious, but the elements that animate it
remain eternally selfsame.

To collaborate in this work we need resolute and combative men, simple
and devoted women, since the spiritual direction that shapes our pedagogical task will require great fortitude in such pitiless times, when men are
judged by their bankrolls. Our school will exert all its strength . . . to
bring about the regeneration of the actor.

Like Jacques Copeau, to whose 1913 manifesto aspiring young
directors regularly tailored their own statements of intention, Dullin set

himself a quasi-religious task. The Atelier was not to be one more business venture but a school, and not one more finishing school but a cradle where people would experience spiritual rebirth, or start life anew "de-bourgeoisified." Just as the bourgeois had despoiled theater of its original integrity, making something complete incomplete and reducing the self-sufficient to domestic servitude, so had they robbed the actor of his birthright, estranging him from himself in having him covet tangible rewards, obey rational precepts, and acquire habits that go by the name of "good taste." Indeed, this manifesto calls to mind an epistolary lecture Elise Toulemon had received from him six years earlier, during the war. "I want you to learn some acrobatic routines," he wrote on that occasion. "I have recently observed, among *le Peuple*, improvisors whose suppleness, whose marvelous instinct haunts me. If you should create Harlequin, then you must begin to do what the Italian actors did—somersault, walk on your hands, and so forth. . . . Stop doing your balletic points and practicing your piano. Work with a real clown. Put your body through the tricks of popular farce actors. Strive to assimilate their way of being, their style of genius. . . . Forget everything that good taste has taught you."

Now that disease had begun to warp him beyond repair Dullin was all the more inclined to seek regeneration in "naïve" forms, to go backward, to reeducate the instrument he could no longer predict and master his body as he had mastered his horse. But if the Atelier grew out of such intimate circumstances, Dullin's commitment to farce and *commedia dell'arte* also mirrored an age in which yearning for the violent simplicity of war, for some lost sense of wholeness saw countless young men (who did not otherwise resemble Charles) scaffold their dreams upon a primitive social order. Wherever "regeneration" became cant language, the word was loosely synonymous with regression. "The mind that plunges into Surrealism relives the best part of its childhood," Breton would presently declare in the *Manifesto of Surrealism*. "From childhood memories . . . there emerges a feeling of being let loose and then *detracked* which I consider incomparably fertile. Childhood approximates 'the true life,' childhood being that time when everything abetted the effective and uncontingent possession of oneself." It was the same vocabulary to which Louis Aragon had recourse in *The Peasant of Paris* when he, whose gloved, well-manicured hand conducted his rhetorical fugues like the schoolmaster's baton marking Latin cadences, portrayed himself as a "peasant"—meaning a child of nature or a savage innocent of the bourgeoisie's intellectual manners.

What Limon had been for the Vieux-Colombier, Néronville would be for the Atelier. Tucked away on the bank of a canal that ran alongside the Loing River through farm country just outside the Fontainebleau Forest, this tiny village, though it lay only fifty miles from Paris, seldom saw Parisians or, indeed, anyone but its own population, until Dullin descended upon it in the summer of 1921 with his band of actors and set up house in a disused barn. Lucien Arnaud, Genica Athanasiou, Jean Mamy, Vassili Kouchitachvili, Magdeleine Bérubet: these (minus young Antonin Artaud, who stayed behind) formed the original "phalanstery," the "ideal corporate organization" that would reconstitute itself again and again, materializing each July, after Paris's season, like a midsummer hallucination to which the peasantry grew more or less accustomed.

For three months, improvisation was not only the basis of a method but a survival technique whereby the theatrical clan made ends meet with such negligible resources as it could muster. Each actor performed a daily *corvée,* chore (Dullin favored the medieval term), now cooking, now gathering wood, now sewing costumes, now building scenery. It was soon brought home to those who had, at best, a passing acquaintance with rural life that to act, if they entertained some hope of doing so, was to invent theater from whole cloth and to create a public from people who never congregated except at mass or at agricultural shindigs.

A fortnight after its arrival in Néronville the Atelier made its first public appearance under conditions with which it soon became familiar. Having received assurances from Magdeleine Bérubet, a young woman whose imagination sometimes ran amok, that Moret-sur-Loing, the nearest town, had a playhouse in need of sweeping but otherwise perfectly commodious, Dullin announced that his troupe would perform there, and on the morning before the performance dispatched a vanguard of two actors armed with brooms. What they found was a structure that seemed as if it had borne the brunt of World War I. The two worked in sheer desperation, improvising benches, hanging expanses of canvas cloth to keep out the wind, building a primitive stage and devising a pulley for the curtain, so that when their comrades arrived the hall looked almost usable. Not until nightfall, however, did it dawn upon anyone that they had no source of light. Bérubet made amends by racing through town shouting "I shall have light! I shall have light!" and dragging from bed several people who lent her hurricane lamps. "The town drum was mobilized to arouse the natives' goodwill," wrote Lucien Arnaud, who emerged as the Atelier's chronicler:

> We ended up with candles, torches, with everything we could lay our hands on, including Moret-sur-Loing's electrical power, which we tapped on the sly. . . . The atmosphere of that evening was quite unforgettable, which is not to say that everything went swimmingly after the performance finally got under way. Certain actors who had called upon wine and alcohol to help them deny their weariness suddenly experienced great difficulties. The candles and tapers lasted through only three-quarters of the performance, which ended in a crepuscular haze with the audience squinting to see us. Everything became slate-colored and the few torches that did last cast fantastic shapes on the canvas and the high walls of the barn.
>
> In the anguish of this finale, Dullin as Harlequin was demonically tearing out his hair and yelling: "We are dishonored! Dishonored!"

When the lights failed on yet another occasion, Dullin's troupe, mindful of General Gallieni's feat at the Marne, pressed into service ten automobiles, arrayed them crescentlike behind the audience, and aimed their headlamps at the stage. Indeed, Arnaud's chronicle is a picaresque saga in which spectators are joined to the cast by some inevitable contretemps, the theatrical event being this hysterical marriage as much as the play itself.

Wherever it went—and presently the Atelier became a regular feature at village festivals held in the southeastern quadrilateral of the Ile de France—a genius for accident ran ahead to make its path uneven, to lay traps or mislay signs, to arrange fortunate little falls that quickened the corporate soul. This genius was all they could rely upon, but it proved infallible, upsetting everything, and not only journeys overland but tours underground. "During those early days, as others bind themselves with blood, we bound ourselves with a bottle. One evening, we buried a bottle containing the names of all who had been present at the Atelier's birth and who had taken the company oath: 'Never shall the aforesworn separate.' We confided our hope not to the sea but to the earth," wrote Arnaud, who adds that an excavation made several years later failed to uncover the buried bottle.

The fact that Dullin needed barely a fortnight to work up a program of comedy including Regnard's *The Divorce*, Courteline's *Les Boulingrins,* and a farce by Thomas Gueulette before he led his ill-coordinated troupe forth from Néronville during their first summer suggests a fundamental difference between the Atelier and Jacques Copeau's communal enterprise. Copeau, as we have seen, found imperfection or disorder abhorrent. The concrete stage, wherever he laid it down, was something like a formal garden that allayed his fear of the surrounding wilderness, a realm in which his actors could not move but that their movement observed geometric patterns elaborated a priori. Of Dullin, on the other hand, it can be said that confusion invigorated him, that he waited upon serendipity as a poet upon a Muse, and the remark Copeau made after seeing the Atelier perform for the first time—"In the Atelier he has kept a bit of the Vieux-Colombier's heart, but where are its spirit and order?"—was no doubt made half-enviously. To infer from this that Charles did not govern what he had wrought would be to misrepresent the issue, for there was in him a Jacques Dullin whose presence, even without benefit of titles like *maître* or *patron*, commanded respect, and a Joseph whose pedagogical gift proved remarkably fertile. "Listening to Dullin's teachings one has the impression of rediscovering old secrets and a whole forgotten mystique of *mise en scène*. The Atelier is at once a theater and a school," declared Antonin Artaud, who came to Dullin by way of Gémier. Lucien Arnaud put it in less hyperbolic terms when he wrote that "there was something very special and engaging about this young troupe of students guided by Dullin whom we never addressed familiarly for all our familiarity, friendship, and fraternity; whom we called, as we have always called him, Monsieur Dullin, though anyone might have taken the liberty of calling him Charles."

Still, an inherent condition of being Monsieur Dullin was that he presided over a rustic mess blending images of Châtelard, the Wild West, the war front, and Old France. Charles never felt more himself than onstage, and a stage was never more *his* stage than when it bore some resemblance to a hayloft, with horses whinnying outside and a whiff of dung exciting his memory. Among other anecdotes in Arnaud's chronicle, the one that best captures "Monsieur Dullin" as he went about the business of furnishing his world touches upon his love for equines. During a *corvée* to find provisions, Arnaud encountered a large herd of asses. When he rejoined the Atelier, he described this unusual encounter—unusual, for asses are rarely seen in herds outside the Charente. Dullin became excited and insisted that they pursue the beasts, although night had already fallen. They set out on bicycle, stopping nocturnal passers-by to ask whether they had not, perchance, seen a herd of asses, and finally found it in Souppes, some miles distant from Néronville, where it had been billeted like a cavalry troop in private stables. "Its herders were staying in the local inn," wrote Arnaud, who was faint with exhaustion but fascinated by Dullin's persistence:

> Dullin held lengthy negotiations with one of them, tearing him away from his white wine, and ended up purchasing a she-ass. We learned in short order what kind of bargain he had struck. . . . The animal, who was given the name Gypsy, would sooner die than trot. Exasperated by her unusual stubbornness, Dullin sometimes let her have it, with childishly cruel digs. Since Madame Dullin forbade anything like a switch . . . he affixed the point of a needle to the end of an innocent-looking reed and when the opportunity presented itself would stroke Gypsy on the sly, "oh, ever so lightly." As a rule guilt did not let him press the point, though once, after he had done so, the animal kicked up her heels and dented the front end of an automobile, to her master's utter dismay. In fact, Gypsy began her antics the very evening Dullin purchased her. We made our way back to Néronville in the dead of night by following the canal—Dullin, the she-ass whom he led by a tether, and I on the bicycle holding a lantern. As I had gotten too far ahead, Gypsy, who would normally go no faster than a walk, started to gallop, for fear of the dark I suppose, while Dullin, flying at the end of her tether like a kite, shouted at me in a tragic voice: "Stop! For heaven's sake, stop!"

Where Jacques Dullin had exercised the right of the lord to bestow whimsical cognomens on his serflike offspring, Charles, who begot no children but nurtured actors and animals instead, gave the latter names emblematic of his own childhood, thus giving his childhood a kind of bestial posterity. "Gypsy" was soon joined by another ass, "Martine," and by horses—"Kiss," "Baby," "Boby," "Mandrin"—in a menagerie whose domestic life became a vital part of the theatrical troupe's. En route to the name "Atelier," had he not paused at "The Anvil" and "The Blacksmith's Vise"? "In the same week I almost lost Martine and Boby, Martine of food poisoning and Boby of colic," Charles wrote to

Pauline in 1929. "Martine has been saved and I think that Boby will pull through. I slept with him last night. There were enormous rats doing gymnastic exercises above my head. I thought about Black and the odor of fermented potatoes that the hay used to have in Châtelard's stable. Do you remember? All that seems so far away." When such calamities occurred during the season, Dullin, in costume, would rush from stage to stable between acts of a play, or else have his cast take turns ministering to the ailing beast. Indeed, *bête de théâtre*, a metaphor used almost synonymously with *monstre sacré* to designate histrionic "naturals," or great instinctual actors, found a literal embodiment at the Atelier.

Dullin's metaphorical beast, his *bête noire*, was perfection—insofar as perfection evoked for him the world of machines, of finished goods, from which he dissociated himself by dubbing his company the Atelier. During the summer, in the country, he would make crude models with the sort of odds and ends little boys fish out of their pockets: cork, string, bits of cardboard, a jagged penknife. "That represented theater for him," Arnaud observed. "Too much perfection was the brief he held against Antoine and against realism in general. Secretly he liked it when things went awry. When they came off as they should, they no longer captured his fancy. Not that he would complicate for complication's sake, only that he preferred what was new, what was fresh."

Had Arnaud paid attention to domains of art other than theater, he might have noted a kindred impulse at work in, say, the "Merz" constructions that Kurt Schwitters built from street refuse, or in Surrealism, whose practitioners occasionally visited the suburban flea market at Saint-Ouen to let fantasy scavenge among *objets trouvés*. That for which bourgeois had no further use became the recycled material of sculpture, of painting, of theater, of literature, with many young artists glorifying trash after the fashion set by Rimbaud, and commemorating Paris's backwaters or its dark interstices in language appropriate to Arcadia. "Gods are no longer worshipped on heights. Solomon's temple has lapsed into metaphors where it shelters swallows' nests and pale lizards. Like blown dust, the spirit of cults has deserted its holy sanctuaries. But there are other places flowering in the midst of men as they routinely go about their mysterious lives. . . . The divinity will soon inhabit them, a new divinity": thus did Aragon open *The Peasant of Paris* in which an old arcade, a pre-Haussmann relic that lay under a sentence of demolition, serves as the podium for a poetic harangue against the city fathers. From debris, barricades arose. Trash cans became receptacles of a new pathetic fallacy. As Macaire had spoken to the Romantics, so Charlie Chaplin spoke to this postwar generation. In conferring exclusive value upon forms and materials to which the bourgeoisie assigned no value whatsoever, the rebel conferred inwardness or soul upon the banal, the dilapidated, the "naïve."

If this was true of a *boulevardier* like Aragon, who has always run with the dogs and couched with the foxes, how much truer was it of Charles Dullin who, when finally he established himself in Paris, would make his home a *théâtre de quartier* that dated to the Bourbon restoration. "Several weeks and very little alteration would suffice to convert most modern theaters into banks, into department stores," he wrote. "For me, they have no soul. . . . But go visit the place Dancourt, have a good look at my theater and you will love it as I do. It is unfit for any service but the one it performs." Unfit for any other service, the soul theater was proof against conversion into an instrument of usury or trade, its anachronistic interior offering its childlike tenants asylum from the well-made world.

Surely nothing could have been less well made, or homemade than the Atelier's first Parisian incarnation at 7, rue Honoré-Chevalier, two blocks south of the rue du Vieux-Colombier. In this quiet, provincial neighborhood dominated by Saint-Sulpice Church, whose flanks were alive with impious bohemians, Dullin found a vacant store just large enough to contain the stage his students had made the previous summer—the summer of 1921—and brought up piecemeal from Néronville. While Firmin Gémier, who felt cramped in his quarters at the Trocadero Palace, was launching the Théâtre National Populaire on a tour of greater Paris, Charles occupied premises that had for some years past housed the local dry cleaner. "Since this shop was narrow, we built a proscenium that jutted out like a prow. And since, in addition, its length did not much exceed its width, the stage all but met the front door. We envisioned a future public seated to port and starboard with our stage cutting through rows like a ship through waves," wrote Arnaud. To accommodate as many spectators as possible in space left unclaimed by the stage was a problem Dullin solved by fashioning tiny play-chairs, twenty of which could seat no more than ten normal buttocks. And to render themselves instantly conspicuous, his minions printed "The Atelier: A New School for Actors" in orange letters on a lapis lazuli façade that might have reminded certain passers-by of the blue that Zola's uprooted heroine Gervaise paints her ghetto laundry. After a season on the rue Honoré-Chevalier, a season that had seen the Atelier perform Regnard's *Divorce* (with Dullin as Harlequin), Cervantes's *The Hostelry*, Max Jacob's *Blackmail*, Molière's *L'Avare*, Lope de Rueda's *The Olives*, Mérimée's *L'Occasion*, and two plays by Calderón, *The Condolence Visit* and *Life Is a Dream* (for which Artaud designed the set), it came to Dullin's attention that a little theater situated halfway up Montmartre on the place Dancourt was available for leasehold.* Its availability did not excite widespread interest because few entrepreneurs beheld ruined beauty with a sympathetic eye and, indeed, the Théâtre Montmartre, like Charles himself, had known better days. One century earlier, when it had stood outside the capital—a charming cameo of a hall decorated by Fragonard's son—villagers would assemble to see apprentice actors perform "hits" they could not afford to see beyond the customs barriers (whence its other name: Students' Theater). On occasion, it transcended its mimetic role, sponsoring the premiere of a melodrama or opera bouffe—Hervé's *Don Quixote and Sancho Panza*, for example—that later won acclaim on Parisian stages. As time wore on, however, it took its toll. Originally white, the theater had turned soot-gray and developed cracks from sagging downhill. Where grime had not obscured its internal embellishments, paint laid on by a heavy hand had done the rest, so that before the nineteenth century elapsed there remained no trace of Evariste Fragonard's frescoes. A shabbier sight was not to be found on the Butte. And yet Paris, though it grew apace, overrunning whatever contradicted the urban imperative, could not wrest from its successive owners this widow of rural Montmartre, which hunched amid latter-day tenements with an air of bereavement, half-theater, half-farmhouse. "It was so pure! and even

---

* As for the preponderance of Spanish plays in his repertoire, Dullin had spent the summer of 1914 touring Spain with Elise Toulemon and conceived a passion for that country all the more keen since his tour, which was interrupted by general mobilization, had come to represent the last summer of youth. But his friend Alexandre Arnoux introduced him to Siglo de Oro literature long before he set foot in Spain. That Copeau largely ignored Spanish theater may have been a further inducement to exploit it as a preserve of his own. In a subsequent chapter, we shall see how Jean-Louis Barrault imitated him.

The Théâtre de l'Atelier (disguised here as the Théâtre de Poitiers for a film being shot in 1979).

more beautifully bare inside its walls than without!" Charles exclaimed years later. Behind a wall hemming it in from the rue d'Orsel, whose name commemorated the defunct village, lay a courtyard, a stable, and a coachhouse surmounted by two haylofts—all in terrible disrepair. Here, oblivious to the shambles, Dullin's she-ass happily installed herself, while up front his students refurbished a long-forsaken stage. The Théâtre Montmartre was born again the Atelier, or—as custom ultimately defeated Dullin's wish that "atelier" replace "theater"—the Théâtre de l'Atelier.

"Refurbish" may suggest a more optimistic picture than actually met the eye. When winter came two months after their arrival, in October 1922, it came as the night had come to Moret-sur-Loing, taking them by surprise. Until Marcelle could unload mementos of her bourgeois past (silverware, furniture) so that Charles could afford a heater, the troupe found itself reduced to thawing its makeup with candles. And the heater, an antiquated contraption of nineteenth-century girth that Charles bought from a flea-market dealer, showed somewhat the same disposition as Gypsy to ignore demands made upon it by its master, which is to say that it would sooner belch smoke than furnish heat. Given such uncomfortable circumstances, it is quite understandable that those who played onstage should often have outnumbered those who sat in attendance. Furthermore, the Atelier's eccentric location discouraged prospective clients. "It took six years of relentless labor before I finally prevailed upon the people from below to undertake the excursion, whereupon my theater became, little by little, a theater indistinguishable from many others, alas!" wrote Dullin. With Charles, the desire for public notice was, and would always be, hampered by fear of the rewards attending it, rewards that demanded he lay his self in forfeit. To the extent that poverty suited him, to that same extent did he view his rural compound as an asylum from what lay down below. "Was it not the ideal shelter for a young troupe of actors firm in their resolve to break with the artificial world of the Theater, actors who sought something other than the accolades of a blasé public and the solicitations of the Boulevard?"

Dullin exaggerated somewhat the length of time it took to attract spectators from below, for if it took six years to create a loyal public, with the help of Jean Cocteau it took only two months to create a stir that put the Atelier on the theatrical map of Paris. Cocteau's *Antigone*, staged in December 1922, was a collaborative effort involving Cocteau himself, Coco Chanel, who made costumes, and Pablo Picasso, who, at the eleventh hour, when Dullin had all but lost hope, conjured up scenery in the form of a shaggy jute backdrop painted violet-blue, with masks surrounding a hole through which Cocteau recited the chorus's lines. "The presence within our walls of Cocteau, of Picasso, of Chanel had alerted Parisian café society, and on the evening of the dress rehearsal, my young stage manager was beside himself with excitement as he told me about automobiles on the rue Dancourt making a racket such as old Montmartrois hanging from their windows had never seen or heard," Dullin recalled. Cocteau's social claque was faithful to him, and so was his literary nemesis, André Breton, who contrived to interrupt one performance before being ejected from the hall. Raymond Duncan, Isadora's philo-Hellenic brother, came accompanied by epigones all dressed in peplums and carrying small bullhorns to toot a protest against Cocteau having defiled Greek antiquity. Such was the hub-bub around *Antigone* that the other play on Dullin's double bill, Pirandello's *The Pleasure of Honesty*, went relatively unnoticed. When the Pitoëffs produced *Six Characters in Search of an Author* four months later, it was already forgotten that Dullin had been the director who first staged a Pirandello play in France.

Having survived its first season, the Atelier took root. Survival remained an issue year after year, to be sure, but Dullin's triumph in a French adaptation of *Volpone*, his marvelous productions of *L'Avare*, and his discovery of Armand Salacrou accounted for several fat years that helped tide him over the many lean. Unlike Copeau, who would periodically feign suicide, Dullin had an indomitable will to stay put, to squat on precarious ledges. "Life never gives us what we demand of it," he told his sister. "We must tear it from it by force." Where Copeau's vision grew increasingly abstract, Dullin's lay in his theater-*cum*-farm, the preservation of which amounted to an act of religious observance or a form of piety upheld against the modern world. Despite his complaint that assimilation had made it banal, never was the Atelier in any serious danger of being indistinguishable from other theaters. Even during its most brilliant periods, when everyone who stood in the limelight of social and literary fashion convened there, under Dullin it always had a scent of the farm or the circus, which was especially noticeable to those who entered it from behind, through a narrow door on the rue d'Orsel. "A courtyard with open sheds; a wooden staircase that led to the *Administration* (now there is a highfalutin word whose letters I cannot write without smiling), to the costume wardrobe, to the atelier in which Dullin's dresser, Jeanne la rousse, held sway, to the venerable premises of the school—a kind of barn—and to the director's office," as Alexandre Arnoux described it. "This courtyard, which was littered with flats, practicals, and bits of timber would get transformed, as soon as spring came, into a set-building yard. Loose straw trailed on the ground. From the first you'd sniff a strange and delicious odor of horse manure. . . . For there was a stable; it was beneath the staircase. In prosperous seasons, when Dullin and Marcelle had film work, that stable sheltered two horses of good stock, devotedly combed and rubbed down."

Nor was there much danger that Dullin himself might ever be mistaken for some other actor. Though arthritis had not yet made him the curled stringbean-like figure he became, with fused vertebrae gathering his whole upper torso into a hunchback, he already walked with a stoop from which he would pull himself erect in brusque movements that caused him pain. The pain was so pervasive as to affect the rhythm of his theatrical delivery, or so it seemed, for he would recite by fits and starts, beginning a soliloquy slowly, gathering momentum, halting when least expected, then rushing forward again. That nothing came easily to him may explain his amazement at the improvisations of a Marcel Levinson. Nature having given him life itself only halfheartedly, he was all the more disposed to believe in, if not to cultify, "naturals." Where others exploited native wealth, he bought everything he owned with indefatigable labor. His virtues were the fruit of his deficiencies. Shortwinded, he rationed the wind he had in his syncopated diction and to such effect that it would carry his voice through long evenings. Hoarse, he made up for threadbare vocal chords with his tongue and teeth, so that his speech, though it would always sound whiny, had a kind of plosive character—what musicians call "attack"—as if he were gnashing into sonority the language he couldn't sing. To watch this slight figure as he chevied Rs by the hour, flushing them out of his throat, was to witness a feat of self-defiance. "Those Rs, especially, which stuck in his throat, which he had to put in his mouth and place in the theater, as high up as the uppermost gallery," wrote Arnoux. "How many times did I listen to him practice his scales *ad nauseam*, fastidious exercises on which he conferred a coarse, baroque vehemence of soul, and which he transformed by zeal and diligence—for he could not utter a syllable without giving it something of his heart—into barbaric incantations, into magical litanies: Gros gras grain d'orge quand te dégrosgrasgraindorgeras-tu? Je me dégrosgrasgraindorgerai." *

His will to bring himself forth, to achieve presence showed clearly enough on his face, which was the image of a peasant economy. All

---

* Dullin evolved a technique of breathing and theatrical diction which are the basis for Artaud's mystical fioriture in *The Theater and Its Double*.

ridges and hollows, it had no flesh to spare, its most generous feature being a sharklike nose. While it entertained many and various moods, there was little room in this terrain for *dolce far niente*. "If one were to imagine a gamut of expressions, at one extreme there would be stupefied horror and at the other infinite, desperate irony," wrote Dullin's friend Jean Sarment, who might have set the limits at mischievous glee and at blind rage—rage that would erupt like *le foutro* of Châtelard whenever the world or he himself weighed too heavily upon him. Vignettes in which his students affectionately recall Dullin acting and directing often show him "working himself up" as though anger at the slights of his ungrateful children served to embolden him, to dispel stage fright. "He would pick a fight with someone—stage manager, another actor, me if I was within reach," noted Jean-Louis Barrault, who practiced artful dodging. "One evening he could not find a pretext. As usual, he was snorting, looking round for prey, for any old thing, and his eye fell on a hole in the curtain. It should be said at once that the curtains had holes everywhere, they were real sieves. 'Who did that?' he half roared. 'Ah! my curtains! I'm ruined! Done for, betrayed, a figure of fun. Well, who is it has torn these curtains?' His anger was rising, rising, he was snorting more and more and then came this sublime phrase: 'Wear out a whole life to come to this!'"

The more famous he became, the more apt he was to quarrel with success, and in quarreling with it, to become the replica of his father joining battle with a world that harbored belligerent designs against him. Debts, with which he was ridden, constituted his only point of contact with the external world; when people from the outside came "to bother me" (as he put it), he felt persecuted and would exclaim, like an umbrageous aristocrat fending off insolent creditors: "How dare they do that to *me*!" According to Lucien Arnaud, he never read the newspapers. "His theater being for him a kind of ivory tower, what took place outside its walls was of no interest to him." *

---

* How like his father he became is apparent in Pauline's recollections of Jacques Dullin held at bay by the bailiff: "Lacking any desire to acquire honors or fortune, he found trade and commerce altogether repugnant, even in his financial dealings. After phylloxera destroyed his vineyards, for example, he applied to the Crédit foncier for a mortgage . . . instead of selling a small parcel of his land. When the interest payment was past due and the bailiff stood at the door waving a sealed paper, the tragic scene would commence. He would tear out his hair and seize his double-barreled shotgun, proclaim-

Charles Dullin (RIGHT) *as Harpagon in Molière's* L'Avare *and* (BELOW) *as Volpone in a production at the Théâtre de la Cité during the early 1940s.* Encyclopédie du Théâtre contemporain

Had he wanted an ivory tower clear and simple, he could have made several films for Fritz Lang, who respected him enormously, and would have earned enough money—some 5 million francs apparently—to purchase his independence. But being debt-ridden enabled him to keep alive a permanent threat of foreclosure, to yearn for freedom as one eternally held prisoner. Could the soul survive without encroachments by the heathen? Its space was defined by a state of siege that pitted native against foreigner, and its time by a state of delinquency that induced lifelong nostalgia for Paradise lost. The lapsed deadline represented the melodramatic frontier all over again, with souls on one side of it and, on the other, mercenaries sworn to drive him from his ramshackle fortress and bring him up-to-date. As Charles imitated Jacques in begetting a theatrical family, so he imitated him in conscripting from down below straight men whose harassments sanctioned his own intolerance of common law, in vilifying the external world the better to exercise a virtuous despotism at home. Even if Lucien Arnaud's memoir had not hinted at Dullin's grandiosity ("faire ça, à moi!"), the roles that showed Dullin at his best—Molière's Harpagon and Ben Jonson's Volpone—would indicate that the chronic debtor served a secret hoarder, that his "war" sustained, however self-punitively, a childhood romance featuring pirates, recluses, saints, healers, woodsmen. "When I follow southward the course of the Rhône, which is *my* river, when I follow it to my little homeland, I recognize perfectly the little boy I was; I see him, I hear him, I 'feel' him in me. It seems to me that the core of one's character does not change very much," he told an audience several months before his death. The core of his character proved the more immutable for having found shelter inside the anachronism on Montmartre, where he staged his fantasy life between 1922 and 1940, or until another German onslaught brought Paris itself full circle, back to an era without modern amenities.

A decade after Dullin bade Néronville farewell, the village survived

ing: 'I am going to blow my brains out! My gun! My gun!' Would he have dared to do it? I don't believe so. But we were petrified and would implore him in the only words that ever came to mind: 'Papa! Papa! . . .' Fortunately, the arbor (the site chosen for his execution) lay quite a ways off so that he had time to collect himself before arriving there. He never knew his credits and debits: the pages of his thick ledger book remained blank. Numbers caused him great vexation. Toward the end of his life, believing himself insolvent, he had fits of muffled despair. 'My God, I am bankrupt, I am dishonored!' "

as a paradigm of Châtelard, a remote birthplace that gave those who had endured the "heroic age" a particular nimbus while enrolling everyone, both veterans and latter-day recruits, in a communal legend. "Family life continued on place Dancourt," wrote Arnaud. "It united actors on the stage and off. There was a dining room, the farmyard, the atelier in which dishes were washed. Our concierge, Madame Verny, made our meals. After work, we would repair to the former carriage house and eat together at a table made of stage planks. The Atelier's 'refectory,' where Beaujolais flowed in abundance, became very popular, not only among our own—Marcel Achard, Valentine Tessier, Michel Simon, Madeleine Robinson, Jany Holt, Henri Guisol, et al.—but among actors from the outside." When Montmartre had all but forgotten what it was to hear the clippety-clop of equine traffic, Charles would get around the Butte on horseback, riding Mandrin up and down the hilly streets with humble contempt for automobiles, not unlike Judge Dullin surveying his Savoyard bailiwick from behind the withers of Black.

By 1921 Dullin and Copeau had ended hostilities. It was under Copeau's aegis that Dullin's troupe first gained wide exposure when Copeau lent it the Vieux-Colombier in June 1921 for a weeklong run of Calderón's Life Is a Dream, the profits from which allowed Dullin to establish himself on Montmartre.* They might have drawn even closer and formed a mutual aid society, or "cartel"—there was talk of it—had Marcelle, who still felt insulted by her expulsion from the Vieux-Colombier, not come between them once again. Whatever else America taught her, it taught Charles's wife to anticipate that any pact with Jacques Copeau would some day yield the posthumous wisdom of a La Fontaine fable; that Copeau could no more treat his confreres as confreres than could the lion resist lording it over other beasts of the jungle. Once a maître always a maître. "Copeau was the great boss," observed Jean-Louis Barrault in recalling the impression Copeau made on him during the early 1930s, when he was serving his theatrical appren-

---

* Dullin had occasion to return the favor, in 1933, when Copeau directed As You Like It at the Atelier.

ticeship at the Atelier. "Even Dullin trembled onstage, like a dog before its trainer, if Copeau happened to be in the audience. He had a way of grasping you by the neck and shaking you affectionately until your head was pressed against his chest as though to make you kiss the feet of Christ. That unnerved me. Nonetheless, we felt veneration for him. He seemed to possess the keys to our mysteries: intelligence, sensibility, vision."

Although the Atelier was, as Cocteau's *Antigone* would suggest, more freewheeling than the Vieux-Colombier had ever been, more susceptible to a twenties mood and rhythm and gregariousness, certain of its features reflected its ideological paternity. Like Copeau, Dullin set store by the notion that the school he ran justified the shows he gave. In due course he started a review entitled *Correspondance* in which he and those whose contributions he solicited—among them Copeau—pleaded for a theater that would synthesize language, gesture, and music. On Saturday mornings, the Atelier became a concert hall where young artists played works by Poulenc, Milhaud, Honegger, Auric. Above all, there was the rebuilt stage.

Dullin did not cannibalize the Théâtre Montmartre with quite the same methodical ardor with which Copeau transformed the Athénée Saint-Germain into a polished skeleton, but his gradual alterations left it sufficiently bare to provoke grunts reminiscent of those emitted by critics in 1913. "Is this the right way?" asked Antoine. "Once the novelty has gone, perhaps it will be seen that these gray walls and sincerely nude vessels take after the Protestant temple, the school auditorium, the railroad station. When set scenes are replaced by neutral drapes, I feel, despite myself, cheated of my pleasure." Antoine's pleasure had always been Charles's bane. Despite his reluctance ever to surrender the liberty of self-contradiction and to confine his enterprise in any one formula, Dullin delivered something like a credo after he saw Meyerhold's production of Ostrovsky's *Forest* in 1931, a production notable not only for the "social masks" previously mentioned but for its montage effects and its *parade*-like division into "episodes," each one introduced by a title projected onto a screen above the stage. "The person who lives in a theater finds nothing more poignant than an empty stage," Dullin wrote in his magazine *Correspondance*.

Our custom of disguising from the public changes of scene and the preparation of the spectacle by means of a curtain raises a barrier between the

drama and its spectators. The atmosphere is continually troubled. With
each change the spectator plunges back into his daily preoccupations. . . .
When the Atelier had just come into being . . . I sought to do away with
the front curtain, but the resistance I encountered was such as to make me
abandon this reform which would have been logical, given my overall position. In the presence of a set that is wed to the drama, that is not an anecdote but a tool, one is held breathless . . . our attention is riveted to the
stage as a believer's in a cathedral to the choir and the apse.

What dictated the starkness that Antoine laid to the account of youthful
perversity (for naturalism had a monopoly on the natural) was Dullin's
animus against all impedimenta that sustained the bourgeoisie's theatrical etiquette. Had another revolution broken out, Dullin would doubtless have celebrated the new era by tearing down the front curtain.* As
it was, he, in collaboration with Léon Barsacq (the same Barsacq who
later designed the cloister set for Copeau's mystery play) did everything short of tearing it down to escape from the little Italian box he
inherited. A rounded apron thrust the playing area into the hall like a
promontory surrounded on three sides by spectators. Boxes that flanked
the proscenium arch became fixed practicals. The raked stage was
made level. And finally, steps provided an easy transition from stage to
audience:

As soon as I took possession of this theater, I had the footlight border condemned; others had done the same before me, but for aesthetic reasons
(the border obstructs the view of some spectators and gives the Italian
stage a doddery *guignol* look). Pursuing my goal, I dreamed of a theater
where actors and spectators would merge, would find themselves on an
equal footing spiritually as well as physically. It was in this spirit that I
founded a little review whose title contains my entire program, for I called
it *Correspondance.*

Theater's *raison d'être* was to cast magic spells rather than to produce aesthetic goods. As in childhood, during the years spent imprisoned at Pont du Beauvoisin, he had made believe that he believed, in

---

* A more recent precedent than that of the *peuple* spontaneously tearing down the
scrim in 1791 was Meyerhold's constructivist-inspired theater. With the production of
Mayakovsky's *Mystery-Bouffe* in 1921, he abolished alike the proscenium and the front
curtain. A series of multilevel platforms connected by steps took up the stage proper, with
a broad ramp sloping down to the front row of seats.

adulthood he became a priest of make-believe, his art his "vocation," his theater his parish church, his audience his communicants, and his family romance his supernal myth. "We don't need a machine to lower Gods from the fly gallery," he asserted, reprimanding once again the commercial "tricksters" outside. "What we need are Gods."

Like his architectural strategy, Dullin's pedagogical method reflected his aversion for barriers, his belief that the actor would remain a vicarious being until he freed himself from artifices as restrictive as the Renaissance box with its border of light. It was essential, he felt, that the actor exhume a pristine spirit buried deep inside the ersatz body culture had molded around him, and this by means of the improvisational method that became gospel at the Atelier. Improvisation would enable him to unlearn responses programmed by his elders, to purge himself of mannerisms that served as a social passport, and receive the lesson constantly offered him by his own five senses. "Exercises are based on the sensations we perceive as we listen, look, taste, touch, smell," wrote Dullin.

> Here are several examples:
>
> Look at at a landscape; follow the flight of a bird in space; lying in the grass, observe an insect. . . .
>
> Listen to the toll of distant bells, to the footfall of someone approaching you, to a muffled conversation.
>
> Sniff an agreeable perfume. Breathe the fresh morning air. Imagine a stench. . . .
>
> This childish lesson . . . aims to have the student contact the external world, which we shall call the *Voice of the World*. . . . The Voice of the World will bring forth the voice that wells up in the interior of the individual, which we shall called the *Voice of Oneself*. And from this confluence *expression* is born. It becomes straightaway apparent that improvisation is binary in its very essence and consequently in its practical application.

During this colloquy between nature and mind, words do not clog the air with preestablished significance. What the improviser apprehends speaks to him not cognitively but sensually, not through the medium of verbal symbols or the mediation of pedagogues but through the orifices of his own body. A "voice" outside instantly calls forth a voice within, as though the human interior were an echo chamber of the world at large. Far from being a dialogue, it is a primal litany, a billing and cooing in which Nature, like the *vox Dei,* fills with sensation every pore of the newborn who receives it. Charles's anagogical nomenclature suggests a discipline calculated to have the initiate transcend time and, in transcending it, feel once again the euphoria induced by lullabies.

How congenial are the religions of Nature and of Art, how readily the *enfant de la nature* who idealizes instinct is able to place his ideal at the service of pure aestheticism, becomes apparent in a complementary set of exercises requiring that the student incorporate masks in much the same way that he incorporated the physical universe. Properly used, the mask would help "depersonalize" the actor, or rid him of his idiosyncrasies, and thus prepare him for a more "objective" art. It was incumbent upon him to study this object in all its aspects, to "live" with it, to make it a "companion," to be its confidant. "A mask has its own life, which is not always the one its sculptor intended to give it," observed Dullin. "Nothing annoys me more than to see a student leap upon it like a draper's assistant grabbing a carnival mask. I feel that he commits a sacrilegious act, for in fact the mask has a sacred character. It summons a public of initiates—not the crowd, which seldom regards it as anything but an instrument of buffoonery; nor schoolmen, who exploit it for academic purposes, wanting to go backward, to restore vanished forms. . . . The use of the mask in modern theater must be created from whole cloth. It lays down conditions for a dramaturgy that has yet to find its poet." Implied here is the idea that a student, having forsworn his elders, should take instruction from an inhuman pedagogue—from a role no longer defined by the hand that wrought it and not yet fashioned to some new dramatic end. If one mode of improvisation had him embrace his unspoiled senses, the other had him identify with an uncreated object, with an icon exempt from historical contingency. As Dullin envisioned it, this symbiosis would not only humanize the mask but reify the actor—by mating his face to a sign, or conferring on his random life an archetypal origin and an ultimate goal. Gordon Craig's *Über-Marionette* prefigured the ideal for which Charles yearned. Though he seldom mentions Craig, his observation that "while here we have witnessed the triumph of naturalism in theater, among Japanese the perfection of technique is, on the contrary, the actor's essential aim; he is not an intellectual being but an instrument whose mechanism must be perfected incessantly. . . . One feels certain that [he] would cease to live if [he] ceased to act" may indicate to what extent he, along with Craig—and despite his animadversions against the machine—cherished the Romantic dream of a technical wunderkind governed by a transcendent power, of an artistic ontology embodied in the puppet who would die if he did not act, or in the character born to live onstage.

As Craig held that theater had fallen from grace when human actors replaced the divine puppet, so Dullin, who crusaded onstage and in *Correspondance* for "pure spectacle," proclaimed that theater would regain its true identity when it ceased to mirror the everyday world and became once again a realm of play for play's sake. Scorning psychological problem-plays, he invoked an innocent past of which clowns, dolls, and toys were the forlorn survivors. Though Dullin did not elaborate anything quite like Craig's creation myth, his writings often hint at the idea that time had defrauded the theatrical enterprise, that over the centuries bourgeois had laid in bondage a once-autonomous actor. "It is in the *café-concert* and in the circus that one may find *commedia dell'arte*'s true descendants," he wrote after engaging Georgius, a popular circus clown, to play the lead in Roger Vitrac's comedy *The Cheap Jack*.

> It is there . . . that the true masks of Harlequin and Scaramouche, Pantalone and the Doctor, Brighella and all the others are reembodied. The dramatic literature produced by poets who found inspiration in the success of these "illustrious players" offers us a highly distorted image of them. . . . If, for the author, the theatrical tradition is recorded in the works of the masters . . . for the actor it is at once oral and experimental. . . . Actors have long been the slaves of words. They have long sacrificed the physical drama, *le jeu dramatique*, to the text. . . . A *commedia dell'arte* improviser created his character as much with his mime-play, his gestures, his entire body as with the dialogue he improvised.

Between the actor and his archetype there had intervened a foreign language laden with the meanings of a class under whose rule he became self-divided. This language forced open the physical or aesthetic matrix he inhabited at the beginning; it visited bourgeois syntax on a vernacular essence; it organized inside his nature a psychological sphere of influence that made him distinguish self from persona. Where the actor originally commanded scenic space with gestures as idiosyncratic as the priest's, now he was a valet to texts, mouthing language dictated by his master. And what would restore him his integrity? "Unbridled farce is what will save us," Dullin proclaimed, echoing the sentiments of his Russian idol, Vsevolod Meyerhold, who had it that "words in the theater are only embellishments on the design of movement."

A tendency to render serious themes farcical characterized Dullin's *mise en scènes* during the 1920s, so much so that one critic wrote in 1926, apropos of Roger Ferdinand's *Irma*, that "Dullin has some very interesting theories of art but is becoming their victim by trying to apply them no matter how inappropriate the circumstances; his hobbyhorse is the circus routine." *Irma*, a play about an old woman enamored of an adolescent boy, was staged as pure burlesque, with entrances choreographed to music written for the occasion by Henri Sauguet, an intermezzo in which actors parading behind a screen became Chinese silhouettes, and decor that evoked Epinal images or rustic lithographs. In Marcel Achard's very free adaptation of Ben Jonson's *Epicene*, for which Georges Auric composed a score that accompanied the precisely cadenced movements onstage, dance and acrobatics and mime all played a part. When it came to Aristophanes' *Birds*, which the Atelier produced during the 1927–28 season, Dullin had a playwright-collaborator named Bernard Zimmer adapt it on the model of a year-end music hall revue. Each applicant to Pisthetairos's utopia—the parricide, the dithyrambic poet, the informer, Prometheus—sang vaudeville-like songs written by Auric, who also composed a blues in place of the flute melody imitating the nightingale and a fox-trot for the exodos. Scrap iron, paper, and oilcloth were the materials from which Lucien Coutaud, Dullin's designer, invented the decor of Cloud-cuckooland.

But Dullin expressed his idea of theater as pure spectacle most clearly through the curtain raisers, or *parades*, that occasionally took place at the Atelier. These called for actors to rig out their personae before the public while improvising sketches in which the troupe openly disported itself as a troupe. In one such improvisation, raising the curtain to a performance of Molière's *L'Avare*, Dullin's dressing room was on the stage. Visitors of the kind who are forever turning up backstage to pester actors filed in one after another. Each created his own character, improvising lines to which Dullin improvised retorts as he was constructing upon his face the face of Harpagon. "Especially memorable

was one scene in which Genica Athanasiou . . . played a young girl
'who wanted to do Theater,' " wrote Lucien Arnaud, a participant in
this happening.

> Dullin . . . asked what text she had prepared for audition. "None," she
> answered. "What I do is plastic improvisation. . . . I can do A Rose for
> you." "Go ahead," said Dullin, whereupon Genica commenced her meta-
> morphoses before the public. . . . It was neither dance nor theater but a
> kind of instinctive translation of the most various things, with the body or
> face bringing it off unaided; neither was it pantomime, since it did not
> spring from a mimetic premise. Rather it was *a display of the corporeal in-
> stinct yielding to sensation* [italics added]. . . . The novelty of this expres-
> sive form and its poetry met with complete success; the public joined in,
> shouting themes like "the sea," "revolution," "fire," "still water," "the
> sun. . . ." If memory serves, Marguerite Jamois tried something of the
> same kind on a separate occasion and did a remarkable "Violet. . . ."
> Such unexpected, highly chastened exercises made spectators who had
> barely emerged from naturalist aesthetics thrill to a new feeling.

Unlike orthodox one-act curtain raisers, Dullin's served not to prolong
an evening whose main feature would have given patrons less than their
three hours' worth but to replace the curtain—to dispel the illusion—
that divided actor from spectator even in dividing the actor from himself. They conveyed as bluntly as the thrust stage Dullin's yearning for a
presence that textual roles could not vouchsafe him, for a density of existence attainable neither in ordinary life nor in the ordinary theater, for
a "hereness-and-nowness" to which Jean-Paul Sartre, whose thought he
found congenial, was to give philosophical expression. The actress who
seems born to improvise, born to live onstage, is locked in a trance that
makes her both witness and performer, or subject and object, without
psychological stratagems distancing her from Nature ("a display of the
corporeal instinct yielding to sensation"). Porous yet self-absorbed, she
embodies the ideal of a theater that is "open" yet hermetic, in which instinct functioning as intelligence dispenses with texts, and abolishes
limits imposed on it by the external world. Had he been given to writing aphoristically, Charles might have formulated some such gnome as
Sartre's "hell is the others," for, turned upside down, the Sartrean
chamber of infernal conflict would produce the undifferentiated hall
where an actor is player, playwright, play, and audience all together.

Sprung free from time, from words, from scruples that sit in judgment over him, only then could he achieve identity. But identity thus conceived was another *huis clos*. "The Atelier possesses a troupe whose character is so pronounced that by introducing any foreign element I could not but destroy its harmony," Dullin declared. Beyond a certain point, the aesthetic preconditions of ensemble theater argued the virtue of a solipsistic community whose text was itself.

Although Dullin did not follow Meyerhold into the Communist fold or Copeau into the Catholic, it became increasingly obvious during the 1930s that he was spoiling for a clamorous rebirth, that his apologies of farce, improvisation, and *commedia dell'arte* bespoke a disposition to welcome all signs of social disorder and to hail as regenerative the ascendancy of primitive theater over bourgeois politics. "Alas, the French are truly exasperating!" he wrote to Pauline in 1936, several weeks after the Spanish civil war had broken out. "They bemoan their fate and do nothing, *dare* nothing. They criticize, they bleat like sheep, they tremble for their savings if they have any, they get all enthused over words but when it comes to acting or following those who act, they lay back. I much prefer a people struck by madness like the Spanish than a sterile breed." Having always set greater value on *action dramatique* (a term that his student Jean-Louis Barrault would adopt for his own mime plays) than on psychological drama, he gave vent to the latent ringmaster who once told Lucien Arnaud that "I should like a theater bigger than the Atelier, a circus with a central track, like the Cirque d'Hiver." As life grew ever more violent outside his theater, what with anti-Fascists battling paramilitary Fascist leagues, he felt increasingly inhibited by a stage unequal to the scope of events that stirred in him Gémier-like ambitions. It was a time not to impersonate characters but to celebrate history's convulsion.

In 1933, the year Gémier died, Dullin produced an adaptation of Aristophanes' *Peace* that witnesses describe as having incited mass hysteria. Though Dullin had not wanted to play Trygaeus and, according to an article he wrote, rehearsed the part mechanically, without giving it much thought, the character suddenly "appeared" before him one evening. After that, he was haunted by this apostle of peace, so haunted, indeed, that during performances he would challenge spectators by asking them if they, too, did not feel a Trygaeus in them, to which the less timid shouted "Yes!" while everyone else present applauded wildly. "One has the impression that the unfaithful, the miscreants, the blasphemers of Peace, should there be any in the hall, are going to rise with an ecstatic air, leap across the rows of the pure, prostrate themselves before Monsieur Dullin, and abjure their sinful ways, as in Negro films," observed Edouard Bourdet, a successful playwright of the period who became administrator of the Comédie-Française three years later and engaged Dullin, among others, to direct productions for him.

> Alone, in my box seat, I was rather humiliated for feeling outside this spectacle of religious delirium. I consoled myself with the thought that I was probably an old convert, a veteran pacifist whereas those around me were neophytes in the full flush of a recent conversion. The ceremony that exalted them left me with the confused sense that I had come to the wrong place, that instead of a play in a theater I was attending a pacifist liturgy in the Sanctuary of Peace.

No doubt Bourdet found especially discomfiting a rope that tied stage to audience like an umbilical cord, or a lariat. At one end of this rope stood the well down which Peace had fallen (in Aristophanes, she is buried in a pit rather than a well); at the other, in mid-orchestra, were actors who exhorted spectators to help him raise the fallen goddess from oblivion. Cries of "Pull! Pull!" resounded everywhere as people took turns grasping the live connection, receiving something akin to an electrical shock, and heaving ho until their labors were rewarded with Peace's climactic manifestation in the shape of a naked young woman.

What deeper significance did *Peace* acquire that Dullin should suddenly have become obsessed by Trygaeus? If a *mise en scène* reveals its director as a text does its author, this one might suggest that the rope (which made "communal bond" a palpable metaphor) led Dullin's imagination round about to another peasant by whom he was haunted, namely Smerdiakov, the parricide who hangs himself after "starting life anew." And perhaps the well from which Trygaeus's divine bride-to-be springs forth exercised the same fascination upon Charles as the millrace in which Pastor John Rosmer consummates his posthumous marriage after abjuring the faith of his fathers. For Dullin, theater was supremely theater when the denouement of dramatic action was an epiphany or a *Liebestod*. Much closer in spirit to Gémier's mystical rallies than to Aristophanes' comedy, his production expressed not a cultic love of peace but, on the contrary, a despair that could not abide the hum-drum world, an emptiness that preached discontinuity, unbridled farce, and collective self-immolation—a preference "for people struck by madness, like the Spanish." Casting himself as the king of peace allowed Dullin to give instinct full reign, to anticipate, with moral impunity, the movement, the mass, the passionate reductionism, the violence of war. Against cityfolk, Dullin-Trygaeus-Christ marshaled a horde that would have made him rejoice in the utmost had it finally burst out of his theater-farmhouse like peasants on a Jacquerie obeying the Voice of the World or "the Trygaeus in each of you," and using the rope to lynch. During this same period he wrote to his sister: "Abandoning everything produces an intoxication of unhappiness that sometimes gives me strength. It seems to me that as soon as he can think and act, man is alone. As he grows older, his loneliness increases. Bonds of affection and sincere tenderness create a kind of happy diversion; passions stir the air and light bonfires; tears and shouts make us believe that we are not alone. But in reality, one dies alone as one has lived alone."

Dullin's preference for people struck by madness was widely shared, so widely shared that a description of all the tracts written in praise of them, of broadsides against the insane asylum, and of systematic attempts upon reason could serve as a useful ancilla to the study of French literary radicalism between the wars. If proverbs minted by Dumas *fils'* Reasoner during the Second Empire still had currency, so did the Romantic myth of Genius inherently at odds with society, of an "absolute" individual victimized by a bourgeois dictatorship. "We shall not tolerate your obstructing the free development of a delirium as legitimate and logical as any other succession of ideas or of human acts," declared the Surrealists in a manifesto published in a 1925 issue of their magazine *La Révolution Surréaliste*. "The repression of antisocial reactions is as chimerical as it is unacceptable in principle. All individual acts are antisocial. Madmen are individual victims par excellence of the social dictatorship; in the name of this individuality which is the nature of man, we demand that all convicts of the sensibility be freed." Antonin Artaud, who acted under Dullin's roof before going on to write the essays that made him the quasi-oracular figure he has since become, was a party to this indictment.

Thus, Dullin did not have far to seek, had he sought like-minded compatriots. But as it happens, the playwright whom he was apt to consider a member of the family—a spiritual alter ego—descended upon him from abroad. In 1922, when the Atelier first gained public recognition by staging *Life Is a Dream* with Dullin cast as the mad Polish prince, a friend, Camille Mallarmé, sent him the manuscript of Pirandello's *The Pleasure of Honesty*. "That morning the trees on place Dancourt were wearing the first leaves of spring; the blue of the roofs lent the Parisian landscape an unreal look that suited my state of mind," he reminisced many years afterward. "I knew very little about this Pirandello, who had just leaped from my mailbox like a devil and therefore began to construct a certain Pirandello who spoke to the facination that Italy . . . had exercised upon me throughout childhood." The Pirandello he constructed was bound up with his memory of letters from Sicilian cousins that would arrive at Châtelard and provide material for endless discussions during the long winter vigil, "especially if they reported cataclysms." He was an amalgam of Charles Vouthier and of the wild *Carbonari* he met en route to school. He was, above all, so much a caricature of the "tormented, jealous, violent" Sicilian that Pirandello, when one fine day he appeared at the Atelier in the flesh, struck Dullin as something of an impostor. "I descended to the courtyard and saw a man of middle age with a white goatee caressing the head of my little she-ass, Gypsy. Surely this could not be my young author (for I naturally imagined him young), but Camille Mallarmé introduced the goateed gentleman as Luigi Pirandello. He knew little French and straightaway embarked on a very Italian pantomime that conveyed his love for the sad sweetness, the profound tenderness of the eyes of little asses."

Tying his favorite themes to Pirandello like ribbons to a maypole and celebrating through The Author a spring homecoming, Dullin reveals by indirection what it was he loved about this dramatic *oeuvre*. If the Pirandellian plot typically begins after some mysterious event has taken place, that mystery deepens with the unfolding of the plot until physical violence or insane laughter ends it all. The event is not an ordinary event but a catastrophe, a Fall that reduces characters to puppets embroiled in an epistemological farce where fact and fancy, mask and face become interchangeable.* Adrift without any common reference, each character perceives a world that reflects his own fugitive image. Pirandello's spokesmen—his Reasoners—are those who preach the surrender of belief in cognition and self. On one hand we have the Father in *Six Characters* stating that "a character, sir, may always ask a man who he is, because a character has really a life of his own, marked with his especial characteristics; for which reason he is always 'somebody,' while a man . . . may very well be 'nobody.' " On the other hand, there is Diego in *Each in His Own Way*, who declares:

> What a joy it is when, caught by the tide of life in one of its moments of tempest, we are able actually to witness the collapse of all those fictitious forms around which our stupid daily life has solidified; and under the dikes, beyond the seawalls, which we had thrown up to isolate, to create, a definite consciousness for ourselves at all hazards, to build a personality of some kind, we are able to see that bit of tide . . . suddenly break forth in a magnificent, overwhelming flood and turn everything topsy-turvy! Ah, at last—a whirlwind! a volcanic eruption! an earthquake! a cataclysm!

The flight into theater almost always begets a play within the play whose twists form a kind of mental crypt that secures the inner cast— the mad—against intrusions by the outer cast of society. Where the outer cast uphold dead forms (rational categories, moral barriers, temporal discriminations), the inner, who exist outside time, have no law but fantasy or desire. Convention binds the social cast, but for the recluses, who enjoy the divine right that belongs to sons of art and creatures of instinct, everything is possible—everything save life offstage. The father in *Six Characters* sleeps with his daughter and kills his son. After twenty years of mad reclusion as Enrico IV, Enrico claims the twenty-year-old daughter of a woman who spurned him, then impales his ever-present rival. And so it goes. In every major play Pirandello

---

* Plays that exploit this theme figured prominently in the Atelier's repertoire. Along with *Life Is a Dream* and two of Pirandello's works, Dullin staged *Monsieur de Pygmalion*, of which its author, Jacinto Grau, wrote that "my goal . . . was to see men and animated marionettes together on the same plane, resembling each other by the fragility of their ephemeral existences." In 1927 the Atelier performed *The Dance of Life* by an English writer, Herman Ould, where, once again, dream and reality intermingle.

wrote, dreamer-playwrights dream with impunity, their dreams—which never age—keeping them eternally young.

This glorification of the playwright-within-the-play led Pirandello to glorify the political *magister ludi*, who confers a heroic purpose upon otherwise aimless lives. "I am antidemocratic par excellence," he declared after visiting New York in 1923. "The masses need someone to form them. Their needs and aspirations do not go beyond practical necessities. Well-being for the sake of well-being, riches for the sake of riches, have no significance or value. Money seen in that light is no more than dirty paper. Here, however, it would serve another purpose and arouse other energies. In Italy wealth would have a spiritual value." His contempt for democratic society pervades *The Imbecile,* a play that Dullin hoped to stage during the 1924–25 season along with *It Is So (If You Think So)* but canceled at the last moment for fear of losing a government subsidy awarded him by Edouard Herriot, who was to attend the premiere.

When Mussolini marched on Rome, Pirandello could not have felt more jubilant had one of his own madmen sprung to life on the larger stage. He told the French press that "a great man's role is to construct reality for the weak who cannot construct these realities themselves." At home, where his black shirt proclaimed his allegiance to the Fascist cause, he was even more explicit, declaring in *L'Idea Nazionale,* "I have always had the greatest admiration for Mussolini and I think I am one of the few people capable of understanding the beauty of his continuous creation of reality: an Italian and Fascist reality which does not submit to anyone else's reality. Mussolini is one of the few people who know that reality only exists in man's power to create it, and that one creates it only through the activity of the mind." However ambivalent his private feelings about Mussolini, his public statements made it obvious that he viewed the dictator's stratagem as his own greatest play. A speech delivered during the Ethiopian campaign, in October 1935 (one year after the Nobel committee had awarded him its literature prize), bears home this megalomanic confusion:

The world should look on it [the African campaign] with admiration but instead it spies on it suspiciously, unaccustomed to a spectacle of real and great beauty. We who are producing this spectacle and living through it at this moment, know how much pain, anxiety, and vigilance, how much daily obedience and moral discipline accompany its beauty, and how much we must exert ourselves not to yield to laziness or cowardice. . . . The Author of this great feat is also a Poet who knows his trade. A true man of the theater, a providential hero whom God granted Italy at the right moment, he acts in the Theater of the Centuries both as author and protagonist.

Embodied by the author-protagonist who has risen above trivial human preoccupations to create a spectacle that the incredulous world outside Italy will not believe, beauty and spirituality find expression not in rational acts—for reason can only delude—but in *beaux gestes*, in crusades, in outbursts of national violence. The feelings that secretly exercised many otherwise respectable middle-class Italians—a hatred for the hard, gray life of every day, a contempt for the established order, a lack of interest in past and future, a nihilistic aspiration to end with a bang this useless and stupid life—was the material from which Pirandello made his well-made farces.

As for Dullin, it would be well to recall what he declared to Elise during World War I—"Aside from . . . beautiful movements dictated by instinct, from spontaneous gestures that lift man well above his condition and his state, I no longer believe in anything. Morality! Duty! Religion! Bah!" Subsequent events indicate that this furious credo, far from surrendering to peace, became part and parcel of a Theater Militant hostile to the individual responsibilities that attend ordinary life. In June 1924, shortly before the Atelier staged *It Is So (If You Think So)*, *Paris-Soir* quoted Dullin as saying: "For those who know how to look, our era is hallucinatory. We therefore need a spectacle of fantasy, a life that will lift us from the doldrums into which we have been plunged by this century of money. . . . Lies are more necessary to man than the truth. Lies are at the core of everything that makes us love life." This contention inevitably led him, as it led Pirandello, to embrace the prospect of another conflagration, another Beginning and End. If lies were more necessary than truth, then the most necessary lie was the illusion that theater alone could give its celebrants: the illusion of obeying decrees formulated by a superhuman mind or of inhabiting a divine body whose movement conforms to natural law. "The theater has a role to play, a very beautiful role, in the forming of a new elite within the bosom of a community which must surmount little egoisms and naïve skepticisms," Dullin proclaimed in 1941, after Hitler's troops had taken command of Paris. He envisioned tribal rites that would elevate man above man and restore him his prehistorical oneness in awakening a "pre-memory." As Pirandello's madmen spoke to this vision, so did Sartre's Orestes, the hero who lives nowhere, who frees Argos from Jupiter (custodian of the past), and who finally tells its citizens: "Everything is new here, everything is to be begun." *

The best measure of Dullin's stature may be the extraordinary roster of actors who served their apprenticeship under him between 1921 and 1940. Taking in strays who were drawn to the Atelier by the communal ideal it represented and by the unorthodox principles taught therein, he fathered an entire theatrical generation, a generation whose number included Marguerite Jamois, Antonin Artaud, Jean Vilar, Madeleine Robinson, Michel Simon, Jean Marchat, Alain Cuny. But it should not be surprising that his most illustrious children were mimes, like Jean-Louis Barrault and Marcel Marceau, who sprang dumbstruck from the dream he never ceased to entertain of an autonomous troupe whose text would be its body and whose actors its playwrights, of a "world outside the world" where children would communicate wordlessly. Although this dream had seen him launch a fairground theater long before the Great War, it flourished in wartime and, afterward, sustained a will never to let the enemy's language penetrate him, never to let the bourgeoisie evict him from his inner Châtelard. "You must change, public!" he declared in 1925. "The war has taught you to distrust words."

---

* Soon after the war, Sartre repeated this message in lectures he gave in Berlin, much to the anger and distress of those who felt that some guilty reflection upon the holocaust would do the Germans more good than Existentialist amnesia.

CHAPTER X

+ + + +

GROWING UP FATHERLESS

The blood of the Barraults . . . comes of pure Burgundian juice. For three centuries wine has flowed in our veins. I feel I am a peasant, and in fact my hands are like big paws," wrote Jean-Louis Barrault in his autobiography. Like the American who takes pride in his foreign extraction, invoking European place-names as if to legitimate himself, to make himself more real, to maintain a line, the Parisian invokes the provinces. When asked who he is, he will as often as not explain where the family came from, echoing an assumption of France's great nineteenth-century novelists that in Paris one does not find oneself, one alters oneself. Identity is soil: it lies among the bones of the dead and inheres in a human mulch. Two hundred years ago, the words "born" and "birth" designated noble lines. The ontological privilege that aristocrats arrogated to themselves has, since the Romantic era, when rootedness and wandering became a central polarity in literature, devolved upon their serfs. Jean-Louis Barrault alleging his rusticity resembles the bastard son suing for his father's patent of nobility. To be a peasant is to be.

As it happens, Jean-Louis's father, Jules Barrault, manicured his fingernails. What is more, he read the works of utopian socialists and, directly the opportunity presented itself, around 1900, left home to study pharmacology, joining that horde of young men in whose flight from the land and enchantment with radical doctrine nationalists like Maurice Barrès, author of *Les Déracinés* (*The Uprooted*), saw France's

337

fatal effeminization. "Home" was Tournus, a town on the southern threshold of Burgundy. The Barraults had lived there since the seventeenth century, rarely traveling beyond Beaune or Mâcon, where they would go to find wives. Tanners and hatters by trade, they, like many local artisans, cultivated vinestock on a sandy slope of the Saône River. Their property, Beauregard, was aptly named, for it offered a view encompassing the pink of Tournus's Romanesque church, Saint-Philibert, the lush green of a plain that extended eastward toward Switzerland, and the white of distant Jura mountainpeaks. In 1850 a Barrault had built a stone house that commanded this view. His son, Henri-Philibert, did nothing but tend the vineyard, which was small but large enough to provide a livelihood. When his wife bore him two sons, Adolphe and Jules, he planted linden trees on either side of the terrace, anticipating that their shade would some day console him for his infirmities. In this he was to be grievously disappointed.

Jules married a Parisian woman, Marcelle Valette, and established residence in a town ten miles west of Paris, Le Vésinet, where two sons were born to them, Max-Henri in 1906 and Jean-Louis four years later. Financial circumstances were so straitened at first that to supplement his income Jules worked in an insane asylum. By 1912, however, he had prospered sufficiently to buy a chemist's shop in Paris, on the avenue de Wagram, near the Arc de Triomphe, and to settle his family nearby with every expectation of seeing it grow still larger. Then the war came. Shortly before his fourth birthday, Jean-Louis was awoken one night by a kiss and vaguely heard his father, who had been transformed into a uniformed poilu, bid him farewell.

The year Charles Dullin joyfully embraced his "destiny," Jean-Louis's little world fell apart. In the shop, where he entertained himself with the labels and bottles, it was now mother who loomed overhead, father having been taken to that other country called the front and become a purgatorial figure not yet dead but no longer quite alive, and accessible only through his mother's mediation. In 1915 Marcelle, risking imprisonment, led Max and Jean-Louis to Saint-Mihiel, a town so near the Verdun line of defense that they could hear cannon fire. During the summer of 1916 Jules was given leave to join his family in Tournus. Although this second reunion took place far from the trenches, it proved more belligerent than the first. Word of Marcelle's infidelity had vaulted the wall of silence by which Joffre isolated the

"Zone of the Armies" from the "Zone of the Rear," and had reached Jules in Flanders. While their parents sat in the parlor at dueling distance, Max and Jean-Louis, who knew that something else had broken, cycled around the house like alarmed birds caught in a storm.

Two years passed before the children saw their father again. By then he had been withdrawn from stretcher duty at the front and assigned to a hospital in Le Havre. Jean-Louis spent two months there. Every afternoon, a nurse fetched him from school and accompanied him to the Kleber barrack whose iron portals swung open after an invisible eye had scrutinized him. He would loiter in the ward for hours, playing with wounded soldiers or staring at beds that repeated one another hypnotically, "like dunes," until his father, who had aged beyond recognition, could visit him on the fly. Night brought no solace. Pretending to sleep, he would observe the lady with whom he boarded stand on her bed in nightshift and woo the military portrait of her dead husband. Then, craving the sleep lost to this ritual nightmare, he would be wakened in the morning by a parrot that shuffled portentously from claw to claw like a parade officer as it issued the command: "Jean-Louis, off to school, quickly-quickly-quickly." Unnerved by his guardian's nocturnal soliloquies and by her parrot's categorical imperative, he was relieved when his sojourn in Le Havre drew to a close.

Toward the end of September 1918, in Tournus, Jean-Louis saw his father for the last time. It was the harvest season. They worked the vineyard side by side and after nightfall sat against the terrace wall confidentially. Jules spoke to him of life and of death, as though sensing that his own end were imminent or unburdening himself of a constitutional sadness belied by his sturdy frame and clear blue eyes.

> Mon coeur est un vieillard assis sur la colline
> Regardant le chemin qu'il vient de parcourir *

he once wrote. Many years before, Jules had often sat against that wall memorizing poems of *The Meditations* and savoring the thought that Alphonse de Lamartine, who came from Mâcon, once boarded in a house that belonged to the Barraults.

---

* "My heart is an old man sitting on a hill / Looking down at the road by which he came."

One month later, in October 1918, Jules died of influenza at the age of forty-two. Since his death occurred during a twenty-four-hour furlough, the War Ministry declared it none of its concern and denied Marcelle Barrault a war widow's pension.

When news of the armistice reached an elementary school on the rue Ampère, the children greeted it in chorus, all except Jean-Louis, who began to weep. Infuriated by his tears, the teacher, a lame veteran decorated with the croix de guerre, brought his cane over the boy's back. The next day Marcelle visited the school, summoned Jean-Louis's teacher, and gave him two smart slaps. It is small wonder that her son should have come to think of her as more "soldierlike" than Jules, as someone whom death itself could not intimidate.

For Jean-Louis, absence had bleached his father of reality even before he died. Experience told him that men can succumb to foreign guises and withdraw behind doors with peepholes, behind "lines" or impalpable effigies of themselves, while women hold fast. At some dreadful juncture men suddenly fail, as though wrought of a fickle substance passed from father to son. On the eve of his fourth birthday he was convinced that during the night he would grow enormous, "like Alice in Wonderland." Needless to say, morning left him disillusioned. His fourth birthday being the first he celebrated without a congratulatory embrace from his father, 1914 announced a lifetime of disproportionate epiphanies (Gargantua, Pierrot, Messalina's stud, Kafka's Joseph K.) that would, each in turn, reiterate his belief, or his fear, that if he grew at all it would not be in the normal course of things but magically, and that magic could as readily make him wane as wax. "An orphan does not succeed in becoming a *real* adult," he later asserted. "As regards the well-known theory of the war between father and son and the conflict of generations, I myself . . . shall have known only the bitterness of frustration."

The parrot dinned home a message he was never to forget, that is, "quickly-quickly." One grew overnight. One disappeared overnight. Lacking the live model against which to test his image, Jean-Louis reconstructed his father from random memories like a paleontologist reconstructing an extinct mammal from scattered bones. Now winged now fossorial, now young now old, now revolutionary now pious, father became whatever he wanted father to be, a convenience for which he would pay endless dues.

"From the foot of the house rows of vines flowed downhill," he wrote of their property outside Tournus. "We still have the house. To us it is sacred, even though there are now only fields there. The vines have been pulled up, undone by the wines of the Midi, by the spirit of speculation, and political deals. This made a lifelong impression on me." Bereft of a father long before he found himself bereft of a vineyard, Jean-Louis felt the deepest affinity to Henri-Philibert, the *petit* having lost his birthright and the *grand* having bequeathed it in vain. Uprooted, he would always seek place, direction, comfort, and resistance from old men. The filial relationship he formed during World War II with Paul Claudel, for instance, was to be a direct consequence of the tragedy that had befallen him during World War I, and Claudel himself an avatar of the grandfather who originally took Jean-Louis under his wing.

"My maternal grandfather was a fantastic specimen. . . . In the scenario of my life, grandfather Valette is a major role, a 'plum,' in theatrical parlance," wrote Barrault, adding that "he was worthy of his own mother." Louis Valette's mother had walked to Paris from the mountains of central France in wooden clogs during the 1850s and found employment as a maidservant. In time she married a mason whose hands might have been enlisted in the labor force building Napoleon III's visionary capital had she not put them to better use building her own material salvation. Many old hotels, she observed soon after she arrived, stood empty of tenants. As the story goes, she prevailed upon her mason to buy one such hotel and, with the skill he had at his disposal, to help her remodel it. Within ten years the Valettes, having bought, remodeled, and sold a dozen derelict properties, were solidly entrenched in the petite bourgeoisie. Posterity did not give Monsieur the recognition to which his labors entitled him. Madame Valette, on the other hand, proved all too memorable. She lived eighty-nine years, observing the golden mean every day by swinging between gluttony and avarice. It was her wont, at family banquets, when her stomach invariably surrendered before her appetite had been appeased, to rally herself for the final course in a manner once employed by imperial Romans. Where the latter brought food up, she flushed it out, attaching a hose to the kitchen spigot. Even *in articulo mortis* this heroine of ingurgitation could not quietly give up the ghost. A physician, after he put his stethoscope to her chest, diagnosed bronchial pneumonia whereupon she replied—these being her last words according to family legend—"Idiot! Those are street noises."

Louis did indeed prove worthy of his mother when it came time to marry. Employed in a small factory whose owner, Monsieur Briy, had three eligible daughters, all of them contending for his favor, Louis, a good bourgeois more interested, apparently, in the golden apple than in the graces, could not distinguish one from the others. At length, he asked his mother's closest friend to have tea at their house, judge them with a practiced eye, and decide which Briy would suit him best. It was a lasting choice. His wife, Hermance, served for half a century, miscarrying three children but bearing two, helping him tend shop, punctually feeding him and always addressing him as "Monsieur Valette," except at dinner when, moved perhaps by the wine to a spirit of communion, she sometimes called him "my little Jesus." Louis, in turn, held that personal feelings deserved a place provided they confine themselves to it and not encroach upon his ledger. Thus, loving Hermance was scarcely reason to join his father-in-law in a bankrupt future. When it dawned on him that industry would one day find a cheap substitute for the inlaid wooden boxes Monsieur manufactured—boxes of the sort that used to encase fine liqueurs—he set himself up as a *marchand de couleurs,* or chandler. The capital that provided him 30 thousand francs' interest a year when he retired at the age of fifty attested to the wisdom of a paradox he would relentlessly urge upon his grandson, Jean-Louis: one made durable fortunes by selling perishable goods.

Louis's full name was Charles Louis Camille Napoleon Eugene Valette—"Louis Napoleon" and "Eugene" commemorating the fact that he had come into this world on the same day as Prince Eugene and thereby acquired, in the emperor, a godfather. As if honorary kinship with the Bonapartes sufficed to stunt a man, he stopped growing at five feet two inches and became a caricature of Napoleon III. Napoleon III was known throughout Europe for his goatee and a mustache waxed to points. Louis Napoleon Valette's goatee and mustache won him comparable renown in the Batignolles quarter of Paris. It was common knowledge that the Head of France found his most ungovernable subject between his legs. So Valette would frequently return to his flat on the rue de Lévis well past midnight, having allegedly spent the evening with *les pupilles de la Nation,* or public wards. After his retirement, he did in fact devote himself to the welfare of orphans and received a medal from the government in grateful recognition. But philanthropy covered a multitude of peccadilloes. When Valette had long since gone to his reward, the family (or his grandson, whose exaggerations are, let us note, of a Rabelaisian order, reflecting the "little man" he has felt himself to be) would boast that at eighty he had cuckolded a neighbor, that age had diminished neither his libido nor his sententiousness. Odd though it may seem for a man of such propensities to have taken cold baths every week and scoured himself with laundry soap, perhaps the martial career required stoic pampering.

This nineteenth-century *force de la nature,* who could no more begrudge an impulse satisfaction than his mother could leave food uneaten, found his petit-bourgeois model in the machine. What greater squander than to let a machine idle? It is itself only when it produces, its idleness is its impotence. At age ninety, feeling intimations of mortality, he asked Jean-Louis if it might be possible to make a bequest of his body. "It's a wicked waste to let such a machine rot." Had Balzac created Valette—and one suspects at times that Barrault's portrait of him was half inspired by *The Human Comedy*—he might have figured in some novel as an embodiment of mercantile heroism, asserting life by haggling with it. When his wife died, for example, he informed the undertaker that nothing would do but a stout coffin, explaining, "I want something solid, something that will last"—then giving way to grief. "The handles and screws are included in the price?" he asked, and further stipulated that his wife's maiden name be engraved on the plate (as Briy contained three fewer letters than Valette, it represented a saving of several hundred francs). Grieving and bargaining by turns, he seized his grandson—once the negotiations were over—and gloated conspiratorially: "See, little fool [a Valettian endearment]? Today I've saved fifteen hundred francs." While earning 1500 francs, he had not only forestalled his own death but made Hermance's less definitive.

Jean-Louis, whose early acquaintance with loss and separation may explain the habit he acquired of perceiving life as a succession of historical coincidences, or of events *déjà vécus,* would have been pleased had he known that underfoot, beneath the cobblestones of the Batignolles quarter where his entrepreneurial grandfather conducted business and where he himself grew up, a vineyard had flourished in the eighteenth century. Until the Revolution, Batignolles—like Monceau, Passy, Chaillot, Roule, Ternes—was a village northwest of Paris, lying between the city and the royal game forest that spread from Montmartre to Saint-Cloud. During Napoleon's regime, speculators bought parcels of it and built a cottage community. In Louis Philippe's time, the cottages were already overshadowed by apartment buildings. Paris having inexorably paved its way to this new outpost of itself, horse-drawn omnibuses called *Batignollaises* assured the connection. After the Revolution of 1848, Batignolles's population swelled with civil servants, tradesmen, retired folk living on a fixed annuity, small investors, and landlords—in other words, with constituents of the petite bourgeoisie fleeing social turbulence. They gave the neighborhood a personality so conservative that it readily lent itself to caricature. In the plays of Scribe and Labiche, in the drawings of Henri Monnier, Gustave Doré, and Honoré Daumier, *le petit rentier de Batignolles,* the "annuitant of Batignolles" who craved security above life itself, won it as a Parisian stereotype. "To spend sixteen hours a day for thirty years in a shop," wrote Alexis Martin, "and live above it in a narrow room, and at great sacrifice accumulate enough capital to bring in three or four thousand francs a year so as to be able to retire to Batignolles: this was in the last century the program of most Parisian shopkeepers." A composite portrait of the *petit rentier* would show him in thick felt slippers, ears plugged with cotton wool, leaning on a cane. He occupied a small apartment of small rooms in which mirrors reflected one another. The parquet floors were waxed, the walls papered. Early to bed and early to rise, he slept in an alcove, or, lacking an alcove, in a four-poster curtained against drafts. Religious images hung over the headboard, for although he had probably lapsed from Catholicism, he was not one to take risks. He entertained himself by playing dominoes twice a week at one of two cafés, the A la grande Marquise on rue d'Orléans or the Au Moka on rue de Lévis, snubbing on his way there the ambulant soup-vendor, whose business came mostly from laborers or Polish refugees (all refugees were "Polish" until proven otherwise). Addicted to snuff, he loathed tobacco. The Sunday dinner *en famille* was "sacred." This regime vouchsafed him a lifespan of seventy to eighty years, his burial plot—preferably in the Père Lachaise Cemetery—having been bought years before he occupied it.

Just as Louis Valette lived beyond the *petit rentier*'s actuarial age limit, so in every other respect did he prove more ample and excessive than an average specimen of the class, without for all that repudiating its values. To be sure, he and Hermance spent three months in Nice every winter (loading their wardrobe into a black leather trunk of Transatlantic proportions); nothing, however, could have induced him to leave before January 15 or to return later than April 15, these being the dates on which his tenants' quarterly rent payments fell due. Rather than join the domino players at Au Moka, he would spend Saturday or Sunday afternoons at his favorite *café-concert*, the Théâtre Moncey, reading his newspaper—a Bonapartist and anti-Dreyfusard one—while listening to a chanteuse sing airs from Offenbach, whose operettas he knew by heart. But the domino players were nonetheless his only friends. Having retired from a business to which he had devoted more or less sixteen hours a day for thirty years, he moved from the apartment over his shop at 55, rue de Lévis to another at number 43; though far better off than most *petits rentiers*, he could scarcely imagine himself living elsewhere than on this bustling market street, where he strode like a gamecock of great local eminence. "*Pas de complications*," as he often put it, sweeping aside whatever stood in his way.

If only history and human nature had cooperated with him instead of complicating matters, Valette would have seen to it that his children felt more at home than he ever could among people of breeding, for the old man, who seized every opportunity to drop Latin phrases culled from the pink pages of his *Petit Larousse*, did not lack social ambition. Marcelle was given piano lessons and sent to an exclusive convent school near the Parc Monceau, where young ladies learned those arcane little graces that distinguished *le monde* from the hoi polloi. After several years, during which her poodlelike classmates would never allow her to forget whence she came, it had been impressed on her many times over that one cracks an egg with the side of one's fork rather than with a knife or spoon, that one sections a cheese before passing it, and that a proper hostess serves herself salad before serving her guests, this in accordance with the culinary adage "politeness [i.e., the dressing] lies at the bottom of the bowl." The product of this education was a young woman in whom manners were so indissolubly wed to rage that she could, like Chaucer's prioress, as easily throw fits of decorum as of temper and, when need be, savage her opponent with points of etiquette. Far from making what Valette would have deemed an advantageous marriage, it was perhaps half to spite him that she married for love an impecunious provincial who sympathized with Socialist ideals.

After Jules departed for the front, Valette's fantasy of refinement came home to roost, bringing along two additional mouths. Though war and its attendant catastrophes—inflation, income tax, a Bolshevik regime that refused to honor railroad bonds in which the French middle class had invested heavily—made him quake for his future, he assumed this charge placed on him so unexpectedly late in life, giving Marcelle an apartment in the tenement he owned on rue de Lévis. His daughter evidently exhausted his generosity by the time his son could profit from it, however. When Robert limped home on legs shattered at the front, Valette drove him away, as though he had seen in him a specter of insolvency. "My lad, you have no excuse," he said. "You are a man now, you must earn your livelihood. I give you a week to find a job; in a week's time you will not be welcome here anymore." His doughty mother had not trudged halfway across France in order that now, two generations later, the family should languish in the cul-de-sac of Batignolles. Where his children ought to have been his crutch, malignant fate made him theirs.

A burden that might have weighed other men down offered certain benefits to the paterfamilias who delighted in playing God to public wards. When Valette loosened the purse strings, a tongue came loose that possessed encyclopedic knowledge of those proverbs the French call *la sagesse des nations*. Money gave him license to dictate, and he brought his dictates to bear in every realm, including, above all, the matter of his younger grandson's education. A precocious child, Jean-Louis, by his own account, had done six grades in three years. At age ten, he reached the crossroads that led in one direction to a Latin school or *lycée*—Carnot—and, in the other, to a school offering no classical curriculum—Collège Chaptal. Where the *lycée* was concerned, some such aristocratic name as Talleyrand might have suited it better than Carnot, for in spirit it stood at an ironical remove from the revolution it nominally upheld. Serving the Plaine Monceau, it richly deserved its snobbish reputation. Marcelle Barrault, who was not about to see the hurt of her own childhood inflicted on her son found, this time around, an ally in Valette.

The latter willingly paid Jean-Louis's tuition (tuition beyond primary school being another barrier maintained by the Third Republic against common people), but he demanded, as one might expect, a good return on his investment. Though Latin was still magic for him, it behooved the orphan whose future had become his responsibility to acquire skills that would help him navigate a world full of reefs and shoals. "Accustomed as they were to living in a universe of monetary stability, they felt bewildered," wrote one historian, Claude Fohlen, about the French population. "Ever since Bonaparte coined the Germinal franc, it had fluctuated only twice, in 1848 and in 1871, so that money had come to acquire a fetishistic value. It was all the more difficult to comprehend this phenomenon because France had emerged from the war victorious. How could a country win and its currency lose? . . . There dawned an age of inflation." Valette therefore sent Jean-Louis to Chaptal in the belief that it reflected its illustrious name more faithfully than did Carnot. As Napoleon's minister of the interior had Jean-Antoine Chaptal not, after all, founded the French Chamber of Commerce? And had Napoleon himself not founded the "lay colleges" with a view to training administrative cadres who would staff his Empire?* "My grandfather . . . resolved that I should have a career in business," wrote Barrault.

Chaptal's curriculum bore no relationship to Valette's notions of it, but neither did Jean-Louis inside school resemble the timorous grandson to whom he gave an allowance on Thursdays, doling out exemplary tales of thrift and financial acumen excerpted from his own childhood. The fears that made life an often incomprehensible trial for Jean-Louis—fears of the dark, of the deep, of elevators, of surprises, of his brother, who bullied him—left him alone in Chaptal, where he drew attention to himself as much by his mischief as by his letter-perfect recitations. "To me school was the best of games. When I felt ill I concealed it, not to miss going there." While the apprentice merchant played hooky, the budding actor discovered that his diminutive size, from

---

* The state subsidized *lycées* and the municipality lay colleges (until the Revolution, religious orders operated all *collèges*). In an imperial decree of 1808 *lycées* were required to teach "ancient languages, history, rhetoric, logic, and the elements of the mathematical and physical sciences" while only "the elements of ancient languages and the basic principles of history and the sciences" were stipulated for *collèges*. By 1920 the lay college, corresponding to the German *Realgymnasium*, had dropped even the "elements," or so it was at Chaptal.

which he otherwise suffered terrible humiliation, could be turned to good account. He took pride in being uncatchable, or caught, uncontainable. When banished from class, he would continue his pranks outside, borrowing the charwoman's broom, for example, and balancing it over a jamb with such cunning that its bristle end, directly an irate teacher threw open the door, fell plumb upon his head. The ovations this earned him from fellow students were easily worth the *pensum*, or copying task, that stood for punishment in French schools. Jean-Louis, as drawn by Barrault, answered the ideal of Harlequin, smaller than others but physically and mentally more nimble, endearing himself to grown-ups but ridiculing them behind their backs with elfin improvisations. It would have been as unthinkable for Harlequin to get expelled from school as to forgo the pleasure of a subversive whim that cost him *le prix d'excellence*, first prize. Winning honors the better to forfeit them, testing the limits of authority as he could not afford to do outside Chaptal, he took calculated pratfalls, or teetered at safe brinks. Chaptal taught him, in Jean Cocteau's excellent phrase, "jusqu'où on peut aller trop loin" ("up to what point one may go too far").

In his autobiography, Barrault portrays the child he was most revealingly in those passages that slight the teachers whose approval he sought, as such disparagement only underlines his allegiance to a cultural myth with which, he has, often despite himself, always been enthralled. "To me, the teachers were, on the whole, a huge joke," he wrote. "One had an enormous beard, another a beetroot where the nose should have been; this one had a lisp, that one, in math class, made us go through gymnastics to teach us 'common factors' and 'common denominators.' . . . So far as I'm concerned, profs are no more responsible than insects that carry pollen. The teacher has no importance." It goes without saying that schoolteachers who enter memoirs rarely leave them unscathed. It is also true that each culture metes out punishment according to its own vocabulary of derision. When Kafka observed that recalling his teachers was as difficult as holding a row of identical blocks pressed between his hands—inevitably one would always fall out and jumble all the others—the Central European memory thus avenged itself on a corps of drillmasters who relied on military discipline to keep students in line. In France, the *professeur de lycée* might have found such oblivion a kinder fate than the commemoration he often received, for his literary stereotype, from Bourget's *The Step* to

Pagnol's *Topaze*, is misshapen, beset with crotchets, and ostracized. There are, of course, those who cut exceptional figures—Louis Guilloux's Cripure, Sartre's Roquentin—but even so he conforms to type, internalizing society's view of him so that he beholds himself, in Sartrean parlance, as *de trop*, or superfluous. His very virtues were social stigmata.

In 1904 Charles Péguy had written this by way of paying tribute to his old teacher Georges Edet:

> The young rhetorician will believe that he was a ceremonious old prof, Latinist and dreary; far from it—he was an admirable man, all heart and probity. Praised be the old university masters; they were *honnêtes hommes*. An *honnête homme* like Father Edet toiled and spent more time pondering the question whether this or that was a solecism (and if perchance it was missing from paragraph 1245 in Riemann, it might be found in paragraph 2171, et cetera—for he could quote the book chapter and verse), he made greater exertions to understand the exact thought of some author in a Latin expression, to conduct his mind exactly, honestly in the realm of the unreal and the potential than do young men nowadays to erect a world system under the aegis of sociology.

Such devotion was not uncommon among *professeurs de lycée*, for they came in the majority from lower-middle-class families and wed classical culture the more ardently for having had to win it. Therein lay their "maladjustment" from the viewpoint of their patrons—of the philanthropists who gave them scholarships, of the dignitaries whose own sons would have disappointed them had they chosen to teach: what they won could not be theirs definitively or intrinsically because they had won it. Marriage, however ardent, could not bring them what the bourgeoisie claimed as its birthright; indeed, ardor and toil were telltale signs of a demi-bourgeois or a cultural parvenu, exertion betraying congenital want. Though a bourgeois might apply himself, the social myth had it that he did so not in order to acquire something from without but to elicit something innate, not to become what he wasn't, but to come into his own. Culture spoke to the bourgeois much the way Pascal's Hidden God spoke to the believer: "You would not have sought me, if you had not already found me." Grace would therefore reveal itself as facility, as a "natural" display of erudition and talent. In his eulogy, Péguy deliberately inverted the conventional image of an *honnête homme*, a gentleman. A gentleman did not, like Georges Edet, lucubrate, puzzle, or agonize. Culture being form, virtuosity was the mark of a man born to it. Culture being impractical, a gentleman made it his sport rather than his livelihood and played not to grow wiser but to grow more supple. "This is the creature that has the art born with him;/Toils not to learn it, but doth practice it/Out of most excellent nature."

Where solemnity—the *esprit de sérieux*—befit the disinherited, a kind of ludic aplomb marked the heir. One took to heart something foreign; the other, in publicizing his emotional distance from it, paradoxically gave proof of his endowment. Student society, which reflected in miniature society at large, observed the cultural schism between gentlemen and scholars. It was incumbent upon the *boursier*, or scholarship student, who in many instances became the *professeur de lycée*, to toil and fret, for patronage demanded of him a sober air. The intellectual ward was perforce the grind, the *fort en thème* who groped for knowledge inasmuch as he lacked the culture of a native. Working by the sweat of his brow, he advanced step by step.

Upon this belief—that a laborer, a farmer, a shopkeeper courted disaster by skipping stages in the process of acculturation—conservative minds like Paul Bourget and Maurice Barrès predicated their literary mission. Indeed, the title of Bourget's once-celebrated novel *L'Etape* (*The Step*, which might also be translated as "The Halting Place"), speaks for itself. While the *boursier*, that slave of temporality, could not skip, the true heir, whose swiftness argued his birthright, his born exemption from "steps," and inherent finesse, could not but skip. The former required teachers to help him bridge his original lacuna, a Fall having condemned him to a laborious ascent. The latter was ineducable, his natural brilliance, ease, and fluency demonstrating that teachers were otiose, that the mind or soul given him to begin with formed a paradigm of the Eternal Model. Since culture resided inside him, his schooling was in the service not of cognition but of re-cognition. "Profs are no more responsible than insects that carry pollen; the teacher has no importance": born gentlemen from Carnot could not have stated this upper-class precept more cruelly, and certainly not more to their own disadvantage, than the *enfant terrible* of Chaptal, who tells us he skipped three grades in three years.

That Jean-Louis beheld himself as an outsider or an exile would serve to explain, in part, Barrault's oft-repeated and poignant expressions of nostalgia for the Latin he was never taught. "I began [in adolescence] to regret not having had Latin. I shall regret it all my life. . . . At Chaptal, we learned neither Latin nor Greek. I have always experienced this as a lack," he wrote, adducing the same reasons to justify—and condemn—himself that Monsignor Félix Dupanloup had pressed home a century before when defending the study of rhetoric against pedagogical reformers whose modernism threatened sacred traditions.

> I have felt this lack in the inadequate knowledge I have of French, my maternal language. I would have been able to express myself with greater facility in my own language had I studied Greek and Latin. So deeply has this lacuna affected me that on various occasions I have sought, unavailingly alas, to learn declensions. I have, however, found a pallid remedy . . . in the method once used in grade school, namely, *The Garden of Greek Roots* and *The Garden of Latin Roots*. After someone recommended these two little books, I set myself the task of memorizing them, "like a donkey." . . . How can one know the language through which the body expresses itself if one doesn't know its roots?

The last sentence suggests the predicament of the youngest child in a family conversant with words unintelligible to him, who remains convinced, against all reason, that they were born eloquent or rooted in a language whose secret will always somehow escape him. Not until he, foreigner that he is, learns what he can never know at first hand will he possess such knowledge or reality as was theirs by nature. And so he seeks the origin of words like a creature deprived of roots, going back to the beginning but mocking himself all the while, as if his doing so were an asinine venture. What hope of salvation could a donkey reasonably entertain? Very little, unless, that is, he belonged to the Atelier where, in due course, Barrault would cultivate the art of silence.

It is hardly a coincidence that in 1924, when the sense of alienation from his "maternal language" first began to exercise him, Jean-Louis found himself deserted once again. Four years earlier, his mother had married Louis Martin, a childhood friend. Educated in the genteel tradition like herself, Martin—who painted pretty watercolors, brought off tolerable renditions of old favorites on the violin, rode horseback, and dressed elegantly—was like herself without any means of earning a livelihood. In a better world his prospects might have equaled his parts, but the France of 1918, to which he had returned broken and broke, had use neither for his personal ornaments nor for the copper window fixtures his father had manufactured during the *belle époque*. Cast adrift, this mild victim of war and economic obsolescence found safe haven on the rue de Lévis, where he courted Marcelle as assiduously as he knew how. Although the courtship caused consternation at home—Max fought it tooth and nail—it soon became apparent that his presence would not seriously disrupt the status quo or redirect lines of power established within the household. "The mere fact that she was basking in love made me happy," wrote Jean-Louis, who identified almost symbiotically with his mother—his mother having addressed him throughout childhood as "my little girl" and encouraged him to regard himself as her daughter in male guise, her tomboy. "We four quickly formed a team of comrades, charming comrades none very sure of himself."

Larger now by one more waif dependent on Valette's charity, the family had just about absorbed its new member when Louis Martin fell gravely ill. Heeding a doctor's admonition that Paris would be the death of him, Marcelle straightaway made arrangements to occupy the house Jules Barrault had left her in Tournus. As for Jean-Louis, it was decided that separation from Mother represented a lesser evil than separation from Chaptal. Max, whose scholastic career had been futile and episodic, accompanied their mother to Burgundy, but Jean-Louis stayed behind in Paris as the ward of his uncle Robert (or Bob; the English diminutive followed him through life). "Bob was given our flat on condition that he provide me with bed and board. I was to have lunch every day at my grandparents'. All this, of course, by fiat of King Valette. So my mother was far away."

How deeply this second break in his young life affected Barrault may best be measured by his need to believe in a Providence that constantly brings life full round through reincarnations and miraculous coincidences, in a telepathic language that tells people, through a "sixth sense," the thoughts harbored by loved ones far, far away. His autobiography, *Memories for Tomorrow*, is fraught with tales intimating the existence of another world where people do not quarrel, separate, or die, and where love endows lovers with ubiquity. Did Marcelle forsake him on Louis Martin's account? She would suddenly return when he, Jean-Louis, fell ill, having learned of his illness "in a dream." Did Marcelle defy the temporal powers when she joined Jules at the front in 1915? Twenty-five years later, during the Phony War, Barrault's own wife would make short shrift of danger and surprise *him* at the front, appearing, quite by chance, on the anniversary of Jules's death. Events combined to unravel his life, and his imagination knit them together with analogy and metaphor, creating a seamless fabric that preserved him from sudden disaster. The need he felt for some principle of inner coherence expressed itself perhaps best in the geometrical figures that offered him pleasure and solace throughout adolescence:

> I had a particular passion for math, and more than once found the solution to a problem in a dream. Above all, I loved solid geometry. To reconstitute in three dimensions an object of which one has the projection on only one plane, to pass from the shadow which is cast to the "thing" turning in the light, is . . . exactly like taking a text printed on paper and making of it a show. . . . I had invented a philosophy, "harmonism," according to which "the drawing of the trajectory of one's life must complete, on the day of one's death, a pretty curve." Even today I have nothing against this aesthetic wake of mine.

Inner coherence derived from a mother's warmth and solicitude. The "pretty curve" suggests that math had come to serve unconscious wishes, rather like *écriture automatique*, with Jean-Louis's doodle forming an abstract diagram of the body in which he dreamed of seeing himself enveloped.

As "dense" as Marcelle made him feel, apart from her he felt "unreal," "hollow," or "weightless," and longed for the vintage season when shadows became the show, when, during his annual sojourn in Tournus, he would barter the immaculate consolations of geometry for the feast of his mother's presence: "She grew more and more bohemian, did my mother. So long as Louis made love satisfactorily, nothing else mattered. Always with a cigarette between her lips, she governed the life of the house. Cats, chickens, rabbits, dogs, and goats lived communally. She prepared a single dish for the lot: a tubful, in the kitchen. . . . I can still see that harmonious confusion of pecking beaks, lapping tongues, twitching nostrils, and snuffling mouths." At times the "peasant" whose hands resembled paws, at other times the "aesthete" whose thoughts fed on death, Jean-Louis was already, in embryo, the director whose repertoire would include theatrical adaptations of Rabelais and of Knut Hamsun's *Hunger*. Succored and starved by turns, he sprang to life or lay fallow according to the season.

His guardian uncle presided over the fallow season, in spirit as well as in body. Were it not for an artist's model, Adrienne, whom he met soon after Valette denied him shelter, Robert might have lost what remained of his courage to survive and made his bed on the riverbank, along with *clochards*, down-and-outers. Instead, he became a vendor at the central wholesale market, Les Halles, selling flowers to florists. He would rise before dawn in order to receive the daily shipment from Holland at five o'clock and come home at dusk exhausted not only by his long day but by nagging resentment of his wasted years. Adrienne, in turn, never quite rose from bed, for even when she had, her eyes went on dreaming of it, or so it seemed to Jean-Louis, who portrays her as a tropical frond overcome by the sheer strain of verticality. "She would sprawl in armchairs, inhaling the smoke from her cigarette of black tobacco with the same withdrawal, the same inner dialogue that would have been hers had she smoked hashish, while her left hand, open and dangling, held a glass of red wine. She was not trying to provoke desire; she was simply there, where chance had set her down." Robert and Adrienne lived together for years without marrying (getting married, when at length they did, mainly to placate Hermance); perhaps they could not, except under duress, bring themselves to solemnize a ménage which they knew would produce no children, to consecrate an arrangement that seemed imbued with a spirit of aftermath. Where chance had set them down, there they coped day by day, enjoying dominical respites from their otherwise lackluster existence in a cottage they owned not far from Paris.

Bob was a painter *manqué*. He loved art, and transmitted his love to Jean-Louis. After dinner, they would often study picture books, recite poetry, or play word games, though never for long, since Uncle Bob could not afford the luxury of staying awake much past nine. During these brief sessions, Jean-Louis, who grew extremely fond of him, may well have heard subversive encouragement to resist Valette, to embody hopes and dreams that he, Robert, had never completely relinquished. "He was not living the life he would have liked. . . . This made a decisive impression on me. Where old man Valette was what he was and accepted himself, not so Bob, who pined for a different way of life, like someone chronically homesick."

This melancholy survivor, Robert Valette, accommodated to perfection the image Jean-Louis had formed of his father, Jules Barrault. His fondness for one *manqué* was inseparable from his nostalgia for the other (*manqué* meaning both "missed" and "would-be"), and nostalgia argued similitude where similitude did not necessarily exist, so that uncle and father became a single figure, posthumous yet alive, whose buried ambitions constituted Jean-Louis's mandate. Barrault would have it that Jules, like Robert, suffered from homesickness all life long. "Deep down, he felt himself to be a poet, which made him faint at the sight of blood when an injured man was brought into his shop. . . . Why did my father choose a chemist's shop—he, a man constantly homesick for the house in which he was born?"

Whatever uncle and father may have been, it is certain the homesick one was Jean-Louis himself, who made loss work to repair loss, creating, with similes in hand, a fraternal order of the exiled, the homeless, the forlorn. Cut off from Tournus "like" Jules, divorced from real life "like" Robert, he found not only companionship but identity in the parallel. Heir to their lost potential as well as to their mortal regrets, he was doubly the heir.

Grandfather Valette also filled a void, and filled it rather too amply at times. Where Robert represented "dream" (to quote Barrault), the old man, like Dickens' Gradgrind, brought home "hard facts." Not a day passed that did not give Jean-Louis some morsel of common sense to digest, for every day he would eat lunch on rue de Lévis, his grandfather materializing at noon when the sun reaches its zenith and the French paterfamilias reigns at the head of the table. "At lunch I sat on his left and he watched me closely. Above us, in the center, a large hanging lamp. Never any butter on the table," Barrault wrote, setting the scene not so much for a meal shared as for a drama in which he felt spotlighted or for a trial in which he stood accused. Jean-Louis could rely on no one but his grandmother to protect him; having been rubbed against by Valette for half a century, she was now beyond abrasion. "In the midst of this whirlwind she had built a nest of her own." At the earliest opportunity, Hermance would retire to her bedroom, draw a hassock under her legs, put on glovefingers, then smoke three cigarettes in quick succession, holding an ashtray against her chest like a bib and rounding her lips to form smoke rings. "What silence, what calm, what affectionate gentleness I found in that room! There, one was in the eye of the hurricane."

It is no wonder that Jean-Louis came to fancy himself a plaything of wanton adults, if not indeed a sport of nature. Toyed with, and travestied, he developed a strong aversion to corners from which he could not escape without revealing himself or being defined. Grandfather Valette was by no means the only inquisitor he knew. Jean-Louis owed explanations to everyone in the family. "Some evenings, we—my mother, Louis Martin, Max, and I—played cards. Whenever I had a good hand, blood would rise to my forehead and even to my ears. When I had not, I would blanch, and my eyes would dull. They, seeing so clearly what my hand was like, laughed themselves silly, while I, not understanding how they knew, became furious," he wrote. That Max hoped to emasculate him might be accounted a normal enough expression of sibling love. ("I was his scapegoat. He would stifle me under the bedclothes. This has made me claustrophobic for life. . . . Max was also my protector, however; I was his own, his plaything, his Nénette."*) But danger lurked even under the otherwise affable surface of Uncle Bob, from whom there would at times spring forth a Mr. Hyde, a predator he could neither anticipate nor defend against:

> Bob sometimes treated me as a joke. On Thursdays, the school holiday, he would look for me in the evening and stare with his dark eyes into mine: "What have you done today?"—I went and played football in the Bois de Boulogne."—"Are you quite sure?" His gaze would take on an inquisitorial intensity. I would begin to blush. "Er . . . yes!"—"And yet someone saw you at four o'clock in the place Pigalle. Don't deny it!" I would go purple in the face. My forehead was covered with sweat. I no longer knew how to answer. I no longer even knew who I was.

When, before long, he became an actor-director, it was himself he played again and again. Whether in Hamsun's *Hunger*, Cervantes's *Numancia*, Kafka's *Trial*, Camus's *State of Siege*, Vauthier's *The Fighting Character*, or Ionesco's *Rhinoceros*, he invariably chose to stage works whose heroes are besieged, trapped, or under sentence of death for a crime as unatonable as original sin.

Meals with grandfather grew more indigestible as time wore on, for as graduation from Chaptal loomed nearer, the prospect of leaving school and entering a trade became increasingly abhorrent. Alternatives

---

* During World War I, women knit tutelary dolls for their soldiers, the male doll being known as "Rintintin" and the female as "Nénette."

to the career set forth for him by Valette flitted through his mind. Now he pictured himself a veterinarian, now a forester or *ingénieur des eaux et forêts*, but the lap of mother nature and God's little dappled creatures lost their charm directly he tried to reconcile them with the idea of earning his livelihood. At length, push came to shove, a family council was convened, and a decision made that Jean-Louis, who acquiesced in it, should become an engineer. Valette would support him until such time as he had absorbed enough higher mathematics to compete for admission to the Ecole Polytechnique, and then, if fortune smiled, see him through university. Jean-Louis, in turn, would observe the Valettian dictum, *pas de complications*.

Only six months elapsed, however, before this program went awry. "My demons were at me," wrote Barrault. Whatever his demons may have been, they showed no disposition to let him follow the path of least resistance, or to go on eating lunch in the glare of justice. He gave so poor an account of himself during his preparatory year that Valette finally lost patience. "My grandfather would not feed me for another year. He cut me off after the second term, telling me that I must now earn my living. I was eighteen."

When his grandfather withdrew support from him, Jean-Louis set out to deliver himself of his newfound freedom by organizing his existence around Robert Valette. Before long he had become a factotum in the flower business and a pupil at the Ecole du Louvre. He would go to Les Halles at 5:00 a.m., work there until noon, attend classes in art history at the museum, dine, fill telephone orders from Parisian florists, sleep, then rise before daybreak, driving himself month after month, "like" Robert, lest doubts as to his scholarly aptitude and creative talent overtake him. While art fascinated Jean-Louis, his artistic vocation, such as it was, was inseparable from his yearning for a life governed by mathematics or by aesthetic law, so that he entered the Louvre each day more in the spirit of religious postulancy than of intellectual apprenticeship. At nineteen, he felt as bewildered as the four-year-old who dreamed himself a giant only to wake up convinced that he would remain a midget forever, that nature had denied him an essential part, that he would grow not from within but through miraculous intervention. "I loved van Gogh, his tragic life; when I thought of him, I would touch my ear. It was still there, but I would have gladly cut it off would that gesture have made me a hero like him. I loved heroes," he wrote.

How could mere knowledge make him "real"? And if, as his poet of the moment, Paul Valéry, proclaimed, "genius is a long patience," how did one acquire the genius to wait upon oneself when fate might strike one dead at any moment? His own drawings bespoke his predicament, for, one infers from what he says about them, they were graphic mimicries, disembodied caricatures reminiscent of the cartoonist Sem's, notations made in shorthand and *en passant* by a young man who had no time to bide. "Quickly-quickly," screamed the parrot. "All my efforts to become a painter failed: at the competition held by the Galerie des Beaux-Arts, four were accepted and I was fifth. I obtained an interview with a famous teacher: Devambez. He scarcely glanced at my portraits, for I had not previously done three years at some academy. In that quarter, life resisted me." After a year of hectic equivocation, Jean-Louis returned to Chaptal as a live-in tutor, a *pion*, his alma mater being the one place from which he could contemplate the future without feeling harried by it.

It was while in this sanctuary that his thoughts alighted on the Théâtre de l'Atelier. Toward the end of January 1931 he sent the following letter to Charles Dullin:

Monsieur,
I am a student, aged 20, a pupil at the Ecole du Louvre for painting; I am a tutor at the Collège Chaptal, where I did my secondary studies. But on the generally repeated advice of the people I know and because of the strong inclination I have long had deep down in me for the theater (or cinema), I would appreciate the opinion, if that were possible, of an eminently competent person. . . . With this in mind, may I ask you to grant me a brief interview? Hoping very much for a favorable reply, though only if it does not cause you any inconvenience, please accept, Monsieur, the expression of my deep and respectful admiration.

Why Barrault, who had by his own reckoning seen only a dozen plays since childhood, should suddenly have found theater so irresistible is a question which in his memoirs he does not broach. "My explanations are inexhaustible. At the time I could only have answered: I wanted it. A vocation is desire, pure and simple." But reasons there were, and the very myth in which he sought to envelop them reveals their outline. It is noteworthy that Marcelle Barrault's dormant fantasy of theatrical stardom—yet another fantasy put to shame by Valette—should have awakened shortly before Jean-Louis sent Charles Dullin the above letter. "While I was at Chaptal and in Paris, my mother, at Tournus, to make her winter evenings rather more cheerful, joined a society that got up shows," he wrote. "Jacques Jacquier, an old actor who had played with Sylvain, was the moving spirit of these. Marcelle had found once again the atmosphere of the amateur dramatic society at Le Vésinet. She acted in comedies and was happy, for to her theater was like a pregnant woman's craving. Which of us would inherit it, Max or I?"

Nearly twenty-five years later, in a personal testament entitled *I Am a Man of Theater*, Barrault declared:

> Only a boundless love of mankind . . . can make possible the marriage of our personal heart with the collective heart, the common heart [*le coeur commun*]—I was about to say the common body [*le corps commun*], thinking of the mystical body. Indeed there does exist a physiological resemblance between the man of theater, the priest, and the sorcerer. While the "commodities" they offer differ in quality—the priest pardons and saves, the sorcerer liberates, the theater succors—the process of communion with others is the same. . . . Only love and even personal desire can attain effectively and authentically that marvelous moment of *collective communion* that exists in churches, magical ceremonies, and in theaters worthy of the name. It follows that the man of theater seeks with all his might to melt into others until he has rediscovered himself in others. As of that moment, he need no longer concern himself with them, but with himself alone, since his soul is perfectly attuned to theirs!

The language of this testament evokes Dullin's assertion that he had not known what it was to act until, with Smerdiakov, his "body and soul" first felt the need "to melt in order to externalize a character." If theater succors, if by means of it an actor enters the mystical body, where but in the Théâtre de l'Atelier could Jean-Louis have found more happily assembled the elements of a personal conjuration? There, on a stage adjoining a farmhouse, he could imagine himself at home in Tournus, where his mother held forth as actress and nurturant queen. Barrault might well have written, as Jouvet did, that "one practices Theater because one has the impression of never having been oneself, of being unable to be oneself, and of having discovered at last the means of being oneself. . . . From the outset of his career, the actor feels an emptiness, and lives on it."

Dullin granted him an audition, for which he prepared two scenes, one from Molière's *Les Femmes savantes* (*The Learned Women*) and another from Racine's *Britannicus*. It took place in the room over Gypsy's stable. What Barrault remembers of it is the fear that had beset him often before, as at table with his grandfather or during inquisitions conducted by his uncle. If it were not terrible enough to face a hunchback whose keen eye gave him no quarter, in the midst of his theatrical exertions he became aware of another, even more redoubtable audience, for outside the window two figures suddenly materialized. "I could make out a couple in the hotel opposite—a hotel that let rooms by the day. They could not see Dullin. They kept pointing at me, whispering to each other, laughing. I must be barmy. I spouted my speeches in front of a pantomime, window to window, across the pavement of the rue d'Orsel." It is unlikely that the young Barrault would have known what sort of establishment stood opposite the Atelier, but no matter: his anecdote indicates how feckless he believed himself to be, how far outside the pale (and yet at its very center?), how incapable of projecting his voice and of impressing judges who held him in contempt. The window might as well have been a mirror, so faithfully did it throw back the image he carried inside his head of Jean-Louis as Nénette.

Dullin saw something else, however. The wiry young creature whose face, with its sharp nose, its eyefolds, its bulbous forehead, and mummylike cheekbones seemed to have descended upon him from elfland, was made for *commedia dell'arte*. He took him in straightaway, and free of charge.

CHAPTER XI

✦ ✦ ✦ ✦

THE EVOLUTION
OF A MIME

Barrault's audition in 1931 was the first of many trials he would endure at the Atelier, where he spent four years learning his trade under a master who toughened him with digs and thrusts, with faint praise and volleys of damnation. Not for nothing did Dullin entertain himself, during summers in the country, by flicking a bullwhip at imaginary targets. During the other three seasons, his newest apprentice served as his whipping boy. "For four whole years I never met Dullin's eye without trembling with awe and the desire to be worthy of him. . . . I was his constant butt, as if he were submitting the boiler of a steam engine to all the explosion tests." *

Unbeknownst to Jean-Louis, who found comfort in the thought that he was somehow uniquely responsible for his mentor's rage—after all, a constant butt resembles a cynosure—everyone, including especially Charles Dullin, filled Dullin with loathing. "I cannot suffer certain social hypocrisies," he wrote to Pauline in 1931. "Most people disgust me beyond words. I understand deep solitude and consider that it alone allows us to breathe at the present time. . . . The stupidity, the uselessness, the upstart arrogance of most people make their presence intolerable. . . . I who have neither religion nor hopes confide myself to nature; I believe in it and would sooner surround myself with trees than

---

* "Dullin had the morphology of a man of great stature," wrote Barrault, in whose mind he was larger than life.

with men." By 1931 his marriage had gone sour. Though Marcelle continued to appear in productions and teach at the school until 1934, when her health failed, Dullin had left her for Simone Jollivet, who wrote plays under the pen name of Simone Camille-Sans. In 1931 the Atelier staged Simone Jollivet's play *L'Ombre* (*The Shadow*), which one critic described as a medieval drama fraught with philosophical considerations clearly indebted to Nietzsche and with psychomythological fioriture involving doubles, androgynes, et al. If ever Dullin had misgivings about her work, they went unrecorded. And it may be that he did not, for just as the peasant boy persuaded himself some years earlier that his elegant fiancée was a born actress, so now the man who had had little in the way of formal education became infatuated with a *femme savante*, an intellectually modish blue stocking.

This blue stocking was cut from no conventional cloth, as one gathers from the portrait of her that appears in Simone de Beauvoir's *The Prime of Life*. When still a girl living in Toulouse, she created for herself a little Pantheon whose principal divinities included Lucifer, Bluebeard, Pedro the Cruel, Cesare Borgia, and Louis XI. Being not only beautiful but precociously well-read (her father, a pharmacist of considerable culture, had acquainted her with Michelet, George Sand, Balzac, and Dickens), she felt that some exceptional destiny awaited her, that her endowments deserved a stage on which she could display herself to her best advantage. Accordingly, she began at the age of eighteen to frequent fashionable houses of assignation and soon made her mark there. Simone de Beauvoir wrote of her:

> Camille [the pseudonym Beauvoir gives her] possessed an acute sense of the appropriate *mise en scène;* while awaiting a client in the room set apart for him she would stand in front of the fireplace, stark naked, her long hair combed out, reading Michelet or, at a later period, Nietzsche. Her cultured mind, her proud bearing, and the subtle technique she brought to her task knocked town clerks and lawyers flat: they wept on her pillow from sheer admiration. Some of them established a more permanent relationship with her, showered her with presents, and took her on their travels. She dressed very expensively, but chose her clothes less from the current fashion than from pictures which happened to catch her fancy.

Furthermore, she held parties in the cellar of her home, which was transformed into the stage set for (as fancy dictated) a black mass, a vignette from Boccaccio's *Decameron,* or, on one occasion when she played a Roman lady of the Late Empire with her guests all wearing togas, for a Lupercalian orgy. Among her numerous devotées was the young Jean-Paul Sartre who, long after she initiated him, continued to regard Simone Jollivet as the ideal concubine, the hetaera Simone de Beauvoir could never replace. No sooner did she arrive in Paris than she set about pursuing Charles Dullin. "Camille admired vast outbursts of passionate devotion, and affected to suffer such transports herself. She became infatuated with Conrad Veidt, and then, after seeing him play Louis XI in the film *The Miracle of the Wolves,* with Charles Dullin," wrote Beauvoir.

Suffice it to say that once she entered Dullin's life in the late 1920s, the shadow Simone Jollivet cast grew longer and longer. His manifestos, his choice of plays, his personal associations, his casting assignments: all these fell increasingly within her editorial province. Holding him spellbound, she stood guard between him and the world, she coddled him, cuckolded him, adapted novels to his stage, encouraged his dreams of magnitude, and finally, when Paris accorded her own *oeuvre* nothing like the recognition to which she felt entitled, she literally thrashed him for it during drunken rages. It was Simone Jollivet at whom Pauline Teillon-Dullin took particular aim, after Charles's death, in writing that "I loved him enough to want to share all his privations. I confess that I was jealous. I hated those women who seemed to love him, but who were incapable of persevering in their love, their fidelity, their devotion. I never believed in them."

Of all this Jean-Louis Barrault remained largely unaware, since his exclusive concern was to pass muster in Dullin's eyes. "You want to do too well. That's why you do so badly," Dullin told him, to no avail. Paralyzed by stage fright, he seldom showed flashes of his comic genius and then only on informal occasions when, offstage, he regaled the company with imitations of *le maître.* "On New Year's Eve we would all see the New Year in together; the scenery would be shoved aside and we would have a banquet on stage. Aided by wine, we would move on to games, improvisations. Two of us used to imitate Dullin—my fellow actor Higonenc and myself. Once, in his presence, we did 'Dullin directing Dullin.' Higonenc played Volpone, I played Dullin directing him. . . . Dullin laughed till he cried."

Besides allowing him to make light of the figure in whose hands he had put his fate, to control Dullin by reducing him to laughter and tears, mimicry bonded them. A postulant fearful of separation from God, who regarded the world outside, which he had so recently left, as uninhabitable, Barrault spent nights as well as days in the Atelier, the fact that he could afford none but the poorest lodgings furnishing him an excuse to sleep backstage (with Dullin's consent). And there, all by himself, he continued his mimicries. One night, for example, after everyone had gone home following a performance of *Volpone,* he ventured on stage with candle in hand, parted the curtain guiltily, and faced the empty seats. "The *silence* of the theater came over me," he wrote. "I was caught in it as though in ice. Frost was all around me and on me. I was soon covered over with a hoarfrost of *silence."* Then he curled up in Volpone's bed, the bed Dullin had just evacuated, and fell asleep.

> I began dreaming. . . . That old theater on the fringe, the life of all those strolling players Dullin had known. . . . At that very moment I was living, was marrying the life of the theater. I came to realize in the course of that night of initiation that the whole problem of the theater is to set that *Silence* vibrating. Unfreeze that Silence. Move upstream. When a river flows into the sea, it dies; its estuary is its deathbed. . . . Ever since then I have been constantly in search of that silence . . . when a thousand hearts are beating to the same rhythm, and mine is beating to the rhythm of theirs. . . . Just as sometimes, in love, we want to delay the marvelous instant in which we are torn apart, I too sometimes want to delay that instant. I sit silently; I have stopped breathing; all of us have stopped breathing. We are palpitating in the motionless.

Dullin voiced the exact sentiments of his apprentice when, some years earlier, he told Pauline that "I would like to remain young and never know the sluggishness of heart and mind called maturity." Rather than enter the grown-up world, Jean-Louis would have made his home a "magic enclosure." Not for mere effect did he call the river's estuary its deathbed: his metaphor evokes Jules Barrault, who died in a city that commands the Seine's estuary. While outside the theater time marched on heedless of the dead, the absent, and the mournful with whom it populated the world, here in this cave where everything conspired to induce a sense of physical beatitude, life was synchronistic. Taking Dullin's place onstage, occupying his bed, inhabiting his persona, stealing his audience, appropriating even his memories, Barrault describes what might appear to be an Oedipal scenario except that silence prevails where one anticipates fiats, soliloquies, triumphant ejaculations: it ends not with an enthronement but with a corporate merger, nor with a conquest of the future but with a return to the womb. "Since that era, my body has become my face," he wrote. "I look with my breasts. I breathe at the level of my navel, and my mouth is at my sex. Were I to represent this impression in painting, I would choose René Magritte's tableau entitled *The Rape.*"

The conversion of his raw mimetic gift into an instrument of great artistic refinement might not have taken place were it not for an older confrere, Etienne Decroux—and, indeed, the harsh face Dullin showed Barrault was due, in part, to umbrage at seeing what authority someone else could exert upon "his" apprentice. Decroux, who had come over from the Vieux-Colombier in 1925, cut a formidable figure. At the Vieux-Colombier, where he sported the large bow tie by which militant Socialists often identified themselves during the twenties, he browbeat fellow students with slogans like "Politics above art!" and "Art is a publicity seeker, truth a saint; a saint should never lower herself, no matter how ugly she may be, before a publicity seeker," thus earning the nickname *l'Orateur.* A former mason, factory hand, hospital attendant, plumber, and butcher's clerk, Decroux had registered at Copeau's school not to become an actor but to learn the diction that would make him an effective political propagandist. Art for him was Socialist Realist sculpture and Georges Carpentier's boxing style. His apostolate of silence began when he first saw Vieux-Colombier apprentices perform improvisations seminude and with masks covering their faces. Struck by the resemblance between what took place onstage and athletic games, he felt impelled to explore the possibility of sculpting "mobile statues," of devising a language—a body language—more inherently theatrical than the spoken word, of inventing an art form predicated on events that occur in everyday life. Creating an illusion of walking forward without moving from one spot, of climbing or descending an imaginary staircase, of scrambling up a nonexistent tree, of kicking an invisible ball, and doing such things convincingly, as if the absence of staircase, tree, and ball were so many hallucinations: this was the task he set himself.

By 1931 Decroux had staged several mime plays—one entitled *Primitive Life,* another *Medieval Life*—and begun formulating the aes-

thetic principles he would impress upon Barrault, who came to him as
Galatea to Pygmalion, endowed with a mimetic intelligence and physical apparatus the likes of which he had never seen. "The mime produces
nothing but presences, which are not conventional signs," proclaimed
Decroux. "If the mime is born of silence," echoed Barrault, "that is
because he is essentially present. . . . It is not a question of making
oneself understood but of being evident." Presence implied "the
present," a dramaturgical present outside time in which movement
speaks only of movement, a present devoid of the "meanings" that
enter consciousness through words. To Decroux, who held that mime
was the "essence" of theater and theater "an accident of mime," words
diagrammed abstract edifices. Mime, on the other hand, was nothing if
not a sequence of present actions:

> The word alone can evoke absent things. The word alone can say what
> was, what one would have life be, whence one came or whither one is
> going, what is happening far away beyond the horizon or behind the wall,
> what one thinks about what someone is doing to us. In short, it alone can
> pronounce an abstraction without which thought becomes almost impos-
> sible. . . . With words one can construct stories, plots; one provokes
> reboundings, bifurcations, reversals, for on the green felt of the concrete
> and physical present, such things as the past, the future, the faraway, the
> abstract are so many ivory balls knocking about. Mime cannot accomplish
> that, nor should it try to. . . . What it does is shine by its manner. . . .
> "The manner of giving is worth more than the gift:" so the manner of
> walking is worth more than the goal, the manner of picking is worth more
> than the flower. . . . Here we have an art in which the only things that do
> not count are facts.

Were the aforementioned "goal" or "flower" invested with significance
beyond the walking or picking, they would have detracted from the
body, whose presence depended on the gratuitousness of its acts and the
self-referentiality of its movements. "To walk" and "to pick" would
then have operated as transitive verbs leading not only outward from
subject to object but forward from present to future, so that the
"sequence of present actions" which characterized mime would have
become a dramatic episode, a mute narrative unfolding, like any spoken
play, in time. The more hermetic its gestural vocabulary, the more
"concrete" the art: this was Decroux's fundamental assumption.

By a path that poets and painters had already beaten smooth, he moved toward that point where formalism and materialism converge, where art for art and the cult of quiddity join to enforce a common terror. "The surface of things would be their face and thus the depth of things. The container would be the contained . . . the manner would be the very idea," he asserted. "As interest in some action increases, perception of its manner diminishes. . . . Actions in themselves do not interest us. We are interested in the interrelationship or in their manner. All the rest is literature." * Calling himself now a sculptor of mobile statues now a vehicle of geometry in motion, Decroux not only shared Copeau's penchant for the impersonal, but proved *plus catholique que le pape.* It was his conviction that true mime should have no face whatever, that theater would become completely "present" when its human agents had become completely anonymous and the stage completely bare. Accordingly, he performed all but nude with a stocking pulled over his head, as if to make himself a tabula rasa, to re-create existence from scratch. Pastless and futureless, innocent of texts and conventional signs, embedded in matter yet reborn as pure style, thus did the New Mime make his appearance. "Unlike Chinese masks, ours was inexpressive. . . . The face alone is immodest since it alone reveals our intimate person, what we are. The body, on the other hand, is capable of tracing through space broad lines that distract from those of our form. . . . When one is nude in a framework that is nude, emptied of language and of music, then style and symbol become obligatory. They alone clothe." Headless in a virgin universe, this creature of silence, half-aesthete half-*enfant sauvage,* would seem to have leapt from Mallarmé's blank page, if not from a Revolutionary scaffold.

Barrault, who could be himself onstage only when he hid his face, gave several mimetic exhibitions with Decroux, including one of *Primitive Life,* and it is as though he were a lifer paroled from the world of words in which he ordinarily felt so ineffectual, not to say discountenanced. His reflections on the subject make it clear that mime came to

---

* The last sentence is a quotation that asserts a connection between Decroux's mimetic enterprise and literary symbolism. It comes from Verlaine's poem "Art Poétique"—"Et tout le reste est littérature," by which Verlaine meant that the purpose of poetic language was not to convey facts or narrate events but to orchestrate its own internal harmonies.

acquire for him quasi-mystical significance. "Mime is an essentially *animal* art; caught in his own space, living in a continual state of siege, man fights to the death," he declared (with the hysteria that often left him speechless before his public).

Our relations with the external world are magnetic. Instinct is a kind of compass; the senses work like radar indicating the direction in which our limbs must move to intercept or to avoid what suits or harms us. . . . Just as the earth is enveloped in an atmospheric layer, man, by virtue of his living radiation, is enveloped in a magnetic halo. The latter, which belongs to every man, *touches* external objects even before the skin does. This magnetic halo varies in thickness according to the vitality or education of a man. It can extend for kilometers, which is why certain sorcerers anticipate your arrival when they have not been forewarned of it. Their magnetic field has been *touched* kilometers away. Though it is said of them that "they have *seen* you," in reality they have been touched. The sense of touch is the divine sense. To be *touched* by grace is not a figure of speech. Nor is God's finger a metaphorical organ. One can readily imagine that saints who see Christ or the Virgin have been put in a "second state" of "vision" thanks to a *real touch.* Touch is the "perforating" sense. It lets us "see" the other side of things, puts us in contact with the unknown, and glimpse the invisible. It is the sense whose range extends "beyond the limit."

The mime must, above all, become aware of this limitless tactility with things. Between man and the external world there exists no isolating layer, no no-man's-land. When man displaces himself he ripples the external world, as a fish ripples water. For man, the external world and the internal world weigh on each other. Walking is pushing. . . .

Weight is not a negligible force: it is the permanent symbol of our final collapse. If we do not remain vigilant, it can slyly cut us down. We must oppose to it our Force of Elevation.

Of the many sorcerers in Jean-Louis's life who wore halos and who exercised magnetic power over him, the most prominent was a sorceress.* When he had fallen ill, his mother had "divined" it from afar through a language physical in nature yet unrestricted by physical li-

---

* Later the crown of light and magnetic scepter would devolve upon his wife, Madeleine Renaud. In his autobiography, the chapter that deals with their courtship is entitled "Three Years of Light."

mits, a silent language that conveyed absolute knowledge and issued irresistible orders. According to this fantasy, he and she were never out of touch, for his every feeling and thought would send ripples across a magnetic field consubstantial with her body. While in the real world he often, throughout his life, felt directionless, loveless, and meaningless, in utopia he could not but move this way or that, as lines of force or "rays" evocative of the puppet's strings tied him to an all-seeing, all-knowing divinity who abolished chance. Unlike the real world, utopia had no mortal boundaries, no Styx, no outside. "Between man and the external world there exists no isolating layer, no no-man's-land." Hermetically sealed against time and encompassed by Providence, here was a plenum in which death, loss, loneliness, incommunicability became unthinkable concepts. Where everyone touched everyone else, sensation would leap from body to body, glutting all of space and obviating words. What need could there possibly be for words? Verbal discourse mediates among individuals: simultaneity of feeling postulates a rigorously homogeneous world, a world coextensive with one inhabitant or one body telegraphing itself everywhere at once and living forever in the present. When he was six years old, Jean-Louis said to his mother that "dans mon coeur on est serré comme dans le métro"—"In my heart everyone is packed tight as in the subway" (the phrase contains an unconscious pun, for le coeur serré also means "distraught"). Fifty-five years later, when he was converting a defunct railroad station, the Gare d'Orsay, into a honeycomb of theaters, he wrote this: "Theater is promiscuity; its premises must be filled with such a load of humanity that one always feels there is no room. In a theater, as soon as there is a stretch of wall that cannot be 'humanized,' death infiltrates, sticks to it, and freezes the place. Stage life is a race against death." Under the spell cast by the mime cum hypnotist, spectators would enter a "second state," transcend individual perception, and merge. Filled with this tangible presence, the theater would become the divine body that crowds out death.

Barrault's thoughts call to mind Jean-Jacques Rousseau's rhapsody on a prelapsarian Voice that could make itself heard everywhere, until men isolated themselves from one another in discrete space, building houses with inner walls and theaters with inner boundary lines. But his description of mime as "animal art" would suggest that another eighteenth-century ideologue—one whose pseudoscientific cosmology was by no means incompatible with Rousseauian doctrine—exercised a more direct influence on him, namely Franz Mesmer, the preacher of "animal magnetism." Barrault's statement about there being "no isolating layer, no no-man's-land" rephrases in twentieth-century terms Mesmer's proposition: "There exists among celestial bodies, the earth, and animate bodies a mutual influence. What conveys this influence is a fluid spread throughout the universe continuously so as to suffer no void . . . a fluid susceptible of receiving, propagating, and communicating all the impressions of movement." Whether Jean-Louis read Mesmer's *Memoir on the Discovery of Animal Magnetism* or knew it at second hand, it is clear that he was introduced to Mesmerist literature by his Surrealist friends, who made occultism their business. When Mesmer, an Austrian physician expelled from Vienna for propagating the notion that there resided within himself an occult force by which he could influence others, arrived in Paris in 1778, his thought found a proper home. During the last years of the *ancien régime* hypnotic séances were all the rage. And after they ceased to be quite so fashionable, mesmerism survived the nineteenth century underground, or on the fringe, moving more toward the center of literary fashion with the Surrealist movement.

Historians have noted that several prominent revolutionaries, among them Marat himself, strongly sympathized with mesmerism when they did not actually serve as officiants of the cult. This "fluid" circulating through the universe like Nature's ichor became the occult authority they invoked against "artificial" institutions, the secret bond that argued a universal brotherhood beneath finite societies, the wordless tongue that bespoke an original unity. Whatever interrupted its flow—and almost everything that constituted culture constituted an obstacle, whether language, art, jurisprudence, etiquette, or scientific laws upheld by the Académie—was thought to be physically insalubrious, if not morally evil. "There exists one uncreated principle: God. There exist in Nature two created principles: matter and movement," wrote Nicolas Bergasse, Mesmer's principal hierophant, who recorded this credo during the 1780s not in words but in symbols, it being said that the Master had received it wordlessly from Nature while wandering alone in the forest for three months (during which time he erased all ideas implanted by society).

Some years before Saint-Just decried "factions" as subversive of the democratic republic, mesmerists would gather around a tub filled with iron filings in mesmerized water and link hands so as to form a "chain" through which mesmeric fluid or virtuous matter could flow unobstructed by the ramparts of personal space or the sentinels of reason. From self-hypnotic séances to hypnotized assemblies, from parlors to public squares was a logical progression, given the abhorrence of voids that characterized this vital element or the will to exercise unlimited power over those with unlimited aptitude for self-abandonment that characterized its discoverer. The Festival of Unity and Indivisibility had not yet taken place when Mesmer sent the French National Convention a treatise (entitled "Elementary Notions on Ethics, Education, and Legislation to Serve Public Instruction in France") proposing that France hold public festivals not only to celebrate the civic religion with athletic contests but to promulgate laws and adjudicate legal disputes. If Nature had two created principles, matter and movement, then decisions made by the body politic assembled en masse would issue from Nature's bosom as oracles from Delphi. "Finally," he wrote, "it will be proven by the principles that form the system of influences or of animal magnetism that it is very important for man's physical and moral harmony to gather frequently in large assemblies . . . where all intentions and wills should be directed toward one and the same object." To devout mesmerists who established the Society of Universal Harmony in 1783, it was an article of faith that time had served to fragment an original whole, that of all the obstacles hindering Nature's free flow, history (and its clutter of institutions, customs, ideas, artifacts) constituted the major one, that Mesmer's theory was the remnant of a primitively recognized truth in which the new social order would anchor itself. The eminent astronomer J. S. Bailly recalled that when the Constitutional Committee of the National Assembly met in December 1789 to prepare a constitution for Revolutionary France, "Bergasse, in order to speak of the constitution and of the rights of man, made us go back to the rule of Nature, to the state of savagery."

It followed from Mesmeric-Rousseauian postulates that the closer a man was to prehistoric life the more harmonious his nature was apt to be (any "space" inside the sentient being would impair health). According to this hierarchy, peasants without any line represented a higher estate than aristocrats of great lineage. "It is especially in the country and in the most indigent and least depraved class of society that my discovery will bear fruit. It is easy there to place man again under the rule of

372

nature's conservative laws," Bergasse declared in Mesmer's name. "The common man, the man who lives in the fields, recovers quicker and better when he is sick than does the worldly man." But the paradigmatic model of utopian society was the rapport that obtained between a nursing infant and its mother. Mesmerists outdid the most domestic bourgeois in sentimental effusion when it came to milk-laden breasts, for at the fount and source, Nature's fluid, flowing as it flowed "at the beginning," mediated the perfect union. Jacques-Pierre Brissot, who passionately championed mesmerist claims until the Revolution gave him another ax to grind (whereupon he became a leader of the Girondins—sometimes known as Brissotins—and lost his head during the Terror), declared that "the state of a nursing mother is a state of perpetual mesmerism—we unfortunate fathers, caught up in business matters, are practically nothing to our children, but by mesmerism we become fathers once again." Although the Revolutionary fuglemen who filled their cups with water drawn from the breasts of Nature before marching across Paris in the Fête de la Réunion did not necessarily attend séances, kindred fantasies begot analogous rites and symbols. The eye of surveillance behind which they paraded calls to mind the eye that exuded hypnotic fluid. Indeed, mesmerism counted among its devotees many somnambulists who claimed that they had seen an image of their own insides, ubiquitous vision or clairvoyance being no less central to the arcana of this faith than to the politics of terrorism.

Jean-Louis Barrault may be said to have come by his mesmeric principles long before he ever heard of Mesmer, for like all French boys and girls he learned them, unwittingly, from that most celebrated of French childhood tales, *Paul and Virginie,* an idyll whose titular soulmates, brought up fatherless on a tropical island, exhibit what nineteenth-century spiritualists called "community of sensation." Somewhat later, when he was old enough to read Balzac, Dumas, Hugo, Lamartine, and Gautier, he rediscovered mesmerism (though still unaware of its being mesmerism) in the cryptic power that these Romantic writers attribute to their heroes—indeed, to one another. Of Balzac, Gautier wrote that "he wanted to be a great man and he became one by incessant projections of that fluid which is more powerful than electricity and which he analyzed so subtly in *Louis Lambert.*" In similar terms Balzac portrayed Vautrin, the dark genius of *The Human Comedy,* the all-seeing, all-knowing amoralist who would ransack Paris and estab-

lish himself on virgin land overseas.* The age that saw technics make
extraordinary advances, harness nature, and enthrone the bourgeoisie
saw mesmerism retreat to another world, to an "elsewhere" of cosmic
ecstasy (such as in Fourier's utopia) or of necrophiliac spirituality. While
its first generation included distinguished scientists for whom the word
harmony had much the same resonance it did in, say, Rameau's music
treatises, after the Terror mesmerism wed Gothic fiction and melodrama. Embodied by the Great Outsider, by the wizard, by the Director
who assumes at will whichever form pleases him, mesmeric power became the instrument of a nature hidden from view and fraught with occult intentions. Drawing man downward, such power could, however,
also draw him upward, as it does in Balzac's *Seraphita* or in Hugo's
Contemplations, where the magnet is God and nature a metempsychotic
underworld that holds spirits imprisoned. Either way it left no room for
neutral expanse. Now satanic, now divine, it *polarized* the Romantic
universe and charged it even beyond the limit of life with presences,
with an animus, with emotion. Eighteenth-century mesmerists invoked
Newton as they communed around tubs; by 1850, when turning tables
were the fashion and communicants were more likely to see ghosts of
the long-departed than images of their own bowels, gravity had acquired a dialectical partner in grace. From Jersey, where *l'ombre du
sépulcre*—"the shade of the sepulcher"—regularly visited him during
séances held at Marine Terrace, Hugo wrote:

> Pendant que l'astronome, inondé de rayons,
> Pèse un globe à travers des millions de lieues,
> Moi, je cherche autre chose en ce ciel vaste et pur.
> Mais que ce saphir sombre est un abîme obscur!
> On ne peut distinguer, la nuit, les robes bleues
> Des anges frissonnants qui glissent dans l'azur.†

---

* Balzac wrote in his foreword to *The Human Comedy*: "Animal magnetism, whose
miracles I have familiarized myself with since 1820; the fine research of Lavater's successor, Gall, and, in short, all who have studied thought the way opticians have studied light,
two virtually similar things, confirm the ideas both of the mystics, those disciples of Saint
John the Apostle, and of the great thinkers who have established the spiritual world."

† "While the astronomer, submerged in rays, / Weighs a globe millions of leagues
away, / I look for something else in this vast, pure sky. / But what a dark abyss is this somber sapphire! / At night, one cannot make out the blue gowns / Of shivering angels who
slip through the azure.

And, in "O Gouffre!":

> Nous épions des bruits dans ces vides funèbres;
> Nous écoutons le souffle, errant dans les ténèbres,
> Dont frissonne l'obscurité;
> Et, par moments, perdus dans les nuits insondables,
> Nous voyons s'éclairer de lueurs formidables
> La vitre de l'éternité.*

Light and darkness represented not the phases of that world-view formulated by eighteenth-century *philosophes,* who beheld history as a rational, progressive adventure, but the chiaroscuro of a haunted universe in which the dead never die.

It could be argued that modernism began with a reversion to animism. Just as literary rebels proclaimed themselves outside bourgeois France by wearing anachronistic garments and glorifying the Dark Ages, so they sabotaged progress by offering hospitality to those who returned from the grave, to revenants who rose or descended at night, like fugitives. Would a bourgeoisie that sent its surveyors into darkest Africa leave any space untriangulated? Hugo's astronomer weighing stars millions of leagues away was the ultimate agent of a colonial enterprise that would take the measure of all Creation. Against an enemy equipped with precise weights and measures, the outsider went forth armed with science's childhood remnants and spoke the language of magic—of numerology, astrology, alchemy. Hugo consulted mediums. Baudelaire followed Swedenborg. Rimbaud studied Eliphas Lévi. Evicted from themselves in a world that had grown infinitely wakeful— a world whose rulers buried as they built, and built, and built—poets of the vanguard (not to mention nonpoets like Allan Kardec, France's most celebrated medium) sought refuge in sleep or in trance, creating verbal edifices no one save the initiate could enter. When Hugo proclaimed *The Flowers of Evil* a "new shiver," he knew whereof he spoke, it seems, for the magnetic fluid that sent night shivers through the *voyant* would attract poetic generation after poetic generation. Verse was to be written in occult communities—communities of sensation— by mandarins who could decipher the world's hidden text. "I simply

---

* "We catch noises in these funereal voids; / We hear the breath, wandering in the shadows, / With which the darkness trembles; / And, at times, lost in the unfathomable nights, / We see glowing with formidable lights / The windowpane of eternity."

wanted to tell you that I have just laid the plan of my entire work, after having found the key to myself, to the center of myself, where I crouch like a sacred spider at the center of a web whose main threads I have already spun from my mind; following these, I shall weave marvelous lacework, which I can divine, which already exists in the bosom of Beauty," Mallarmé wrote to Aubanel in 1866.

Some twenty years later, when his Symbolist web was near completion, Mallarmé would dwell on The Book, "persuaded as I am that there is but One Book—the orphic explanation of the Earth, which constitutes the Poet's sole duty and the literary game par excellence, for the very rhythm of the book, impersonal and alive down to its pagination, conveys the equations of my dream or Ode. . . . I have always sought to accomplish this dream, sacrificing all vanity and satisfaction for it, even as the alchemist burned his furniture and the beams of his roof to feed the furnace of the Great Work." Like the magnetic field, the web is a physical language that translates a dream of intransitiveness, of omnipotence, of divine impersonality. As mesmerists claimed they could see their own insides while entranced, so the Symbolist would have figured as subject and object or actor and spectator in a theater without "other." To spin from inside oneself Beauty's preconceived design was to behold oneself from the impersonal center of one's own exoskeletal universe.

When, after World War I, André Breton predicated his apostolic mission on "automatic writing," he had Mallarmé very much in mind. Although Surrealists held that they took dictation from the Unconscious or from Nature, rather than from the Idea, and although Breton's fiat that "Beauty will be erotic-convulsive or will not be" would have left Mallarmé's Platonist followers aghast, in whichever guise Beauty materialized she conferred Orphic eloquence on her protégé, reinventing the world for him alone and guiding him through it by an infallible compass.* "The mind of a man who dreams is fully satisfied by what is hap-

---

* One is also reminded of the round house or "tower" that Carl Jung built for himself in Bollingen, beginning in 1923. "From the beginning I felt the Tower as in some way a place of maturation—a maternal womb or a maternal figure in which I could become what I was, what I am and will be. It gave me a feeling as if I were being reborn in stone. It is thus a concretization of the individuation process, a memorial *aere perennius*. During the building work, of course, I never considered these matters. I built the house in sections, always following the concrete needs of the moment. It might also be said that I built it in a kind of dream. Only afterward did I see how all the parts fitted together and that a meaningful form had resulted: a symbol of psychic wholeness."

pening to him. No longer does the tormenting question of possibility arise. Kill, fly more quickly, love as much as you please. And if you die, are you not assured of waking up among the dead? Let yourself be led, events will not allow you to postpone them. You have no name. The ease of everything is priceless," wrote Breton in the *Surrealist Manifesto* of 1924, where Surrealism is defined as follows: "Surrealism resides in the belief in the superior reality of certain forms of associations hitherto neglected, in the omnipotence of dream, in the disinterested game of thought. It tends to ruin definitively all other psychic mechanisms and to substitute itself for them in the resolution of the principal problems of life. Proof of ABSOLUTE SURREALISM has been given by . . . [nineteen names follow]." Surreality abolished externality. In dream, the pure aesthete playing disinterested games of thought combined with the child of nature whose mind was a virgin enclave, like Paul and Virginie's island. Whether dream came from Mallarmé crouched spider-like in his web or from Breton, who portrayed himself as a fish soluble in its own medium (*un poisson soluble*), both pure abstraction and pure flux spoke to the ideal of a plenum, of a hermetic paradise made for one.

Surrealism brought mesmerism full circle, which is to say that with Surrealism mesmerism accomplished yet another revolution, engendering a new species of terrorist. Surrealists did not march across Paris after raising goblets to Nature's breast, but they did the equivalent in their magazine *La Révolution Surréaliste*, the first issue of which (1924) featured a nude Madonna garlanded by snapshots of each initiate, eyes shut tight as during a séance. "*Libre à vous!*" declared Louis Aragon, "there is no morality but the morality of the Terror, no liberty but the liberty of implacable domination: this world is like a woman in my arms. There will be irons for liberty's enemies. Man is free, but not men. There is no limit to the liberty of the one: liberty for all does not exist. . . . Herewith ends the social history of humanity. . . . The mind has a right and a left. And it is liberty that pulls the needle of this compass toward magnetic north." Fascination with the Terror led Antonin Artaud, another prominent Surrealist, to call for outdoor spectacles, for a "Theater of Cruelty" in which the spirit that attended revolutionary festivals would once again convulse the crowd and hurl masses forward as one Being impelled by a force stronger than will or intelligence. Theater, he asserted, would not recover its necessity until, obliterating the conscious mind, it plunged men "into love, into crime, into war, into madness." It was Artaud who wrote that "belief in a fluidic materiality of the soul is indispensable to the actor's métier." And it was at Artaud's urging that Jean-Louis Barrault, when the two became acquainted round about 1934, began to study occult literature.

What Decroux and Barrault called "corporeal mime" sprang from the same impulse to "cleanse" art that sustained the Surrealist movement. Their obsession with problems of physical grammar, with the development of a formal vocabulary serving no end but motion itself, evokes Mallarmé's *poésie pure*, and, indeed, *pur* was a word to which they often had recourse. "Had I been asked at that time what my opinion was of the art of Mime, I should have said that . . . it is one of the two extreme points of pure theater, the other extreme point being pure diction, wrote Barrault." * If *pur* translated, among other things, a will to guard against meanings imposed from the outside by "culture," and a belief that such meanings constituted artifices or bodies foreign to one's nature, then action and language could not be absolutely pure unless absolutely devoid of social context. Walking without advancing, walking but walking nowhere, the silent, faceless mime embodied the gratuitousness of *art pour art* and the innocence of somnambulism. At once technician and dreamer, aesthete and nudist, he was above all—or would have made himself—a hermetic nature. The hermeticism that Barrault and Decroux cultivated onstage in exercises like the *sur place* ("same spot"), which took them weeks to perfect, with each criticizing the other, imbued every aspect of their lives. They ate only "natural" food, for example; abstaining from meat, like Albigensian Perfects observing Lent all year long in the belief that anything sexually begotten is impure, they survived on fruit, vegetables, lemon juice, kippers, and boiled semolina. "Decroux was a puritan revolutionary. He cultivated the more-than-perfect," wrote Barrault when they had gone their sepa-

---

* Some thirty-five years later, during the student insurrection of 1968, "pure action" and "pure speech" would figure as cant phrases in the vocabulary of radical dissent.

rate ways, alluding to all that made Decroux the sort of man who would name his son Maximilien, after Robespierre.*

By 1934 Barrault had grown more confident of himself, confident enough, at any rate, to leave the Atelier after dark and take shelter in the Bateau Lavoir, that labyrinthine tenement on place Ravignan, which was already past decrepitude when Picasso, Max Jacob, and Juan Gris lived there during the decade before World War I. "Day by day I could feel myself becoming a young male: glances that I tried to make profound, hair disheveled, clothes and accessories artfully negligent, the gait of a wild animal, something between a puma and a wolf. The esoterism of the East, the new American literature and certain Scandinavian writers attracted me. I was enlarging my field of influences." Although Decroux had all but kept him under lock and key, this new tyranny, to which he had lent himself, had had the virtue of distancing him from Dullin, who was nonplussed by his gyrations in a loincloth and his zeal for animal art.

Barrault's zeal for animal art, which took him further afield than his mentor thought wise, reflected the larger "field of influences" he had begun to cultivate. On boulevard Saint-Germain, where the *Tout Paris* of avant-gardism gathered in bars and cafés, animal art was all the rage. There, Picasso's drawings of himself as a horned god circulated like common coin. Monsters invented by Dali, Ernst, and company filled the glossy pages of *Minotaure*, a Surrealist review, whose editorial gray eminence was none other than André Breton. With Montherlant's play *Pasiphäe*, bestiality found a heroine who did not suffer anything like the guilt that beset and killed her Jansenist daughter in Racine's masterpiece. Bushmen paintings exhibited at the Salle Pleyel inspired one young intellectual, Georges Bataille, to write: "What we have become so incapable of experiencing sensually, the blatant heterogeneity of our being with regard to the world that gave it birth, seems to have been, for those among us who lived in nature, the very basis of all represen-

---

* Decroux never forsook his conviction that "art is a publicity-seeker, truth is a saint." He gave public performances as he conducted rehearsals, repeating steps *ad nauseam*, with undisguised contempt for the audience. To complaints about his appearing on the stage practically nude, he would peevishly answer: "Am I to blame if the public is evil-minded enough to find nature ugly? One does not go naked because one is handsome, but rather to become it." Rousseau did not put it better when he declared that if his head were made of glass, and his innermost thoughts visible, he would walk abroad unashamedly.

tation: elephants and zebras seem to have had the same eminent role in their lives that houses, administration buildings or churches occupy in ours."

Against urban culture, Paris's native intelligentsia marshaled zoomorphs of every description. Reviling the bourgeosie for having cut them off from nature, they envisioned a society in which "the return of the repressed" would abolish all norms, in which instinct would have its shrine and primitives—the madman, the killer, the sexual pervert—be given an honored place. While on the Butte Jean-Louis ate vegetation, in the Latin Quarter he was a wolf among wolves and a puma among pumas. Sublime up above, down below he belonged to the chorus that echoed protagonists like Antonin Artaud when Artaud called for the restoration of totemic ritual, or Georges Bataille when Bataille, who edited a review entitled *Acéphale* ("Headless"), condemned bourgeois justice as dehumanizing in comparison with the justice meted out in societies still given to cannibalistic *mana* worship:

It is inadmissible that society smite criminals otherwise than in broad daylight. It is inadmissible that men be slaughtered at dawn and on the sly, like animals in a slaughterhouse. . . . The time has come to shout . . . that the system of repression now in force is the most monstrous and degrading that man has ever applied to man. This system has completely lost the passionate element without which social repression could never have arisen. The sentiments a Chinese has for a criminal under torture seem human compared to those a European has for people he serenely jails or executes. In China, the liver of a man who died while demonstrating pride under torture is eaten by another man who admired him and would appropriate his value.

In one century the melodramatic world-view had traveled from the Boulevard of Crime back to the center of Paris, where Surrealists and neo-Surrealists held forth as Sade's posterity, as Jacobins of the Id ready to behead those who dared to constrain virgin nature. "This revolution struck me as an extraordinary cleansing operation, beginning with the brains," Barrault observed. "Automatic writing, waking dreams, hallucinations. To blow up the Others lock, stock, and barrel did not suffice. Real courage consisted in blowing up oneself lock, stock, and barrel."

A fairground atmosphere pervaded Saint-Germain. Animals were very much in vogue, but so were harlequinades, though now Harlequin took *inner* voyages around the world. The world beyond France became (for habitués of Les Deux Magots) codimensional with an irrational underground or an esoteric depth. Under the Old Regime Harlequin had kept abreast of the travelogues that brought to light previously unsuspected peoples and lands. In 1935 he studied Marxist ideology and Oriental religion to be *à la page.* The Bhagavad-Gita, Tantric Yoga, Hatha Yoga, the Upanishads and Milarepa, the "golden verses" of Pythagoras, Trotsky: Jean-Louis Barrault omnivorously devoured whatever his avant-garde acquaintances fed him.

The work that made a decisive impact on his life arrived not from the East, however, but from America, slipping in behind translations of Whitman, Thoreau, Melville, Hemingway, Dos Passos, and Steinbeck. "*As I Lay Dying* was a revelation, a tearing of the veil, a kind of vision, a window opening in the mountain mists," wrote Barrault. "It seemed to me that with its help, I might be able to pull together all the ideas and feelings I had about theater." His enthusiasm was by no means singular. While the critical fraternity of New York and London generally endorsed the judgment rendered by one reviewer that Faulkner's "cosmos" was "awry," in Paris this novel about hillbillies who, at her request, transport their dead mother from the Mississippi countryside to Jefferson, the city of her birth, found an ardent public among Left Bank literati. Depicting the America civilization had not yet rationalized, the primitive world still ruled by *Magna Mater,* it spoke a dialect perfectly comprehensible to Romantics preoccupied with the Great Mother, with incest, madness, death, the Unconscious, who, had they lived in post-Revolutionary France, might have made cult books of Chateaubriand's *René* and *Atala.* "We can, without parodying the novel, transpose it into an episode of epic dimensions: the episode of a funeral procession of the Homeric queen Addie Bundren, conducted, in accordance with her final wishes, by her husband Anse, and by her children, the princes," wrote Valery Larbaud in an essay that accompanied the French edition. Barrault had no sooner read it than he embarked upon the project of transposing it. To him Faulkner's novel suggested a silent epic, or an epic silence, in which he could readily imagine himself onstage demonstrating alike his mimetic skill and his own wordless mythos. After four years with Dullin he had had more of supernumerary existence than he could bear. Once again his fantasy of growing huge had matured after four years, as though an inner clock told him that it was 1914 and time for father to disappear.

In May 1935, one month before he staged the *action dramatique* based on *As I Lay Dying*, Barrault wrote that "this kind of mime, I believe, has nothing to do with pantomime, education, or aesthetics (or that disagreeable thing the *tableau vivant*); it is an attempt to be purely animal. For example, the face becomes a natural mask, concentration being respiratory." The expression "purely animal" would apply to Addie Bundren's bastard son, Jewel, with whom Jean-Louis identified completely. Barrault's idea for a mime play took hold of him and crystallized when he read this extraordinary passage:

> When Jewel can almost touch him, the horse stands on his hind legs and slashes down at Jewel. Then Jewel is enclosed by a glittering maze of hooves as by an illusion of wings; among them, beneath the upreared chest, he moves with the flashing limberness of a snake. For an instant before the jerk comes onto his arms he sees his whole body earth-free, horizontal, whipping snake-limber, until he finds the horse's nostrils and touches earth again. Then they are rigid, motionless, terrific, the horse backthrust on stiffened, quivering legs, with lowered head; Jewel with dug heels, shutting off the horse's wind with one hand, with the other patting the horse's neck in short strokes myriad and caressing, cursing the horse with obscene ferocity. They stand in rigid, terrific hiatus, the horse trembling and groaning. Then Jewel is on the horse's back. He flows upward in a stooping swirl like the lash of a whip, his body in mid-air shaped to the horse. For another moment the horse stands spraddled with lowered head, before he bursts into motion. They descend the hill in a series of spine-jolting jumps, Jewel high, leech-like, on the withers.

Were Faulkner's language not sufficient in itself to excite a mime, what must have made his centaur image all the more compelling for Barrault was the symbolic environment in which horse fuses with mother and "pure animal" with "pure spirit." "Jewel's mother is a horse," says Darl, the mad, insightful son. Jewel stands apart from his brothers and sister, embodying his mother's secret passion. Gotten on Addie Bundren not by her husband Anse but by a preacher, the Reverend Whitfield, he sprang from a woman half-winged half-hoofed who willingly coupled with no man but God's surrogate during her lifetime and after death has herself laid beside her father in a funeral procession *cum* nuptial voyage that restores her her virginity. "My children were of me alone, of the wild blood boiling along the earth, of me and of all that lived; of none and of all. Then I found that I had Jewel."

Rotating from inner voice to inner voice, with each chapter an isolated monologue, the novel stops at Jewel only once, as though his language were the language of his body and his movement his thought. While Darl, whom Addie Bundren spurned, loses himself in words, Jewel the Chosen One never gets lost. It is he who keeps the funeral procession on course, rescuing Addie from a flood and straddling her coffin when fire threatens to consume her ("the glittering maze of hooves"). Inarticulate, he emerges in his very dumbness as her self-begotten child, as the offspring of an "I" whose narcissistic rage spends itself on words:

> So I took Anse. And when I knew that I had Cash, I knew that living was terrible and that this was the answer to it. That was when I learned that words are no good; that words don't ever fit even what they are trying to say at. When he was born I knew that motherhood was invented by someone who had to have a word for it because the ones that had the children didn't care whether there was a word for it or not. I knew that fear was invented by someone that had never had the fear; pride, who never had the pride. I knew that it had been, not that they had dirty noses, but that we had had to use one another by words like spiders dangling by their mouths from a beam, swinging and twisting and never touching, and that only through the blows of the switch could my blood and their blood flow as one stream. I knew that it had been, not that my aloneness had to be violated over and over each day, but that it had never been violated until Cash came. Not even by Anse in the nights.
> He had a word, too. Love, he called it. But I had been used to words for a long time. I knew that that word was like the others; just a shape to fill a lack. . . . Cash did not need to say it to me nor I to him.

It is easy to imagine with what force such language struck Jean-Louis. Here the contestants do not stand so neatly opposed as they do on the Hill of Ares in Aeschylus's *Oresteia,* for if Addie Bundren would be an Athene, the Goddess delivered from her father's head (she has herself buried near her father), Athene doubles as a Fury who arbitrates her own quarrel with man in proclaiming that "my children were of me alone." The raped virgin turns rapist. The schoolmarm imparting knowledge through words hates the words that come between her and children whom she whips into consanguinity. Language is nonself. Created from "lack," it sustains a world of objective time and formal

Jean-Louis Barrault as Jewel in Autour d'une mère, *his stage adaptation of William Faulkner's novel* As I Lay Dying. *1935.* Collection Roger-Viollet

relationships, an outside that the titular "I" would internalize by impregnating it with sensation. Finally, Addie Bundren has the last word. As her children carry her across hill and dale, they rot in her wake. Enveloped in the stench of a body to which Cash, who built her coffin, ascribes "animal magnetism," they become pariahs, exiles fallen from their hill, amputees unfit for independent life. When they reach Jefferson, Cash with only one leg and Jewel—robbed of his winged horse—with only two, the circle closes, Addie having dragged her favorite children halfway underground. For them, the endless funeral procession led not forward but round about, from womb to tomb. "My aloneness had been violated and then made whole again by the violation: time, Anse, love, what you will, outside the circle," said Addie in her autobiographical reverie.

Barrault envisaged an adaptation of *As I Lay Dying* that would show theater "in its primitive state," with no text save two lyrical monologues (one quoted above) spoken by Addie Bundren. The actors would disport themselves in *cache-sexe* on a bare stage and conjure up their environment through physical language, miming the sun, a river, rain, the flood, fire, buzzards, fish, a city, the circulation of traffic. Although he had a Mexican composer named Tata Nacho write choral chants to be accompanied by tom-toms, the action would otherwise unfold silently, or wordlessly. "It is 'speaking' theater in which people say nothing. If their breathing makes a sound, if their footsteps beat time, so much the better." Sacrificing psychological nuances along with language, he designed his choreography around movements or dances calculated to foster an atmosphere of collective ritual. Before the death march (in which he employed *sur place* technique), there was the death itself. "The mother is nearing death. Her eldest son is making the coffin. The wheezings from her chest fit in with the raspings of the saw. All the rest of the family, like an enormous jellyfish, contracts and relaxes in unison with the mother and the carpenter. The whole theater is in death throes—a pump rhythm, an octopus rhythm—and all of a sudden, at the climax of a breath: total stoppage. The mother's hand, which had been raised as when someone wants to look out into the distance, falls slowly in the silence, like a water level going down." As Addie Bundren recited monologues after her death, so her breath, in the form of musical wheezings and soughings, cadenced the funeral procession, like an animus driving her pallbearers. The significance Barrault attached to this pneumatic communality, to this "pump rhythm," became clear, or clearer, in a memoir he wrote on his own mother's death, which took place four years after the spectacle.

> "My children, if you only knew how good one feels! It's wonderful"— those were her last words. She had no more suffering at all. Her small respiratory forge had taken on a regular rhythm, like the engines of a ship that has started on a long journey. This went on for another day and two nights. I was no longer doing anything, I was attached to my mother's breath, as I once had been to her breasts full of milk. . . . At dawn on the second day she gave her last sigh. . . . That summer . . . I made a pilgrimage to the Chauvigny Gorge, cradle of my mother's side of the family. There the old parish priest gave me a photograph of my mother at the age of fifteen. I asked for a genuine Mass. . . . With the help of his server, he took us into the real regions of the sacred, of prayer: a rite as strong and primitive as if we had been in the middle of a tropical forest among witch doctors. Rhythm is the only thing that can take us out of ourselves.

Breath becomes confused with milk, gasping mother with suckling infant, cradle with grave. In the fluid medium that nourished his ideal of symbiotic union, it was perhaps inevitable that Barrault, once he grew weary of Decroux's plotless maneuvers and set out on his own, should have choreographed an eternal return. Rehearsals for the journey, for the march outside time, had begun long before this *action dramatique*. They had begun as early as the war, when Marcelle led Jean-Louis across the threshold that divided war zone from civilian zone. With his first directorial effort, he switched roles and, playing Jewel, guided Addie Bundren to the world beyond.

Though various and sundry misfortunes befell him in due course, nothing could distract Barrault from his goal. He worked on the horse scene every morning, executing wild leaps on the forestage while cleaners down below did their chores. "They and I were living our own lives, like the characters in the novel. . . . I moved like a somnambulist." Indeed, obstacles served him well, as they forced him to improvise solutions that straightened the course he set for himself and made the spectacle he eventually produced more idiosyncratic than it would otherwise have been. Gallimard refused to let him borrow the title *Tandis que j'agonise,* so he coined another, *Autour d'une mère* ("Around a Mother"), which lent itself quite conveniently to the abusive wordplay of Parisian wags, who circulated it as *Autour d'une merde* ("Around a Turd"). Actors deserted him, whether for fear of exposing their bodies—even pseudonymously—or of damaging their careers, so he found substitutes on whom he could rely. And when, only two days before the premiere, his Addie Bundren called in sick, he resolved to play the mother himself. Transforming Addie into a totemic figure, the artist Félix Labisse designed for him a skirt of broad ribbons, an enormous black wig that came down to his thighs, and a mask made of cheesecloth, with steel buttons for eyes. To complete the effect, Barrault stripped to the waist. By altering several scenes, he could play both parts, or all three, counting the horse, which symbolically amalgamated mother and son. Now man, now woman, now beast, he would reduce the other actors to attendants in a display of magical self-transformation whose scenario was, if not as archaic as theater itself, as old as Jean-Louis.

In early June 1935 *Autour d'une mère* was given four performances at the Atelier, which Barrault rented with money left in trust by Jules. Banking on a *succès de scandale* that would warrant him a place in revolutionary annals alongside Alfred Jarry, he planned to have the cast recite Rimbaud's poetic diatribe against the bourgeoisie, "Les Assis" ("The Seated"), when all hell broke loose. Hell did not break loose, however. (And had it done so, "The Seated" would scarcely have shamed an audience in which Saint-Germain-des-Prés outnumbered Paris's straitlaced constituencies.) There was, to be sure, some rowdy laughter at first sight of Addie Bundren beribboned and bewigged, but the public fell silent immediately afterward and brooded from afar until Barrault won it over with his rendition of Jewel mastering a wild horse. Aficionados claimed never to have witnessed such mimetic virtuosity. "In Jean-Louis Barrault's spectacle there is a kind of wondrous *centaur-horse,* and great was our emotion on seeing it, as if, with his appearance as a centaur-horse, Jean-Louis Barrault had restored magic to our lives," wrote Antonin Artaud in a review published by the *Nouvelle Revue Française* and subsequently appended to the essays that make up *The Theater and Its Double.* "This spectacle is magical the way the incantations of African sorcerers are magical when the tongue clicking against the palate releases rain upon the countryside, or when the witch doctor seeing a sick, wasted man gives his breath the form of a strange discomfort and with his breath purges the illness. Thus does a whole chorus of sounds spring to life in Jean-Louis Barrault's play when the mother dies. . . . Up till now only the Balinese theater seemed to have preserved a living trace of this lost spirit." Artaud, with his customary hyperbole, may have exaggerated the spell that *Autour d'une mère* cast upon the audience, but this was the version that gained credence among absentees hospitable to the legend of a prodigy birth. Jean-Louis's ten minutes on horseback might have been Paganini's *moto perpetuo* and Jean-Louis a wunderkind executing it flawlessly for all the notice he received from people who had hitherto looked right through him. Louis Jouvet invited him to stage a matinee performance of *Autour d'une mère* at the Théâtre des Champs-Elysées. A young cineast named Marc Allégret (who was André Gide's companion) gave him his first opportunity to act before the camera with a part in the otherwise unmemorable film *Happy Days.** And on the boulevard Saint-Germain, he became a figure as respectfully greeted as Louis Valette was on the rue de Lévis. While Barrault does not say what Valette himself thought of all this, perhaps the old man considered that his grandson had made amends for failing to become a veterinarian by succeeding as an animal.

Success being success and humans human, Barrault's tour de force earned him not only love but resentment. Decroux, for one, condemned the philistine use to which he had put the techniques of a quasi-sacred art. In his view, Barrault had defrocked himself. "I consider you pretty well sunk," he wrote. "It is essential: 1. that you admit you have wasted your time; 2. that you now change from top to bottom the company you keep; 3. that until further orders you give up acting the great man and acting period."

Dullin was apparently of two minds about *Autour d'une mère*. Though sufficiently intrigued by it to peek at rehearsals from the fly gallery, where creaking boards betrayed his presence, several hours before the first performance he threw a temper tantrum, declaring (as Barrault remembers it): "I shall not attend this evening. It's completely mad. Everything that I detest. Compared with this, Artaud is Boulevard! It's like monkeys in a zoo. And that father is just gaga." Perhaps he did in truth find Barrault's direction slipshod, his theories ponderous, and the nakedness too naked. Then again, it must have been very dif-

---

* Several years later, Barrault played the terrorist in Allégret's cinematic adaptation of Joseph Conrad's novel *Under Western Eyes.*

ficult to anticipate with perfect equanimity a future that would see him
stoop lower and lower while the young man down below leaped higher
and higher. If he understood what role he played in the genesis of Jean-
Louis's horse, even so, theatrical fatherhood was small compensation
for the ills that afflicted him. Seven years earlier, when he made his
third film, *Maldonne,* which Jean Grémillon shot on location near
Châtelard, Dullin rode all the way from Paris to his native province in a
buggy, stopping at inns to rub down his horse. Now, at fifty, he could
not have endured one full day on the road, much less a fortnight. And
when his hump did not tell him that he was unfit for "roles in which
one looks at the sky," youth drove home the point none too tactfully.
"Of course the father is gaga," Jean-Louis riposted. "He's fifty."

The last remark proved to be a Parthian shot. Dullin forgave it
soon after Jean-Louis made it, but neither of these youngest children
could really forgive the other his place in time. Once *Autour d'une mère*
finished its brief run, Jean-Louis rejoined his mother in Tournus, where
he spent the summer wondering what to do with himself come September. Merely to consider leaving Dullin was to revive all the fears and
guilt that attended the thought of separating from father. To continue
living on Montmartre in the Bateau Lavoir, on the other hand, was to
make a graveyard his home and walk among ghosts, to inhabit the shell
of Dullin's artistic generation, like a post-Revolutionary Romantic
squatting in some ruined monastery of the *ancien régime.* An ultimatum
sent by Dullin July 26, 1935, helped him make up his mind, though even
then he could not allow that he had had any choice in the matter, or
that the choice had been his. It was, he wrote four months later, his
"animal" that drove him to it, as if the horse had subdued the mime. "I
left everything that had caused the Atelier—preceding generation,
theories, et cetera, a time of peace. What then did "my animal" want?
. . . I have come to see that the movement of real life, at the present
day, has no relation with the movement in which I was living. Does this
movement really exist? Is it merely in me? I don't know. . . . What I do
know is that this movement is what "my animal" was after and so is
now living more happily. . . . I have a physical conviction that I am
beginning life."

The adage which has it that he who ignores history condemns himself to relive it would hold true here, and not only for Jean-Louis but
for the world at large. Dullin had claimed his independence in the aftermath of war; Barrault began life "anew" in the same aftermath.

✦ ✦ ✦

Putting the Seine between himself and his past, Barrault moved to the Left Bank where, at 7, rue des Grands Augustins, a sixteenth-century building whose other tenants (among them the Bailiffs' Union) occupied it only by day, he found a flat of three rooms with huge uncovered beams as old as the structure itself. The first, which measured forty-six feet by twenty-six, he took as his workroom and gave shows there. The second, fifty feet by thirteen, became a common room for sleeping, dining, and storage. The third, twenty-six by thirteen, he reserved for himself, though so halfheartedly that when he came home late at night, it was often to find every bed taken. One gained access to his baronial garret by ascending a spiral staircase on which Balzac had conferred something like landmark status, for literary archaeologists agreed that it had been this very staircase Pourbus climbed, in *The Unknown Masterpiece,* to paint pictures nobody understood. Before long it would accommodate another painter of genius. When Barrault eventually left what he called the "hayloft"—the *grenier des Grands Augustins*—it became the residence of Pablo Picasso, who, requiring more and more space for his work in progress, annexed a weaver's studio on the floor below. His work in progress was *Guernica.*

If Barrault sought "the movement of real life," he did not have far to seek. Equidistant from Saint-Germain cafés and from the Sorbonne, he could, in one direction, join a veritable who's-who of avant-garde society at the Brasserie Lipp, the Café de Flore, or Les Deux Magots, and, in the other, observe youthful militants as they fought for territorial advantage on the streets of the Latin Quarter.

Since February 1934, when an anti-Republican rally threatened parliamentary government, the Latin Quarter had come to resemble a proving ground where every ideology had its student phalange, every *faculté* its political hue, and every wall combative slogans. On rue Saint-André-des-Arts, right around the corner from rue des Grands Augustins, stood an outpost of the Ligue d'Action Française, the Catholic-royalist organization that had won hegemony over this neighborhood during the Dreyfus affair and patrolled it with weapons in hand. Rue de Condé, several blocks south, was the turf of Jeune Patrie, a private militia whose founder, Pierre Taittinger, would see his patriotic dreams come true several years later, under Pétain. Antifascist students staked out the territory east of boulevard Saint-Michel, which thus became a borderline, its odd-numbered side commanded by leftists distributing tracts or hawking newspapers such as *Le Populaire,* and its even-numbered side by the *camelots du roi*—the bully boys of Action Française—who wore rubber-padded berets, brandished yard-long canes issued (in lieu of swords) by their parent organization, and carried sidearms for good measure. To advertise one's cause conspicuously was to invite trouble from across the street:

> We had a very simple tactic [wrote Henri Noguères, head of Socialist Students]. We would send a small group down the boulevard Saint-Michel with minimal escort. Beginning at rue Soufflot and walking on the odd-numbered side, we would sport our three-arrowed insignia and loudly peddle *L'Etudiant socialiste, Le Populaire,* or *Le Cri des jeunes.* Our reinforcement party would meanwhile be laying back, on the even-numbered or "bad" sidewalk: a dozen sturdy militants from TPPS (*Toujours prêts pour servir*) who sometimes got help from Frontists or members of LICA (*Ligue Internationale contre l'anti-sémitisme*). . . .
>   . . . . Classically, our peddlers were set upon opposite the Source, a café frequented by *camelots* who would storm across with canes or truncheons at the ready and execute a maneuver in which they had considerable experience, some ripping up the newspapers, others attacking the escort. Our reinforcement party would then take them unawares (traffic on boulevard Saint-Michel was still light enough to permit lightning-quick dashes to and fro), and deliver a blow before the police arrived.

When, as often happened, some "incident" led the belligerents beyond their border skirmishes, it had repercussions throughout Paris. Late in 1935, for example, Action Française and Jeune Patrie staged violent demonstrations at the Law School to protest courses given by Gaston Jèze, a noted jurist who had helped Haile Selassie argue his brief against Mussolini before the League of Nations. Earlier that year, when Action Française called upon physicians to strike until the government passed laws excluding not only foreigners but even residents of foreign extraction from the medical fraternity, there took place a veritable pogrom which saw right-wing thugs run amok through the Latin Quarter and burn Léon Blum in effigy. Still another "incident," the gravest such incident to occur during this period, affected Léon Blum in person. On February 13, 1936, Action Française turned out a large crowd for the funeral procession of its most distinguished intellectual, Jacques Bainville. *Camelots* swept in squadron force to boulevard Saint-Germain, creating a traffic jam that embroiled, among others, the Jewish leader of the French Socialist Party. Pulled out of his car by several *camelots* who had recognized him, Blum was beaten bloody and might have been lynched had some laborers, witnessing the scene from a construction scaffold overhead, not intervened.

Blood called for blood. "Photographs of Léon Blum with his head swathed in bandages threw us into a murderous rage," wrote Noguères, who—along with fellow Socialists—spent the entire evening and night scouting Paris with a view to bashing in the head of anyone hawking Action Française's newspaper, reading it, or wearing a fleur-de-lis boutonniere. Another, far more effective reprisal took the form of a protest march held three days later. Organized by the parties that constituted the Popular Front—Socialist, Communist, and Radical—it drew something over five hundred thousand people, who flowed in a human tide from the Panthéon, down both sidewalks of the boulevard Saint-Michel, across the Saint-Michel Bridge to the place de la Nation at whose center stood Dalou's huge statuary group, *Triumph of the Republic*. In April, this same throng would rejoice when the Popular Front won a legislative majority and, in June, would celebrate the prime ministership of Léon Blum, who lost no time dissolving paramilitary leagues.*

With the Popular Front, France became once again a country "on the march." The years 1936 through 1938 were marked not only by legislation that offered the laboring class room for movement upward but by rituals that mobilized Frenchmen en masse, by gatherings and displacements of a collective nature. Young people set out in far greater numbers than ever before on treks around France, as youth hostels multiplied under the aegis of a government whose assistant secretary for Sports and Leisure declared, evangelically, that "youth hostels are one aspect of the great experience we are pursuing to transform the human condition." The month's paid vacation engendered special trains that conveyed workers at reduced fare to seaside towns, where party guides hailed them with close-fisted salutes, this exodus producing a counterexodus of bourgeois fleeing what they considered a plague sent upon their summer nation.

---

* These private armies remained intact, under different guises, and after 1940 merged into the Vichy militia.

Even more significant than the movement away from cities, however, was the swarming that took place within them, and particularly within Paris, whenever Communist and Socialist leaders enjoined the faithful to assemble for a show of strength. "France of the Popular Front was, first and foremost, the cortege of militants in all its diversity and anonymity," wrote one historian. The "cortege of militants" resembled nothing so much as a general mobilization for war, with tens of thousands of workers from the *banlieue* jubilantly converging on the capital by metro, by bus, by car, by van, or on foot. Several days before a march, *L'Humanité* and *Le Populaire* would have begun to diagram it in detail—its order, the composition of its eight or ten major groups, the site at which each formed up, the roster of leaders—lest chaos ensue, though chaos was there as an ever-present threat, as a Voice raised above the city's workaday hum. Wherever marchers marched they made themselves heard, singing songs that evoked the revolutionary past and the utopian future. "From the minute we set out to the minute we dispersed (many hours later for those among us who brought up the rear), we would shout and sing ourselves hoarse," wrote Noguères. The "Marseillaise" marched in counterpoint with the "Internationale." From the midst of Soviet songs introduced to France via Chant du Monde records ("Komintern," "The Partisans," "Long Live Life") music of the French Revolution would ring forth, especially the "Carmagnole" and the "Ça ira," which accommodated innumerable variations on topical themes.

What direction the crowd took was dictated by circumstances, or by the nature of the event that brought it forth. Demonstrating against Action Française, people overwhelmed the Latin Quarter. Mourning Henri Barbusse, the novelist who had died in Russia, they followed his casket up Ménilmontant to Père-Lachaise Cemetery. Commemorating the assassination of Jean Jaurès, they assembled at the Panthéon. Asserting solidarity with Spain's Frente Popular, they took the royal road of popular vociferation, which led from place de la Nation to place de la Bastille. But in any event the crowd beheld itself as a virtuous army and Paris as its Champs-de-Mars. "As others reminisce about their campaigns, the veterans among us—who were not necessarily the oldest—would learnedly compare a demonstration which had just taken place with its predecessors, evaluating the number of marchers, enumerating the 'stars' they had seen, appraising the behavior of police (both police in uniform and police in civilian clothes)." Not since 1793 and 1794 had such multitudes gathered on so many occasions. Indeed, one mass demonstration was held to commemorate another as the mass became increasingly self-absorbed and the cortege an end in itself, transcending its pretexts. Demonstrations pullulated, like the logos or acronyms that all by themselves tell the sociopolitical story of France during the so-called "thousand days."

If many Parisians who lived through them remember the thousand days as one prolonged holiday, with students roaming the streets, workers occupying factories, Socialists holding rallies in Luna Park, converts to Bolshevism meeting underground like primitive Christians awaiting God's Advent, and everyone marching, it was on official holidays that Paris of the Popular Front showed itself at its most apocalyptic. On July 14, 1936, for example, people were overcome by zeal, and not only the zeal that informed a million or more voices singing the "Internationale," but the zeal that fueled the rhetoric of ten thousand or more intellectuals who lavished praise on le Peuple while quoting words spoken by Saint-Just in 1793:

We marched, we sang with our comrades [André Chamson, Jean Guéhenno, and Andrée Viollis collectively declared]. Our voices were a bit cracked, perhaps, but we had with us a youthful generation that sang, and sang in tune, our common hopes. Marching in one row between two hedges of crowd, underneath windows from which flags were waving, we looked at the faces. And if we are so joyous this evening, we owe our joy to the fraternal spirit borne home by the smiles and friendly glances of unknown men and women. . . . Saint-Just used to say that happiness was a new idea. Today we have breathed, in the air of Paris, the newness and the youth of that idea.

That "oceanic" feeling which Romain Rolland equated with religiosity in his letter to Sigmund Freud did not sweep everyone off his feet. Some, even some men of good will who resisted Fascism by other means, stayed away from place de la Bastille on July 14. But if they ventured to join the fête, they may have thought it wise, after seeing what they saw, to avoid its denouement late that night at the Alhambra Theater, where audience became cast during the greatest performance ever given of Rolland's July 14th. July 14, 1936, was a day on which cautious men did not reflect in public that virtuous crowds and good sidewalks

had a melodramatic affinity to evil crowds and bad sidewalks.* The day
on which the People rose was Rolland's day rather than Freud's, and
Freud's sober observation in *Civilization and Its Discontents* would not
have been suffered gladly—that "the truth . . . which people are so
ready to disavow is that men are not gentle creatures who want to be
loved, and who at the most can defend themselves if they are attacked;
they are, on the contrary, creatures among whose instinctual endowments is to be reckoned a powerful share of aggressiveness. . . . *Homo
homini lupus*, 'Man is a wolf to man.' "

Freud's day lay at hand, however. Less than a week after the *fête*,
Franco's troops invaded the Spanish mainland, setting the stage for a
civil war in which Communist freedom fighters slaughtered their Socialist brethren while Spaniard cut down Spaniard. A month later, news
from "the land of socialism" told Frenchmen of show trials and purges
implemented on a vast scale by Stalin's special confidant, N. I. Yeshov,
who had replaced Yagoda as head of the NKVD. Nearly a year later
Léon Blum waxed lyrical in an address given just before the inauguration of the 1937 World's Fair, as though he had not perceived the stone
colossi that flanked the Soviet and Nazi pavilions, or as if, perceiving
them, he did not believe that these cosmocrators, whose identical musculature represented "beauty" in the popular eye, would endeavor to
conquer mankind. "I no longer recall who defined the poet's specific gift
as one that allows him to forge beauty from difficulty," he told foreign
journalists who had gathered in Paris, where the newly constructed Museum of Man and Palace of Discovery attested to an optimistic faith in
human evolution. "We have attained the moment in which difficulties
overcome will at last become something beautiful. So let us cease . . .
to complain, let us cease to shout and decry. Let us take pride in presenting to the universe the work, the work difficult and beautiful as a
poem, that Paris and France have just created."

So long as Barrault lived at 7, rue des Grands Augustins, its staircase was a vertical tributary of the rushing street and its garret loft a
pocket where flotsam collected. Antonin Artaud, who proclaimed the
need for theater embodying "myths that hold sway over massive collec-

---

* So it was with nature as well. Not only Socialists but Fascists pressed nature into
the service of a new order. "With Doriot," wrote Pierre Drieu la Rochelle, "the France of
camping-out will vanquish the France of the apéritif and party congresses."

tivities," often dropped by, before he sailed to Mexico on January 10, 1936, in quest of the solar religion practiced by Tarahumaras Indians. So did Georges Bataille who, besides editing *Acéphale*, founded a Society of Collective Psychology that occasionally met in the garret. André Breton paid several memorable visits, as on January 21, 1936, when he, together with his diminished band of apostles, gathered to commemorate Louis XVI's execution. The erstwhile Surrealist Robert Desnos befriended Barrault and introduced him to Jacques Prévert, who brought others in turn. Seldom did Jean-Louis find himself alone. His door stayed open as a gesture of hospitality extended to all (or almost all) and all alike. On Wednesday evenings, the commune—for the loft was in fact a communal pad with beds set up in every corner—mustered its slender resources to conjure up a banquet whose aroma attracted stray cats from far and wide. "They were so successful, these Wednesdays, that we didn't know half the people there," wrote Youki Desnos, Robert's wife (who otherwise amused herself by swimming naked in the Seine).

I remember one particular Wednesday when Jean-Louis was dead broke and our friend in charge of festivities, Blanche Picard, told me that all she could put together was three hundred francs. Not much for food and booze even in prewar days. I suggested we buy those little cuttlefish called *calamars* which cost ten sous a kilo, and so we did. What a pain it was, peeling twenty kilos of the little beasts, and onions in the bargain. Simone and I spent all day at it, but the result was an immense tubful swimming in tomato sauce flambéed with cognac. We cheerfully lugged it over to rue des Grands Augustins, Blanche Picard and I. Simone followed with cheese and bread. La Maison Nicolas delivered a case of its cheapest wine. . . . That evening thirty guests arrived unexpectedly from the restaurant Cheramy, where word had spread that there were free eats at number 7. My culinary amour-propre was really flattered that day, for by the time Jean-Louis Barrault and Robert Desnos returned from their radio broadcast,* nothing remained but several squares of cheese neglected by the thirty guests contentedly installed around the table.

---

* To survive, and help his friends in the process, Desnos wrote radio commercials for Information et Publicité, an agency run by Paul Deharme, who evidently valued his knack of matching great poetry with banal products. One such commercial had Barrault reading excerpts from Walt Whitman's *Leaves of Grass*.

Guests got more than food served up to them. After everyone had eaten his fill, attention would shift from the common table at one end of the loft to a stage on which Jean-Louis performed mimetic improvisations, improvising either alone (and often to music by avant-garde composers like Edgar Varèse) or with fellow actors who would certainly have figured among Dullin's original recruits in Néronville had they been fifteen years older. "Gymnastics, rhythm and breath exercises, voice projection, animal imitations, readings from little-known texts, ideas bandied back and forth. This *grenier* des Grands Augustins was a beehive, a school that had sprung from the enthusiasm of Barrault's comrades. The latter originally came to find shelter but they stayed to work," Youki recalled. Where stage and offstage became obsolescent categories, with people acting, sleeping, and eating en masse in one unpartitioned room, life had a "wholeness" irreconcilable with bourgeois space, which is to say that his hayloft answered Barrault's notion of the ideal theatrical environment. Not yet called upon to direct, but no longer obliged to follow directions, he improvised himself at will in a halfway house of which he was both proprietor and protégé. Like the stocking pulled over his face, the communal incognito sanctioned the name he had begun to make for himself. "What I remember from this period . . . is the effervescence, freedom from care, and complete liberty of my behavior. . . . Anarchy is a form of nobility," he wrote.

If nobility required that he occasionally join battle on the Left, Barrault proved himself virtuous by appearing at Trotskyist meetings, where he would improvise gestures to Robert Desnos's improvised poems, and by associating, however informally, with Groupe Octobre, a theatrical troupe for which Prévert wrote sketches and revues. Like Antoine's original company, Groupe Octobre consisted of amateurs from the lower class—laborers, seamstresses, clerks, teachers. Unlike the Théâtre Libre, Groupe Octobre, whose name bespoke its loyalties, had mobilized for a specific ideological purpose, to wage war against capitalist society after the fashion of German Communist "shock theater." Where Antoine loved crowd scenes in plays by Shakespeare or Schiller, Groupe Octobre's director, Lou Tchimoukow, served a supratheatrical institution. As was the case with other such groups born of ideological warfare, this one had no home except within the faith, no repertoire but political circumstance, and no aesthetic pieties apart from the "party line." Performing at protest rallies, at working-class shindigs, at factory gates, or at syndicalist meetings, it addressed issues of the moment in makeshift theater that relied on songs, on what Meyerhold called "social masks," and on spoken choruses. In *Citroën*, for example, a chorus enumerated the grievances of workers striking the automobile factory. *Hitler's Advent* was put together in one night and presented the day after Hitler's appointment as chancellor. For *Follow the Druid*, a revue that mocked the tourist-poster image of Brittany, Groupe Octobre sailed to its performance on carnival floats bearing grotesque, Genet-like impersonations of Queen Margot and her favorites, Duchess Anne, the General Staff, and the ecclesiastical hierarchy. In Prévert's *Long Live the Press*, capitalism held the stage along with its entourage of newspaper-courtiers, each reading obnoxious excerpts from itself, until a Communist daily, *L'Ami du Peuple*, stepped forth to lead a chorus that spoke as follows:

> Beware, comrades, beware
> To die for the country is to die for Renault
> For Renault, for the pope, for Chiappe
> For the meat merchants,
> For the cannon merchants. . . .
> Here children play with tuberculosis in the gutter. . . .
> Work is hard, badly paid, very hard, very badly paid
> And when you go into the street, the street is not yours.
> The street belongs to the cops,
> The street belongs to the priests. . . .
> Look toward Russia, comrades,
> Russia where there are men and children who laugh,
> Men like yourselves
> Who call you and shout to you:
> Proletarians of all countries, unite.

These and other revues earned Groupe Octobre not only a preeminent position among its brother companies in France but first prize at a theatrical Olympiad in Moscow.

Groupe Octobre never came closer to literary theater than it did shortly before its demise in 1936, when Barrault got Jacques Prévert to adapt Cervantes's *Wonder Show*, a jovial little play that oddly anticipates some of Pirandello's favorite conceits. Two gypsy mountebanks named Chanfallo and Chirinos induce the dignitaries of a provincial town to attend a "wonder show" whose biblical scenes will be visible only to the pure Christian legitimately born. As Chanfallo and Chirinos describe one scene after another, those whom they have lured assert their pedigree first by ornamenting the narrative and then (in a sixteenth-century version of status-climbing) by climbing onstage to embrace nonexistent personae. The spectators become the spectacle, which continues madder and madder until a simple man brings everyone to his senses.

What Barrault obviously saw here was a vehicle for the mime seeking opportunities to improvise, for the bastard or family outcast welcoming pretexts to avenge himself on *les grandes personnes*, and for the mesmerist. Prévert, in turn, could not resist a satire ready-made for the ideological vocabulary on which he scaffolded so many of his poems, film scripts, and theatrical revues. Among Communists, "ghost" was a code word synonymous with "bourgeois" while "real" was indissolubly linked with "proletariat." Prévert's play *Ghosts*, which Groupe Octobre staged in 1934 at the opening of the Karl Marx secondary school in Villejuif, spoke for itself. And Meyerhold, in his Sovietized production of *The Government Inspector*, used every device to portray as unreal the provincial burghers who dupe themselves through an impostor of their own creation. Indeed, Meyerhold's production may well have enhanced the idea of modernizing Cervantes; for such was the impact it made on Paris when it ran at the Théâtre Montparnasse in 1930 that the avant-garde community proclaimed it a wonder show. Meyerhold divided Gogol's play into separate titled episodes or vignettes. These took place on a small truck stage inside the larger stage, which had been enclosed by an imitation mahogany screen. Each time the truck stage glided out of the darkness with actors frozen in *tableaux vivants* that suddenly came alive, it was as if a picture at some nineteenth-century exhibition had leapt from its polished frame to imitate the quick for one brief instant, before freezing again. "Crystal sparkles, blue and translucent; heavy silk, gleaming and flowing; the dazzling black hair and dazzling white breast of a grand stately lady; a dandy, drunk as only a Hoffmann could imagine, romantically gaunt, lifts a cigar to his languid lips with the movement of a somnambulist," wrote one critic, Sergei Radlov, about the scene in which Khlestakov the impostor drunkenly rhapsodizes on his Petersburg exploits: "A silver bowl filled with pieces of fat, succulent watermelon. Enchanted objects, wobbling slightly, float from hand to hand, passed by servants in a trance. Huge splendid divans, like elephants carved from mahogany, stand poised in majestic slumber. What is this—*Caligari* in slow motion by some lunatic projectionist?"

Applause was not universal: at the premiere in Montparnasse, a section of the Russian émigré community demonstrated against Meyerhold's "mutilation" of Gogol. But it can fairly be said that this production—with its acrobatic *corps de ballet* of provincial sycophants, its complex musical score, its expressionist strategies (as in one vignette, where eleven hands emerge from the mahogany screen offering Khlestakov wads of banknotes, which he collects like a mechanical doll)—went on to haunt the decade. Those who saw it included Jouvet, Picasso, Dullin, Cocteau, Eluard, Derain, Baty. "And when the performance ended," recalled Ilya Ehrenburg, "these people, gorged with art—one would have thought—and in the habit of carefully measuring out their approval, rose to their feet and united in an ovation." *

Prévert's *Wonder Show* was first produced *en famille* at 7, rue des Grands Augustins. From there it circulated through Paris under the direction of Tchimoukow, who had the play-spectators perform on a revolving staircase whose revolutions served to disorient audience and cast. In the role of gypsy impresario, Barrault followed Groupe Octobre wherever it went, miming for the benefit of unemployed workers at the Mutualité convention hall, for women strikers at the Louvre department store, in the warehouse of another department store, Samaritaine. What seems especially noteworthy in retrospect was not *The Wonder Show* itself but the relationship that this playlet fostered between Barrault and Prévert, a relationship destined to bear far more important fruit seven years later, after all else had been lost, in the film *Children of Paradise*.

Just as anarchism gave Charles Dullin an "ism" when no other philosophy could reconcile the various gods he had to placate as a young man, so Barrault's plea of anarchy dignified otherwise irreducible con-

---

* One image undoubtedly born of Meyerhold's production is to be seen in Cocteau's film *Blood of a Poet*, where disembodied arms, holding torches, extend from a wall.

tradictions in his life. The half-dozen films he made between 1936 and 1939 (including *Under Western Eyes*, *Drôle de Drame*, *The Puritan*) assured him an income to which he could not easily confess. While the "bourgeois" part of him bankrolled handsome fees, the bohemian side kept up appearances by refusing to count it. Despite its discomfort, this arrangement may have furnished him the best of both worlds, for if money brought certain obvious satisfactions—among them, Valette's esteem—to identify with the little, the rebellious, and the disinherited was to claim the prerogatives attendant on virtue. Whether or not Picasso ever said that "I like living poor with lots of money," Barrault found the sentiment eminently congenial. How well it suited him he himself first came to realize after he met Madeleine Renaud in *Hélène*, a film produced in 1936 by Jean-Benoît Lévy.

Even as make-believe lovers, Madeleine Renaud and Jean-Louis Barrault formed a paradox. Where Barrault had no reputation outside the intellectual Left Bank, Renaud, who was ten years older than he, had been widely admired ever since she took first prize in comedy at the state Conservatoire. First prize had led directly to the Comédie-Française, on whose stage and behind whose scenes she acquitted herself so successfully that by 1928 she had become a *sociétaire*, or tenured member of the company. "My line, my manner, and my size all combined to recommend me for the role of ingenue. As luck would have it, there were no competitors, so that I ended up playing all of Molière's Henriettes, Angéliques, and Mariannes," she wrote. Her mother, who had raised her on that island of gentility known as Passy and allowed her to study acting only with the utmost reluctance, could not have invented a more capable duenna than the classical repertoire. For French theatergoers, Madeleine Renaud was the eternal Agnès, a creature so wonderfully consubstantial with Molière's virgins that her appearance in some other guise would have seemed an imposture.

Agnès year after year, Agnès she remained until *sociétaires* of the Comédie-Française, whose professional lives were governed by a contract that Napoleon had formulated in 1812, won the right to appear in films, whereupon Madeleine Renaud entered theatrical womanhood. Through films such as *La Maternelle*, *Jean de la Lune*, *Dialogue of the Carmelites*, Ophuls's *Le Plaisir*, *Remorques*, *Maria Chapdelaine*, and, finally, *Hélène*, people who could not imagine her operating outside classical conventions discovered her remarkable versatility. She achieved stardom, and lived like a movie star, with a swank roadster, a villa in Normandy, and a town house in Passy, not far from the apartment building on boulevard Henri-Martin that had been her girlhood domicile. "And so I went to see her," wrote Barrault, recalling the audience he was given after Jean-Benoît Lévy suggested that Madeleine Renaud consider this tyro for her romantic lead in *Hélène*. "She lived in a superb house, decorated with pink cushions and modern glass trinkets. I had shaved, that was all. . . . Though nervous, I was determined not to give up my 'puma' style. As it turned out, the conversation was delightful. She asked me what I thought of the decoration of her drawing room. I replied, frankly, that I detested it. I dragged in some literary quotations, and it was her turn for some gentle mockery. She was charm itself, with her Angel of Reims smile and her large, heavily lidded nut-brown eyes. I was above all attracted by her forearms, which seemed to me as appetizing as two warm brioches."

If Jean-Louis wasn't all that bestial, neither was Madeleine Renaud all that angelic. Having lost her father at four, she had made good her loss at twenty by marrying Charles Granval, an actor twice her age. What little we know about Granval suggests that Madeleine Renaud was swept off her feet by a man she could dominate, that the child bride had more mettle in her than the surrogate father who taught her stagecraft, armed her against intrigue, groomed her for art, and got her with child. "Granval belonged to a third generation of actors," wrote Barrault. "A greenhouse flower is a brittle flower: early broken, early bruised, soon discouraged. And moreover, Granval had against him the very thing that made him superior: a more or less complete culture." He exemplified, or so it would seem, the predicament of the heir crippled by his inheritance. Though Granval, like Madeleine, had taken first prize at the Conservatoire, graduating from it in 1902, he contrived to remain a *pensionnaire* or untenured member of the Comédie-Française until 1920, when finally, and half despite himself (for a *pensionnaire*, hired by the year, was always free to escape the consequences of a *gaffe*), he became a *sociétaire*. "The problem is to remain on terms with knowledge. Granval's capacity for initiative was held in check by all the knowledge he had acquired at the Comédie-Française, since it deprived him, in his own eyes, of the right to make mistakes," Barrault observed. Afraid to fall but equally afraid to rise, unable to fully "join" the company which he disparagingly called *la pharmacie centrale* (hypochondria was endemic) but unable to gain purchase outside it, Granval hid his vulnerability beneath an erudite, mordant persona in which some people saw an aristocrat, and others a superannuated *enfant terrible.*

It was inevitable that Madeleine should have become the victim of his perfectionism as well as the beneficiary of his theatrical culture. Not only did he endeavor to help her refine herself intellectually but he would inspect his creature for wrinkles and fret over them more than she. His marriage succumbed to the same fear that made him thwart professional success. When she grew more mature, he grew more platonic. When she acquired fame, he sought refuge from it as the bohemian *pensionnaire* in a marriage of convenience. Tied to each other by bonds that were filial rather than conjugal, they lived separately, she with their son Jean-Pierre, and he alone. Madeleine had spent many years rehearsing for independence. Indeed, the rehearsal had begun long before she ever met Granval. "Being brought up by women—by my mother and grandmother—influenced me deeply. It made me unhappy to see my mother suffer for being materially dependent on my grandmother. Very early on, I swore that I would learn a métier." The spirit behind this resolution is what Barrault had in mind when he called his future wife "a real little soldier."

Barrault's living arrangements after 1936 indicate that love followed a more tentative course than his avowals of mystical union with Madeleine Renaud might lead one to suppose, or else that the course it followed led, by seeming indirection, to a childhood address. Madeleine felt ill at ease on the Left Bank. While she was by no means a snob, and visited Jean-Louis despite her mother (who had always given her to understand that proper young women did not cross the Seine except in emergencies, and even then, never alone), still, a communal loft demanded more of love than love could bear. At her behest, Jean-Louis left 7, rue des Grands Augustins and took a studio right around the corner from it, on place Dauphine, where he lived by himself, commuting between the Latin Quarter and Passy. Late in 1937 he quit the Left Bank for the Right so as to be nearer Madeleine's town house, which now occupied the center of his thoughts. "I set up in the hameau Boulainvilliers in Auteuil; Granval came to live with me for a while. Our lives were becoming inextricably mixed. I encountered another bohemian life, a gilded one. . . . Madeleine remained protected by the bastion of her town house. At night, I'd walk figure eights in the street while waiting for her signal, a light in the bedroom window."

At length, trust prevailed over past experience, and Madeleine put her "bastion" up for sale and joined Barrault on a voyage that began in yet another luxurious bastion. "That evening we went to stay at the Grand Trianon Hôtel in Versailles. . . . Some time before, I had bought a superb little Danish caravan, which I towed behind a Ford roadster designed to go everywhere. It looked like a small mahogany railway carriage. The surprise of the staff at the Hôtel Trianon—pages, waiters, porters, receptionists—was worth seeing as they watched me arrive with my caravan in front of the main entrance and carry off my *sociétaire*, like a gypsy eloping!" Having entered her world, he came equipped with a carapace, a mobile version of the poor artist's garret, a "little" house in which he made believe that he had not really deserted *la vie de bohème*. After Versailles, they drove north to spend several months in Normandy, where Jean-Louis would camp out near the villa that accommodated Madeleine, her husband, son, and retinue of servants.

This scheme proved so mutually agreeable that when summer had drawn to a close, they duplicated it as best they could in Boulogne-sur-Seine, just beyond Paris's city line. "In September 1938 we took a modern house, with a garden and a small lodge. . . . I was to live in the lodge; Madeleine and Jean-Pierre in the main house, surrounded by flowers and pine trees." No doubt propriety had a hand in keeping them apart, but even when, several years later in Paris, they settled under one roof as husband and wife, Jean-Louis's special domain would be a maid's room where he could ignore the affluent avenues of Madeleine's native quarter. Playing poor in the lap of luxury, inwardly distancing himself from his own good fortune, scaling himself down to the environment of *le menu peuple* while figuring among the great, he conducted himself rather like Jean-Jacques Rousseau, who fled Madame de Warens' large house to dream about her in her one-room hermitage outside Chambéry.

The plays he staged during his courtship were all variations on the theme of virtuous martyrdom. Cervantes's *Numancia*, in which a Spanish city besieged by Scipio Africanus commits mass suicide rather than leave the Romans any human trophy, was ideal material for Barrault, who read it as a "collective" play that would speak to current events yet support his own vision of militant mime. "I had found what I was looking for, a classic off the beaten track. On the social plane I would be making my contribution to the Spanish Republicans. . . . On the plane of theatrical metaphysics I would be plunging headlong into the world of the fantastic, death, blood, famine, fury, frenzy." With the panic energy generated by a conviction that *Numancia* (translated as *Numance*) would conquer Madeleine or else bring disgrace upon him, that the outcome of his exertions would be life or death, he began mobilizing all the friends and resources at his disposal. André Masson agreed to design costumes and decor. A French-Cuban, Alejo Carpentier, whom he met at the *clubs nègres* he frequented on rue Blomet, helped him arrange musical accompaniment. Charles Wolff, the celebrated musicologist, made available his library of rare recordings. And Madeleine offered such moral support as her own qualms allowed her to muster. "She was somewhat surprised—at once disappointed and touched—to find herself living a love affair with a maniac who would come and collapse exhausted at her side on the bed in the little studio." Young Roger Blin, who later became Samuel Beckett's brilliant *metteur-en-scène*, joined a cast that included not only veterans of *Autour d'une mère* but six young men recruited from a gymnastic club to play the Roman army. As is obvious in notes he made afterward, Barrault set particular store by the gymnastic choreography of his *mise en scène*:

> *The decor*: Happy arrangement thanks to the wall that opened and shut solely by the will of the characters. Machinery belonging essentially to the drama. Nothing in excess and what there was was dramatically telling.
>
> *Costumes*: *Numance* is a collective play. By the different values playing on each other Masson gave an impression of numbers. The masks corresponded exactly to the symbols; the attributes were correct. The bull's head, *Numance*'s emblem, had the desired tragic grandeur.
>
> *Groupings*: . . . Stylization of a collective gesture to suit a collective character. I gave the Roman soldiers not an individual gesticulation but something chosen from the collective gestures of troops on the march and in this way the six of them resembled a whole batallion.

Numance was doubly pertinent, for while it made a political statement about Spain, it also made one within the terms of a civil war that had long raged in France between "Romans" and *infantes*, between those who upheld the classical culture and those who defined themselves outside its pale. Ever since the Romantic era, Spain had been a source of inspiration to Frenchmen at war with officialdom, a peninsular night-world in which rebels, whether Catholic or anticlerical, sought asylum from the rationalism of bourgeois France. Thus, for example, Dullin, when he launched the Atelier, did so under the auspices of Calderón, deliberately invoking a seventeenth century other than Louis XIV's. Barrault did likewise and endeared himself, with *Numance*, to the far right as well as to the extreme left. On the right stood Paul Claudel, who would, in due course, authorize him to stage his "Spanish" plays—*Break of Noon* and *The Satin Slipper*. On the left was Georges Bataille, who lauded him in *Acéphale*, declaring, among other things, that "what gives *Numance* its tragic grandeur is not the death of a certain number of men but the entrance into death of an entire city: we do not witness the death throes of so many individuals but of a people." Barrault's production, he wrote, recognized death to be the real basis for mankind's common activity. "No one believes that the reality of a common life depends on the pooling of nocturnal terrors and of that ecstatic tensing death provokes."

Numance, notwithstanding its "collective" nature, may also have reflected the circumstances of Barrault's personal existence. Even as he was laying siege to Madeleine's "bastion," he was producing a play in which he stood foremost among the besieged. And when finally he had given Madeleine (herself a "Roman," a "real little soldier") proof that he could wage a successful campaign by filling the Théâtre Antoine for fifteen performances in June 1937, he emerged from battle not the victor but the neophyte, as though his victory had at all costs to be diminished lest it bring about a separation. "My voice had not yet found its pitch. My acting was nervous, taut, cramped. I could not apply all my lovely theories. I was hardly an actor at all. A pupil in his second year at the Conservatoire, whom I should have despised some years before, was ten times more skillful than myself. . . . I had before my eyes the outstanding example of Madeleine Renaud, who seemed to me more and more the very prototype of the professional actor." If this autocriticism had some basis in fact, its cruelty suggests a self-administered hazing or a pitch for martyrdom more than an objective appraisal. Could any proof he gave have been proof enough under such circumstances? Or is it that he felt his place was secure provided his place were the gardener's lodge, the caravan, the maid's room?

Barrault's affinity to works in which death occupies center stage

manifested itself once again in 1938 when, during his summer with
Madeleine, he undertook to adapt for the stage Knut Hamsun's great
novel *Hunger*. Starvation is once again the predicament, though here it
afflicts not a city under siege but a destitute writer trapped in the city.
Where *Numance* honors patriots who would rather die Spanish than
survive Roman, *Hunger* shows the artist adrift among burghers like a
patriot without a country or a martyr without a God. He is not that
starving artist mythologized by Romantics but the artist whose vocation
is starvation. What he would express in words he expresses far more
eloquently in an ascetic discipline that sees him pawn his few posses-
sions, lose his room, forfeit his civil identity, and empty his mind of everything except fantasies induced by hunger. The would-be genius becomes a would-be saint who exults in his painful body, if not a
would-be terrorist who turns his hatred of bourgeois society against his
own person. To quell hunger when he has nothing left to pawn for
food, he sucks wood shavings and stones, or chews words of his own
invention, nonsense words that are uniquely his for being incomprehensible. It is as though his mouth were his incognito, for he delights in
presenting himself to people under fanciful aliases that conceal his dire
need and, by the same token, craves a language that would render him
impenetrable, omnipotent. "Up in heaven God was sitting, keeping an
open eye on me, and taking care that my defeat proceed after the correct rules of the art, evenly and slowly, with no break in rhythm even as
in the pit of hell the evil devils roamed around bursting with rage
because it was taking me so long to commit a mortal sin," declares this
hero whose name is never revealed.

The emotions Hamsun's novel awakened in Barrault led him back
to early adolescence, when he himself was a hunger artist of sorts,
hungering for a mother who abandoned him and translating his rage
into images of pure form. "*Hunger* gave me the chance to put over on
the stage a fever that consumed me for years and that I sometimes tried
to calm with quinine," he wrote, the fever in question having first beset
him at Chaptal.

Quinine had given me acute noises in my ears; while the fever revealed to
me the sharp beating of my heart. "Hunger," which was not unknown to
me, had caused me to undergo those periods of hallucination that struck
me as being so dramatic and owing to which the subject sometimes

borders on waking dream. Finally Knut Hamsun's theme gave me the opportunity of attacking my art from its most extreme, if not impossible side. One man and his double at grips with a cruelly organized collectivity. With that theme I could throw a challenge at the very substance of drama; it was a theme that touched the limit of the theater's possibilities, a borderline case. But in mathematics, don't we often discover solutions along these lines?

Imbued with the sense that he had no place, that he fell outside all known genres, that his own identity was borderline, Jean-Louis had found in mathematics not only a self-referential language that prepared him for Decroux's instruction but a stoic home from which thoughts and impulses he would collectively nickname "my beast" were excluded. Avowing his kinship with the latter but denying it his name and humanity, he came to regard himself as two people, one besieged by the other, or as a bone of contention worried by occult powers.

Barrault had read other writers obsessed by the "double" and, for example, knew by heart Baudelaire's *pensée*: "At all times there exist in every man two simultaneous postulancies, one drawing him toward God, the other drawing him toward Satan. The invocation of God, or spirituality, is a desire to climb upward; that of Satan, or animality, is the joy one finds in descent." But there is no doubt that *Hunger* addressed the matter of doubleness in terms peculiarly compatible with his own view of life as visceral siege warfare. For Barrault, to starve was to frustrate both the predatory world intent on prying him open and a predator within himself. "We live in a body as in a house," he observed. "We shut the eyelids as one lowers a Venetian blind. Opening them again, there one is at the window. Do I close my lips? The door to the inner courtyard is shut. My nostrils are two chimneys. In our carcass of bones and blood, we can stand a siege. And yet a mere fork planted right in the middle of the eyes would be enough to extract from us the inner animal, as you do with a snail." Exchange between the inside and the outside being fraught with danger, he elaborated theories that invariably show him obsessed by the need to guard against invasion through his orificial organs, to wrap his eyes and mouth in a stratagem of hermetic discourse. As in *Hunger* Hamsun's character uses shibboleths along with stones and wood to exclude the outside world, so in Barrault's writing the mouth is a fortification and the brain a sentinel

that regards everything entering and leaving it as metaphorically collu-
sive. Food, air, and words are coefficient agents of exchange whose passage demands the utmost vigilance.

What Barrault wrote about breathing—and during this period he
wrote about it at some length in an essay entitled "Alchemy of the
Human Body"—may therefore be read with reference to his *mise en
scène* of *Hunger*:

> Let us observe breathing more closely: the chest dilates, it *receives* air. It
> contracts: it sends the air out again, it *gives*. It can also clench: it *holds the
> breath*, it suspends the circulation of exchanges. Let us call this *retention*.
> There you have the primitive ternary of life: Receiving, Giving, Retaining.
> The ternary of breathing is: Inspiration, Expiration, Retention. For the
> moment we are not thinking; indeed we shall not ever "think."
>
> But the sensuality of life makes it easy for us to understand that receiv-
> ing is the feminine time, giving the masculine, retaining the neuter. There
> you have the cabbalistic ternary. Of course it is not a matter of women or
> of men: whichever our sex, we are all made up of the tenary of life. The
> dose varies according to the sexes, *and in the artist the whole thing is con-
> fused. . . .*
>
> Just as Being is double, so there are two kinds of breathing: unconscious
> breathing, which keeps up biological life, the "self"; and conscious, that of
> the Persona, who establishes contact with the Other. . . .
>
> In spite of me, against my will, the exterior forces me to breathe in. This
> inspiration is therefore "passive." I am forced to absorb air that does not
> suit me. It could just as well be an idea. . . . When I can't stand it any
> longer, I assemble my will and, with all my energy, expel by "active" expi-
> ration what someone or something tried to impose on me. Then I shut
> down. But soon, on pain of asphyxiation, air comes in again against my
> will, and so on.*

With mouth and sex confused, the metaphor that confuses breathing,
eating, and speaking has an ever wider field of play: extended downward, it confuses genders as well. If one ventured to extrapolate from
this occult treatise an interpretation of the spectacle Barrault ex-

---

* That these thoughts are based on a section of *The Theater and Its Double* entitled
"An Affective Athleticism" does not make them any the less revealing of Barrault's intellectual and emotional life. On the contrary, his theoretical mimicries underscore his apostolic vocation.

trapolated from Hamsun's novel, one might suggest that through *Hunger* he endeavored to dramatize not only the artist's social alienation but problems of identity with which he in particular had been beset since childhood. Whatever else it may have signified, hunger was sublimation carried to a suicidal extreme. Promising ultimate deliverance, it created the perfect enclosure.

Barrault's *mise en scène* hinged on the introduction of a double, played by Roger Blin, who did double duty, now engaging the protagonist in conversation, now leading a chorus that enacted the protagonist's thoughts and deliria. There were simultaneous scenes, nonsense scenes, cries, long silences, wheezings, chants intoned through closed lips, wild dances, and at least one mimetic cadenza in which Barrault walking on a horizontal plane with lights playing over him conveyed the impression of climbing a circular staircase. "To the dramatic action as a whole I applied a method of plastic interplay which considerably increased the possibilities of changing the location, of rapidly establishing an atmosphere. . . . This plastic material was a means, a freer and broader means towards dramatic movement." Those who knew him well could already anticipate certain devices or effects that had come to form his directorial signature, and not least among these effects a musical amplification of the psychophysical drama. In *Autour d'une mère* he had had everyone march to the rhythm of a tom-tom beating as a heart. In *Hunger* he carried the idea even further with music scored for piano, trumpet, bassoon, ondes Martenot, and drums. The hunger artist's auditory hallucinations became universal. His cramps, nausea, and emotional anguish were borne home on a volume of sound that left no room for thought.

The theater he filled in the spring of 1939 was the same theater in which, eight years earlier, he had given an audition that curiously set the stage for this spectacle. He had, it will be recalled, prepared two scenes. What is more, he had learned all the parts himself because he knew nothing about auditions and came to the Atelier without anyone to feed him cues. Playing himself and his interlocutor, he could not, on that occasion, project his voice across the street to a naked couple who saw in him—so he imagined—a figure of fun, a jest, a pantomimic divertissement. *Hunger* gave him his revenge, even if nothing could finally avenge insults he would live again and again through his art, or give him such attention as he craved. The spectacle ran for something over two months, on a bill that included Laforgue's *Hamlet*, with Barrault playing the title role in an adaptation directed by Granval. It made a great impression on the young, to judge from Simone de Beauvoir's memoirs:

> He could not resist the temptation to introduce several bravura touches
> . . . at one point, for instance, he climbed an imaginary staircase by
> "marking time," an exercise that stuck out from the over-all pattern of the
> production and disrupted its rhythm. I was far more appreciative of those
> moments when gesture per se became a genuine mode of dramatic self-
> expression. There was one scene conducted wholly in dumb show, where
> the hero, through sheer physical debility, failed to possess the woman he
> desired: this was strikingly successful, and though daring, contained not
> the slightest hint of coarseness. . . . After *Numance* and *As I Lay Dying*,
> this production . . . suggested that Barrault might well give the theatre
> just that fresh lease on life which it so badly needed.

Letters of praise came from the older generation as well, however. Paul Claudel congratulated him heartily. Decroux took back his bitter adieux. And Dullin felt reassured that in Barrault he had found a worthy *dauphin*.

For by 1939, after seventeen seasons at the Atelier, Dullin felt cramped in it, despite tours that took him and his company through the French provinces nearly every year. Having long entertained the dream of presiding over a large theater, as had Firmin Gémier, he found one near the place Clichy, where movie palaces attracted great crowds, and entered into negotiations with its proprietor. "The moment has come when I *must* address a larger audience," he exhorted himself. "Since we first opened, our public, which comes from every class of society, has grown larger and larger. The general public has demonstrated the most touching loyalty. For twenty years I have had two crutches: the general public and French youth." The elation he had known as Trygaeus in Aristophanes' *Peace* sufficed to argue down all reasons for staying put, for growing old in the house he had brought alive after World War I. A new theater meant, among other things, a reprieve from the imminence of senility.

His mantle thus fell on Barrault, who would, according to plans they laid in 1938, become director of the Atelier beginning in October 1939. Indeed, *Hunger* sealed and celebrated this agreement. But Barrault had no sooner begun warming to the prospect of sleeping in Volpone's bed when events combined to ruin his precocious achievement. In January 1939 his mother learned that she had terminal cancer. For six months Barrault went about rehearsing and performing *Hunger*, while Marcelle grew more and more emaciated. By June it had become apparent that she would die at any moment. "My grandfather was brought, after being told what was happening. Perhaps expecting to set eyes on her for the last time, he had dressed in black, ready for the funeral. He looked like a poor old lost animal. When she recognized him she quickly raised her arm across her face, as though in self-protection. A moist cry of 'Baby darling' came from between the mustache and small beard, now thin with age, and he went away: the leave-taking between daughter and father was confined to that. A strange settling of accounts." The end came on June 14, 1939, after a priest administered Extreme Unction with holy water she had kept hidden in her linen closet and a sprig of boxwood brought from Tournus.

Having lost his father one month before Armistice Day, he lost his mother as the storm was gathering over Europe once again. News of general mobilization reached him in Pennedepie, near Honfleur, where a bill posted on the town hall advised him that his regiment would form up at Dijon on August 31. After agonizing farewells, Madeleine drove him to the railroad station in Trouville, then returned to the villa to hear her ancient grandmother mumble: "What a pity you fell in love with that boy. But for him we wouldn't have a soldier in the family; we'd be nice and quiet."

CHAPTER XII

* * * *

CHILDREN OF
PARADISE

Along with several million other Frenchmen torn from civilian life, Jean-Louis Barrault spent nearly a year dawdling at the front waiting for something to happen. His adventures in limbo would be comical had they not belonged to that tragic scenario known as "the Phony War," which cost him months and months of intense boredom. To judge from Barrault's diary, the French were defeated by sheer ennui long before Germany invaded France. "We are doing nothing, nothing, nothing," he wrote. "A September day, fog which the sun is taking a long time to pierce. The boredom is pouring softly, like a spring with a regular flow. Boredom has set out on a long spell. It surely knows it will last for a good long while. It has its small, even, terrible rhythm." Caught in a military machine that worked around the clock killing time while waiting for human raw material to arrive, Barrault was shunted all over Alsace, like a migrant laborer. At Dingsheim, where German soldiers across the Rhine had spread out a huge streamer imploring Alsatians not to fire on "your brothers," he cleaned the officers' quarters. At Reipertswiller, in central Alsace, he milked cows left behind during the civilian exodus. At Soucht, he distributed tobacco in the living room of an abandoned farmhouse. Elsewhere, he was given a forage wagon with three famished horses, which promptly dropped dead. This menial tour might have taken him even further afield if not for influential friends arranging to have him join the Third Engineers at Suippes. There, in northeastern Champagne, he suddenly found himself among artists, sculptors, and architects who had been brought together for the purpose of devising new camouflage techniques. "We were made to 'put on our thinking caps' about the problems involved. I remember one project for protecting Paris by altering the course of the Seine, using municipal sprinklers to scatter soap bubbles: at night, enemy aircraft would be misled by the reflections!"

In the early spring of 1940, it having become abundantly clear by then that the ideas emerging from Suippe would not help France confound her enemy, Company F1 was relocated near Ermenonville, with instructions to protect the famous château. Barrault occupied himself watching the swans, gathering morels in the forest, communing at Rousseau's tomb on the Ile des Peupliers, and reading *The Reveries of a Solitary Walker*. So deep was this bucolic lull that war, when finally it came for real, struck him like a bolt from the blue. Of course it had taken everyone unawares, including the French General Staff. "I admit that this was one of the greatest surprises I have had in my life," wrote Winston Churchill after General Maurice Gamelin confessed on May 16 that he had no strategic reserve to parry the German thrust toward Paris. From one day to the next, French soldiers and civilians invaded Barrault's forest lair pell-mell in what soon became a flood of panic-stricken humanity retreating southward. On June 10 the French government departed the capital. On June 11 Barrault slipped onto a truck bound for Chartres and hid under the tarpaulin.

However sincere his vituperations against war, war excited him as did no other circumstance in life. With the future a shambles and society reduced to a primitive horde, he embraced uninhibitedly the myth by which he had set store since early childhood, the myth, that is, of a stalwart presence working underneath appearances to chart his course as the Unconscious charts the somnambulist's. When life seemed most incoherent, it was, he asserted, unfolding with rigorous logic. One coincidence after another furnished proof that he was not a waif lost in the wilderness but an object of divine solicitude, a universal protégé who could never lose his way as home encompassed him wherever he went. Baudelaire's cryptic lines from the poem "Correspondances"—"In nature man passes through forests of symbols that observe him with familiar looks"—made perfect sense to Barrault.

Providence manifested itself the moment he emerged from hiding on June 13 at Châtillon-Coligny, for among the first faces to greet him was that of Madeleine Renaud, who had been swept up by the cyclone and miraculously deposited in this village near the Loire. Stranger still, several weeks earlier, when neither had had any notion that the Germans would launch an offensive, they had published the bans and planned to marry in Paris on June 14. Their marriage took place as scheduled. A captain administered the vows, whereupon bride and groom went separate ways, Madeleine southeast to join her mother in the Creuse, and Jean-Louis south with a ragtag batallion that fetched up in the town of Miramont-de-Quercy. They would not see each other again until August, during which interval a further obstacle came between them, the "line of demarcation" separating German-occupied France from a "free zone" governed (theoretically without German intervention) by the Pétain regime in Vichy. When remnants of the French Army disbanded after the armistice, Barrault traveled to Toulouse, where he loitered for some time, along with countless others who had no safe-conduct, or *Ausweis*, to see them across the line of demarcation.* "As at Dijon nearly a year before, I began to haunt the railroad station, watching for, not believing in, the arrival of Madeleine. At last I had news of her. She was in Brittany. I waited, half-mad with despair. Then, out of desire to be reborn to my country as to an ancestral womb, I went to the municipal library and steeped myself in French history."

It was there, in the public library, that chance arranged yet another providential encounter—this one not with Madeleine Renaud but with Monsieur Fleury, treasurer of the Comédie-Française, who had apparently come to shepherd home *sociétaires* and *pensionnaires* stranded south of the border. He informed Barrault that the Comédie-Française would open its doors earlier than usual, on orders issued by Vichy. Fleury brought him even more startling news. The Comédie's interim director, Jacques Copeau, had decided that Barrault, if he could be found, should be invited to join the Comédie as a *pensionnaire*. Barrault leaped for joy. The prospect of rejoining Madeleine and becoming a student again dispelled the murk in which he had been groping a moment before. Copeau was no longer the autocrat who once unnerved him by grabbing his head, as if to make him "kiss the feet of Christ,"

---

* The line of demarcation ran an undulating course from the Jura mountains in eastern France to just south of Tours in the West, then swept southwest, parallel with the Atlantic coast to the Spanish border.

but the Savior who had lifted him from despair. "I was returning to school and, what is more, to the school of Jacques Copeau, the creator of the Vieux-Colombier, the instigator of the whole modern theater movement." Fleury procured an *Ausweis,* which got him into Occupied France at Vierzon and afforded him his first glimpse of the green uniforms that would make hunger and siege his lot for the next four years.

If Barrault owed this mixed blessing to Jacques Copeau, Copeau in turn owed the authority he wielded to Edouard Bourdet, a skillful playwright who had become *administrateur général* of the Comédie-Française in 1936. Under Bourdet's administration, the reformist spirit of the Popular Front was brought to bear on the company. Where *sociétaires* had traditionally run roughshod over *administrateurs,* Bourdet, enjoying as he did the full support of Jean Zay, an education minister of Malrauvian rigor, imposed himself on his temperamental servants. He taught them to see him at fixed hours. He intercepted appeals they made over his head. He had senior actors and actresses who clung to heroic roles as to an illusion of eternal youth surrender their illusion in the interest of verisimilitude. He disciplined malingerers and abolished certain byzantine privileges. He staged what he saw fit to stage, preempting an actors' committee—the *Comité de lecture*—which traditionally had the final say. Above all, he worked hand in glove with four men—namely, Jacques Copeau, Charles Dullin, Louis Jouvet, and Gaston Baty—whose appointment as official *metteurs en scène* of the Comédie represented a consecration of the avant-garde.* Once a week he would have them gather at his house for lunch where, far from the theater and safe from eavesdroppers, this camarilla would exchange ideas in general or discuss the presentation and cast of future spectacles. While internecine warfare raged between "Bourdettistes" and "anti-Bourdettistes," Bourdet carried on as though oblivious of the wounded sensibilities that lay in wait for an opportunity to destroy him.

Their opportunity did not present itself until 1940. Resuscitating a

---

* Although this arrangement met with his satisfaction, it had been proposed in the first place not by Bourdet but by Louis Jouvet when the latter, who was Jean Zay's first choice for *administrateur,* declined Zay's offer.

moribund institution had won Bourdet such prestige in Paris that sur-
reptitious campaigns failed to dislodge him even after his political
guardians, Jean Zay and Léon Blum, had fallen from power. The stroke
that finally brought him low was delivered by accident, outside the
Comédie-Française. In February 1940, when blackouts made it more
than usually dangerous to cross Paris streets at night, an automobile
struck him on the avenue des Champs-Elysées and crushed one of his
legs. Surgery saved it, but phlebitis eventually set in, forcing him to retire for the interim and appoint a substitute. Baty, Jouvet, and Dullin
turned him down, whereupon Bourdet, despite severe reservations he
had about the man, addressed himself to Copeau, who was lecturing
abroad. Copeau had no sooner taken office on May 14 when he issued
an *ordre du jour* written in the hortatory, bombastic style that had long
since become second nature to him:

> We have been receiving terrible blows for several days now. These blows
> have inflicted painful wounds. I do not believe that words can mollify
> them, but it is with words that one strives, in one's misery, to sustain con-
> fidence, courage, dignity.
>
> Let us all keep our dignity constantly in mind. Let us be men and
> Frenchmen. In such dire circumstances, it is not shameful, it is natural for
> each of us to be concerned with himself and especially with those near and
> dear to him. Some people have more mettle in their natures than others.
> That is why we must endeavor to help one another, the stronger coming to
> the aid of the weak.
>
> Strong or weak, let us not lend an ear to alarmist rumors many of which
> are false and most of which are exaggerated or distorted by enemy pro-
> paganda. Let us defend ourselves according to our means, as the comba-
> tants defend themselves according to theirs. What are our sufferings in
> comparison with their trials? It is pusillanimity that causes suffering.
> Courage strengthens the soul and pacifies it.
>
> Let us apply our courage to work, to good works. Let us think about
> our métier, which is threatened, about our House, which is threatened,
> about our intellectual and spiritual patrimony, which is threatened. Let us
> constitute ourselves defenders of the Fatherland and of Civilization.
>
> I have confidence in you. And I place this confidence while invoking the
> memory of the combatant Charles Péguy, whom we shall celebrate Satur-
> day next.

The company scattered a fortnight later, on the same day that the government left Paris. Copeau went to Pernand in Burgundy and then, after
the armistice, to Vichy.

"Why should the Comédie-Française take me on at this point, when I am run down, out of training, and have forgotten everything I ever knew?" Barrault asked himself. While men at war often fear that memory has failed them, that they have been forgotten and have forgotten, in Barrault's case this fear was especially pervasive, for World War II brought him full circle, tearing open a wound inflicted during *la grande guerre*, when he knew very little indeed. His "amnesia" was, furthermore, an earnest of good behavior, a plea of innocence calculated to propitiate gods who might hold against him the rebelliousness he displayed yesterday, in his "animal" phase. Until 1939 the desire to start from scratch had seen him flirt with Communism and play iconoclastic games organized by his Surrealist comrades-in-arms. In July 1940 starting from scratch meant embracing for dear life the traditions, institutions, and values he formerly derided. With everything he ever knew "banished from mind," he dove headlong into the "ancestral womb" of French history, getting "reborn" even before he was enjoined to do so by a regime whose motto would be "work, family, fatherland" and whose thurifers would proclaim Marshal Pétain the embodiment of France's guardian principles.* "I love the ceremony of the table," Barrault wrote in his autobiography. "To me a meal is a quasi-sacred rite: another attitude bequeathed by my ancestors. I love customs. . . . Those of the Comédie-Française delighted me from the first. . . . The first thing that enraptured me . . . was the smell of the boards, the time-worn mellowness of the vaulting, the extraordinary impression conveyed by a place 'where work is done.' " It was the waif in search of a bastion who presented himself to the dean of actors at the Comédie-Française—a prodigal son.

Reduced to noviceship once again, he was beset once again by the ineducable demons that had made him miserable a decade earlier, during his first year or two at the Atelier. Then he spent nights in a bed designed for Charles Dullin. Now he found himself clad in garments that hung like sacramental robes tailored not for him but for a race of giants. Reciting four lines from Corneille's *Polyeucte* entailed upon him a bronze breastplate "lined with saltpeter deposited by the sweat" of

---

* Among these guardian principles was the superiority of the Latin curriculum, which Vichy lost no time reestablishing. During the last years of the Third Republic, legislation had favored scientific disciplines. In addition, Vichy repealed laws that had made *lycées* tuition-free since 1930.

great predecessors like Edouard de Max, whose name he found written
on a label beside the inventory number. As the guard in Molière's *Misanthrope*, he wore a period costume, undergarments and all, so heavily
embroidered with pearls that just standing still sufficed to exhaust him.
"The timidity of my earliest days again took hold of me. The Comédie-
Française teems with awe-inspiring *Shades*," he confessed. "The bench
in the concierge's office . . . still bears the traces of de Max's Shade.
And in the Café de la Régence there survives the thundering Shade of
Paul Mounet. And near the stage there is the bust of Worms. And the
corridors still re-echo with Silvain's exquisite repartees." Paul Mounet,
Edouard de Max, Silvain, Gustave Hippolyte Worms: these were the
"Romans" who straddled *fin-de-siècle* Paris, the vocal athletes who
competed in range of voice like discoboli hurling discs, the "sacred
monsters" of whom Dussane, another *sociétaire*, wrote that they upheld
an epic dream and "knew how to make it plausible, or, better yet,
manifest." In evoking their memory, Barrault vested the Comédie-
Française with the weight of his grandfather's generation, with the body
of an age that gloried in its embonpoint, with the *capacité* of a nineteenth century whose legendary feats had first been impressed on him at
table. By what magic could a hunger-artist prove worthy of such company? How insubstantial he felt emerges quite clearly from a self-
portrait drawn under the guise of an object lesson for theatrical novices:

Take a match, but don't be content to look at it. See it, feel it—its fragile
slenderness. . . . "I am wood, but more like a thread, a memory of wood;
I come from a Swedish forest. What is left of my health? I am thin! and
long! and my fibers have been bruised in the torture that thinned me out;
my whole being is split, I crack under the least pressure: my wood cracks.
But those who use me mean something else when they say: strike a match.
In that event, it's my head that blazes, for my entire flame is in the head. I
live in a congested state: my forehead burns, my ears are all red. . . . My
fate is to die the instant I give life, heat, light. It's my virtue that consumes
me.*

---

*As a director, Barrault liked to construct roles around a symbolic object that
reified the character's state of mind. In portraying his stage fright, he wrote: "The presence of the audience terrified me. In *Volpone*, dressed as a sbirro, I could feel my body
becoming as thin as my halberd; my wig seemed to be perched on a broomhandle." He
was a broomhandle (or match); Dullin, on the other hand, "belonged to the race of
oaks."

Where the Great Shades could not sweat without their sweat congealing into mineral evidence, he could only aspire to physical life. Where they were made of Corneillean mettle, he was made of stuff that consumes itself without leaving a trace.

Among other *gaffes* committed by Copeau during his brief regime at the Comédie-Française, perhaps the most flagrant was the decision he made to mount a new production of Corneille's *Le Cid* with Barrault in the title role. If Barrault cut a matchstick-like figure, Copeau would not have had it any other way, since his production called for a set that put people in mind of the fairground rather than of the Spanish court. It was as though he meant to dominate the Comédie-Française, whose ornaments he couldn't strip, by reducing its aesthetic scale to the Vieux-Colombier's, by creating a puppet enclave within the palace walls. "All he could do was do again what he had done during the audacious era of the Vieux-Colombier and retrace his memory across the mist of three decades," wrote Cardinne-Petit, secretary-general of the Comédie-Française. "But he made a bad copy of his memory image, or, if you will, betrayed it by transposing it from the exiguous, ill-equipped stage of the Vieux-Colombier to the immense frame of the Comédie-Française. He could not fill that frame." Giving Barrault center stage on the most visible platform in France and having him play the classical *ubique victor*, Don Rodrigue, was not so much a compliment paid the newcomer as it was a willful gesture designed to further ambitions utterly divorced from reality.

That Barrault did his bidding need hardly surprise us. Men less impressionable than he had spoken of the "magnetic" power Copeau exerted over those around him. But in addition, Copeau's bidding coincided with Jean-Louis's own desire to transcend the waif in him, to take Madeleine by storm, to prove that he could grow large overnight, without benefit of Conservatoire training. This fantasy of inflation saw him enact once again what had become a kind of ritual scenario. During the first rehearsal, he felt so unqualified to stand among his new confreres (especially Jean Hervé, whom he evicted from the role), so unequal to the task of projecting himself and filling the cavernous theater with a voice on which he could not rely, that he lost his breath. "After the third line I was drained dry. My lungs were emptied as if they had been sucked in by the huge and monstrously dark theater. What had become of my First breathing and my Second breathing? What had happened to all my fine theories? I stopped and shamefacedly asked if my lines could be skipped." Only later, when everyone had left, did he regain his composure.

I dived down into the metro like everyone else. I had my ticket punched and was waiting for my train when suddenly a flood of love swept up into my breast. . . . I ran up the stairs again, four at a time and plunged into the Théâtre-Français, which was not yet shut, and slipped into the auditorium. I was in the Darkness and Silence of that well of exacting demands. The identical self-recollection of my night at the Atelier, the same potential faces, the same creakings, the same interior murmurings, the same secret whisperings all around me. Only the size of the setting was different. It was bigger, which was natural after ten years.

Withdrawing from the fray tongue-tied and breathless before recovering tongue and breath in a burst of staircase wit, Jean-Louis might have consoled himself with the thought that Don Rodrigue likewise won his battle by taking the enemy unawares. But in fact he was, as soon became apparent to the public, more a closet Cid than a shrewd Rodrigue. Marie Bell playing Chimène and Jean Hervé Don Diègue made him look woefully adolescent. While these two warhorses demonstrated their heroic manners, he went scurrying between them in a vain attempt to establish his presence as hero by sheer nervousness. The passionate aplomb of Corneillean verse got flustered and the drama along with it. "Le Cid was a total flop despite the generous exertions of Marie and Jean-Louis Barrault: for all his pluck, the latter couldn't even approximate Rodrigue," wrote Cardinne-Petit. Barrault put it more succinctly: "It was disastrous."

A novice ceased to be a novice once he realized that only half the battles fought within the Comédie-Française—and not necessarily those on which advancement hinged—were devised by Corneille and Racine, that the period undergarments he wore in Le Misanthrope figured less importantly in the drama of institutional life than the dirty wash aired backstage. As state employees bound by law to serve the Comédie-Française for life, sociétaires spent their leisure time, a good part of it, savaging one another like aristocrats imprisoned at Versailles. Though Madeleine Renaud must have regaled Jean-Louis with tales of intrigue as soon as they met, not until he joined the troupe did he fully understand why its members liked to say, "We're just one big family—the Atridae," or appreciate that this stale jest dignified with classical lineage a world the more vainglorious for having none but mock titles of nobility.

Then again, Madeleine Renaud could not have told him what sinister turns the feud between Bourdet's friends and foes would take after September 1940, when France herself became embroiled in internecine warfare. Among *sociétaires* leagued against Bourdet, sentiment ran high for Pétain. Many indeed were the anti-Bourdettistes who anticipated that a regime led by a grand old hero would sympathize with their grievances, punish their *bête noire*, and restore them their erstwhile prominence, that all the insults Bourdet paid them would be repaid him tenfold. Vichy did not disappoint these petitioners. Vengeance materialized in the person of a hack journalist named Alain Laubreaux, whose rabid anti-Semitism and flair for ideological cliché earned him the freedom to assassinate with impunity any character he disliked. Availing himself of information provided from inside the Comédie-Française by several embittered *sociétaires*, he waged a vigilante campaign against Bourdet in collaborationist papers such as *Le Petit Parisien* and *Je suis partout*. Vintage Laubreaux reads as follows:

> A certain côterie has not given up hope of witnessing the return of Edouard Bourdet to the Comédie-Française. This intrigue is one of the multiple ramifications of the vast plot being woven by Jewry's revenge-seekers who, even now, endeavor by every means and in every domain to sew confusion under cover of which the most poisonous creatures of the Old Regime would make themselves virgins once again. Let us not forget that M. Edouard Bourdet was named administrator of the Comédie-Française by M. Jean Zay. His appointment took place at the dawn of the Popular Front, in the drunkenness of the electoral victory won by Léon Blum and his fellow Jews.

In exchange for information, Laubreaux, who had designs upon the directorship of the company himself, assuaged his informants with a conspiratorial explanation of the disgrace into which they had fallen several years earlier.

Thus, Bourdet was a neo-Dreyfusard pure and simple, a Freemason, a "foreign agent" whose administration, far from restoring the national theater's health, corrupted its soul. A foreign agent could not have done otherwise than corrupt souls, since "foreign," in Laubreaux language, stretched beyond geographical boundaries to denote a shadowy realm that contained everything depraved, irrational, and malevolent. During Bourdet's regime (so the argument goes), policy was formulated in the underworld. While invoking meritocratic principles to legitimate himself, Bourdet, who took office in "drunkenness," presided over a saturnalia that confused day with night, paupers with princes, and dirty Jews with clean Frenchmen. Heinous as it was (the argument continues), this debauch was only one, local manifestation of a plot against France herself. Had Pétain not contended that France's moral fiber went slack long before 1940? that responsibility for its defeat lay with those schoolteachers of the Popular Front era whose socialist-pacifist lessons suborned national virtue? that France's nemesis was not Nazi Germany but the alien within? Laubreaux merely visited Pétain's sermon on the Comédie-Française—denouncing artistic reforms as seditious acts, and reformers as traitors who would, by hook or crook, impede France's regeneration unless driven from the national stage. To conspire against their ilk was to expiate sins and purge demons.

And purged they were. In January 1941 there prevailed an atmosphere of permanent intrigue at the Théâtre-Français where, with few exceptions, one met blank faces and eyes that looked askance. One could not breathe without smelling the toad's broth simmering behind closed doors. Otherwise unflappable sorts would tense directly they entered the place. "Jean Hervé, who felt compelled to sneer whenever he saw me, would emphasize his tragedian's rictus with gnashing, onomatopoeic sounds placed 'in the mask,' as singers say," Cardinne-Petit recalled. "He could not help publicly priding himself in having 'gotten' Bourdet, any more than he could help proclaiming his vow to 'get' Bourdet's creatures, one of whom I had the honor of being." When Bourdet announced in November 1940 that he had mended sufficiently to take charge of the Comédie-Française, Vichy's minister of public instruction requested that he tender his resignation. Though enraged by such ingratitude, he would, in time, be able to count himself lucky, luckier at any rate than, say, Jean Zay, whom Vichy's militiamen captured and murdered several months before the Liberation.*

Jacques Copeau played a characteristically ambiguous part in these

---

* Zay, who was not a Socialist but a moderate ("Radical Socialist"), figured as prominently as Léon Blum on the hate list of French anti-Semites. Céline used to spell *Je vous hais* ("I hate you") *Je vous Zay.*

events. Though he gave the impression that he stood above the battle, those who found him suspiciously humble did not have long to wait for evidence confirming their suspicions that he, Bourdet's deputy, viewed himself as Bourdet's successor.

A trip to Vichy apparently confirmed him in his ambitions [wrote Cardinne-Petit]. As soon as he returned . . . he became another man. The rustic gave way to a dictator who spoke with curt, sullen authority. He hatched long-term projects and made himself very much at home. Close collaborators of Bourdet watched in amazement as his office underwent a radical transformation. An enormous, low-slung oak table replaced the elegant Louis XV desk, massive bookshelves covered the Gobelin tapestries, cartons of books arrived from Copeau's house in Burgundy. Our chief electrician was ordered to devise a system of signals that forbade admittance to the director's office when a red bulb lighted up.

This transformation of an urbane salon into a monkish cell was a proprietary reflex that augured the transformation of the national stage into a pulpit from which Copeau at frequent intervals delivered *obiter dicta* on the marvelous prospects for faith and virtue occasioned by hard times. "I don't pity you," he told an audience of students. "You will be happier than we because you will have received, at the threshold of your life, a grand and painful lesson, because you will have witnessed, before reaching the prime of life, one of the greatest upheavals history has ever recorded." Adversity constituted Copeau's bread and butter. As despondent as he had usually felt in "bourgeois" France, this penitent land strapped for every material resource and cut off from the world outside brought light to his eyes, warmth to his heart, and homilies to his tongue. How, indeed, could he not conclude that history had at last vindicated him when the new regime set out to organize social and economic existence around corporate ideals he had been preaching since 1913? No longer did he cry alone in the wilderness. With work camps for young men springing up throughout France and Vichy consecrating the Barrèsian philosophy that France's salvation lay in reverence for *la terre et les morts*, Copeau was understandably inclined to behold his Vieux-Colombier as a paradigmatic model of France redeemed, his flight from Paris as a biblical departure for which the state owed him investiture in high office, and Bourdet's mantle as a cassock that justified his machinations against Bourdet.

Had he had only one master, the Comédie-Française might have had only one *administrateur général* during the next four years, but Copeau was answerable to a Nazi Propagandastaffel whose authority proved, in his case, more onerous than Vichy's. Soon after he took office, the Propagandastaffel ordered him to appear at 52, avenue des Champs-Elysées with a list of Jewish actors employed by the Comédie-Française (Jews having been banished from the stage). At Cardinne-Petit's suggestion, Copeau submitted a complete roster of actors in the company, hoping against hope that the Germans would take him for deaf or dumb and make no further demands upon him. As they did not take him for deaf or dumb but reiterated their demands day after day, he found it ever more difficult to mask a widening rift between the ambitions he cherished and the moral precepts he urged on the world at large. While Cardinne-Petit waffled with the Propagandastaffel, who declared that they would pillage and board shut the theater unless satisfied, Copeau held himself aloof in his monastic study, waiting for he knew not which, either doomsday or a *deus ex machina* capable of saving him from this repugnant dilemma.

A *deus ex machina* finally came. As it turned out, all he needed to defeat his scruples was circumstantial evidence that someone, probably a *sociétaire*, had already given the Propagandastaffel the list they sought. Presented with strong hints of a *fait accompli*, he knuckled under, requesting affidavits of Aryan lineage from actors upon whom suspicion had fallen and even demanding that a young *pensionnaire* undergo a penis check. Marie Ventura, who had come to the Comédie-Française from Rumania (which made her *ipso facto* indecipherable), received one such request for proof of lineage. "In accordance with your demand, I repeat the declarations I made aloud concerning my racial situation and reinforce them with my parents' marriage certificate, which proves that they were joined by an Orthodox priest according to Christian rites," she protested in a letter that brings to mind Cervantes's *Wonder Show*.

You are not unaware that in the Orthodox religion, Jews may not receive the sacraments of the church. My father's family being one of the most ancient in Rumania—his mother was born Princess Rosetti—I can affirm that his lineage, as far back as the Crusades, is of pure Aryan stock. . . . He died having received the sacraments of the Orthodox Church and was buried in Christian ground. In Rumania there are special cemeteries for Jews. . . . I should like to draw your attention to the fact that my native country has a tradition of virulent anti-Semitism. There has always been a law forbidding Jews from occupying public office and civil-service positions. Never has a Jew been admitted onto a national stage, and my mother was a *sociétaire* of the National Theater of Bucarest. Her father was a professor of history in a state *lycée*. . . . As for myself, I was director of a theater subsidized by the Rumanian state, and I gave a long series of performances in the National Theater of Bucarest, receiving accolades from students well known for their anti-Semitic campaigns.

If Copeau thought that his capitulation, however belated and grudging, would appease the Propagandastaffel, or that the deeds of his son Pascal, who had joined the Resistance, would not be reckoned against his own eligibility for high office in Vichy France, then he was soon to learn a rude lesson about Nazi accountantship. On December 30, 1940, Vichy named him Bourdet's successor, pending confirmation from "the occupying power" which could, according to terms of the armistice, veto any such appointment. A week or so later, word came from 52, avenue des Champs-Elysées that he was to vacate his post and leave the Comédie-Française within twenty-four hours or be expelled *manu militari*. Except for his confidant, Jean Debucourt, no one, not even Cardinne-Petit, knew what had befallen him until the following appeared on a bulletin board, at the Comédie-Française:

Ladies and Gentlemen, *Sociétaires* and *Pensionnaires* of the House of Molière:
Because my son occupied a conspicuous post in the French propaganda bureau during the war;
Because I did not collaborate closely enough with the German propaganda bureau during the Occupation;
Because I showed too much moderation toward Israelites, the Kommandantur required my resignation from the directorship of the Comédie-Française. I gave it. But I do not wish to leave without bidding you farewell and thanking those who showed me consideration and affection. From 12 May to 10 June, and from 20 July until now, 7 January, I sought to serve you, to serve our art with you and through you. My effort is in abeyance. I hope that yours may continue brilliantly. I regret not being with you to celebrate Molière's birthday.

I found myself involved with your company in difficult and even critical circumstances. Do not forget me completely.

J.C.

By the time *sociétaires* and *pensionnaires* read his valediction-in-self-defense, Copeau was already quite some distance away, beyond reach, and what he said acquired something of the force and sanctity of a posthumous message, or suicide note. Although the Nazis gave him no choice, in other respects this flight was a redundant act that saw him follow tracks he had made years earlier, when the order to leave Paris came not from outside but from within, not from a German overlord but from a would-be seer. Now as then his flight started in the city and ended on a hilltop in Burgundy. Now as then it put between parentheses that which he could not reconcile with his public image, and effaced witnesses who might testify against him. It had all taken place before and, for all the wisdom it brought him, might have taken place again had he had another life to live. "Return to reality after eight months among ghosts in that monument of vanity and insincerity, the Comédie-Française," he wrote in his journal on January 29, 1941. "How rich the world becomes as soon as one rediscovers the freedom to offer it one's heart. Fortunately, the vanities that exercise men have almost no effect on me. How easily I slough them off!" Five months later he would tell Roger Martin du Gard that "I am entering a new life. . . . I am writing a Mystery of Saint Francis and each day commit several lines to a notebook."

Barrault was likewise adept at starting life anew after each fresh debacle. His recuperative powers together with instruction he received from Madeleine Renaud in the art of survival helped him survive his inauspicious debut as the Cid. Indeed, by May 1942, he had become France's most illustrious *pensionnaire*. The portrait Gide drew of him that month contains no shadows of doubts but only the glitter of an ascending star: "Admirable visage, exhaling enthusiasm, passion, genius. Next to him Madeleine Renaud effaces herself with exquisite modesty. Their grace and unaffected manner put me at my ease. . . . Barrault instantly invites me to finish for him my translation of *Hamlet*; and such is my confidence in him that I would like to start work immediately. I learn with keen pleasure that he is close friends with Sartre. In the presence of these people, I feel rejuvenated."

During the 1942 season, Barrault played Hamlet in a production (directed by Granval) that won general acclaim, and might have won it even if Parisians, most of whom came on an empty stomach, had known enough Shakespeare to second Simone de Beauvoir's observation that "this lean, bony, neurotic prince was nearer Laforgue's pastiche than the character Shakespeare conceived."* *Phèdre*, which he directed at the request of Marie Bell, who played the title role, earned him additional renown while furnishing him an occasion to bone up on Racinian prosody. "I made a study of the symphonic movements in *Phèdre*. I took its metrical craft to pieces, as one might do with a Greek tragedy. I studied it so closely that one day, in a Dominican monastery, I was able to recite it from memory, all 1654 lines."

Having found the stage of the Comédie-Française an incomparable springboard, Barrault leaped beyond it at every opportunity—to read dramatic verse on radio, to lecture schoolchildren, to mount open-air extravaganzas. In 1941, for example, he directed a production of Aeschylus's *Suppliant Maidens* that would have done Firmin Gémier proud, what with its multitudinous cast disporting itself in the Roland Garros Stadium (a large soccer stadium just west of Paris) to incidental music by Honegger, and a curtain raiser glorifying athletic games. *The Suppliant Maidens* engendered another, even larger spectacle when Vichy's minister for youth affairs, Jean Borotra, who fervently preached moral reeducation through sports, asked Barrault to help organize a Festival of Youth on behalf of the new order:

Barrault accepted with enthusiasm [wrote Cardinne-Petit]. The impresario he was knew no bounds: he saw things writ large and his zeal, which made him chafe at the modest budget allocated him, did wonders in the manipulation of masses. All the youth leaders and monitors of physical education participated in the open-air demonstration at Bagatelle [in the Bois de

---

* Claudel, who found his interpretation "magnificent," dispatched a critique that included these suggestions: "1. People reproach you for scurrying about too much. Given your conception of the role, that is not my opinion. But there are moments in which one must feel more *the Prince*; . . . 2. Not enough variety in delivery. There are moments when you must *change register*; in the flute scene, for example, you must play the dunce, the clown; 3. You always come out at a gallop."

Boulogne] which unfolded after the fashion of the national revolution, with fanfares, choruses, parades, ensemble movements, all to the rhythm of the popular hymn "Maréchal, nous voilà!"

Barrault omitted this episode from his memoirs, but the fact remains that he became a pageant master under Pétain long before he became a master of avant-garde ceremonies under Charles de Gaulle. "I like to obey, perhaps from weakness of character," as he put it, and during the regime that held sway after 1940 his weakness for spectacles incorporating men in an heroic myth or apotheosizing a national parent guaranteed him civic employment and official recognition. What he obeyed above all else was a dream of fusion whose inherent grandiosity compelled him to manipulate ever-larger masses on ever-bigger stages, to glut the void with emotion, with magnetic fluid, with music, with God. Far from representing a departure, the Festival of Youth amplified features of his own directorial *oeuvre*, and not only the gymnastic sequence that had made *Numance* noteworthy but the funeral procession he choreographed for *Autour d'une mère*.

Toward the end of 1942 Barrault learned that *sociétaires* would—after a meeting to be held for the purpose of considering his credentials—in all likelihood, offer him full partnership. The prospect filled him with mixed emotions. Although he stood foremost among the disgruntled *pensionnaires* who, several months earlier, had submitted to the Administration Committee a list of grievances (including one in which they stated that "at the time of our appointments, the previous *administrateurs* led us to believe that we could not and should not remain *pensionnaires* for long"), when success beckoned, he fell into a quandary. Should he accept the appointment, he would sign a contract from which nothing could release him except old age, incompetence, or death. "To stay at the Français was to confine myself in an aesthetic citadel." On the other hand, confinement in an aesthetic citadel seemed, on and off, preferable to freedom in the prison house outside its walls. While soldierly pluck demanded that he create his own enterprise, that he pull down bastions, that he imitate Robert Desnos, for example, and join the Resistance movement, self-preservation told him to seek shelter under what he considered an aesthetic alibi rather than risk the worst by entering "the social fray" or "the battle of ideas and politics." (Desnos was arrested by the Gestapo in 1944 and sent to a concentration camp in Czechoslovakia, where he died.) Then, too, there was

Madeleine, who sat among his judges. "*Wilfully* moving away from Madeleine, when life had miraculously reunited us . . . was tempting Providence. Still, my demons were upon me and gave me no rest." Can it be that these demons struggled to preserve the middle ground between his garret and her manor house? Reluctant to "move away," he was equally reluctant to move closer when to move closer involved an oath that would, as he saw it, make him his wife's institutionalized eunuch. "So the choice was: art for art's sake, exclusively, or the life of the artist for its own personal pleasures? The monk or the anarchist?"

On the horns of this dilemma, he had recourse to friends whose advice could not but skirt an issue he himself could not clearly formulate. "I think a man like you, who has at least one new idea per day, who is made for trying out new things in all directions, ought to be his own master and every time to commit only himself," wrote Sartre. "You mention struggle and fighting, but I see in a work of art not so much a fight as an achievement. My fear is that you will have to fight a great deal and achieve little." Dullin also advised him to set out on his own, though rather more cautiously than Sartre. "Reread La Fontaine's adorable fable 'The Wolf and the Dog' and, knowing me as you do, you will get my point," he wrote. "The form of theater I have always defended is perhaps the one nearest to all those that the Français ought to be defending, and yet the furthest away because of the constraints imposed by false traditions and a state conformism. It is very good that at your age, in the prime of life, you should carry the struggle into the citadel itself. But every concession you will be obliged to make will turn against you even more harshly than in your own theater, unless your ambition turns merely toward your skill as an actor, which, obviously, you can exercise with a maximum of security." The dog of La Fontaine's fable is a sleek mastiff who touts the rewards of servitude to a hungry wolf. In return for chasing beggars and fawning over your master, he says, you get your fill of chicken bones. The wolf has all but decided to apply for this sinecure when he notices a collar around the mastiff's neck. "Oh, yes," the dog explains nonchalantly, as if it were a detail of no consequence, "I spend my days chained to a post," whereupon the wolf lopes away, resuming his hand-to-mouth existence with a sigh of relief. It had been with a sigh of relief that Dullin resigned from the Comédie-Française after Bourdet's dismissal. But, for Barrault, the issue was far more complex and the gamble more redoubtable.

Barrault solved his dilemma by playing wolf, dog, and wolf in swift succession. Just before the electoral committee met, he told the dean of actors, André Brunot, that he would not accept the tenured appointment, and joined a friend at the Brasserie de l'Univers opposite the Comédie-Française. They were toasting Jean-Louis's newly won independence when suddenly Jean-Louis felt panic-stricken. Now that he had made good his escape from the bastion, he viewed himself as an exile or an orphan unable to cope with life on his own. Life was there, across the square, and he had rejected it in the service of a future that now seemed "amateurish," "artificial," "intellectual and naïvely pretentious." To his friend's bewilderment, Barrault crossed the square at a run, took the stairs of the Comédie two by two, and had a uniformed attendant inform the committee that if it should see fit to confer upon him membership in the *sociétariat*, he would accept it. After five minutes, the *sociétaires* emerged tearfully to welcome him into the fold— this a breach of custom—whereupon Barrault, weak from having relived so much of his life in a flash, collected himself once again. "Abruptly I drew away from them, with my back against the wall, and, shaking my fist cried: 'Mind you, beginning today, I'm going to make you foam at the mouth!' "

He could scarcely forgive such judges the weight he placed on their judgment. Nor would he let a grandfather who succored wards of the State sit him down at table and exact from him promises of good behavior in exchange for a weekly consideration.

The *Cromwell* that enabled Barrault to impose himself, or "carry the struggle into the citadel" was Paul Claudel's *Le Soulier de Satin* (*The Satin Slipper*), a play monstrously long and complex even by Hugolian standards. Though Barrault first proposed to stage it one year before he became a *sociétaire*, not until 1943 did he surmount obstacles the least of which was its author's belief that what he had written could suffer no abridgment. Wood for sets and fabric for costumes proved more difficult to obtain than Claudel's cooperation in shortening *The Satin Slipper* by one-third. A dilatory censor held up work month after month. When at last rehearsals got under way, *sociétaires* who found the play incomprehensible boycotted them. But nothing could distract Barrault from a project on which he had, characteristically, staked his all. "I, too, am burning to see the outcome of this project," he wrote to Claudel, "for I tell you once again that *my fate at the Français is bound and remains bound to that of* THE SATIN SLIPPER. Under no circumstances will I release my prey." Between periodic trips across the demarcation line for *pourparlers* with Claudel, who lived near Lyons, he orchestrated a Catholic circus in which he was not only God's martyr, Don Rodrigue, but a ringmaster attending to the stage business of his clowns, to the movement of his mimes, to the music being written by Honegger, to the set designs of Lucien Coutaud, to the idiosyncratic diction that Claudelian verse required of his actors. He wheedled, wept, threatened, and raged from January 1943 until November 26, when the five-hour spectacle had its premiere.

To say the least about *The Satin Slipper,* which takes place in the late sixteenth or early seventeenth century (but occasionally swims out of time), is to say that it revolves around Don Rodrigue, a latter-day Cid who rules as the Spanish king's viceroy, and Doña Prouhèze, a woman made in the mold of Claudel's apostolic *femmes fatales*, who lives with her husband on Mogador, an island fortress off the Moroccan coast. They desire each other from either side of the ocean. Having fallen in love after one brief encounter, Prouhèze implored the Virgin to help her resist temptation and left a satin slipper at the icon so that, if she found her adulterous impulse irresistible, she should "go to evil limping." Separated by the Christian king, they serve him in different hemispheres at the expense of their dream. Only once does Prouhèze attempt to communicate with Rodrigue, and her letter takes ten years reaching him. When Prouhèze's husband dies, the king would, for political reasons, have her marry someone other than Rodrigue. And she obeys him, knowing that her frustrated passion serves a cause not of this world. After one more encounter with Rodrigue, she dies during the Muslims' assault upon Mogador. Rodrigue, in turn, becomes a global conquistador. He conquers the Philippines. He loses one leg in an invasion of Japan. And finally, before dying, he retires from the world scene to become a destitute artist, a *naïf* who paints and peddles his images of the saints.

As in the case of Faulkner's *As I Lay Dying*, here again one detail hooked Barrault on a work to which he felt instinctively drawn long before he perceived its shape and nature. "It would be both childish and untrue to pretend that *The Satin Slipper* first appealed to me by its form. No; it was the play's sheer power and the elevation of its subject that had held me for so many years," he wrote. "Everyone knows that the action takes place largely at sea. The necessity of catching the motions of the sea was the detail that excited me. Indeed, I began my study of this difficult play with the scene in which Doña Sept Epées and La Bouchère . . . are swimming in the rippling sea."

The Satin Slipper was in fact that detail writ large, for the feeling associated with wave motion was upheld by a drama that billows through space until it fills the whole, and by discourse that commits any solecism it must in order to sustain its momentum. "Movement is all," Claudel declared in *Art Poétique* (echoing the preface to *Cromwell*, where Hugo wrote that "the human mind is always on the march or, if you will, in movement, and languages move with it. . . . Languages are like the sea, they undulate ceaselessly"). Every digression on this theme reinforced Barrault's belief that he had found in Claudel an orator who spoke for him better than he could speak for himself, a magus who gave the *disjecta membra* of his own thought shelter inside a venerable body. Movement expressed a congenial obsession with the fluid, the oceanic, the total. "Human being is total, it is complete, and each of its faculties, such as the Creator made it, is indispensable to it," wrote Claudel in *Improvised Memoirs*.

> It is generally admitted that there exists a kind of telegraphy, a nervous current set in motion when, for example, one touches some part of the body, and that this telegraphic impulse or nervous current runs from the affected part to a central post that records it. Sensation is "afferent." I, on the contrary, believe that being is *continually in a state of vibration*, that it bears comparison to a violin whose string is set in motion by the bow, and that the note—in other words, knowledge—results from the modification of this continual current running from center to circumference.

This continuous emission of nervous fluid was, in his view, a continuous birth of Being. "There is," as he put it, "a certain form that can be represented only by a circle; it continually fills this circular territory, doing so by a vibration that does not cease, not even for an instant."

Claudel's theater dramatizes his platonic ontology. In *The Satin*

Slipper as in *Le Partage de midi* (*Break of Noon*) a love affair between lovers unable to consummate it results in a world of starved feeling, a globe pregnant with emotion, a catastrophe from which they emerge reborn through Christ. Vanquishing the New World because he cannot vanquish the *belle dame sans merci* appointed by God to implement His divine purpose, to bait men with desire for ultimate bliss, Don Rodrigue moves ceaselessly, borne outward on a sea that symbolizes alike emptiness and plenitude, separation and merger. The more he possesses of this world, the more bereft he feels of that which he cannot possess. As his power grows until it encompasses the entire earth, so does his sense of universal exile. Unlike the Corneillean hero, after whom Claudel named him, he cannot achieve heroism by force of arms. Serving an Absence whose realm is limitless rather than a Christian king whose kingdom has definite boundaries, he becomes Viceroy, or Cid, en route to the fall that heralds his epiphany outside time and space. Over this birth woman presides as God's midwife. Where Chimène, in *Le Cid*, would have Rodrigue prove worthy of the name he bears, Claudel's Prouhèze would have Rodrigue strip himself bare. Where Chimène rallies a warrior, Prouhèze swaddles a martyr. "Strip yourself! Throw away everything! Give up everything in order to receive everything!" The stoic virtue she enjoins upon him has its physical correlative not in aristocratic mettle but in water, and finds its ultimate reward not in self-affirmation but in self-dissolution. "Let me begin my penitence in the bosom of these eternal delights," she exclaims, after describing herself as a sea. "Let me be the drop of water that joins these delights to your heart! Let me have no more body so that I may no longer have a wall to your desire! Let me have no more face so that I may penetrate to your heart! . . . I hear the endless Sea breaking on these eternal shores!"

Such paeans to oceanic merger invariably come from a woman's mouth. After Prouhèze dies, her apostolate (as well as her androgynous nature) devolves upon her young daughter, Doña Sept Epées, who shows the mystical stuff of which she is made in the scene that riveted Barrault. "It is delicious to dip in this liquid light, which transforms us into divine and suspended beings . . . glorious bodies," she says as she bobs on the waves. "You no longer need hands in order to grasp and feet to travel. Like anemones you move forward by breathing, by the simple swelling of your body and the thrust of your will. . . . There's something that joins you in blessed unity to everything else, a drop of water associated with the sea! The Communion of Saints!" The "circular territory" allotted to each swells into this final vision of the universe as a bowl with God's spirit moving over the waters, of a plenum that has no outside and no interstices separating man from man. The Satin Slipper abounds with exiles, refugees, prisoners, and orphans, but the faith it propagates promises to bring everyone home. Its very abundance—its babel of dialects, its hodge-podge of cultures—redounds to the glory of the One that transcends accidents of time and space.

Claudel dedicated The Satin Slipper to José-Maria Sert as one painter of immense neobaroque frescoes speaking to another. And yet, despite its scope, The Satin Slipper might pass for a bloated miniature, a pageant of supermarionettes who ride melodramatic storms and execute worldwide leaps on a stage operated by ten fingers overhead. Never did Harlequin justify metamorphoses more implausible or styles more jarring than those Claudel permitted himself in the name of Oneness. People dance naked under the same roof as Platonic shadows. Low slang follows hard on classical inversions, and Wagnerian bombast on vulgar jokes. History mingles with fantasy and era with era in a medium so fluid as to be incapable of supporting firm barriers. What Claudel has Rodrigue say toward the end of The Satin Slipper—"There is no wall and barrier for man other than Heaven! All that is earth on earth is his to walk upon and it is inadmissible that any parcel of it should be foreclosed"—expresses not only the childish arrogance of a character "born to live onstage" but the megalomania of a dramatic enterprise that would seem to have required either Earth itself or, lacking even one parcel of it, the fairground booth. When Claudel wrote in his preface that he imagined his play performed during Mardi Gras, at four in the afternoon in a big hall "heated" by some previous spectacle, and celebrants abuzz with excitement, he clearly had in mind those descendants of the fairground that stood side by side on the Boulevard du Temple, swallowing a public that streamed in from every quarter come Mardi Gras.

"The whole, whole, whole of Paris was there," wrote Barrault, and indeed, ministers of state, ecclesiastics, courtesans, ambassadors, poets, academicians, and high German dignitaries all came to witness this petard he hoisted inside his prison house. The spectacle had not yet begun when a voice wailing air-raid instructions above Honegger's overture announced that confusion would be the order of the day. If Claudel envisioned "an immense masquerade, a tragic mélange half-mystical half-farcical," then Barrault's production of *The Satin Slipper* more than did it justice. Interludes of slapstick featuring, among other anomalies, a fish dressed in petticoats alternated with flights of high romance. A Negress baring her bosom while dancing a samba brought the Folies-Bergère smack into a drama whose tergiversations clothe the bisexual nature of a heroine modeled after Saint Joan (Prouhèze wears male attire). Scene changes were pretexts for *lazzis*, or banter between stage-hands and a carny who wandered in and out nonchalantly, like a comic hyphen. Whenever the action grew huge and ponderous, a whimsical episode would advene, as if to let Claudel's run-on sentences catch their breath, to give the public relief from an argument that might otherwise have driven it mad, or to foster promiscuity for its own sake. "I had put the whole works into it: mime, nudity, madness," wrote Barrault. How successful he was became quite apparent within a fortnight, or by December 10, when the *administrateur général* wrote to Claudel that "the box offices are besieged by a crowd so avid and demonstrative that on certain mornings the police have been obliged to intervene." Though some, like Paul Léautaud, lost interest as soon as the Announcer declared in a preamble that "what you don't understand is what's most beautiful, what's longest is what's most interesting, and what you will not find amusing is what's most droll," Barrault's gallimaufry seduced others who had not expected to like it. "We had objected to a good many things in this play when we read it a few years before; but we had admired Claudel for successfully containing heaven and earth in a love affair," wrote Simone de Beauvoir in *The Prime of Life.* "Ever since he had written his *Ode au Maréchal* we had found him utterly sickening; but all the same, we were curious to see his play and find out how Barrault had dealt with it. . . . His production was a wonderful medley of styles. The motions of the sea he indicated by means of human gestures, a happily inspired borrowing from Chinese theatrical convention. There were other devices which recalled Barrault's innovations in *Hunger.* Yet more than once the curtain rose on a set that might have been designed by Châtelet." Sartre and Beauvoir walked out asking each other which aesthetic "line" among the many that converged in this production Barrault would ultimately decide to follow.

Dullin's was the response that pleased Barrault most deeply. The La Fontaine fable had made him feel ashamed of himself; but when, in

June 1943, Dullin produced *The Flies*, which Sartre had written at Barrault's instigation and with every assurance that Barrault would stage it
after quitting the Comédie-Française, his shame had grown even more
acute. While his erstwhile master braved the powers-that-were on behalf of a play about tyranny by a young intellectual, he had committed
his interpretative energies to the *summum* of an old man who endorsed
Generals Franco and Pétain. It therefore came as an immense relief to
hear Dullin say, in a letter written immediately after the premiere:
"When I have told you that I was very moved by the performance . . .
I have told you the essential thing. . . . I found your contributions
quite staggering, like a block that hit me all at once, a visceral blow, a
family achievement. . . . I have recognized also that you were right in
seeking to create your work in that house." Barrault must have known,
furthermore, that between its lines this letter made a poignant confession: that Dullin, in deserting the Atelier for the Théâtre Sarah Bernhardt, where he felt quite lost, had, unlike Barrault, chosen the wrong
house.

No one who attended the Comédie-Française—neither Beauvoir
nor Sartre, nor Dullin, nor, indeed, Barrault himself—suspected that
posterity would remember Barrault under the Occupation less for *The
Satin Slipper* than for a role he had created on a different stage even as
he was organizing the *mise en scène* of Claudel's cosmological drama.
In June 1942 he had gone south with Madeleine Renaud, who had been
cast in Jean Grémillon's film *Lumière d'été*. Barrault commuted between Saint-Tropez and Nice, where French cinema made the Victorine
Studios its summer capital. One day, on the Promenade des Anglais, he
encountered Jacques Prévert and Marcel Carné. Prévert and Carné were
inseparable collaborators, the one writing screenplays, the other directing them. After seven films, they were, as Barrault learned over apéritifs,
at their wits' end looking for yet another subject that would command
financial support and not rub Vichy the wrong way. Story followed
story when Barrault related an anecdote that suddenly made his friends
lean forward. "It had to do with the mime Deburau," Carné recalled.
"As Barrault told it, Deburau was strolling on the Boulevard of Crime
one day, arm in arm with his mistress, when a drunkard began to hurl
abuse at the young woman. He didn't know her and had no reason to
act as he did. Deburau, who had restrained himself, finally lost all control and dealt the man a blow with his cane, killing him straightaway.

. . . What made the incident enthralling was this: that all Paris attended the trial at Assizes Court *just to hear Deburau speak.* The idea bowled us over." Their enthusiasm may well have sprung, in part, from a realization that this subject, sufficiently picturesque or *démodé* to pass through Vichy's board of censorship unimpeded, could convey a subversive message. The boulevard on which cultural outsiders foregathered in nineteenth-century Paris might symbolize an exiled nation and Deburau's trial articulate the indignation of Frenchmen living under a regime of silence imposed on them by *concitoyens.* In Barrault's case, however, other thoughts were at play. He who always felt accused had always craved a language that would not only plead his innocence but hold people spellbound. Struck dumb by fears he expressed in siege after siege and trial after trial, he, the eternal captive, longed to be a law unto himself, an occult force, a prodigy exempt from covenants that govern social existence. But now, just before he entered the *sociétariat,* he was more than ever inclined to entertain renegade fantasies. Recoiling from the prospect of life imprisonment among "Romans," his imagination suggested that he follow his "beast" outside bourgeois Paris and lord it among bohemians.

The film born of this encounter was originally to have been entitled "Les Funambules," but as the subject grew during the months that followed, it grew beyond Deburau's trial and became increasingly a romantic evocation of nineteenth-century bohemia, with the Boulevard du Temple its protagonist. Soon after the conversation in Nice, Carné visited Paris and found pictures in the prints department of the Bibliothèque Nationale that fleshed out a world he had never quite been able to visualize and reinforced the impulse given him by Barrault's anecdote: pictures showing boulevard theaters and bistros, dives in La Courtille, profiles of street merchants who exercised what were known as "the little trades of Paris." At a bookstore on the rue de Seine, he discovered Jules Janin's theater criticism, which taught him that the *menu peuple* of nineteenth-century Paris called the cheap seats "Paradise." Laden with this precious documentation, he headed south again. "I had no sooner arrived in Nice than I threw my photographic documents on the table that separated me from Prévert and said, triumphantly: 'The whole film is right there!' " Prévert, for his part, had begun to formulate a plot that would embroil Deburau, Frédérick Lemaître, and peripheral characters such as Lacenaire, the multiple murderer *cum* dandy, whose trial was a sensational event in France of Louis Philippe's era. They agreed that the title should be *Children of Paradise*.

Children of Paradise was made, at a halting pace imposed by political circumstances, between August 1943 and December 1944. Creating the set Barsacq designed would have been difficult even in peacetime, but during war it required logistical genius and feats of persuasion. Carné had scaffolding transported by the truckload from Paris. Three hundred and fifty tons of plaster were needed to sheath the façades and five hundred square meters of glass to make panes for three hundred windows. After bulldozers leveled an immense terrain adjoining the Studios de la Victorine, construction proceeded in earnest, with fifteen carpenters, fifty machinists, twenty plasterers, and innumerable handymen laboring round the clock for three months. Once they had finished, another crew laid cobblestone-like plaques over two thousand square meters of ground and transplanted trees on a strip several city blocks long. By August 1943 Carné's dream street stood complete, whereupon the work began of bringing it alive.

Eager to escape dismal Paris and act in a film that promised rewards of every sort, Barrault, Pierre Brasseur, Etienne Decroux, Marcel Herrand, Maria Casarès, Arletty, and Louis Salou had long since accepted the parts offered them by Carné. Pierre Renoir joined the cast belatedly, as a replacement for Robert Le Vigan, who fled France (in the company of Louis-Ferdinand Céline) when the Allied armies began to close in, knowing that after Vichy fell the anti-Semitic broadcasts he had made since 1940 would, in all likelihood, earn him a prison sentence.

This brilliant troupe thus convened on a Boulevard of Crime built for one last go at the hated Romans. "I would like to play comedy," Prévert's Frédérick Lemaître (Pierre Brasseur) declares to the manager of the Funambules. "Comedy!" the director rejoins:

> But my poor friend, you've got the wrong theater. Here one doesn't play, one doesn't have the right to play comedy. "We" must enter the stage walking on our hands! On our hands! Do you understand, on our hands. And why? Because they persecute us. And why is that? Because they fear us. They know that if comedy were performed here, they—the beautiful, grand, noble theaters—would have to put the key under the door and close up shop. In their world, the public dies of boredom. They put it to sleep with their museum plays, their antiquarian tragedies, and their wretched

Jean-Louis Barrault as Jean-Gaspard Deburau playing Baptiste in one of the mime scenes in Children of Paradise. Film Archives, Museum of Modern Art

mummies who come wrapped in peplums, stand stock-still, and bawl for all their worth, like "Romans" if you please! While here, at the Funambules, it's alive, things leap, things stir. Pure enchantment, right! Appearances, disappearances, just as in life! The worn-out shoe, and then the wand—just as in life. And what a public! It's poor, of course, but it's made of pure gold, my public. Look at them up there, in paradise!

From the above pronouncement to the final sequence, in which Deburau finds himself engulfed by white-clad Pierrots dancing farandoles as far as the eye can reach, *Children of Paradise* celebrates exiles with nowhere to move but up, prisoners who resist a society that erects barriers between class and class, stage and audience, theater and reality, men and childhood. Above all, this fable of occupation celebrates the people's street. After its mortal vicissitudes in Paris, the street ignominiously buried by a ruthless city-builder got resurrected on the Côte d'Azur by a cinéaste. Through the miraculous intervention of film, nineteenth-century bohemia became an Outside idealized forever, and, miracles begetting miracles, the sainted mute a *sociétaire* of the Comedie-Française. So far as Barrault was concerned, it did not much matter whether he played Rodrigue here or Deburau there, for in any event the last line of *The Satin Slipper* provided a fluent transition from rue de Richelieu to the set of *Children of Paradise: "Délivrance aux âmes captives"*—"Deliverance unto captive souls."

Two scenes from Children of Paradise. (ABOVE) *The reconstruction of a Boulevard du Temple theater; Frédérick Lemaître, played by Pierre Brasseur, is guying the part of Robert Macaire in a melodrama entitled* The Inn of Les Adrets. (BELOW) Mardi Gras *on the Boulevard du Temple.* Film Archives, Museum of Modern Art

EPILOGUE

✦ ✦ ✦ ✦

MAY 1968

By 1945 Charles Dullin looked much older than his sixty years. The Occupation had taken its toll, and the Liberation brought no relief. "One feels a bit discouraged with the present state of things," he told his sister in January 1946. "Doing anything of the slightest interest seems futile. One is caught in this atmosphere of confusion, equivocality, ugliness, hypocrisy. In a word, one has no desire to work." After the municipal government, which owned the Théâtre Sarah-Bernhardt, made him leave it in 1947, he acted in two films and directed several plays, including Armand Salacrou's *Archipel Lenoir,* but seemed to function by sheer will power. A tour of southeastern France with *L'Avare* in 1949 finished him. He came back to Paris from Marseille on his last legs and died of stomach cancer at the Saint-Antoine Hospital, departing this world two months after Jacques Copeau, and two years before Louis Jouvet. It was what Barrault called "an exodus . . . that removed, one by one, all those who had made me more or less what I am."

To wonder, as Simone de Beauvoir did, which "line" Barrault would ultimately follow was to assume that the shuttlecock could declare its independence of the battledore and side against the net. His game forbade it. In 1946, when a ministerial commission formulated new statutes for the Comédie-Française, Barrault and Madeleine Renaud resigned from the Society, availing themselves of a special dispensation granted by Charles de Gaulle's government. Along with several other fugitives, they founded their own company and quartered it at the Marigny—a theater of modest proportions just off the Champs-Elysées—that enjoyed no great distinction in histrionic annals, apart from it having been the scene of Jacques Offenbach's first popular success. There they remained for ten seasons.

From the outset, Barrault entailed a filial claim on the mantle of Copeau and Dullin. He started a review (*Renaud-Barrault Notebooks*), he held poetry readings, he sponsored Pierre Boulez' efforts on behalf of modern music, and, in general, did his utmost to take the public constantly by surprise, staging now Aeschylus now Offenbach, now Feydeau now Stravinsky. He did not, however, establish a school. Though the Marigny begot a Petit Marigny, an experimental theater-within-the-theater where several young playwrights had their debut, Barrault's diffidence and grandiosity, his intolerance of limits and anguished impatience made it hard for him to teach. "*Mal mais vite,*" he would say, only half in jest. "Badly but quickly." The eternal student, he became a world-class sprinter, leading his companions on tours that took them round and round the globe, from Paris to Anchorage to Tokyo to Saigon to New Delhi to Jerusalem.

By 1959 he had achieved quasi-ambassadorial status, whereupon André Malraux urged him to become director of the Odéon. "To hand ourselves over to 'officialdom' was risky," he wrote. "Would we not be sucked in? By becoming Théâtre de France would we not, in the eyes of many people, be 'academicizing' ourselves? Was it not a trap, the prelude to some kind of betrayal? What did my 'double,' the libertarian, think of it all? But there was Malraux and, behind him, de Gaulle. I like men who have dimension."

During his administration, the Odéon was transformed into a stage that consecrated those who had been brought together under the rubric of "absurdist theater." Reconciling the bohemian image to which he owed allegiance with his need for "dimension" or grandpaternal support, he produced Beckett, Pinget, Ionesco, and finally Genet, whose *Screens* was the cause of much tumult and ballyhoo. After nine years, he began once again to feel that death had caught him up, that a patina would soon encase him unless he kept moving, that the Odéon was, as Copeau put it years earlier, the threshold to Père-Lachaise. Even if May 1968 had passed uneventfully, Barrault would sooner or later, and most likely before his sixtieth birthday, have ridden free of officialdom on his ever-contentious beast. But May 1968 did not pass uneventfully. There took place what came to be known as "the events." With Prime Minister Georges Pompidou out of the country, students rose in protest against the educational and social policies of Charles de Gaulle. Their protest soon became a general insurrection against Gaullism involving the powerful trade unions.

The *événements* culminated in a general strike on May 13 that saw hundreds of thousands of people parade from the Gare de l'Est south across central Paris to the place Denfert-Rochereau while singing the "Internationale," shouting slogans, and brandishing red and black flags. Before the demonstration was over, several prominent militants arranged a meeting for the purpose of devising a sequel, of doing whatever could be done to sustain the spirit they had felt emanating from masses on the march. And what had that spirit been? "A spirit of fervor, of liberation, of dialogue entered and embodied itself in this throng," wrote Patrick Ravignant. "Perfect strangers challenged one another, addressed one another in the familiar form, shared and gave; for the first time in generations communication among individuals was no longer that goal toward which one wends one's way through a labyrinth of complexes and frustrations; it was a basic fact, burstingly evident. *One felt that something unheard of was occurring* [italics added], that suddenly nothing seemed impossible any longer."

The same spirit prevailed among the conspirators, according to Ravignant, who evokes their meeting in terms reminiscent of Chamson and Guéhenno celebrating the advent of Happiness on July 14, 1936, or of Péguy describing the collective fit of virtue induced by Kaiser Wilhelm's visit to Tangiers in 1905, or of Revolutionaries toasting the Fountain of Regeneration in 1793. Most of these men had never met one another, but—he observed—they emitted an identical "vibration":

> A single conception of life bound them closely. What had to be abolished was the feeling of sin, the spirit of culpability that derived from Christian civilization . . . that old separation, erected by our society into dogma, between intellect, feeling, emotion, sex, etc. . . . . All inclined toward a vision of man integrated, reintegrated . . . no more "intellectuals," "artists," "manual workers," no more "cultural" as opposed to "noncultural." . . . Art must be everywhere, or not be.

Not only complexes and frustrations but the entire psychosocial edifice that makes individuals individual would be laid waste in an orgy of collective rebirth. Like eighteenth-century Revolutionaries who thought to jettison original sin, along with other unwanted legacies, when they declared 1792 Year I, these militants experienced the march as a break in time, as a beginning or end, as a baptismal *fête* repealing the laws that structure daily life. To be was to lose oneself in a throng whose feelings argued its inherent virtue. Reborn en masse rather than individually, marchers constituted the "human" nation outside a "consumer society" intent on reducing people to objects or imprisoning them in abstractions. Their intimacy-at-first-sight bespoke their beatific integration. Liberated from all that had kept men separate under the Old Regime—patronymics, métiers, titles, memories—they became members of a single festive organism celebrating its nativity, of a clan joined in passionate namelessness. The magic Schiller once ascribed to joy—"Your magic ties back together what custom sternly separates"— now devolved on instinct. No longer bound by social consuetude, men rediscovered the *"grand élan créateur,"* the great creative urge, which had hitherto been obliged to express itself by circumlocution, to lie low, and slave for profit. In the absence of censors, speech became "pure speech" and art an instinctual imperative.

The Latin Quarter was strewn with debris from a pitched battle between students and riot police that had raged two nights before, on the "Night of the Barricades," after which de Gaulle decided to adopt conciliatory tactics. The people who met on May 13 agreed, toward dawn of the fourteenth, that the "cultural revolution" should take hostage some state institution outside the university and that that hostage should be the Odéon. Strategic advantages recommended it, for the Odéon stood near the Sorbonne, which insurgents had just occupied. But strategy went hand in hand with arguments that clothed aggressiveness in psychophilosophical cant. The Odéon was said to have incriminated itself by fabricating a consumerist art that represented a "dangerous factor of alienation." That it staged "leftist" or avant-garde plays made it doubly pernicious, since avant-garde theater constituted a "reassuring abscess of fixation," an "exutory": make-believe revolution served to discourage real revolution. It was this line that prevailed in discussions held at Censier, a branch of the university that functioned as a combination recruitment center, headquarters, and forum of the student movement. When several young actors otherwise sympathetic to the movement dared to defend Barrault's theater, they found themselves verbally set upon by a young firebrand who had renounced a theatrical career out of—in her own words—disgust for its artificiality. "Your métier could be among the most marvelous, and it has become the most degrading because they make stars of you, that is, consumer objects essential to the masturbation of millions of spectators!" she declared, inviting her audience to go in the street, to improvise, to help people express themselves, create, and overcome their servitude to publicity and gadgetry. "You have something important to do, but no longer can it be done by acting on stages before a docile, slavish public," was her envoi. Such flights of rhetoric proved irresistible. While those who had laid plans for the occupation would have waited until May 16, on the fifteenth (or one day after de Gaulle haughtily went flying off to Rumania) a tumultuous mob formed at Censier and demanded immediate action. All plans crumbled.

Alerted by telephone that "they were there," meaning the students, Barrault set out for the Odéon at around 11:00 p.m., with instructions from the Ministry of Cultural Affairs to "ouvrez-leur les portes et entamez le dialogue," ("open the doors and engage them in discussion"). Parliamentary practice did not, however, obtain at the Roman circus in which Barrault presently found himself. His contention that "theater is promiscuity—its buildings must be filled with such a load of humanity that one always feels there is no room" came home very much at his expense, demonstrating that roomlessness constitutes the most insuperable barrier to dialogue. There reigned an atmosphere reminiscent of the Terror, when the Committee of Public Safety baptized the Odéon "Theater of the People" and had it reconstructed as an amphitheater in accordance with the decree that performances given there be given "by and for the people." Twenty-five hundred bodies occupied space that normally accommodated less than half that number. The stage swayed beneath the weight of another three hundred demonstrators, mostly youths. From the stage, where a hostile throng was jostling him, Barrault spied Julian Beck, whose Living Theater he once had hosted at the Odéon, and, evidently unaware that Beck had figured in the original conspiracy, cried: *"Salut, Julian, wonderful happening, n'est-ce pas?"* When his attempt at light-heartedness earned him thunderous disapproval, he threw in his lot with the insurrection and declared:

> It's not a question of theater, but of a revolutionary movement, a movement of youths who want to transform society. I am wholeheartedly

behind this movement. You can do what you wish in this theater. I ask only that you let us perform in the evening. It does not even concern *me*, for right now the Odéon is the Théâtre des Nations and Paul Taylor's ballet the featured company. We aren't earning a cent of revenue. Let me remind you that Paul Taylor has danced in Cuba: he is with you, he is a revolutionary!

He was only shouted down again. "You must definitively repudiate the labels of *metteur en scène* and actor. Our movement welcomes all; you may join it provided you come as an ordinary individual," he was told by militants on the stage. "Yes, yes!" he stuttered. "I am no longer a director, I am no longer an actor, I am no longer anything!" Had Madeleine Renaud not stood nearby, fear might have prompted him to make public confession of his guilt. As it was, the "little soldier" showed herself to be just that, and enveloped herself in contempt for the howling mob.

During the next month, Barrault's nooklike office in the Odéon became his lonely redoubt. Ostracized inside by militants and outside by André Malraux, who had heard about his endorsement of the revolutionary movement, he wandered through his theater aimlessly, as a prisoner condemned to see the ideal of fusion he had always upheld against bourgeois society grotesquely fulfilled. Beginning with the second week of occupation, the Odéon became a shelter for the capital's nomadic population. By June waifs, tramps, and starvelings were there in force, colonizing not only the cellar but the loges and backstage area. Whatever they could lay their hands on, they took. Costumes were used as garments or cut up to serve as blankets. Girls adorned themselves with all the bracelets and diadems in the prop store, so that the disaffected theater was soon swarming with a Mardi Gras crowd got up in strange disguises. Any swatch of black or red material—including the stage curtain—was requisitioned for the fabrication of flags. "Backstage became a veritable dormitory with bodies piled on top of one another and muffled up in blankets, curtains, rags," wrote one observer. "In this glutinous, dusty mass of sleepers, couples made love side by side." The costume ball included a constabulary which had armed itself with helmets, swords, and pikes—these, too, looted from the prop store. "Something like eight to ten thousand persons per day were milling about in the corridors, dressing rooms, auditorium, and on the roof. And the words kept drooling. Impression of hell," Barrault noted as he watched it all unfold despite himself, and despite evacuation orders given him by the Ministry. Hell seemed to exercise such fascination on him that he could not tear his eyes away from it, and, indeed, collaborated as a martyr, exposing himself to insult by speaking up at the ideological filibuster that took place on what had recently been his stage. When one of Malraux's subalterns requested him to have the Electricité de France darken the theater, he would not obey.

While couples held orgies in the basement and sentinels stood guard on the roof, orators discussed utopia in the playhouse. Of the innumerable proclamations and edicts that came flowing from the Odéon and Censier, one deserves to be singled out. Under the title, "Join the Revolutionary Commune of the Imagination," it called for:

> occupation of all the theaters in the Latin Quarter, and their utilization as operational bases for transforming outside space into a vast stage with infinite possibilities, on which each person becomes both actor and author of collective social-dramatic events. . . .

> occupation of all movie houses, art galleries, and dance halls and their conversion into operational bases for taking over all urban space: walls, sidewalks, streets, roads, rivers, and sky, as settings for images, sound, and plastic expression, in a huge sketch based on permanent invention available to everyone. . . .

> APPLICATION OF THE IMAGINATION TO THE SERVICE OF THE REVOLUTION

Three days later, police surrounded the bastion and expelled its occupants, some of whom would presently find refuge in the faubourgs where proletarian theaters—theaters collectively designated *le théâtre hors les murs*—began to multiply. The city's cultural walls had withstood yet another assault, though behind them, in bourgeois habit, were many who remembered nostalgically the promiscuous adventures, the suspension of verbal etiquette, and, above all, the spectacle of fire and desolation that had prompted Ernest Mandel, Trotskyist Fourth International leader, to exclaim from atop a barricade on May 13: *"Ah! Comme c'est beau! C'est la révolution!"*

+ + + +

REFERENCE
NOTES

CHAPTER I
ON BOURGEOIS THEATER

pages

2. "We visited the Louvre": Mark Twain, *The Innocents Abroad*, New York, 1966, 100
3. "A writer for the official bulletin": S. C. Burchell, *Imperial Masquerade*, New York, 1971, 128
3. "My dear Sir": ibid., 126
4. "Oh Lord": ibid., 170
4. "Government exists in order to": J. M. Thompson, *Louis Napoleon and the Second Empire*, Oxford, 1954, 233
4. "The government loans": ibid.
5. "France is like Molière's miser": Edmond and Jules de Goncourt, *Journal*, I, Paris, 1956 (June 15, 1857), 371
6. "Fould counts": Burchell, 174
8. "There is no longer a race": Adeline Daumard, *Les Bourgeois de Paris au dix-neuvième siècle*, Paris, 1970, 120
8. "The Second Empire was for French cuisine": Jean-Paul Aron, *Le Mangeur du dix-neuvième siècle*, Paris, 1973, 80ff
9. "The Café Anglais sells": Goncourts, *Journal*, I, 1212
9. "The talk of the town": ibid., I, 456
10. "When seven o'clock": Aron, 191
11. "Marvelous thing, wealth": Goncourts, *Journal*, II (May 31, 1867), 347
12. "If it were possible": ibid., I (August 28, 1955), 202
13. "When it comes to mounting": Jean-Pierre Moynet, *French Theatrical*

Production in the Nineteenth Century, American Theatre Association, 1976, 66

13. "The machinist's art": ibid., 111
14. "Money is a very big thing": Goncourts, I, 1157
17. "To write an oration": Antoine Prost, *L'Enseignement en France 1800–1967,* Paris, 1968, 52
19. "Our bourgeoisie, even the most humble": ibid., 267
19. "The students are not to say": ibid., 53
20. "The ruling classes will always be": ibid., 332
20. "Children think, imagine": ibid., 65
22. "Humanity is so weak-minded": Ernest Renan, *La Vie de Jésus,* Paris, 1976 (folio ed.), 51–55
22. "It does not seem to me": Régine Pernoud, *Histoire de la Bourgeoisie en France,* II, Paris, 1962, 486
22. "Our conscientious distinctions": Renan, 51ff
24. "To form, through the universities": Renan, cited in Pernoud, 560
24. "The Church made the mistake": ibid., 559
25fn. "You discovered simply this": Paul Valéry, *Occasions,* Princeton (Bollingen Series), 1970, 34
25. "Let us learn": Prost, 248
26. "I had a strong prejudice": Alexis de Tocqueville, *Recollections,* New York, 1970, 34
26. "Woman was the giver of life": Esmé Wingfield-Stratford, *The Victorian Cycle,* New York, 1935, 224 in *The Victorian Sunset*
27fn. "The Gospel was the supreme remedy": Renan, 229–30
27fn. "Today there is a barrier": Prost, 268
27. "Of all the avenues": Pernoud, 491
28. "Young girls are reared": Prost, 268
30. "You will use any weapon": Othenin d'Haussonville, *Réponse au discours de M. Alexandre Dumas,* Paris, 1875, cited by Maurice Descôtes in *Le Public de théâtre et son histoire,* Paris, 1964, 329
31. "They quote his repartees": Hippolyte Parigot, *Théâtre d'hier,* Paris, 1893, 239
31. "When he mints": Emile Zola, *Nos Auteurs dramatiques,* Paris, 1881, 138
31. "Who in this book": Gustave Flaubert, *Oeuvres,* I, Paris, 1958 (Pléïade edition), 666
32. "A painting admirable": ibid., 661
32. "The statues of great men": Pernoud, 482
36. "The railroads, exercising a bizarre": J. J. Weiss, *Le Théâtre et les moeurs,* Paris, 1889, 121
36. "Railroads were created": Alexandre Dumas *fils, Théâtre Complet,* I, Paris, 1896, 26

37. "Writers, painters, sculptors": "Les Artistes Contre la Tour Eiffel," *Le Temps*, February 14, 1887

38. "If a woman is allowed to go": Dumas *fils*, I, 50

CHAPTER II
THE SPEECHLESS TRADITION

42. "Spectators have become": J. J. Rousseau, *La Nouvelle Héloïse*, II

43. "There, everyone mingles": Henri Lagrave, *Le Théâtre et le public à Paris de 1715 à 1750*, Paris, 1972, 253

45. "His Majesty": Emile Fabre, *La Comédie-Française*, Paris, 1942, 13

46. "Eyes open all over": John Wolf, *Louis XIV*, New York, 1974, 166

46fn. "As he is of a rank": Warren Hamilton Lewis, *The Splendid Century*, New York, 1945, 28

47. "Not only to divert": Jules La Mesnardières, *La Poétique*, Paris, 1640

49. "He wishes to observe": cited in Lewis, 27

56. "It seems as if Nature": Theodore Besterman, *Voltaire*, New York, 1969, 133

56. "The effect of exquisite": Le Pere Bouhours, *Maniere de bien penser dans les ouvrages de l'esprit*, Paris, 1683, cited in Maurice Descôtes, *Le Public de théâtre et son histoire*, Paris, 1964, 136

56. "This purity of writing": Le Père Rapin, *Réflections sur la poétique*, Paris, 1674, cited in Descôtes, 136

57. "Versification, good or bad": letter of Jean Chapelain, April 23, 1668

57. "Those stormy times": cited in Descôtes, 138

57. "*Atreus* is a tragedy": ibid., 155

57. "Our facile taste": ibid., 171

58fn. "I have seen warriors": this and other fairground verse quoted in Maurice Albert, *Les Théâtres de la Foire*, Paris, 1900

59. "To labor with all care": the Abbé A. Fabre, *Chapelain et nos deux premières académies*, Paris, 1890, 181

60. "Moved to enthusiasm": quoted by Jean-Claude Chevalier, "La Linguistique, Discours pour l'Inégalité," in *Qu'est-ce que la culture française*, essays collected by Jean-Paul Aron, Paris, 1975, 75

61. "Where language is concerned": Michel de Certeau, inter alia., *Une politique de la langue*, Paris, 1975, 302

61. "Probity, virtue": ibid., 312

62. "The Nation is too vain": John Lough, *Paris Theatre Audiences in the Seventeenth and Eighteenth Centuries*, Oxford, 1965, 263

66. "Despite the great lessons": Maurice Albert, *Les Théâtres des Boulevards*, Paris, 1902, 48

67. "The play has had extraordinary success": Lough, *Paris Theatre Audiences*, 235
67. "Monstrous pantomimes": Descôtes, 210
68. "Any citizen can establish": Albert, *Les Théâtres des Boulevards*, 67
68. "If this goes on": *Journal des Spectacles*, July 16, 1793
69. "The performers at every one": ibid.
70. "The famous decree": Albert, *Les Théâtre des Boulevards*, 76
71. "These gentlemen": Marvin Carlson, *The Theatre of the French Revolution*, Ithaca, 1967, 170
72. "The totality of the child's existence": Robespierre, *Textes Choisis*, Paris, 1957, II, 174
72. "To love justice and equality": ibid., III, 117
72. "Half the globe": ibid., III, 156
74. "The small theaters": Carlson, 182
75. "This great and superb spectacle": J. J. Rousseau, *Lettre à d'Alembert*, Droz, 1948, 105
76. "Man is the greatest object": Robespierre, III, 176
77. "So that the sun's first rays": David Dowd, *David: Pageant Master of the Republic*, Lincoln, Neb., 1948, 111
78. "In one stroke": Georges Pillement, *Paris en Fête*, Paris, 1972, 224
80. "During the entr'actes": Carlson, 163
80. "The theaters are still encumbered": quoted by Romain Rolland, see Eric Bentley, ed., *Theory of the Modern Stage*, London, 1968, 467
80. "Into a circus": ibid., 466
82. "In democracy": Alexis de Tocqueville, *Democracy in America*, II, New York, 1945, 87

CHAPTER III

THE BOULEVARD OF CRIME

83. "The taste for theater": Descôtes, *Le Public de théâtre et son histoire*, 214
84. "Our boxes and orchestras": *Le Décade*, March 30, 1796
88. "Pixérécourt's theater": Descôtes, 224
88. "The entire people": Charles Nodier (critic), in *Le Publiciste*, January 13, 1804
89. "We want an order": Robespierre, *Textes Choisis*, III, 112
90. "From October 15, 1825": Descôtes, 229
90. "I write for people": ibid., 220
90fn. "Melodrama purified": John Lough, *Writer and Public in France*, Oxford, 1978, 274

93. "The celebrated Cartouche": Robert Mandrou, *De la culture populaire aux dix-septième et dix-huitième siècles*, Paris, 1975, 127
97. "The coarse populace": cited in Descôtes, 221
97. "The ladies of *new France*": ibid., 222
98. "My friend, you must not": Max Aghion, *Le Théâtre à Paris au dix-huitième siècle*, Paris, 1926, 258
98. "I note with pleasure": Albert, *Les Théâtres des Boulevards*, 215
99fn. "Barras did me a service": *Memoirs of Napoleon I*, compiled by F. M. Kircheisen, London, no date, 47
100. "The more I study Voltaire": ibid., 253
102. "The *maximum* number": Albert, 220
103. "Gymnastic games": ibid., 233
104. "I am informed": ibid., 235
104. "This spectacle is necessary": ibid., 236
106. "France's mission": Daumard, *Les Bourgeois de Paris au dix-neuvième siècle*, 343
106. "The father was a peasant": Pernoud, *Histoire de la Bourgeoisie en France*, II, 482
107. "I have always considered": ibid., 409
109. "Workers are outside political society": Daumard, 283
110. "Workers are as little duty-bound": Louis Chevalier, *Classes laborieuses et classes dangereuses*, Paris, 1958, 233
111. "The circumstances that oblige": ibid., 233
112. "If you dare": *Le Globe*, January 1, 1825
112. "If the effect": Tocqueville, *Democracy in America*, II, 85
113. "Never would a low word": Descôtes, 262
113. "The thinking men": Robert Baldick, *The Life and Times of Frederick Lemaître*, London, 1959, 136
116. "The people have so lost faith": ibid., 152
116. "Ladies and gentlemen": ibid., 103
116. "To the lamppost": J. Lucas-Dubreton, *Louis-Philippe*, Paris, 1938, 257
117. "Civilization is sleeping": ibid., 258
119. "When one sees": S. Kracauer, *Offenbach*, London, 1937, 29
119. "I looked at it": Gustave Flaubert, letter of May 1, 1845, to Le Poittevin
120. "My hero is gracious": Jules Janin, *Oeuvres Diverses*, V, Paris, 1881, 76
120. "He sired a new species": ibid., 68ff
123. "The ignoble theater": ibid., 179ff
125. "From the foot of Belleville": Tristan Rémy, *Jean-Gaspard Deburau*, Paris, 1954, 203
125. "It's extraordinary": Maxime Leroy, *Histoire des Idées Sociales en France*, III, Paris, 1950, 75

125. "At 8:30 a.m." Roger Price, *1848 in France*, Ithaca, 1975, 114
125. "The struggle these last few days": ibid., 117
127. "The parvenus who emigrated": Daumard, 209
129. "Like other middle-class Parisians": Elliot Paul, *The Last Time I Saw Paris*, New York, 1942, 145
129. "No 29a is the Théâtre Moderne": Louis Aragon, *Nightwalker (Le Paysan de Paris)*, Englewood Cliffs, N.J., 1970, 86

CHAPTER IV
A SAVOYARD BOYHOOD

132. "My vocation": Charles Dullin, *Souvenirs et Notes de Travail d'un Acteur*, Paris, 1946, 27
132. "Far from everything": Pauline Teillon-Dullin and Charles Charras, *Charles Dullin ou Les Ensorcelés du Châtelard*, Paris, 1955, 28
133. "He always wanted to command": ibid., 85
134. "My father would not tolerate": ibid., 113
134. "Well, you know": ibid., 49
135. "See here": ibid., 78
135. "Give me my handkerchief": ibid., 77
136. "Father lent himself": ibid., 81
136. "He attended the fittings": ibid., 82
138. "I am returning": ibid., 90
138. "The only laws he knew": ibid., 101
139. "One day he made me burst into tears": ibid., 98
139. "He did the poor no harm": ibid., 99
140. "Father decided one day": ibid., 94
140. "While taking care of him": ibid., 107
141. "Frail in appearance": Alexandre Arnoux, *Charles Dullin*, Paris, 1951, 44
142. "During lessons": Teillon-Dullin, 127
143. "It was my joy": Dullin, 18
143. "I myself gave him a missal": Teillon-Dullin, 174
144. "As to my 'religious vocation' ": Dullin, 22
145. "On the night of her death": Teillon-Dullin, 72
146. "Despite all our sorrows": ibid., 201
146. "A freethinker": ibid., 110
147. "The night my mother died": Dullin, 16
147. "He's a sweet chap": Teillon-Dullin, 190
147. "Charles was famous": ibid., 192
148. "Enfant de la montagne": ibid., 195
148. "He occupied an . . . atelier": Henri Béraud, *Qu'as-tu fait de ta jeunesse?*, Paris, 1941, 78

149. "Our farces": ibid., 86
150. "We listened": ibid., 88
151. "The course took place": Dullin, 24
152. "At the heart . . . of our dream": Béraud, 101
152. "I have not changed": Teillon-Dullin, 220
152. "I am destined to live": ibid., 224
153. "We spent the night": Béraud, 105

CHAPTER V
THE BOHEMIAN FRINGE

157. "All that sustains these old houses": Pierre Mac Orlan, *Montmartre*, Brussels, 1946, 17
159. "Sitting before a fire": André Salmon, *Souvenirs Sans Fin*, Paris, 1955, I, 183
160. "He was unknown": Roland Dorgelès, *Au Beau Temps de la Butte*, Paris, 1963, 72
161. "When I can afford to bring you": Teillon-Dullin, *Charles Dullin ou Les Ensorcelés du Châtelard*, 209
161. "I've found a little room": ibid., 210
162. "I have a good friend": Teillon-Dullin, 212
164. "At these balls": Emilien Carassus, *Le Snobisme et Les Lettres Françaises*, Paris, 1966, 416
164fn. "Stretching his limbs": Colette, *La Vagabonde*, Livre de Poche edition, 50
164. "Yesterday evening": Teillon-Dullin, 208
166. "Everyone left": Paul Poiret, *En habillant l'époque*, Paris, 1930, 232
166. "You know that the bourgeoisie": Teillon-Dullin, 208
167. "What does it matter": Laurent Tailhade, *Entretiens Politiques et Littéraires*, Paris
167. "Steal from the wretched poor": ibid.
167. "You know, I am taken": Teillon-Dullin, 209
168. "It's bloody cold in Paris": ibid., 214
168. "Uncle Joseph was right": ibid., 213
169. "This afternoon, it was so cold": Arnoux, *Charles Dullin*, 14
169. "The luxurious Paris of Passy": Victor Serge, *Memoirs of a Revolutionary*, Oxford, 1963, 21
172. "A king of tragedy": Dullin, *Souvenirs et Notes de Travail d'un Acteur*, 31
173. "One practices theater": Louis Jouvet, *Le comédien désincarné*, Paris, 1954, 41
173. "I used to smile": Dullin, 29
174. "The poets, my old uncle": ibid., 27

174. "The drama of my life": Arnoux, 85
174. "Though it made me laugh at first": Charles Dullin, *Ce sont les dieux qu'il nous faut*, Paris, 1969, 142
175. "When I was with the Théâtre Montparnasse": ibid., 44
176fn. "The Théâtre de Grenelle had survived": Béraud, *Qu'as-tu fait de ta jeunesse?*, 128
176. "I see the flaws": Teillon-Dullin, 211
176. "Yesterday I had fire in my guts": Teillon-Dullin, 212
176. "My Paulin! Victory!": ibid., 214
178. "The intimate . . . necessity": *Encyclopédie du Théâtre contemporain*, I, Paris, 1957, 37
179. "During the past ten years": quoted in Denis Gontard, *La Décentralisation Théâtrale*, Paris, 1973, 23
179. "The theater is marked": ibid., 24
180. "The people is instinct": Elise Jouhandeau, *L'Altesse des hasards*, Paris, 1954, 222
180. "I have discovered a genuine actor": ibid., 221
181. "I would certainly have been a monk": ibid., 207
181. "One day, my heart torn by doubts": ibid., 92
183. "My anarchist": ibid., 177
184. "On April 5, 1911": Dullin, *Souvenirs*, 40

CHAPTER VI

JACQUES COPEAU'S NAKED STAGE

189. "Along with Rimbaud": Clément Borgal, *Jacques Copeau*, Paris, 1960, 24
190. "At twenty-seven, he seems": André Gide, *Journal 1889–1939*, Pléïade edition, 1965, 167
190. "Copeau, supple mind": ibid., 151ff
192. "Yesterday evening": ibid., 199
192. "Copeau came yesterday": ibid., 369
193. "From the first": Roger Martin du Gard, *Oeuvres Complètes*, I, Pléïade edition, 1957, LXIX
194. "About nothing": letter to Louise Colet, January 16, 1852
194. "We cannot repeat it": Borgal, 34
195. "The classical form": ibid., 39
195. "At an age when I needed to believe": Yette Jeandet, "Copeau fondait le Vieux-Colombier," *Nouvelles Littéraires*, October 29, 1938
195. "If I could not bring to bear": Jacques Copeau, *Souvenirs du Vieux-Colombier*, Paris, 1931, 19
196. "We shall propose that the classics": Jacques Copeau, "Un essai de

rénovation dramatique: le Théâtre du Vieux-Colombier," *Nouvelle Revue Française*, September 1, 1913, cited in Borgal, 94

197. "I sought": Jacques Copeau et le Vieux-Colombier (catalogue of Copeau exhibition at Bibliothèque Nationale), Paris, 1963, 9

197. "To detested realities": Copeau, "Un essai de rénovation dramatique," cited in Borgal, 90

200. "There is a puritanical pall": Borgal, 98

202. "It would charge no tuition": Copeau, "Un essai de rénovation dramatique," cited in Borgal, 86

204. "So imbued was he": Martin du Gard, I, LXVI

204. "Stripping the stage bare": Bibliothèque Nationale catalogue, 16

205. "One must encumber": Jean-Louis Barrault, *Memories for Tomorrow*, New York, 1974, 291

205. "This triumphant success": Gide, 421

206. "Work is my companion": Copeau, *Souvenirs*, 84

206fn. "We were all unjust": Berthold Mahn, *Souvenirs du Vieux-Colombier*, Paris, 1926, XII

206. "We are all counting": *Correspondance Roger Martin du Gard-Jacques Copeau*, edited by Jean Delay, I, Paris, 1972, 143

207. "Good God, man": ibid., 146

207. "I would sometimes plant myself": Jouhandeau, *L'Altesse des Hasards*, 203

207. "It will always be a source of chagrin": *Correspondance*, 166

207. "He appears younger": Gide, 474

208. "It's barbarism!": Borgal, 111

208. "We are giants": Maurice Kurtz, *Jacques Copeau*, Paris, 1950, 57

209. "But, dear old chap": *Correspondance*, I, 229

209. "For solidity": Borgal, 114

210. "We must not predicate": ibid., 115

210. "I would like to put": Kurtz, 118

210. "I have in mind": Borgal, 117

210. "Our action": Bibliothèque Nationale catalogue, 18

211. "In 1889, Lyceum Theatre": Denis Bablet, *Edward Gordon Craig*, New York, 1966, 12

212. "Mr. Craig, it is certain": Bentley, ed., *Theory of the Modern Stage*, 138

214fn. "But although the man": Bablet, 83

215. "The most important thing": ibid., 120

216. "I want to remove": ibid., 123

216. "He set out to cleanse": ibid., 139

216fn. "In order to lighten": Konstantin Stanislavski, *My Life in Art*, New York, 1963, 514

217. "The Beginning": Gordon Craig, preface to *A Portfolio of Sketches*, Florence, 1908
217. "He took rooms": Edward Craig, *Gordon Craig*, London, 1968, 261
218. "Craig took a house": ibid., 267
218. "If you could make your body": Gordon Craig, *The Art of the Theatre*, Chicago, no date, 70
219. "Form broke into panic": ibid., 89
219. "In Asia lay": ibid., 86
220fn. "Forty years later": Edward Craig, 59
221. "Napoleon is reported": Gordon Craig, *The Art of the Theatre*, 80
222. "I want to study the theatre": Edward Craig, 261
223. "First and foremost": ibid., 289
223. "No member of the School": ibid., 288
224. "There was one subject": ibid., 292
225. "He speaks about nothing": *Correspondance Martin du Gard-Copeau*, I, 187
225. "It answers to a tee": Kurtz, 61
225. "There is something": *Correspondance*, I, 187
226fn. "Got a card from Copeau": Gide, 507
226. "It consists of three parts": P. B. Ingham, "Eurythmics," *Encyclopaedia Britannica*, 14th edition, 1937
227. "There is a definite affinity": *Correspondance*, 188
227. "First we would render": Copeau, *Souvenirs*, 93
228. "The mask is a perfect symbol": Borgal, 127
228. "We liked to believe": Copeau, *Souvenirs*, 93
228. "I would like to form": *Correspondance*, I, 211
229. "I foresee": Kurtz, 68
230. "I must record it": Martin du Gard, I, LXXI
231. "Morning session at the *N.R.F.*": Gide, 529
231. "I dream of a spectacle": *Correspondance*, I, 211
231. "I carried the idea": Martin du Gard, I, LXXV

CHAPTER VII

FROM ABSTRACTION TO RELIGION

233. "For France above all": Raoul Girardet, *Le Nationalisme Français*, Paris, 1970, 94
234. "If I heeded": *Correspondance Roger Martin du Gard-Jacques Copeau*, 223
234. "This tour in America": ibid., 226
234fn. "Her activity is fantastic": ibid., 249

235. "My personal impressions": ibid., 241
235. "You see, my dear Gaston": ibid., 247
236. "Our friends will say": Borgal, *Jacques Copeau*, 141
237. "Blueprints of the Garrick": *Correspondance*, I, 260
238   *"Je m'en fous!"* ibid., 263
238. "And his thought": ibid., 260
239. "In the cab": *Correspondance Martin du Gard-Copeau*, II, 830
241. "I became increasingly": *Correspondance*, I, 260
241. "In my musings": ibid., 274
242. "What I call my ideal": ibid., 281
243. "In Paris, I shall definitively": ibid., 282
243. "One of my pet projects": ibid., 294
243. "If someone told you": Borgal, 150
244. "Right now it can be said": *Correspondance*, I, 282
245. "We must create": Borgal, 165
247. "Because it is little": Kurtz, *Jacques Copeau*, 79
247. "The Vieux-Colombier would no longer be for me": Borgal, 201
248. "Copeau allows himself": *Correspondance*, II, 864
248. "Everything, everything": ibid., 863
249. "Everything he organizes": ibid., 865
249. "We were witness": Borgal, 220
250. "Journalists expected": ibid., 230
251. "This *No* play": Copeau, *Souvenirs du Vieux-Colombier*, 99
251fn. "He appalls me": Gide, *Journal 1889–1939*, 1021
251. "I left my theater": Copeau, *Souvenirs*, 104
251. " 'The Birthplace'—flop": *Correspondance*, I, 384
252. "You have rightly sensed": Borgal, 235
253. "What was perishing": Copeau, *Souvenirs*, 108
253. "I had only myself": ibid., 107
253. "Write to me, I implore you": Copeau to Claudel, *Cahiers Paul Claudel*,
        no. 6, Paris, 1966, 123
254. "Yes, one must become Christian": ibid., 117
254. "I've just returned": ibid.
254. "Conversion is not a matter": ibid., 122
254. "What happiness!": ibid., 126
254. "Yesterday I saw Isabelle": ibid., 130
255. "My friend, do not misconstrue": ibid., 131ff
255. "Give thanks to God": ibid., 132
256. "A platform and five": ibid., 134
256. "Instead of a good rest home": Copeau, *Souvenirs*, 107
257. "A mixture of fatigue": ibid., 104

258. "Everything he wrote was dry": Borgal, 230
258. "When you return": *Cahiers Claudel*, 134
259. "Already in Limon": Jean Croué, "Copeau fut toute ma jeunesse," *Opéra*, November 2, 1949
259. "Pernand is beautiful": *Cahiers Claudel*, 137
260fn. "I would like so much": Gide, 1021
260. "Imagine the drama": Borgal, 238
260. "It is true my life": *Cahiers Claudel*, 136
261. "A week from now": ibid.
262. "Once more I am a victim": Borgal, 239
262fn. "In all the Mediterranean villages": John Ardagh, *The New French Revolution*, New York, 1969, 284
263. "What interests us": Albert Camus, *Essais*, Paris, Pléiade edition, 1965, 1700
263. "Lunch with Pierre Fresnay": *Correspondance*, II, 474
264. "I fear for you": ibid., 476
264. "I am immediately writing": *Cahiers Claudel*, 159
265. "I was upset": *Correspondance*, II, 477
266. "The methods were very simple": Borgal, 256

CHAPTER VIII
ACTORS AT WAR

270. "We are living": Jouhandeau, *L'Altesse des hasards*, 197
270. "I'm fed up": ibid., 204
270. "The Anarchist turned": ibid., 215
271. "Every last one of us": Charles Péguy, *Oeuvres en prose*, Paris, Pléiade edition, 1968, I, 852
272. "One doesn't give a damn": ibid., II, 1245
272. "France is not only": ibid., 1264
273. "We do not know whether": ibid., 1241
273. "Familiarity with danger": Jouhandeau, 225
274. "There was something ugly": ibid., 235
274. "I would like to have you share": ibid., 213
274. "The war has above all": ibid., 232
275. "It's a rough school": ibid., 232
276. "I am a bohemian": ibid., 239
276. "I would like to remain young": Teillon-Dullin and Charras, *Charles Dullin ou les Ensorcelés du Châtelard*, 225
277. "They were remarkable": Dullin, *Souvenirs et Notes de Travail d'un Acteur*, 56

278. "I am proud": Bibliothèque Nationale catalogue of Copeau exhibition, 49
278. "Those who think, who see": Teillon-Dullin, 221
278. "Acting is not always a function": Dullin, *Souvenirs*, 90
279. "The actor-hero": Dullin, *Ce sont les dieux qu'il nous faut*, 154
279. "Ah! Here I am at last": Stendhal, *La Chartreuse de Parme*, ed. Garnier, 43
281. "I can no longer bear constraints": Teillon-Dullin, 224
281. "Oh, how I should love to show you": ibid., 222
282. "I should like to have": ibid., 224
283. "Copeau . . . pretended": Jouhandeau, 102
284. "Perhaps you know": *Correspondance Martin du Gard-Copeau*, I, 294
286. "It was less impressive": Firmin Gémier, *Le Théâtre*, Paris, 1925, 274
287. "There is not in any given": Gontard, *La Décentralisation Théâtrale*, 44
288. "At the very origin": ibid., 43
289. "Indeed . . . I have never": Samuel Waxman, *Antoine and the Théâtre Libre*, New York, 1968, 95ff
290. "I feel a vast dramatic poem": Maurice Descôtes, *Romain Rolland*, Paris, 1948, 114
292fn. "I had sent him my small book": Sigmund Freud, *Civilization and Its Discontents*, New York, 1962, 11ff
292. "It seems at times": Gémier, 65
292. "There is perhaps nothing": ibid.
293. "Dramatic geniuses are the painters": ibid., 56
294. "Present-day houses": ibid., 75
294. "People have often mocked": ibid., 66
295. "I shall organize": Paul Gsell, *Firmin Gémier*, Paris, 1921, 29
298. "Among ancient Greeks": ibid., 24
302. "I am striving": Gémier, 279

CHAPTER IX

THE ATELIER

304. "The name I have chosen": Charles Dullin in *Le Petit Parisien*, Nov. 25, 1941
305. "Seated beside Charles Dullin": Lucien Arnaud, *Charles Dullin*, Paris, 1952, 20
305. "The Atelier, A New Actor's School": ibid., 24ff
306. "I want you to learn": Jouhandeau, *L'Altesse des hasards*, 110
306. "The mind that plunges": André Breton, *Manifestes du Surréalisme*, Paris, 1963, 54 (collection *Idées*)
308. "The town drum was mobilized": Arnaud, 28

308. "During those early days": ibid., 31
309. "Listening to Dullin's teachings": Antonin Artaud, *Oeuvres Complètes*, III, Paris, 1961, 118
309. "There was something very special": Arnaud, 38
310. "Its herders were staying": ibid., 45
311. "That represented theater for him": ibid., 221
311. "Gods are no longer worshipped": Aragon, *Nightwalker (Le Paysan de Paris)*, 9
312. "Several weeks": Dullin, *Souvenirs et Notes de Travail d'un Acteur*, 72
312. "Since this shop was narrow": Arnaud, 33ff
313. "It was so pure": ibid., 49
315. "It took six years": ibid.
315. "Was it not the ideal shelter": ibid., 50
315. "The presence within our walls": Dullin, *Ce sont les dieux qu'il nous faut*, 277
316. "A courtyard with open sheds": Arnoux, *Charles Dullin*, 66
317. "Those Rs, especially": ibid., 28
318. "If one were to imagine": Jean Sarment, *Charles Dullin*, Paris, 1950, 88
318. "He would pick a fight": Barrault, *Memories for Tomorrow*, 63
318. "How dare they": Arnaud, 220
318fn. "Lacking any desire": Teillon-Dullin and Charras, *Charles Dullin ou les Ensorcelés du Châtelard*, 83
320. "When I follow southward": Dullin, *Ce sont les dieux*, 267
321. "Family life continued": Arnaud, 111
321. "Copeau was the great boss": Barrault, *Memories*, 64
322. "The person who lives in a theater": Arnoux, 166
323. "As soon as I took possession": Dullin, *Ce sont les dieux*, 128
324. "We don't need a machine": Dullin, *Souvenirs*, 73
324. "Exercises are based on the sensations": ibid., 110ff
325. "A mask has its own life": ibid., 122
325. "While here we have witnessed": ibid., 61
326. "It is in the *café-concert*": Charles Dullin, *Le Journal*, September 27, 1936
327. "Dullin has some very interesting": Quoted by Sollis Schub in "Charles Dullin et son influence sur le théâtre contemporain," Sorbonne doctoral thesis, unpublished, 1953
327. "Especially memorable was one scene": Arnaud, 38
329. "The Atelier possesses a troupe": quoted by Schub
329. "Alas, the French": Teillon-Dullin, 227
329. "I should like a theater": quoted by Schub; also, Arnaud, 116
331. "We shall not tolerate": *La Révolution Surréaliste*, no. 3 (1925)
332. "That morning the trees": Dullin, *Ce sont les dieux*, 269

332. "I descended to the courtyard": ibid., 270
334. "I am antidemocratic": Gaspare Giudice, *Pirandello,* Oxford, 1975, 143ff
334. "A great man's role": ibid.
334. "I have always had": ibid.
334. "The world should look on it": ibid.
335. "The theater has a role to play": Charles Dullin, *Le Gerbe,* July 31, 1941
336. "You must change": newspaper article quoted by Schub

CHAPTER X
GROWING UP FATHERLESS

337. "The blood": Barrault, *Memories for Tomorrow,* 15
341. "From the foot of the house": ibid.
341. "My maternal grandfather": ibid., 16
347. "Accustomed as they were": Claude Fohlen, *La France de l'entre-deux-guerres,* Tournai, 1972, 34
347. "To me school": Barrault, *Memories,* 26
348. "To me, the teachers": ibid.
349. "The young rhetorician": Péguy cited in Prost, *L'Enseignement en France 1800–1967,* 373
351. "I began to regret": Barrault, *Memories,* 36 and *Comme je le pense,* Paris, 1975, 110
351. "I have felt this lack": Barrault, *Comme je le pense,* 111
352. "We four": Barrault, *Memories,* 22
352. "Bob was given": ibid., 25
353. "I had a particular passion": ibid., 26
353. "She grew more and more bohemian": ibid., 37
354. "She would sprawl": ibid., 30
354. "He was not living": ibid.
355. "Deep down": ibid., 15
355. "At lunch": ibid., 27
356. "I was his scapegoat": ibid., 23
356. "Bob sometimes treated me": ibid., 30
357. "My grandfather would not feed me": ibid., 38
358. "Monsieur": ibid., 45
358. "My explanations": ibid.
359. "While I was at Chaptal": ibid., 35
359. "Only a boundless love": Jean-Louis Barrault, *Je suis homme de théâtre,* Paris, 1955, 16
359. "One practices": Jouvet, op. cit.
360. "I could make out": Barrault, *Memories,* 46

CHAPTER XI
THE EVOLUTION OF A MIME

361. "For four whole years": Jean-Louis Barrault, *Reflections on the Theatre*, London, 1949, 12

361fn. "Dullin had the morphology": Barrault, *Memories for Tomorrow*, 51

362. "Camille possessed": Simone de Beauvoir, *The Prime of Life*, New York, 1966, 58

363. "On New Year's Eve": Barrault, *Memories*, 59

364. "The *silence* of the theater": ibid., 60

365. "Since that era": ibid., 58

366. "The mime produces": Etienne Decroux, *Paroles sur le mime*, Paris, 1963, 144

366. "If the mime is born": Jean-Louis Barrault, *Nouvelles Réflections sur le Théâtre*, Paris, 1959, 76

366. "The word alone": Decroux, 135

367. "The surface of things": ibid., 158

367. "As interest in some action": ibid., 149

367. "Unlike Chinese masks": ibid., 17

368. "Mime is an essentially": Barrault, *Nouvelles Réflections*, 76 and 80ff

369. "Theater is promiscuity": Barrault, *Memories*, 291

371. "Finally, it will be": Robert Darnton, *Mesmerism and the End of the Enlightenment in France*, Cambridge, Mass., 1968, 147

371. "Bergasse, in order to": ibid., 118

371. "It is especially in the country": ibid., 121

374. "I simply wanted to tell you": Henri Mondor, *Vie de Mallarmé*, Paris, 1941, 214

375. "Persuaded as I am": Stéphane Mallarmé, *Ecrits pour l'Art*, Paris, 1887

375fn. "From the beginning I felt": Carl Jung, *Memories, Dreams, and Reflections*, New York, 1963, 225

375. "The mind of a man who dreams": Breton, *Manifestes du Surréalisme*, 23

377. "Belief in a fluidic materiality": Artaud, *Oeuvres Complètes*, 1964, IV, 157

377. "Had I been asked": Barrault, *Reflections on the Theatre*, 26

377. "Decroux was a puritan": ibid., 23

378. "Day by day": Barrault, *Memories*, 63

378. "What we have become so incapable": Georges Batailles, *Oeuvres Complètes*, II, Paris, 1970, 117

379. "It is inadmissible": ibid., 135

379. "This revolution struck me": Barrault, *Memories*, 78

380. "*As I Lay Dying* was a revelation": ibid., 66

381. "When Jewel can almost": William Faulkner, *As I Lay Dying*, New York, 1957, 12
381. "My children were of me alone": ibid., 167
382. "So I took Anse": ibid., 163
384. "My aloneness had been violated": ibid., 164
384. "It is 'speaking' theater": Barrault, *Memories*, 67
384. "The mother is nearing death": ibid.
385. "My children, if you only knew": ibid., 101
386. "This spectacle is magical": Artaud, IV, 68
387. "I consider you": cited in Barrault, *Memories*, 58
387. "I shall not attend": ibid., 70
388. "I left everything": ibid., 72
390. "We had a very simple tactic": Henri Noguères, *Front Populaire*, Paris, 1977, 90
393. "We marched, we sang": ibid., 26
394. "The truth . . . which people": Freud, *Civilization and Its Discontents*, 58
395. "I remember one particular Wednesday": Youki Desnos, *Les Confidences de Youki*, Paris, 1957, 190
396. "What I remember": Barrault, *Memories*, 79
397. "Beware, comrades": *Premier Plan*, no. 14, 72
398. "Crystal sparkles": Edward Braun, *Meyerhold on Theatre*, New York, 1969, 216
399. "And when the performance": ibid., 240
400. "My line, my manner": cited in Paul-Louis Mignon, *Le Théâtre d'aujourd'hui*, Paris, 1966, 212
401. "And so I went": Barrault, *Memories*, 90
401. "Granval belonged": Barrault, *Reflections*, 74
402. "Being brought up by women": Mignon, 212
402. "I set up": Barrault, *Memories*, 95ff
403. "That evening": ibid., 98
403. "In September 1938": ibid.
403. "I had found": ibid., 89
404. "She was somewhat": ibid., 95
404. *"The decor"*: Barrault, *Reflections*, 71
405. "My voice had not yet found": ibid., 72
406. "Up in heaven": Knut Hamsun, *Hunger*, New York, 1967, 54
406. *"Hunger* gave me the chance": Barrault, *Reflections*, 79
407. "We live in a body": Barrault, *Memories*, 48
408. "Let us observe breathing": ibid., 84
410. "He could not resist": Beauvoir, 281
411. "My grandfather was brought": Barrault, *Memories*, 100

CHAPTER XII
CHILDREN OF PARADISE

412. "We are doing nothing": Barrault, *Memories for Tomorrow*, 106
413. "I admit": Winston Churchill, *Their Finest Hour*, New York, 1948, 46ff
414. "As at Dijon": Barrault, *Memories*, 113
415. "I was returning to school": ibid., 115
416. "We have been receiving": R. Cardinne-Petit, *Les Secrets de la Comédie-Française*, Paris, 1958, 145ff
417. "Why should the Comédie-Française take me on": Barrault, *Reflections on the Theatre*, 88
417. "I love the ceremony": Barrault, *Memories*, 118
418. "The timidity of my earliest days": Barrault, *Reflections*, 92
418. "Take a match": Barrault, *Nouvelles Réflexions sur le Théâtre*, 48
418fn. "The presence of the audience": Barrault, *Memories*, 54
419. "All he could do": Cardinne-Petit, 190
419. "After the third line": Barrault, *Reflections*, 94ff
420. "*Le Cid* was a total flop": cited in Barrault, *Memories*, 119
421. "A certain côterie": Cardinne-Petit, 207
422. "He could not help publicly": ibid., 206
423. "A trip to Vichy": ibid., 189
424. "In accordance with your demand": ibid., 171
425. "Ladies and Gentlemen": ibid., 202
426. "Return to reality": *Correspondance Martin du Gard-Copeau*, II, 628
426. "I am entering": ibid., 627
426. "Admirable visage": André Gide, *Journal 1939–49*, Paris, Pléïade edition, 1954, 118
427. "This lean, bony neurotic prince": Beauvoir, *The Prime of Life*, 403
427fn. "People reproach you": Claudel, *Correspondance Paul Claudel–Jean-Louis Barrault*, Paris, 1974, 89
427. "I made a study": Barrault, *Memories*, 121
427. "Barrault accepted": Cardinne-Petit, 256
428. "At the time of our appointments": ibid., 210
428. "To stay at the Français": Barrault, *Memories*, 124
429. "*Wilfully* moving away": ibid., 124
429. "So the choice was": Barrault, *Reflections*, 102
429. "I think a man like you": cited in Barrault, *Memories*, 125
429. "Reread La Fontaine's": cited in ibid.
430. "Abruptly I drew away": ibid.
431. "I, too, am burning": *Correspondance Claudel-Barrault*, 92
431. "It would be both childish": Barrault, *Reflections*, 139

432. "Human being is total": Paul Claudel *Mémoires improvisées*, Paris, 1969, 230ff
433. "Strip yourself!": Paul Claudel, *Théâtre*, II, Paris, Pléïade edition, 1956, 844
433. "Let me begin my penitence": ibid., 799
433. "It is delicious": ibid., 923
434. "The whole, whole": Barrault, *Memories*, 148
435. "I had put the whole works": ibid.
435. "We had objected": Beauvoir, 446
436. "When I have told you": Barrault, *Memories*, 149
436. "It had to do with the mime": Marcel Carné, *La Vie à Belles Dents*, Paris, 1975, 219ff
438. "I would like to play": screenplay published as nos. 72–3 *L'Avant-Scène du Cinéma*, 22

EPILOGUE
MAY 1968

442. "One feels a bit discouraged": Teillon-Dullin and Charras, *Charles Dullin ou les Ensorcelés du Châtelard*, 118
443. "Would we not": Barrault, *Memories for Tomorrow*, 666
444. "A spirit of fervor": Patrick Ravignant, *La Prise de l'Odéon*, Paris, 1968, 31
444. "A single conception of life": ibid., 36
446. "Your métier": ibid., 43
446. "It's not a question": ibid., 60
447. "Backstage became": ibid., 195
447. "Something like eight": Barrault, *Memories*, 318
448. "Occupation of all the theaters": Alain Schnapp and Pierre Vidal-Naquet, eds., *The French Student Uprising*, tr. by Maria Jolas, Boston, 1969, 444
448. "Ah! Comme c'est beau!" Patrick Seale and Maureen McConville, *Red Flag, Black Flag; French Revolution, 1968*, New York, 1968, 87

INDEX

✦ ✦ ✦ ✦

Bourgeoisie, French (cont.)
theater vs., 41; postrevolutionary recovery of, 105–106; in the Second Empire, 4–12, 21–24; slumming on Montmartre, 163–64; toughmindedness as the elitism of, 21–23; Surrealists vs., 379; as urbanites vs. provincials, 127; women's role and education in, 25–33; working class vs., 108–11
Bourget, Paul, 348, 350
Brasseur, Pierre, 438
Break of Noon (Claudel), 253n, 258n, 405, 433
Breton, André, 160, 267, 306, 316, 375–78, 395
Briand, Aristide, 176, 286
Brieux, Eugène, 194
Brissot, Jacques-Pierre, 372
Brosses, Charles de, 60
Brotherhood of the Passion (Confrérie de la Passion), 42–43
Brothers Karamazov, The (Dostoevski), 183–86, 195, 259, 261, 281
Bruant, Aristide, 158, 160, 163, 164; bruandailles of, 163
Brunot, André, 430
Bruscambille (buffoon), 44
Buffoons, 44, 50
Bulletin of Laws (1807), 102
Buret, Eugène, 110
Burton, Sir Richard, 55
Butcher, The, 178

Cagliostro, Alessandro, 64
Cahiers de la quinzaine, Les, 270
Cahiers du Vieux-Colombier, Les, 245
Calderón de la Barca, Pedro, 313, 332, 333n
Callot, Jacques, 215
Camelots du roi, 390–91
Camille (Dumas fils), 36, 38
Camille-Sans, Simone, see Jollivet, Simone

Camus, Albert, 263, 356
Capucins, The, 69
Carco, Francis, 155–56, 159
Cardinne-Petit, R., 419–25
Carné, Marcel, 436–37
Carnot, Lazare, 87
Carnot, Sadi, 150
Carnovsky, Morris, 261
Carolina-la-Laponne (dwarf), 105
Carpentier, Alejo, 404
Casarès, Maria, 438
Caserio, Sante, 150
Castelvestro, Ludovico, 47
Catechism of the Holy Council, The, 260
Cauchy, Augustin-Louis, 25
Caussidière, Louis, 125
Celestina (Rojas), 262
Céline, Louis-Ferdinand, 422n, 438
Censier (branch of university), 445–46
Censorship, theatrical: abolition of, in 1906, 39; Counter-Reformation and, 47; euphemistic code language vs., 56; under Louis XIV, 46–47; plebeian theater vs., 42; Restoration on, in 1835, 119; under the Revolution, 61; of scatological references, 53–54; of speaking in Harlequinades, 52–53; of Théâtre Italien, 47
Cervantes Saavedra, Miguel de, 313, 356, 397–98, 403–405
Cézanne, Paul, 33
Chairs, The (Ionescu), 230
Champfleury (Jules Husson), 125
Chamson, André, 444
Chanel, Gabrielle "Coco," 315
Chapelain, Jean, 57
Chapelier, Isaac-René-Guy Le, 68
Chaplin, Charlie, 312
Charterhouse of Parma, The (Stendhal), 100, 275, 279
Châtelard, Le, 132–37, 175
Chekhov, Anton, 248n
Cheap Jack, The (Vitrac), 326
Childlike innocence, 306–307

ABOUT THE AUTHOR

Frederick Brown is a professor of French at the State University of New York at Stonybrook. Besides *Theater and Revolution*, he has written *Jean Cocteau: An Impersonation of Angels* and *Père-Lachaîse: Elysium as Real Estate*, and is currently at work on a biography of Emile Zola. His articles have appeared in many publications, including *Harper's, The New York Review of Books, The New Criterion*, and *The New Republic*.